Zhivago's Children

Vladislav Zubok

Zhivago's Children

The Last Russian Intelligentsia

The Belknap Press of Harvard University Press
Cambridge, Massachusetts, and London, England   2009

Library of Congress Cataloging-in-Publication Data

Zubok, V. M. (Vladislav Martinovich)
Zhivago's children : the last Russian intelligentsia /
Vladislav Zubok.
p. cm.
Includes bibliographical references and index.
ISBN 978-0-674-03344-3 (alk. paper)
1. Intellectuals—Soviet Union—History. 2. Soviet Union—
Intellectual life. 3. Soviet Union—History—1953–1985.
4. Soviet Union—History—1985–1991. 5. Social change—
Soviet Union—History. 6. Socialism—Soviet Union—History.
7. Pasternak, Boris Leonidovich, 1890–1960. Doktor Zhivago.
8. Pasternak, Boris Leonidovich, 1890–1960—Influence.
9. Stalin, Joseph, 1879–1953—Influence. I. Title.

DK276.Z83 2009
305.5'52094709045—dc22   2008053107

To the memory of my son Andrei
(1984–2008)

Contents

Zhivago's Children

The Fate of Zhivago's Intelligentsia

N DECEMBER 1955 the Russian poet Boris Pasternak, from the austere study at his country house in Peredelkino, near Moscow, exulted in a letter to a friend about the novel he had just finished: "You cannot imagine what I have achieved! I have found and given names to all this sorcery that has been the cause of suffering, bafflement, amazement, and dispute for several decades. Everything is named in simple, transparent, and sad words. I also once again renewed and redefined the dearest and most important things: land and sky, great passion, creative spirit, life and death."[1] Those themes were tragically connected with Pasternak's own life, and with the fate of thousands of Russian intellectuals and artists in the era of Soviet revolutionary violence and terror.

Boris Pasternak was born in Moscow into an assimilated Jewish family in 1890. His mother, Rozalia Kaufman, was a gifted pianist and his father, Leonid Pasternak, a prominent artist. The Pasternak family belonged to the creative milieu of Moscow, and young Boris grew up surrounded by professional musicians and artists, but also novelists and poets. His mother counted among her friends Sergei Rachmaninoff and Alexander Scriabin. Leonid Pasternak, who was acquainted with Lev Tolstoy, produced one of the finest portraits of the great writer. The parents saw their artistic endeavors as part of the larger civic and cultural mission of the Russian intelligentsia. The intelligentsia, a cultural phenomenon that had emerged in tsarist

Russia by the middle of the nineteenth century, was not a specific social group with distinct boundaries or definable characteristics that could be measured. As a rule, those who identified with the intelligentsia in the early twentieth century stood in opposition to the tsarist state and welcomed the revolutions of 1905 and 1917. Many Russian intellectuals and artists believed that the emancipation of society from the authoritarian state would usher in an era of unparalleled creativity.[2] Like the majority of intellectuals, artists, and university students in the early 1900s, the Pasternak family longed for the social and cultural emancipation of Russia from the absolute autocracy of the tsars and the power of a corrupt bureaucracy. Leonid Pasternak, despite his cultural assimilation, refused to renounce his Jewish roots and be baptized. Little Boris, however, accompanied his Russian nanny Akulina, a deeply religious woman, to Orthodox church services.[3] He imbibed the mystical Byzantine atmosphere of old Moscow, with its hundreds of cathedrals and little churches, its black-cloaked, bearded priests and monks, the long Orthodox liturgies, the beautiful choral singing, and the languorous effect of incense. He never lost that early connection to the world of Byzantine-Russian faith, which many years later was to save him.

Pasternak studied German philosophy in Marburg and had begun to write poetry by the time Russia entered the war against Austria-Hungary and Germany in 1914. After an initial outburst of patriotic fervor, the mood of the country turned to anger against the tsarist regime as the carnage mounted. The Great War sealed the fate of those who, like the Pasternaks, identified with the Russian intelligentsia. When revolution broke out in Petrograd in March 1917, cheering crowds of people welcomed it as "the dawn of freedom." The Pasternak family, like many of their friends, believed that Russia not only would win the war but would join the family of Western democracies. Soon, however, these dreams were crushed by the stark reality of anarchy, mob violence, and economic disintegration. In October 1917 a group of socialist extremists led by Lenin and Trotsky toppled the well-meaning and liberal, but ineffectual, Provisional Government. In Boris Pasternak's eyes, the Russian Revolution represented an extension of natural forces, the awakening of the people's spiritual strength, and a leap into the unknown. But as Russia descended into bloody chaos, Pasternak remained above the fray. In 1921 he published a book of love lyrics, written in a strikingly new language and employing brilliant and original verse forms. Seen as according with the revolutionary times, the poems met with acclaim from the best Russian poets, including Anna Akhmatova, Marina Tsvetaeva, Osip Mandelstam, and Vladimir Mayakovsky.

As the Bolshevik rulers moved to consolidate the new order in Russia, they began to destroy the most essential components of Pasternak's milieu: freedom for individual creativity, sources of nonstate support for intellectual and artistic undertakings, and opportunities for civic solidarity and intellectual dissent. The Bolsheviks arrested, murdered, and forced into exile thousands of nobles, clergy, bourgeois, and educated professionals—the groups from which the intelligentsia had emerged. Even more than the tsarist government, Lenin and his associates regarded the intelligentsia as a social class and as a dangerous political opposition movement. The early Bolshevik years, marked as they were by terror, civil war, and rampant violence at every level of society, took a terrible toll on Russia's intellectuals and artists. Petrograd, the capital of Russia before the Revolution, suffered especially heavy losses. By 1923 half the membership of the Russian Academy of Sciences had died, emigrated, or been expelled by the regime. From 1921 to 1923 Lenin's government, apprehensive about the intelligentsia's capacity to generate anti-Bolshevik sentiment, expelled a sizable number of intellectuals, university professors, philosophers, economists, writers, and journalists from Soviet Russia.[4] Others emigrated to return to normal life and continue their education—among them Pasternak's sister Josephine, who moved to Berlin. In September 1921 Pasternak's father, mother, and younger sister Lidia left for Germany as well. In 1923 Pasternak stayed with them in Berlin, but then returned to Moscow. He would never see them again.

Waves of arrests among intellectuals who did not support Bolshevik rule continued, despite the advertised liberalization of the New Economic Policy (NEP). At first, it seemed possible to live outside politics and maintain a relative cultural autonomy from the regime. Also, many young artists were attracted to the cultural projects that Bolsheviks had initiated and supported. These projects sought to promote a new proletarian culture and build a bridge between the "bourgeois" cultural legacy of the old Russia and the masses. The state-sponsored "enlightenment" policy received enormous social support from workers who had tasted the fruits of knowledge and were eager to express themselves in novel artistic forms within the revolutionary cultural framework. The people from these movements, usually party members, enjoyed the patronage of intellectuals in the Bolshevik Old

Guard, among them Nikolai Bukharin, Anatoly Lunacharsky, and Georgy Chicherin. Pasternak and many young intellectuals and artists who had been educated in prerevolutionary universities and nurtured in a "bourgeois" milieu remained under the powerful spell of the revolutionary mystique. They believed they were witnessing the "birth of a new world." Emigrating, escaping to the safety of the "old world," from their point of view meant cultural death. Boris Pasternak, however distressed he was by the separation from his family, believed that only in the "new" Russia could one create authentic forms of cultural expression. The dream of the new Russia, articulated in a number of ideological schemes, from Eurasianism to Fabian socialism, caused many Russian émigré intellectuals to return to Soviet Russia in order to join the Great Experiment. Prince Dmitry Sviatopolk-Mirsky, a brilliant scholar of Russian literature who was born in the same year as Pasternak, was a striking example of this phenomenon. Mirsky fought in the White Army against the Bolsheviks and fled from Russia in 1920 after its defeat. In 1932, after years of scholarly research and lecturing in Britain, France, and the United States, he returned to the Soviet Union a devoted communist. He wrote, "An émigré intellectual who wishes to remain alive must either lose his nationality or accept the revolution in one way or another."[5]

Instead of the new Russia, however, the Soviet Union emerged, a totalitarian multiethnic empire. When Stalin consolidated his hold on power in the early 1930s, official tolerance for cultural autonomy and pluralism came to an end. The Stalinist regime sponsored ultraleft professional educational groups and restructured the scholarly and scientific elites. It used writers and journalists to create a mythology that masked the existence of mass terror, famine, and a slave economy.[6] Eventually, Stalin sought to gain total control over the substance and direction of cultural and intellectual production. The regime categorized all people of culture involved in education and science as Soviet intelligentsia. It became one of Stalin's pet projects, no less than the secret police and the army, to marshal the intellectual and cultural resources to glorify his regime, prepare for war, and call upon the population for sacrifices.

The ideals of self-cultivation and self-improvement through high culture, intellectual work, and scientific knowledge were the official requirement for all Soviet citizens. The "Soviet intelligentsia" became necessary for the production and propagation of these ideals (of course under the guidance of the party leaders).[7] In exchange, the state granted educated professionals privileged access to scarce goods, beginning with food. In 1934 Stalin authorized the establishment of "creative unions," state-sponsored guilds for writers and literary critics, musicians, artists and architects, filmmakers, and theater people. Simultaneously, scientists and scholars were incorporated into the state-sponsored academy and academic institutes. Literature, once the "teacher of life" for the intelligentsia, now became the most important staple of the Stalinist arts. Stalin flattered writers, characterizing them as "engineers of human souls." With great cunning, the Soviet leader let writers themselves construct their intellectual and aesthetic prison. Maxim Gorky presided over the establishment of the new cultural doctrine of socialist realism, announced with great pomp at the First Congress of Soviet Writers in 1934; but in practice the doctrine soon became the reflection of Stalin's personal preferences. The innovative formalist vanguard was repudiated, and state-sponsored art promoted Soviet patriotism and mobilized the populace for the inevitable outbreak of war. All the "Soviet intelligentsia" had to submit to the infallible Stalin's judgment of cultural works.[8]

The authorities bowdlerized Russian culture, excising from it everything judged to be "reactionary." At the same time, the regime appropriated the greatest figures of classical Russian culture, from Pushkin to Tolstoy and Chekhov, as well as select figures from the revolutionary vanguard, like the poet Vladimir Mayakovsky. All of them took their place in the Stalinist literary pantheon. In a macabre paradox, during the height of Stalin's terror, the entire country celebrated the hundredth anniversary of Pushkin's death. Every town, every collective farm, and even the smallest shop had to honor the aristocratic Russian poet with lectures, readings, and performances. This cult of Pushkin became emblematic of the linguistic and aesthetic norms that defined for millions the shape of socialist realism.[9] Only shortly before, Stalin's new Soviet constitution had decreed that everyone who had an advanced education or worked in the professions belonged to the Soviet intelligentsia, a vague "intermediary layer" (*prosloika*) in the Stalinist social cake, between those of the allegedly "hegemonic" workers and of the collectivized peasants. State co-optation of intellectuals and artists—along with their social milieu, their cultural symbols, and their very language—had reached its apogee.

Few options remained for Russian intellectual and cultural groups that had not been in the Bolshevik camp. Even earlier, during the 1920s, they had had to choose between cooperating with the revolutionary victors or finding niches outside the public sphere and forming semiprivate circles, in order to preserve an ethos of free discussion and cultural interaction. The first option meant becoming "fellow travelers" of the regime out of necessity, and thus compromising cultural independence for the sake of new opportunities. Often this was a slippery slope leading to forced collaboration with the secret police and denunciations of colleagues. The second option entailed intellectual and artistic marginalization, poverty, oblivion, and eventual elimination. The growing realization of that ineluctable outcome triggered a wave of suicides among artists who had earlier believed that the Russian Revolution was synonymous with cultural and spiritual emancipation.

Stalin's regime was successful in incorporating many members of the prerevolutionary educated elites into the state-run cultural institutions. Not only intimidation, the secret police, and the gulag contributed, but also many artists and intellectuals' willingness to accept an autocratic order in preference to famine, violent death, or emigration. And the rewards were considerable. The state fed and clothed the Soviet intelligentsia, which it placed high in the distribution hierarchy. Stalin's creative unions afforded the educated elites unique benefits and privileges, while millions in the Soviet Union lived in misery and destitution. Unionized writers, artists, scholars, and scientists received better food supplies at a time of universal shortages, enjoyed free vacations at the unions' guest houses and hotels, and dined in subsidized union restaurants that were closed to the general public. The most loyal, successful, and sometimes even talented were awarded big monetary prizes, dachas, chauffeured cars, and scarce luxury goods.[10]

Stalinism attracted intellectuals by identifying the Soviet modernization project with the agenda of the Russian Revolution, and the goals of social and cultural transformation espoused by generations of the Russian leftist intelligentsia. Stalinism not only subverted the revolutionary message but also manipulated the intelligentsia's traditional values of self-improvement, social activism, and commitment to being an agent of historical progress. The alternative to becoming part of the Soviet intelligentsia was too bleak to contemplate. Marginalization entailed the virtual impossibility of creative work and social recognition. Many members of the old intelligentsia, overwhelmed by traumatic changes, allowed themselves to be caught up in the current of history—that is, they served the regime. Some became informers for the secret police. Some even managed to perceive Stalin as the embodiment of History itself. Cultural and intellectual life in the Soviet Union during the 1930s resembled the two escalators of Moscow's metro, moving in opposite directions. On the escalator going down stood people who were disillusioned, cynical, broken, and resigned. On the escalator moving up were those who were still young, ambitious, optimistic, full of smug idealism.[11]

The Great Terror of the 1930s marked a point in time when the logic of fear and survival among intellectuals and artists provided a powerful corrective to their interests and pursuits. Even those who had enthusiastically joined the Revolution and served the Bolshevik regime during war communism, NEP, and the first years of Stalinist transformations felt trapped. The regime demanded individual approval of terror from each and every member of the Soviet intelligentsia, whether in the form of "indignant" speeches at rallies or a signature under collective letters published in Soviet media. Thousands of intellectuals destroyed their archives, burned their diaries, in fear of arrest and interrogation. The personal files of the secret police archives are closed, but it is safe to conclude that practically every professional in the scholarly, scientific, educational, cultural, and engineering spheres had a dossier filled with denunciations. It was the time when intellectuals devoured one another, sacrificing colleagues for the sake of survival. Anybody with ancestors from "former classes," like the nobility, clergy, merchants, or kulaks, was vulnerable. Dmitry Likhachev, a student at Leningrad University, was arrested in 1928 for belonging to a circle of philosophers, lovers of Russian culture. After two years in a concentration camp on the Solovetsky Islands and at the "correctional works" of the Belomor Canal, he was allowed to return to Leningrad (as the city, formerly St. Petersburg or later Petrograd, was now called). Aware of his chronic vulnerability, he found an inconspicuous job as a proofreader at the Academy of Sciences Press. There, all the staff members were people from "former classes" who could not find better employment. After the murder of Kirov in 1934, Likhachev learned from a woman who worked in the personnel department that she was making a list of members of the nobility and he was on it. In fact, Likhachev did not belong to the noble estate. He offered to retype the list at his own expense and thus saved his life. All people on the list disappeared without a trace. In 1938 Likhachev began to work at the Institute of Russian Literature (Pushkin House) in Leningrad. He found there an "apocalyptic" atmosphere of mutual treason, and only a few people of integrity among the hordes of "scoundrels."[12]

Boris Pasternak, like many others, was fascinated by Stalin's power to transform Russia. And he felt, like many, the collectivist urge to leave the "rotten" humanism of the old intelligentsia behind. The meaning of the Russian Revolution for modern European history, for the fate of Russia, and for his generation captivated his mind. Yet his talent, integrity, and religious faith saved him from illusions about the nature of Stalinism. He saw the Russian countryside destroyed by Stalin's collectivization, peasants begging for food, carloads of peasant families dragged from their homes off to Siberia. In 1933, after Hitler came to power in Germany, Pasternak wrote to his parents in Berlin comparing the Nazi regime to Stalinism: "These two movements act in tandem and have the same characteristics. To make matters worse, one feeds off the other. These are the right wing and the left wing of one materialistic night." As Stalin's terror spread, Boris Pasternak was in despair and on the brink of suicide.[13] He was horrified when Stalin offered him public recognition as "the number one poet" of the Soviet Union. The Kremlin leader allocated to him one of the first state-built country houses in Peredelkino, a village converted into a relatively comfortable ghetto for "Soviet writers and poets." Pasternak stopped writing poetry and devoted himself to doing translations of Shakespearian tragedies, as well as Goethe's *Faust*. He refused to read Soviet newspapers, which were filled with news about executions. In 1937 he stayed away from the official celebration of Pushkin's centennial. In that year many of his friends perished; some took their lives, and some died in labor camps. When Stalin and his secret police began to arrest and murder famous Old Bolsheviks, all members of the Soviet intelligentsia had to affix their signatures to petitions praising executions and demanding more of them. Pasternak refused to sign, saying: "Nobody gave me the power of life and death over other people." He confessed to his friend Kornei Chukovsky that he would die rather than sign in support of such "baseness." The officials of the writers' union, appalled at Pasternak's defiance, forged his signature.[14]

Pasternak surmounted the temptation to commit suicide by rediscovering his Orthodox Christian faith. The Great Terror, paradoxically, freed him from the fear of being marginalized. He realized that his infatuation with the Russian Revolution and attempts to "align himself" with the Soviet project had brought him to the brink where the destruction of humanist values meant the death of an artistic and moral self. Pasternak rejected the totalitarian temptation, without fear of the consequences. He began to write poetry again, but no longer in an experimental formalist, "revolutionary" style. His language became simpler, more lucid. The writer Alexander Afinogenov, who lived in Peredelkino in September 1937, wrote in his diary: "My conversations with Pasternak will forever remain in my heart. He comes to you and immediately begins to speak about big, interesting, genuine issues. Art alone is his main concern. He loves people and suffers for them, yet he does it without weepy sentimentality. He has the gift of peering into the future, of separating the wheat from the chaff."[15]

The Great Terror left many writers, artists, and intellectuals disastrously isolated and demoralized. After the orgy of mutual denunciations, they could barely trust one another. Former members of the Russian intelligentsia who had supported the Bolshevik regime during the 1920s and enjoyed the political patronage of Bolshevik politicians now felt isolated and abandoned. According to a secret police file, the writer Mikhail Svetlov said in 1938, "We are just the pitiful remnants of the epoch that has died. Nothing is left of the old party; there's a new party, with new people. They have replaced us."[16] Indeed, there were no more Bolshevik intellectuals like Nikolai Bukharin, or authoritative cultural figures like Maxim Gorky, connoisseurs and patrons of art and literature. The new recruits in the party and state apparatus, many of them from a blue-collar or peasant background, treated intellectuals and artists as a class in the service of the regime. The only patron of art and culture was now Joseph Stalin.

The German attack on the Soviet Union on June 22, 1941, and the subsequent tragic developments overshadowed not only the previous years of terror and upheavals, but even the Bolshevik Revolution itself. The country was fighting for its life, and the people, after months of defeats, desertions, cowardice, and disarray, began to rally around the Soviet flag under the slogans of the "holy" and "Great Patriotic" war. The war decimated the remaining cultural elite, as it did every other group in Russia. The German siege of Leningrad in 1941–42 took a particularly horrifying toll: most of the old city dwellers who had grown up in the prerevolutionary culture died of famine. People burned libraries, to keep from freezing to death. At the same time, the war raised the morale of intellectuals and gave a new meaning to their personal destinies. Scientists, including those under arrest, worked to design new weapons. The regime mobilized artists and writers, who served in various capacities to inspire people to sacrifice and heroism with national patriotic slogans. This was the moment when the defunct ethos of the old Russian intelligentsia, which had been trampled underfoot, appeared to be returning. It was especially true for the writers, poets, and musicians: people turned to their verse and songs for direction. Vera Sandomirsky, a Russian émigré in the United States, wrote in 1943 that the word *rodina* (Motherland) "became the highest symbol of unification, the banner of a whole nation." The remaining members of the old intelligentsia and the young intellectual iconoclasts alike realized, under wartime duress, that they owed loyalty not to the Revolution, but to the country and the Russian people. The war restored a mutual trust, a sense of national identity, and the feeling that Soviet citizens were a "band of brothers" risking death at the hands of the brutal enemy.[17]

Pasternak was unfit for military service. He, like most other poets and writers, was evacuated by train to eastern Russia when German armies approached Moscow. When he returned, months later, he found his city apartment vandalized. His books and manuscripts, as well as the works of his father, had vanished. He also grieved at the suicide of his dear old friend Marina Tsvetaeva, the great Russian poet who had recently returned to the Soviet Union from emigration. These were drops in an ocean of war-related disasters and tragedies. Pasternak began to read Soviet news, and he empathized with people's heroism and tenacity. In 1943, after the victory at Stalingrad, he traveled to the front line as a military journalist. He wrote in his notes about the ruined Russian cities and German atrocities against civilians, yet also prophetically remarked that if one had "to change the political system" to rebuild Russian cities and restore the country's well-being, "this sacrifice would not be made. Instead, they would sacrifice the whole world to save the system."[18]

As Pasternak's religious and mystical inclinations deepened during the war, they reinforced his view of human existence as a duel between life and death, whose ultimate stakes were spiritual resurrection. He summarized his spiritual experience in "Dawn," a poem later included in his great novel as one of the "poems of Yuri Zhivago."

> My life owed everything to you.
> Then came the war and devastation.
> You vanished from my sight and soul,

Even your name became unmentioned.
Now, after many, many years
I heard your voice with trepidation.
All night I read your testament
And was awakened back to action.[19]

Pasternak seemed to ignore the nationalist and racist hatred around him, including rampant anti-Semitism. Other writers and poets of his generation did not share his spiritual detachment. Ilya Ehrenburg, who came from an assimilated secularized Jewish family of the same Moscow milieu as Pasternak, joined the Bolshevik party at a very young age. He welcomed the Revolution but soon left the party in disillusionment and emigrated to Paris, Brussels, and other European cities, to live the life of an avant-garde artist. With the rise of fascism and Nazism, however, Ehrenburg returned to Moscow and became Stalin's informal ambassador-at-large in charge of international propaganda, using his extensive contacts among those on the European left to mobilize the antifascist coalition. During the Great Patriotic War he became a member of the Jewish Antifascist Committee, a vehicle to mobilize support for the Soviet cause in the United States. At the same time, the entire Soviet army learned to worship Ehrenburg, who put hatred against the Nazi invaders into cruel language. He wrote: "Kill the German— that is your grandmother's request. Kill the German—that is your child's prayer. Do not let him through. Kill!"[20]

The poet Konstantin Simonov's main theme during the war was his love for a woman who was waiting for his return. Simonov was born in St. Petersburg to a Russian noble family; his mother was Princess Obolenskaia, and his father, a general, perished in World War I. Young Kirill (that was Simonov's birth name) was raised by his stepfather, a tsarist officer who joined the Red Army. Simonov grew up accustomed to the discipline and unswerving loyalty of the military caste. During the 1930s he plunged into the furnace of the cultural revolution in which "new Soviet people" were being forged. Like many others who were products of that era, he "aligned" his life with revolutionary history. Between 1937 and 1939 he began to write poetry intended to mobilize youth to serve the state in the impending epic battles of World War II. In 1939 he graduated from the Institute of Literature and became a war journalist. The Nazi assault on the Soviet Union changed his life. He began to write about the real tragedies of the Russian people—soldiers in grim retreat and peasant women left to the mercy of the enemy. Millions of soldiers at the front and their relatives back home quoted Simonov's poem:

> Wait for me, and I'll be back.
> Wait the best you can.
> Wait when sadness overwhelms
> You in the yellow rain.
> Keep on waiting even when
> All of them give up.[21]

The poet Alexander Tvardovsky celebrated the simple patriotism and sturdiness of a Russian peasant soldier. He belonged to the cohort of talented people of peasant background who joined the Soviet intelligentsia during the 1930s. His father had been dekulakized and the family exiled. Alexander, under threat of arrest, had to separate himself from his family. He joined the Russian Association of Proletarian Writers.[22] In his autobiography, published in 1951, Tvardovsky admitted that he suffered from the lack of a "serious cultural background," a crucial problem for his literary generation.[23] It took him less than a decade to compensate for his peasant "backwardness" through determined all-night self-education sessions: in 1936 he became a student at the Institute of Philosophy, Literature, and History (IFLI). Two years later he published a poetic saga about the end of a naive peasant's dream to find a country with no communists or collective farms. In 1941, on the eve of the war with the Nazis, Tvardovsky received the Stalin Prize for literature. By that time, feeling more secure, he had found his family in exile and brought them to back to their homeland. Yet the stigma of having a "kulak" father continued to beset him for the rest of his life.[24] When the war with Germany broke out, Tvardovsky became a military journalist and wrote a cycle of poems about war, whose lack of officious pathos and sincere tone won readers' hearts. His main protagonist, the soldier Vasily Tyorkin, became a hero to the army. Tyorkin, who was known and loved by millions, joined the gallery of Russian national characters previously created by Ivan Turgenev, Lev Tolstoy, Anton Chekhov, and Ivan Bunin. Stalin also liked Tyorkin, and bestowed further awards on Tvardovsky.[25]

During the war, hopes soared for a better life after victory, and the end of the repressive regime. Wartime transformations—the abolition of the Communist International, the opening of churches, and other measures taken by the regime—left intellectuals musing about the future. Some voiced remarkably frank opinions in private conversations that were registered by the secret police and its ubiquitous informers. One writer said in 1943: "In the near future we will have to permit private initiative, a new NEP, without which we won't be able to restore and revive the economy and circulation of goods." A journalist was heard by a secret police informer to say, "My sympathies have always been on the side of the democratic powers. . . . In the event of victory for Soviet power, there is only one thing left for me, an old democrat—suicide!" Another writer said, "The Revolution has not justified the forces and sacrifices expended on it. We need reforms, transformations. Otherwise, we won't be able to rise out of this abyss, out of the devastation the war has cast us into." Others continued to adhere to the Soviet communist project or remained pessimistic about the possibility of changes in the future. At most, they expected the end of terror and alleviation of the bureaucratic management of cultural affairs. They hoped the regime would allow them to write their books, make their films, and stage their performances. There were people who welcomed the Russian nationalist patriotic themes and wanted to evict the Jews from the ranks of the "Soviet intelligentsia." The Jews, by contrast, dismayed by the growing anti-Semitism, felt vulnerable and sought a return to the internationalist Bolshevik traditions of earlier years.[26]

In May 1945, after millions of casualties and indescribable suffering, the Soviet Union won the war. Instead of instituting reforms, however, Stalin mobilized the country for a cold war against the Western powers. New waves of terror ensued. Remarkably, Stalin and his secret police did not arrest the members of the Soviet intelligentsia who had raised reformist and liberal voices during the war. Instead, a campaign to rein in the "cultural front" commenced. It became known as *Zhdanovshchina*, after Stalin's lieutenant Andrei Zhdanov, who voiced the leader's opinion. The party decrees of 1946–1948 humiliated and denigrated, among others, the most original and autonomous artists from Pasternak's milieu: the writer Mikhail Zoshchenko and the poet Anna Akhmatova, the composers Sergei Prokofiev and Dmitry Shostakovich, and the filmmaker Sergei Eisenstein. It was the signal to all creative voices: align with the regime's policies or perish. The Stalin-Zhdanov decrees of 1946 that gave the party direct control over culture killed genuine creativity, caused self-censorship to metastasize, and opened the door to mediocrities, careerists, and intriguers. Some literary hacks, in collusion with the party censors, invented the "theory of the absence of conflicts," as a way of emasculating and banning literary works and essays that focused on social and economic problems. Many writers began to compose for an audience of one person, Stalin himself, in works catering to his whims and tastes, and seeking to win his favor. Indeed, the despot remained the ultimate judge of what was good or bad in literature. He could even, at times, overrule the oppressive dictates of his minions and their literary assistants.[27]

Zhdanovshchina and the Cold War ended the hopes of intellectuals and artists in Soviet Russia to resume contact with the outside world and regain their freedom to travel abroad. During NEP these contacts and travel had become a privilege, available only to supporters of the regime and trusted "fellow-travelers." It had still been possible to obtain individual permission to emigrate.[28] During the 1930s, however, the borders closed completely, and it became very dangerous to have foreign friends and contacts. And after World War II Stalin, concerned with the effects that exposure to foreign lands might have on the Soviet army and society, unleashed a campaign against "genuflection before the West." Special "courts of honor" were created to stigmatize international cooperation and contacts in science. All forms of cultural exchange came to a halt. The almost complete isolation of Russian intellectuals and cultural figures from the rest of the world lasted for at least two decades under Stalin. It had traumatizing and sometimes curious effects. The Oxford scholar Isaiah Berlin, who visited Moscow and Leningrad in 1946 and 1956, observed that even the most sophisticated and knowledgeable people in Moscow and Leningrad knew nothing about contemporary culture, lifestyle, and living standards in the West and remained unaware of the problems high culture faced in societies characterized by mass consumption and marketing directed toward the lowest common denominator.[29]

Stalin's postwar policies reflected a growing suspicion of Jews as "the agents of American and British imperialism." Antagonism at the top coincided with the dangerous growth of anti-Semitism in the bureaucracy and in society as a whole during the war. After the establishment of Israel in 1948, anti-Semitism became a state policy used to unify and cement Soviet Russian nationalism: Yiddish cultural institutions were shut down, and leading Jewish poets and actors, members of the Jewish Antifascist Committee (JAC), were arrested and murdered. The campaigns against "cosmopolitan influences," aimed at Jews assimilated into Russian-Soviet culture, became the most divisive and traumatic experience of the late Stalin years, culminating in the Kremlin's Doctors' Plot accusations and purges of January 1953. At one of the anticosmopolitan meetings at Moscow State University, a professor of history asked a colleague what the reason for this campaign could be. The answer was: "War. People must be prepared for a new war." During the anticosmopolitan campaigns, colleague denounced colleague, students humiliated their own professors, and writers, poets, literary critics, academic scholars, and many others had to attend the public sessions of *prorabotki* ("criticism and self-criticism") that degraded and decimated the intellectual and cultural milieu in which they worked.[30]

Again, as during the 1930s, the members of the "Soviet intelligentsia" who had jobs in state-sponsored institutions were caught up in an orgy of mutual recrimination and self-castigation. All of them became executors of the regime's policies, among whom, according to a cruel Stalinist logic, were the popular literary heroes of the war years. Ehrenburg, because of his Jewish background, was under attack, but Stalin decided to keep him in his "literary court." From 1946 to 1952 Ehrenburg helped the Soviet Union organize the Soviet-led "peace movement," and he was as effective then as he had been ten years earlier during the antifascist Popular Front. Ehrenburg was the only member of the Jewish Antifascist Committee who survived its tragic end. Had Stalin lived longer, Ehrenburg would have faced a terrible dilemma: whether to participate in the cover-up of a Jewish pogrom or to perish.[31] Simonov, like Ehrenburg, became part of the literary court Stalin created, and his propaganda "ambassador." In early 1946 Stalin sent Simonov to the United States and later "recommended" that he write a play portraying "dark forces" in America plotting a war against the USSR. Stalin then made use of the play and film script *The Russian Question* in marshaling forces for the Cold War. Simonov had to preside over the public humiliation of the writer Mikhail Zoshchenko, whom Stalin viciously attacked in August 1946 as a "literary low-life." Later, Simonov obediently led the attack on Jewish writers, many of whom were his friends.[32]

It was at this time, during a new descent from hope into despair, that Boris Pasternak began to write his novel *Doctor Zhivago*. During World War II, Pasternak lost his parents: they died in London after fleeing there from Nazi Germany. He also grieved over the death of twenty-year-old Adrian Neigauz, the son of his second wife, Zinaida. And the first years after the war brought him a new personal drama. He fell in love with the young and charming Olga Ivinskaia, who worked for the literary journal *Novy Mir*. After two years of an intense romantic relationship with him, Ivinskaia was arrested and sent to labor camps. As he had during the Great Terror, Pasternak staggered under the blow. He regained his creative stamina, however, and a new theme emerged in his writings, the tragic demise of the Russian intelligentsia in an era of revolutionary violence.

On March 5, 1953, Stalin died. Millions mourned his death. Very few noticed that the great Russian composer Sergei Prokofiev had died on the same day. It was a bad omen for the future of Russian culture. Among the Soviet intelligentsia, no level of creative autonomy, not to mention separation from the regime, was possible in public or even in private. All possible outlets for intellectual and artistic endeavor were controlled by the state and the secret police. Even more significantly, intellectuals and artists had been fatally vitiated, consumed by their own venom, including ideological fanaticism and anti-Semitism. Writers and poets seemed to have forgotten how to think and write freely. Artists could not express their true feelings on canvas or onstage. Filmmakers were conscripted to shoot crude propaganda and slapstick comedies. The ideal of civic solidarity among intellectuals seemed a hopeless pipe dream. And the mission of improving and reforming Soviet society and its government seemed definitively buried. Yet the decade that followed proved that the obituary for the intelligentsia was premature.

Pasternak's novel was the first defiant challenge to the postwar cultural silence. In *Doctor Zhivago* a mystical poet, a sensitive idealist, a doctor who saved people's lives, finds supreme meaning and resurrection in love. In the novel, Yuri Zhivago has lost both his parents as a child and grown up in a family of educated and assimilated Jews, similar to the Pasternaks. Zhivago's milieu too worshipped classical Russian culture and welcomed the Revolution against the tsarist regime. Yuri marries Tonia, a daughter of the people who adopted him as a child. A series of mysterious events, however, leads him to meet a young woman, Lara, who becomes his true love. Yuri is not particularly interested in politics and has no inclination to participate in the Revolution. Yet the Revolution sucks him into the vortex of outsize and tragic events, along with his family and his love. Fate gives Zhivago only a few weeks of happiness with Lara, during which he composes the "poems of Yuri Zhivago" in a country house, to which the couple has escaped from the surrounding turmoil. Soon the Civil War separates him from Lara, and later she seeks to emigrate from Russia and disappears from Zhivago's life forever. Yuri himself is at the brink of death several times, but each time Providence saves him. In the novel's poignant concluding scene, which takes place in NEP Russia at the end of the 1920s, Yuri, sick and unrecognized, believes he sees Lara from the window of a crowded streetcar. He rushes out to greet her and instantly dies of a heart attack.

Doctor Yuri Zhivago belongs to the Russian intelligentsia, an imagined community that existed for seven decades in Russian society.[33] Zhivago's fate in the chaos and violence of the years that follow emblematizes the destruction of the social milieu and ethos of the intelligentsia. Pasternak describes, through the eyes of this doctor, the fratricidal, often senseless, and always dehumanizing nature of the Russian Revolution and Civil War. Pasternak writes about the crimes committed by the Reds and the Whites, which mirrored and reinforced one another. Yuri Zhivago, having been forcibly drafted into a peasant army, is in a position to observe both the ideological rigidity of communist fanatics and the desperate ruthlessness of the White Army leaders. Many atrocities, in his view, were committed by simple peasants and soldiers who "needed no encouragement to hate intellectuals, officers, and gentry with a savage hatred." Pasternak remarked that the enthusiastic left-wing intellectuals greatly valued such people. "Their inhumanity seemed a marvel of class consciousness, their barbarism a model of proletarian firmness and revolutionary instinct."[34] Pasternak seems to argue that the ideologies that the Revolution unleashed and the principles and values that Stalinism appropriated and exploited in lethal fashion were all dehumanizing dogmas, not worth the loss of Russia's cultural and spiritual treasure trove. Though many intellectuals were culpable, he deplores the disappearance of the intelligentsia's cultural milieu, which he compares to "frozen music." In the final pages of *Doctor Zhivago*, after Yuri Zhivago's death, his friends, survivors of war and terror, meet the only child of Yuri and his beloved Lara. That child, Tania, has grown up as an orphan among peasants, separated from the world of high culture. She has no opportunity to inherit the tradition of freethinking, spirituality, and creativity that her father embodied. Pasternak does not tell us Tania's fate. Her cameo appearance in the book makes the readers wonder whether the cultural continuity of the Russian intelligentsia has been irreparably broken.

In 1956 Pasternak sent the manuscript of *Doctor Zhivago* out to several foreign publishers, and despite heavy pressure from the Soviet authorities, conspired with those publishers to have his novel published abroad. Even before its publication, however, party authorities began to blackmail the writer. Olga Ivinskaia, Pasternak's lover and the prototype for Lara, had just recently returned after seven years in labor camps and in exile. Imploring Pasternak to give up his dangerous project, she told him that not only his life but also her own was at stake.[35] Pasternak resisted. "If the truth that I know must be redeemed by suffering," he wrote to the boss of the party department of culture, Dmitry Polikarpov, "I can accept any suffering." The atheistic bureaucrat could hardly appreciate Christian parables and sentiments, and party leaders were deaf to Pasternak's appeal: "How can anyone think that someone's passionate and focused creation can be concealed from the world simply by sealing it as one seals a bottle with a cork?" The writer continued by assuring them that "the only way to calm the storm" would be "to leave [him] and this theme in peace."[36]

On November 23, 1957, *Doctor Zhivago* came off Feltrinelli's presses in Milan. Overnight it became a worldwide literary sensation and was translated into virtually every major language.[37] In October 1958 the Swedish Academy voted to award Pasternak the Nobel Prize for Literature. In the United States the translated version topped the *New York Times* best-seller list for over half a year. Nikita Khrushchev, who had taken over the leadership of the Soviet Union after Stalin, was enraged. He and his associates had learned from members of the Union of Soviet Writers that the poem "denigrated" the Bolshevik Revolution and blamed it for the destruction of Russian cultural heritage. Khrushchev and his political lieutenants never bothered to read the novel, but they decided that the brouhaha surrounding it was a Western Cold War provocation. The party presidium assessed the novel as "a tool of international reaction" and ordered "a collective letter from the most prominent Soviet writers" to be issued condemning Pasternak. *Pravda* denounced Pasternak as a "literary weed in the service of international reaction."[38] In a nationally broadcast speech, Vladimir Semichastny, the head of Komsomol, the communist youth league, said that Pasternak was an "internal émigré," worse than a pig, which "never makes a mess where it eats and sleeps."[39] Pasternak found himself under tremendous domestic pressure to repent, while thousands of intellectuals and public figures from all over the world expressed their solidarity with the beleaguered writer. In January 1959 he responded to the witch hunt with another poem, published abroad:

> What was my fault?
> Did I commit a murder?
> I have just written about my beautiful land
> And made the whole world commiserate.[40]

Pasternak's defenders included such world-famous writers as John Steinbeck, Graham Greene, Aldous Huxley, Somerset Maugham, Ernest Hemingway, André Maurois, and Alberto Moravia. Eleanor Roosevelt and Prime Minister Jawaharlal Nehru of India both appealed to Khrushchev not to expel Pasternak from the Soviet Union.[41] Khrushchev decided to rescind the sentence exiling the poet. On November 1, Pasternak, under enormous pressure, agreed to write to Khrushchev renouncing the Nobel Prize. According to some observers, Olga Ivinskaia, fearing arrest, served as the tool of the regime by helping fabricate letters of repentance that were published in *Pravda* and attributed to Pasternak. The poet was not defeated in spirit, however. Privately, he announced his verdict on the Soviet regime: "It is doomed. One cannot live like this."[42]

In Pasternak's novel numerous people, recognizing Dr. Zhivago posthumously as a figure of great talent and inspiration, attend his funeral. When Pasternak died, only a brief mention in the newspapers signaled the death of "a member of the Literary Foundation, B. L. Pasternak," on May 30, 1960. But many admirers of the poet experienced a moment of revelation the day they learned of his death.[43] Some went to the village of Peredelkino to bid him farewell. The authorities had clearly discouraged attendance at the funeral, and KGB agents took photographs of those who were present at the graveside. Nevertheless, Pasternak's funeral was the occasion for the first sizable demonstration of unofficial civic solidarity in Soviet Russia, and as such it was symbolic. The funeral procession, later described by many witnesses and memoirists, as well as KGB agents, consisted of five hundred mourners who made their way from the poet's dacha to a church cemetery on a nearby hill. Speeches were given at the newly dug grave.[44] According to one witness, the very fact that hundreds of people ignored official disapproval of the public funeral march showed a "crystallization of new civic notions" that were "stronger than the usual fear."[45] Although many of Pasternak's friends and admirers did not show up, for fear of losing official

Boris Pasternak, who wrote *Doctor Zhivago* about the vanishing milieu of the old intelligentsia, which he described as "frozen music." His funeral in 1960, however, marked the birth of a new community of Russian intelligentsia (Courtesy of Memorial, Moscow).

public standing and privileges, many others, including some people who had betrayed Pasternak during his ordeal, came to his funeral, perhaps to atone for their betrayal.

The death of the poet, who had belonged to the spiritual milieu of the old intelligentsia, was the moment at which another spiritual and civic community emerged in the popular mind. The young people who identified with that community had a vastly different social background and life experience than Pasternak had, and many of them did not share or even understand his spiritual world. At the same time, they too were striving for intellectual and artistic emancipation, as the dead poet had. And they viewed themselves as the descendants of the great cultural and moral tradition that Pasternak, his protagonist Yuri Zhivago, and his milieu embodied. Thus, they were Zhivago's children, in a spiritual sense.

These people did not belong to a single generation, if one defines a generation by age. The oldest of them were born in the 1920s—the Russians who fought against Hitler's armies in World War II. Pasternak had high hopes for the war veterans. In his novel he attributed to them "fabulous, astounding qualities," including a readiness "for great, desperate, heroic exploits," and called them "the moral elite of this generation."[46] Yet the survivors were few, for many of their peers had perished in the carnage of war.

The larger cohorts of Zhivago's children were younger. They were born in the 1930s or early 1940s and were the generation that entered the universities of Moscow and Leningrad after the war. There, they met the veterans, and their feelings of solidarity united them in one "extended" historical generation that transcended the boundaries of age.

Zhivago's spiritual children were born into a society where everyone was supposed to absorb the Soviet way of life as naturally as the Russian Orthodox had their faith, in church. They walked under the Kremlin's red stars and learned Soviet songs. Many of them grew up without fathers, because of the lives lost to war or to political terror. In a sense, "Comrade Stalin" became their substitute father. Some of them were taught to love Stalin more than their parents. The beneficiaries of the Soviet enlightenment project, they were the graduates of the best universities, above all in Moscow and Leningrad, and were destined to become the highly educated group that Stalin cynically called the Soviet intelligentsia. In reality, they were intended to be cadres totally loyal to Stalin's agenda and the party line: scientists and engineers, physicians and educators, elite youth in the military, security, propaganda, and cultural institutions who were destined to become apparatchiks in the state and party bureaucracies. This cohort of young intellectuals and artists grew up in isolation from the world, in a country of closed borders and "captive minds." Meeting a foreigner was less likely than seeing a total solar eclipse. Foreign travel was unimaginable. Comparison between the Soviet experience and life in other countries was almost impossible.

Yet something remarkable occurred. The years of war, violence, and misery tested the spirits of the "extended" generation of Zhivago's children who grew up during that time and gave them extraordinary experience. They broke loose. The educated cadres trained for Stalinist service turned out to be a vibrant and diverse tribe, with intellectual curiosity, artistic yearnings, and a passion for high culture. They identified not only with the Soviet collectivity, but also with humanist individualism. This was the unintended result of the Stalinist educational system, the ideals of self-cultivation and self-improvement, and the pervasive cult of high culture that it propagated. These ideals, once intrinsic to the ethos of the Russian intelligentsia, now provided the codes for its revival among the young educated cohorts of the post-Stalin era. The remnants of the old intelligentsia in literature and liberal arts, with their memories of the truncated past, were still around and, despite their abdication to the Stalinist mainstream, provided a compass to pre-Soviet ethical and aesthetic ideals, behavior, and language. Likewise, remnants of the romantic revolutionary idealism and optimism that had powerfully motivated the founders of the Soviet regime lingered on, despite the colossal moral and physical losses among its agents in the first half of the twentieth century. This idealism and optimism, although manipulated and corroded by the regime, still had the vigor to confront cynical conformism and docile passivity. The prestige of science and scientists, boosted by the exigencies of the Cold War, grew to an unprecedented degree in the USSR. The relentless search for "objective truth" placed scientists in the position of supreme intellectual oracles, autonomous from the party and ideology.[47]

As a result, these people who had grown up under the unifying press of Soviet conformism and censorship would succeed in presenting a dazzling array of ideas and attitudes.[48] In 1987 Joseph Brodsky spoke in his Nobel Prize acceptance speech about his generation of writers, artists, and intellectuals:

> The generation born precisely at the time when the Auschwitz crematoria were working full blast, when Stalin was at the zenith of his Godlike, absolute power, which seemed sponsored by Mother Nature herself—that generation came into the world, it appears, in order to continue what was interrupted in those crematoria and in the anonymous common graves of Stalin's archipelago. The fact that not everything got interrupted, at least not in Russia, can be credited in no small degree to my generation, and I am no less proud of belonging to it than I am of standing here today. Looking back, I can say again that we were beginning in an empty—indeed, a terrifyingly wasted—place, and that, intuitively rather than consciously, we aspired precisely to the recreation of the effect of culture's continuity.[49]

This tribute might well be addressed to all Zhivago's children, the different groups from that complex extended generation whose view of the uses of the mind and spirit rekindled the intelligentsia's dream of a just and humane Russian society.

We fulfilled our duty during the war,
And we wanted our rights in peacetime.

—David Samoilov, 1979

The "Children" Grow Up
1945-1955

AFTER WORLD WAR II a remarkable surge took place in the educational and cultural life of Russia. Schools and universities in Moscow, Leningrad, and other Russian cities filled up with new cohorts of students. The city youth, those who did not drown the stresses of war in drunkenness, gambling, and crime, plunged into reading and study. Soviet libraries registered a burgeoning demand for detective and adventure stories, and even for fairy tales. Yet a minority of readers had more serious educational aspirations—acquaintance with world literature, history, poetry, and philosophy.[1] The number of university students that graduated during the postwar years was no more than a million and a half. It was a small group by comparison, for instance, with college graduates in the United States, where eight million people graduated from universities as a result of the G.I. Bill alone. Still, it was the largest group of educated young men and women that had ever emerged in Russia—six times as large as the entire "Zhivago generation," the university graduates in the last decades before the Revolution.

Aside from quantity, these students exhibited a special quality. During the first two decades of their lives they had acquired extraordinary memories and social experience. Their youth and childhood had been interrupted by the Nazi invasion. Their soul and spirit absorbed the worst impressions of inhumanity as well as sublime moments of patriotic sacrifice and national unity. Many years later, the young Russian filmmaker Andrei Tarkovsky attempted to translate these impressions in his first internationally acclaimed film, *My Name Is Ivan,* the tragic story of a Russian child in wartime obsessed by feelings of vengeance. Western critics, shocked by the film, regarded the portrayal of its protagonist as an exaggeration. Yet after the four years of war, famine, and privations on an unimaginable scale, the postwar students remained scarred by the slaughter and inhumanity of the recent cataclysm. The immediate postwar years had brought more hardship and malnutrition. Moscow, Leningrad, and other cities were filled with tens of thousands of teenage orphans, crippled veterans missing limbs, and desperate prostitutes. In spite of all this (or perhaps because of it), the students of the postwar years felt tremendous optimism and passion for life.[2]

The presence of young war veterans at universities and in urban life was an important factor in the postwar educational boom. The Soviet Union had nothing analogous to the G.I. Bill, yet war veterans could enter universities, including the best ones in Moscow and Leningrad, virtually without entry exams or competition and could study for free. Most of these people were noticeably older than the postwar youth, sometimes by a decade. They had already commanded troops, sent people to their death, seen untold evil and destruction, liberated Europe, and returned home in triumph. Having come back to university halls and library desks, they were determined to make up for the "lost years." Many of them later chose a party or administrative career instead of intellectual and cultural pursuits. Others, however, became a vital addition to the postwar generation of intellectuals, indeed perhaps the most crucial one.

This generation had been brought up in the Stalinist system of education designed during the 1930s. In the early postwar years this system became ever more conservative. Boys and girls went to separate schools, and everybody had to wear uniforms. The postwar students included sons and daughters of the highest party leaders: Stalin's daughter Svetlana and the children of Viacheslav Molotov, Georgy Malenkov, and Nikita Khrushchev. Yet social elitism did not define the ethos of the postwar students. On the contrary, they turned out to be not only a numerous and dynamic group, but also a remarkably egalitarian and democratic-minded generation. Despite vast distance separating the children of the privileged party and state nomenklatura and the kids who came from the impoverished provinces or destitute countryside, they all were convinced that they were equal, and that great opportunities lay ahead of them.

Idealists and Veterans

Certain members of this generation were directly descended from the old Russian intelligentsia. They were not only those from the families of professors, doctors, writers, journalists, scholars, scientists, artists, and so on—those who had shared and tried to preserve the intelligentsia's ethos, habits, and values. Quite a few of them came from "common," uneducated families but had had a chance to grow up in downtown Moscow or Leningrad, where a concentration of intelligentsia types remained even during the 1930s, despite arrests and deportations. One such area of Moscow was the Arbat district, a lovely maze of crooked lanes lined with ancient mansions and turn-of-the-century apartment houses, located in the vicinity of the Kremlin and many government institutions. Before the Revolution, when democratic-minded intelligentsia, educators, artists, and physicians had lived side by side with gentry and other groups, the district had acquired a certain renown. After the Revolution and during the 1930s the population of the Arbat became even more diverse: thousands of people from all parts of the Soviet Union moved in, compressing the available space in communal apartments and filling the courtyards with their children. Many of these people belonged to the emerging party elites and had been able to move to Moscow because of their service to the Bolshevik regime. Among them were many Jews, but also Georgians, Armenians, Latvians, and people of other ethnic origins, some of them educated and assimilated into the Russian culture, some of them not. Most remarkably, the melting-pot of the Arbat did not reject the old culture of the intelligentsia, but rather absorbed and preserved it. The "children of Arbat" went during the 1930s to schools where most teachers were still of prerevolutionary vintage. Most communal apartments in the Arbat were tiny, yet overflowing with books from old private libraries. The "culture of the Arbat," as one scholar of this district describes it, was the traditional culture of the rank-and-file intelligentsia of the late nineteenth century, somewhat influenced by the "Silver Age" trends in art and music. This culture presupposed aversion to nationalism and to anti-Semitism. It was also based on romantic relations between genders, and above all the conviction that "history is reasonable and develops in a good and positive direction." The kids from the Arbat district also inherited another cardinal principle from the old intelligentsia: a sense of social duty, of responsibility for the country, and a need for personal engagement.[3]

The Arbat was, of course, not the only locale where the cohorts of young postwar intellectuals and artists grew up. There was the Institute for Philosophy, Literature, and History—a Soviet analogue of the Ecole Normale Supérieure in France. There was also the Institute of Literature in Moscow, where mature writers and poets taught seminars to aspiring youth with an interest in the humanities, preparing the best of them to become the shapers and creators of culture. Other university-level institutions of higher learning were re-created in the 1930s as workshops for educated Soviet elites. Yet those elites—the Bolshevik vanguard, the majority of the Old Bolsheviks, Red Army marshals and generals, numerous "Red professors," and hundreds of leftist writers—perished in the dungeons of the secret police, in the camps of the gulag, and in mass graves on execution fields. That great bloodletting deprived the revolutionary and Soviet past of its heroes and replaced them all with the towering effigy of the Great Leader, Stalin. The terror destroyed and erased from public memory the role models of their youth—among them Nikolai Bukharin, Marshal Mikhail Tukhachevsky, and the writers Isaac Babel and Boris Pilniak. Most of the survivors of the terror at universities and other cultural institutions were, paradoxically, the professors who did not share the communist idealism. They, who had instead been brought up in the nineteenth-century traditions of liberalism and humanism, could not help passing on to their students their manners, habits, ethical standards, and aesthetic attitudes—while keeping their political views to themselves.

Among the students at IFLI and the Institute of Literature, passion for Russian fine arts coexisted with the desire to transform Russia and the world. A few of these students were talented poets who later became the voice of the postwar and post-Stalin generation. Among them were Jews whose parents had moved to Moscow and abandoned their Jewish roots in the interests of adopting the new Soviet "motherland" and identity. David Kaufman (alias Samoilov) came with his family from Vilno. Pavel Kogan came from Kiev. Some were Russians whose parents had belonged to the peasantry or the provincial lower-middle class: they also left the "old Russia" behind and fervently identified with the new Soviet Russia. Sergei Narovchatov, a blue-eyed poet from a Russian town on the Volga, stood out among them. The most profound ambition of these revolutionary romantics was to sacrifice themselves in the coming battle with fascism and Nazism and to continue the great spiritual transformation of mankind that, as they believed, had begun with the Russian Revolution. They looked for kindred souls and found them, surprisingly, at the Moscow Institute of Law. At a time when Soviet jurisprudence and "socialist law" justified the extermination of "enemies of the people," Konstantin Simis, Boris Slutsky, Vladimir Dudintsev, and other law students attended a literary circle run by Osip Brik, a friend of famous poet Vladimir Mayakovsky. They invited poets from the Institute of Literature to a session. Slutsky, an aspiring poet from Kharkov, especially impressed them with his organizational skills, unusually broad erudition, and fervent belief in the world revolution.[4]

In 1940 this group of young people were passionately engaged in endless conversations about the future of the world, the imminence of a great war, and the duties of poets and intellectuals. They quickly proclaimed themselves the vanguard of their generation, at the very moment when the madness of Stalin's great terror was beating their predecessors to a pulp. Samoilov's private diary recorded his dismay at the devastating arrests and executions. Some of the young poets' classmates lost their parents in the purges and were harassed and ostracized as "children of enemies of the people." The young poets faced deeply troubling questions. Why did Vladimir Mayakovsky, the greatest bard of the Bolshevik Revolution, commit suicide? Why did the revolution from above cause famine in the countryside and necessitate the introduction of rationing in the cities? How could those who surrounded Lenin stoop so low as to become, as their death sentences stated, allies of fascists and Nazis against the Soviet Union? In 1939 came the shock of the Molotov-Ribbentrop Pact, which allied the Soviet Union with the Third Reich. Then came the Soviet Union's war of naked imperialism against Finland. Samoilov's diary during his teenage years reveals an inner struggle to refashion his soul and become fit for the future struggle, despite these seeming contradictions. Samoilov loved the Russian high culture of the nineteenth century, yet in the spirit of the times he tried to reject its humanism. He admired Lenin and Stalin, and feared he was not yet "up to standard" for joining the Komsomol. To be a person of action and sacrifice meant to defeat within oneself the "vagueness, nervousness, and hysteria" characteristic of non-Soviet intellectuals.[5]

Growing up in the prewar intellectual atmosphere of the Moscow districts and learning about Russian culture and art from their professors had left an indelible cultural mark on the group. Oleg Troianovsky, another IFLI student (from 1938 to 1941) and a future diplomat, recalls how during official demonstrations on May Day or the anniversary of the October Revolution his group of classmates, marching with the columns toward Red Square, would always shout out, at an agreed-upon spot, "Long live Boris Pasternak!"[6] This was several years after the Soviet press had criticized Pasternak and he had fallen out of favor with the authorities. Students in Moscow wanted to worship both Russian literature and the Revolution, and they saw no contradiction in that attitude. Yet above all they remained intoxicated with their youthful radicalism. The young poets of IFLI and the Institute of Literature did not want to escape to the margins of history. They were still convinced that Stalin and his regime constituted the only revolutionary force of the times. Instead of doubting Stalin and the Soviet state, the students in the group hoped to offer their services to them.[7] The coming war against Nazism, they believed, would be a battle between good and evil on a truly millenarian scale. There was no time for individual introspective reflections and doubts. In his diary Samoilov points out that "others," skeptics and realists, "felt contempt for our passion and fervor." In return, Samoilov wrote, "we disliked them."[8] From the fraternity-like atmosphere of this circle emerged the most important Soviet lyrical "message of this generation"—the poem "Brigantine." Kogan, its author, was a highly romantic, passionate, strong-willed, and doctrinaire member of the circle. He rhapsodized about "fierce and unyielding" young revolutionary fighters, those who "spurned comfort and tranquillity" in the name of sacrifice, adventure, and struggle. Kogan also wrote a poem calling on his generation to fight in every battle, "to reach the Ganges," and to "expand the motherland from England to Japan."

The Nazi invasion and the Great Patriotic War seemed to validate the views of the group, but it also endowed them with unimaginable experience. Many boys from the Arbat and other districts of Moscow and Leningrad immediately volunteered to fight. Yesterday's idealistic prophets shared the sobering and awful experience of military and social collapse in 1941–42, which included the sight of retreating troops, the rigidity and ineptitude of the Stalinist high command, German superiority in the skies and on the battlefield, and widespread panic in Moscow at the enemy's approach. They also experienced a historic reversal in the course of the war and rising waves of patriotism in the army and in society as a whole, as the Soviet army halted the Germans at Stalingrad.[9] During the war, the educated volunteers were inspired by the verse of older poets and writers, among them Ilya Ehrenburg, Konstantin Simonov, and Alexander Tvardovsky. As young officers, they learned to see the qualities as well as the limitations of their soldiers, Russian muzhiks from the collectivized villages, and saw things for which, as the older poet Ilya Selvinsky put it, "a language is as yet not created": Nazi concentration camps, ditches filled with Holocaust victims, scenes of senseless murder.[10] Finally, they participated in the conquest of Europe, which especially in Germany, Austria, Czechoslovakia, and Hungary displayed its splendid material civilization and cultural richness even in the midst of war's devastation. They never believed that they had participated in an occupation of Eastern and Central Europe. On the contrary, they felt that they had been part of a great liberating force, bringing much-needed social and political reforms. Slutsky was one of those who helped divide landed estates among the peasants in Romania and Hungary, thus overhauling the societies that had spawned Nazism and fascism, and helped organize "people's democracies." The pride of the victors was palpable. Nikolai Inozemtsev, an artillery intelligence sergeant and future director of the Institute for World Economy and International Relations in Moscow in the 1970s, wrote in his diary in July 1944: "Russians are the most talented, gifted nation in the world, with boundless capacities. Russia is the best country in the world, despite all our shortcomings and deviations." And on Victory Day he wrote, "All our hearts are overflowing with pride and joy: 'We Russians can do anything!' Now, the whole world knows it. And this is the best guarantee of our security in the future."[11]

In Europe many Soviet officers and soldiers did not live up to their image as liberators. They turned into marauding beasts. They pillaged houses of helpless German, Austrian, and Hungarian owners, and sent home war booty, from silk stockings and wrist-watches to tapestries, bicycles, and pianos. By contrast, the educated idealists brought home books—literature and philosophy—and precious vinyl records of classical music. In Prague and Belgrade, the cultural centers of the Russian émigré intelligentsia, Slutsky discovered the richness of Russian cultural heritage preserved there in libraries, numerous journals, and Russian churches. In dismay, some of the educated lieutenants and captains of the victorious army watched the frenzy of rapine, property destruction, murder of civilians, and rape on a mass scale.[12] Military journalist Grigory Pomerants, a former student at IFLI, was shocked at the end of the war by "the ugly things committed by heroes who had walked through the fire from Stalingrad to Berlin." If only the Russian people had the same energy to demand civil rights![13]

The war mercilessly mowed down the youth educated before the war, volunteers from Moscow, Leningrad, and other cities. About nine out of every ten who had volunteered did not return home. The cultural environment shaped by the old intelligentsia shrank disastrously. Leningrad, where over a million died during the Nazi siege—in addition to the tens of thousands lost during the Stalinist terror—suffered the greatest social and cultural damage. The Arbat district in Moscow became a rough place, invaded by social "outsiders" with little appreciation for its traditions.[14] The group of poets from IFLI and the Institute of Literature had been decimated. In 1942 Pavel Kogan was killed at the front. "Where young forest stood, only trees and stumps remained," wrote Slutsky later. Those who survived felt they had to live with special meaning and intensity—not only their own lives, but vicariously those of the friends who had perished. Initially, the survivors hoped that they would be able, with all their energy and skills, to reform and improve life in Russia. In 1945 some educated high-minded officers in the Soviet Army felt like the Decembrists, the young Russian officers who had returned to Russia from the war against Napoleon imbued with political liberalism and had later organized a military insurrection to introduce constitutional rule. One Soviet officer later recalled: "It seemed to me that the Great Patriotic War would inevitably be followed by a vigorous social and literary revival—like after the war of 1812—and I was in a hurry to take part in this revival." The young war veterans expected the state to reward them for their suffering and sacrifices "with greater trust and increased rights of participation, not just free bus passes."[15] Slutsky expressed this postwar mood in a curt formula: "Bow to no one!" Like the poets of the Proletkult after the Revolution, he dreamed of blending poetry and power to bring about change in Russia.[16]

The passion for poetry did not abate after the end of the war: from 1945 to early 1946, Pasternak, Akhmatova, and other poets spoke before large audiences in packed halls. Educated people in Russia continued to believe in the power of the word and the idea. A group of veterans became philosophy students at Moscow State University (MGU), men of insatiable curiosity. Yuri Levada, a student from the class of 1952, recalled: "It seemed as if there had never been such interesting people there before or since." Boris Grushin, a student from the same class, remembers that war veterans invigorated students by teaching philosophy "with new perceptions and assumptions, with a new vision of life, of the world." Similar to Slutsky, Samoilov, and the poets, this group of philosophers felt that it was their mission to discover the laws of human development not only in the books of Marx, Engels, and Lenin, but also in the writings of classical German and French philosophers. There were some who "spent the war with a volume of Hegel."[17]

The postwar years presented a serious test for the prematurely gray young intellectuals. In 1946 Stalin launched a vicious attack on what he considered the habit of "laxity" and attributed it to Western influences. Georgy Shakhnazarov, a young war veteran and a postgraduate student at the Moscow Institute of Law in 1949, later came to believe that the target of the *Zhdanovshchina* campaigns was not so much old cultural elites as postwar youth. Stalin realized that the war veterans "believed they were entitled to live as they deserved" and decided to thwart them. His solution was "to destroy their political innocence, to engage them in a pogrom against Jewish 'cosmopolitans' in university departments, party meetings, publishing houses, and other institutions of the ideological establishment."[18] The young idealists were slow to realize what was coming. Slutsky, Samoilov, and Sergei Narovchatov did not know how to interpret Zhdanov's attacks. The only reasonable explanations seemed to be a necessity to mobilize society for the Cold War. Samoilov recorded his conversations with Narovchatov. "The period of agreement with [Western] 'democracies' must inevitably come to an end," because prostrate Europe had become the theater of struggle between the Soviet Union and Western powers. The young theorists naively expected that Europe would become "socialist" and that the Communist International, disbanded by Stalin in 1943, would be restored, to promote world revolution.[19] Instead, Stalin chose great-power chauvinism, Russian nationalism, and anti-Semitism as his tools in restoring total control over Soviet society. Instead of offering advice to a company of attentive and understanding leaders, Slutsky had to earn a living by writing such shows for state radio as "People of the World Praise Their Great Leader." To make ends meet, Samoilov had to translate the Albanian poem "Stalin Is with Us" and similar propagandistic rubbish. The very air these young intellectuals breathed was filled with menace, terrifying enough to make them cringe at the sound of passing footsteps outside their door.

Still, the friends continued to meet and debate. Samoilov married in 1947, and the living room in his communal flat on Sretensky Boulevard in Moscow was often filled with guests. Among them were not only poets, but also physicists, economists, and historians. At the end of 1949 both Slutsky and Samoilov found a second home in an apartment owned by Yuri Timofeev, a student at the Institute of International Affairs. Yuri had a rich library, and a fine collection of medieval armor. Above all, he was a collector of human talent, of brilliant men and women. Besides Samoilov and Slutsky, the guests at Timofeev's gatherings included other poets and writers, scholars, playwrights, people in radio and film, actors and actresses, as well as other young people of quick wit and erudition who shared a love of high culture. As they had in the prewar years, the guests still liked to generate and discuss sweeping concepts and universal truths. Alexander Kazhdan, a young professor of Byzantine history at Moscow State University, shared his research findings. The physicist Lev Landau explained quantum mechanics, which was banned in the USSR as a "bourgeois science." Samoilov and Slutsky read poems that could not be published. Everybody sang songs they had brought home from the war or learned in the streets. Their idealism had survived the war, but no one was ready any longer to die on the battlefield for the creation of a universal "Soviet race." Fear inhibited discussion of politics. Instead, the conversations were about science, literature, and poetry, interspersed with humorous banter, music, and flirtations. One of the guests recalled, "We wanted to compensate ourselves for the four years that the war took away from us." Another profound and hidden motive was the desperate need to escape from the shabbiness and uniformity of contemporary Soviet life.[20]

In Stalinist Moscow during the years from 1949 to 1952, those informal and boisterous meetings were a wondrous oasis in the desert of Soviet repression for the hundred or so young men and women who frequented them. In early 1953 the Stalinist pogrom was about to erupt on a national scale after the arrests of the Kremlin doctors, many of them Jews. Most guests at Timofeev's gatherings felt danger breathing down their necks. Samoilov's father-in-law, Lazar Fogelson, was a Kremlin doctor, the only one who was not arrested, but it was only by accident. The secret police summoned both Samoilov and his wife, a student at the Institute of Foreign Languages, and tried to recruit them to inform on their friends.[21] In 1951 Slutsky could still tell Samoilov that he "liked Stalin on the whole." But a year later he also began to feel that his firm faith in the party and Stalin had been built on sand. He was convinced that there could be no future for him and the people in his circle.[22] He suggested disbanding the group, which was becoming too dangerous. Even a single report to the secret police could

The intellectual Yuri Timofeev, who was listed in Stalin's 1953 police file as the "leader of a Jewish terrorist center." In reality he was a collector of human talent—brilliant men and women from the postwar generation (Courtesy of Isay and Yevgenia Kuznetsov).

have landed many of the young participants in mortal danger. Many years later, it turned out that there had indeed been informers among that band of joyous friends. The secret police had started a file on "Y. P. Timofeev, leader of a Jewish terrorist center."[23]

It was a great loss for Russia that the energy and creativity of the young war veterans found no outlet. Slutsky, Samoilov, and dozens of other talented veterans could not publish anything while Stalin was alive. Their "truth from the trenches," their brilliant erudition and humor, remained untapped and unrecognized. Yet at least they remained alive, escaped Stalin's terror, and were able to wait for better times.

Postwar Students

Younger men and women born during the 1930s populated Moscow and Leningrad high schools and universities. Their youth had been scarred by war—it had left unforgettable wounds but also incomparable moments of remembered joy, such as Victory Day in 1945. Like the older educated intellectuals, the war veterans, these men and women were passionately patriotic and in many ways shared the universalist ideals and dreams of the prewar years. Leonid Gordon, who was a history student in the MGU class of 1953 and would become a sociologist in the 1960s, recalled, "All of us in our generation had a strong faith in socialist values, contempt for wealth and everything that we considered bourgeois. Our Soviet patriotism was strong."[24] Nail Bikkenin, a future adviser to Mikhail Gorbachev, who in 1947 was a student of philosophy at MGU, remembered that students "had faith in their country and its proclaimed ideals, in the sacred memories of the war, and [in the idea] that the USSR was a country of enormous possibilities and we had a lot of work ahead of us."[25] Ludmilla Alexeyeva became a history student at MGU in 1945. During the war, determined to volunteer at the front, she quickly obtained certification as a nurse, but she was not accepted because of her tender years. In her memoirs she wrote that the war had taught her to take responsibility as a citizen. She modeled herself on the wartime patriotic icon Zoia Kosmodemianskaia, a teenage Komsomol girl who was tortured to death by the Nazis in November 1941. Alexeyeva was ethnic Russian, yet when the anti-Semitic campaign began in the Soviet Union, she felt dismayed and confused. She asked her uncle how it could be compatible with the internationalist principles of Marxism-Leninism. Her uncle replied, "International principles, Marxism-Leninism—that is for fools like you. There is a band of brigands. They have power. And they use it." Alexeyeva told her husband, after the uncle left, "He is a wonderful man, but his thinking is primitive." She believed that all good educated people must join the party to improve it from within. She herself joined in 1951, at the age of twenty-four, and persuaded her husband to do the same.[26] She and others like her continued to measure the value of their lives by their ability to construct a better "socialist" society. Alexeyeva and her classmates flocked to university auditoriums in the expectation that their generation would master the knowledge necessary for constructing a true communist society and bringing about radical improvement of people's lives. Khrushchev's daughter, Rada Adzhubei, a student at MGU in the early 1950s, recalls, "The most important thing was that we were victorious and came out alive from the terrible war. We looked to the future with optimism. We believed that we could do everything, that in our country everything would turn out all right."[27] These feelings would stay with the postwar students as they grew up and began to occupy a prominent place in the intellectual and cultural life of Russia in the 1960s.

The openness of universities to all groups and the social and geographic diversity of university students remained impressive. Students came from industrial cities in the Urals, from faraway Siberian towns, and even from collective farms. One of them was nineteen-year-old Mikhail Gorbachev, the future leader of the Soviet Union, from a village near the Northern Caucasus, who became a student in the MGU law department in 1950. His wife, Raisa Titarenko, who had been born into the family of a railroad worker in a small town in the Altai Mountains, in the heart of Eurasia, became a student of philosophy at MGU in 1949. The MGU dorm was a "little Soviet Union," populated by students from many regions and many ethnic backgrounds. For all of them, life in Moscow, with its symphony orchestras and art galleries, the Bolshoi, and the Moscow Art Theater, offered the first encounter with high culture and the fine arts. Gorbachev in his memoirs recalls a student club at MGU, where famous classical actors and singers performed for the student audience. "This was a remarkable tradition of a creative intelligentsia going back to the prerevolutionary era."[28]

The boundless, sparkling optimism of this group contrasted with the postwar misery, famine, and devastation around them. Even Moscow, the capital city, was in reality a far cry from the idealized images of propaganda. Students who lived in Moscow, with a few exceptions, never had a room of their own to study in; usually, because of urban overpopulation and the lack of large-scale housing construction in Stalin's Russia, they slept, ate, and studied in the cramped conditions of deteriorating communal flats. Behind and above them loomed several pompous skyscrapers constructed on Stalin's orders by gulag prisoners to adorn the victorious capital. One of them, hidden in scaffolding until 1953, was a monumental university building that towered over Moscow from Lenin Hills. Meanwhile, the MGU dormitory where all incoming students lived, 32 Stromynka Street, was a huge barracks with a mile-long quadrangle of corridors, common facilities, and crowded rooms where at least six and often up to sixteen students lived together.[29]

It was common to see students dressed in secondhand war dungarees, rumpled jackets and pants, or high-school uniforms. The residents were satisfied with their living conditions and did not perceive them as inadequate—especially in the context of widespread misery following the war. Students lived off the stipend the state paid them and even managed to send some rubles to their relatives. The material benefits of studying and taking up a profession were not discussed: the majority of students wanted to devote themselves to high culture and the life of the spirit. Considerable prestige attached to intellectual professions after the war. The state, reacting to the great deficit of educated people and scientists, raised salaries for professors sharply, along with stipends and scholarships for postgraduate studies at privileged colleges. The first postwar generation of students would provide the initial pool for supplementing the remnants of educated cadres that had survived the purges and the war. These newcomers were convinced that they would be the vanguard of an fair and egalitarian society. Many of them would later benefit from incredible upward social mobility, similar to that experienced by the cohort of Stalinist appointees during the 1930s.[30]

The rapid onset of the Cold War and the confrontation with Western democracies, recent allies in the conflict against Nazi Germany, produced no noticeable doubts or rifts among students. The creation of "people's democracies" in Eastern Europe, the communist revolution in China, the Korean war, and the seeming advance of communist forces in Western Europe appeared to prove that communism represented the wave of the future. A Polish student who came to MGU in 1953 recalled that nobody around him felt any guilt about the Soviet partition of Poland in 1939 or later crimes against the Poles; quite the opposite: everyone expected the Poles to be grateful to Soviet Russia for liberating them, establishing new Polish borders in the West, and helping set up "the progressive social order" in Poland.[31]

The anti-Semitic campaigns of 1948–1953 affected students, especially those from Muscovite Jewish families, and some Jewish professors, but these campaigns did not alter the mainstream students' optimism. No anti-Semitism was apparent at the grassroots level. Some of the students believed that the campaign was a bizarre deviation, perhaps an error that would eventually be corrected. "The great majority of students from my class were conformist," one former history student from the class of 1953 later recalled. "We not only thought, we firmly *knew*, that our country was the vanguard force of mankind, evoking the admiration and envy of the entire world." Zdeněk Mlynář, a Czech student who lived in the same dorm room as Mikhail Gorbachev, recalled, "We both had been supporters and proponents of Communist ideology in the form in which it had existed in Stalin's time. And that left its mark on the process of our formation as individuals." Most of the MGU students continued to trust Stalin and all his declarations, even during the anti-Semitic campaign.[32]

Fear was present, of course, but it was not the predominant motivation, and it is almost absent from the recollections and diaries of the majority of the postwar students. (By contrast, it was *the* motivating factor in the behavior of the Jewish student minority.) More important still, the youngest among the students only vaguely remembered the Great Terror of the 1930s and learned to look elsewhere when arrests took place—to ignore the dark side of Soviet reality. Mainstream students during the Stalin era formed a seemingly happy brotherhood of the young, espousing the ideals of equality, justice, truth, and hatred of racism and militarism. Yuri Burtin, a future literary critic for the journal *Novy Mir,* and in 1951–1953 a student of philology and literature at Leningrad State University, recalled in his memoirs that he partook of this common identity. "Since childhood we had lived in a totalitarian society and knew no other. It was the norm for us, and few argued with the norm."[33] Burtin also remembered the "militarism of mentality that fed on the logic of the Cold War." Like other students, he was convinced that the state and society were more important than the individual, and that the Soviet leadership, Stalin in particular, knew best in which direction everyone should move.[34] This revolutionary-romantic identity, however, made the postwar students malleable clay in the hands of the totalitarian regime.

The students' daily existence was outwardly politicized. They attended numerous Komsomol meetings, where they were allowed to simulate "political democracy" by nominating their candidates and arguing about their agenda (although the party and Komsomol leaders always called the shots). Students went to official rallies on Red Square, read Stalin's "Short Course" on party history, as well as his articles on linguistics and political economy, and discussed the content. At the same time, the dictates of ideology began to exist separately from real life in their minds. This bifurcation allowed students to combine common sense and total faith in the Soviet regime and its propaganda.[35] "We lived in an absolutely congested, regulated world," recalls Rada Khrushchev-Adzhubei, "where it was absurd and criminal even to think about any kind of criticism of Lenin and Stalin. We were born into it and believed in it without asking questions."[36] As had been true of children of enemies of the people in the 1930s, students whose relatives were in prison or in the camps sought to "erase" the fact from their consciousness and redoubled their efforts to merge with the mainstream. The existing order became the accepted structure. As far as one could judge, students of the late 1940s–early 1950s increasingly diverted their energy into nonpolitical activities: active tourism, with tents and backpacks, field trips to distant areas of the Soviet Union, work on archeological sites, outdoor sports such as soccer and cross-country skiing, and, of course, dancing and dating.

Still, the disquieting trends and events of the last years of Stalin's life could not avoid raising eyebrows even among the mainstream students. They could not help wondering when the entire country seemed to genuflect before the "great leader" during Stalin's seventieth birthday celebration in December 1949. Huge pharaohlike statues of Stalin were erected around the empire. In Moscow overzealous officials transformed the Museum of Fine Arts, opened with the support of the intelligentsia in the late nineteenth century, into the collection of presents that a grateful population had sent to Stalin. The deafening crescendo of acclamation in the cult of Stalin grated on the ear and insulted the general sense of propriety. Even more perplexing were the "scientific discussions" and campaigns of 1948–1951 against "idealism and Western influences" in philosophy, biology, physics, and linguistics. Such world-famous physicists as Einstein and Bohr were attacked, along with their theories. T. D. Lysenko, an autodidact-agronomist and the sworn enemy of genetic studies, "routed" all his academic critics with Stalin's support, and the Soviet media began to call genetics "a paid servant of imperialism." The same vulgar anti-Western label was attached to a new discipline of "cybernetics," which the American Norbert Wiener defined as a study of control and communications systems in machines and organisms. In June 1950 Pravda published Stalin's article "On Marxism in Linguistics," which criticized the dominant scientific school, and the entire discipline immediately reversed itself, praising Stalin as a choryphaeus of science. Students had to memorize the article by heart.[37]

The Kremlin doctors' affair in January 1953 dismayed anyone who was not deaf and blind. Those who believed in Stalin's infallibility were asked to credit that the doctors were indeed poisoning people for political purposes. Rada Khrushchev's classmate and husband, Alexei Adzhubei, had just graduated and begun to work for the newspaper Komsomolskaia Pravda. On January 13, 1953, Alexei was told to write an editorial about the "Doctors' Plot." When he saw the names of the indicted doctors, he momentarily passed out: one of the doctors was a family physician of the Khrushchevs, a gentle and straightforward person.[38] Yet Adzhubei's faith in Stalin's wisdom did not waver, and terror of dissenting made most others of that generation turn a blind eye to the enormity being perpetrated.

Rebels and Jazzmen

Among the youngest of the "children" growing up in the last years of Stalin's life were some who carried their youthful idealism to its logical conclusion. They had learned at school about the heroes of the nineteenth century, the resisters and victims of political repressions, including the People's Will terrorists who had assassinated the tsar. And what students saw at schools and universities, and in their families, convinced them that the revolution had been "betrayed," and that their own teachers and parents were servants of the repressive regime. A few fearless youngsters organized secret societies to prepare a "revolution" against the "tyrannical Stalinist regime." Secret police files and other documents about their underground activities reveal that these rebels had grown up naive Stalinists, true believers who were passionate about their Komsomol membership. They reacted to the state-sponsored cynicism, misery in the countryside, the privileges of the party apparatchiks, and above all to the corruption, crass materialism, and conformism of the bureaucracy, which they likened to the prerevolutionary petty bourgeoisie (meshchanstvo). They were too young and romantic to conceal their doubts and blend in. The groups never lasted long, and their members met with a cruel fate, either long terms in the labor camps or execution.[39] The phenomenon of "naive Stalinism" was especially strong among youth of Jewish descent, children of privileged officials, and those who had been inspired by the Russian literature of the nineteenth century. Naum Korzhavin, a student at the Institute of Literature who was arrested in 1947 by the MGB (a predecessor of the KGB), recalled, "I believed that the atmosphere of the triumphant petty bourgeoisie around me was killing the ideals of communism. Everything around me seemed to be phony, above all my teachers (nothing surprising: they were afraid). It seemed that the bourgeois-minded bureaucrats had seized power and honest communists got arrested."[40]

Many more young men and women did not risk their lives by going underground. They, like the guests at Timofeev's place, gathered in small groups with the aim of *escaping* from the mortal danger of politics into high culture and science. Some of them realized the futility and suicidal nature of struggle against the regime. Others, who still wanted to trust Stalin, did not even dream of such a struggle. The official educational curriculum did not satisfy their intellectual and artistic curiosity. The rapid shrinking of permissible cultural choices as a consequence of *Zhdanovshchina* left all the schools and styles beyond the pale except those prescribed, such as socialist realism and "Soviet patriotic art." The campaigns to root out entire disciplines and fields of science and art, the disappearance of many banned books from public libraries, and other repressive measures evoked covert resistance among those young men and women. They had acquired a great appetite for forbidden cultural and intellectual fruits, and so they coalesced in groups of trusted friends, functioning as informal literary and musical societies. A truly extraordinary group of students from the Academy of Art and the department of philosophy at MGU wrote "reports" for one another on theosophy, genetics, and other disciplines banned in the Soviet Union. In public these students posed as an innocent band of carefree youth, drinking, and composing and singing student songs. A bunch of Leningrad students discussed music by Sergei Prokofiev, Dmitry Shostakovich, and Vano Muradeli, the composers selected for party criticism after 1947.[41]

The tightly controlled Soviet cultural sphere and the squalidness of everyday life only increased the search by urban youth for entertainment and their own, "generational" music and styles. Stalinist policies were not consistent in this regard. On one hand, after some hesitation, the state authorities authorized partial release of German and American films captured in Europe. These were mostly musicals, light-hearted comedies, and soap operas, films with Glenn Miller's orchestra, the *Tarzan* series with Johnny Weismuller and *His Butler's Sister* with Deanna Durbin.[42] On the other hand, in 1948, as the anticosmopolitan campaign in Soviet propaganda turned shrill, the Soviet media and propaganda apparatus lashed out against "aping of Western styles and fashions" among the "unstable part" of Soviet youth. The attack's main targets were *stiliagi*—"style apers."

According to the Soviet behavioral canon, young men had to dress conservatively and frugally, and young women could never use makeup. Defying these conventions, reported the Soviet satirical magazine *Krokodil,* was the main aim in life for the *stiliagi.* The magazine's cartoons and caricatures showed young men between sixteen and twenty-one years old who resembled American zoot-suiters of the 1940s: they wore extremely narrow trousers, very broad-shouldered jackets, huge ties, and high platform shoes, and often sported a bobbed hairstyle. All items of clothing, especially the tie, were of fantastic tropical design and color. The *stiliagi's* female partners dressed in similarly provocative fashion and wore wild hairdos and large amounts of makeup. Although Soviet students were supposed to dance the way their parents danced, to tuneful orchestral pieces, *stiliagi* mimicked the American "dirty dances" of the 1940s, such as the jitterbug and the boogie-woogie, to the sound of jazz. They had obviously learned them from a privileged few who had traveled abroad with parents who were Soviet officials. Stories and caricatures depicted style-mongers as deviants, above all as social "parasites" and "spongers" off their parents' income.[43]

Many *stiliagi* were children of the state and military elite, top engineers, and secret police officials. Despite, or rather because of, the campaign for cultural regimentation and eradication of "decadent" Western influences, a freer style in clothes, music, and behavior became irresistible to a minority of the postwar generation. Everyday Russian life was threadbare, bleak, and uniformly dingy—devoid of anything bright and colorful. Soviet people were wretchedly dressed after the war, in ugly, ill-fitting clothes. But was this the only reason for the phenomenon of *stiliagi*? Their emergence pointed also to important social and psychological changes, which the *stiliagi* picked up on. It became "hip" to relax and enjoy life. In the absence of new and fascinating ideas in the late 1940s, there were fresh and fascinating things to see and to possess. Postwar students saw "trophies" that veterans brought back from Europe, including American-made radios and vinyl records with American jazz. And the famous four parts of *Tarzan* created a sensation among Moscow and Leningrad school kids. Joseph Brodsky, the future poet and Nobel laureate, was fascinated by the American "trophy" items as a kid in Leningrad. He also recalled, with the exaggeration of hindsight, that Johnny "Tarzan" Weismuller's guttural jungle yell "did more for de-Stalinization than all of Khrushchev's speeches."[44] Vasily Aksyonov, the future Russian writer who was a style aper in the city of Kazan in those years, recalled the effect of the first postwar screenings of Hollywood films. "There was a time when my peers and I conversed mostly with citations from those films. For us it was a window into the outside world from the Stalinist stinking lair."[45]

The style apers were not as antipatriotic as their officious critics claimed. There were those among the fans of style who dreamed of overthrowing the Stalinist regime. Yet most of them accepted Soviet realities as a given and just wanted "to have fun." In their eyes Soviet propaganda films could not compete with musicals from Hollywood and Europe. Music and songs by Isaac Dunaevsky and other Soviet composers attracted them less than the works of Glenn Miller, Benny Goodman, Duke Ellington, Louis Armstrong, and Ella Fitzgerald. "Sun Valley Serenade," "Chattanooga Choo-Choo," and "My Melancholy Baby" became tribal mantras for this contingent of urban youth.

Passion for jazz became the most conventional route for the transition from the Soviet mainstream to the world of Western "style." Jazz was banned in the USSR after 1948, and numerous teenagers who had already fallen in love with it during the war and after suddenly found themselves in the cultural underground. The party's propaganda attempt to ostracize both jazz and those who listened to it began to alienate these youngsters from the regime and quite often from their parents, who were its loyal servants. Alexei Kozlov, who loved jazz from childhood, recalled that his "dissent" began in the early 1950s when he expressed his displeasure about the Soviet ban on jazz to his parents. Alexei's father, a true party believer and well-established university professor, "trembled with wrath when he heard the hoarse voice of Louis Armstrong on the radio." Paradoxically, the same father, whom his son viewed as a "fanatic," procured everything Alexei asked for, including a shortwave radio set, one of the first tape recorders, and even U.S.-made clothes and boots—the last obtained in the special stores for privileged officials.[46]

The anti-*stiliagi* publications and cartoons as well as the party propagandists who guided them committed a grave error. They publicized the new youth "counter-elite." Instead of tabooing the style phenomenon, *Krokodil,* the satirical magazine, with its extensive circulation, introduced the *stiliagi* to a large audience. A growing trickle of imitators appeared at dance parties and in the streets. Komsomol gangs hunted *stiliagi* down and beat them severely. The Komsomol activists and vigilantes fought them, cut their tight slacks, and broke their records. In some cases groups of *stiliagi* ambushed the Komsomol patrols and paid them back in kind.[47] The more *stiliagi* became the target of public hostility, however, the more they appeared to be the vanguard of a new wave. They even adopted the mocking term "style apers" as their sobriquet, to be worn with pride. An important goal caused their attributes and behavior to stand out amid the drab Soviet crowd: to look "American," or at least foreign. Of course, no part of the young rebels' elaborate wardrobe could be obtained in Soviet stores. "Specialists" remodeled Soviet-made clothing and shoes into "made-in-the-States" articles. Then there was the way the style apers behaved and talked among themselves. They used their own slang, full of new words, with the aim of making this jargon impenetrable for their parents as well as for others among the uninitiated. *Stiliagi* had their "Broadways": a downtown segment of Gorky Street in Moscow, part of Nevsky Prospect in Leningrad, and main streets in other Soviet cities. They had an elaborate code of behavior, whether in their "cafés" or at parties. The gatherings of style-mongers were extremely exclusive and male-dominated; their girlfriends clearly occupied a lower tier in their milieu, although they were indispensable to social life, especially dancing and casual sex. The right kind of girlfriend had to love jazz, dance the foxtrot and the boogie-woogie, and at least pretend to be available for an uncomplicated sexual relationship.[48]

Naturally, all the elements of this imagined "style" generated a considerable demand for money and stimulated resourcefulness; not everybody had obliging and well-to-do parents. No wonder that, aside from the growing cultural rift with the mainstream, the young *stiliagi* would later come to challenge the basic economic wisdom and values of Soviet "socialism," the society where money was not supposed to be a fundamental value. More among them questioned the code and ideals of the "builders of communism" as their emphasis on the material aspects of style brought them into an acute conflict with the majority of their own age group as well as the rest of the Soviet public. For many of the rebels, the rejection of the "common life in misery" led to mockery of publicly proclaimed social justice and egalitarianism. The British journalist and historian Edward Crankshaw was surprised when, in casual conversations shortly after Stalin's death, he heard "charming, highly-educated youngsters speaking of the masses of the proletariat to whom the country is supposed to belong with a callousness and brutality which I have not encountered in the countries of Western Europe for many decades."[49] The representatives of the "working masses" replied with unmitigated hatred. There was clearly no love lost between the self-fashioned "elite" and the "plebeians."[50]

The young style apers created an imaginary America and an imaginary West, all that represented the antithesis of Soviet society. Alexei Kozlov became a friend of the high-flying Felix, whose privileged apartment looked right onto the courtyard of the U.S. Embassy. From there Kozlov was able to take a peek into "American territory" for the first time. Behind the high fence he glimpsed "cars of never-seen beauty, and children playing unknown games and speaking American." Later Kozlov recalled his anguish: he was looking at "the unachievable dream, at an unreachable planet." The two friends often sat on the windowsill, peering into the courtyard and "feeling a passionate love for all things American."[51] Joseph Brodsky observed that he and his friends tried to be "more American than the Americans themselves."[52] This "American dream" and the passionate belief in the existence of a "better world" on the Western side were the direct consequences of the Iron Curtain and would play a crucial part in the evolution of many intellectuals and artists from this generation. The imaginary West accompanied many postwar students as they grew up, and lasted into the 1960s, until some of they managed to go abroad for the first time.

From the start, the admirers of American style and jazz, as well as their broader following of imitators, engendered a dual conflict: between children and parents and between them and Soviet institutions, especially the school and the Komsomol.[53] At the same time, identities were not black and white. Most jazz lovers and famous future guitar balladeers, among them Vladimir Vysotsky, Yuri Vizbor, and Alexander Gorodnitsky, had never been style apers, although they absorbed some of their language and manners. And some of the Komsomol oppressors of *stiliagi* would later become avid advocates of Western-style openness and liberalization. American cultural influences did *not* lead automatically to anti-Soviet views among the young. Paradoxically, many of them recalled that love of jazz and fashionable clothing coexisted with unquestioning acceptance of the cult of Stalin. Yet the fans of American style were distanced from the romantic Stalinism of many of their peers; they created themselves in a different image from the rest of Soviet society. And this incipient alienation encouraged some of them to begin not only to have fun, but to think independently.

Stalin's Death and the Thaw

Stalin died on March 5, 1953, just when the stage had been set for an orgy of arrests, possibly a repetition of the Great Terror of the 1930s. Had it happened, this would inevitably have swept away many of the young intellectuals, not only war veterans, but also numerous students that were under the surveillance of the secret police and its informers. From March 6 to

March 8, 1953, Stalin lay in state in the Hall of Columns in the House of the Soviets, a former palace of Field Marshal Prince Dolgoruky near the Kremlin. Huge crowds rushed from all directions to this location, creating a terrible congestion in the narrow old streets of the capital. It was the first spontaneous appearance of the masses in Soviet streets since the Victory Day festivities. Then, the crowds had celebrated life and their survival. This time, the mass outpouring of energy ended in tragedy. The police and the military had neither experience nor instructions on how to prevent a stampede. Instead, the authorities made the stampede worse by stationing dozens of trucks to block the back alleys and lanes along the main streets where people accumulated. Hundreds of people were crushed and maimed.

The friends from Timofeev's gatherings did not go to the House of the Soviets. On March 9, 1953, while Stalin was being buried in the mausoleum next to Lenin, Samoilov and many of his friends were celebrating the birth of his first son. They merrily discussed the future. Their intuition told them that the worst was behind them.[54] Many from the "children's" generation went to bid farewell to Stalin. At the news of Stalin's death, anguish and uncertainty seized thousands of young educated men and women. The familiar order began to crumble when the Red pharaoh suddenly turned out to be mortal. "What would happen now?" One future dissident, then a senior philosophy student at Leningrad State University, was "suffocated by tears." The slogan "For the Motherland! For Stalin!" was not jarring to his ears.[55] Some, including even children of the victims of repression, suggested that the best students should now join the party, to support it as had been done in the wake of Lenin's death.[56] Even many Jewish students and young intellectuals, the targets of Stalin's last campaign, felt gripped by apprehension and wept, not knowing what the future would bring.

In Moscow many students risked their lives in the stampede to see Stalin lying in state. Mikhail Gorbachev stood for more than thirty hours in line and managed to view the dead leader.[57] The young poet Yevgeny Yevtushenko, a student at the Institute of Literature, was caught in the mob and realized with horror that it was crushing people against streetlights, telephone booths, and military trucks stationed to control the crowd. He survived only because he was tall, whereas short people, women, and adolescents suffocated or were dragged down. The sides of trucks were slick with blood. Police and young soldiers watched helplessly from the trucks, since they had no instructions. In an episode Yevtushenko described later in his

Precocious Autobiography, he undertook to act on his own, organizing a chain of strong young men that began to restrain the mob and save dying women. At that moment he felt a savage hatred for everything that had given birth to that criminal stupidity of the authorities.[58]

Bronislav Kholopov, an MGU sophomore, and his young girlfriend escaped from the stampede only to make another attempt to get to Stalin's body the next day. The scene of the previous day's tragedy was littered with innumerable buttons and galoshes. A woman wandered around the square, looking for a lost shoe; the entire back of her fur coat was torn away. Half-dead of frost, Kholopov and his fiancée made it to the House of the Soviets, where they saw Stalin in his coffin and many of the Kremlin leaders. After returning to the university they shared their experience with hundreds of students in a gigantic hall. Everyone wept. People said, "Lucky you. You buried Him. You will remember this all your life." Forty years later, Kholopov remarked, "The system and the secret police could mold such people in any way they wanted."[59]

Postwar students and many intellectuals were still mourning Stalin when the first shocking revelation came in April 1953: the Kremlin Doctors' Plot was bogus, a fabrication by the secret police, and consequently the entire anti-Semitic campaign was a sham as well. The official announcement acknowledged, for the first time, that the "confessions" of the doctors had been extorted under torture. On June 23 came another shock: Lavrenty Beria, Stalin's right-hand man and the head of the secret police, had been arrested as an "agent of international imperialism" and, more specifically, a "British spy." This was the beginning of a political awakening and an existential crisis for MGU students. Ludmilla Alexeyeva found herself "haunted by the image of our leaders around a dinner table, guzzling wine and vodka and plotting whom to kill next."[60] Party agitators tried to explain to students at the Stromynka dormitory that the party had made mistakes but had found the courage to admit them publicly. When the authorities themselves began to acknowledge their fallibility, the romantic cult of Stalin among students began to crumble. Fundamental changes were afoot.[61]

Yet students remained confused about the direction and nature of the changes. Many people were shocked to read criticism of the "cult of personality," along with the information on Beria's arrest. They could not understand why, after constant daily praise for the Great Leader, Stalin's name suddenly disappeared from newspapers, radio, and public discussions. The first anniversary of Stalin's death on March 5, 1954, came and went without mention in the media. Young intellectuals felt cheated, even offended by this omission. At the Stromynka dormitory they showed, as part of the Women's Day ritual, a Soviet film about a simple peasant woman who met Lenin and became a member of the Bolshevik government. When, in a final scene, Stalin enters a great hall to thunderous applause, the students of MGU also rose and began to applaud. An MGU student of philology, Igor Dedkov, suggested during a lecture that the audience should stand and commemorate Stalin's memory. These were the last gasps of reverent and romantic Stalinism. Yet, more significantly, it was the beginning of a genuine public self-expression that was out of step with the official tune.[62]

The fans of "style" were the second group among Soviet students after the Jews to begin to reflect on the changes. When one of them heard the news of Stalin's illness over the radio, he was struck by the phrase about the urine test. The great Stalin urinated like the rest of mankind! From that moment on the myth of Infallible Leader was shattered for this young man.[63] The *stiliagi* and jazz fans had special and immediate reasons for optimism: jazz music was in the air again. In November 1953 Yuri Gendler, a teenager from Leningrad, listened to a concert from the House of the Unions commemorating the anniversary of the Bolshevik October Revolution. After sections of pompous performance and classical music, the conductor's baton passed to Leonid Utesov, the Soviet jazz legend. And Utesov declared: "We are opening the second section with a tango, 'Splashes of Champagne.'" Decades later Gendler would remember his shock. For years the word "tango" had been banned, along with jazz and other types of Western music. Two months after Stalin's death the "splashes" sounded almost like an act of emancipation. Gendler astutely realized that big changes were under way. Indeed, with the disappearance of the Great Leader, the ban on jazz performances miraculously disappeared as well. For a while the noisy public campaign against the *stiliagi* also quieted down.[64]

Many in Moscow remembered the first years after Stalin's death, among other things, for the spectacular proliferation of *kompany*—circles of friends, informal groups consisting mostly of educated people in their twenties and thirties. It was common for a circle to number twenty, thirty, or even fifty people. Also, it was common for these circles to include professionals from different vocations: physicists and other scientists encountered novelists, poets, and artists; university professors and people in the

liberal arts met physicians and lawyers. Timofeev's parties lost their uniqueness after 1953. By comparison with Western student groups, *kompany* of
educated Soviet youth had far greater significance. The sociologist Vladimir Shlapentokh, who grew up in Moscow in the 1940s and 1950s, concludes that American society simply had no equivalent term to describe
"friendship among adults." Russian companions shared a passion for sport
and music, but also for ideas and the fine arts. Alexis de Tocqueville wrote
in his *Democracy in America* (1831) that Americans had learned to offset
their individualism by forming voluntary associations. In the Soviet Union,
where the regime sought to turn young people into obedient functionaries
and loyal professionals, many groups of friends functioned as substitutes
for nonexistent voluntary associations. Ludmilla Alexeyeva considered that
the bands of friends of the 1950s had sprung up as a social institution, serv-
ing this generation by fulfilling "a psychological, spiritual, perhaps even a
physiological need to discover their country, their history, and themselves."
What had been mortally dangerous only recently under Stalin now became
tolerated by the regime.[65] The large groups of friends became a substitute
for "publishing houses, salons, billboards, confession booths, concert halls,
libraries, museums, counseling groups, sewing circles, knitting clubs,
chambers of commerce, bars, clubs, restaurants, coffeehouses, dating agencies, and seminars in literature, history, philosophy, linguistics, economics,
genetics, physics, music, and the arts."[66] Some of these groups traced their
origins to the self-education groups of the late 1940s but were larger, more
diverse, and more open than these. The *kompany* also bore striking resemblance to the *kruzhki* (circles) where the Russian intelligentsia had developed in the 1840s and where in the first decade after the Revolution the
followers of that vanishing tribe had entrenched themselves, preserving
their intellectual and cultural habits and interests.

For a while, the biggest problem for these groups was where to meet.
One legacy of Stalinism was a terrible shortage of private space, and an extreme scarcity of cafés and other public venues for informal gatherings.
Among the *stiliagi* the designated meeting points were the Nord café in
Leningrad and the Cocktail Bar on Gorky Street in Moscow. Those who
lived in separate apartments (not communal flats) became extremely valuable assets for their companions. Andrei Mikhalkov-Konchalovsky recalls
that many members of his elite companies came to spend evenings in his
spacious apartment, owned by his privileged father, a high functionary in

the Union of Soviet Writers. They occasionally stayed overnight in the dining room, sometimes even sleeping on the floor under the old piano.[67]

The rise of such circles of friends, with their intense networking, offered alternative gathering points for human interaction, including relationships with the opposite sex. Groups of young companions were natural centers of dating and matchmaking. Countless young men and women met their partners there. Yet the absence of private space and life in communal apartments discouraged or undermined many romantic affairs. Allegedly, among bohemian *stiliagi*, many of whom had privileged parents possessing separate apartments, one could find a sex partner more easily, or so it was believed. Many, however, had to limit their courtship to dancing, long walks, and endless conversations. Mikhail Gorbachev recalled that he fell in love with Raisa in an instant and she soon shared his feelings, but the couple

Yuri Timofeev (left) and his friends in one of many *kompany* in Moscow during the Thaw. He told his little daughter that one day she would be proud to live in the country where the communist experiment had played out (Courtesy of Isay and Yevgenia Kuznetsov).

could only meet in the Stromynka dorm or at a student club. This obstacle hampered their intimacy.[68] At the same time, sex was not the center of the intellectual *kompany;* they offered deeper relationships. Male friendship, in particular, provided a crucial sociopsychological bond for the groups of young people of the 1950s.

The predominance of men in the bands of companions continued for many years after the war. Often a core group consisted of a few men who trusted one another absolutely and consulted one another on all important issues. The psychological distance between the members of this group was minimal; they felt they could spend an eternity together.[69] Intellectual *kompany,* in contrast to the rest of the society, also offered equality and respect to many educated young women. In general, Russian women had a very hard time of it, because Stalinism promoted male chauvinism and because twelve to seventeen million men had been lost during the war. Many women had to raise children alone, without male assistance or alimony.[70] Foreign visitors until the early 1960s described young Soviet women as vulgar, badly dressed, and lacking in feminine charm. In intellectual circles, women flourished and found freedom from household chores. Ludmilla Alexeyeva was one of them. After her graduation from Moscow State University, she entered into a marriage of convenience and had children "like everybody else." At the same time, she and her friend Natasha met a group of older men who had been imprisoned in 1946 for forming a mock association, "brotherhood of penniless sybarites." In the safer environment of the Thaw those men formed a vibrant circle of friends. Each woman contributed her erudition or professional expertise to the group's pool of knowledge. Ludmilla produced "reports" on what she found in the numerous volumes of Lenin's work and old Bolshevik papers she read at that time, in an attempt to trace the transformation of Bolshevism into Stalinism. Natasha, an expert on Spain and Cuba, told the group what she read in Spanish-language press and learned from Spanish ex-pats who had moved to the Soviet Union after the Spanish Civil War. Alexeyeva found her true love and intellectual partner among the "penniless sybarites" and divorced her husband. Her children stayed with her.[71]

A major social function of the circles was to provide an environment that would foster self-education. A handwritten student journal, *In Search,* produced in October 1956 by the philology students at Ural State University, described this motive well. "The humanities have been destroyed in our country, stripped to the bone during the last twenty sorrowful years. There is nobody to restore them, except ourselves. What should we do? Our teachers cannot give us everything. We are in the need of self-education."[72] As the atmosphere was gradually oxygenated with hope and initiative after 1953, young people avidly sought to form new connections and friendships. People struck up conversations, and subsequently relationships, while waiting in long lines for much-coveted books, or to buy tickets to much-discussed theater plays, or by sharing literary news in a library reading room. Alexeyeva found new opportunities for friendship and intellectual interaction in the basement of the Lenin Library in Moscow, where people discussed articles in the literary journal *Novy Mir* from 1953 to 1955—and often disagreed over them.[73]

As the site of informal discussion clubs, student dormitories played an extraordinary role in those years. Graduates of Moscow State University in 1954–55, Gorbachev among them, recalled that the lights in the Stromynka dorm stayed on during the night. Students stayed up all night long, exchanging ideas and discussing literary news. Mikhail and Raisa met in a dorm room with their young classmates, philosophers and jurists, among them Merab Mamardashvili, a Georgian, and Yuri Levada, a Russian. Mamardashvili would later become an original interpreter of neo-Kantian philosophy; Levada would revive Russian sociology and launch Russia's first independent public opinion center. Back then, they were still orthodox Marxist-Leninists; but what counted more was that in circles of intimates they were "normal"—that is, sincere and honest friends and associates, not hacks or informants. In the first sign of departure from the totalitarian identity of the 1930s, post-Stalin youth culture began to consider any reporting on informal student life as a betrayal. Openly "anti-Soviet" political remarks were still the exception in these kinds of companies, but most of the time the perpetrator would be reprimanded by the members of the company itself and the indiscretion would be concealed from the authorities.

Seeking Honesty in Literature

Between 1953 and 1955 this growing world of circles of friends, where the postwar generation of students and young intellectuals socialized, eagerly welcomed every signal of change and liberalization following Stalin's death.

It was a time of renewed hope and of social and intellectual awakening in Russia. Hundreds of thousands of men and women began to return from the concentration camps and rejoin society. The World War II veterans whose expectation of a better and freer life after the victory had been shattered by Stalin got their second wind. Russian cultural, scientific, and educational institutions mushroomed, fed by the influx of postwar university students and graduates. Those years later came to be known as the Thaw, after a novel by Ilya Ehrenburg published in May 1954. It was a metaphor that transformed the idea of time and change. Whereas Stalinist propaganda had presented the postwar years as a time of red-hot dynamism and feverish progress, Ehrenburg's phrase equated them with the long winter and paralyzing frost. It hinted that the melting of the old order that had repressed society and culture had already begun and might—or might not—turn into spring.

Anatoly Cherniaev, a war veteran and a classmate of poet David Samoilov, wrote in his memoirs that in the years after Stalin's death "everything honest, healthy, ethical that had been surviving for several decades in this deceived and maimed society began to boil like geysers under the surface of the dead sea, attracting everybody's attention. And as it had been the case many times in Russian history, the leader and avatar in the liberation of minds was literature."[74] By the early 1950s, Russian literature seemed a lifeless landscape. The officious pseudoliterature of socialist realism degenerated into a form of propaganda that concocted an imaginary "ideal" world populated by archetypes of Soviet people, not by thinking men and women with hearts and souls.[75] As Trofim Lysenko created a powerful faction in biology that marginalized and harassed talented geneticists, Soviet literature underwent a similar process. The Lysenkos of literature were hacks elevated by the regime to the position of watchdogs of socialist realism. The monumental enterprise of socialist realism, however, had significant flaws. The pseudoliterature it created was low-quality pulp fiction, pretentious and artificial. It promoted the middle-class virtues of comfort and conformism along with conservative aesthetics and imperial chauvinism.[76]

Most writers reacted to Stalin's death in the same way as the rest of the society. Konstantin Simonov felt that some part of his life had ended. He sat down to express his feelings in verse but, unexpectedly, burst into tears. He later recalled: "I did not cry out of sorrow or out of pity for the deceased: these were not sentimental tears, they were the tears that result from shock."[77] An editor of the *Literaturnaia Gazeta,* he penned an editorial of encomium: "Now, for many years ahead, our Soviet literature has one major task—to recreate the image of Stalin, the greatest genius of all times and peoples, in all its fullness." This editorial infuriated Nikita Khrushchev, the new leader of the party secretariat, so much that he demanded that Simonov should be fired. Another talented poet, Alexander Tvardovsky, also wept privately over the death of the "great man," and was later morally troubled by the sudden silence about Stalin in the media. Tvardovsky had had to distance himself from his family when it was exiled during the collectivization, and he felt ashamed of it. So many years after the fact, he must have felt that a renunciation of the late leader would have been an indication of moral cowardice.[78]

Soon, however, the rumor of changes began to spread through the Union of Soviet Writers. Some writers believed that head of state Georgy Malenkov supported cultural liberalization. In August and September 1953, Alexander Fadeev, the head of the union, sent two secret letters to the new Kremlin leaders seeking clarification. He admitted that there was no longer vibrant literature in Russia. He wrote: "How is it possible that during the last century and a half of the existence of the old Russia, despite the ferocious resistance of the most reactionary tsarist regime to everything progressive, there emerged plenty of writers, composers, actors, and artists in every decade, distinguished not only during their time but also many decades later. And in our day, when the socialist order in the USSR has been in existence for almost half a century, with the communist leadership being the most progressive power, we have had allegedly only one great poet, Mayakovsky, and after him literature came to a grinding halt."[79] Fadeev cautiously suggested that Stalinist regimentation in cultural affairs was excessive: it throttled creative efforts. The existing system, he wrote, gave too much power to the army of half-educated bureaucrats: editors, publishers, directors, bureaucrats in the creative unions and in the Ministry of Culture, and regional party bosses. Many of them, he complained, were too "unqualified, ignorant, and rude" to handle the delicate task of controlling culture. Fadeev, never a liberal in cultural affairs, suggested establishing a "special connection" between the Kremlin leadership and the leading writers and artists. If the top leadership "could take under its immediate observation and guidance ten to fifteen of the best writers in the country and would deal with the ideological and creative dynamics in the writers' union in its entirety, then our Soviet literature would make great strides forward."[80]

No response to Fadeev's letters was forthcoming. Yet on November 27,

1953, *Pravda* published an article, signed by the anonymous "Spectator," which defined socialist realism as broadly as it had originally been defined in 1934 by Gorky and Bukharin: as a principle that allowed "unbelievable freedom of development" for a plurality of literary schools and "preserved the artist's right to independence." This article sent a signal of hope to the cultural elites. Some writers, musicians, and artists began to speak about a possible repeal of the *Zhdanovshchina* decrees. People who had suffered during the anticosmopolitan campaign began to talk about "some kind of ideological NEP," alluding to the period in the 1920s, which in retrospect appeared as the time of unimaginable freedoms. And Fadeev began to inquire whether one could declare amnesty for all the writers attacked and ostracized after 1945.[81]

Alexander Tvardovsky, the editor of a leading Moscow literary journal, *Novy Mir,* decided to help the party leadership by initiating a discussion on cultural policies and the task of culture. With his connections in the party apparatus, he knew about the uncertainty and disagreements among the Kremlin leaders.[82] Tvardovsky also had his own hopes for a better future. He leaked the news that he was finishing a sequel to Tyorkin's saga. This time he put the Russian folk hero into "another world," an imaginary life after death, where Tyorkin, to his amazement, found just the kind of institutions, norms, and rules that had prevailed in Stalin's state and society. Only Tyorkin, a spontaneous personality, was alive in this kingdom of "dead souls." Even as Tvardovsky continued to mourn Stalin's death, his innate honesty, humor, and irony led him in the direction of de-Stalinization.

In December 1953 Tvardovsky launched the most significant public discussion of the issues with a series of essays by Vladimir Pomerantsev in *Novy Mir,* entitled "On Sincerity in Literature." Literature, Pomerantsev argued, cannot exist without talent and honesty on the part of the author. Prefabricated books that "varnish reality" are above all boring; they contradict their readers' common sense and offer nothing to their minds and souls. Literary critics, instead of testing the patriotic and ideological credentials of the author (a jab at the anticosmopolitan campaign), should stick to their actual business, criticizing bad books and helping talented writers. The conflicts and "vulgarities of life" should be the focal point of literature. Pomerantsev's unassuming style and his Socratic manner of argument contrasted with the bombastic and cliché-ridden literary essays produced by Stalinist critics. In the postwar years Pomerantsev lived in East

Germany, working for the Soviet Military Administration. Even there, he seemed to breathe air less stale than that in Moscow.[83] In a society debased and defiled by Stalinism, his essays calling a spade a spade produced a sensation. It was as if one suddenly came upon a normal mirror in a hall of twisted reflections. The term "varnishing of reality" challenged the established literary hierarchy of late Stalinism.

It was not the quality of Pomerantsev's essays and other Thaw publications that made literature the herald of liberalization. Rather it was the special role of Russian literature in general in the worldview and education of the postwar generation. During World War II a bond had already been forged between them and talented writers and poets. Tvardovsky's poems about Soldier Tyorkin, Simonov's lyrics, and Ehrenburg's fiery reporting survived the postwar crackdown. Some exceptions also punctuated the grayness of late Stalinist literature toward the end of the 1940s. Certain novels about the war provide at least some presentiment of the true tragedy and complexity of life, such as *Star,* by Immanuel Kazakevich, *Front-Line Stalingrad,* by Viktor Nekrasov, and *A Story about a Real Man,* by Boris Polevoi. Many students also devoured the Russian classics, including works by Pushkin, Gogol, Tolstoy, Chekhov, and Herzen, as well as by Vladimir Korolenko and Konstantin Paustovsky. The works of Fyodor Dostoevsky, Sergei Yesenin, and numerous poets and writers of the past were banned from Soviet libraries. Some students got banned books from their home libraries. After 1946 the poems and novels of Akhmatova and Zoshchenko, denounced by Stalin, continued to be circulated in handwritten and typed copies. Small groups of young, well-educated Russians found refuge in the libraries, reading any world classic that could be found there. It was customary for young book lovers in those days to enter lengthy excerpts of the books they read, along with their thoughts about them, in their diaries.[84]

Pomerantsev's article gave numerous bands of students a welcome focus for discussion. They linked the dismal state of the arts in the USSR with economic and social problems. There still was no political framework for addressing this issue. Pomerantsev, however, proposed a moral framework: Why could the people who had won that monumental war not be treated like adults and told the bitter truth? Should the class struggle justify dishonesty and "varnishing" of reality? During the first months of 1954 the universities in Moscow, Leningrad, Sverdlovsk (Yekaterinburg), and other cities were abuzz with talk about "sincerity in literature." Discussions among students resembled the debates about Nikolai Chernyshevsky's articles in Russia's "progressive society" a hundred years earlier. At MGU a group of graduate and postgraduate students expressed their solidarity with Pomerantsev in a collective letter. Among them was the astronomer and future dissident Kronid Liubarsky. It is worth noting two other students of Moscow State University, roommates in the dormitory on Stromynka Street, for their participation in those debates. One was the Czech student Zdeněk Mlynář, who would become a leading figure in the Prague Spring of 1968 and later a human rights advocate. Another was Mikhail Gorbachev, the future Soviet leader.[85]

Yet the hopes ended as abruptly as they had arisen. In the Kremlin, at the top of the party pyramid, no unity existed, and certainly no will to abolish Stalinist control over literature. Malenkov's influence began to slip. His rivals, Nikita Khrushchev and Viacheslav Molotov, criticized him at the time for lack of ideological firmness and for attempts to increase his popularity in Soviet society at their expense. Cold War tensions grew, exacerbated by the nuclear arms race.[86] Sensing the chill wind emanating from the Kremlin, the secretary of the writers' union, Alexei Surkov, once a gifted poet and now an experienced apparatchik, published a critique of Pomerantsev's article and the whole discussion of "sincerity in literature" as expressions of ideological vacillation in the face of external threat.

On July 23, 1954, the party secretariat condemned the "errors" of *Novy Mir* and pressured Tvardovsky to recant. Khrushchev, who also knew and liked the Tyorkin poems and identified with Tvardovsky's peasant roots, sharply disapproved of the *Novy Mir* discussion of "sincerity." He believed that the postwar suppression of literature and the fine arts, the implicit target of the discussion, was the correct party line, dictated by the emerging Cold War situation. And how could Soviet literature be "dishonest"? Also, Khrushchev might have been displeased with Tvardovsky's recent publication of a poem about Stalin, commemorating the anniversary of his death. In it the poet called himself an orphan.[87] Tvardovsky refused to repent; yet, he still had complete faith in the wisdom and fairness of the party and in his own ability to work with its leadership for the "socialist cause."[88]

The year 1954 ended with the convening of the Second Congress of Soviet Writers in Moscow. By comparison with the first congress, which had taken place twenty years earlier, this gathering, given lengthy coverage in the Soviet media, testified to the huge losses that literature had suffered under Stalinism. Hundreds of the most talented authors were gone, killed or ostracized by the regime. What remained was an assembly of aging, largely cynical men and women delivering sterile speeches, deceiving others and themselves. There was no infusion of young blood, no influx of fresh talent. Critical minds viewed the congress as the funeral of a once vital, complex, and idealistic literature. A professor of history from Moscow State University, Sergei Dmitriev, noted in his diary that the situation of literature was so disastrous that it would be best to "disband the writers' union, avoid creating a new one, and stop convening any congresses of writers."[89]

Although critical thoughts and discussions were suppressed and the official literature was in profound crisis, one "geyser under the surface of the dead sea" continued to gain strength. It was poetry. The Great Patriotic War had already produced a phenomenal demand for lyrics to embody the longings, desires, and profound sentiments of Russians whose individual feelings had long been suppressed.[90] The renewal of this suppression after 1946 only whetted the appetite for intimate verse. Between 1953 and 1955, responding to this demand, even Soviet newspapers, usually turgid and sterile, began to publish poetry almost daily. Astonishingly, in April 1954 the journal *Znamia* published, without much ado, ten beautiful poems by Boris Pasternak, which he had written in 1946–47 for his *Doctor Zhivago*. The political and literary censors, and most of the public, completely missed the fact that Pasternak had written these poems about the resurgence of his love for God. His "second birth" into mystical Christianity had helped the poet survive years of suicidal despair.

David Samoilov and Boris Slutsky, already in their midthirties and still without a single publication, felt renewed inspiration. Slutsky in particular believed that his time had finally come. Slutsky was convinced, and tried to convince others, that the "poetic renaissance" that had followed Stalin's death was an omen of better and greater things to come. The core of his political philosophy remained the same as in 1940 or in 1945: it was a Marxist-Leninist revolutionary philosophy, but now it stood in opposition to the anti-Semitic and anticultural policies of the Stalinist "ruling class." In Slutsky's opinion the Great Patriotic War was a period of redemption for communist ideas; and the party, once it had been purified of careerists and time servers, would again become the proper vehicle for global historical changes. He, a party member, wanted to be a commissar of the "progressive" literature of the future.[91] In his poems about Stalin, "Boss" and "God," circulated in handwritten copies among friends, Slutsky sought to break Stalin's terrible spell over his generation. He portrayed him as "another God, more cruel and clever than Jehovah," who responded to worship and love only with "somber, grim hatred" toward his slaves. In his poem "Jews," Slutsky, whose relatives had perished in the Holocaust, wrote about living "under the curse of a wretched race." Citing his own war record, he dispelled the Nazi slander, adopted by Soviet anti-Semites, that Jews had let others fight for them.[92]

The poet Yevgeny Yevtushenko remembered a conversation he had had in the first half of 1954 in the group of students from the Institute of Literature. Yunna Morits, an eighteen-year-old poet, whose parents were still in the camps, said to the twenty-one-year-old Yevtushenko, "The Revolution is dead, and its corpse is stinking." Another teenage student, with a round childish face and a thick red plait, Izabella Akhmadulina, her sloe eyes flashing, retorted, "You ought to be ashamed of yourself. The Revolution isn't dead; the Revolution is sick, and we must help it."[93]

Yevgeny Yevtushenko had been born in 1932, the son of young and romantic geologists, in Zima, a stop on the great Trans-Siberian Railway. His parents soon split up, and only later did he learn a family secret: both his grandfathers had vanished during Stalin's Great Terror. He grew up a naive Stalinist, like many others. His early patriotic poems, published in a sports tabloid, were his ticket to the Institute of Literature in 1953. The tragic stampede during Stalin's funeral shattered Yevtushenko's blind optimism, yet the romantic core remained intact. He did not want to stand outside the mainstream, he wanted to direct its course. Yevgeny enjoyed his role as a public personality, and he was a natural fighter. His considerable dramatic talent turned his poetic evenings into emotional mass performances. Tall and lanky, with the jaunty smile of a pop star, in his tweed jackets and bright ties, he could be mistaken for a *stiliaga*. Akhmadulina, later known as Bella, would soon become the brightest female light of the new poetic generation. She had been born into a family of low-ranking Soviet officials in Moscow.[94] As a student, she was an idealistic Komsomol activist. At the same time, she had a profoundly private side; her literary taste was shaped by Marcel Proust. Beautiful, frail, exuding immense feminine charm, Akhmadulina rivaled the most famous actresses when she was onstage. In the opinion of many later admirers, she had "a completely un-Soviet expression" on her face and a look of "perpetual, quivering astonishment" in her gaze.[95]

Bella (Izabella) Akhmadulina, who became a nationally known poet after Stalin's death. She said in 1954, "The Revolution isn't dead; the Revolution is sick, and we must help it" (Courtesy of Memorial, Moscow).

Soon after their conversation about the ailing Revolution, Yevtushenko and Akhmadulina were married. In a few years, moreover, their poetry came to symbolize the yearning for change and spiritual liberalization. In 1955 Anastas Mikoyan, then a member of the Politburo and Khrushchev's most important ally, noticed a crowd blocking the way of his government limousine. On inquiring what all the commotion was about, he received one word in reply, "Yevtushenko." When he inquired who that was, the answer was, "A poet." Mikoyan later admitted: "I saw people queuing up for poetry, not for food. I realized that a new era had begun."[96]

During the decade that followed, literature, especially poetry, would become the main outlet for the creative energies of the new generation. The search for a fresh style and individual self-expression, heralded by the appearance of the *stiliagi*, would continue in the sphere of the fine arts. From the ranks of the war veterans, as well as the maturing students of the immediate postwar period, would emerge the heirs to the socially concerned intelligentsia that had nourished the poets and writers of the Russian past. The eagerly awaited words of these "children of Zhivago" would serve as an inspiration to the rapidly burgeoning numbers of young artists and intellectuals, scientists and engineers, philosophers and journalists. On the ruins of the old intelligentsia young shoots began to sprout—a change at first as gradual and imperceptible as the Thaw that had produced them.

I built my house on sand
That seemed so recently to be a rock.
So is it still for some. For me
It split asunder, fell to bits.

—Boris Slutsky, 1952

Shock Effects
1956-1958

O N THE morning of February 25, 1956, Nikita Khrushchev walked up
to the Central Committee podium to read the most important speech of his
life. He faced thousands of delegates to the Twentieth Congress of the Communist Party of the USSR, gathered in the long, cavernous Hall of the Supreme Soviets in the Kremlin. In the speech he castigated Stalin as a tyrant
and a murderer of many "honest communists." Based on previous investigation, the report he delivered unmistakably indicted Stalin as the master-
mind of the destruction of party and state elites during the 1930s. Quickly
dubbed the secret speech, Khrushchev's report would soon become anything but secret for tens of millions in the Soviet Union and hundreds of
millions around the world.[1] Khrushchev edited the report to suit his communist beliefs and political purposes. He did not mention in the report that
between 1937 and 1938 alone Stalin's secret police arrested 1,548,366 people. Of these, 681,692 were executed. He did not mention the atrocities of
the Revolution, the deportation and death of millions of peasants during
collectivization, the elimination of gentry, clergy, intellectuals, and artists—
crimes that had occurred before 1937–38. He also omitted to mention later
crimes, including those in which he was personally involved, such as the
infamous Katyn massacre, in which 22,000 Polish officers were murdered
by the NKVD in 1940.[2]

Still, the enormity and cold cynicism of the Stalinist crimes, revealed by Khrushchev, produced profound and lasting shock among the communist believers and many educated idealists who believed in the Soviet cause. Even the people who had seen much cruelty and injustice in Soviet society were shattered by the revelations. Thirty-two-year-old Alexander Yakovlev, a war veteran and young party apparatchik (he would later become one of the fathers of glasnost under Gorbachev), was lucky enough to obtain a guest ticket for the concluding day of the congress. Ten years earlier, soon after his demobilization from the army, he was standing at the train station of his hometown observing cars filled with Soviet POWs traveling from German camps to Soviet camps in Siberia, when he suddenly began to notice other harsh realities of Soviet life—starving children, the confiscation of grain from peasants, and prison sentences for trifling violations. "It became increasingly obvious that everybody was lying," he recalls, referring to the public triumphalism after the war.[3] Still, for him the shock at Khrushchev's report "was incredibly profound." He felt a terrible chill inside. Khrushchev's words "canceled out everything" he lived for. His faith was "exploding in shrapnel like a grenade shell." Thirteen hundred delegates to the congress felt the same. Nobody applauded at the end of the speech. People left the hall bowed down, as if crushed by the unfamiliar knowledge. During the intermission an IFLI graduate and war veteran, Igor Chernoutsan, stood smoking in the corridor with poet Konstantin Simonov. He later wrote: "We already knew a lot, but we were stunned by the way the truth caved in on us. But was it the whole truth?"[4]

For idealistic, educated Russians, the shock of the "secret speech" was comparable to the outbreak of World War II. Just as then, a world of certainties came to an end, now that core beliefs and commonly accepted wisdom had turned to dust. The shock effect was especially strong on the cohorts of young university graduates and on those university students who were just entering social and cultural life. Confronting the enormity of Stalinist crimes, admitting the criminal nature of the man who had led the Soviet Union to victory during the war, and toward superpower status afterward, required a mental revolution. Whom now to trust? Where to turn? The Soviet project and their own existence, professional and personal, suddenly lost their moorings.

Catharsis and Trauma

Khrushchev did not have the vision or the intellectual ability to turn de-Stalinization into a consistent policy after the secret speech. It was as if he had pushed a huge boulder down a mountain and could not comprehend the magnitude of the avalanche it produced. Educated Russians learned about Khrushchev's speech in a peculiar way. On March 5 the party Politburo (at that time called the presidium) approved Khrushchev's edited copy of his speech, and later it was issued to all party committees, to "inform all the Communists and Komsomol members, and also nonparty activists including workers, white-collar personnel, and collective farmers." Party functionaries read the speech aloud behind closed doors at universities, colleges, and even high schools. It was relatively easy even for nonparty members, including university and high school students, to familiarize themselves with the speech. William Taubman found that altogether "up to seven million Party and eighteen million Komsomol members had the speech read to them in the weeks that followed."[5]

Lidia Chukovskaia, the daughter of a famous literary critic from the prerevolutionary intelligentsia of St. Petersburg, described in her notes how the reading of the speech went at the office of the writers' union in Moscow. "We suddenly saw that all the people standing quietly in the corridor trickled into the conference hall. We entered with them and sat at the long table. A young, pretty woman in a green suit locked the door and sat down at the head of the table. She read very distinctly, in a style typical of the intelligentsia. The reading lasted for two hours and a half." Some women cried. There was no discussion after the reading, and the audience filed out of the hall, each left with his or her own feelings and thoughts.[6] Chukovskaia and some others who had known the truth about Stalin's repressions or had secretly hated the tyrant and his regime rejoiced. Yet many more were overwhelmed and even appalled. Ehrenburg recalled that he "was shaken" by the speech, "as it was not given in a circle of friends by one of Stalin's victims but by the first secretary of the party."[7]

Party committees and propagandists, as well as the secret police (transformed in 1954 into the KGB), were painfully unprepared for the new situation. The absence of any explanation or guidelines for discussion of the speech produced a virtual state of paralysis in the party and the state propaganda apparatus.[8] Party organizations, expecting to receive detailed instructions from above, delayed their regular meetings. Weeks passed, and still the Kremlin was silent. The delay only magnified the wild rumors circulating in Moscow and Leningrad.[9] The KGB and party organizations also reported rumblings of discontent from Ukraine, Estonia, Central Asia, and the South Caucasus. From March 4 to March 9, a nationalist mass uprising exploded in Georgia, even before the secret speech was read there: crowds consisting mostly of students and members of the Soviet intelligentsia "defended" Stalin against what they perceived as Khrushchev and Mikoyan's conspiracy. The Georgian mutiny was put down by the army at the cost of dozens of casualties.[10]

Among students and young intellectuals in Russia the first reaction to the speech was often one of collective catharsis. Vadim Medvedev, a student at Leningrad State University (he would become a Politburo member under Gorbachev), recalled that in the complete silence of the university conference hall somebody whispered, "Something is rotten deep down inside our party." In the spring of 1956, strangers and even opponents could freely tell one another their real thoughts about the Communist Party and the Soviet past. "Such conversations would have been unthinkable a few weeks earlier," recalled Alexeyeva. "Something extraordinary is happening," one student told Ehrenburg. "Everybody is arguing—and moreover, absolutely everyone is beginning to think."[11] Great numbers of students could not immediately digest the terrible news revealed by Khrushchev: they were angry at him and blamed him for ruining their youthful idealism. Those naive Stalinists persevered in their faith. Yet for others, especially those whose parents and relatives had perished in the Great Terror, the facts were undeniable, and Stalin "was a great malefactor." These students asked: Who created the cult of personality? If there was only one personality, what did the rest of the party do? The obvious answer was that the cult of personality was not the dictatorship of only one man. Every party committee in every region, district, and area had its petty Stalins. And if there were many executioners, where did they come from, from what dark realm had they emerged? Where were the guarantees that past crimes would not be repeated? Spontaneous, unguided discussions began to erupt among the student youth of Moscow, Leningrad, and other Russian cities in late March and April. After a presentation of the speech at the Moscow Regional Pedagogical Institute to professors, graduate students, and some undergraduates, "many considered it as manifest proof of the degeneration and bureaucratization of the party."[12]

An avalanche of desperate signals from disoriented party propagandists reached party headquarters, reporting on "antiparty activities" in places with a high concentration of professionals and educated groups. Confusion was widespread: What to do with Stalin's portraits and statues? Should all his works be removed from propaganda and teaching schedules and materials? Students in Moscow high schools began to tear Stalin's portraits off the walls. At the party meeting of the Dubna Thermo-Technical Laboratory, a secret lab near Moscow working on the development of atomic reactors under the aegis of the Soviet atomic ministry, a spontaneous discussion of the speech took place. The young physicist Yuri Orlov, a war veteran and an MGU graduate (class of 1952) felt an irresistible urge "to get cleaned up from all this filth and blood." At a public discussion of the speech Orlov spoke about the dictatorship of "a gang of crooks" in the country. He denounced the tyranny of "careerists and conformists" in the bureaucracy, the scientific establishment, and state media. The vast majority of the audience, primarily young physicists, applauded. Other speakers deplored the absence of freedom of information and free speech. Some of them demanded an end to jamming of the BBC and other Western radio stations. The anger of the young discussants increasingly focused on the *present* leadership. Stalin was dead. But what about his accomplices who were still in power?[13]

The tumult provoked by Khrushchev's speech began to alarm the party leaders. The pressure grew for Khrushchev to define the content and limits of de-Stalinization. On April 5 *Pravda* published a piece severely criticizing the "antiparty remarks" of young scientists at the Thermo-Technical Laboratory. Yuri Orlov and three other young scientists who supported him were fired (there were no arrests). The Politburo decided to convene a party plenum to address "the task of improving ideological efforts." The Soviet leader still seemed inclined to deliver further attacks against the cult of Stalin. He put his favorite speechwriter and adviser, Dmitry Shepilov, in charge of the preparations. Khrushchev's ally Marshal Georgy Zhukov, the minister of defense, prepared materials on Stalin's errors during the war. The plenum was never convened. The text of the speech was leaked to Israeli intelligence, and then to the CIA. The U.S. State Department published the speech, and soon American-funded Radio Liberty and Radio Free Europe began to broadcast it, to the dismay of communists in both the East and the West. This unexpected development altered Khrushchev's calculations. Suddenly, the entire communist world, and especially Soviet satellites in Eastern Europe, were in turmoil, and this strengthened the opponents of rash de-Stalinization in the Kremlin.[14] On June 30, 1956, *Pravda* finally published a Central Committee resolution titled "On the Cult of Personality and Its Consequences." It explained Stalin's crimes as caused not by flaws of personality, but by "historical circumstances," such as the war and the presence of enemies within and surrounding the USSR. The resolution also explained that the party could not criticize Stalin, because people already associated socialist victories with him. The Kremlin belatedly sought to set boundaries for de-Stalinization. There was the blatant contradiction between the secret speech, which condemned Stalin's crimes, and the party resolution, which did not. And that discrepancy only provoked additional passionate debates among young Soviet intellectuals and students.

With the secret speech, the Thaw not only returned, but rapidly evolved into a much more radical and divisive phenomenon. Khrushchev was mistaken in thinking that Soviets could easily remove Stalin from the Soviet and communist worldview and move on. The revelations about Stalin's use of terror against party members dealt an irreparable blow to the teleological view of Soviet history. Stalinism implied a constant expansion in time and space; it recognized no reversals, and "each step was a step forward, every stage an absolute achievement." The past was only the springboard for another leap into the future. In contrast, Khrushchev was now asking people to return to the past. This request meant that despite the bloodshed and sacrifice of millions, the communist "train" had been moving in the wrong direction.[15] Given the quasi-religious faith that communism was the wave of the future, such a realization implied that perhaps Soviet society could no longer be seen as being in the forefront of global progress.

Some older intellectuals and artists, especially the victims of Stalin's repressions and those who had just returned from the gulag, greeted the speech with quiet satisfaction but felt uneasy about the passions it had unleashed. The poet Anna Akhmatova, a victim of communist and Stalinist repression, was thankful to Khrushchev for liberating her only son Lev, who had spent years in the camps. She began to call herself a Khrushchevist. At the same time, she remarked on March 29, 1956, "What if each and every one started to draw conclusions from Khrushchev's report and, most important, added his or her own considerations and experience? It would be disastrous." Bitter experience made Akhmatova worry that moderate liberalization from above might again generate a vicious cycle of radicalism and repression.[16] The radicalization Akhmatova feared did indeed begin to emerge in university classes and dorms. The reaction to Khrushchev's bombshell reactivated the traditional alienation between the "thinking" segment of the younger generation and the ruling class. This kind of tension had given rise to the Russian intelligentsia a century earlier. Moreover, the questions of who was to blame and what was to be done were the same "accursed" questions that had tormented and fragmented educated circles in Russia earlier. Indeed, a small but growing number of young writers, intellectuals, artists, and numerous circles of friends would soon pursue exactly the same road that the nineteenth-century intelligentsia had taken before them: they would question the existing regime in the name of universal ideals of justice and human rights.

The more idealistic young intellectuals and students were, the more they felt shocked by the secret speech. At Moscow State University, the most intense discussions took place among students in the humanities: historians, philologists, philosophers, and journalists. Such young men and women had the intellectual and cultural ammunition to discuss social and political issues. Among students of physics, chemistry, geology, and biology, ideological unrest was marginal. But even some of these students quoted Trotsky, criticized the party, and compared the KGB to the Gestapo.[17] At some schools the student movement was more visible: the Institute of Literature and the Institute of Cinematography (VGIK) in Moscow, the Institute of Mining Engineers and the Institute of Technology in Leningrad, and so on.[18]

The secret speech alienated the idealistic students of 1956 from Stalin but also from Stalin's successors. Socialist romanticism was the political credo of these students, and justice, equality, and internationalism were their ideals. These students did not differ much in their beliefs from the postwar students and the educated war veterans of the 1940s and early 1950s. In other words, they were part of one extended historical generation. One student of Moscow State University, arrested in 1957 for "anti-Soviet crimes," recalled, "For me, and also for the majority of the politically engaged youth, Marxism-Leninism remained the unshakable foundation." He admitted he "could not conceive of a society, first, without a socialist order

[and], second, without a politically centralized organization—that is, the party."[19] Mikhail Krasilnikov, a student of philology at Leningrad State University arrested in November 1956, would later acknowledge that at the time of his arrest he preserved a completely "communist" mentality: he read John Reed's sympathetic account of the Russian Revolution and despised capitalism and consumerism.[20] Commenting on the viewpoint of the educated majority during the Thaw, a Russian sociologist wrote about the paradox: a profound hunger for personal freedom coexisted and clashed with a sincere belief in the Holy Grail of collectivism.[21]

For such students, the first reaction to Khrushchev's revelations was sympathy for the victims of the Great Terror—the Old Bolsheviks. Many of the younger generation had either lost their parents and relatives during that time or knew someone who had. The most politically engaged not only read Marx, Engels, and Lenin, far beyond the required curriculum, but also managed to read Bukharin and Trotsky, whose works were banned from Soviet libraries. Yet their main inspiration came from Alexander Herzen and other Russian socialists of the nineteenth century. The young radicals came to the conclusion that the existing regime was a horrible deviation from revolutionary ideals. It had come to represent the injustice of tyranny by a bureaucratic apparatus over the working masses. Pimenov, a young mathematician from Leningrad State University, wrote several romantic dramas and poems about non-Bolshevik revolutionaries. His heroes were the idealistic terrorists of the nineteenth century: Andrei Zheliabov of the People's Will, the organization whose militants assassinated Tsar Alexander II in 1881; Georgy Gapon, a priest whose fiery socialist agitation among workers triggered Bloody Sunday of January 1905 and the first Russian revolution; and Ivan Kaliaev, a suicide bomber from the paramilitary wing of the Socialist Revolutionary Party.[22]

The young idealists of 1956 had already witnessed three years of political changes since Stalin's death, zigzags in propaganda, and discussions about a literary Thaw. Some of them were free of the paralyzing fear that muzzled the older intellectuals. Across the country, students raised embarrassing questions in front of older party members and propagandists. How could you allow the cause of the Revolution and the ideals of communism to be defiled and diverted? Why did you not stop Stalin? The ability to think independently and hold unauthorized public discussions about Stalinism led by logical progression to public protest. At the end of May the students at

Moscow State University decided to boycott a canteen at the Stromynka dorm. The canteen was notorious for its bad food and for the regular theft of produce and meat by the personnel. Young women from the MGU department of philology came up with the initiative to picket the canteen. Students from the departments of history, biology, and journalism jumped at the idea. Slogans emerged: "If you do not want to be fed like cattle—support the boycott!" "We will rock Lenin Hills!" These hills, across the Moscow River from the city center, were the location of the newly opened university campus. But the obvious political pun (the reference to Lenin) rattled party and state officials.[23] Right under the nose of the Kremlin, the students at the most elite Soviet university were engaged in a spontaneous protest.

Baffled authorities at first blamed the boycott on foreign students from "people's democracies" who resided in the MGU dorm. There was a search for the "enemy forces" that had instigated Soviet youth. Yet instead of a crackdown, a directive came from the Kremlin to negotiate with the students. A number of speakers from the Moscow Party Committee and the KGB came to MGU and the Stromynka dorm, in an attempt to pacify protesters and answer their questions. The Komsomol organization at MGU was caught off guard by the novelty of the situation and paralyzed by indecision over how to respond. In fact, many Komsomol activists sympathized with the student protest.[24]

Another important development was the students' exercise of direct democracy. In spring 1956, during the discussion of the secret speech, students replaced the old Komsomol organizers, usually appointed from above, with new "natural leaders" from their bands of companions. Many of these people supported the boycott. The Komsomol meetings turned into ever more radical discussions. At the department of philosophy, students openly questioned the curriculum. "Marx and Engels are banal," they said. "Lenin is outdated. Let us read Bukharin," and "The party Central Committee is not an icon." In what reads like a roster of future stars of Gorbachev's glasnost, the list of speakers included Yevgeny Plimak, Yuri Kariakin, and Anatoly Butenko.[25] At the department of journalism the new Komsomol bureau headed by Igor Dedkov, Valentin Chikin, and Bronislav Kholopov "crushed Stalinist dogmas" at student meetings. Freedom of speech was typically one-sided. The audience hissed and booed if anybody tried to defend Stalin and his era. Dedkov got into the habit of putting a

Igor Dedkov, who in 1956 was an activist in the student movement against bureaucracy and in favor of a "return to Leninism." Later he became a literary critic for *Novy Mir* (Courtesy of Memorial, Moscow).

black porcelain cat on the presidium table whenever a speaker turned out to be "reactionary"—it was the sign for him or her to leave the podium.[26]

Student activism withered in June, as exams started. The party and university authorities believed that the whole affair was over and were prepared to sweep it under the rug.[27] However, the national revolution in Poland, triggered by bloody reprisals against labor riots in Poznan on June 28, reignited the student movement in Moscow, Leningrad, and other urban centers.[28] Many students stopped attending lectures and seminars in the struggle to gain a "free schedule." Students rushed to buy Polish-language dictionaries as well as Polish newspapers—soon these disappeared from the press stalls. With the support of the newly elected Komsomol committees, student activists began to issue wall newspapers and self-published journals without the approval of the authorities—a startling break with Stalinist regulations. Most of these newspapers dealt with issues of interest to students, such as the curriculum, but toward the end of October some articles began to discuss Impressionism, Postimpressionism, and other trends in Western art—a taboo subject since the late 1940s, when the monopoly of socialist realism was established. At the Institute of Technology in Leningrad, a group of young poets and "style apers"—Yevgeny Rein, Dmitry Bobyshev, and Anatoly Naiman—posted a number of articles on Western art in general and Picasso in particular for the institute's wall newspaper *Kultura*. Students at the Herzen Pedagogical School in Leningrad posted a number of articles "burying socialist realism" in their wall newspaper

Lit-Front. Similar publications appeared at MGU and a number of Moscow institutes as well as at other universities in the Soviet Union.[29]

And like their predecessors a hundred years earlier in tsarist Russia, the disaffected and alienated students turned to literature for guidance. They focused their attention on one novel that had appeared in the literary journal *Novy Mir.*

Not by Bread Alone

Most Soviet writers were as unprepared for the secret speech as anybody else. The public discussion of Khrushchev's speech at a party meeting of the Moscow writers provides a glimpse of their public reaction. Alexei Surkov, the secretary of the Union of Soviet Writers, delayed the regular meeting of the writers, who were members of the party, until March 29, 1956. In his opening speech he avoided the topic of Khrushchev's report.[30] Then other writers in the audience took the floor to initiate an unauthorized and passionate discussion of Stalinist crimes and the responsibility of Soviet writers. So many writers wanted to speak that the meeting lasted for three days. None of the "old intelligentsia" writers spoke. Moreover, writers and poets who had won national fame and prizes under Stalin, such as Simonov, Tvardovsky, and Ehrenburg, were notably absent or silent.

Most outspoken were those who called themselves Old Bolsheviks, the survivors of the purges. Also active were those who had joined the "socialist intelligentsia" during the 1930s but then became the target of various Stalinist campaigns. Their pent-up fear found release in a spate of vitriolic and emotional anti-Stalinism. Alexander Avdeenko, a worker-turned-writer whom Stalin first elevated and then ostracized, was quick to explain his lack of literary achievements by pointing to "the stifling cult of personality."[31] Avdeenko was very close to Khrushchev in his social background and views. He expressed great happiness that "we liberated ourselves from the General Tutor of Soviet literature who acted like the tsar, rewarding some and executing the others."[32] Another speaker, Pavel Bliakhin, the author of the twenties best seller *Red Daredevils,* about the Civil War, asked Soviet writers to admit that by helping create the cult of personality, they had enabled Stalin to become "an autocrat comparable to any Russian tsar in the past." To great applause from the audience, he criticized the bureaucratization, corruption, and great inequality in society and in the union.[33] The greatest emotion erupted among the audience when Bliakhin raised the issue of the recent anticosmopolitan campaign. From 1953 to 1956, people of Jewish background still made up almost a third of the membership of the Moscow writers' organization. The lack of resistance against the persecution of Jews in the union, Bliakhin said, "cast a dark spell on us Russian party members." Several other speakers, including war veterans, condemned Anatoly Sofronov, Nikolai Gribachev, and other literary hacks, who had zealously organized the purge of Jews from the Soviet literary scene several years earlier.[34]

Avdeenko and Bliakhin defended the "cult of Lenin" as "the cult of humanism, the cult of great ideas that transform the world." This quickly became the public consensus at the meeting. The writer Vasily Ermashov extolled members of the Bolshevik old guard who allegedly, on the eve of their execution, "spoke truth to the despot's face." Stalinism, as he summed it up, was "the entire system of anti-Leninist views." His appeal to begin a long and difficult struggle for "the return to Leninism" elicited prolonged applause from the audience.[35] Raisa Orlova (Liberson), a graduate of IFLI and former "naive Stalinist," recalled in her memoirs that the audience burst out singing "The Internationale." Orlova was overwhelmed with emotion. "Finally, the true and pure revolutionary ideal has returned, something you can give yourself to without doubts. It was us against them, Stalinist goons. The world once again was becoming simple and black-and-white in a new way."[36]

The Revolution and the Russian tradition of revolutionary sacrifice remained unquestioned ideals throughout the discussions of Stalin's crimes by most the literary figures of the time. At a meeting of Moscow literary critics with the collective of the *Literaturnaia Gazeta,* one critic declared, "We all know that during the last twenty or so years the history of Russian populism, of Land and Freedom, of the People's Will, was scandalously downplayed."[37] In the next twenty years, the study of these revolutionary predecessors of Lenin's party attracted increasing attention from Soviet idealists. De-Stalinization did not mean the end of the communist ideal. To the contrary, it meant a rejuvenation of the idealism and the intellectual identity of the pre-Stalin period.

The official de-Stalinization rekindled Boris Slutsky's idealism, which had been shattered by earlier events. Slutsky believed that the Twentieth Party Congress gave new life to the communist experiment, by cleansing it of Stalinist anti-Semitism and chauvinism. He felt responsible for the future of the revolution.[38] Slutsky's star was on the rise. In July 1956 the established literary veteran Ilya Ehrenburg published an enthusiastic review of Slutsky's poetry in the *Literaturnaia Gazeta*. He advertised the stern, honest poetry as speaking in the vocabulary and intonations of his contemporaries. "He is able to perceive what others can only dimly glimpse."[39] Slutsky's friend David Samoilov also agreed that it was necessary to recover the lost revolutionary and internationalist values, yet he was less optimistic. He wrote in his diary that Stalin had brought to power the anti-intellectual lower-middle classes *(meshchanstvo),* the embodiment of provincial benightedness and crass materialism. This new caste that dominated the bureaucracy, secret police, and propaganda apparatus "forced art, science, and the press to serve its interests." After June 1956 Samoilov already viewed Khrushchev as "the agent of the ruling class" and suggested that official liberalization had peaked. He concluded that the task of "everything honest in our literature" should be to oppose and denounce this new caste.[40]

Samoilov was not alone in such broodings. In the early morning of May 14, 1956, Alexander Fadeev, the former omnipotent head of the Union of Soviet Writers, committed suicide. In his farewell note to the party Central Committee Fadeev wrote, "The most sacred thing, literature, was allowed to be torn to pieces by bureaucrats and the darkest elements of the people." The fifty-six-year-old writer recalled that his generation had entered the field of literature under Lenin with a great feeling of liberation and a sense of the world's openness, with unlimited inspiration to create art. Instead, writers became whipping boys for the party, and now "only a few preserved the sacred flame in their soul." Fadeev concluded that his own great and "profoundly communist" talent had been exploited, mistreated, and finally rejected by the party bigwigs. "The arrogance of the new bosses speculating on the great Leninist teachings has resulted in my complete mistrust of them. They are even worse than the satrap Stalin. He at least was educated, and these types are ignorant."[41] The KGB confiscated the letter and reported it to the leadership. It was buried in the party safes, but the Kremlin's angry response was discernible in the official obituary that ascribed Fadeev's suicide to alcoholism.

Other writers in 1955–56 continued to hope for a "literary renaissance" under the Kremlin tutelage, and there were promising signs that it might take place. Since early 1955, even before the party congress, Khrushchev and his supporters had been following a policy of "peaceful coexistence" with the West. Part of this course was demonstrating the open and "peace-loving" nature of Soviet society, and a "public diplomacy" of people-to-people contacts.[42] The Kremlin's new foreign policy opened up opportunities for the liberalization of domestic cultural life. In 1955 a group of Soviet writers and journalists was instructed to travel to the United States, to observe, study, and write about the country. They brought back not only their American observations, but numerous proposals on how to reform and improve Soviet journalism, foreign policy propaganda, diplomatic practices, and even airport services. The leaders of the writers' union even petitioned the Kremlin for permission to join PEN, an international literary organization. The petition was rejected in 1955, but resubmitted after Khrushchev's secret speech. The authors of the petition argued that PEN would be an excellent platform for spreading Soviet influence among "progressive" writers and "significant groups of the intelligentsia" in the West.[43] Last but not least, the Kremlin gave a secret command from to the department in the party apparatus in charge of culture to look critically at the repressive Stalin-Zhdanov measures of 1946–1948 against writers, musicians, and artists. One of the apparatchiks in the department of culture was Igor Chernoutsan, a graduate of IFLI with broad connections in Moscow literary and artistic circles.[44]

During the breaks, the delegates to the Twentieth Party Congress could buy an almanac, *Literaturnaia Moskva*, a collection of works selected by a group of prominent writers, among them Konstantin Paustovsky and Veniamin Kaverin. It contained the masterpieces of Anna Akhmatova, Nikolai Zabolotsky, and Boris Pasternak, as well as the works of Viktor Shklovsky and Kornei Chukovsky. It was the first attempt on the part of writers since the early 1930s to act as a group of co-workers and select literary works according to their own aesthetic and ethical judgment. In this way writers tried to reclaim and restore the traditional duty of the old Russian intelligentsia to define the criteria of art and culture. In the more open atmosphere after the secret speech, the appearance of *Literaturnaia Moskva* did not create a sensation. The second issue of the almanac appeared in the summer of 1956. Its editors rejected Pasternak's *Doctor Zhivago* as "too voluminous." Yet the book contained many more talented works, which contrasted with the insipid offerings in the Soviet literary journals. The true public sensation of the second issue was "The Levers," a short story by

Alexander Yashin. When Yashin had tried two years earlier to submit it for publication, he was told to burn the manuscript or hide it in a safe. The story described the phenomenon of double thinking and dual behavior among Russian peasants on a collective farm. Privately, they spoke in plain language and with sincerity about everyday problems, but the moment they began to speak at a party meeting, they ceased to be kind and honest people and turned into "levers" in the gigantic party machinery. This story brought back the theme of sincerity and the impact of ideology on behavior and culture, which had been raised by Pomerantsev in December 1953.[45]

The season of literary sensations, however, was only beginning. Konstantin Simonov, Tvardovsky's successor as editor of *Novy Mir,* was determined to turn this journal into a vehicle of the cultural Thaw. In the spring of 1956 Simonov was reading two potentially explosive manuscripts. One was *Doctor Zhivago* by Boris Pasternak. The other was *Not by Bread Alone* by Vladimir Dudintsev, a young jurist and war veteran. It did not take Simonov long to decide not to publish *Zhivago.* He quickly concluded that the novel negated his own life, its meaning, ethos, and pathos. As for Pasternak's Christian allegories, they simply fell on deaf ears, since Simonov was an atheist.[46] Dudintsev's novel, by contrast, took as its holy script the Bolshevik Revolution.

Dudintsev belonged to the older cohort of "children." He had first tried his hand at literature as a young romantic from the poets' circle at the Institute of Jurisprudence. After the Nazi invasion he volunteered for the army and witnessed the military disasters of 1941 and the inadequacy of the Soviet political and military leaders. Dudintsev recalled watching a couple of Luftwaffe fighters shoot down several dozen Soviet aircraft one by one. "How could this happen? A question churned in my mind."[47] He decided to write a book and search for answers. Unlike Pasternak, Dudintsev did not deplore the death of Russian culture, humanism, and individualism in the wake of revolutionary chaos and state terror. His goal was to unmask new "enemies of the people," the bureaucrats and careerists who had thwarted the great revolutionary experiment. Thirty-three years later Dudintsev expressed this goal with the same clarity. "In 1917 the Revolution took place, and all the people, if you allow me this metaphor, landed on a new uninhabited island. And some people became 'parachutists,' who came from the destroyed world to settle down amid the Soviet realities. The entrepreneur and the egotist nestled in their souls. They looked around and realized they could live well if they accepted the new rules of the game. They concealed their real selves and began to shout along with the others, 'Long live world revolution!' And because they mimicked sincerity and yelled louder and more emphatically than others, they rose quickly, assumed leadership positions, and began to struggle for their own personal well-being."[48]

At the party plenum in July 1956 Khrushchev blamed governmental "bureaucratization" as the barrier to the unbridled innovative energy of the masses. Simonov, a participant at the party plenums, decided to make publishing Dudintsev's novel a priority. A friend recalled that he "fully realized what a brouhaha the appearance of Dudintsev's novel would cause. He savored in advance the role answering phone calls and letters, being attacked by interviewers, and speaking at various readers' conferences, where, responding to the applause of the majority, he would defend his decision before the [party] stalwarts."[49] He hoped to counteract the negative fallout from his March 1953 homage to Stalin and regain Khrushchev's trust.

As expected, the publication of Dudintsev's novel in *Novy Mir* in August through October set off a public furore. The novel became a manifesto for those who took the secret speech as a call for new thinking and action. Simonov was elated. Other experienced "generals" of the literary establishment seemed to be in the same camp with him. Many writers on the editorial board of the *Literaturnaia Gazeta,* the official publication of the Union of Soviet Writers, praised Dudintsev's novel to the skies. Ivan Frolov, a postwar philosophy graduate of MGU (and a classmate of Raisa Gorbachev) said: "Our literature simply has not had such outstanding characters; the writer rises to a tremendous level of universality." Valentin Ovechkin, an early advocate of "sincerity in literature," concluded, "It is time to apply the tools of literature" to unmask the "covert enemies of Soviet society, [who] have set us back by five to ten years." Pasternak's friend the writer Vsevolod Ivanov asserted that the novel would enjoy "enormous success in the countries of people's democracies [in Eastern Europe] that also suffer from bureaucratization."[50] The Moscow branch of the Union of Soviet Writers scheduled a public discussion of *Not by Bread Alone* for October 22, 1956.

What exactly happened at this historic discussion at the Central House of Writers in Moscow can be established only from private recollections and unofficial minutes. All the witnesses unanimously recall agitation and high feeling swirling around the event. Special detachments of mounted Moscow police had to control the crowds that wanted to enter the building located on Vorovsky Street. In the discussion hall, Dudintsev recalled, people even sat on the floor, but the front seats, reserved for dignitaries, remained unoccupied. Then "solid-looking people," probably from the KGB, appeared, and some "brave lads cleared the way for them. They occupied those front chairs and, poised to listen, took out their pads and golden pens. For anybody with eyes and ears this was enough to sound the alarm calling for maximum caution."[51]

At first the public discussion went smoothly and calmly. A number of writers, including the top officials of the writers' union, took the floor to defend the novel as the new beacon of "truly Bolshevik literature" in the spirit of the Twentieth Party Congress. Then Konstantin Paustovsky, an old and respected Russian writer, took the floor and recalled that in July 1956 he had taken part in the first Soviet cruise around Europe aboard the luxury liner *Victory*. Among the passengers were many privileged members of the Soviet high bureaucracy (party nomenklatura), traveling first-class but forced to mingle with others. The old writer was appalled by their arrogance and undisguised contempt for "simple folk" who were traveling in other classes. The privileged passengers were also rabidly anti-Semitic. They were exactly like Drozdov, the dark main character in Dudintsev's novel, a crafty apparatchik who had no revolutionary ideals and who throttled innovation and progress. "There are thousands of those Drozdovs," Paustovsky stated, "an entirely new social stratum . . . a new group of acquisitive carnivores brought up and encouraged to gratify their lowest instincts. Their weapons are betrayal, calumny, character assassination, and just plain murder. These types dare to claim the right to represent the people without the people's consent." The time was near, he warned, when the people would "mercilessly sweep away the Drozdovs." He concluded, "We must fight this battle to the end."[52]

The audience, especially the students up in the galleries, applauded furiously. The script of the discussion, prepared by cautious advocates of the Thaw, was swept aside. Konstantin Simonov realized that Paustovsky's words could be interpreted as an attack against the party authorities. In the concluding speech at the meeting he sought to steer the meeting in a politically correct direction. The enemies of socialist idealism, he said, could be found in all groups in Soviet society, not only in the upper bureaucracy. "Drozdovs, if one can speak about the cruise ship *Victory*, exist at every level: they travel in any class, including the one where the writers traveled."

Simonov distanced himself from those who were prepared to use Dudintsev's novel "for malicious purposes" and present this literary work as criticizing "whole strata of the party and state apparatus."[53]

Just over a week later, on October 30, at a national conference of teachers of literature, Simonov delivered an inspired and robust defense of Dudintsev's novel. Undaunted by the conservatism of the audience, he declared that the Stalinist decrees on theater and music should be revised or repealed. He also deplored the anticosmopolitan campaigns in literature and culture, as well as xenophobia and isolationism in the guise of "Russification" of culture. The majority in the audience were teachers from provincial schools who felt greatly surprised: just a few years ago Simonov had expressed the opposite opinion. Apparently, some concluded, the new policy he was voicing had been approved in the highest spheres. Simonov pursued the same "revisionist" line in his "Literary Notes," an essay that would soon appear in *Novy Mir*.[54]

Meanwhile, on October 23, 1956, an anti-Stalinist national revolution had suddenly begun in Budapest. The revolution in Hungary, one of the Soviet satellite countries of Eastern Europe, grabbed the attention of numerous university students in Moscow and Leningrad. Some of them attempted to organize public meetings for November 4 in solidarity with the Hungarian rebels. During the official celebration of the anniversary of the Bolshevik Revolution in Leningrad a few days later, the poet and style aper Mikhail Krasilnikov was arrested after shouting slogans expressing solidarity with the Hungarians.[55] Lev Krasnopevtsev, a graduate of MGU, decided to organize a secret group of junior faculty members to conduct revolutionary propaganda among Moscow university students. The Hungarian events, he recalled, "turned us upside down." The Hungarian Revolution radicalized thousands of students who deplored Stalin's subversion of the values of "true socialism" and wanted "glasnost" and an end to the tyranny of the bureaucracy.[56]

According to the KGB and party informers, "anti-Soviet agitation" was brewing at MGU, the Moscow Conservatory, the Institute of Literature, the Institute of Cinematography, the Institute of Mining Engineers, and the Institute of Energy. In the Archangelsk region a young man was caught distributing leaflets comparing the Soviet regime to the Nazis'. The leaflet read, "Stalin's party is a criminal and antinational [organization]. It has degenerated and turned into a closed group consisting of degenerates, cowards, and traitors."[57] The future dissident Vladimir Bukovsky dreamed of acquiring weapons and going to Budapest to support the insurrection or storming the Kremlin.[58] Igor Dedkov, a Komsomol activist at the department of journalism at MGU, recalled that for him "the revolution had been betrayed. We underwent a very distinct alienation from the authorities and even opposition to them." A delegation of students, including Dedkov, visited the rector of MGU and threatened to protest "the executions in Budapest" publicly. Even Khrushchev's granddaughter Yulia, a sophomore student on the editorial board of a student newspaper, sided with the radicals and informed them about "the moods at the top."[59]

In this new context, Dudintsev's novel became in the eyes of many a call not for reforms, but for revolution. At Leningrad State University the crowd of students, as one of them later recalled, expected the writer to become their leader, "the one to point them toward some actions."[60] The Ukrainian writers' union in Kiev received an anonymous letter that read, "Dudintsev is a thousand times correct. There is a whole group in power, a product of the terrible past." The author of the letter was "a representative of a quite sizable stratum of middling Soviet intelligentsia that grew up in the 1930s to 1940s." After the secret speech, the writer said, "[we] opened our eyes, we learned to tell the truth from a lie. There could be no return to the past. The edifice of lies that people like you helped erect is falling apart."[61]

These radical voices notwithstanding, many other students were not prepared to reject the foundations of the system and denounce Soviet policies. The Russian provinces remained quiet and conformist. Alexander Bovin, a future "enlightened" party apparatchik, had transferred to MGU from provincial Rostov and found himself the most moderate among his classmates. "I was not ready for such a high-pitched democratic and anti-Stalinist mood." Bovin disagreed with the criticism of the party and of the entire Soviet system; he defended the Soviet policies in Poland and Hungary. Other students interrupted and booed him.[62] Reports in Soviet press that a Hungarian "fascist" mob was lynching communists in Budapest cooled students' sympathies toward the Hungarian rebels. Still-recent memories of the war and the Battle of Budapest at the end of 1944, which had cost the Soviet army tens of thousands of lives, also influenced many. For the vast majority of Zhivago's children, the Soviet tanks in Hungary were "our tanks." At MGU one war veteran and professor of history cut off students in his seminar when they began to question the Soviet invasion: "Discussion is inappropriate at a time when Soviet soldiers are spilling their blood over there."[63]

The invasion of Hungary was the point when the radicalized students began to feel alienated not only from the Soviet regime, but also from the society. Boris Pustintsev, one of the 1956 protesters, recalled later, "In this country we were completely alone. The masses were possessed by absolute chauvinism. Ninety-nine percent of the population entirely shared the imperial aspirations of the authorities. Even many anti-Stalinists then approved of all the twists and turns of the regime."[64] The rest of urban society, above all workers and the lower classes, as well as peasants in the countryside, did not join the anti-Stalinist movement. The shocks of 1956 did not break through the solid home front. Yet even a limited student movement represented a threat to the party leadership. It responded with repression.

Crackdown and "Consolidation"

At first, the Kremlin did not know what to do with the students' activism and the discussions on literature and culture. The presidium appointed a commission to work on the issue.[65] On November 12, the newly established Party Bureau of the Russian Soviet Federated Socialist Republics adopted a resolution, "On Measures to Improve Ideological Work in Institutions of Higher Education." There was still no talk about repression, but the momentum was building in that direction.[66] On December 1 a memo from the party Central Committee, party department of culture, mentioned Simonov's proposal to abrogate the party decrees on literature. "Com. Simonov's speech contained some correct critical remarks. At the same time, the very fact of his criticism of the CC [party Central Committee] resolution in front of a nonparty audience must be recognized as inadmissible for a communist."[67] The last word, however, was Khrushchev's to speak, and the Soviet leader was busy with more pressing issues.

Writers were not sure how the events in Hungary would affect the Thaw. Sixty-six writers signed an "open letter" to their French colleagues justifying the invasion of Hungary. Among them were Ehrenburg, Tvardovsky, and Paustovsky—the most prominent supporters of the Thaw. By siding with the authorities politically, they probably intended to save the literary "renaissance" that, as they hoped, might still continue.[68] On November 21 Simonov sent a long memorandum to Khrushchev urging him to repeal

Stalin's postwar censorship of literature. Promoting xenophobia and re-pressing famous writers, he argued, stifled opportunities to recruit new friends in the West and thwarted innovation and progress. Referring to Khrushchev's recent speech promoting scientific and technological innova-tion, Simonov wondered why innovation should not be promoted in the cultural arena as well.[69]

The response from the Kremlin finally came: it was a resounding no. On December 6, Dmitry Shepilov, Khrushchev's lieutenant, invited Simonov and other prominent writers to "a conference on issues of literature" at party headquarters. Shepilov read the order from above: Soviet writers should not desert the party ranks and promote cultural liberalization dur-ing the acute Cold War struggle. Instead, they should help the party to build a firewall against the Western campaign to undermine Soviet society by ideological and cultural means.[70] The majority of the invited writers eagerly accepted the new line and opened fire on Simonov's *Novy Mir* and Dudin-tsev's novel, as well as on the almanac *Literaturnaia Moskva* and Yashin's *Levers*. The previously cautious supporters of the Thaw joined the chorus of critics. The writer Boris Polevoi urged his colleagues, "Stop taking pride in this lousy liberalism; stop indulging in this desire to show that we stand above the fray." Alexei Rumiantsev, a young editor of *Kommunist,* the par-ty's "theoretical" journal, denounced "the Trotskyite notion about the emer-gence of a new bourgeoisie, some kind of new class that exploits the work-ing class of our country." Simonov tried to stick to his guns and defend his position.[71] But hopes for a "literary renaissance" lay in ruins.

The Hungarian Revolution convinced Khrushchev that even a literary debate could spark a conflagration. The KGB reported that the revolution in Budapest had begun with literary discussions at the Petöfi Circle, a club of nonconformist Hungarian writers. One of Khrushchev's old friends, the Ukrainian literary hack Alexander Korneichuk, denounced the group of writers who published *Literaturnaia Moskva*. He explicitly compared them to the Petöfi Circle. Such a denunciation only recently could have led to ar-rests. On the same day the "conference" with the writers opened, Khru-shchev asked menacingly at the party presidium what should be done with anti-Soviet elements. He linked the student turmoil to literary publications. Just a few months after denouncing Stalin's repression, the Kremlin leader-ship was talking about the need to investigate, arrest, and try internal political enemies.[72] The KGB and local authorities sprang into action. In

Moscow and Leningrad, the authorities began to remove from the local Komsomol organizations those activists who had been elected in the spring and those who had encouraged the student glasnost and free speech. On December 1 the KGB arrested two students of the Institute of Cinematography. In Leningrad on December 21, 1956, the KGB learned that a few students planned to gather on the Square of Art to discuss the Picasso exhibition that had recently opened at the Hermitage. Hundreds of KGB plainclothes officers, police, and sleuths surrounded the square, after clearing it of pedestrians. Arrests of students followed. A number of students in provinces were expelled from universities on spurious charges of challenging the principles of socialist realism in literature and art.[73] By the spring of 1957 thousands of students and other "troublemakers" would be expelled from schools and arrested. During 1957 almost twenty-five hundred people, among them not only students and intellectuals, but many workers and collective farmers, were indicted for counterrevolutionary crimes—the biggest spike in repressions since 1953.[74]

The editors of *Literaturnaia Moskva* were not arrested, but the almanac was shut down. A long and vicious official campaign against Simonov and Dudintsev announced the end of the Thaw to thousands of educated readers of *Novy Mir*. At first, Simonov behaved with dignity, offering his resignation from the journal.[75] Soon he went into semiexile in Tashkent, where he stayed for two years. At the same time, following the party orders, Simonov publicly renounced his earlier appeals for cultural liberalization and his views on Dudintsev's novel. That ended his short-lived career as the spiritual leader of the younger generation of educated Russians. David Samoilov referred in his diary to Simonov as "that son of a bitch."[76]

The crackdown of 1956 did not last, however. Khrushchev did not and probably could not return to full-scale Stalinist practices. In June 1957 Khrushchev emerged triumphant, having foiled a coup against him at the party plenum. He ousted his enemies Molotov and Kaganovich (but also Malenkov and Shepilov). And he tried to repair the damaged relationship with the Soviet intelligentsia, especially writers. In his usual populist manner, he organized his "appearance" before writers in the least formal way, at an outdoor party with food and drinks. The party took place on May 13, 1957, in one of Stalin's former dachas, sixty miles outside Moscow. His assistants prepared a carefully balanced text for him, but, as was his habit, he cast it aside, driven by his instincts and gradually by excessive amounts of alcohol, and began to speak off the cuff. Rada, his daughter, remembered her growing dismay as Khrushchev spoke: "Everything was wrong."[77] Khrushchev contradicted himself hopelessly and began to explain why he both "respected and condemned Stalin." He called Dudintsev a "chicken," a pawn in the hands of those who "wanted to seize political initiative from the party." He went on: "All the reactionary foreign press lionizes Dudintsev. They want to undermine us ideologically. They want to influence you, writers, and thereby demoralize our society."[78]

Those writers who had come in the hope of finding in Khrushchev an ally for the literary "renaissance" were appalled. Khrushchev's zigzags undermined his authority as a statesman among Stalinists and anti-Stalinists alike.[79] He was incapable of being the architect of the Soviet cultural paradigm. "Tsar Nikita" was woefully undereducated. He looked like a tipsy satyr, not an omniscient teacher. No matter how Soviet writers, intellectuals, and artists had suffered under Stalin, they still regarded him as a significant presence, almost as a mystical force. Khrushchev's behavior left them amused and humiliated at once. His power over writers and culture, now desacralized, began to resemble oppression, but also nonsense.[80] This view of Khrushchev quickly spread through the entire generation of younger educated Russians. Many could watch the Kremlin leader on television. In one televised appearance, speaking to the Congress of Soviet High School Teachers, Khrushchev apologized for his speech. He looked like a guilty schoolboy standing in front of the blackboard. On another public occasion, during the inauguration of the huge Lenin Stadium in Moscow, Khrushchev jabbered on so long that the audience of students and Komsomol activists began to jeer him.[81] The poet Samoilov saw Khrushchev close-up in April 1957 and thought he was a parody of a ruler; his behavior was "a cheap circus, philistinism expressed in state categories."[82]

Sensing his failure to communicate with intellectuals, Khrushchev turned to writers from a plebeian background, who could better understand him. Paradoxically, one of them was Alexander Tvardovsky, one of the original promoters of the Thaw. In July 1957 the Soviet leader invited him to become once again the editor of *Novy Mir*. Khrushchev also left everyday cultural matters, including literature, art, philosophy and history, to the officials of the state bureaucracies in charge of culture, education, and propaganda. This network included the divisions of the party apparatus, the ministries of education and culture, the subdivisions of the KGB, the secretariats of professional unions, and the presidium of the Academy of Sciences. For all its centralization and duplication, it was not monolithic. Some of the key bureaucratic players were determined to control the cultural output.[83] Others, among them Khrushchev's well-educated assistants Igor Lebedev and Igor Chernoutsan, harbored a personal passion for the arts and favored the gradual liberalization of artistic and intellectual life.[84]

Gradually, the number of arrests among students and intellectuals diminished.[85] The post-Stalin leadership expected to win over educated youth, not to terrorize them. During late 1956 and 1957 the party leaders and lecturers, as well as KGB functionaries, regularly gave speeches to students at Moscow State University. These functionaries sought to restore trust in Kremlin policies.[86] The KGB officials stressed that they would never return to Stalinist excesses and spoke about "socialist legality."[87] At the same time, the authorities restored some practices from the early 1930s, to pacify the students. In particular, they again introduced quotas on the number of children of intellectuals to be admitted to universities and took measures to increase the numbers of "children of workers and peasants" in the student body. Also, high school graduates could not enter the university without two-year "working-class experience," that is work at a factory or a plant.[88] The new policies made membership in the Komsomol obligatory for all college and high school students. By 1958 Komsomol ranks had soared to 18.5 million members. In 1962, membership reached 19.4 million—the numbers just could not grow any further.[89] These policies, the authorities hoped, would prevent educated youth from imitating their radical predecessors from the prerevolutionary intelligentsia.

The students and young intellectuals who had been politicized by Khrushchev's denunciation of Stalin and the Hungarian Revolution of 1956 graduated and dissolved into Soviet society. Some of them, like Igor Dedkov, were blacklisted and could not be employed in Moscow or other major cities, despite summa cum laude diplomas. A much greater number, however, continued to study at the universities in Moscow and Leningrad and cause headaches for the party nomenklatura and KGB. At Moscow State University, the departments of history, biology, and physics were especially volatile and "unreliable." Memories of the secret speech, the Stromynka boycott, the literary discussions of 1956, and the Hungarian Revolution continued to influence the mood of students and faculty. Many of them believed in pursuit of justice and wanted to fight for their rights. The students of the Institute of Cinematography organized a lecture boycott to protest the arrest of two of their classmates. They elected a commission to investigate the causes of the arrests and sent a letter of protest to the Supreme Soviet. The arrest of Krasnopevtsev's group by the KGB in August 1957 sent thousands of MGU students into a state of shock; some perceived it as a "return to 1937."[90]

The hopes for further liberalization did not come to an end. From the issues of power and politics the attention of educated young people moved to the search for new forms of cultural and personal self-expression. In February 1958 the head of the party organization at the history department complained that it was hard to defeat "revisionism" among students. There were just too many of them. During 1959 party functionaries in the MGU physics department complained that senior students rooted en masse "for freedom, for any kind of freedom. Even girls are for free love, for freedom of the arts, of abstract art. Somebody keeps shaping their views. Who does it? We in the party organization have no idea."[91]

Zhivago's Passions

Boris Pasternak, the author of *Doctor Zhivago,* was the only Russian writer in 1956 who did not wait for liberalization to come from above. He simply acted as if no censorship existed. Pasternak wrote to Konstantin Paustovsky: "Only the unacceptable should be published. Everything acceptable has long since been written and published." In May 1956 Pasternak distributed the manuscript of his novel to Polish and Czech publishers. He also asked an Italian visitor, Sergio D'Angelo, to pass the manuscript along to Giangiacomo Feltrinelli, a young Italian communist and aggressive publisher. Pasternak did not want to listen to the objections of his wife, who was fearful of the consequences.[92] In the commotion following the secret speech, when many foreign visitors to Pasternak's dacha came and went, the manuscript crossed the Soviet border. By September, the news that Pasternak had written an "anti-Soviet novel" and sent its manuscript abroad reached the KGB and the head of the party department of culture, Dmitry Polikarpov. About that time Simonov, after consultation with the authorities, sent a letter to Pasternak explaining that *Novy Mir* could not publish *Doctor Zhivago*. On September 1, 1956, a memorandum from the leaders of the writers' union to the party leadership concluded: "Pasternak not only comes out against

the socialist revolution and the Soviet state. He breaks with the core traditions of Russian democracy, [and] declares every word about the bright future of humanity, about the struggle for the people's happiness to be senseless, false, and duplicitous." At that point all the parties still wanted to
prevent a bigger scandal, and to dissuade Pasternak from publishing his
work abroad.[93] The Soviet authorities asked Pasternak to demand the return of the manuscript of *Doctor Zhivago* from Feltrinelli. The Russian
writer and the Italian editor were both, however, determined to publish the
novel. At that time Pasternak openly acknowledged that his earlier romantic infatuation with the Russian revolutionary movement and political radicalism had been a tragic mistake. He planned to use the royalties from the
novel to set up a foundation to restore destroyed churches and help the
families of victims of Stalinist repressions.[94]

After the novel was published in the West and received the Nobel Prize
in October 1958, the scandal triggered by Khrushchev's denunciation of
Pasternak quickly began to spiral out of control. Never before had a writer
living in the Soviet Union been the cause of such international political
storm. As had happened during the show trials of the 1930s, the authorities
set off an organized mass hate campaign, this time against the "unpatriotic"
Pasternak. The formula "He who is not with us is against us" presented him
to the Soviet people as a Western agent who had sold his "Soviet pride" for
Nobel Prize money. Workers and peasants who had previously never heard
of him demanded his expulsion from the USSR and even his execution.
The poet's family expected him to be deported any day. Adding insult to
injury, all Soviet publishers and editors broke their contracts with Pasternak, he no longer received any money, and his mail was stopped.[95]

The "Pasternak affair" sharply divided the Russian educated public and
cultural circles. Even those writers who championed cultural liberalization
and admired Pasternak's poetry decided against supporting him. Fear was
a major factor in their decision. Many convinced themselves that it was
madness to oppose the Soviet state. Some of Pasternak's old friends renounced him or feared to get in touch with him. Pasternak's Christian faith
and his firm belief in art free from ideology or politics irritated and infuriated many of his colleagues; they saw his stance as arrogance, his refusal to
back down as egotism, childish individualism. Even Vladimir Dudintsev,
whose name had been emblazoned on the banners of the 1956 movement
for liberalization, distanced himself from Pasternak and allowed the au-

thorities to use his name in the campaign. A high official of the Union of Soviet Writers and the author of the Soviet national anthem, the poet Sergei Mikhalkov, proposed to extradite Pasternak from the USSR.[96] Most strikingly, the students of the Institute of Literature in Moscow signed a letter supporting this motion. On October 27, 1958, the board of the Union of Soviet Writers voted unanimously to expel Pasternak from the union's ranks. On October 31 a general conference of Moscow writers voted in favor of the proposal to the government to send Pasternak abroad.[97] Among the speakers, unexpectedly, was the poet Boris Slutsky. He felt that Pasternak had become a tool of Western propaganda in the Cold War confrontation. He also felt responsible for the literary "renaissance" that Pasternak's individual revolt seemed to threaten. As he explained later to his oldest friend, "Had I refused [to denounce Pasternak], I would have been forced to renounce my party membership. After the Twentieth Party Congress I neither could nor wanted to do that."[98]

At the same time, a minority of writers, artists, intellectuals, and students viewed Pasternak as a hero, a victim of a monstrous and ignorant bureaucratic regime. David Samoilov wrote in his diary about *Zhivago,* "The significance of this book is far superior to its qualities." He remarked on Pasternak's "fascinating freedom of mind and seriousness in approaching the fundamental issues of our time."[99] Yevgeny Yevtushenko publicly insulted Slutsky by handing him "thirty coins," in an obvious comparison to Judas. A few students of philology and fans of futurism from Leningrad State University painted on the walls of the Peter and Paul Fortress in huge letters, "Long Live Pasternak!"[100]

This division was replicated among the broader reading public. Nobody could read Pasternak's novel (except a few who had seen it in manuscript and some who heard the excerpts on Western broadcasts). This fact did not prevent many people from expressing sharply divergent opinions about *Doctor Zhivago* and the author. They based their judgment on the selected fragments that *Literaturnaia Gazeta* had published. In November 1958 the newspaper had received 423 letters from its readers on the Pasternak affair. Of these, 338 expressed complete solidarity with the official denunciation of the "antipatriotic acts of B. Pasternak." Aside from the letters of collective "indignation," a group of people believed that Pasternak was wrong in his interpretation of the Russian Revolution as a cultural catastrophe, as an orgy of bestial energy that had destroyed Russian culture. They viewed the

Revolution as an enormous awakening of the repressed majority's self-worth. Only 43 letters, roughly 10 percent, supported Pasternak. By contrast with many denouncers and critics who had been witnesses to the Revolution, these defenders were younger educated people and students, the same audience that had applauded Dudintsev's novel two years earlier. For them Pasternak and his hero Zhivago could not be wrong, especially because they had been targets of an official campaign.[101]

The years of shocks produced an ambiguous impact on Russian intellectuals. An articulate minority of the young educated public felt prepared to oppose the party's decisions in the domain of culture, if not in other areas. This minority emerged largely during the events of 1956, which presented the younger generation with unexpected choices. The shock effect of Khrushchev's secret speech in particular was profound and lasting. Suddenly, the old idols lay shattered, and the new leadership's explanations of the past crimes were manifestly inadequate. The ideological commotion and unrest among students was palpable, for the first time since the advent of Stalinism. Some Soviet writers sought to reclaim their traditional Russian role of public moral leaders, raising "accursed questions" about who was guilty and what was to be done. The party leadership initially favored cultural liberalization but, under the impact of revolutionary events in Eastern Europe, returned to repression and reasserted control over the cultural sphere. Established writers, faced with pressure from above, capitulated and acted as servants of the regime. Only Boris Pasternak behaved in 1956–1958 in the tradition of the democratic "old intelligentsia" and defied the Soviet authorities. His novel *Doctor Zhivago* was a leap toward individual freedom and the outside world.

The momentum of emancipation from below continued. Facing the impossibility of radical democratization, young idealists placed their bets on cultural revival and self-expression. These familiar reflexes of Russian intelligentsia, squashed by the Bolshevik regime and Stalinism, began to reappear. Of course, this emerging contingent, for all its similarity with the "old intelligentsia" of the nineteenth century, belonged to a strikingly different society and a different era.

Frontiers are in my way. It's awkward
Not to know Buenos Aires or New York.

—Yevgeny Yevtushenko, 1955–56

three

Rediscovery of the World
1955-1961

KHRUSHCHEV'S course of "peaceful coexistence" presented new opportunities for travel abroad and interaction with foreigners. The Kremlin
envisaged a rapid expansion of cultural exchange with Western countries,
including ballet tours, concerts and music competitions, book and art exhibitions, and scientific and scholarly conferences. This policy was based on
the optimistic expectation that the Soviets could use the appeal of Russian
culture and science to offset the scary images of Soviet militarism and belligerent communism that had been the hallmark of U.S. Cold War propaganda.[1] The Soviet state began to tell Soviet citizens to "conquer" the hearts
and minds of foreign guests with hospitality and love.[2]

In opening up foreign tourism to the USSR and cultural exchange with
the West, Khrushchev incurred a risk. Thousands and eventually millions
of Soviet citizens—including scientists and artists—were drawn into this
enterprise. In 1955–56 artists, art exhibitions, performers, and just plain
tourists rushed into a previously hermetically closed Soviet society. On
June 2, 1957, Khrushchev, appearing on the popular CBS program *Face the
Nation,* provocatively called on Americans to "do away with your Iron Curtain." The Foreign Ministry followed up with formal proposals for a more
broad-scale exchange of technical, industrial, scientific, and artistic groups.
"Working with foreigners" became a growing cottage industry, involving
hundreds of institutions and hundreds of thousands of Soviet citizens.

Although Soviet authorities hoped that they had the means, beginning with the secret police, to keep "cultural diplomacy" under their control, this soon proved to be an illusion. Educated young Russians had grown up in a closed society, in an atmosphere permeated with xenophobia and anti-Western propaganda. After Soviet soldiers had marched across Europe and liberated it from the Nazis, Stalin rang down the Iron Curtain. Everything Soviet and Russian was extolled; everything foreign and especially Western and American fell under suspicion. Even during Stalin's life this policy backfired, producing spontaneous resistance from the *stiliagi,* the young men who turned foreign material culture and art, especially American jazz, fashion, and dances, into a cult. And when the post-Stalin leadership ended the period of xenophobia and cautiously began to open the country to the world, the Western cult begun by a few became a major trend.

Frederick C. Barghoorn, an American scholar from Yale University who was one of the first Western scholarly "paratroopers" to land behind the Iron Curtain, quickly noticed that Russian society was more vulnerable to Western penetration than American society was to communist influence. The American CIA understood it, as well, and considered educated young Russians targets of opportunity. The Kremlin acknowledged the point, albeit in an unconventional way. In October 1963 the KGB arrested Barghoorn on a trumped-up charge of espionage.[3] The future, however, proved that Barghoorn was right. Western "soft power," not the KGB, was a winning weapon. The growing exposure to foreign influences began, very slowly, to shape the minds of larger groups of educated Russians, especially youth in Moscow and Leningrad.

Glimpses through the Curtain

The isolation of the Soviet society from the world was imposed not only by the Iron Curtain, a physical barrier maintained across the eleven time zones with barbed wire, KGB border guards, and barking dogs. A psychological wall existed inside the hearts and minds of the vast majority of citizens of the Soviet Union. Some compared Soviet fear of everything foreign to a kind of mental illness that Stalin exploited. In the years from 1953 to 1955, recollects one Russian writer, that wall seemed to have been built "for life."[4]

Yet there were loose bricks in that wall. In 1955, as two young fans of

Western "style," the jazzman Alexei Kozlov and his friend Felix, kept their worshipful watch over the U.S. Embassy courtyard from the window of a Moscow apartment, other Russians began to gain glimpses through the Iron Curtain in ever greater numbers. The first layer of the Iron Curtain that Russians might penetrate, the first boundary to cross, took the form of the border with the "fraternal" countries of the Soviet bloc. After 1955, newspapers from "people's democracies" were available on some news-stands in Moscow and Leningrad, including on university campuses; those papers provided the first alternative source of information to reports in the Soviet media. At the same time, Soviet tourism to Eastern Europe grew rapidly; in 1957 more than half a million Russians traveled to Poland, Ro-mania, China, East Germany, and other communist countries.[5]

Poland was especially important. One linguist and poet from Moscow recalled that "for a certain part of intelligentsia in the Soviet Union, Poland after 1955–1956 served as a bridge to Europe, to European culture—begin-ning with the general culture of ideas and ending with political culture." Some poets and other writers, budding intellectuals, and scholars learned Polish before they learned other foreign languages. Polish newspapers and books on philology, art, philosophy, and sociology were like a second-hand version of the Western original, yet they provided a good start. Some American and European authors, such as William Faulkner, Franz Kafka, and James Joyce, were banned from Russian libraries, yet available in Polish translation. Even Polish publications on Marxism-Leninism had more depth to them, for their authors were aware of the plurality of European Marxist and social democratic thought. Besides, Polish and Russian culture and history were inextricably linked. A Russian student of Polish ancestry who studied at Moscow State University observed, "Everything that took place in Poland reverberated in Moscow. Why? The Poles have always been very close to us. We share a common history, a common experience."[6] Both the Polish and the Russian intelligentsia had idealistic, romantic, and revo-lutionary roots; in both countries the intelligentsia collapsed as a result of the repression, violence, and mass massacres during World War II and the Stalinist period. And in both the Soviet "metropolis" and the Polish "satel-lite" late Stalinism did everything to extinguish the specter of cultural au-tonomy and freethinking. The Poles, however, managed to preserve more of these precious qualities.

The next and most coveted boundary to cross allowed entry to countries outside the Soviet bloc. Yugoslavia, Greece, Italy, France, and a host of other attractive tourist destinations were virtually off-limits, for they belonged to the hostile parts of the world. For years, only a select few members of "Soviet intelligentsia" like Ehrenburg and Simonov were able to travel there, always with Stalin's personal approval. Khrushchev changed that. He and other Soviet leaders began to go abroad, starting with a trip to Yugoslavia in May 1955, "like Renaissance princes, accompanied by a retinue of top performers—ballerinas, singers, and pianists were taken along."[7] In June 1956, on its maiden voyage, the luxury liner *Victory* took a large group of high-placed Soviet officials, but also journalists, writers, musicians, and artists, around Europe for the first time in their lives. (It was this trip which led Paustovsky to think about a new privileged class in Soviet society.) The ship sailed from Odessa to Turkey, Greece, Italy, and France—altogether eleven countries—and returned to Leningrad. The liner's passengers saw Mount Etna on Sicily, visited Capri, and saw the museums of the Vatican and the Louvre.

Every traveler abroad had to be approved for an "exit" visa from the USSR. This meant obtaining approval from a host of authorities at the person's place of work or study—the Komsomol, party, management, trade unions—and then being vetted by the KGB and the "exit" section at party headquarters. A candidate for a trip abroad had to have an unblemished "moral and political face," at least from the point of view of the screening committees. Any one of them could close the exit gates at any moment. For many who left the USSR for the first time, the trip became an intense, almost religious experience, a tale to share with all friends and acquaintances.[8] Onboard the *Victory* liner, a young writer "discovered new worlds" for the first time. "It is impossible to set down on paper the beauty of those landscapes, the sultry breeze and warmth, and the feelings that overwhelmed us." Another passenger, a journalist for the party organ *The Communist,* swore half a century later that the voyage had "shocked him even more than Twentieth Party Congress." He explained, "I saw cultures and ways of life that we could not even dream about."[9]

The leaders after Stalin encouraged privileged journalists and other writers to publicize their impressions about the outside world, provided that those impressions were ideologically correct and patriotic. In the fall of 1955 seven Soviet journalists and writers took a tour across the United States. The group included Khrushchev's son-in-law, Alexei Adzhubei, who was the editor of *Komsomolskaia Pravda*. The journalists traveled around the United States for two weeks on a lavish spending account and attended numerous meetings, rallies, and parties. The Soviet visitors tried hard to conceal their culture shock with invocations of Soviet patriotism. After the trip they told Khrushchev that most Americans were friendly and open. The leader of the group, the head of the international department of the Union of Soviet Writers, sent several memoranda to the party Central Committee with recommendations that took aim at xenophobic traditions in Soviet diplomacy, the rigidity of the Soviet media, and the propaganda machinery. The memos also proposed reaching out to American writers, and publishing the works of Ernest Hemingway, William Faulkner, and Arthur Miller in the Soviet Union. Foreign correspondents working in the Soviet Union, according to one memo, should not be treated as foreign spies and "bandits of the pen."[10] A series of articles (later transformed into books) appeared in millions of copies, informing educated Russian readers, among other things, that Americans owned fifty-five million cars, that the United States had high-quality roads and services and comfortable hotels and motels.[11] All this was a great revelation to Soviet readers.

Another memo from the writers observed that 8 to 10 percent of American citizens had family roots in tsarist Russia but that at the height of the anticosmopolitan campaign, they had no longer been able to communicate with their relatives in the Soviet Union. The memo recommended lifting restrictions on such family correspondence, so that thousands of Soviet citizens, "with the assistance" of Soviet and Komsomol organizations, could write back to their American relatives and dispel "legends about the Iron Curtain." Of course, the memo continued, the correspondence would be controlled, and harmful epistles would simply be intercepted.[12] In the next few years the propaganda authorities and the KGB disagreed on the issue of private correspondence. Yet tens of thousands of families in Russia again began to receive letters and postcards from their relatives living abroad.

No foreign tourists had arrived in the USSR by the time Stalin died. In Moscow in 1954–55 a tiny foreign colony remained, consisting mostly of journalists and men who had married Russian women and decided to stay. In the population of Moscow, just a tiny fraction was left of the once-extensive community of foreign communists, their families, lovers, friends, and acquaintances: it had been destroyed by the Great Terror and the subsequent anticosmopolitan campaigns.[13] At the same time, the growth of the

Soviet empire produced a new international crowd: exchange students from "fraternal" countries. University dorms hosted thousands of young men and women from Poland, Czechoslovakia, Hungary, Romania, Bulgaria, East Germany, China and Mongolia, and Albania. Later, students came from Yugoslavia, France, and Italy, and Egypt, Syria, and other Arab countries with "progressive" regimes. Many of them made substantial contributions to the endless, sometimes stormy debates students had about political, social, and cultural developments in the USSR. Particularly strong was the cultural and intellectual influence of Polish and Czech students. Mikhail Gorbachev developed a close friendship with Zdeněk Mlynář, a Czech student. Friendship with foreigners opened up new comparative perspectives and eroded the customary xenophobia, dogmatism, and chauvinism among students. Many still believed that the "Soviet way is always the best," but a few others began to harbor doubts. Eastern and Central European literature and fine art, once discovered, dispelled the myth of Russian and Soviet cultural superiority.[14]

In 1955 Moscow, Leningrad, Stalingrad, Rostov, and a number of other Soviet cities opened their doors to Western tourists and their once-dreaded cosmopolitan influences. The tourist infrastructure and logistics dismantled in the 1930s were restored. A few hotels in Moscow and Leningrad, among them the Moskva and Sovetskaia, were spruced up and elevated, at least in the Soviet imagination, to Western standards of service.[15] A number of Soviet intellectuals and artists took advantage of Khrushchev's secret speech to invite their colleagues from abroad as well as Russian artists who had emigrated to the West after the Russian Revolution. Members of the old intelligentsia, separated for decades, could meet again. In May 1956, the famous linguist Roman Jakobson, an émigré from Russia who was a professor at Harvard University, returned to visit his friends. Isaiah Berlin also visited from Oxford for the first time since 1945.[16]

Foreign visitors became the object of tremendous attention from Russian students. During the summer of 1957 the future CIA analyst and historian Raymond Garthoff met with hundreds of students in Moscow and around Russia. In one instance, Garthoff and his colleague met spontaneously with 150 students from an agricultural college outside Leningrad. As soon as it became clear that the Americans spoke Russian, a large circle gathered around each of them. Students were so excited and grateful for the opportunity that they even escorted the guests in a ceremonial march to the train station.[17] The KGB could not monitor every contact young intellectuals had with foreigners, although it watched them closely.[18]

The appearance of foreigners on the streets of Moscow, Leningrad, and other Soviet cities after 1955 provided a boost to the *stiliagi* movement. The fans of "style" met their role models, real Westerners, for the first time. An American college student who traveled to Russia late in 1956 talked to many Moscow teenagers. Some of them proudly told him which wavelengths enabled them to hear the Voice of America. The American student noticed their contempt for the authorities and the police and perceptively observed that "in their general hatred of their own life, they have built up an over-glamorized picture of life outside the Soviet Union." The *stiliagi* tried to buy everything he was wearing.[19] The immediate result of the reappearance of foreign tourism was the practice of buying and selling of foreign clothes, sometimes secondhand. At first style apers just wanted to buy foreign-looking articles that were fashionable and of high quality for themselves. The search for individual bargains quickly developed into a new kind of black market, one in highly prestigious "Western products" that were not available in Soviet stores.[20]

Culture Shock

From October to December 1956, in addition to the Hungarian crisis and the heated literary discussion surrounding *Not by Bread Alone,* another event excited tens of thousands of people in Moscow and Leningrad: the Cubist art of Pablo Picasso, the prolific Spanish genius, was on display for the first time in the Soviet Union, at the Pushkin Museum of Fine Arts in Moscow, and then at the State Hermitage Museum in Leningrad. Under Stalin, Picasso's art had been banned in the USSR as "formalist," despite the fact that Picasso was a member of the French Communist Party and his dove was the symbol of the pro-Soviet international peace movement. The ban on formalist art was not lifted after Stalin's death and was even strengthened by the Cold War cultural offensives, as the American government promoted abstract art as a proof of freer artistic self-expression in the West.[21] Last but not least, power in the Union of Soviet Artists and the Soviet Academy of Arts was completely in the hands of the established "masters of socialist realism"—in other words, those who controlled the gigantic and highly profitable production of artifacts for party propaganda ranging from pompous paintings to statues and busts of Stalin and Lenin.[22]

The opening of the Picasso exhibitions was the result of Ilya Ehrenburg's clever scheme. He had known and liked Picasso since the 1920s, when they met in the bohemian circles of Paris. Ehrenburg played on the Kremlin's eagerness to reach out to the broader intellectual and artistic circles of Western Europe. The French Communist Party supported Ehrenburg and greatly enhanced his lobbying power. Additional support came from many younger Soviet artists who in 1955 began to raise their voices against the complete subjugation of art to the goals of state propaganda. They looked for an opportunity to rehabilitate artists who had been victims of Stalinist purges and campaigns after the early 1930s.[23] On the eve of the exhibition opening in Moscow, a large group of artists organized a reception to celebrate Picasso's seventy-fifth birthday. When Ehrenburg entered the reception, they gave him an ovation. By contrast, most shunned the confused and sweating Alexander Gerasimov, the president of the Academy of Art.[24]

On October 25, 1956, the day of the opening, crowds of people gathered around the Pushkin Museum. Ehrenburg asked those who were pushing forward through the police cordon to remain patient: "You waited for this moment for twenty-five years. Now please wait a few minutes more."[25] Many young Soviet artists considered the exhibition to be the most important single event of their artistic lives. Indeed, it marked a breakthrough. It became possible after the Picasso exhibition to bring back from oblivion the names of other artists banned and ostracized during the Stalin years. The fans of Western "style" and aesthetic rebels who made it to the exhibition recognized Picasso's art as truly revolutionary, as their ally against the ossified Stalinist culture.[26]

Many other educated visitors to the Picasso exhibition, however, were not prepared for what they saw. Confronting Cubism was an unnerving experience for the culture-hungry audiences in Moscow and Leningrad. Debates about Picasso flared up right in front of his paintings and became the second most important discussion after the 1953 debates on "sincerity in literature." The journals of visitors, kept in the archives, bear the traces of profound stupefaction and the most often repeated exclamation was, "We cannot understand anything!"[27] The centrality of the fine arts in Russian consciousness, combined with decades of isolation of educated Russian society from the multitude of the world's cultural trends, contributed to the shock and the subversive power of the Picasso exhibition. In the Soviet Union of 1956 it was as much a symbol of radicalism as was support for the Hungarian Revolution. Soviet students, scientists, teachers, physicians, engineers, and other professionals had a certain idea of what high culture was and believed that Soviet educational experience had equipped them with a sufficient understanding of what was "good," "progressive," and beautiful and what was not. Now another certainty had been shattered. Which art was "progressive" and which was not? What did "socialist realism" mean?

Other questions emerged in 1956. Which system, capitalist or Soviet, provided better conditions for cultural growth and self-expression? The Kremlin's new approach was implicitly based on its sense of cultural superiority. The Soviet leaders wanted to demonstrate to the world the "great achievements of Soviet culture" as well as the well-preserved traditions of prerevolutionary Russian culture. Performances by the Bolshoi and Kirov ballet groups, the Moiseyev Dance Company, or the spectacular virtuosi Emil Gilels, David Oistrakh, Leonid Kogan, and Mstislav Rostropovich never failed to fill Western concert halls.[28] Yet this had to be a two-way street, along which American and Western European musicians and artists could now travel to perform in Moscow and Leningrad. And educated Soviet audiences could now watch, listen, and compare.

The first wave of performers from the United States opened in December 1955 with a sensational presentation of Gershwin's *Porgy and Bess* by the Everyman Opera Company in Leningrad. Truman Capote, who covered the trip as a correspondent for the *New Yorker,* described the culture shock Russians experienced. About a thousand Leningraders came to greet the cast at the train station: they stared at the exotic visitors, mostly black, "with immense silence, an almost catatonic demeanor." At the same time, Russian ballerinas rolled their eyes appreciatively and sighed as they gazed at the visitors' shoes, touched their dresses, rubbed silk and taffeta between their fingers. Thirty thousand people flocked to the Marinsky (Kirov) Theater to hear the performance. Most of them were scandalized and astonished by the unabashed eroticism of the production. During the scene when Crown attempts to rape Bess, "he grips her to him, gropes her buttocks, her breast; and ends with Bess raping him—she rips off his shirt, wraps her arms around him and writhes, sizzles like bacon in a skillet." At that moment "areas of the audience suffered something like a blackout." After Leningrad, the cast went to Moscow, where, on the eve of the Twentieth Party Congress, the Kremlin leaders attended and applauded the performance.[29]

Soviet journalists and writers who traveled to the United States in 1955 reported that the United States was not only a fascinating material civilization. Americans also enjoyed many wonderful museums, theaters, and a flourishing cultural scene.[30] The excellence of American classical music performances in Moscow and Leningrad in 1956 also shook the smug sense of Russian cultural superiority.[31] In January 1956 the newspaper *Soviet Culture* published the glowing account of the Soviet violinist David Oistrakh, who performed in the United States for the first time. Oistrakh highly praised the Philadelphia Symphony Orchestra under the conductorship of Eugene Ormandy, as well as many American violinists he met during his tour. American cultural influence on educated Russians increased through another prestigious channel: literature in translation. In 1955–56 Moscow publishing houses printed millions of copies of translations of books by various American authors previously unavailable or forgotten in the USSR.[32] Many American authors, such as Theodore Dreiser and Upton Sinclair, were selected because of their criticism of American capitalism. Publication of other authors required intense lobbying. Ehrenburg successfully fought for Hemingway's novel *The Old Man and the Sea,* and it was published in March 1955 in *Inostrannaia Literatura* (Foreign Literature), a recently launched and highly popular journal for the intellectual and cultural elite. The works of Hemingway had been popular among young romantics in Russia in the late 1930s, and he immediately became a cult author among students during the Thaw. Other authors remained to be rediscovered. One of them was John Steinbeck, who had disappeared from the Soviet list of "progressive writers" after he published an honest account of his trip across the Soviet Union in 1947.[33]

The inroads made by American cultural influence produced an immediate counterattack. Reacting to Oistrakh's article, the party's department of propaganda and agitation warned newspaper editors that only the Soviet Union could be advertised as a world leader in classical music.[34] In 1957 *Literaturnaia Gazeta* published a series of articles by Alexander Kazem-Bek, an aristocrat and Russian right-wing nationalist who had returned to the Soviet Union after 1945. The author denounced the United States as "a country without [high] culture," in contrast to the Soviet Union and Europe with their great cultural and intellectual heritage. American capitalism and commercialism, Kazem-Bek warned, paid for mass entertainment and did not need the fine arts or masterpieces of poetry and fiction. The newspaper editor, a passionate Stalinist, welcomed the article as a salvo against "cosmopolitan forces" inside the Soviet cultural establishment.[35]

Ilya Ehrenburg, an informal leader of the "cosmopolitan forces" in Soviet society, countered, convincing the Soviet leadership that Kazem-Bek's article was harmful to Soviet influence in the world peace movement. "It should be obvious to everyone that we cannot appeal to our Western fellow-travelers without showing some kind of initiative inside our country. Even during the [Great Patriotic] war nobody here wrote about German culture in the tones Kazem-Bek has written about American culture." Ehrenburg's argument had its effect: the party leadership instructed the newspaper to publish the rejoinder.[36] Ehrenburg wrote that America was a country of great culture and that many "progressive" writers and musicians lived there.[37] The polemics Kazem-Bek and Ehrenburg engaged in provide an early look at the growing rift between the nationalist-xenophobic and internationalist trends among Soviet intellectuals and cultural figures. This rift would only grow in the next decade, rendering the official policy of consolidation of cultural elites null and void.[38]

For educated and socially conscious Russians the Thaw was a time of rediscovery of art films offering a complex treatment of history and social issues. Audiences that had grown up with the images of Stalinist comedies and patriotic blockbusters, *Tarzan*, and *The Great Waltz* were stunned by a series of drama-packed Italian neorealist films by Vittorio De Sica, Roberto Rossellini, and Luchino Visconti. Later, *La Strada* and *The Nights of Cabiria* by Federico Fellini, starring Giulietta Masina, conquered the hearts of many Russian viewers. Postwar Polish films, above all the films of Andrzej Wajda *(Kanal; Ashes and Diamonds),* presented recent history in tragic and unusually nuanced ways. This is not to say that the culture-starved Russian public preferred "serious" films to blockbusters and entertainment. Cinema was the most powerful vehicle of American and Western influence during the Thaw. Many of the best-known American films (by Elia Kazan, Cecil B. DeMille, and Alfred Hitchcock) did not reach a broad Soviet audience, owing to party censorship. Still, rates of purchases and releases of foreign films increased considerably according to official statistics, from 46 in 1954 to 71 in 1955. The secret speech emboldened cinema critics, film directors, and above all the Ministry of Culture to lobby for more. The ministry's main interest was economic: every foreign film automatically became a blockbuster with the cinema-starved Soviet audience and brought millions of rubles into the ministry's budget. In May 1956 the minister of culture suggested that the party secretariat delegate the business of selecting foreign films to ministerial experts. In June the secretariat, prompted by the CC department of culture, rejected this initiative, thus retaining its right to screen "alien" ideological and cultural film productions.[39]

Some signs seemed to indicate that the educated Soviet public was longing for new cultural icons reflecting the spirit of a new era. The twenty-year-old actress Liudmila Gurchenko, a swarthy beauty from Ukraine, became the first national movie star in 1956–57. As Gurchenko would recall in her memoirs, on her way to the Moscow film studio every day she saw "billboards announcing the arrival of foreign artists, the jazz orchestra of the famous Benny Goodman, singers from Sweden and Germany, ballet groups from India, the United States, and France. We learned to appreciate our value on a different scale."[40] Foreign artists competed with the Russian ones for the sympathies of the young public. Concerts in Moscow by the French actor and chansonnier Yves Montand in late 1956 created a sensation. Even earlier, many intellectuals in Moscow and Leningrad had become fans of Montand and signed up in droves to learn French, just so they would be able to understand the lyrics to his songs. After the Soviet invasion of Hungary, the vast majority of Western visitors decided to cancel their trips to the USSR in protest. Montand allowed Soviet diplomats to convince him to defy the Western cultural blockade.[41]

In Moscow a red-carpet treatment awaited him: he even met personally with Nikita Khrushchev, and on December 15, 1956, sang at the newly opened Luzhniki Sports Arena, the largest performance venue in the USSR. The appearance of the dark-eyed and dashingly elegant French actor in a tight-fitting black sweater was a tremendous success. His lyrical songs, including the hit "Les feuilles mortes," made older audience members weep. Montand's concert was the first occasion of mass hysteria produced by a Western pop star. Soviet fans, especially young women, behaved like their Western counterparts at the concerts of Elvis Presley: they tore buttons off the singer's coats, wept with joy, and danced in rapture on their seats. "This was not enthusiasm—it was something wild," recalled one Komsomol official indignantly. Montand's songs and appearance "generated immense anxiety among us young people for a beautiful life" outside the boundaries of the Soviet Union, recalled a Leningrad art student.[42]

In April 1958, the Texas-born pianist Van Cliburn unexpectedly won the Tchaikovsky International Piano Competition in Moscow, another new encounter in the Soviet cultural offensive. The twenty-three-year-old American played Tchaikovsky's First Concerto with more depth, élan, and feeling than his Russian competitors.[43] After Van Cliburn's performance the elite Moscow audience stood up and chanted, "First prize! First prize!" Not only foreigners on the jury, but the composers Dmitry Shostakovich and Dmitry Kabalevsky as well as the piano stars Genrikh Neigauz, Sviatoslav Richter, and Emil Gilels gave the young American their full support. The patriarch of the Russian piano school Alexander Goldenweiser called Van Cliburn "a new Rachmaninov." Public pressure forced the Ministry of Culture to appeal to Khrushchev for permission to award the first prize to the American pianist. Khrushchev, himself a victim of the young lanky American's charm, gave his consent.[44]

Not only did Van Cliburn touch the Russian soul with his music, but he turned into the first international star on Soviet television. Six feet tall, seemingly delicate, with elegant hands and incredibly long fingers, a child-like smile, and a crown of wavy hair, he replaced the French singer as a male icon among refined Russians. Van Cliburn's personality generated a quasi-erotic response in many, especially the educated female audience, sensitive to romantic and spiritual influences. One woman wrote in her diary, "My soul is turned inside out by the playing of this American young man. How beautiful and inspired a man can be!"[45] American diplomats observed that Van Cliburn's appearance generated "a kind of mass hysteria," especially among "females between the ages of 15 and 65." Young Muscovite women shrieked, "Vania, Vania!" threw flowers, offered him jars of jam and winter socks, tugged at the pianist's clothes, and stood in front of his hotel for hours. Many women sent love letters to the Moscow Conservatory, urging "Vania" to marry them and stay in Russia.[46]

"Vania" remained a hero of the postwar generation. Hundreds of thousands of Soviet parents made sure that their children would take piano lessons. In December 1987, when the aged Van Cliburn performed at the White House for honored Soviet guests Mikhail and Raisa Gorbachev, emotions overpowered all three. They embraced with tears in their eyes.

Kremlin All-Nighter

The public emotion evoked by Picasso, Montand, and Van Cliburn paled in comparison to that elicited by the event that took Moscow by storm, the World Youth Festival in July–August 1957. Komsomol leaders, together with the Committee of Youth Organizations, had obtained Khrushchev's authorization for this event in 1955, the year of public diplomacy. At first, the Kremlin expected to conduct the festival on the most restricted budget possible. The initial budget was estimated at around three hundred million rubles, most of it to be covered by a special festival lottery.[47] As was the case with many initiatives of the Khrushchev era, the organizers failed to foresee the scale and expense of the festival. The Kremlin leaders expected great propaganda gains. For this reason Soviet authorities advertised the event globally, to ensure maximum international participation, even after the danger of an international boycott over the Soviet invasion of Hungary had subsided. Eventually the plan to get "the most bang for the fewest rubles" was discarded. The youth festival in Moscow had to be bigger, better, and jollier than any previous event of its kind.

Alexander Shelepin, the head of the Komsomol, created special head-quarters for the preparations. Shelepin, who was a graduate of the famous IFLI, had quickly become a party careerist. He mobilized Komsomol youth for war, but he never saw battle himself.[48] A tough administrator and a stern disciplinarian, Shelepin put all gears in motion. His team planned a huge mobilization campaign. The Komsomol called on "boys and girls of the Soviet Union," especially of Moscow, to start creating new parks, planting trees along streets and on squares, and constructing sports arenas and play-grounds. Young Muscovites were encouraged to learn at least one foreign language, to memorize foreign songs, dances, and games. The Kremlin directed many ministries to help with Shelepin's preparations. The Ministry of the Interior, Ministry of Foreign Affairs, Ministry of Communications, and of course the KGB became closely involved in the preparations. Chinese, English, German, French, and Spanish language classes were broad-cast on Soviet television.[49]

Soviet authorities anticipated that eighty-three thousand young men and women from all over the Soviet Union would visit the festival. The number of foreign guests was limited by quotas for each country, but, as would become evident, these could not be predicted with precision. The organizers estimated that 7,000 guides, including 3,290 interpreters, would be needed, "to work with the festival participants." Hectic recruitment of guides began among senior students at universities and technical schools in Moscow and Leningrad. Directors of all educational institutions, as well as many state enterprises, were ordered to allow their students and employees who were involved in the festival organization and activities to go on paid leave for thirty-five days' duration.[50]

Preparations took two years and required a truly titanic effort. For a quarter of a century the Soviet Union had remained virtually closed to foreigners; there was no tourist infrastructure in place. The organizers had to tackle such issues as the squalid appearance of most urban areas, the inadequacy and scarcity of hotels, and the lack of good advertising, clothing, carnival costumes, paraphernalia of attractive quality, fast-food places and ethnic restaurants, and shopping opportunities. Shelepin and his people groaned as they confronted, at every step along the way, further manifestations of the backwardness of Soviet society and the economy.[51]

Yet they scored impressive achievements. Moscow authorities, with the Komsomol's assistance, constructed at breakneck speed the Luzhniki Sports Arena. In addition, they built the Winter Stadium and several large covered swimming pools, a luxury previously unknown in the USSR. They renovated Moscow hotels and installed foreign tourist facilities, such as the currency exchange offices and equipment for international telephone calls. The service economy in Moscow was doubled, including an upsurge in the number of trained staff, the production of tourist souvenirs, openings of self-service or fast-food restaurants, cafés, shoe repair shops, and laundry services, and the manufacture of a wide variety of youth "couture" (vests, trousers, T-shirts, and so on). And the Komsomol organized rallies, carnivals, fireworks, singing contests, and more for the avalanche of youth they expected to come to Moscow. They even chose a hit song for the festival, "Moscow Nights," which soon would become known around the world. Most spectacularly, a number of the festival events were planned to take place inside the Kremlin. The old tsarist castle had remained closed to the public since 1918, when the Bolshevik leadership moved there from Petrograd. Stalin and other members of the leadership had lived inside its walls with their families, and the Politburo held its sessions there. In March 1955 the party presidium, at Khrushchev's initiative, decided to reopen the Kremlin, and in July a large portion of it became public space.[52]

A wide array of carnival items were now produced for the festival, including even Venetian masks. Drab Moscow began to take on a new look, at least in downtown areas and in the neighborhoods assigned to host festival events and offer residences for foreigners. Many dusty streets, cracked facades, rank alleys, and garbage-filled courtyards were spruced up, cleaned, painted, washed. Balconies on which people had heretofore only hung out clothes to dry or grown vegetables were festooned with flowers. Still, the last-minute improvisations in tourist service could not produce enough hotels. The existing ones would have to accommodate four to five foreign guests in every room. Soviet guests were lucky to sleep in dormitory units and school classrooms, each housing twelve or even fourteen persons.[53]

The authorities assumed that the festival, like any Soviet mass event, would proceed under the control of state and party authorities and their agents. "If they [the festival guests] were to be surrounded by thieves and *stiliagi,* then they would leave with a bad image of our country," said one top organizer. The Ministry of the Interior began to clear Moscow of "undesirable elements," including Gypsies, prostitutes, beggars, and homeless orphans. At the same time the authorities mobilized, in addition to numerous policemen and security agents, thirty-two thousand volunteers from the Komsomol organizations, to meet and help foreign guests.[54] Up to the last minute, fears of Western "provocation" haunted the organizers. A good number of Social Democratic, Catholic, and other anti-Soviet youth institutions abroad denounced participation in the Moscow festival as immoral. The KGB warned that among foreign youth were some "people with hostile attitudes toward the USSR, as well as spies and saboteurs."[55] In order to preempt the expected hostility of the guests, the festival organizers appealed through newspapers to Muscovites. They told them "to embrace foreign guests with love."[56] In a word, the Soviet regime brought foreign youth to Ivan and Masha with instructions for them to fall in love.

The transition from the USSR's complete isolation to limited, controlled openness produced unexpected mass exhilaration. Analogies with hermits coming out of isolation, or divers rising rapidly to the surface spring to mind. Russians, whose only large-scale encounter with foreigners had occurred during the last war, suddenly saw trains full of friendly and sympathetic young men and women, some of them from other countries, coming to Moscow from Brest, Odessa, and Leningrad, and other ports of entry. Muscovites felt overwhelmed and overexcited, intoxicated as if by an excess of oxygen. Crowds, applauding and throwing flowers, gathered at every station along the way to Moscow. They were no doubt "organized" by local authorities, yet they expressed spontaneous and boundless joy. Many of the Komsomol volunteers and young policemen who were supposed to keep the festival under control felt transported like everybody else.[57]

Three million people in Moscow, and other Russian guests, most of them under thirty, had fervor enough to turn the festival into a true carnival, rich with affection and spontaneity. They met thirty-four thousand foreign guests who came from 130 countries. Soviet authorities were unprepared for the scale of the enthusiasm. On the opening day the triumphal procession from the exhibition of Soviet economic achievements to the Luzhniki Stadium took four hours instead of one: people blocked the route, and the police were helpless to stop them. Tens of thousands of hands were stretched out to foreign guests to convey ice cream, drinks, cakes, and coins "for luck."[58] Even the organized events were imbued with a fresh and exhilarating sense of liberation. The Kremlin flung its doors open to the youthful crowds, and thousands danced at "Kremlin parties." There was even a torchlight parade.[59] By the second day of the festival, official reports from Komsomol observers as well as from agents of the Ministry of the Interior mentioned "peculiar spontaneous meetings" in the streets of Moscow. Thousands of young foreigners roamed freely around the Soviet capital, meeting strangers. Inevitably, a crowd of Russians would surround the foreigners, and with the help of impromptu translation and vivid gestures a dialogue of civilizations began.

Russian xenophobia and fear of secret police informers virtually evaporated during the festival. Police reports mention specific cases of young Russians loudly complaining about supervision and control in front of foreign guests. The absence of fear was remarkable in the light of the recent arrests during the crackdowns of late 1956. Many of the foreigners were invited by Muscovites to their homes for a chat. Some Muscovites brought milk and meat from their homes as refreshments for foreigners.[60] Russian crowds extended their exuberant affection even to Americans, some of whom came to Moscow bristling with their own ideological self-righteousness and prepared for Cold War polemics. The jazz musician Kozlov recalls, "Americans were depicted in two ways—either as poor, unemployed, gaunt, unshaven people in rags or as big-bellied bourgeois in tuxedos and top hats, with a fat cigars in their mouths. And there was a third category—hopeless Negroes, all of them victims of the Ku Klux Klan."[61] Now Russians saw freethinking young men and women, dressed in simple but stylish clothing. Their Cold War stereotypes lay in ruins. Many people simply left their workplaces and offices, eager to see as many events as possible. Among them was Khrushchev's daughter Rada, the editor of a scientific journal.

She recalled the festival as a moment when "the world opened up" and the long-expected bright future suddenly came to Moscow streets and squares. Rada's husband Alexei Adzhubei wrote in his memoirs that downtown Moscow "practically did not sleep during all fifteen days of the festival."[62]

The festival was a time of revelation and, for a brief moment, liberation for Russian fans of "style," especially young musicians and artists. In their eagerness to demonstrate the diversity and creativity of "Soviet life," the party and Komsomol authorities suspended the ban on "Western" and formalist styles in music and pictorial art for a week, and suddenly Moscow was jolted by Scottish bagpipes, Spanish and Hawaiian guitars, and jazz saxophones. On Pushkin Square, in the middle of Gorky Street in the center of the city, bands from different countries played, day and night. Americans and other Western youth taught Russian volunteers how to dance rock-and-roll and boogie-woogie, dances that were forbidden in the USSR and practiced only at the style apers' private parties. Russian formalist and abstract artists, the persecuted underdogs of the Soviet art world, were able to participate in international art competitions and publicly display their works. The variety of artistic styles contrasted sharply with the customary oppressive monotony of official Soviet art.[63] The traditional Russian-Soviet cultural hierarchy with its top and bottom, the refined and the vulgar, began to erode. The idea of a multiplicity of cultures, and cultural pluralism, which had been excluded by socialist realism, returned.

For the first time, real American jazz bands played in the concert halls of Moscow and even in the streets. There was a jazz competition, and Russian bands, mostly consisting of Moscow's students, took part in it. Jazz concerts sparked enormous curiosity among the public, since Soviet ideologists had for years treated jazz as "enemy art," a tool of the United States in the Cold War. For Soviet jazz musicians such direct exposure to live American jazz improvisation and musicians from another world brought nothing short of catharsis, not to mention an indispensable professional update.[64]

Nonrealist Russian painters experienced a similar catharsis. Artists who had been working for years beyond the pale of officially recognized art, in tiny, cramped basement studios, took part in the festival's international art exhibition in Gorky Park and worked side by side with young American and West European artists in the festival's art studios. When American artists, in imitation of Jackson Pollock, began to sprinkle and drip colors on their canvases, their Moscow colleagues were mesmerized by a sense of freedom. Anatoly Zverev, at twenty-six years old a phenomenally talented artist, immediately responded to the American challenge. Within an hour, working at a furious tempo before the eyes of the fascinated crowd, he painted an entire partition wall of the studio in "drip" style. He and some other underground artists received prizes and medals from the festival's international jury.[65]

The Komsomol reports smugly announced that "the majority of Soviet youth quickly figured out the reactionary essence of bourgeois culture and art." The encounter with Western cultural demons, the reports continued, merely "helped our youth better appreciate the beauty and national character of Soviet art."[66] But even the official reporters had to admit that "a small stratum of young people became visible during the festival, mostly students and representatives of the young intelligentsia, who enthusiastically embraced bourgeois culture and, froth on their mouths, defended the abstract art before those who did not understand it. A certain part of our youth began to ape the loose mode of behavior demonstrated by some delegates from Western countries." To the propagandists' regret, the entire country saw televised images of young people dancing American-style during the Kremlin ball. A crowd of *stiliagi* and other sympathizers broke through the police cordons, crashed the gates, or just sneaked into the concert hall assigned for a jazz competition.[67]

The festival transformed some fans of "style" into underground entrepreneurs who got involved in illegal exchange of money and sales of much-coveted foreign clothing. The attractive black market price of the ruble (which contrasted with the overrated value of the ruble at the official exchange rate) ensured that many young foreign tourists would try to add to their funds in Moscow by turning to private buyers. Soon improvised exchanges and sales of Western jeans, shirts, and other fashion items began on a large scale. The underground entrepreneurs competed successfully with the Komsomol officials who had organized official purchase centers to curb the black market. A group of students from Moscow's Institute of Foreign Languages organized an illegal currency exchange; when the police arrested them, they had already bought thousands of U.S. dollars at thirty rubles to the dollar.[68] Another group of young businessmen who exchanged money and purchased foreign clothing continued their operation for years after the festival, and by the time the KGB arrested them, they were living the life of secret millionaires.[69]

During the festival a few freethinking young men and women contacted foreigners to ask for printed information and books, and to reveal their opposition to the Soviet regime. Soviet authorities and the KGB suspected that American delegates wanted to establish contacts with such people. Among the casualties of Soviet vigilance was Daniel Schorr, the first CBS correspondent in Moscow since 1947, for the office of the broadcasting company was closed down. Komsomol "information" reported on August 7, 1957, that Schorr had passed instructions from the U.S. Embassy to a group of young Americans in the festival delegation. Later the Ministry of Foreign Affairs revoked his visa; he has been persona non grata in the USSR ever since.[70] Nevertheless, there were simply too many contacts for the KGB to shadow. Garthoff remembered in his memoirs that one young man displayed an insatiable appetite for the magazines that the American had brought with him to the USSR. His name was Alik Ginzburg: like the famous American beatnik poet Allen Ginsberg, he was also a fan of cultural freedom, but he had to be more resourceful to achieve it in Soviet society. He would play a distinguished role in the Russian intellectual and human rights movement in the next two decades.[71]

Other young Russians, more interested in democratic socialism than in Americanism, sought contacts with the young festival delegates from Central and Eastern Europe. The Poles and Hungarians arrived fresh from the experience of the national revolutions that had, for a brief moment, overthrown the structures of Stalinist states. The frequency of these contacts is hard to measure, but the Komsomol authorities and the KGB worried about them. In one documented case, members of an underground political group of university professors and students headed by Lev Krasnopevtsev attempted to use the festival to exchange information with Polish journalists. They managed to meet with Eligiusz Lasota, an editor of the Polish literary magazine *Po Prostu,* who had been very active during the "Polish October" of 1956.[72] These contacts were detected by KGB agents. Alexei Adzhubei, Khrushchev's son-in-law and a member of Shelepin's team of festival organizers, warned Lasota in blunt terms, "Listen, in Poland you can do what you want, but keep in mind that it rubs off on us here as well. You come and spread this plague, [you want to] subvert us. We will not allow this to happen."[73] Soon after the end of the festival, Krasnopevtsev and most members of his group were arrested.

Soviet police reports described the behavior of the Hungarian and Polish delegates as "provocative." Fortunately for the hosts, there was no solidarity between the sons and daughters of two Eastern European countries. The Poles cursed the Hungarians (who preferred to keep their mouth shut) for their reluctance to admit that there had been a revolution in Hungary, called them cowards, traitors, and stooges of Moscow. It almost came to a scuffle. Even more pronounced was the sense of superiority tinged with nationalist contempt that some young Poles felt toward Russian youth. This attitude did not encourage rapprochement. Besides, some Poles and Hungarians, instead of engaging in the "discussion clubs" set up for them by the Komsomol activists, brought suitcases full of cheap underwear, makeup, and other items, and tried to sell them on the black market.[74]

In fact, the youth from Africa, Asia, and Latin America made a much greater impression on the Russians than their "socialist cousins" from Eastern Europe. The sympathies of Russian students, male and especially female, belonged to the tall and handsome Africans from Ghana and Kenya, as well as Indians and delegates from the Arab countries. In the eyes of the Russians their appearance and dress were exotic, and they were surrounded by the aura of the anticolonial liberation movements. In 1957 they electrified young Soviet intellectuals and students in the same way that Third World radicals would galvanize leftist Western students ten years later.

The festival was also a significant event for Soviet Jews. The Israeli delegation represented the first public appearance of Zionists in Moscow since 1948, when the Israeli Ambassador Golda Meir had arrived in the Soviet capital. In the October War of 1956, Israel had been the target of blistering criticism in the Soviet press. Many Soviet Jews denounced Israeli aggression against Egypt.[75] Although the Israeli group at the youth festival included some delegates from the Israeli Communist Party ("democratic" delegates), the real furore emerged around the "Zionist" section, mostly young veterans of the recent war, whose demeanor, dignity, fearlessness, and above all pride in being Jewish were new and astonishing to Soviet Jews.[76] Official reports about the festival were replete with alarm signals. "Zionists continue to distribute among Moscow Jews the literature they brought," read one report. "The workers of a Moscow cinema studio have been filming only the Zionist part of the Israeli delegation for two days." Jewish Muscovites gathered in crowds around theaters and hotels, invited the young Israelis to visit their homes, and complained about their tribulations in the USSR. Several thousand Jews came to listen to an Israeli performance during the international-music concert at the Ostankino concert hall. A crowd of young men who could not get tickets to Israeli performances and films crushed the cast-iron fence in front of the Mossovet Theater and stormed into the performance hall. Despite years of anti-Zionist propaganda, the festival enabled an increasing number of well-educated and urbane Jews to rediscover their Middle Eastern "homeland."[77]

The prevalent feeling at the festival was a passionate, often erotic desire to "merge" with the outside world through its messengers who had arrived in Moscow. Suddenly, during the festival, spontaneous love affairs between young Russians and foreign guests sprang up like wildfires in a dry forest. Young Russian men did not miss the first opportunity to date foreign women. Yevgeny Yevtushenko could never forget the moment when, "for the first time in my life, my socialist lips touched so-called capitalist lips, because I kissed an American girl, breaking Cold War rules. Not only I did it. Many of my friends, too, were doing the same in the streets of Moscow, in all the parks."[78] Russian women also took advantage of the festival's romantic opportunities. According to Alexei Kozlov, every night "crowds of young ladies from all over Moscow converged on the places where foreign delegates were staying—various student dorms and hotels on the outskirts of the city." Then, without too much "wooing" or "fake coquettishness" couples formed and quickly headed into the dark, into fields and bushes, "knowing perfectly well what they would soon be doing."[79] Memories of a "sexual minirevolution" that had occurred in Moscow parks and courtyards, especially in the vicinity of student dorms and the residences of foreign guests, continued to circulate. The real scale of libertinage is impossible to assess.[80] The knee-jerk reaction of some Komsomol vigilante squads was to apprehend the guilty girls on the spot and shave their heads.[81] Some foreigners and Russians announced their plans to marry; most of the couples wanted to leave the USSR, but some wanted to stay.[82]

Thus, sexuality emerged as a threat to Soviet values from the minds of a concerned conservative majority, parents, and officialdom, and as spontaneous acts of liberation in the eyes of educated Russian youth. If Soviet morality was Victorian in the wake of Stalinism, young members of society were not. Among them, the metaphor of sexual love betrayed the longing to give away one's "socialist virginity" for the sake of connection with the forbidden "capitalist West," and even more with the exotic and recently discovered Third World.

Shelepin and the Komsomol officials declared the festival a smashing success. Indeed, the festival did create thousands of lifelong friends of the USSR and did a great deal to offset the negative images of Soviet tanks in Hungary in 1956, as well as the xenophobic Soviet past.[83] Millions around the world learned the tune of "Moscow Nights." At the same time, the Iron Curtain had been irrevocably breached during the festival. The young and enthusiastic Soviet television announcers and journalists devoted ten hours every day to reports on the festival events. Millions spent fifteen days (July 28–August 11) glued to their television sets. After the end of the event, thousands of guests from various countries left by train and on their way home made stopovers in Leningrad, Stalingrad, Odessa, Kishinev, Tashkent, and other cities.[84] Of course, one event could not break the spell of Cold War images and xenophobia over the masses of Russian people. Still, the festival marked the beginning of the slow opening of the "Soviet mind" toward the outside world. The festival also propelled idealized images of the outside world, until then present only in the imagination of a few elite intellectuals and passionate style apers, into the awareness of much larger groups of Soviet citizens.

Under direct impact of the festival, some of the old taboos on youth styles were lifted. The public campaign against *stiliagi* continued, but the authorities came to a novel realization: if the project of communism were to succeed in its appeal to the urban youth, it had to reflect their cultural needs. The Kremlin decreed the development of the entertainment sphere, directed textile industries to produce fashionable clothes for the young, and encouraged composers to write light, jazzy, rhythmical songs and music. Moscow began to lose its dingy monotony and drab provincialism and began to transform itself from a "big village" into a metropolis. A great number of cafés and fast-food places opened in Moscow, Leningrad, and later other cities. They had cheerful, nonideological names, such as Smile, Spring, Breeze, Chamomile, and Lily of the Valley. In September 1962 the head of the Komsomol, Sergei Pavlov, admitted, "We now wear the same tight slacks for which we would have had shaved heads five years ago. Fighting against tight slacks belongs to the past. A new time has come: we are now struggling for the inner world of the individual."[85]

The festival was a big milestone for the postwar generation of educated Russians. Many intellectuals, artists, and especially admirers of Western "style," jazz fans, and cosmopolitan-minded youngsters compared its transformative impact to that of the secret speech. Vladimir Bukovsky recalled that after the festival "all this talk about 'putrefying capitalism' became ridiculous."[86] The film critic Maia Turovskaia believed that Russians at the festival had been able to touch and smell the outside world for the first time after three decades. "The generation of the sixties would have been different without the festival."[87] Alexei Kozlov, the jazz musician, even declared that the festival "was the beginning of the collapse of the Soviet system. It made the fragmentation process of Stalinist society irreversible." The festival, he continues in his memoirs, "changed even the Komsomol functionaries. From then on, they lived a double life: while professing loyalty to the system, they realized the inferiority of the Soviet way of life."[88]

When Khrushchev received the final bill for the festival, he was shocked. He refused to allocate resources for another extravaganza, a World Exhibition in Moscow.[89] Forgetting his anger, however, Khrushchev entered into other commitments that would make the Iron Curtain ever more penetrable. The Soviet cultural offensive around the world and cultural exchange with the West continued. The success of the first Sputnik launch on October 4, 1957, seemed to boost Khrushchev's overconfidence into the stratosphere. In the same month the Soviet state signed agreements on cultural exchange with France. In January 1958 a similar agreement was reached with the United States. The Soviet leader could never grasp the full impact of Soviet cultural engagements with the world on the minds and souls of the younger generation.

America and Other Worlds

In 1957 Shelepin wondered at a meeting of top Komsomol officials why many Soviet young men and women expressed admiration for the United States, despite all the efforts of Soviet propaganda to highlight the economic and racial inequalities in American society. The majority of the two million students in the USSR studied free and received stipends from the state. Yet they failed to realize how privileged they were by comparison with American students, who had to work to pay their education expenses.[90] Shelepin's bewilderment pointed up the main problem for the Soviet regime. It had been spending ever greater sums trying to bring up a new educated class of dedicated communists who would wage and win the Cold War against the United States and "world capitalism." Instead, quite a few students of the late 1950s were of two minds about "Enemy Number One." In search of an explanation, Shelepin observed that the new generation "did not pass through the stern school of revolutionary struggle, unlike the older generation, our fathers, mothers, and older brothers."[91]

Jazz music remained by far the greatest source of American "soft power" inside the Soviet Union. Many young people developed the habit of listening to Voice of America (VOA) radio programs, almost exclusively because of American jazz and rock-and-roll programs. American jazz, broadcast on German, Polish, Turkish, and other shortwave stations, could be heard every night in the dormitories of Moscow State University.[92] The number of shortwave radios in Soviet homes grew from half a million in 1949 to twenty million in 1958. Toward the end of his life Stalin ordered a cessation in the production of shortwave radios by 1954. Instead, after Stalin's death Soviet industry began to produce four million of them annually, primarily for commercial reasons.[93] Particularly popular was VOA's *Time for Jazz*, whose disc jockey, Willis Conover, "the world's richest bass-baritone," was a secret hero of many Moscow and Leningrad students. They sang, or sometimes just mimicked without understanding the lyrics, songs by Benny Goodman and Glenn Miller. They listened to Ella Fitzgerald, Louis Armstrong, Duke Ellington, and Charlie Parker. Later came the era of Elvis Presley. Recordings of American music stars were not available in stores; therefore, any chance to obtain a foreign-made vinyl record was considered a miracle. By the late 1950s the appearance of better and cheaper tape recorders broadened the exposure to Western music.[94]

For the Soviet authorities a total ban on Western music was no longer an option; thus, they desperately tried to produce Soviet-made versions of new cultural phenomena that came from the West. After the youth festival, jazz could no longer be considered, as the propaganda cliché went, a "dance of the fat bourgeoisie." For the second time in fifteen years jazz music was rehabilitated, but on the condition that it was distinctively Soviet-style jazz. The masters of Russian jazz were told to develop "native" compositions. In the fall of 1958 the first jazz club opened in Leningrad with the authorization of the local Komsomol authorities. It was closed after a year. After 1961, however, jazz appreciation clubs and jazz fans began to emerge again, first in Moscow, then in other cities.[95]

Because of the Cold War, only a few young Russians could discover America in the flesh. In 1957–58 U.S. leadership, recovering from the effects of McCarthyism, missed a great opportunity to tear down the Iron Curtain even further. Since 1955 Eisenhower had nurtured the idea of inviting ten thousand Soviet students annually to the United States, in exchange for a corresponding number of American students' traveling to the USSR. Unfortunately, various reasons, above all opposition in Congress and the anticommunist paranoia of the FBI's J. Edgar Hoover, led Eisenhower to abandon the plan.[96] Still, he proposed a modest program of student exchange to the Soviet leaders. Khrushchev accepted the proposal and in 1958 the first group of seventeen Soviet students, only one of them a woman, arrived in the United States to study at some of the best universities (Columbia, Harvard, Berkeley, Chicago, and George Washington). Some of them would later make their careers in the party propaganda apparatus or the KGB.[97] For the rest of the educated young Russians America remained an imagined and heavily mythologized country. The sounds of jazz accorded well in their imagination with the Hollywood films they could see on Soviet screens, and also with the colorful photo spreads from the journal *America,* which had been distributed in the Soviet Union by the USIA through the U.S. Embassy since 1955. Most of the copies went to the families of Soviet nomenklatura officials. The journal became a much-cherished commodity on the growing black market for foreign products.

It was, therefore, another cultural shock for Russians when America came to Moscow and the artifacts of its civilization went on display for all who wanted to come and see them. In fall 1958, Soviet and American authorities agreed to exchange national exhibitions "devoted to the demonstration of the development of their respective science, technology, and culture." In June 1959 a Soviet exhibition opened in New York, inaugurated by Vice President Richard Nixon and Khrushchev's first deputy Frol Kozlov. The American exhibition opened a few weeks later in Sokolniki, a recreational park in the northeast corner of Moscow. Khrushchev, buoyed by the rapidly growing economy and the huge success of Sputnik, was not afraid to show American achievements to Soviet citizens. On the eve of the opening of the Sokolniki exhibition, he shared his opinions with the leader of the German Democratic Republic, Walter Ulbricht: "The Americans believe that the Soviet people, looking at their achievements, will turn away from the Soviet government. But the Americans do not understand our people. We want to turn the exhibit against the Americans. We will tell our people: Look, this is what the richest country of capitalism has achieved in one hundred years. Socialism will give us the opportunity to achieve this significantly faster."[98] The Soviet leader personally threw the Soviet propaganda machine into the battle by wrangling with Vice President Nixon inside an American model kitchen at the opening of the exhibition. Khrushchev was unabashedly boastful and bombastic.

For all Khrushchev's bravado, the Soviet propaganda chiefs anticipated the American plan to stun Soviet visitors with the superiority of the American lifestyle and awaken their consumerist envy. The party and Komsomol officials had learned from their oversights during the youth festival and had planned a staggering amount of propaganda designed to counter public impressions from America in Sokolniki. The Soviet press was full of stories about the "awful life in the United States"—the hunger, unemployment, persecution of blacks, fires at schools, criminality among minors, and similarly gloomy subjects. "If one believes Soviet newspapers, all that the American exhibition shows is hogwash and propaganda," wrote one observer in his diary.[99] Soviet officials staunchly resisted American plans to have a jazz band play on the exhibition ground. They also vetoed free distribution of American cosmetics for Russian women and plastic toy cars for men. After much haggling, only the free distribution of Pepsi to exhibition visitors was agreed on.[100]

During forty-two days in July and August, when the American exhibition was open, about 2.7 million Soviet citizens from Moscow, Leningrad, and other cities and localities stood in line for many hours to see American artifacts. Young people, especially students, visited the exhibits many times, either by procuring tickets or by sneaking over or under the fence. It was three times more than the number of Americans who had gone to see the Soviet exhibition in New York. Although the U.S. Congress, typically, had failed to realize the potential of American "soft power" behind the Iron Curtain and kept the funding of the exhibition to a minimum, gifted management and donations from American corporations saved the situation. Another impressive addition was the selection of seventy-five exhibition guides, American college students, some of them children of Russian émigré families, who spoke Russian and volunteered to go to Moscow. Hundreds of party and Komsomol agitators worked at the exhibition, heckling the guides and "directing" the discussions into politically correct channels. The American guides, however, evoked universal sympathy, and visitors brushed off the propagandists and hired hecklers.[101]

On average, Russian visitors displayed enormous curiosity, far surpassing the curiosity of their counterparts overseas about Soviet culture and achievements. This attitude expressed itself in endless questions for the American guides and in the public's insatiable appetite for the information distributed at the exhibition. Especially irksome to Soviet authorities was the constant pilfering of books and any other kind of printed media from the book section of the Sokolniki exhibition. At the same time, America in Sokolniki revealed a generational and cultural divide among Russians. Older and more conservative Russian visitors expressed criticism that bourgeois trivia, not the tools and achievements of industrialization, were displayed at the exhibition. These viewers were the first to criticize the exhibition's defects and to argue that Pepsi-Cola did not taste as good as Russian kvass, a traditional malt beverage.[102] The young Russians, by contrast, were fascinated. They came to the exhibition again and again to touch the huge cigarlike cars, look at pictures, even flip through books, and experience different colors and smells. For many it was the experience of a lifetime. Many years later people showed off the exhibition button with pride.[103] Russian young men gasped at the incredibly long American cars with huge fins and polished chrome parts. Large crowds gathered around the Chevrolet Impala and another car, the color of "a splash of burgundy." The exhibition had even more to offer to Russian women, society's habitual experts in consumerism. Rather cleverly, American planners responded to Khrushchev's penchant to compete in the sphere of space technology by choosing a field in which American superiority over the Soviets was overwhelming: the fully equipped modern kitchen and other objects of consumer desires. Some male visitors even complained that the exhibition was intended "more for women's eyes than for men's."[104]

Walter Hixson concluded that "for its cost—$3.6 million in federal appropriations—the exhibition arguably offered a greater return than any single Cold War initiative since the Marshall Plan. The six-week display of 'America in Sokolniki' could not shake the foundations of the Soviet regime, yet the response that it provoked was a harbinger of the mounting appeal of Western culture." The enthusiasm of many visitors did express "the growing desire to access consumer goods" and "attain middle-class status."[105] Most important was that the United States played the role of a "measuring stick" of progress and advancement for Soviet citizens.[106] In 1957 the Soviet leader had come up with a slogan, "Catch up and surpass America," that would be the cornerstone of his program for the construction of communism over the next twenty years. Whatever Khrushchev's intentions may have been, the long-term effects of his bragging were rather destructive for Soviet anti-American propaganda and communist ideology. Khrushchev's erratic rhetoric and the American exhibition helped plant in the mass consciousness the image of the United States as a cornucopia—a myth rivaling the Soviet one about a future consumerist paradise.

Khrushchev unwittingly provided Soviet society with an explicit frame of comparison. Gorbachev's classmate the future Czech communist reformer of 1968 Zdeněk Mlynář perceptively observed many years later, "Stalin never permitted comparisons of socialism or communism with capitalist reality because he argued that an entirely new world was being built here that could not be compared with any preceding system." This attitude led to autarky and isolation, yet also ensured that communist ideology could be judged only by its own criteria. Khrushchev's new slogan directed the worldview of Soviet citizens away from ideology, toward an economic race. As a result, over the course of many years, people continued to compare their lives and standard of living to Americans'. One generation after another recognized that in reality American living standards were infinitely higher than those in the Soviet Union. "Whoever searched for the reason for this might easily come to the conclusion that the main obstacle was the existing economic and political system. That is, the opposite of what Khrushchev intended occurred. He wanted to strengthen people's faith in the Soviet system but in fact the practical comparison with the West had the opposite effect and constantly weakened that faith."[107]

The growing popularity of the idealized United States should be seen in the broader historical context. It would be simplistic and wrong to speak about a reversal of the American image from negative to positive. The erosion of the "enemy" image of the United States and the West was a complex phenomenon; among mainstream students and young intellectuals, fears of American nuclear power and anticapitalist and anti-American clichés coexisted in a peculiar way with the memories of Lend-Lease during World War II and their sympathies for all things American, especially music. And it would be wrong to assume that the majority of the younger generation of educated Russians at the end of the 1950s was prepared to recognize the superiority of the American way of life. Raymond Garthoff remembered the youth he met and talked with in 1957 as falling into several categories. Those who had recently graduated from secondary school believed the propaganda about the United States. Their older peers could be divided into "believers," precocious cynics, and "golden youth" that found escape from the dullness of Soviet cultural life in unabashed Westernism and Americanism.[108] The believers were in the majority. The communist myth had yet to exhaust its appeal to the hearts and minds of younger educated elites. Many postwar students and war veterans still assumed that Lenin's Revolution had set their country on the correct historical path.

America was not the only country rediscovered by the postwar generation during the Thaw. Others included the countries of Eastern Europe, China, and the Third World. In Eastern Europe, Polish cultural influence continued to grow after 1955–56. Not only politicized young intellectuals, poets, and artists, but also the broader educated public began to read Polish journals of news and fashion and to appreciate Polish entertainment and "light" music. Russian readers rediscovered older Polish literature, such as the historical novels of Henryk Sienkiewicz; they also began to read the science fiction of Stanisław Lem and the plays of Sławomir Mrożek. And they began to learn the biting aphorisms of Stanisław Jerzy Lec such as: "Whom should Freedom marry, to make it procreate?"

The exposure to Yugoslavia during the brief Tito-Khrushchev reconciliation in 1955–56 also opened new cultural horizons for the Russians, for whom its attraction was the "Yugoslav model of socialism." Interest in this model shaped the careers of many Russian social scientists and philosophers of that time, among them Gennady Lisichkin, who graduated from the Moscow State University in the mid-1950s. He volunteered to go the "Virgin Lands," where he briefly worked as the head of a collective farm. Lisichkin read in Soviet newspapers about the Yugoslav experiments with "workers' councils" and decided to study them. Like many socially motivated students of his time, he passionately believed that the main obstacle to a productive socialist planned economy was uneducated bureaucrats. After a field study trip to Yugoslavia, he would become a prominent advocate of democratization of the Soviet centralized economy in the early 1960s.[109]

In contrast to those who dreamed of America, many thousands of young specialists from Moscow, Leningrad, and other Russian cities who yearned to see other "socialist" countries, like China, could travel and work there. They went to provide "fraternal assistance" to the "progressive regimes" and national liberation movements of Asia and Africa. In the 1950s the educated members of Russian Soviet society resembled their predecessors of the 1920s in that they regarded the countries of Asia, Africa, and the Middle East as new frontiers for revolutionary socialist experimentation.

Indeed, Soviet assistance to some of these countries was generous, enthusiastic, and comparable in scale to the American Marshall Plan for Europe.[110] Various young specialists, emissaries, and aid workers in China, India, Indonesia, the Middle East, and Africa returned with experience and impressions that shaped them for life. The collective experience and memories about other socialist countries were remarkably varied and at least as important as exposure to Western culture. Often exposure to the Third World validated Soviet ideological convictions and generated faith in a bright socialist future. In China young Soviet professionals and scientists were fascinated by the sight of masses of people working at giant construction sites; some Soviets felt as if they were vicariously experiencing the Soviet industrialization of the early 1930s—something they had only known from books and films. The optimism and enthusiasm of the "working masses" in China spread to these Russian specialists, and the Spartan simplicity and accessibility of Chinese Party leaders provided a striking contrast to the Soviet bureaucracy.[111] Yelena Bonner, the future dissident and wife of Nobel Peace Prize winner Andrei Sakharov, worked in 1959–60 in Iraq on a Soviet medical team to fight smallpox. Khrushchev gave assistance to Iraq after the pro-American and pro-British monarchy there was replaced, following a bloody coup, by the "progressive" regime of Abd al-Karim Quasim. Bonner did not lose her romantic socialist beliefs there, but she began to perceive existing Soviet society as one among many, and perhaps not the best.[112]

Since 1959 the Cuban revolution had boosted the "left" romanticism among the younger educated Russians. Almost everything about the Cuban revolution captivated the young audience: the heroic descent of a small band of bearded young men from the Sierra Maestra, their triumphant march into Havana, the defeat of the counterrevolutionaries trained and funded by the CIA, and last but not least the exotic land itself, where people seemed to dance, sing, and make love around the clock in all four seasons. Intellectuals and students began to hang portraits of Fidel Castro and Che Guevara on the walls of their apartments. On April 16, 1961, Castro proclaimed the Cuban Revolution to be "socialist," but several months earlier Soviet public opinion had already embraced it as "our revolution." During the May Day rally on Red Square in Moscow in 1960, the marchers mistook the military delegation from Ghana for Cubans and enthusiastically cheered them.[113] In May 1960 a metallurgical engineer from Magnitogorsk in the Urals wrote to *Komsomolskaia Pravda,* "I am convinced that our generation will witness the greatest advances in perfecting human society. The yoke of capitalism will collapse under the pressure of the subjugated people who seek freedom." Another engineer from a forest plantation near Tomsk in Siberia sent his "best regards to the Cuban people." He regretted that he could not "go there as a volunteer. We are all under the spell of Fidel Castro! Long live Cuba!"[114]

The simplicity and grace of the Spanish language, the rhythms of the tango and the samba, and the bold monumental paintings of Latin American artists brought back memories of Sergei Eisenstein's romance with Mexico, and the passionate Soviet support of the Republicans in the Spanish Civil War. Antibureaucratic rhetoric and the populism of Castro and his friends resonated with the antibureaucratic student movement in Soviet Russia in 1956.[115] Yevtushenko became the Soviet Union's informal poetic ambassador to Cuba. Armed with his self-taught Spanish, he met Castro and received an invitation to go on a fishing expedition. He even managed to read his poems to a crowd gathered at a stadium in Havana, where Castro staged a "dialogue" with the Contras captured during the botched Bay of Pigs invasion. From the island Yevtushenko wired back his exalted stanzas about young *barbudos* and the supreme morality of the Revolution. In December 1960 the magazine *Yunost* (Youth), read by hundreds of thousands, published Yevtushenko's request, "Fidel, accept me as a soldier in your Army of Freedom!"[116] Yevtushenko even wrote a script for the film *I, Cuba,* eulogizing the liberation of the island from the greedy and corrupt regime, as well as from American financial interests.[117]

A host of Moscow and Leningrad professionals, recent university graduates, applied to work in Cuba. The Komsomol sent three hundred of them to the "island of liberty" to provide technical assistance, teach Cubans how to create a medical system and engineering schools, and even to work in Cuban agricultural cooperatives. All of them quickly learned to speak fluent Spanish, and shared their anticapitalist and anti-American fervor with the Cuban revolutionaries. In August 1961, one thousand Cuban students came to the Soviet Union to study agriculture in the Krasnodar and Stavropol regions, in Tbilisi, Tashkent, and Ukraine. In Stavropol their host was the charismatic deputy secretary of a regional party committee, Mikhail Gorbachev.[118]

Less than a decade after Stalin's death, the Iron Curtain around Soviet society was irrevocably breached. The glimpses and impressions of educated

Russians were diverse and confusing, yet in general many Russians once again had an ability to see other worlds and develop a comparative framework for their culture and way of life. Yet assessing the impact of this development on the intellectual and cultural history of Russian society is not easy. Indeed, even a cursory glance reveals that the transition from extreme xenophobia to relatively restricted and controlled access to the outside world produced highly ideological and neurotic responses among educated Russians, especially the younger generation.

The psychological "wall" between some educated Russian people and foreigners, especially Westerners, continued to exist, despite many chinks. And it produced vastly different reactions, from envious admiration and an inferiority complex to defensive nationalism. Many would still try to convince themselves of the superiority of the "Soviet way of life." Others would feel trapped in the "Soviet prison," allowed only to glimpse "freedom" beyond its borders.

The other worlds beyond Soviet Russia would play a crucial role in shaping the self-consciousness of the Russian intelligentsia during the 1960s. Inadvertently, Khrushchev's policies of peaceful coexistence and cultural competition, as well as his rhetoric, helped resurrect a major phenomenon familiar to the older Russian intelligentsia: the idea of the outside world, above all the West, as a measuring stick for Russia's progress or backwardness. The United States reassumed the central place in the Soviet imagination not only as a Cold War enemy, but also as an object of emulation when it came to technological and material development. The imaginary America would continue to play a central role in the cultural battles of the postwar generation of Russian intellectuals and the artistic community. At the same time, the revolutions and national liberation movements in the Third World offered educated Russians other powerful and diverse forms of exposure to the world that counterbalanced Western influences. The popularity of socialist ideas and practices in Asia, the Middle East, and Africa appeared to revalidate the place of the Soviet Union and its educated elites in the vanguard of progress. The discovery of other worlds was still linked in the minds of many intellectuals to the future of the Soviet communist experiment, its progress or failure.

This generation of Soviet people will live to see
the victory of communism!

—Nikita Khrushchev, 1960

four

Optimists on the Move
1957-1961

IN OCTOBER 1957 the launch of Sputnik created a worldwide sensation
and turned the Soviet Union into the leading power in space exploration. In
1959 the Soviet leader, Nikita Khrushchev, declared that the Soviet Union
had completed the "full and final construction of socialism." Capping the
years of optimism, in April 1961 the Russian Yuri Gagarin became the first
man to orbit the earth in a spaceship. The Soviet way of life seemed to be
the wave of the future again, transforming nature and conquering space,
liberating Russia from poverty and malnutrition. Georgy Shakhnazarov,
later a leading political scientist and adviser to Gorbachev, remembered the
late 1950s and early 1960s as a time of enthusiasm fed by strong faith in
the great experiment—constructing a fair society with opportunity for
all. "The Twentieth Party Congress seriously shattered that faith but did not
topple it."[1]

Optimism and youth are always neighbors, and at the end of the 1950s
the majority of people in Soviet Russia were the young and very young. In
fact, those aged thirty and younger constituted 55 percent of the population, and only 10 percent were older than sixty.[2] World War II left gaping
holes in the number of middle-aged people. The country teemed with young
people everywhere: in university auditoriums, on the streets, at construction sites. From 1955 to 1960, hundreds of thousands of young men and
women, among them university graduates, volunteered to work and live in

the Virgin Lands in Kazakhstan. Many huge industrial plants and river dams appeared, as if by miracle, in Siberia.

Large groups of younger educated Russians continued to be imbued with social optimism and communist idealism. The belief was widespread that with the help of better state policies and social activism the mistakes of the past could be rectified, and the Soviet Union would be once again on the historically correct path. Above all, the original promise of the communist project—transforming nature with the help of science, and perfecting human society and institutions with the aid of culture and education—still appealed to many.[3] Sophisticated observers realized that the hope of achieving a material paradise within the lifetime of a generation, as Khrushchev had famously promised, was utopian, yet they did not doubt that the future belonged to some kind of socialist society, and not to capitalism. This was the main message conveyed in newspapers and on radio and television at the time. Millions believed that scientific progress would help solve most social, economic, and political problems within their lifetime and bring about the final stage of communism. Scientists both fostered and shared this mood: they appeared to be independent-minded and knowledgeable about the future. This optimism shaped the outlook and expectations of the postwar cohorts of educated Russians, including those who had begun to think independently and question the wisdom of the party and Soviet propaganda.

Khrushchev's "New Deal" and the Sputnik Effect

Khrushchev, despite his repressive policies in 1956, did not plan to return to Stalinist terror. He was a true believer in socialism and did not want to compromise it with blood, mass arrests, and slave labor. According to post-Stalinist ideological innovations, "enemy groups" no longer existed in Soviet society. All of them, including the clergy, descendants of the former nobility, and the kulaks had an equal right to reach the communist paradise. The secret police, re-created in 1954 as the Committee for State Security (KGB), seemed to have been tamed and forced to observe "socialist legality" under party supervision. The special commission created by the party presidium continued to rehabilitate the victims of Stalinism. "Deviant elements" were now to be corrected within society, increasingly with the help of public organizations, the Komsomol, trade unions, and cultural associations.[4]

Khrushchev wanted to prove that the Soviet model could produce a happy society of creative and highly educated people. From 1953 onward the Soviet government sharply reduced work hours and taxes, while increasing investment in public housing, education, mass culture, and health care. In November 1955 abortion, banned since 1936, was legalized. The state began to invest massively in urban infrastructure and consumer-oriented industries, which had been neglected or sacrificed during the Stalin years. Russian and foreign economists agree that after the liquidation of harsh enforcement and of the labor armies of the gulag, the economy began to grow more quickly.[5] In 1956 the workers' uprisings in Poland and Hungary gave the Kremlin leadership another convincing reason to launch a "New Deal" to alleviate the misery in Soviet society. Daniel Schorr, the CBS correspondent in Moscow, observed, "In the Soviet Union itself the regime seemed to be trying to head off trouble by making life a little easier for its citizens."[6]

In early 1959 Khrushchev proclaimed at the party congress that the USSR should begin preparations for the final leap to socialism. He told his presidium colleagues: "I believe that after we work for a five-year term or two, we will be able to transfer as much food to people as anyone wants. We will have enough bread, and—in two five-year plans at the most we will have enough meat—please, eat!" Khrushchev identified kindergartens and pension plans as bulwarks of communism.[7] Other "spotlights of communism" in Moscow and major cities included free daycare and kindergartens, free school education, and tuition-free colleges. The growing public transit system adopted the honor system: nobody would check passengers' tickets. The Soviet leader instructed a group of speechwriters in preparation for the new party program. The final product was an overweening, sky's-the-limit plan of catching up with the United States and "completing the construction of communist society" in the Soviet Union within two decades. In July 1961, in a speech to the Central Committee, Khrushchev promised that the next generation of Soviet people would live in a communist paradise. The Soviet Union, the leader boasted, would "rise to such a great height that, by comparison, the main capitalist countries will remain far below and way behind." After a national "discussion," in which 4.6 million people took part, the Twenty-second Party Congress unanimously adopted the program in October 1961.[8]

His lack of realism notwithstanding, Khrushchev introduced some policies that had far-reaching social effects. Khrushchev's New Deal established the foundations of a better-off society with social safety nets and of a state with greater responsibility for material standards of its citizens. The Russian historian Elena Zubkova notes that by the end of the 1950s the Soviet leadership had "worked out a broad system of social security, introduced passports in the peasant villages, shortened the work day, increased vacation time, and built more vacation facilities and sanatoria for factory workers. Government policy, it seemed, did in fact turn its face to the people."[9]

The ambitious social policy also entailed continual investments in education. From 1928 to 1960, the number of university graduates in the USSR grew twelvefold. The postwar cohorts in 1946 through 1955 numbered 1.8 million, according to Soviet statistics. During the next five years alone, 1.5 million more joined the ranks of Soviet citizens with university and other advanced diplomas. The number of university-educated professionals increased from 233,000 in 1928 to 3.5 million in 1960. The staff of scientific and academic institutes and university faculty doubled in size between 1950 and 1960 and reached 350,000.[10] The students who graduated during the 1950s represented the *majority* of Soviet educated classes. And they joined the workforce during a period of unprecedented job expansion, fueled by the Cold War, the scientific-technical revolution, and Soviet enlightenment projects. A huge gap separated these young people, numerous, optimistic, and fresh, from their predecessors, who had been decimated by the war and Stalin's terror and whose authority was tarnished by their Faustian bargains with the regime.

Massive housing construction, neglected under Stalin, became one of Khrushchev's priorities. The idea was to mass-produce prefabricated five-story apartment buildings equipped with minimal facilities. Poorly constructed and ugly by any standards, Khrushchev's urban developments nevertheless produced a clearly visible increase in living standards and provided a huge boost to the consumer-oriented economy. From 1956 to 1965 about 108.7 million people moved into new apartments distributed by state authorities, trade unions, and other Soviet institutions. In 1958 the government allowed cooperative housing projects, a significant ideological concession; by the mid-1960s these projects would generate five to six million square meters of living space annually.[11] The provision of new housing developments was accompanied by the mass construction of hospitals and clinics, nursery schools and kindergartens, school complexes, and sports facilities. A forest of five-story apartment buildings began to sprout up, first in Moscow, then in other cities. For millions of Soviet people an opportunity emerged, for the first time in their lives, to have a living space completely to themselves—and privacy that they had previously lacked. One witness to this process, an art historian in Leningrad, recalled the change from the communal apartment to a private one as a psychological revolution. The habit of living in a fishbowl began to disappear. The long-forgotten sense of privacy and human dignity began to return. The social space that had helped generate "ordinary Stalinists"—among them secret police informers and Soviet vigilantes—shrank. And the social space available for companionable circles of students and professionals grew rapidly.[12]

While seeking to make life under "socialism" better for the people, Khrushchev remained a firm believer in revolutionary collectivist methods of industrial and agricultural development. In 1954–55 Khrushchev came forth with his project to develop the Virgin Lands, hundreds of millions of acres in the steppe of Kazakhstan. Peasants had never before lived there; thus, it was a perfect place for social and economic experimentation.[13] Khrushchev's son-in-law Adzhubei recalled that the horizon of the Kazakh steppe was ablaze with fires, which demarcated the tent cities. During the day "combines advanced like tanks in attack formation."[14] In the summer of 1956 the Virgin Lands campaign already had thirty-three million hectares under cultivation and four hundred agrocities. New cities and hundreds of new towns and Soviet collective farms sprang up. This giant agricultural project was based on the Komsomol's mobilization of hundreds of thousands of "volunteers." From 1954 to 1960 entire classes of university students and high school students from Moscow, Leningrad, and other major cities were sent to work in the Virgin Lands. For them it became the largest experience of collectivist effort, something analogous to the war for their elders (although much less lethal). Several million Russian youth went through the Virgin Lands experience, among them many who would figure prominently on the intellectual and cultural scene of the 1960s.

Science and scientists became great beneficiaries of Khrushchev's New Deal. Under Stalin, the growing prestige of science was the by-product of the successes of gigantic rearmament projects that relied on discoveries in nuclear physics, chemistry, mathematics, ballistics, and so on. In 1955 the physicists and engineers from the Soviet atomic project successfully ended the American monopoly on thermonuclear weapons. Tens of thousands of young professionals, graduates of the major universities of Moscow and Leningrad, found immediate employment in jet aviation and rocket technology, space programs, and related areas, such as electronics, computer science, and aerodynamics. Dozens of secret installations were being constructed and expanded, and entire cities were populated with scientists and their families, as well as technicians and engineers of the military-industrial complex. The nuclear program continued to play a special role and underwent spectacular growth.[15] In 1955 the first nuclear lab in Sarov (Arzamas-16) was cloned; a twin lab opened in another secret city, Snezhinsk. Yet another secret city near Krasnoiarsk in Central Siberia began to produce weapons-grade plutonium in 1958. The reactors and twenty-two workshops were located in a huge artificial cavern beneath the earth; the complex had its own subway system and high-quality urban infrastructure that serviced and housed several thousand scientists, engineers, and workers. All the secret cities were constructed as islands of "developed socialism": the state took care of all basic social and cultural needs for those who worked there. They enjoyed stable employment, relatively high salaries, and generous benefits; their families could rely on a free and efficient system of health care, and day care and schools for their children.[16]

In March 1957 Khrushchev authorized the construction of a "city of science" (Akademgorodok) near Novosibirsk, beyond the Urals. One of the authors of this idea, the academician Mikhail Lavrentiev, was influential at the Kremlin as a leading expert in the mathematical modeling of explosives and as a strong advocate of computerization.[17] To attract young scientists, the state authorities created thirty new positions at the level of full academician and corresponding memberships for those scientists who would agree to leave Moscow and Leningrad for the northeastern frontier. The state also allocated billions of rubles to create a comfortable environment for scientists who migrated and their young families. By state decree, scientists retained their old residency rights and apartments in Moscow and Leningrad when they moved.[18] In 1960 the new city, Akademgorodok, already consisted of seven institutes for basic research. Eventually, seven more institutes would be created. They became the main hub for the Siberian branch of the Academy of Sciences. In addition, eight research institutes opened in Irkutsk, as well as smaller research conglomerates in Krasnoiarsk, Vladivostok, and Sakhalin.[19] The project, widely advertised in the Soviet media, combined the social cult of science with the romantic vision of the era in a grandiose development scheme for northern Russia and Siberia. Between 1957 and 1961 Akademgorodok came to house the largest concentration of scientific minds in the Soviet Union, after Moscow and Leningrad.

A lasting "Sputnik effect," a widespread belief in emerging Soviet technological and scientific superiority, fed the faith that science and technology could help resolve social and economic problems and contradictions. Those nuclear scientists who emerged from the obscurity of the secret programs into the public realm became objects of veneration. They had accomplished vital defense tasks, so could they help resolve other burning issues through the use of scientific methods? The Sputnik effect received powerful validation on April 12, 1961, when Soviet radio and television announced that a Russian man, Yuri Gagarin, a major in the Soviet Air Force, had become the first man in space. Together with the adoption of the party program of communist construction the previous year, this event marked the apex of Khrushchev's New Deal. A shared joy and pride united the regime, scientific elites, educated urban youth, and the population in general. Spontaneous demonstrations by elated citizens filled the streets of many cities. A young American witness in Moscow saw "genuine joy on Russians' faces! All the shortages, the sacrifices, the consumer goods and gadgets they gave up so that their country could have a man in space. Strangers kissed one another, old women did jigs, young people cheered, students walked out of their classes."[20] In Leningrad, recalls Mikhail German, "natural, spontaneous demonstrations proceeded along Nevsky Prospect," the main street. "I have not seen such faces, lit up with delight, since the Victory days." In Moscow, as the motorcade made its way from the airport to the Kremlin, an enthusiastic man darted out toward the open limousine where Gagarin and Khrushchev sat and thrust a bunch of flowers into the hands of the first cosmonaut. The police and KGB, ignoring the possibility of a malicious attack, let the man through unaccosted.[21]

Before long, disastrous errors and bureaucratic follies in other areas began to overshadow the victories in space and the successful policies of Khrushchev's New Deal. Khrushchev alienated many Russians, especially in the countryside, when he launched a campaign of militant atheism, with the goal of eradicating any form of organized religion or private worship. The Soviet leaders were incensed to learn from secret reports that in 1958 half of all newborn children in Russia were being baptized. In October 1958 the party leadership issued secret instructions to start "an offensive against the atavistic remains of religion among the Soviet people."[22] The theorists of official atheism observed that "overcoming the remaining superstitions" could be accomplished "without state repressions, by spreading scientific knowledge." They started the journal *Nauka i Religia* (Science and Religion), to promote scientific atheism. Yet the major methods of the campaign were administrative and economic repression against churches, and violence and intimidation with regard to believers. In 1961 the Council of Ministers passed legislation allowing regional authorities to close religious institutions, without the possibility of appeal to the central powers. The Russian Orthodox Church suffered severely. It lost fourteen hundred parishes in 1961 and almost sixteen hundred parishes in 1962. Thousands of cathedrals and church buildings were closed and torn down by overzealous local officials. Many seminaries, the centers of religious learning, were closed. From 1961 to 1964 Soviet courts sentenced 1,234 persons "for religious reasons." In provinces, many attempts were made to jail Protestant "sectarians" and even place their children in the custody of the Komsomol or orphanages.[23]

The majority of young urban professionals, intellectuals, and artists after the war grew up as atheists, and not many of them lost sleep over the state persecution of religion. By contrast, Khrushchev's experiments with agriculture left many of them puzzled and frustrated. In the summer of 1958 Alexei Kozlov joined the labor armies in the Virgin Lands of the Kazakh steppe with his entire class from the Moscow Architectural Institute, to collect the harvest. For all his skepticism about Soviet organized collective life, the enthusiasm was contagious and affected him as well. He saw "happy faces, songs, music, enthusiasm, genuine faith in a bright future." He went on to describe the "really enthusiastic work of tractor drivers, combine mechanics, truck drivers who collected the gigantic harvest." Very soon, however, the waste and disorganization he observed confirmed his preexisting doubts about the Soviet regime. "It was in the Virgin Lands that I found my animosity toward Soviet propaganda, toward all this pompous mendacity, confirmed. Even the most immature and unengaged young people left the Virgin Lands with the feeling of some kind of absurdity."[24]

While increasing the harvests on the barren steppes with one hand, Khrushchev destroyed Russian agriculture on traditional farmlands with the other. In 1957 the authorities closed the small cooperatives in the countryside that supplied urban markets with fresh produce, fish, and meat. In August 1958 the government of the Russian Federation, the largest republic of the USSR, imposed a ban on private ownership of cows and pigs by those who lived in provincial cities and towns and were not members of collective farms. The Kremlin cut down on the size of state-sanctioned private plots for peasants. The consequences of all these innovations were devastating. From 1953 to 1958, years in which Stalin's agricultural taxes were slashed, agricultural production increased by 50 percent and the yield for livestock raising and cattle breeding grew by 24 percent.[25] By contrast, in 1959–60 private livestock holdings plummeted. Local party officials, seeking to meet Khrushchev's plans "to catch up and overtake" the United States, purchased private livestock from peasants and slaughtered it to fulfill the wildly exaggerated pledges for meat production.[26]

Although collective farmers still constituted more than half the population of the Russian Federation, Khrushchev's forced modernization schemes led to accelerated urbanization and a rapid decline among the peasantry. People in the towns, no longer tethered to their cows and private plots of land, moved to bigger cities in search of employment. In villages, people still had no right to move wherever they chose. Yet young men took advantage of a loophole in Soviet practices: they could make a choice following their service in the armed forces, and many of them moved to urban centers. For the second time since the early 1930s, Moscow and other big cities were flooded with uprooted young peasants.[27] In summer 1958, milk and cheese disappeared from stores in Leningrad, the second-largest urban center after the capital. Over the next two years fresh fish disappeared, too. In 1961–62 city newspapers stopped advertising fish and meat. Quality meat, dairy products, and confections quickly became scarce everywhere except in downtown Moscow. Mikhail German, an art historian from Leningrad and the son of a famous writer, was astonished, when he visited his Moscow relatives, to find "thick slices of pastrami and ham, expensive bologna, cheese" on their plates.[28] Central Russia was the most affected by the food crisis. By October 1961 most of the Russian provinces were without meat.[29]

The contradictions so apparent in Khrushchev's New Deal shaped the evolving consciousness of young members of the intelligentsia. They observed the growing anger among the workers and peasants, the increasing frustration caused by the gap between Khrushchev's promises of material abundance and actual living standards. The thirty-two-year-old sociologist Vadim Olshansky almost became a victim of this frustration in October 1961. A graduate of Leningrad State University and a party member, he applied for postgraduate studies at the Institute of Philosophy in Moscow. The advice he received was to study workers' attitudes, by working "undercover" at a factory. Olshansky, following the institute's recommendations, signed up as a technician at the Lenin Plant in Moscow. Soon a group of workers discovered his false identity and cornered him, with the obvious intention of beating him up, as a "mole" of the administration. When he explained he was a scholar, a worker attacked him with a question: Do you believe in communism? Olshansky decided to take a principled stand. "Yes, I do." Clearly about to pummel him, the worker shouted in his face: "And we do not!" In the remaining split second before violence broke out, Olshansky responded to the challenge. He told the workers that the vile mess around them had nothing to do with communism, that Khrushchev had turned the notion into a meaningless shell. Still, he insisted, communism meant something honest, elevated, and beautiful. The workers listened. Then one of them brought a glass of diluted spirit (a cheaper substitute for vodka). "Drink! You are one of us!"[30]

Many decades later Olshansky questioned whether he had been completely honest in this confrontation with the workers. Yet his socialist beliefs, defying the ambivalent reality, were typical of the cohorts of educated younger Russians in the late 1950s and early 1960s. Apparently, communism remained a positive idea, synonymous with a happy and secure life of abundance. Many among the postwar educated elite, despite their knowledge and observations, continued to identify with socialist values and collectivist projects. Anatoly Cherniaev experienced the same feelings of ambiguity. In the spring of 1961 he returned to Moscow from Prague, where he worked for *Problems of Peace and Socialism,* the journal of the international communist movement. Among his intellectual and artist friends, he would have never argued that "we would catch up and overtake America and would be able to build everything that Khrushchev's program pledged." Still, some core belief made him "wish Khrushchev success."[31] Yuri Timofeev, a friend of many writers and artists, continued to take communism very seriously. He told his little daughter that one day she would be proud to live in the country where this great experiment had played out.[32]

On balance, Khrushchev's New Deal and the Sputnik effect encouraged socialist thinking on a grand scale among younger educated, intellectual groups. This thinking was not the "alignment with history" of the 1930s, driven by blind, unquestioning optimism or by fear of marginalization and repression. The liberating shocks and doubts of the Thaw had had their effect, although they were often absorbed into everyday routine. Still, the dominant assumption was that the existing order needed to be not dismantled and rejected, but rather transformed and reformed. There was a widespread belief that the Soviet Union, once restored and liberated from Stalin's dark legacy, could become truly a beacon of "progressive humanity," a great world power. The ambiguities of this "reformed communist" worldview, a mixture of bitter knowledge of the past, optimism about the future, and incipient freethinking, were manifest in the mindset of two groups of younger educated Russians at the center of public intellectual ferment: scientists and journalists.

Optimistic Scientists

Scientists became the first group of highly educated people in the late 1950s and early 1960s whose influence on society and cultural life far surpassed their professional competence. Although the public veneration of science was a feature of Russian public opinion well before the 1950s, the end of that decade marked the zenith of public awareness of scientific achievements, which was boosted by the Sputnik effect and by nuclear programs.[33] This public awareness was part of Khrushchev's New Deal. The research center in Dubna, fifty miles to the north of Moscow, became the first declassified center of nuclear physics in 1956 to attract enormous public attention. The Dubna center served as a window onto the Soviet "peaceful atom" program; physicists there dreamed of developing sustainable solar plasma as a potential source of unlimited energy for peaceful uses. This goal perfectly corresponded to the official formula of communism, "Soviet power plus electric power." The Soviet press wrote about a giant cyclotron, the largest in the world, built in 1957 in Dubna as a tool essential to the future communist cornucopia.[34] In October 1958, as Soviet newspapers heaped opprobrium on Pasternak's Nobel Prize for Literature, *Pravda* lionized the physicists Igor Tamm, Ilya Frank, and Pavel Cherenkov, who had received the Nobel Prize for Physics. Periodically, the Soviet press published brief communiqués about state awards to an anonymous group of scientists "for their achievements in strengthening [our] national defense."[35]

Physicists in secret labs, researchers at the Dubna center, and the scientists in the freshly constructed Novosibirsk academic city and other new institutes acquired not only access to a wide array of foreign professional publications, but also—despite the resistance of the KGB and ideological censors—increasing access to popular and political Western periodicals. The Dubna center eventually housed the United Institute for Nuclear Studies, where scientists from twelve Soviet bloc countries worked.[36] Numerous scientists, along with the best artists and performers, regained the privilege of traveling abroad, under the aegis of "public diplomacy," to support the antinuclear movement in Western countries. In July 1957, at the initiative of the American industrialist Cyrus Eaton, who had a special relationship with the Kremlin, a select group of American and Canadian scientists concerned with the nuclear race met with several Soviet scientists in the Canadian town of Pugwash. The Academy of Sciences of the USSR created the Soviet Pugwash Committee, which legalized regular communication between leading Soviet scientists and their foreign colleagues—for the first time since the 1920s.[37]

The recently acquired fame of some scientists, as well as the secrecy that continued to surround many others, only increased public curiosity and fortified the cult of science. For the young Vladimir Vysotsky, the bard who would achieve international fame, "the words 'physicist' and 'young scientist' stood for 'magician.'" In those days, "it seemed that physics was going to unveil some ultimate secrets to humanity—and then right away cosmonauts would fly to the planets and stars, and the entire universe with its treasures and other civilizations would reveal its mysterious depths."[38] The actor Alexei Batalov recalled much later how excited he was in 1960, when he featured in a film about the life of nuclear physicists. "Filming took place in a world no one had known about before. No one had seen these installations and labs." For Batalov as well as the other actors and the film director, Mikhail Romm, it was like making a picture about Martians. "No one knew" how these secret scientists lived, "how they worked, what they talked about."[39] This mystique of secret, empowering knowledge, combined with great job opportunities, attracted many university students. From 1950 to 1965 the number of scientists and jobs in scientific research in the Soviet Union grew faster than anywhere else in the world, increasing from 162,500 to 665,000.[40] At MGU and Leningrad State University the number of students in basic sciences—chemistry, biology, mathematics, physics—increased exponentially, a reflection of social trends and high status as well as new job opportunities. The best and the brightest went into physics, "the queen of sciences" at that time. The joke in Moscow was that young women switched their preferences from military men and diplomats to physicists, who became the latest epitome of the desirable male companion.

In September 1959 the newspaper *Komsomolskaia Pravda* published an exchange between the writer Ilya Ehrenburg and a Leningrad student, "Nina S." She complained that her boyfriend Yuri, a workaholic engineer, believed that art and lyrical poetry were outdated in the "space age." Ehrenburg expressed complete solidarity with Nina, stressing that art and poetry were necessary to the cultivation of human souls. Several weeks passed, and the newspaper published a letter "in defense of Yuri," signed by the "engineer I. Poletaev," which declared that the time when writers and poets could be "engineers of human souls" was over. The author wrote that science and technology "shape the face of our epoch, increasingly influence the taste, customs, and behavior of human beings. Like it or not, poets have less and less sway over our souls and have less and less to teach us. The most fascinating tales are told by science and technology, by precise, bold, and merciless reason."[41] This was a revolutionary claim for the supremacy of science as a cultural form, replacing the previously dominant poetry and highbrow novels.

Igor Poletaev was not an "engineer," but a mathematician and the author of *Signal,* the first popular Soviet book on computers, published in 1958. Also Poletaev was a party member and war veteran, who had worked in the United States in 1945 as part of a trade delegation. There he took a strong interest in Norbert Wiener's "science" of mathematical regulation of complex information systems. When the study of cybernetics was banned in the Soviet Union, Poletaev became even more passionate about it; he felt safe because he worked in the secret labs of the military-industrial complex. After Stalin's death he joined the informal circle of cybernetics enthusiasts, an influential group that quietly began to lobby for the rehabilitation of cybernetics. Members pointed to the spectacular American progress in computer technology and the vital role that the technology played in nuclear and missile projects.[42] More than any other branch of scientific exploration, cybernetics seemed to offer Soviet optimists a fresh and truly universal intellectual framework. "Soviet cybernetics," concludes Slava Gerovitch, "emerged as a project of reforming Soviet science—politically and intellectually—after the years of Stalinism." Yet its cultural significance extended far beyond the sciences. In the opinion of its advocates, cybernetics created a universal language. It was more modern than the lyrical murmur of poetry and more precise than the imperfect historical and human reflections in Russian novels. And above all it was a powerful tool against the dogmatic and demagogical manipulators of Marxism-Leninism, the phony priests of dialectical materialism, who supported Lysenko and other pseudoscientists. At the same time, cybernetics did not represent a rejection of socialism as a futuristic project. On the contrary, Poletaev and his colleagues believed that cybernetics would be a crucial instrument for helping Soviet society move in the direction of the communist dream. In his book *Signal*, Poletaev wrote that the computer "forces man to be honest, precise, rigorous, and ready to accept the truth, however unexpected and bitter this truth might be." The use of computerized language, as Poletaev and his allies hoped, would eliminate ideological verbiage from sciences—because it was "not amenable to formalization." In fact, adepts of "cyberspeak" like Poletaev hoped that this language of objectivity would inaugurate social and economic reforms in the Soviet Union. Computers and computer science would curb, correct, and gradually replace the cumbersome, corrupt, ideology-laden bureaucracy that hindered the experiment to build a communist society. Computerization would help to bring about decentralization and provide greater feedback from scientists to the ruling institutions of the party and the state. In short, cybernetics, reinforcing communist idealism with the technocratic dream of a harmonious society, became a new outlet for that idealism.[43]

Poletaev did not reject the role of poetry and classical literature in Russian-Soviet culture. He read voraciously, adored classical music, and played many instruments himself. He did, however, believe that the role writers, poets, and artists had played in Stalin's day under state censorship had destroyed their right to be the intellectual and cultural vanguard of society on its way to emancipation from Stalinism. Poletaev believed that the Stalinist regime would have been impossible without "writers, and other humanitarians of poor quality who only lied and settled personal accounts." For this reason, he regarded Ehrenburg's appeal to "plough virgin souls" by means of classical art and literature as a dishonest attempt to support "the rotting authority" of the compromised literary elite.[44]

The polemics between Ehrenburg and Poletaev set off a great public debate over whether the language of fiction and poetry or the universal

Ludmilla Alexeyeva, an idealistic student at Moscow State University during the last years of Stalin's rule. In 1951 she joined the party, to improve it from within. Yet her true allegiance was to a circle of friends (Courtesy of Memorial, Moscow).

language of science would guide the society along the road to the communist future. This debate became known as physics versus lyrics. It raged for months in universities, academic centers, scientific laboratories, libraries, and numerous circles of friends. Poletaev, much to his surprise, was drawn into its vortex; his colleagues, military intellectuals from one of the defense sector institutes, "stopped working for two or three days, and argued until they lost their voices." Hundreds of thousands of educated Russians became polarized between the two camps. Often married couples split up because they found themselves on opposite sides. In some circles of educated friends in Moscow, recalls Ludmilla Alexeyeva, the discussion proceeded like this. Those who sided with the "physicists" said: "All this blather about social justice, democracy, equality, 'the people,' proletarians-of-the-world unite. Look what it got us . . . We are up to our throats in shit, and you are still chitchatting." And the "lyricists" responded: "You've counted up all your atoms, your neutrons and shmeutrons, what does it mean to us? How's a person to live?" On December 24, 1959, Ehrenburg summed up the public discussion with an article, in which he sought to reconcile the camp of "feelings" with the camp of "reason."[45]

The public passions that were roused in the "lyrics versus physics" debate pointed up again the growing prestige of scientists and the need that the younger educated public felt for fresh intellectual leadership. Nobody claimed victory in the debate, yet it showed that scientists had become paragons of objectivity in the eyes of the educated public. Because the people of the postwar generation grew up believing that religious faith and organized religions were destined to fade away, they imagined a new temple of science, where modern and highly rational priests of mathematics and physics initiated the public into the mysteries of nature and space. Scientists had knowledge, resources, and powerful connections that writers and others in the liberal arts lacked. And scientists seemed to combine a sense of intellectual freedom with a sense of civic duty, of moral responsibility for the fate of world civilization. The scientific head of the Soviet atomic project, Igor Kurchatov, warned Kremlin leaders that a thermonuclear race could eventuate in a war that would destroy the world. Until his premature death in 1960, he lobbied for termination of ground nuclear tests. In 1957 the thirty-six-year-old physicist Andrei Sakharov, fascinated by genetic discoveries, wrote a study about the long-term biological effects of nuclear tests on human beings. His conclusions had "moral and political" implications: termination of the tests would save the lives of hundreds of thousands of people for many centuries into the future.[46] Even the select physicists who belonged to the Pugwash Committee and served Soviet "public diplomacy" impressed their Western counterparts with their earnest desire to prevent a nuclear war. Quietly, they began to promote an agenda of arms control and disarmament for both Western and communist camps. Encouraged by their Western friends and by the ideas they had gleaned from international scientific literature, some Soviet physicists began to develop pacifist ideas, as well as technocratic schemes to use the power of science to achieve cultural and political liberalization.[47]

Poletaev and other influential scientists acted on their hatred of "party philosophers" and pseudoscientific careerists and demagogues. The most notorious target was Trofim Lysenko, the archenemy of genetics, and his numerous and powerful protégés and allies. The struggle against Lysenkoism became one of the most dynamic and socially important movements among scientists in the history of Russia.[48] The anti-Lysenko coalition cut across scientific disciplines and included computer mathematicians, many prominent physicists, such as Pyotr Kapitsa and Lev Landau. They sent collective letters to the party presidium, pressing for legalization of genetic studies and greater autonomy from ideological dictates for the hard sciences.[49] When the young nuclear designer Andrei Sakharov arrived at the prestigious Academy of Sciences, along with a group of nuclear physicists, he joined an informal coalition there struggling against Lysenko's allies to achieve a greater scientific freedom. The party apparatchiks were quick to notice that none of the young academicians were party members and that most of them (although not Sakharov) were of Jewish background. The attempts of the party department of science to get a number of its candidates, Lysenko supporters, into the academy failed miserably; they did not receive enough votes.[50]

During the Thaw, when writers failed to take literary matters into their own hands, some scientists succeeded in emancipating their theories from state censorship. They created informal self-education circles and "academies" that were autonomous from party control. An informal academy emerged around the geneticist Nikolai Timofeev-Ressovsky at the biological station of Miassovo Lake near the Ural Mountains. In summer 1959 he conducted a workshop on genetics, the first one in the USSR in ten years. Poletaev attended the workshop and brought his son with him. The audience consisted of biologists, physicists from Sverdlovsk, Moscow, and Leningrad, biochemists and chemists, mathematicians, doctors, and even artists. Rank and formal status were not observed. When the summer heat became unbearable, the "colloquia" moved to the beach, and discussions took place in the waters of the lake.[51]

Aside from Ressovsky, a few scientists who managed to organize such independent workshops became role models for scores of colleagues, most of them still in their thirties and forties. Soon, with the help of young journalists and television producers attracted by the spontaneous brilliance of the scientific milieu, some of these scientific figures became role models for the broader educated public as well. They exuded intellectual freedom, missing from the worlds of culture and art. The most famous was Lev Landau, a favorite student of Niels Bohr. He was born and raised in a Jewish family in splendid, cosmopolitan Baku, and during the 1930s he was an ardent communist. In 1938 he was arrested, along with other young physicists who had written an anti-Stalin leaflet. Only the intercession of his boss, the world-renowned physicist Pyotr Kapitsa, saved his life. His illusions shattered, Landau returned emaciated, sobered by his brush with death. He was forced to participate in the Soviet atomic project, but after 1953 he tried to distance himself from the business of making nuclear bombs for a regime he considered oppressive.[52] After Stalin's death Landau, like many other intellectuals, believed that "true socialist values" could be restored. In 1956 he read with admiration Dudintsev's novel and Paustovsky's speech with their denunciation of the ruling Soviet bureaucratic class. Above all, he valued intellectual and scientific freedom. The Soviet invasion of Hungary destroyed his dreams again. According to his KGB file, he said in November 1956, "Our system remains fascist and simply cannot change. It is ludicrous to hope that this system can lead us to something good." He even said at some point, according to the KGB informer, "If our system cannot collapse peacefully, then a third world war with all its horrors is inevitable. Therefore, the issue of a peaceful dissolution of our system is the vital issue for the future of all humankind."[53] Thanks to his genius, Landau remained free to do his scientific work, but he was never allowed to travel abroad. Not only were his lectures and seminars brilliant, but they broke with Soviet academic rules and conventions. He liked to think aloud and taught innumerable young scholars to do the same. Any student could join his workshop, but only after passing a number of tests on theoretical physics. Landau took those exams lying on his sofa at home. "Dau" was unconventional in everything, including his personal lifestyle. Similar to Alexandra Kollontai and some other communist intellectuals of the 1920s, he espoused the philosophy of free love. Husband and wife, he argued, should have total freedom to meet with other partners, provided that they took care of their children. Dau's jokes, pranks, and escapades became legendary. He remained, despite his disillusionment with the Soviet regime, an incurable optimist.[54]

Another brilliant physicist and free spirit was Andrei (Gersh) Budker. He was born in the Jewish Pale of Settlement. Like Landau, he initially embraced the spirit and ideals of the Bolshevik Revolution, but Stalinist crimes and oppression dampened his enthusiasm. After graduation from Moscow State University in 1941 he took part in World War II, after which he was conscripted to work on the Soviet atomic project. In 1952 he fell under suspicion with Lavrenty Beria, the feared chief of the project, but was not arrested. During the Thaw Budker became a leading scientist in the field of controlled thermonuclear synthesis (fusion). He also pioneered research on sustainable solar plasma that could yield unlimited amounts of energy. In the fall of 1958, at the age of forty, the theoretician went to Novosibirsk, to start a new institute of nuclear physics there. This institute became the most liberalized part of Akademgorodok. Like Landau, Budker despised the Soviet regime and bureaucracy and posed as a natural democrat in science. His institute was designed in such a way that scientists could "constantly bump into each other, inspiring daily interaction." There, scientific work and discussion proceeded in the total absence of hierarchy or bureaucratic administration. According to Budker, "scientific workers should not accord power to the administrative apparatus." Jokingly, he proposed to fire all Soviet bureaucrats and send them to a resort with full pay and privileges. Both science and the economy would function more efficiently as a result.[55] One of his colleagues recalled that Budker had "a romantic soul" and always looked on the bright side. Although he was highly critical of the Soviet system, he preserved the optimistic core beliefs of his postrevolutionary youth. For him, the best model for an equal and just society was a community of physicists, devoted to the beauty of their discipline.[56] Numerous talented scientists flocked to Budker's institute to do theoretical physics, but also to become "citizens" in his minisociety.

People like Poletaev, Landau, and Budker did not think about waging protests or struggles for political liberalization. Yet they inspired the Thaw intellectuals to emancipate themselves from the Stalinist dogmatism and xenophobia, to experiment and explore, to connect the Soviet Union with the outside world through a universal scientific language and ethics. Such scientists knew that in the West the social sciences had grown in status, also boosted by the successes of computerized mathematical analysis and research on artificial intelligence. By the early 1960s, the same people who had fought against Lysenkoism and promoted freedom of scientific interaction also began to promote liberalization in the humanities, including literature and art. Scientific institutes and labs were the first to offer patronage to innovative poets and artists. Scientists also supported a new cohort of Russian linguists who were struggling to free themselves from Stalinist tenets. One such linguist was Viacheslav (Koma) Ivanov, the son of an established writer from the old intelligentsia, a close friend of Boris Pasternak. In 1958 the son had the courage to defend Pasternak publicly during the Nobel Prize affair and as a result lost his position at Moscow State University. His friends found him another job at the Institute of Precise Mechanics and Computer Technology, where Poletaev worked. Ivanov remembered how inspired he had been in the late 1950s by cybernetics: "We were tired of the phraseology of the official philosophy. We wanted to deal with precisely defined concepts and with terms that were defined through rigorously described operations." At that time "linguistics was the only field in the humanities that developed sufficiently precise methods, and the influence of official ideology was virtually absent. Not surprisingly, many talented young people rushed into this field."[57]

Koma Ivanov was not alone in thinking that the realm of science was preferable to that of literature and the other humanities, maimed by party control and self-censorship. Dubna and Akademgorodok appeared at the time to be exemplars of an intellectual commune, a brotherhood of equals where all worked according to their abilities and received according to their contributions to the common cause. The scientists from the independent workshops of Timofeev-Ressovsky, Landau, and Budker appeared to be prototypes for a civil society otherwise nonexistent in the Soviet Union. Even the literary vanguard during the Thaw seemed to recognize the supremacy of scientists. For all their personal candor and linguistic experimentation, the young poets of the Thaw could not and did not offer a universal and global alternative to the discredited official ideology in the way cybernetics seemed to do. In fall 1959 Boris Slutsky admitted as much, in a poem that quickly spread around Moscow. "Looks as if physicists are in, looks as if lyricists are out. Nothing Machiavellian—nature's law, no doubt." Slutsky reproached the lyricists for the weakness of their ideas. The power of words, he concluded, was weaker than the nascent power of "sign and number."[58]

In 1960 two young writers, the brothers Arkady and Boris Strugatsky, wrote a novel describing a technoscientific utopia. The heroes of their book were "magicians" from a secret scientific laboratory, most of them in their twenties and thirties. The authors deliberately placed them in a setting with wizards and witches from classic fairy tales, which gave the book an entertaining aspect, but also derailed the censors. Boris later recalled that it was a book about "the best of our contemporaries—our friends and loved ones." At that time, Boris recalled, "we sincerely believed in communism as the highest and ultimate stage of human society's development."[59] The youthful world of scientists, full of improvisation, scintillating humor, and unflagging optimism, accorded with the brothers' vague but very passionate socialist orientation. The eggheaded scientists, they wanted to believe, would succeed with computers where revolutionary romantics with Lenin's slogans and commissars with shotguns had failed.

The "Honest" Journalists

Journalists who worked in the Soviet media remained employees of the state propaganda apparatus. Soviet radio, newspapers, publishing houses, and other media channels were subject to strict and multilayered censorship. The party leadership, intimidated by the revolutions in Eastern Europe, resisted any liberalization in this sphere. Yet an increasing number of journalists, for the first time since the war, began to develop a new consciousness. Their main audience, instead of the party leadership and the censors, became the educated public, known in Russian as *obshchestvennost*.

The new technology and, surprisingly, the Cold War propaganda competition encouraged this transformation. Under Stalin the main medium for the transmission of state propaganda was not the printed press, but radio. "Black plates," wired receivers that broadcast only one program, were installed in many towns and villages. It was forbidden to turn them off during the daytime. Still, some areas were impervious to the spread of radio propaganda. After the war, wireless radio broadcasting had emerged, relying primarily on medium- and shortwave transmission.[60] This in turn made Soviet broadcasting vulnerable to foreign intrusion. After 1953, however, shortwaves quickly became the main weapons in the psychological warfare between Western countries and the Soviet regime. In August 1958 a commission of experts reported to the Kremlin that the jamming of radio stations to suppress propaganda broadcasts by the West cost more money than Soviet domestic and international broadcasting combined. "Despite the billions spent," the report continued, "jamming does not achieve its goal." It blocked foreign broadcasts only in Moscow and a few other big cities, while anyone just a few miles away could listen freely to them. "Radio intervention by the imperialist states," they concluded, "has been doing great harm to our ideological work. It even can cause serious damage to the combat readiness of this country."[61] Western propaganda radio stations, including VOA and Radio Liberty (until May 1959 it was called Radio Liberation), gradually became an alternative source of information for educated and news-hungry Soviet citizens.

Another way to respond to this challenge was to turn to more credible and informed print media, newspapers that people would be willing, even eager to read. A group of war vets and fresh graduates of universities who came to journalism during the 1950s believed they were up to the task. In their opinion the spread of knowledge was an important mission, a vehicle for social and cultural change, a means to overcome the Stalinist legacy. Rada Adzhubei, the daughter of Khrushchev, began work at a scientific journal with this conviction. She preserved it for her entire life.[62]

The boldest and most successful of that cohort of journalists was Rada's husband Alexei Adzhubei. Tall and handsome, artistic and talented, impatient and temperamental, he was among the first MGU journalism majors, graduating on the eve of Stalin's death. Adzhubei had been raised by his mother, a fashion designer who made couture clothes for Politburo wives and famous actresses. A member of the postwar generation of students who was too young to have witnessed hostilities, Alexei at first wanted to be an actor and even studied the Stanislavsky method at an acting school. Then he transferred to MGU, where he conceived a lifelong passion for journalism and for Khrushchev's daughter. They married in 1949, and as Khrushchev was ascending toward the pinnacle of power, Adzhubei swiftly climbed the journalistic career ladder. From 1955 to 1958 he rose from being in charge of the sports section of *Komsomolskaia Pravda* to being editor of the newspaper. In May 1959 he was appointed editor in chief of *Izvestia,* the second-most-important newspaper in the Soviet Union after the official party mouthpiece, *Pravda.* He was only thirty-five years old.[63]

Overnight, *Izvestia* was transformed from the dullest Soviet newspaper into the most innovative one. Adzhubei was a fantastic media organizer. At his first meeting with the staff, he told the journalists to take out of their drawers "the best and most important material" they had written but could not publish.[64] "The state does not need journalists to be its defenders or prosecutors," Adzhubei told the staff of *Izvestia* in June 1959. "We must fight for innovations in industry, agriculture, and science. Fight in earnest!" Let *Pravda* be the mouthpiece of the party leadership; *Izvestia* should become the newspaper of the intelligentsia, in order to support "fresh, clever people" in the society who wanted to improve, renew, and reform medicine, education, theater, services, retail, and social life. Adzhubei spoke about the problem of boosting "morale, courage, and decency" in society.[65] The newspaper, Adzhubei continued, should reach out and send correspondents to every remote corner of the USSR but also invite "scientists, actors, and innovators of industry" to write to the newspaper. It should advertise new films and propagandize discoveries. He proposed to hold meetings with creative people every Friday. "All we need is one enthusiast" to help arrange them. The new editor in chief also spoke about the need to disseminate more information about the world, to write "critical" and "honest" commentaries on foreign news, to satisfy the voracious hunger of Soviet society for international news.[66]

For years the interpretation of foreign and domestic developments was the monopoly of the Politburo and the foreign ministry. When Adzhubei's colleagues reminded him of this fact, his response was, "The newspaper must be a policymaker, as well as a mirror of policy." One journalist interjected, "One has to have the right to do it." Adzhubei replied, "We cannot just go to the Central Committee and say: Give us the right! We need to show them our materials—once or twice, and we will obtain this right."[67] Adzhubei's instructions to his journalists could be summed up in five principles. First, a newspaper should not tell the readers what to think, but should engage them in a conversation and the process of thinking together. Second, every issue should contain a "bomb" (sensational material) or a "nail" (a lead story) to attract the reader. Third, a journalist must write about what really grabs his or her attention. Fourth, a newspaper should sift through society for opinions and debates and immediately respond to them. Fifth, all articles should firmly rest on reliable evidence.[68]

Adzhubei followed up on his optimistic intentions. His daily contact with Khrushchev and excellent connections with the Komsomol and the KGB leadership allowed him to raise the sycophantic Soviet newspaper almost to the status of the "second power" next to the party. He never took no for an answer from the party ideologues or state censors. *Izvestia*'s journalists began to travel to numerous closed areas and secret installations in the USSR, including missile launch grounds and sites of military exercises. Censors vetted *Izvestia* articles faster than they did the communications in *Pravda* and TASS. Adzhubei used the secure high-frequency state phone, another perquisite of his privileged position, to call ministers and party officials, asking for access and plane tickets for his correspondents as well as for interviews and information.

After Gagarin's space flight in April 1961, the newspaper put together an illustrated book about the first Soviet cosmonaut in just twenty-four hours. Three hundred thousand copies sold immediately. *Izvestia* became not only the most popular but also the most profitable of all Soviet papers. In the early 1960s *Izvestia* branched out: it published a weekly of domestic news, *Nedelia* (Week), and a weekly of foreign news, *Za Rubezhom* (Abroad), named after a magazine suspended in the 1930s. It expanded its publishing capacities, bought the best publishing equipment in West Germany and Japan, and built cooperative houses and resorts for newspaper staff, correspondents, and their families.[69]

Adzhubei felt condescension and sometimes even contempt for the party ideologues, old Stalinist cadres of limited cultural background, imagination, and talent. They responded with jealousy and hatred. The party secretary Mikhail Suslov threw a monkey wrench into Adzhubei's media enterprises whenever he could. Having lost some battles, Adzhubei aimed at winning his campaign for the redefinition of cultural policies. In the divisive politics of the Thaw, especially while Khrushchev's personal position was not clarified, Adzhubei yielded to his artistic bent: he was much more liberal in matters of culture than in politics. The newspaper supported young talent in poetry and art. Adzhubei once brought a book of poetry back from Paris, one by Nikolai Gumilyov, the former husband of Anna Akhmatova, who was executed in 1921 for conspiracy against the Bolsheviks. Adzhubei showed the book around during an editorial meeting and asked his staff, "Could we do anything to rehabilitate him?"[70]

Izvestia attracted excellent writers and unconventional minds. The most remarkable among them was Anatoly Agranovsky, perhaps the best practitioner of "honest" and "thinking" journalism in the Khrushchev era. His father, a Bolshevik from a Jewish family, had worked as a journalist for *Izvestia* and *Pravda* during the 1930s. He was arrested in 1937 but released after the war started. Agranovsky felt he was continuing his father's mission to turn socialism into a fair and humane social system. The journalist had a unique talent for looking beyond the obvious in investigating the forces and motives that corrupted, degraded, or delayed "socialist progress."[71] In a famous essay published in 1962, when he was forty, Agranovsky told about his trip to the faraway Altai region, where German Titov, the second Soviet cosmonaut in space, had been born. In contrast to numerous other journalists who sang the hero's praises, Agranovsky investigated Titov's family background. The question he had was what had enabled a son from a peasant family to become a space explorer. Agranovsky's answer diverged from the usual clichés, such as "the Soviet system of education" or "the party's care for people." He wrote that Titov had grown up in a family that had benefited from constant cultural enrichment, thanks to an enthusiastic teacher who had organized the May Morning commune in the village where the Titov's parents lived. The entire village read and discussed Tolstoy, Turgenev, Gogol, Gorky, and other classic Russian writers. They also delved into the books by Ibsen, Molière, Heine, Maupassant, and Maeterlinck. There was even a peasant orchestra at May Morning. All this existed until the mid-1930s, when the local party authorities accused the commune leader of being a "hidden enemy" and shut the commune down. Agranovsky interviewed the person who had denounced the idealistic teacher and remembered that his father had tried to defend the local experiment in *Pravda*. From the vantage point of the early 1960s Agranovsky wondered who had won—the educator or his antagonists? His message was this: Stalinism had unleashed ignorant bureaucrats and aggressive party vigilantes against the intelligentsia. And the space flights of Gagarin and Titov proved that the intelligentsia—everyone from space designers to village educators—had triumphed in the end. Without the intelligentsia, Sputnik and the feats of those first cosmonauts could never have happened.[72]

Agranovsky's articles were a shot in the arm for many creative individuals, among them Sviatoslav Fyodorov, an ophthalmologist who invented the operation for artificial cornea implants, early glaucoma surgery, and a method to correct nearsightedness.[73] Agranovsky managed to articulate on the pages of a mass-circulation Soviet newspaper read by millions the main theme of Thaw literature: socialism could not be built through violence, fear, submission, and bureaucratic omnipotence. It could only be constructed by creative and dedicated individuals, and those individuals should find their own solidarity, become a genuine, not an official, intelligentsia. Humanizing the pages of Soviet newspapers and making people reflect on the complex facts of life were the main missions of the "new journalism" promoted by Adzhubei and Agranovsky.[74] *Izvestia* was like the fresh wind blowing through the stuffy premises of the overregulated Soviet media. Other newspapers and magazines had to follow the leader, at their own speed, for fear of losing their readers.[75]

The new journalism provided cover for the resurgence of sociology and studies of public opinion, disciplines completely banned under Stalin. In *Izvestia*, Adzhubei created a new approach to readers' letters. Special staff read and analyzed the letters to the editor and used the analysis to establish an interactive relationship with *Izvestia*'s growing audience. "One pointed and colorful letter," Adzhubei said to his staff, "can save a man from execution and prevent a factory from production stoppages. It can make policy." The number of letters to *Izvestia* increased from thirty thousand in 1952 to half a million in 1964. The newspaper began to serve as an intermediary between its audience and the authorities: most of the mail from readers concerned fixing problems, curbing local bureaucrats, or checking up on how local authorities were following through on their promises. The correspondents, reacting to whistle-blowers and pleas for help, undertook investigations. The very mention of *Izvestia* was enough to make many provincial or mid-ranking bureaucrats tremble before such investigative journalists.[76]

In May 1960 a group of journalists from *Komsomolskaia Pravda* took a revolutionary step—they launched the Institute for the Study of Public Opinion, the first in the Soviet Union. All the investigators in the group were MGU graduates, had absorbed the energy and ideas of the Thaw, and wanted to help improve society. They armed themselves with mathematical statistics, sociological questionnaires, and increasingly fashionable theories of cybernetics. The initiative to study public opinion stemmed from the raison d'être of "honest journalism": transforming Soviet media into the intermediary between the intelligentsia and the state. One person in the group, Boris Grushin, acknowledged four decades later that the first goal of the institute was "the spread and inculcation into mass consciousness of the values and norms, the types of consciousness and behavior that constituted the corpus of the communist education of the youth." *Komsomolskaia Pravda* received an enormous volume of mail, sixteen thousand to seventeen thousand letters every month. This made it imperative to find out more about the authors of the letters, categorize their opinions, and seek to establish a dialogue and a relationship of trust with them. At the same time, Grushin said later, the new institute provided him with ample opportunity to pursue his sociological research using the relative freedom provided by the newspaper.[77]

Grushin and his group conducted the first public poll from May 10 to May 14, 1960, on the eve of Khrushchev's trip to Paris, where he was to take part in a summit with the leaders of the United States, Great Britain, and France. Gary Powers had just been shot down in his U-2 reconnaissance plane above the Ural Mountains on May 1, but there were still hopes that this incident would not prevent President Eisenhower from coming to the Soviet Union. The poll included three questions: Will it be possible for mankind to prevent a war? What is your opinion based on? What should be done above all to strengthen peace? Grushin's group deliberately selected ten localities along the thirtieth meridian passing from Murmansk through the vicinity of Leningrad down to southern Ukraine. Many people along this meridian had lived under German occupation during World War II. Out of a thousand people polled, 72 percent (and in some localities as much as 90 percent) had lost close relatives in the war. The staggering losses and lingering pain seemed to provide a clear answer to the first question—no. Soviet people had "bleeding memories" of the Great Patriotic War and consequently supported Khrushchev's course of peace and negotiations with Western powers. The young pollsters counted the results in just one day.[78] They appeared in *Komsomolskaia Pravda* on May 19, by which point the agenda of the Paris summit was in tatters and Khrushchev was delivering threatening harangues against Western "militarists."

While providing the presummit propaganda, Grushin and his young colleagues had an independent research agenda. They wanted to determine how fears of war correlated with hopes about the future. The results amounted to a paradox: the Soviet people, victims of war, had "seemingly boundless optimism" and a "more than confident look at their own future and the future of mankind." Most respondents wrote, sometimes quite enthusiastically, about their confidence in a peaceful future. The optimism of the Soviet public, Grushin noted, had a vigorous, excessive quality to it, "with a touch of exalted theatricality." One-fifth of the people polled declared their intention "to strengthen peace" with "their own labor," "overfulfill state plans," and "meet the obligations to the state." The results of the poll redirected Grushin in his research. Although he shared the optimistic mood of the times, he was struck by the deficit of individual critical thinking and by the reliance of the Soviet public on the state propaganda slogans.[79] This phenomenon had definitely played a crucial role in the establishment of Stalinism.

Another group of talented journalists who worked at *Izvestia* and *Komsomolskaia Pravda* made unexpected discoveries during those years. They were "agrarian" reporters, most of them with peasant backgrounds and a love for the Russian country lifestyle. One member of this group was Yuri Chernichenko, the son of an agronomist, who had spent his childhood among the Kuban Cossacks in the Northern Caucasus during the dreadful famine caused by Stalin's food requisitioning. "I could have been kidnapped and eaten there" by local cannibals, he recalled later. Instead, he graduated from Kishinev (Chişinău) University in literature and philology. In the mid-1950s he volunteered to go to the Virgin Lands and lived there for six years, writing for Moscow newspapers, working as a professional tractor driver, and trying to develop an intimate grasp of Soviet agriculture. At first, Chernichenko was fascinated by Khrushchev's grandiose idea. Yet he

and his colleagues quickly became appalled by the waste and disorganization, the lack of storage facilities for the rotting crops, the shortage of tractor fuel and spare parts, the inefficient ways of plowing the fragile steppe
soils, and the penchant of the local authorities for fraud and Potemkin villages. The agrarian reporters, including Chernichenko, blamed the local
bosses but also Nikita Khrushchev for the errors and disorganization. What
they saw in the Virgin Lands made them look with fresh eyes at the tragedy
of Stalinist collectivization in the early 1930s and the famine of the late
1940s, at the destruction of Russian peasantry.

At the same time, the source of unresolved ambivalence for the "honest"
journalists during Khrushchev's Thaw was that they remained firmly em-
bedded in the party propaganda machinery. Both flagships of the new journalism, *Izvestia* and *Komsomolskaia Pravda,* continued to publish editorials
and op-ed articles dictated by the party leadership. Adzhubei is the best
example of the paradox: he was at once a brilliant, innovative journalist and
a party careerist. He could not move outside the circle delineated by Politburo policies and Khrushchev's own ideas and preferences. In fall 1959 Adzhubei organized a very effective campaign to promote Khrushchev as a
world statesman by producing a glitzy and extremely popular book about
the "discovery of America," Khrushchev's visit to the United States in
September 1959. Adzhubei never missed a chance to demonstrate Soviet
superiority over the United States whenever he could.[80] A passionate West-
ernizer in the tradition of Peter the Great, Adzhubei welcomed Western
technological innovations but opposed political democratization and Western liberalism. He firmly believed in the authoritarian model and saw no
alternative to the party and KGB controls. In the early 1960s Adzhubei considered himself one of the "children of the Twentieth Party Congress," those
who wanted to reform the Soviet system, not destroy it. As he wrote in his
memoirs, "we used to finish our meetings with indispensable slogans about
the victory of communism. We had no feeling of failure, deadlock, or stagnation. I would like to stress: there was still a reserve of energy; many remained optimistic."[81]

Adzhubei pushed for a limited kind of glasnost, yet the core of his policy
was to propagate communist romanticism and patriotism. The "new" Soviet media created through Adzhubei's power and energy encouraged and
articulated a certain kind of public opinion—Soviet, patriotic, enthusiastic,
and optimistic. Back when Adzhubei was still working at *Komsomolskaia*

Pravda, he had proposed a newspaper "action"—a team of correspondents would go to a train station in Moscow where forty years ago in 1919 workers had allegedly worked for one week without pay, thus setting an example of "communist labor." The journalists' initiative, supported by Khrushchev, quickly became a nationwide campaign for communist labor, encompassing factories, collective farms, scientific labs, and even universities and high schools. The Soviet media informed readers daily about its "new ventures" and "achievements."[82]

"Agrarian" reporters revealed critical impulses and lamented the disastrous lack of genuine cooperative movement or respect for individual creativity in Russia. At the same time, their discoveries still did not amount to a fresh perspective. Their fundamental assumption was that Soviet socialism could and should be built and improved within the existing system. The agrarian reporters were hesitant to question the wisdom of the Virgin Lands enterprise. They tried to convince themselves that the Virgin Lands saga, despite its terrible wastefulness, had not been in vain, and that Khrushchev sincerely wanted to offer a better life to the long-suffering people, to put more food on their tables.[83] The honest journalists in this field were unwilling, as well as unable owing to censorship, to see that private initiative in agriculture could hardly emerge without the lifting of the Soviet ban on private farms and ownership of land. And although the writers understood the follies of the planned economy and collectivized agriculture, they had very limited and partial prescriptions for countering them.

The rise of honest journalism appealing to the educated and thinking audience was even more dramatic in the electronic media than in the printed press. Television was very new, with a young, highly educated staff, on the cutting edge of scientific-technological programming, and initially almost uncensored by the state. Soviet Central Television began to broadcast daily in 1951, when there were only about 2,500 television sets in the USSR. The military-industrial complex, which had a monopoly on the production of television sets, produced only one model for the civilian market. It had a seven-inch screen, and the image was magnified by a big lens filled with distilled water.

The new electronic media benefited from Khrushchev's social programs, but also from the challenges of the Cold War technology race. The party commission dealing with the challenge of foreign broadcasting concluded in 1958 that the development of Soviet television would diminish the effectiveness of Radio Liberation and other enemy radio stations.[84] The next year, the vice president of RCA, Thomas Digen, wanted to bring a color television studio to the Sokolniki exhibition, on the condition that the Soviets would later purchase it. Soviet authorities replied, arrogantly and falsely, that the equipment "was of no interest to the Soviet Union," where "significantly more advanced equipment" had already been created.[85] Eventually, another American company, AMPEX, brought its color television studio to Sokolniki. Standing in it, Khrushchev boasted that Soviet color television was even better. Again, he lied. Yet the rapid growth of Soviet television with the help of state investments was undeniable. In 1959 twelve new models—one million units in all—appeared in stores, with larger screens and a sleeker design. And Khrushchev's bravado pushed Soviet authorities to erect a 540-meter-high television tower in the Soviet capital, the tallest in the world. They also made plans to produce fifteen million television sets and expand television broadcasting across the whole of Soviet territory by the mid-1960s.[86]

At first, television broadcasting seemed to be the perfect tool for the regime's propaganda. On May 1, 1956, the Moscow television station broadcast a military parade and an organized mass demonstration on Red Square for the first time. The quality of television journalism was poor. Stern and rigid women and men appeared on the screen reading the text placed before them in stentorian voices. All this, however, began to change when a host of young men and women came to work for the state television company.[87] They arrived just in time to prepare the coverage of the Moscow Youth Festival. This event, watched by millions around the country, revolutionized television journalism. It boosted dynamic, spontaneous TV reporting. Television programs offered the public a huge advantage over print media, in that they had to be aired live and, in the absence of recording and editing technology, could not be censored. Everything depended on TV journalists, overwhelmingly young—on their reaction and intelligence. When the festival began, a news anchorman and his cameraman were about to launch into a report on the festival procession from a television bus. Suddenly, part of the department store above them collapsed under the weight of the many Muscovites on its roof. The anchorman lost consciousness for a moment, and when he came to, he had to go immediately to Luzhniki Stadium to report live on the festival's opening ceremony. "My clothes were in tatters, my head was bleeding," he recalled. "After the paramedics fixed me, I went on air to the great surprise of my comrades, who thought I had been killed." He reported for an hour and a half and received three shots of analgesics to keep him on his feet.[88] The festival preparations allowed a group of young actors and composers to launch the first entertainment program with audience participation, called "An Evening of Funny Questions." Eventually, an enthusiastic crowd consisting of fans of the program took the television studio by storm, and in September 1957 the party leadership canceled the show for "aping the worst methods and customs of bourgeois television." The director of the Moscow television center lost his job over it, but the audience loved what it saw.[89]

Bolstered by state resources and the creative spirit of its educated staff, Soviet television began to transform itself into something more than a mere vehicle for political and ideological propaganda. On April 14, 1961, television channels broadcast live from Red Square the scenes of national jubilation after Gagarin's historic flight. Millions of viewers all over the USSR could see the smiling cosmonaut walking toward Khrushchev along the red carpet. Later Khrushchev and Gagarin climbed Lenin's Tomb and waved to the ecstatic Muscovites. Here was immediate, unedited, unvarnished "reality" being revealed to millions—something that writers steeped in socialist realism and print journalists, long hobbled by censorship, could only dream about. Everybody could see that the most famous man in the world had one of his shoes untied. Again, as during the youth festival, the instantaneous connection between the new hero, cause of spontaneous demonstrations, and millions of viewers was an exhilarating experience for those who produced this technical miracle. The literary critic and television enthusiast Vladimir Sappak wrote, after the event: "I seemed to see how millions of eyes grew kinder—people saw Yuri Gagarin on their television screens. Our contemporaries, with their painful search for the ideal, sometimes asserting their egos in extreme ways, need such signal personalities today."[90]

Sappak was the first to notice that television was a frontier where a genuine intelligentsia could emerge and gain in strength sufficiently to replace the official "Soviet intelligentsia." A graduate of the Institute of Literature from the same age cohort as poets Slutsky and Samoilov, he had avoided the trenches in World War II only because he was afflicted with severe asthma. His malady confined him within the four walls of his apartment but allowed him to discern that the TV screen could be as important to the battles of culture and ideas in the Soviet Union as were high literature, theater, and cinema. His book *Television and Us,* written at that time, oozed with romantic optimism. He saw television not as a propaganda medium, but as a powerful device for fostering "sincerity" in public life, education, and social reform. For Sappak, the rapid growth of the television audience portended not only the beginning of a communications revolution, but the emergence of a new form of democratic art. He hailed the appearance of the first "television artists," among them Van Cliburn and Yuri Gagarin. Soviet television, he announced, awaited "its Eisenstein." According to Sappak, television was above all a humanizing and thought-provoking art form, featuring "intellectual" men and women, along with famous writers, scientists, and theater directors. Turgid bureaucratic obfuscation and pathos would go up in smoke before the merciless "Tele-Eye": "It is impossible to cheat television! It is a documentary witness operating with facts and images of reality itself. Television in the future will reveal itself as an art with supreme moral potential."[91]

Indeed, the Soviet television of the early 1960s took over from radio and cinema as the primary vehicle for dissemination of high culture to the Soviet masses. Even Soviet authorities initially viewed television as "a technical attraction bringing art to households." Concerts, films, theater plays, and discussions of books and poetry appeared on television programs as often as did sports. Television paid good money to film producers, playwrights, and actors, as well as composers, musicians, singers, and dancers.[92] In December 1961, television producers launched the first weekly news program, *Estafeta Novostei* (News Relay). The anchorman interviewed cultural celebrities live, and they in turn brought their friends to the television studio the next time around. Sophisticated, erudite conversationalists, famous composers, and ballet dancers graced the "blue screen." As television veterans recalled, "people began to converse among themselves in the studio, looking at each other instead of at the camera. The less they cared about the camera, the more viewers cared about them."[93] This program and a growing number of other television programs came to be modeled after the *kompany,* the circles of students, intellectuals, scholars, and artists discussed earlier. These shows brought to the Soviet television screen an informality reminiscent of the ways of the old intelligentsia and preserved only in rare enclaves of Soviet society. Young directors and editors of television programs did their best to invite people from these circles—as well as their talented friends and acquaintances—who embodied the new spirit and trends of the Thaw. Last but not least television assisted radio in spreading the norms of civility, new fashions, and normative educated language— commodities that were still in short supply even in Moscow at that time.

At that time, however, many intellectuals did not take television seriously but treated it as light entertainment, in contrast to "serious art." Sappak's premature death in late 1961 left electronic media without their most far-seeing and enthusiastic promoter among intellectuals. At the same time, it was a great stroke of luck for Soviet television that party and state officials shared this underestimation of television's liberating potential. Advance vetting of the content of the programs and careful selection of prospects to appear on the blue screen were almost nonexistent at that time. Of course, the young television journalists faced the same dilemmas and unresolved

Alexei Adzhubei, the editor in chief of the Soviet newspaper *Izvestia* and Khrushchev's son-in-law, preparing for a live appearance on Soviet television. Behind him are portraits of Russian and Soviet cultural and intellectual icons: Maxim Gorky, Ivan Pavlov, Vladimir Mayakovsky, and Mikhail Sholokhov (Courtesy of Sergei Smirnov).

paradoxes that their colleagues at *Izvestia* confronted. And for a while they successfully combated them. Some of the journalists could mock the ostentatious, propagandistic aspects of their work. The beginning of the television news program, for instance, was announced by these pompous words: "People of the five continents—we address you. Let the planet Earth flourish in friendship, freedom, and peace! The dawn of communism is rising over the planet."[94] And yet as long as they remained optimists themselves, the announcers did not feel any duplicity in repeating the slogans of the program.

Power of Marxism

The "accursed" questions that had emerged for hundreds of thousands of intellectuals and students in 1956 did not fade away. They continued to surface in everyday encounters and situations. Who is to blame for the past? Why are there so many holdovers from this past at all levels of state and society? And what can educated, socially conscious people do? And yet these questions at the end of the 1950s did not dispel the general mood of optimism and romanticism that prevailed among even the most sophisticated of intellectuals. A powerful force sustaining this mood, aside from sheer youthfulness and the feeling of broadening horizons, was the tenacious belief in the Marxist, and Leninist, logic of historical development.

The Thaw and increased freethinking did not reduce the grip of Marxism and Leninism on Russian intellectuals. On the contrary, it only grew stronger. Zhivago's children did not doubt that Marx had discovered "laws" that guided the historical process. While cybernetics led society into the future, Marxism could explain why the Russian Revolution had transformed itself into the Stalinist regime.[95] Many anti-Stalinist intellectuals during the Thaw thought that a "return to Lenin" could help reveal the truth about the past. For a decade after 1956 some of them would search for "a flaw in the original design" of the Bolshevik state by exploring history, philosophy, sociology, and political economy from a Marxist-Leninist perspective. Others would propagate the idea of "genuine" revolution and honest and "moral" revolutionaries, including Lenin (as opposed to Stalin and Stalinists), in theater, cinema, art, and literature.[96] Ludmilla Alexeyeva, whom we met in the first chapter, read Lenin's works in their entirety and reported on her findings to her intellectual friends, the "penniless sybarites." Another member of her group did the same with the writings of Marx. He also studied the works of Marx's German followers Karl Kautsky, Rosa Luxemburg, and Eduard Bernstein.[97]

With the gradual opening of the Iron Curtain and with Western propaganda efforts, Russian-Soviet intellectuals were exposed to unfamiliar shades and versions of the Marxist creed. And the young thinkers still took pride in knowing that Soviet Russia remained in the eyes of the world the first place where Marxism had been tested. Foreigners who visited Moscow and Leningrad noticed that even those who professed their opposition to the Soviet regime could not accept that the capitalist free market and unplanned distribution of goods were more efficient than a centrally planned economy. When the physicist Lev Landau spoke in 1956–57 about the need to destroy the Soviet regime in order to save humanity from a nuclear war, he was still in the grip of Lenin's theory of war and imperialism. And he still believed in a possibility of combining some kind of genuine socialism with intellectual freedom. Most of Landau's students, along with most other intellectuals of the postwar generation, were convinced that human, social, and cultural progress was linked with the "inevitable transition" from capitalism to some kind of socialism. Even those who admired the American exhibition in Sokolniki in 1959 continued to believe that capitalism was eventually "doomed." Some politicized young intellectuals still predicted "a new revolutionary situation" in Russia and awaited the outbreak of a workers' strike. Even the rudiments of liberal-democratic thinking were encased in the logic of Marxist and Leninist ideas sharply differentiating between bourgeois and socialist democracy. Bourgeois democracy figured as shallow and even fraudulent in their eyes. The socialist form of democracy stood as a goal to be attained in the process of overcoming the Stalinist legacy.

The polls conducted by *Komsomolskaia Pravda* in 1960–61 reveal the strong connection between the mood of optimism among young intellectuals and the basic Marxist worldview they held. In January through March 1961, the Komsomol newspaper posed twelve questions to readers who were under thirty years old. Among them were the following: What do you think about your generation? What do you like and dislike about it? Do you have a goal in life? Do you think you will reach it?[98] For 96 percent of respondents, life had a purpose, and 82 percent were confident they would achieve it. The poll found that even educated respondents who did not parrot the official ideology but spoke about their individual goals viewed the Soviet Union as on a path of inexorable progress.[99] The majority of this group regarded education and knowledge as the most important prerequisites for the fulfillment of their goals. Virtually nobody mentioned money or a large salary as part of their professional motivation.[100] Those who had doubts were almost defensive about them. One respondent wrote, "Our fathers entered the Revolution together with Lenin; they led armies, commanded construction sites, and directed research institutes at the age of twenty-five. They were true Leninists, and their heartbeat should have passed to the hearts of their sons. Yet they were arrested as enemies of the people. This was the origin of our doubts, and everyone knows that doubt corrodes souls."[101]

The political awakening in 1956 of some of the "genuine" Marxists and Leninists led them to the idea of underground struggle against the bureaucratized regime. During the crackdown after the Hungarian Revolution, many such people ended up in the camps. In August 1957 the KGB arrested members of an underground political group of Marxist-minded university professors and students headed by Lev Krasnopevtsev. When they arrived at the camp of Dubrovlag the following spring, they were astonished at the numbers of young political prisoners who met them—whole groups from Moscow, Leningrad, Kiev, and other leading universities of the Soviet Union. Also present at the camp were a great number of former Komsomol activists, who had been politicized by Khrushchev's denunciation of Stalin and the events of 1956—those who had begun to express the idea of a "purification of Marxism and Leninism from Stalinism." Even camp wardens derisively called their prisoners Marxists.[102]

Some "genuine" Marxists remained believers in underground political struggle against the regime. Just when Krasnopevtsev's group was arrested, Valery Ronkin, a student at Leningrad Institute of Technology, came to the conclusion that true socialism did not exist in the Soviet Union. There was no classless society, but there was a ruling class—the party-state bureaucracy. When Ronkin began to work as a technician in an industrial plant, he tried to talk workers into going on strike.[103] In the early 1960s Ronkin and his friends founded an underground group called the Bell, after the famous nineteenth-century journal edited by Alexander Herzen in London. Later the KGB arrested this underground group as well. The secret police files reveal that Ronkin and his friends, just like many other political dissidents arrested, had been model members of Komsomol, idealistic builders of communism.[104]

A much larger group of genuine Marxists and genuine Leninists, however, decided to contribute to reforms through everyday legal activities. The fundamental belief that the Soviet state and society had to be reformed and liberated from the Stalinist legacy led many educated people, intellectuals who were not careerists or cynics, to join the party. Virtually all "honest" journalists, philosophers, and sociologists during the Thaw were party members and true believers. Many were the children of Bolshevik and communist functionaries who were arrested and murdered during the Stalin era. Khrushchev's secret speech validated their choice. They even began to regard themselves as "children of the Twentieth Party Congress." One of them was Len Karpinsky, who came from a family of Old Bolsheviks. His father, the editor of the communist newspaper *Bednota* (Poor People), had known Lenin personally and named his son after him. Although his father was killed during the Great Terror, Len was able to study at Moscow State University. After his graduation from MGU in 1952 with a degree in philosophy, he had, in his own words, "absolute faith in the correctness" of Marxist social and economic theory. He could "kill" party ideologists with unorthodox citations from Lenin. Khrushchev's policies restored Len's romantic idealism. He believed in the power of the intellect and in his ability to help Khrushchev fight for reforms, while overcoming the resistance of the bureaucracy created under Stalin. He spent several years editing the theoretical journal *Young Communist.*[105]

A more serious and mature group of genuine Marxists and Leninists in the party ranks consisted of war veterans. Among them were the poet Slutsky, the philosophers Plimak and Shakhnazarov, and the historian Cherniaev, a future foreign policy assistant to Gorbachev. Cherniaev deserves a detailed introduction. He had become a student at Moscow State University before the Nazis attacked, but he graduated only after fighting for four years in the war. During the Thaw he taught history at MGU and was a member of circles of Moscow intellectuals during the Thaw. His oldest friend among them was the poet David Samoilov. In politics, Cherniaev liberated himself from Stalin's spell early on. After World War II he marched with the column of university students on Red Square during the May Day demonstration. When the public stampeded, he turned and saw the "fat bottom and the military boots of Stalin who was waddling upstairs" to

Lenin's tomb. At that moment he was struck by an aesthetic disconnect: "All that culture which came from Tolstoy and Chekhov, from Shakespeare and Anatole France, fell victim to brutal, ignorant force, absolutely alien to my inner world." During the Thaw Cherniaev, like many other intellectuals, was passionately interested in Marxist-Leninist philosophy. Lenin was his hero—the man of action and, he believed, the antithesis of Stalin.[106]

For many Marxist and Leninist intellectuals inside the party, the Thaw was a fascinating and rewarding time, when they could contribute to social change. As it happened, Len Karpinsky was appointed to go to Poland with a top Komsomol delegation in 1956, and he impressed his bosses with his polemics against Polish intellectuals. In 1959 he became one of the secretaries of Komsomol responsible for cultural and ideological work. Anatoly Cherniaev received an invitation the same year to join the central party apparatus and work at the department in charge of science and humanities. Other passionate Marxist-Leninists used party connections and consulting jobs in the Komsomol to undertake various social projects. Yuri Levada, a classmate of Karpinsky's at MGU, began to rehabilitate sociology, the discipline Stalinism had destroyed. During the Moscow Youth Festival of 1957 Levada organized discussion clubs with foreign youth. In 1959 he led a group of young sociologists in monitoring the American Exhibition in Sokolniki and later presented to Komsomol and party officials an analytical memorandum about the reactions and attitudes of Soviet visitors. Boris Grushin, a student of Marxist epistemology and logic at MGU, used his connections and work at the newspaper *Komsomolskaia Pravda,* as we have seen, to organize the institute for the study of public opinion, the first in the Soviet Union. All these intellectuals hoped that their analyses would reach the party leadership and influence its policies.

At the end of the 1950s the genuine Marxists and Leninists emerged as a distinct reform-oriented group inside the Komsomol hierarchy. They encouraged various forms of activities which, although they were under the Komsomol aegis, reflected the students' search for fresh and meaningful experiences. Under Len's leadership, the Komsomol began to provide material support and protection for the theater studios, poetry groups, and amateur art circles that sprang up like mushrooms on university campuses. At first, they enjoyed a relative degree of freedom to decide on their offerings. Other autonomous student associations included the first environmental groups, singing clubs, and societies supporting scientific and technical creativity.[107]

In the party hierarchy the genuine Marxist and Leninist intellectuals were still a tiny minority. They had to work among people seasoned by bureaucratic work under Stalin and shaped not so much by ideas and formal education as by the experience of survival and intrigue. In fact, the lack of formal education was quite striking in the higher structures of the party, including its central headquarters. Even Stalin had been concerned at the end of his life that in contrast to the first generation of Bolsheviks the new party staff did not "have a deep understanding of Marxism. The majority of them were raised on quotations, not the study of Marx and Lenin."[108] The new party intellectuals believed that with their superior knowledge of Marxism-Leninism, they had a leg up on the old-timers. They also felt alienated by the lack of culture (nekulturnost) among the majority of party apparatchiks and viewed it as the source of conservative and reactionary behavior of the party bureaucracy. These apparatchik-intellectuals were determined to succeed the compromised generation of "party philosophers" of Stalin's day and to apply their superior theoretical knowledge to the task of rejuvenating the party's guiding role in the society.

Party journalism, speechwriting, and contacts with foreign communists became the areas where the genuine Marxists-Leninists within the party visibly excelled by comparison with their more experienced but less educated colleagues. After 1957 some of the Marxists spent a year or more in Prague, working for the theoretical journal of the Moscow-dominated international communist movement Problems of Peace and Socialism. This journal was set up as a replacement for the disbanded Cominform and became an international workshop where Western communists and Soviet party intellectuals socialized, debated, and became friends for life.[109] This was an experience that the communist intellectuals in the USSR did not have after the 1920s. Anatoly Cherniaev went to Prague after a brief stint in the party apparatus. He believed that his time there (1959–1961) transformed his life and mindset no less than the war experience had done earlier. The milieu of communist intellectuals did something that the party apparatchiks did not: they took ideas and culture seriously and debated in a naturally egalitarian and democratic environment. They held discussions in the editor's office, in lobbies, in the canteen over lunch, or at a nearby pub over a Prozdroj beer. They visited one another's apartments. Relatively young, thirty-five to forty years old, they freely discussed the most sensitive issues of Soviet society in that circle. And they believed that reforms in the Soviet Union were inevitable and that they would come soon.[110]

Even though Khrushchev made too many unrealistic promises and his New Deal was bound to suffer a backlash, it contributed to the mood of optimism during the late 1950s. Other factors, such as the Sputnik effect, the cult of science, and the abiding faith in the Marxist laws of history, produced the widespread feeling among Moscow intellectuals that the legacy of Stalinism could be gradually overcome and reforms could set the Soviet Union on the right track. Many intellectuals, so-called genuine Marxist-Leninists, still believed that the party and its leadership could be the vehicle for reform and change. Above all, they believed that their expertise and the forces of enlightenment and knowledge would inevitably prevail over the "uncultured" and conservative majority in the bureaucracy. The values and outlook typical of the Russian intelligentsia reemerged in the most unlikely places, including the totalitarian party and Komsomol structures. Optimistic scientists, journalists, and thinkers inside and outside the party believed in progress, culture, human reason, and moral revival. Many of them tasted bitter disappointments in 1956 that dampened their expectations. At the same time, they had witnessed considerable social, scientific, and technological achievements that the previous generation could only dream about. And this progress boosted the faith that the forces of education, science, and high culture would prevail over the entrenched group interests of the Soviet bureaucracy, and that honest presentation of the "truth," through various media from literature to TV, would render people self-aware and morally healthy. David Samoilov recalled that the optimism of the late 1950s and early 1960s was "possibly beneficial and necessary. We had to heal the burning wounds in our minds. We had to heal the wounds of fear." In that optimistic environment, Zhivago's children "slowly recovered."[111] Part of this recovery process was a revival of the idea of an intelligentsia, of a civic community that could become a moral and cultural vanguard for society.

The old intelligentsia no longer existed, but we wanted to believe that we would be able to recapture its intellectual and spiritual exaltation. Our goal was to lay claim to the values left by the social stratum that had been persecuted by the czars and destroyed by the revolution.

—Ludmilla Alexeyeva, recollections
   in *The Thaw Generation*

five

The Intelligentsia Reborn
1959-1962

T HE BEGINNING of the sixties marked an extraordinary moment in Russian intellectual and cultural history. After only a few uncertain years of the Thaw, of partial opening to the outside world, under the conditions of a still-powerful post-totalitarian regime and a decimated, traumatized, and fragmented society, a small but growing number of educated Russians began to develop a common self-awareness, distinct from that of the Soviet mainstream. In a quasi-religious phenomenon, they were able to revive the notions and values of the Russian intelligentsia. The idea of this community, which earlier only a few aging representatives of the older, pre-revolutionary generation of scholars, artists, and teachers had shared, began to spread among the younger people brought up and educated during the late Stalinist period and the Thaw.

The optimism, illusions, and social developments of the 1950s formed the ecosystem which made this revival possible. The optimism had been boosted by the rapid growth in the number of university graduates and others holding scholarly degrees—the likely social base for a community of the intelligentsia. At the same time, the exponential growth did not by itself generate the ethos of the intelligentsia. Rather, it was the search for meaningful social roles and moral values, to replace those which had been shattered and defiled after Stalin's death. The most talented and energetic men and women in the postwar generation sought not only to express themselves professionally, in science, mass media, the liberal arts, and so on, but to create a new language of civic culture—a framework of social and moral responsibility, truth and sincerity. The emerging community also directed its energy toward clearing room for a private social life separate from the official public realm that had held their parents' lives in thrall. They looked toward the creation of more humane ethical and aesthetic norms among themselves, in their circles and bands of friends.[1]

The revival of the intelligentsia began in Moscow, the capital of the Soviet empire, but also the main center of the Russian cultural and intellectual life, and thus most affected by the post-Stalin Thaw. Alexeyeva recalls that in 1959–60 her friends already proudly referred to the old notion of the *Russian* intelligentsia—making a sharp distinction between this and the official category of Soviet intelligentsia.[2] The established Soviet cultural elites, whose moral bankruptcy became apparent during the Thaw, served as an essential negative "other." At the same time, members of circles of companions differed in their social background and ideological beliefs from the old Russian intelligentsia as well. The belief system of the nascent community was in traumatic transition from the Stalinist idealism of youth to something different, yet that set of beliefs remained by and large Soviet, and in many instances communist. The ethos of Moscow freethinkers was to be conceived as the opposite of the Stalinist dogmas and lies, yet based on the values of the Revolution and socialism. The revival of the intelligentsia, they hoped, would mark the incipient humanization of Soviet society, not its destruction. They were not inspired by the prerevolutionary alternatives to Bolshevism, defeated and rejected in the course of the Russian Revolution. A great number of them, perhaps a majority, had no clear understanding of Western notions of freedom, democracy, and the rule of law.

Still, the drive for intellectual and cultural emancipation was important in itself, considering the foregoing Soviet history. Most important, the idea of a "genuine" intelligentsia helped many intellectuals and cultural figures develop a new civic solidarity and a collective identity. They wanted to distinguish themselves from the discredited Soviet intelligentsia even in temporal and generational terms. In December 1960 a young literary critic, Stanislav Rassadin, wrote for the first time in the literary magazine *Yunost* (Youth) about the *shestidesiatniki,* "the people of the sixties," as a new community that had "the ability and desire to think, to reflect about life and its complexities." They sought to understand the reality "behind every word."

People of the sixties were the men and women who would not be deceived again by lofty slogans and would not march in lockstep at the state's behest.[3] The *shestidesiatniki* perceived de-Stalinization and cultural emancipation, just like the Thaw, as a natural phenomenon, an inevitable historical evolution.

Older Mentors

Revival of the intelligentsia's ethos and community could not help embodying an act of creative imagination, of symbolic reunification between post-Stalinist and pre-Stalinist cultural and intellectual history. The funeral of Boris Pasternak in 1960, described at the beginning of *Zhivago's Children*, provided the symbol. It brought together people from the two different worlds: old people such as Konstantin Paustovsky, survivors of the milieu of those who still heard Pasternak's "frozen music"; and the aspiring composers of a new community ethos, among them David Samoilov and Lev Kopelev. Two other writers from the second group, Andrei Siniavsky and Yuli Daniel, carried the lid of the Pasternak's coffin.[4]

Most young people who attended Pasternak's funeral hardly knew or understood his outlook on the recent Soviet tragedy. A Western scholar correctly guessed that Pasternak's Yuri Zhivago, almost a Christlike figure, might seem incomprehensible, if not completely alien, "to many of the young generation of Soviet Russians, brought up on the heroes and martyrs of the revolution."[5] Indeed, even the few of those young people who had access to Pasternak's novel were emotional and ideological atheists and could hardly understand the "religious symphony" of Zhivago's life and death. True believers in the Marxist view of human progress, they could hardly have realized that Pasternak repudiated the Revolution "not as a political movement to which he opposes another movement, but as a salient manifestation of the lie in which contemporary society is enmeshed."[6]

For many of Pasternak's young worshippers, he was the last victim of Stalinism-after-Stalin, and a martyr to cultural emancipation. Yet their view of this emancipation was quite limited. Many of them wanted to rediscover and revive the cultural and intellectual traditions of the first postrevolutionary decade, which had been crushed and distorted by Stalinism. They looked for cultural heroes and guidelines in the futurist-revolutionary poetry of Mayakovsky, the vanguard theater of Vsevolod Meyerhold, in con-

Yuli Daniel, a poet of the post–World War II generation. In 1957 he and his friend Andrei Siniavsky began to publish their short stories in the West. In 1960 they attended Pasternak's funeral (Courtesy of Memorial, Moscow).

structivism, suprematism, and other "isms" that had flourished during the NEP years. A few aging men and women who had preserved those traditions became living repositories of their spirit: in literature, Anna Akhmatova, Konstantin Paustovsky, Vladimir Mayakovsky's widow Lilia Brik, Nadezhda Mandelstam, and the former literary critic Kornei Chukovsky; in theater, the actors of Konstantin Stanislavsky's Moscow Art Theater, followers of Vsevolod Meyerhold and Yevgeny Vakhtangov. An intellectual from Leningrad recalled the interaction of the two generations in idealized terms. The prerevolutionary intellectuals "had waited a long time for someone in this world who still had any need for their *non-Soviet* upbringing and worldview, had grown tired of waiting, and had almost lost hope, and we . . . threw ourselves at them and greedily absorbed, over at least three decades, their experience, their stories, their opinions, their schools, their libraries, their samizdat, and, of course, the incomparable atmosphere of their everyday lives."[7]

The people "from the past" had been hopelessly marginalized just a decade earlier. During the Thaw, however, the tribulations suffered during Stalin's era gave them enormous moral credibility.[8] Those of the young intellectuals who already felt alienated from Soviet role models and social environment found in the representatives of the old intelligentsia what they had been looking for—ethical and sometimes aesthetic alternatives. Manners, behavior, and figures of speech that had been considered ancien régime now appeared irresistibly charming. Sergei Averintsev, a philosopher, poet, and linguist from Moscow who was a scholar of Byzantine culture and theology, felt that charm when he met with the academician Dmitry Likhachev, a historian of Russian medieval literature who had been shaped by the cultural milieu of the St. Petersburg prerevolutionary middle class. For Likhachev the ethos of Russian intelligentsia was as natural as the air he breathed. He was also an Orthodox believer and cherished Russia's ancient religious roots—something that the new generation, brought up as atheists, could not comprehend.[9] Many of Zhivago's children later expressed gratitude to their professors, the old standard-bearers of culture. Mikhail German wrote in his memoirs: "I have been thinking a great deal about those people who saw the war and the Great Terror. . . . They lived by the motto 'Better to light a candle than to curse the darkness.' And they tried to light the matches for us, one by one. When those matches went out, they lit another, often burning their fingers. And this helped us to begin to see something in the dark."[10] Without these survivors from Zhivago's generation, thousands of whom were still around in Moscow and Leningrad during the late 1950s and early 1960s, the rebirth of the intelligentsia would have been unimaginable.

Privately, some of old cultural mentors no longer feared to voice their noncommunist and anticommunist views to their trusted young friends. Some of the remnants of the old educated classes had abhorred the Soviet regime since its very beginning, before it reached its Stalinist phase. At the same time, they had prudently decided long ago that resistance was suicidal and that the only option was to hunker down and wait. Some even learned to play little games, to protect themselves and those they loved. Quite a few survivors, educated and trained before the Revolution, had developed a philosophy of pragmatic cynicism. Talented artists who had practiced free art earlier painted Stalin and Lenin on the canvases that hung all over revolutionary museums and Soviet institutions. There were even closet monarchists and Russian Orthodox believers among them, yet in public they presented an impeccably Soviet facade. Mikhail German described one of his mentors, a historian of art and music, who escaped into the past. This person cultivated "the forgotten values of the high intelligentsia," possessed enormous cultural erudition, yet never blushed to write a propagandist opera or book. "Render to Caesar what is Caesar's" was his motto.[11]

The vast majority of young intellectuals, however, were not yet alienated from the Soviet project and could not fully appreciate the bitterness and wisdom of mentors from the pre-Stalin past. The re-creation of the intelligentsia's community and ethos required a public space and a public discussion. Moreover, it called for the people whose values and beliefs had been nourished by the hope and promise, not by the hatred and fear, of the Revolution. The most influential mentor of this kind was Ilya Ehrenburg. He was not only a highly visible living link to the cultural past, but he had the determination to tell millions about it. Ehrenburg had been known in Western intellectual circles since the 1920s as a Russian European. He had survived Stalinism by using his extensive connections to promote Stalin's "peace" campaign among the left-leaning European intellectuals. At the same time, after Stalin's death Ehrenburg passionately sought to disconnect Russian literature and liberal arts, whatever remained of them, from the Stalinist legacy and regenerate their European origins. He began to write his memoirs, which he titled "People. Years. Life." This became a monumental project to restore the heritage of numerous Russian writers, artists, and intellectuals who had been forcibly erased from Stalinist public culture. In April 1960 Ehrenburg sent the first volume of his recollections to Tvardovsky's *Novy Mir;* in the fall of that year, after months of procrastination by the censors, the memoirs appeared in print.[12] Vail and Ghenis summed up the memoirs' significance: "Not only Western, but Russian, culture had been waiting for its rediscovery. And Ehrenburg rediscovered it with gusto." Maximilian Voloshin, Marina Tsvetaeva, Osip Mandelstam, Andrei Bely, Isaac Babel, Vsevolod Meyerhold, and many others "entered the consciousness of Soviet readers through Ehrenburg's 'encyclopedia,' which was more complete than the *Big Soviet Encyclopedia*."[13] High culture was a secular religion for Ehrenburg, and he would not let it die. Speaking at the end of his life, in 1966, he said: "We all should rehabilitate consciousness. This can be done (after the rejection of religion) only through art." In the same vein, he supported the officially banned, underground art of the time as much as he could.[14]

Ehrenburg, however, was not the person to lead the effort to re-create the ethos of the intelligentsia. His leftist European cosmopolitanism did not relate to Russia's "accursed questions": Who is to blame? What is to be done? It also did not appeal to the sense of Russian national identity, awakened during World War II. The poet Alexander Tvardovsky, the son of a Russian peasant, was a better candidate for the task. In August 1958 Khrushchev, who liked Tvardovsky's poetry, invited him to the Kremlin and reappointed him the head of *Novy Mir.* Tvardovsky was forty-five.[15] His private diary of the late 1950s and 1960s, published by his children decades after his death, is the testimony of a tormented man.[16] In the public realm, he was a senior Soviet official, a member of the party Central Committee. He had access to the halls of power, spoke with high-placed authorities over a secure phone line, and enjoyed a level of familiarity with the officials from the party's upper bureaucracy, including Khrushchev's assistants, that very few writers did. Tvardovsky remained a believer in the Russian Revolution and in the basic principles of Soviet socialism. He took part in the competition for a new Soviet anthem, at which he spent countless hours. For a long time he could not rid himself of the Bolshevik and Stalinist habit of dividing the world into "us" and "them"—the latter including not only anticommunists but also pessimists, griping and spiteful critics, and non-Soviet "Philistines."

At the same time, the past and especially the time of Stalinist collectivization, when the young Tvardovsky had had to reject his "kulak" father in order to begin his Soviet career, came to haunt him.[17] Despite his party privileges, Tvardovsky remained a Russian muzhik: his heart was in the countryside. The tragic fate of the Russian peasantry and the death between 1929 and 1953 of the traditional Russian way of life weighed heavily on his conscience. Gradually, he began to face the truth about the misery and destruction of the Russian peasantry from the 1930s to the 1940s and its death throes during the 1950s.[18] He felt that it was immoral to cover up the past and all its victims.[19] He also had learned much about the gulag from writers who returned from it. The most painful revelation, however, emerged from a chance encounter with a countryman, the chairman of a collective farm, from whom he learned that his village, formerly populated with robust, joyous, hard-working people, was now almost deserted, depopulated and destitute. The best memories of his peasant childhood, "the golden, purest spot in [his] heart," had been destroyed. In 1957 he began to plan his autobiography, *Pan Tvardovsky,* a tribute to his father and, indirectly, to life in the Russian countryside.[20]

After Khrushchev reappointed Tvardovsky to lead *Novy Mir,* the propaganda boss Dmitry Polikarpov gushed, "You are the first poet! Khrushchev is interested in you more than in any other writer in the country!"[21] Khrushchev's assistant Igor Lebedev, who wanted to be seen as a connoisseur and supporter of literature, became a vital link between the "first poet" and Communist Number One. Thanks to Lebedev, Khrushchev, who normally never read literary journals or recent novels, got involved in the affairs of *Novy Mir* and often supported Tvardovsky's editorial decisions. Until Khrushchev's downfall, Tvardovsky used his access to Khrushchev and Lebedev to circumvent the censors, the Ministry of Culture, and the party's Central Committee departments.

The party's lies and pomp disgusted Tvardovsky. His curious and reflective mind recognized many things that others overlooked. As a Central Committee member, he had access to a variety of Western sociological and historical studies, as well as Russian émigré publications, that had been unavailable under Stalin and were by then published in "special editions" for the party nomenklatura. Armed with this knowledge, he felt a civic responsibility to help rejuvenate the party and the socialist experiment. Tvardovsky was especially concerned by the failure of ideological education "that transformed great teachings [those of Marxist-Leninism] into boring pages in an obligatory textbook."[22] If the current generation of educated youth failed to become believers in communism, then the cause of the Revolution was lost. And then all the casualties, the enormity of the ruin and sacrifice, would be in vain.

Moved by these reflections, Tvardovsky decided to turn *Novy Mir* into a vehicle of moral and social revival. Russian literature, his main vocation and passion, was for him the means to accomplish this task. As a senior literary bureaucrat and party apparatchik, he realized what a huge challenge it would be. The party authorities and censors had quickly crushed previous attempts by Moscow writers to collect and publish almanacs of the best literary works—that is, to assume the right to define the criteria of "good" literature and true culture. In the Soviet Union since Stalin's times the bureaucratic institutions in charge of cultural and propaganda affairs had held a monopoly in this sphere, and they zealously continued to protect it. Still, he was ready to devote the remainder of his active life to the struggle to restore the role of Russian literature as a great ideological and moral teacher. Tvardovsky's personal agony and determination turned *Novy Mir* into the journal that for a decade acted as the main and the only public embodiment of the intelligentsia's ethos and mentality in post-Stalinist Russia.

In Search of Self-Expression

The cultural language and style of the original Russian intelligentsia came from the great nineteenth-century literature. Even as Stalinism was destroying the intelligentsia's ethos, the intelligentsia's icons were canonized by the regime. Prose and poetry by Pushkin and Gogol, Herzen and Belinsky, Tolstoy and Dostoevsky, Chekhov, Nekrasov, and Blok remained an essential part of Soviet education, even if the ethical and philosophical ideas in them contradicted Soviet practices. These works, in many ways prophetic, acquired fresh meaning during the Thaw, when they were staged in theaters and interpreted in films. In 1956 the classical Maly Theater in Moscow performed Tolstoy's tragedy *The Power of Darkness*. The leading actor later confessed that he suffered from an intense split consciousness. As a Soviet citizen, he believed in a set of ideological assumptions. He was horrified to discover that many of them did not stand up to the profound revelations of Tolstoy's art. In an article in *Literaturnaia Gazeta* and later in his memoirs, the actor explained: "I couldn't betray Leo Tolstoy, nor could I betray contemporary Soviet ideology. At one point I was so torn between the two that I turned the part down." The cause of his anguish was the play's main message: the absence of God meant darkness; salvation lay in the human soul. Such views had been forgotten in Russia after many decades of Soviet rule.[23]

At the same time, the tragic events of the recent past infused the Russian classics with poignant contemporary meanings. In 1957 Dostoevsky's novel *The Idiot* appeared onstage in Leningrad and became an instant sensation. Innokenty Smoktunovsky, the actor who played Prince Myshkin, had no illusions about how cruel state and society could be. Born into a peasant family, he had had to flee collectivization and famine. He had been a prisoner of war, and worked in Siberia, next to labor camps. As he began to grapple with his role in *The Idiot*, he noticed a man standing alone amid the bustle on the stage set, absorbed in his book, noticing no one. It turned out to be an intellectual who had returned from Stalin's camps. The actor had found a true Myshkin: here was a believer persecuted by the very people his philosophy had taught him to love.[24] Many in the theatrical audience were struck by Smoktunovsky's portrayal, yet how many could understand its message?

For Zhivago's children the meaning of the Soviet experience was still hazy, and the idealized images of the Revolution, the Civil War, and the NEP cultural vanguard prevented uncompromising self-searching about what Russia had experienced since 1917 and what role the cultural-intellectual elite had played in that experience. Toppling the state-controlled cultural canon of socialist realism became the immediate goal of the younger generation, the task that consumed most of its energy. And young intellectuals believed that the best weapon was a "contemporary style," an uncontrolled stream of "sincere" consciousness. In that sense, they were no different from Allen Ginsberg and Jack Kerouac in New York's Greenwich Village during the 1950s, or the German, French, and Italian New Wave artists in later times. The emphasis on style and form was a historical continuation of the jejune aesthetical rebellion of *stiliagi* in the late 1940s and early 1950s. In fact, those style apers who became poets, writers, and artists during the Thaw continued to cherish the memories of their *stiliagi* youth. They recognized one another by the *stiliagi* jargon, the ability "to speak modern."

Poetry was one of the cultural realms where the contemporary style emerged. Vladimir Mayakovsky was the guru for the cultural iconoclasts, a revolutionary poet who had taken his life during the initial years of Stalinism. He was a great innovator with language who inspired a host of imitators among the post-Stalin generation. His verse was syncopated, rebellious, uncompromising, and coarse. His private life was unconventional as well: he lived with the woman he loved and her husband in an unhappy ménage à trois. Mayakovsky concealed his wounded soul beneath public revolutionary convictions, and his suicide in 1930 demarcated perfectly the boundary between the romanticized era of NEP "leftist" culture and reactionary Stalinism.[25] In 1959 the Moscow officials unveiled a monument to Mayakovsky on Gorky Street, half a mile from the Kremlin, and in the next few years tens of thousands of poetry fans and onlookers congregated at its pedestal.[26]

Most of those who gathered around Mayakovsky's statue believed in the revolutionary legacy and communist principles and wanted to change the Soviet regime, "without destroying it down to its [socialist] foundations." One of them recalled that "the struggle for Soviet power meant the struggle against lies within the party, against the corruption within."[27] Addressing large audiences with emotional rhymes had the effect of glasnost, of a quasi-religious catharsis. There was an enormous need to say publicly what had long remained private, hidden, and banned. This included even the language of friendship and love, intimate feelings and doubts, and tragic experiences.[28] Soon, the gathering place at Mayakovsky's statue became known as Mayak (Lighthouse), a place where lonely intellectuals could gain a sense of civic togetherness. Mayak gradually became a meeting place where young men and women exchanged information, passed around typed or handwritten copies of poems, and shared reading materials.[29] What had begun as an official celebration of a poet canonized by Stalin evolved into a site where words and ideas were liberated from fear and dogma.

The rise of the young poetic contingent to national prominence was meteoric. Its members displayed a talent for public reading and for addressing crowds in student auditoriums, rather than reading to select connoisseurs in exclusive salons. The leaders of this cohort were Yevgeny Yevtushenko and Andrei Voznesensky. Each of them expressed distinct feelings and aspects of the emerging community of sixties intelligentsia.[30] Yevtushenko's lyrics appealed above all to romantic, revolutionary optimism, the sense of expanding horizons. He avoided an existential and moral crisis of belief in 1956 by divorcing the idea of communism from Stalinism, the humanist ideals of collectivism from state practices. In an early autobiographical poem he wrote:

> Blind love for Russia we don't need.
> Instead, we need an open-eyed and contemplating love.

Yevtushenko addressed the anxiety of young men and women who had lost their certainty about the past:

> Don't worry. Yours is no unique condition,
> Your type of search and conflict and construction.
> Don't worry if you have no answers ready
> To the lasting question.
> Hold out, meditate, listen.[31]

Yevtushenko decided to use poetry as a moral remedy to rescue society from corrosive cynicism. One of his poems in 1960 was entitled "Consider Me a Communist." In it he compared his personal "war" against bureaucrats and hidden admirers of Stalin and his empire to the Russian Civil War and the Great Patriotic War.[32] Yevtushenko was a tireless educator of the public, reaching out even to those who never read poetry: he translated complex cultural and historical phenomena into the simple vocabulary of communist romanticism. His young audience preferred his fiery interpretations of international developments to *Pravda*'s dry pronouncements.[33]

While Yevtushenko created the image of a new generation and its surroundings, Andrei Voznesensky sought to invent a novel language for the

Yevgeny Yevtushenko, a poet who translated the sixties using the lexicon of communist romanticism. He believed that his poetry offered the moral remedy that could save Soviet society from corrosive cynicism (Courtesy of Memorial, Moscow).

intellectuals. He became a favorite poet of those who wanted "to feel and speak modern." Influenced by Pasternak's early poetry (Voznesensky had also known Pasternak personally), his book that was published in 1960 was an instant success. In his poems, Voznesensky tried to bring lyrics and physics together, and his architectural degree helped him to achieve that end. He wrote that the linear Stalinist logic of history was now broken, and "Predictions, regulations have no power / Over history, love, and art, / Which move along a parabolic path!" He exclaimed: "Long live fantastic anti-worlds, / The antidotes to boring words!"[34] Voznesensky became especially popular among scientists, those who wanted to combine the ethos of the intelligentsia with modernity and technology, cybernetics and space exploration.[35]

This contemporary poetry of the day was brave and optimistic; it addressed the past with subtle irony and stern judgment. Yet many felt a strange nostalgia for their personal past, if not the denounced Stalinist past. They recalled the shattered peaceful years of childhood, the wartime hardships and certainties. The current generation needed its own unifying myths situated in that idealized personal time, imbued with honesty and integrity, and separate from the Stalinist era. The singer Bulat Okudzhava created those myths in his poetic songs. Okudzhava was born in Moscow's Arbat district and grew up in its cosmopolitan atmosphere. His own family was of Russian-Georgian-Armenian origin, and his parents, communist idealists, vanished during Stalin's terror. After fighting the war in the Caucasus and studying literature in Georgia, Okudzhava worked as a schoolteacher in a provincial Russian town. When his dead parents were "rehabilitated" by Khrushchev, he was able to return to Moscow and began to write poems, which he performed as songs with a guitar accompaniment. His voice seemed to express the spirit of war veterans and the younger generation. Recorded on tape, his poems spread much faster than his name. Okudzhava's songs, like Pasternak's last poems, were remarkably simple. They were about the beauty of a woman, love for life, and the tragedy of war. They also displayed an "inner freedom" unusual for the poets of his generation, who were concerned with specific events and the search for "modern" forms of self-expression. His verse on the communist romanticism of the past was nostalgic, yet tinged with irony:

> I knew a soldier—he was brave
> And handsome as a hero.
> Yet he was only a child's toy,
> And he was made of paper.
> He had a dream to change the world,
> To make all humans happy.
> Yet people pulled him by a string,
> For he was made of paper.[36]

At the same time, Okudzhava discovered a refuge from cynicism in love and hope. He sang about the "last blue trolley car," which he took when he had abandoned all hope. He sang about an idealized community of friends who had grown up in the Arbat district of Moscow, educated by teachers from the old intelligentsia, but also streetwise and patriotic. The heroes of his songs went to war against Hitler to defend their "small fatherland," and many died there. Okudzhava performed a vital task: his Arbat became an important symbol, a "small fatherland" for the resurgent intelligentsia, within historical and geographical reach of educated young Muscovites and compatible with a revolutionary and socialist romanticism that many of them still shared.[37]

Bulat Okudzhava, who sang about hope and created the mythology of Moscow's Arbat intelligentsia. His idealism was tinged with irony and sadness (Courtesy of Memorial, Moscow).

Members of the reviving intelligentsia, however, did not talk in rhymes among themselves, in their circles of friends. The continuing search for honest and genuine language that contrasted with the official spiel had led the generation that had risen from the ashes to mistrust the literature of socialist realism. Young intellectuals looked for a contemporary literature that would express their doubts and anguish. In 1959–60 this literature came from the West, in the novels of Erich-Maria Remarque, J. D. Salinger, and Ernest Hemingway. These writers were not of the same caliber as Tolstoy, Dostoevsky, and Chekhov but were contemporaries of the young Russians and responded to the brutal challenges of the age.

Ernest Hemingway had already been popular in the Soviet Union before World War II. After 1945, however, his books disappeared from libraries and stores. His *Farewell to Arms* and *For Whom the Bell Tolls* remained officially banned. When a freshly translated volume of Hemingway's novels, including these works, appeared in Soviet bookstores in 1959, the bearded American quickly became the guru of Russian romantic intellectuals. Hemingway's life matched his writing style and resonated with the post-Stalin generation. He had fought on the side of the Spanish Republicans against Franco and the fascists; he was a leftist but also a bohemian, and he intensely disliked Stalinists. He lived as he wished: hunted, fished, braved the open sea, killed bulls, enjoyed good food and wine, loved numerous women, and was loved by them in return. Hemingway was a romantic but not starry-eyed, experienced but not cynical, manly but not crude. This was the perfect combination for the *shestidesiatniki* in Russia. The writer's outward appearance—rough turtleneck sweater, pipe, and beard—set the fashion for hundreds of thousands of his Russian acolytes.[38] In October 1959 the weekly *Literaturnaia Gazeta* published Hemingway's letter to the Union of Soviet Writers expressing his wish to come to the USSR.[39] Unfortunately, Hemingway took his own life in July 1961. His tragic end only burnished his myth. Hundreds of thousands of students and young intellectuals in Russia called one another Old Man, sported beards and turtlenecks, and tried to mimic "Papa Hem" in every other way.

Remarque's *All Quiet on the Western Front, The Arch of Triumph,* and *The Black Obelisk* especially addressed themes of war and postwar fatigue, disillusionment, destitution, and deformation of social life that echoed the recent experience of educated Russian readers. These novels focused on people whose youthful enthusiasm and naïveté were manipulated and abused by warring states and who learned to treat everything around them with skepticism and irony to defend their scarred souls against the injustices of the world. J. D. Salinger's *Catcher in the Rye,* along with his short stories, appeared in Russian in 1959. The confrontation of the American teenager Holden Caulfield with the "phony" world of social conventions and insincerity struck a chord with many Soviet students who were questioning the conventions and hypocrisies of their upbringing for the first time.

After the appearance of Remarque and Salinger on Soviet bookshelves, novels and plays about "angry adolescents" invaded Russian literary journals and theaters. The most successful author of this genre was Vasily Aksyonov. His novel *A Ticket to the Stars,* published in July 1961, was about a group of Moscow teenagers who fled from their parents and explored life without adult interference. In the opening paragraph of the novel the older brother of one of these adolescents confesses that he cannot understand the motives of the youth. "I am a loyal person. When I see a red light, I stop. With my younger brother Dimka it's a different matter. Dimka always crosses at a red light." The public knew what Aksyonov was hinting at. His teenagers not only escaped from Moscow and parental control; they also resisted the collectivist mentality and rules.[40] Aksyonov had experienced alienation and an angry adolescence himself. Aksyonov, who was born in Kazan into a family of communist true believers, saw his parents arrested in 1937. After World War II he went to the Kolyma camps to visit his mother, and that trip had opened his eyes to the realities of the labor camps. He joined the *stiliagi* movement, worshipped American jazz, and became a passionate admirer of Hemingway. Aksyonov described in his novels the youthful intelligentsia's behavior, appearance, and speech in imitation of Hemingway. In this way, the culture of *stiliagi* was disseminated and, in turn, imitated by hundreds of thousands of readers.

"Nonrealist" visual forms of art became another powerful source for the young artists' self-expression. And again, the discovery of contemporary European and American art was the trigger. Western artistic influences penetrated the Iron Curtain in many ways during the Thaw. The Picasso exhibition in Moscow and Leningrad in 1956 was the first big ripple in the pond of socialist realism. Then, at the American exhibition in Sokolniki, the paintings of Edward Hopper and Georgia O'Keeffe, Mark Rothko and Jackson Pollock, exhibited in the USSR for the first time, stunned Russian art connoisseurs, and inflamed young intellectuals. Some of them became vocal advocates of modernism in Soviet art.[41] Vittorio Strada, a young Italian scholar of Russian history and a member of the Italian Communist Party, was one of many foreigners who became private ambassadors for contemporary art in Moscow. He came to Moscow during the World Youth Festival and was introduced to Pasternak. He helped Pasternak to pass his messages to Feltrinelli, which led to the publication of *Doctor Zhivago*. He also met Slutsky, Yevtushenko, and the literary critics from *Novy Mir* and *Yunost*. Strada returned to Moscow in 1959 and studied there for two years. In the process, he not only married a young Russian woman but also became a member of several Moscow *kompany*, where many *shestidesiatniki* socialized. During his trips back home he bought albums of Vasily Kandinsky, Kasimir Malevich, Marc Chagall, and other formalist artists, which he brought to Moscow.[42] Thanks to Strada and other foreign visitors, Zhivago's children learned that Russian painting from 1900 through the 1920s had been in the vanguard of European art, and had had a great impact on Italian, German, and French design and advertising. In Soviet Russia, however, the same vanguard had been rejected, suppressed, and forgotten.

The discovery of the Russian-European art vanguard generated turmoil in the Moscow branch of the Union of Soviet Artists. Its younger members associated the return to the legacy of the first three decades of the century with the rejection of Stalinism and the restoration of artistic links to Europe.[43] In the forefront of this movement were the artists of the so-called severe style, who sought to depict reality without the pomp or saccharine gloss of socialist realism. The focus of the severe style was not only on a new form, but also on the discovery of contemporary Soviet men and women, the modern builders of communism. The artists traveled to remote corners of the Soviet Union, lived with geologists and workers constructing power grids, painted industrial landscapes in the Far North and Siberia. They fought to take control over the union from the "stalwarts," a group of old, cynical, and very powerful men, who controlled the highly profitable business of serializing sculptures and portraits of Stalin, Lenin, and other communist leaders.[44] In the spring of 1960 the stalwarts were in visible retreat. On May 24, 1960, painters in the Moscow union came to a general gathering to elect delegates to the First Congress of Artists of the Russian Federation. At this meeting the advocates of vanguard art argued against election of the most notorious producers of Stalinist artifacts. As a result, some of the old academicians, whose art had become synonymous with Stalinist era, were voted out. This initial success allowed the incoming cohort of artists to occupy posts on various committees that decided whose works would be exhibited and that controlled considerable funds flowing to the painters' union from the state budget.[45] In April 1960 Georgy Nissky, one of the older art academicians, published an article supporting the modernist rebels. He argued that younger artists' search for fresh visual forms adapted the method of socialist realism to changing realities and the "progressive ideas of our time." He wrote that the art of the Russian and the Western vanguards expressed the spirit of modernity better than Stalinist art had, and proposed a traveling exhibition in which great classical artists would be displayed alongside Picasso and Matisse, to bring their art to the young workers of the Urals and Siberia.[46]

This suggestion had a historical precedent: the Wanderers, a group of Russian artists who considered themselves to be part of the Russian democratic intelligentsia, had tried one century earlier to use their art for the enlightenment of the Russian people and the advancement of progressive social reforms. Shortly, a group of members from the Soviet Union of Artists decided to repeat the Wanderers' experiment. Eli Beliutin, a professor at the Moscow Institute of Printing and Book Production (a successor to the art school where Pasternak's father had taught), organized the first genuinely autonomous community of painters since the early 1930s and called it New Reality. The name was a jaundiced allusion to the reigning official art doctrine. Beliutin, a tall, elegant, charismatic man in his thirties, seemed to find a way to work with the authorities. His wife Nina worked as an art consultant for the party's Central Committee and helped introduce the artists into the corridors of power. Beliutin's group practiced "instantaneous reaction," a kind of Stanislavsky method in painting that revealed the individuality of the artist. In 1958 the group exhibited its works in Gorky Park. By 1960 New Reality consisted of 250 painters. During the summers of 1961 and 1962 Beliutin rented riverboats exclusively for his artists; they sailed from Moscow down the Oka and Volga rivers, drawing and painting Russian landscapes and towns, and debating art with the provincial public. Beliutin's idea was, in the spirit of Russian intelligentsia, to "go to the people," both to draw them and to show them unorthodox works of art. To the artists' regret, however, the provincial Russian public did not favor their newfound visual forms. There were even attempts at vandalism.[47]

By contrast, the New Reality and modern art became a sensation among Moscow's scientists, writers, and filmmakers. An increasing number of intellectuals and students empathized with the avant-garde art as the symbol of social progressivism, an expression of a "contemporary" style.[48] Poet David Samoilov later wrote about the broader social and cultural meaning of the "rebellion of form" in the visual arts: "The young who had barely liberated themselves from the burden of old superstitions, yearned for at least novel forms of life and art." The formalist trend became a universal expression of the yearning for change and liberalization, a social symbol of progressivism. Moreover, as modernism swept through Western art, it seemed to be more than just a way to overcome Russia's xenophobia and isolation. It finally appeared to be the ideal weapon, a cultural battering ram to break down the walls of Stalin's cultural "project."[49] The rebellion of form and style was not limited to visual arts. In classical music, younger artists returned to the search for "contemporary" forms that had been interrupted by Stalin in the 1930s. The composers Alfred Schnittke, Sofia Gubaidulina, Edison Denisov, and Andrei Volkonsky contributed to the "rebellion of form" that coincided with the rebirth of the idea of the intelligentsia. In 1961 the public in a small hall of the Moscow Conservatory applauded furiously to "Mirror Suite," after a poem of Federico Garcia Lorca. The composer was the twenty-eight-year-old Andrei Volkonsky, a fan of dodecaphonic music.[50] The avant-garde wave reached even the game of chess. During the Stalinist era it was the second most popular game after soccer, and it was propagandized by the regime as the manifestation of Soviet superiority.

Everyone was shocked when the twenty-four-year-old Mikhail Tal defeated Mikhail Botvinnik, a living symbol of Stalin-era Soviet predominance in chess. Botvinnik's calculating style led Western analysts to compare Stalinist foreign policy moves to chess gambits and endgames. Tal, by contrast, dazzled the chess world and millions of Soviet chess fans with his unpredictability. He was a genius of improvisation who viewed chess as an art form. Every game for him was as inimitable and invaluable as a poem.[51]

Imagining the Intelligentsia on Stage and Screen

Theater and cinema produced innovative images that profoundly shaped the ethical and aesthetic worldview of the upcoming educated cohorts. In 1956 a group of creative actors, recent graduates of Moscow Theater Institute, had launched a new theater—Sovremennik (the Contemporary). It was the first theater since the 1920s to be initiated from below, by the artists themselves. The theater's social program, writes the Russian art historian Anatoly Smeliansky, was "in a word, anti-Stalinist." Oleg Yefremov, the Sovremennik's leader, was an idealist who took his principles with deadly seriousness. In his student days, Yefremov had vowed to re-create the social significance and mission of Stanislavsky's Moscow Art Theater—the major theater of the prerevolutionary Russian intelligentsia. He had put his oath in writing and signed it with his own blood. During the Thaw, Yefremov came to view Russia as a country suffering from a form of serfdom, imposed by the ruling Stalinist bureaucracy. Yet like the great majority of the young intellectuals and artists, Yefremov believed that the Russian Revolution and communism had nothing to do with this serfdom. The Revolution and its ideals had been betrayed by the Stalinist state. He had joined the party immediately after Stalin's death, determined to try to make things better. When the party authorities forced the theater to perform "obligatory" plays about Lenin, Yefremov and his actors did their best to present the Bolshevik leader and his comrades as the genuine paragons of revolutionary principles, in contrast to their successors, the cynical bureaucratic timeservers. Some of the Sovremennik's plays were banned, but the state censorship only confirmed their convictions.[52]

Almost all the early plays performed at the Sovremennik were written by playwrights who had grown up in families of communist idealists, assimilated Jewish revolutionaries, and educated professionals executed or black-

Oleg Yefremov, the founder and head of the Sovremennik Theater in the early 1960s. He was an idealist in the mode of the revolutionary intelligentsia and was deadly serious about principles (Courtesy of Memorial, Moscow).

listed during Stalinism. These plays sought to restore the spirit of war communism, meanwhile overlooking most of its cruelty and violence. They contrasted the ascetic rigor, passion, and great promise of the early revolutionary days with the stagnation, rigidity, and boredom of Stalinist and post-Stalin Russian society. A range of young iconoclasts walked the Sovremennik's stage, most of them disgusted by the quiet spread of "bourgeois" amenities into Soviet life, such as material comfort, good furniture, personal cars, and even simple household gadgets. In one of the plays, staged in 1957, the young hero had pulled his grandfather's Civil War saber off the wall and hacked up a piece of the costly furniture that was regarded at the time as the exclusive privilege also of the party and state bureaucracy, the "class" that had betrayed the Revolution. The spirit of the performance accorded well with the traditional anticapitalist stand of the left flank of the old Russian intelligentsia.[53] The Sovremennik audience that viewed this play knew perfectly well that it attacked the ruling regime. At the same time, the Sovremennik productions told the people of the sixties what they wanted to hear. The fear of selling a free soul for material comfort, of betraying the ideals of the young and egalitarian circles of companions, of becoming like the bureaucratic strata of the regime and the established cultural timeservers, developed into part of the ethos of the emerging intelligentsia.

The Sovremennik became the first theater for and by the intelligentsia in this latest avatar. Between 1959 and 1962 the actors reenacted onstage all the principal hopes and illusions of the Thaw. The audience, whose members had read the novels of Remarque, Salinger, and Aksyonov, would immediately recognize in the Sovremennik's performances characters that reminded them of these authors and their style and language. By coincidence, the theater faced the square in which Mayakovsky's statue stood and where improvised poetic readings took place. The Sovremennik thus became the center of the cultural ecosystem for the *shestidesiatniki*. Aspiring poets, together with musicians, critics, writers, and painters gathered there. Late at night, after rehearsals, this enthusiastic crowd migrated to a modest nearby café. It was hard to tell which aphorisms, ideas, and remarkable insights emerged inside the theater, and which entered it from the broader intellectual-artistic milieu.[54]

Cinema, once the main propaganda tool of the Stalinist regime, began to produce remarkable films featuring unfamiliar protagonists, intellectuals who espoused anti-Stalinist ethical and aesthetic principles. A cohort of young and talented directors, most of them in their midthirties, began to make their first films. These filmmakers were replacing the older colleagues who, having begun their careers after the Revolution, had been forced to compromise their artistic freedom and principles during the Stalin era.[55] The young filmmakers, mostly graduates of the Institute of Cinematography in Moscow, had, as students, experienced the revelations and the turmoil of 1956–1958. In the words of one of them, Yakov Segel, "the common quality of our generation is intent attention to the individual, his fate, personal problems, and details of life. At the same time we continue to pay close attention in our art to social reconstruction, social issues." Another filmmaker, Marlen Khutsiev, agreed: "The distinctive features of our style emerged in reaction to the pompous and false movies from the period of the 'cult of personality.'"[56]

This group sought to revive the cinematic language of Sergei Eisenstein, Yakov Protazanov, Vsevolod Pudovkin, Boris Barnet, and other masters of the revolutionary cinema of the 1920s. Also, contemporary European cinema, especially the films of the Polish director Andrzej Wajda and the Italian neorealist cinema of Vittorio De Sica, Giuseppe De Santis, and Federico Fellini, greatly influenced young Soviet filmmakers. Fortunately, they did not have to wrestle the old elite for authority and resources. By contrast with the Union of Soviet Artists, the cinema experienced no generational rift. The atmosphere there was relatively open-minded and innovative. The influential "cinema generals" were not afraid of the young, but instead helped them in any possible way. They used their connections to obtain state funds for experimental film studios where their students could make their first films.[57]

In 1956 some young filmmakers, working together with writers, attempted to express anti-Stalinist and antibureaucratic messages on the screen. After the invasion of Hungary and the cultural crackdown, these attempts came to an end.[58] Under pressure from the authorities and the censors, filmmakers had to abandon politically charged contemporary themes and turn largely to the "historical" dramas of the Revolution, the Civil War, and the Great Patriotic War; however, they sought to give their own twist to these themes, in trying to remove the Stalinist propaganda varnish from them and fill them with human emotions, individual tragedies, and agonizing personal choices—something they hoped would resonate with the educated contemporary audience. Grigory Chukhrai, a war veteran and a communist true believer, at thirty-five launched his cinematic career with a remake of an old civil war classic, *The Forty-first,* on the brief love affair between Mariutka, a Red sharpshooter, and a White officer. In contrast to the first version, made thirty years earlier by Protazanov, Chukhrai's version makes his heroes' love for each other seem to transcend the "class" divide. The relationship between Mariutka and the White officer falls casualty to human insanity and violence. Remarkably, Pasternak was developing a similar theme in *Doctor Zhivago* at around the same time. In 1959 Chukhrai continued his exploration of individual fate in the midst of a great war: his second film, *The Ballad of a Soldier,* became a cultural sensation in 1960. The film's protagonist, a peasant boy and soldier in World War II, Alyosha Skvortsov, is rewarded with a few days of furlough and makes the long trip home to see his mother; however, he gets sidetracked on numerous occasions and helps other people caught in war's tragedies. The film critic Maia Turovskaia wrote in *Novy Mir,* "Alyosha Skvortsov's road to his native village becomes his road to himself."[59] Alyosha becomes a true war hero, unlike characters in pre-Thaw films, which too often glorified Stalin as a war leader.

The filmmakers took advantage of Khrushchev's "public diplomacy" and growing cultural exchanges to publicize their cutting-edge films all over the world. The Soviet authorities allowed Soviet filmmakers to participate in the Cannes Film Festival and other international events. Chukhrai's films received awards and enjoyed a popularity within the Soviet Union that was matched by their warm reception abroad. The fame and recognition filmmakers won became a bargaining chip in their negotiations with the state.[60] It gave them more resources and the clout to expand their artistic freedom. In 1959 Moscow hosted the first International Film Festival, attended by numerous star directors, actors, and actresses from the West and other parts of the world. In contrast to "academic" art and sculpture, Soviet cinema returned to the European and indeed the world stage, and it did so with triumph.

Gradually, instead of the typical people's heroes of Stalinist cinema—shock workers, tank drivers, air force pilots, and collectivized peasants—intelligentsia types appeared on the screen. Several old filmmakers expressed a special interest in portraying the generation that had defeated Hitler and overseen the crumbling of the cult of Stalin. Among them was Mikhail Romm, one of those artists who in Stalin's times had offered his talents to the party, unable to distinguish between the regime and revolutionary ideals. Even though he remained a communist idealist to the core, Romm wanted to comprehend how the revolutionary ideals he worshipped had ended up in the service of the hordes of criminals, cynics, and paper-pushers.[61] The public debate on physics versus lyrics inspired Romm to explore in film the topic of the new intelligentsia. He used his social contacts to meet nuclear physicists who were engaged in secret state work. Among his friends were nuclear physicists, including Lev Landau, who obtained permission for Romm's crew to film a still-secret cyclotron. Romm even invited students from the Moscow Institute of Physics to re-create onscreen the environment of their *kompany* and their optimistic faith in the ability of science to transform human life. Romm's *Nine Days of One Year* was the first film to focus on the feelings and thoughts of the post-Stalin generation of intellectuals. Two young, handsome, and brilliant physicists, played by Alexei Batalov, and Smoktunovsky, introduced the viewer into the temple of science. The film featured little action but much reflection and gave utterance in fascinating monologues and dialogues on cutting-edge issues, including the atomic bomb, the arms race, bureaucracy, humanism, and human evolution. Romm's scientific community was a microcosm of a civil humanist society. His scientists theorized, suffered from their complex romantic entanglements, displayed courage, and, above all, remained honest and genuinely believed in what they were doing. The film, after some controversy with the authorities, was released in 1962 and viewed by twenty-four million people.[62]

In 1961 Marlen Khutsiev, a filmmaker of the new generation, decided to create a cinematic portrait of Moscow students.[63] He borrowed the idea of his film from *Kino-Eye,* the 1920s avant-garde classic of Dziga Vertov (Denis Kaufman). Khutsiev and his crew followed the two twenty-year-old protagonists of the film, Sergei and Anya, with a camera around Moscow's social and cultural hubs, showing the emerging Russia of the 1960s through the eyes of these young people. In search of authenticity, Khutsiev wrote the film script with a young coauthor, a student at VGIK, who was a member of Moscow *kompany.*[64] The film showed youthful Moscow intellectuals and artists in the same nuanced and complex way that Aksyonov had portrayed them in his novels. In general, the youth culture was patriotic and optimistic. Among the film's highlights were scenes of the May 1, 1961, public rally to celebrate International Labor Day, when the exuberant students celebrated the recent space flight of Yuri Gagarin. At the same time, Khutsiev's film presented a circle of friends in Moscow, meeting in the private apartment of a high-ranking official, as sophisticated, ironic, and taking nothing at a face value. The hero of the film, twenty-year-old Sergei, having lost his father in the war against the Nazis, has grown up with his mother and felt haunted by uncertainty about the meaning of his life. When his father visits him in a dream, Sergei, ridden with doubts, asks for his advice. The father vanishes, however, without answering the question. For Sergei's generation, the answer has to come from the sons, not from the fathers. Khutsiev's own answers can be found in the title of his film *The Ilyich Gates.* The reference was to a district of Moscow named after Vladimir Ilyich Lenin and hinted at the revolutionary origins of Soviet power. The film invoked a time when the party was still democratic and the state had not yet been hijacked by Stalin and his bureaucrats. Khutsiev and many other children of Zhivago still regarded the Bolsheviks as the legitimate heirs of the Russian Revolution and still romanticized the early years of communist regime.[65]

The film culminates with a poetry recital at the Polytechnic Museum in downtown Moscow, next door to the KGB headquarters. Khutsiev's camera catches the glowing faces of numerous students in the audience, listening to their favorite poets: Yevtushenko, Voznesensky, and Okudzhava.[66] Khutsiev's message to the film's viewers was: See how many young, intelligent, idealistic people have civic consciousness and a sense of individuality! These people are the future of Russia. Khutsiev's audience listening to poetry was the same as the young May Day crowds. It consisted of romantics, optimists, and idealistic professionals. These young men and women have just tasted the fruit of the tree of knowledge. They speak in the language of Hemingway but also believe in the promises of Lenin and the values of the Revolution.

The "contemporary" theater and cinema of the late 1950s and early 1960s created and reflected the language and style of the young intelligentsia. Their social message conveyed young intellectuals' search for individual meaning in life, and their desire for a more humanistic environment. At the same time, the contemporary heroes in the Sovremennik's plays and the intellectuals and students in the films that were coming out continued to advocate the original ideals of the Soviet regime, and a return to the revolutionary foundations of Soviet society and culture.

Marching Out of Lockstep

Gaining public cultural space was essential for revitalizing the intelligentsia. Yet an increasing number of young intellectuals already understood perfectly well that any public activity entailed compromise with the authorities and loss of autonomy. Determined not to allow their creativity and free speech to be limited by state censorship and party cultural policies, some resorted to more clandestine methods. From 1959 to 1962 an innovative cultural venture came into being. The term samizdat, which derives from words meaning "self-publish," was invented by the poet Nikolai Glazkov. In 1960, having arisen from below, it became a rapidly expanding cultural movement, unconstrained by the state and defiant toward the official cultural realm.[67]

This phenomenon snowballed. In a country where even a postcard had to be vetted by the Main Directorate of Printing Affairs (Glavlit), samizdat was a truly revolutionary development. The authorities, who understood it well, interpreted it as a great danger. It began among young people in Moscow who read and shared their poetry at Mayak gatherings. In the words of one participant, the gatherings around Mayakovsky's monument became "a catalyst that started the process of crystallization. People met there, found each other, and formed some sort of a nucleus."[68] From the open-air club at the statue of Mayakovsky young men and women migrated to private apartments, some of which became meeting places for enthusiasts of underground culture. Natasha Gorbanevskaia, a poet and future editor of the first samizdat human rights newspaper, was at that time a member of a circle of about fifty people. They usually sat on the floor of a private apartment and recited poetry continually. Joseph Brodsky came from Leningrad and read his poems to them. "There were no organized poetic evenings; rather it was everyday life. People drank, conversed, not only about literature, but also about history, philosophy, and economics."[69]

The best-known informal cultural hub was the apartment of Alexander (Alik) Ginzburg near the Tretiakov Gallery in Moscow. Ginzburg, only twenty-four in 1960, already had a rich past. Alik, whose father had died in one of Stalin's prisons, studied at Moscow State University and experimented with several professions, but he quickly lost every job, because the KGB found his frequent meetings with foreigners and his independent views objectionable. Ginzburg behaved like a free man, not concealing his dislike for the regime.[70] The writer Vasily Aksyonov, who met him in June 1960, was struck not only by his views, but also by his genuine American jeans, "which were then a miracle equal to the remains of a U-2." They were strolling in Gorky Park, where a recently shot-down American reconnaissance plane was on view, when Ginzburg said, "It is a new environment, in which they [the KGB] can no longer shadow all of us. There are just too many of us. This generation has turned out that way—too many are marching out of lockstep." Ginzburg's freckled face glowed, and his mane of red hair stood on end as if electrified.[71]

Ginzburg was a live link between the cultural underground and those who, like Aksyonov, were about to gain official recognition. One frequent visitor to Ginzburg's flat observed: "Every day there were hordes of people of all ages. No police presence. Money also had no power there. Artists brought their paintings as gifts, and girls transcribed poems out of sheer enthusiasm."[72] Among his friends were established writers, linguists, and translators of foreign literature. Ginzburg was a frequent visitor to another

The statue of Vladimir Mayakovsky, a revolutionary poet, in downtown Moscow, 1959. It became Mayak (the lighthouse), a symbol of the new intelligentsia and the hub of the cultural underground (Courtesy of Memorial, Moscow).

community that belonged to Moscow's underground culture: the "Lianozovo group" of artists and poets. Lianozovo was one of those places near
Moscow where former gulag prisoners without authorization to live in the
capital could reside. The leader of the group was the artist, poet, and philosopher Yevgeny Kropivnitsky, a survivor from Pasternak's generation and
another natural mentor on the ethos of the prerevolutionary intelligentsia.[73]
Kropivnitsky's son Lev, released from the camps in 1956, was part of the
circle, which sought to restore the organic continuity of Russian cultural
life. The Lianozovo group also continued the traditions of the formalist experimental art vanguard of the 1920s, in which Yevgeny Kropivnitsky had
participated. This kind of experimentation had been banned in the Soviet
Union in the 1930s, just as "degenerate art" was in Nazi Germany.[74]

At the end of 1959 Ginzburg and the poets from the Lianozovo group
issued the first samizdat literary journal, *Syntax*. Samizdat, whose main
weapon was the typewriter, was fueled by enthusiasm and defiance of the
official culture. Young women, members of numerous bands of companions, contributed their typing skills to the fledgling movement. They had
to put eight to nine sheets of thin paper into a German-made Eureka typewriter. After hammering away at the keys with all their strength, they could
produce eight to nine copies of barely legible typewritten text. In the dissident movement later, women would continue to play a critical role as typ-
ists and disseminators of samizdat materials in their free time. Indeed,
free time and the ability to duplicate materials were two key factors in the
growth of the cultural underground. A third was the existence of social networks based on mutual trust and of skepticism toward the official culture.[75]
It was easy to progress from exchanging unpublished poetry to sharing officially banned books and political pamphlets.[76]

Samizdat destroyed the Stalinist boundary between private thinking and
the public social sphere. What could only be whispered or written in a secret diary was now part of the informal yet public culture that growing
numbers of people shared. The first coup for samizdat was Pasternak's *Doctor Zhivago*. At first, the manuscript was available to a narrow circle of the
author's friends; but the circle grew, and the people who passed the banned
novel to trusted friends in their *kompany* soon numbered in the hundreds, and then in the thousands. Another document that circulated was
the unofficial record of the meeting of Moscow writers at which they demanded that Pasternak be thrown out of the writers' union and expelled

from the Soviet Union. People began "to write for samizdat" in the same way they used to "write for the drawer" (of their desk, that is).[77]

From Moscow, this innovation spread to Leningrad, where, in the decade after Stalin's death, the cultural temperature hovered around zero. In this city that had suffered most from the Bolshevik and Stalinist repression, there existed no preconditions for a cultural thaw, no publication analogous to *Novy Mir*, no equivalent of the Sovremennik Theater, no organized groups of modernist artists.[78] The survivors from the old intelligentsia, scarred by endless repression, lived in constant fear of arrest and reprisals. At the same time, Leningrad was teeming with precocious literary talent. From 1955 to 1959 "literary-creative societies" flourished. Such groups, created to keep the budding literati under surveillance by the Komsomol and the state, were attached to Soviet cultural institutions. Especially promising was the literary-creative society at the Institute of Mining Engineers, until the authorities shut it down after the Hungarian Revolution and burned the society's collection of publications in the courtyard of the institute.[79] No wonder that the intellectuals, writers, and poets of the former cultural capital of Russia were avid readers of samizdat materials. Joseph Brodsky, the poetic genius from Leningrad, became known in Moscow's underground cultural circles through his verse in samizdat almanacs. Without those publications, Brodsky's life might have turned out differently, and his path to international fame and the Nobel Prize might have been rockier.[80]

The samizdat poets and underground artists, except for Brodsky and a few others, may not have outstripped their publicly recognized colleagues in talent or skill. At the same time, their very existence presented their colleagues who belonged to the Union of Soviet Writers and Artists with an ethical challenge. Here were people who did not have to bow to the authorities, who owed nothing to the regime. They did not have to live a double life, and their sole allegiance was to their art. Mikhail Romm, who helped support one underground artist, recalled how the painter lived: "There was nothing in the studio, only his wife and baby daughter on a worn-out mattress. He sat on the edge of a chair and painted. They had no possessions—only bread, hot water for tea, and milk for the toddler."[81] Most underground artists received some assistance from their supporters in the intelligentsia. Otherwise, they could not officially even buy oil paint and canvases, since those were sold only to members of the Union of Soviet Artists. Soviet legislation also forced independent artists to seek some kind of gainful employment, to avoid persecution as "vagabonds" and "antisocial elements." Many of them worked part-time in boiler rooms, unloaded cars at depots, and did other types of menial labor.[82] This life, reminiscent of the asceticism of medieval religious believers or Russian revolutionaries (as they were idealized), evoked respect and even veneration among young intellectuals. The underground artists sacrificed material comfort for freedom and individual self-expression. They lived an ideal that the majority, especially those with established positions in Soviet institutions, could never attain.

A few people went even further in their search for intellectual freedom. The example of Pasternak's publication of *Zhivago* created the phenomenon of *tamizdat,* which can be translated as "publish-it-over-there"—that is, in the West. Two Moscow writers who owed the uniqueness of their literary voice to *tamizdat* were Andrei Siniavsky and Yuli Daniel. Both considered Boris Pasternak their true teacher, in literature and values. Siniavsky, with his background in the Russian gentry, grew up concealing his beliefs. The Soviet regime and Soviet life were repugnant to him. Still, he managed to make a decent career in Soviet literary studies. His first articles were on the aesthetics of Mayakovsky and Maxim Gorky. He contributed literary essays to *Novy Mir.* Yet he wanted to write as a free man. And he knew early on that he was a *Russian,* not a *Soviet* writer. Beginning in 1956, Siniavsky began to send his literary works abroad for publication under the pseudonym Abram Tertz. His friend the French citizen Hélène Zamoiska-Pelletier had helped Pasternak spirit *Doctor Zhivago* out of the Soviet Union. She performed the same service for Siniavsky.[83]

In his essay "On Socialist Realism," published in France in 1959, Siniavsky wrote that the Russian intelligentsia was not only a victim of Stalinism, but also its unwitting accomplice and creator. He recalled the intellectuals who had waxed enthusiastic about Bolshevism and Stalin's "revolution from above." The ideal of communism, he concluded, provided the intelligentsia with a higher and more romantic sense of life and creativity than democratic liberalism ever could, and socialist realism had become an "aesthetic-religious system" central to the self-concept of almost every Soviet intellectual. Siniavsky's optimism about the future was moderated by caution and realism. Stalin's death had "dealt an irreparable blow" to the aesthetic-religious system. Yet Siniavsky did not believe that art and literature after Stalin would be able to create another deity "capable of inspiring humanity for a new historical cycle." Scoundrels and hypocrites, he warned, had already begun to scavenge among the ruins of the great utopian project. Siniavsky possessed a wise realism still unique among the writers of his generation. This essay made "Tertz" famous in Western intellectual circles. The text appeared in samizdat as well, although nobody knew the real name of the author.[84]

Yuli Daniel, a son of a Yiddish-language Jewish writer (an ardent believer in the Bolshevik regime), grew up a romantic Stalinist and was wounded in combat against the Germans. The postwar Stalinist xenophobia and anti-Semitism, however, dampened his idealism. As a Jew, until 1956 he could not find a job in Moscow and worked as a schoolteacher in the provinces. Khrushchev's secret speech awed and emancipated him. He and his wife, the future dissident Larisa Bogoraz, were able to move to Moscow and earn money thanks to literary translations. Similar to Yuri Timofeev, whom we met in Chapter 1, Daniel had a great social talent for attracting people and gathering them around him. His Moscow apartment became a bohemian headquarters for the emerging intelligentsia. Crowds of poets came to see him and read poetry.[85] Daniel's close friend Siniavsky shared information with him about his *tamizdat* second life. Daniel began to publish abroad as well, under the pseudonym Nikolai Arzhak. Debates in his bohemian circle gave him material for a few short stories, one of which—"This Is Moscow Speaking!"—became famous. In this story, a group of young artists and intellectuals hear a radio announcement that Sunday, August 10, 1960, will be, by state decree, "the day of open murders." The members of the company, unfazed by the surreal nature of the decree, begin to discuss in earnest what they should do. The hero of the novel imagines himself with a machine gun or a hand grenade, killing the top party leaders and secret police executioners in the manner of the Hungarian revolutionaries in 1956. Yet in the end, he decides that he does not want to shed any more blood. Killing the Stalinists would mean becoming a bit like them, and this contradicts the ethos of the resurgent intelligentsia.[86]

The whimsy, fantasy, and irony in the works of Siniavsky and Daniel were still extremely rare at the time. Like Pasternak in *Doctor Zhivago*, these two younger authors were in search of fresh ways of thinking that were still out of reach for most of their educated contemporaries. The preponderance of intellectuals and artists born under Stalin could not yet imagine that art could exist for art's sake, that cultural liberalism was incompatible with the

Soviet regime, or that de-Stalinization would lead not to the restoration of revolutionary romanticism, but rather to its destruction. Only later would they begin to realize that asserting such civic norms as nonviolence and human dignity was the most important task, the supreme act of disobedience against the regime—and an act of emancipation.

Pasternak's death marked a symbolic turning point, when the language and ethos of the budding intelligentsia, seconded by the survivors from the old Russian intelligentsia, began to take shape and achieved public prominence. The new community of the imagination turned out to be very different from its predecessors. Yet even those who did not march in lockstep did not necessarily oppose the ideals of socialism. Most of those who adhered to the idea of the intelligentsia worked inside the Soviet structures, where they partook of revolutionary mythology. Their "contemporary" style and language emerged in reaction to the official public sphere, with its "phony" language and outdated aesthetics, but they did not represent a renunciation of Soviet "socialism." Nor did the rejection of the Stalinist legacy indicate a repudiation of the Bolsheviks, who were still viewed as the creators of the Russian Revolution.[87] Pasternak's lyrics touched the hearts of members of the post-Stalin generation, but Pasternak's beliefs did not speak to their minds. Not accepting *Doctor Zhivago*'s philosophy, the majority of younger intellectuals and artists believed they could remain loyal to Pasternak's art as well as to the revolutionary legacy that Pasternak had denounced at the end of his life.

The Soviet regime could have tried to incorporate their energy and pathos, and use their language and style to promote Khrushchev's new frontiers. The Soviet authorities became alarmed, however. In July 1960 the KGB reported to the Kremlin on "groups of people interested in abstract art and in the so-called leftist trend in poetry. In these groups pessimistic, anti-Soviet sentiments found articulation."[88] The regime, as before, did not want to encourage an autonomous civic spirit or share its control over the cultural sphere with intellectuals, writers, and artists. The authorities, on detecting signs that instead of playing by the rules for the Soviet intelligentsia, intellectuals and artists were beginning to think and act like an autonomous community, viewed them as an intolerable threat.

As far as art and music go, we have the same views
as Stalin had. We will support those who are close
to us. As for the others, we will strangle them.

—Nikita Khrushchev, December 1, 1962

six

The Vanguard Disowned
1962-1964

O N THE morning of December 1, 1962, Nikita Khrushchev, surrounded
by the party bigwigs, unexpectedly appeared at the State Exhibition Hall in
Manege, the former tsarist stables near the Kremlin. It was the day after a
group of innovative and abstract artists had received an invitation to display some of their paintings there. Khrushchev, on surveying the exhibition, dismissed the paintings and brutally attacked the group of innovative
artists. He described them as "faggots" and their work as "dog shit" and "ass-
hole art." He repeatedly threatened to expel the artists from the union and
the party, send them to Siberia, kick them out of the Soviet Union, and
even throw them into prison. The KGB chief Alexander Shelepin, who accompanied the party leader, told him, "There are 2,600 of these types living
in Moscow, and most of them do not work." He had in mind the underground artists, whom he deliberately lumped together with the more innovative members of the official Union of Soviet Artists.[1]

The sculptor Ernst Neizvestny bravely resisted Khrushchev's onslaught.
Neizvestny was born in the Urals into a Russian doctor's family. His father
rejected the Revolution, but Neizvestny grew up a Soviet patriot, volunteered to fight in World War II, and was wounded seriously in battle. In
the postwar years he studied art and simultaneously majored in philosophy
at Moscow State University. He became an admirer of contemporary sculpture, especially that of Henry Moore. In 1955 Neizvestny joined the Union

of Soviet Artists, and two years later he won a prize for the best sculpture at the World Youth Festival in Moscow.[2] He was legendary in Moscow circles for his bravery and original thinking. Yet the watchdogs of Stalinist art blocked Neizvestny's promotion and stole his ideas. Now, in Manege, the artist blocked Khrushchev's entrance into the hall with his sculptures and tried to challenge him. He told the party leader that he was a war veteran and a party member, not a "faggot." He proposed that Khrushchev furnish him with a woman on the spot to test his sexual orientation. This suggestion gave pause to even the earthy Khrushchev. Neizvestny then asserted that Western communists appreciated his work. At this point Khrushchev brushed him off: "You will not weigh me down with your authority." He added with disarming simplicity, "Don't you understand? All foreigners are our enemies."[3] The party leader then continued to condemn the exhibition of abstract artists.

The crackdown that followed Khrushchev's outburst in Manege resembled the Stalinist campaigns of the 1930s and 1940s against "formalist deviations" in art, literature, cinema, and theater. It was also reminiscent of the worst moments of the assault on Pasternak after the publication of *Doctor Zhivago*. Perplexingly, the backlash occurred just a little more than a year after the Twenty-second Party Congress, where Khrushchev had spoken out vehemently against Stalin and his supporters. Some Western experts at the time interpreted Khrushchev's attacks as a conflict between father and children, a preemptive reaction by the aging party leader against the young vanguard of the Thaw. Yet that characterization was more myth than reality. The crackdown showed, rather, the reaction of party hardliners and various groups within the Soviet cultural establishment against the growing influence of the artistic avant-garde and the very idea of artistic autonomy and sincerity.[4]

Viewed from the remove of many decades, it seems absurd that an exhibition of abstract art could produce such a brouhaha. Yet the confrontation between the innovative artists and their antagonists needs to be seen also in international context. At a time of escalating tensions in the Cold War confrontation, this domestic drama was based on mutual misperceptions. The abstract painters themselves, as well as their intellectual and artistic admirers in Moscow, were convinced that they were helping Khrushchev rebuff the forces of conservatism. And Khrushchev, taken up with the Cold War crises in Berlin and Cuba and laboring under the impression that those people were trying to undermine his leadership at a pivotal moment in his Cold War brinkmanship, lashed out against the abstract artists and the entire "contemporary" orientation in the arts. By that act the Kremlin leader destroyed a chance for a common cause between himself and Zhivago's children aimed at reforming the Soviet project and overcoming Stalin's legacy.

The Thaw in a Time of Brinkmanship

From 1960 to 1962, Nikita Khrushchev shifted back and forth several times between promises of détente and nuclear blackmail. While reiterating his peaceful intentions regarding economic and cultural competition between the Soviet Union and the United States, he practiced a form of brinkmanship that bolstered fears of war around the world. In June 1961 Khrushchev scuttled the summit meeting in Vienna and then, after two months of missile-rattling, decided to build the Berlin Wall. And in May 1962 the Soviet leader made the highly risky decision to send Soviet missiles to Cuba and extend the Soviet nuclear umbrella to the Caribbean island, protecting it from a possible American invasion. In 1960–62 the KGB, headed first by Alexander Shelepin and then by Vladimir Semichastny, bombarded Khrushchev and the presidium with belligerent proposals and alarmist reports, including information on the Pentagon's planning for a preemptive nuclear attack on the Soviet Union.[5]

At the same time, the KGB moved to solidify the domestic front by cracking down on ideological laxity and "rotten elements" operating among students and the educated elite. On July 6, 1960, Shelepin suggested measures to stop the "formalist" assault on the edifice of socialist realism. The memo mentioned "hostile activities" by Alik Ginzburg and warned about "groups in Moscow and Leningrad that became adept in abstract painting and the so-called leftist trend in poetry." Some of them, the memo continued, were known to "establish contacts with representatives of capitalist countries and seek to use these contacts against the Soviet Union." The KGB also reported on the suspicious attitudes of the playwrights who wrote for the Sovremennik Theater. A KGB source quoted Oleg Yefremov, the director of the Sovremennik, as saying, "They [the leaders] say that everything is going well in our country. And from the stage we should respond with a subtle message: 'Really?'" Also on the list of suspects were Kropivnitsky and his associates, the Lianozovo group of artists, who sold the "samples of underground Soviet art" to foreigners. The KGB chief suggested acting on a number of measures to eradicate the "rot" within the "Soviet intelligentsia."[6]

Early in 1961 the KGB, in cooperation with the Komsomol leadership, decided to put a stop to the poetry gatherings around the Mayakovsky statue in Moscow. The security forces were beginning to regard the Mayak group as the nucleus of an anti-Soviet political organization.[7] The guards and plainclothes secret police heckled and beat up the Mayak activists. In September 1961 the KGB arrested a group of young underground poets who had gathered at the Mayakovsky statue. An investigation revealed that they had distributed leaflets for "anti-Soviet agitation," organized "discussions," and "expressed terrorist intentions in their circle with regard to the head of the Soviet government." Indeed, one erratic member of the group had announced his readiness to assassinate Khrushchev. His friend, convinced that such an act would end reforms in the Soviet Union, denounced the young "terrorist" to the secret police.[8]

Khrushchev, however, had no clue what specific guidelines were appropriate for cultural and ideological policy in a rapidly changing society. His actions in this area, as in every other, were chaotic and unpredictable. Economic performance, especially in agriculture, continued to deteriorate. Aware of his compromised credentials, Khrushchev produced another political earthquake at the party congress in October 1961 by railing again at Stalin and his policies. Khrushchev sought to prevent the resurgence of his defeated Politburo rivals by reminding everyone of Stalinism's awful legacy. He was also eager to strike back at Mao's cult of personality and neutralize domestic critics from the Stalinist "old guard" (including the exiled Molotov, Kaganovich, and Malenkov). In contrast to the secret speech, the latest spate of revelations about Stalinist crimes did not precipitate a national catharsis. Still, Khrushchev's second unexpected attack on Stalin and his crimes threw the enemies of the Thaw off balance—or so it seemed.

Moscow intellectual and artistic circles did not understand Khrushchev's zigzags. At the same time, they celebrated a "second Thaw" and hoped that it would be followed by a Moscow Spring.[9] Despite the KGB crackdowns and arrests, the public space for cultural and artistic diversity continued to expand in Moscow. In 1961 the city Komsomol inaugurated a few "youth cafés," named Youth, Aelita, and Bluebird. They were democratically managed by councils that included Moscow jazzmen, such as Alexei Kozlov.

These councils decided on the entertainment program and invited their friends. Jazz musicians were happy to emerge from the underground and came to the cafés every evening to play for free. Kozlov recalled, "After the jazz introduction, poets read their poetry, painters showed their paintings. This kind of interaction among people who did not know each other, in a public place, was such a novel and exciting phenomenon. I remember a special exalted mood, a feeling of lightness and freedom." In the fall of 1962, the Moscow Komsomol organized the first jazz festival, and the winners were allowed to travel to Poland to participate in an international jazz competition there.[10]

Another development during the second Thaw that opened opportunities for cultural diversity and openness was Khrushchev's international public diplomacy. In 1961 and 1962 he intensified it, in an apparent attempt to deflect negative impressions of Kremlin brinkmanship. Delegations of Soviet writers toured the United States, Italy, France, and other countries. Soviet filmmakers attended the Cannes and Venice film festivals. Soviet musicians and dancers made a triumphal tour of several Western capitals. The Bolshoi group went to Paris in June 1961 after the collapse of the Vienna summit. In May 1962 Benny Goodman visited the USSR and gave thirty-two concerts in Moscow, Leningrad, Kiev, Tashkent, Tbilisi, and Sochi. Among the 180,000 people attending them in Moscow was Nikita Khrushchev, who saw a performance at the Sports Palace of the Soviet Army on May 30. The Soviet premier, whose musical preferences never extended beyond patriotic songs and folk music, left the performance at the first break. Still, reviews in the Soviet media were favorable.[11] In Leningrad, Goodman's big band gave only one performance, and tickets were distributed through party and Komsomol channels to members of the nomenklatura and officials with connections. The first rows looked like the window of a luxury store: black fox boas hung around the thick necks of women; their smug husbands sat next to them, Soviet deputy badges on their broad chests, hands folded, double chins swelling over the big knots of broad ties. When the band started, this part of the crowd listened with condescension, frowning back toward the youth shouting from the upper rows. One witness recalled, "The old jazzman, facing the frozen front rows, grew furious, the music spiked. The stunned audience reluctantly began to give in to the unfathomable power of the musician. Heavily made-up mouths opened in enthusiastic gasps, feet began to stomp, awkwardly out of sync, beefy hands began to clap. The audience gave up its smug imperviousness, lost self-control, shrieked."[12] The complete "rehabilitation" of jazz, which had been banned under Stalin, seemed to open the way to the removal of ideological Cold War barriers and to the authorization of other modes of contemporary cultural expression. Optimists could see the light at the end of the tunnel again: the repeal of the Stalin-Zhdanov decrees, the end of party hegemony in the sphere of culture, perhaps even the suspension of censorship in literature and media.

Meanwhile, the figures from the post-Stalin literary vanguard were gaining increasing public prominence. Young poets often appeared on radio and television. In fall 1962 Moscow Komsomol authorities followed suit and, together with the Sports Committee, organized poetic evenings in the Luzhniki Sports Arena. There, Yevtushenko, Voznesensky, Okudzhava, Bella Akhmadulina, and Robert Rozhdestvensky performed before thousands of young poetry fans who thrilled to the novelty of listening in public to the brave new words of their favorite poets in the largest arena of the country. On one night the poets attracted a crowd of fourteen thousand.[13] The leaders of the new intelligentsia seemed to be replacing the Stalinist old guard and the hacks of socialist realism. In April 1962 the Moscow branch of the writers' union held its secret election. As a result, the Stalinist veterans were voted out of its governing board; the incoming board included Yevtushenko, Voznesensky, and the *Novy Mir* columnist Alexander Mariamov. That year, almost every issue of *Novy Mir* and *Yunost* introduced a fresh face and a new novel. Once it was no longer in the hands of the Stalinist fanatic Vsevolod Kochetov, *Literaturnaia Gazeta* became—albeit very cautiously—a showcase for literary creativity and a forum for the discussion of ideas and values central to the intelligentsia's ethos. Although the authorities kept the circulation of these journals artificially limited, they still reached millions.[14]

Forgotten names of figures banished from Russian culture were rediscovered, and unfamiliar literary lights were introduced to the public. In September 1962 *Literaturnaia Gazeta* introduced millions of its readers to Arseny and Andrei Tarkovsky, father and son. The poet Arseny Tarkovsky, then fifty-five, had just published his first book, *Before Snow*. In fact, the galleys had been destroyed in 1946 because of Stalin's attack on Russian literature and poetry. Tarkovsky, like Pasternak, belonged to the vanishing breed of the old Russian intelligentsia. His son, thirty-year-old Andrei

Tarkovsky, making his international debut with the film *Ivan's Childhood,* received the Golden Lion award at the Venice Film Festival. The appearance of father and son together in print was another sign that the link had been restored between the old Russian culture and contemporary art.[15]

Another promising step in this direction was the publication of the literary almanac *Pages from Tarusa.* In 1961 the writer Konstantin Paustovsky and his young friends decided to publish the best literary works of Pasternak's generation and its current successors. *Pages from Tarusa* contained Okudzhava's first novel, poems by David Samoilov, and works by other talented young authors. The almanac also included some poems by Marina Tsvetaeva, a brilliant Silver Age poet who took her life in 1941 after returning to the Soviet Union from emigration, and an essay by Nadezhda Mandelstam, widow of the poet Osip Mandelstam, who had died as a victim of Soviet repression. Paustovsky's plan was to publish the book in an obscure place outside Moscow and away from the watchful eyes of the censors. When this trick did not work, he appealed directly to Khrushchev's assistant Lebedev to facilitate publication. Finally, on the eve of the party congress in October 1961, *Pages from Tarusa* came off the press. After vigilant local officials destroyed over half the printed copies, the rest reached Moscow bookstores and were sold in an instant. The collective of authors celebrated its victory over monolithic cultural censorship.[16] The volume was another step toward restoration of the continuity of Russian high culture, battered by Stalin's terror and socialist realism.

The renascent Russian literature, for the first time since *Doctor Zhivago,* attracted international attention. On September 19, 1961, Yevtushenko achieved his breakthrough to world fame when *Literaturnaia Gazeta* published his poem "Babi Yar." The poem commemorated the extermination of Kiev's Jewish population by the Nazis in a ravine near the city. It was the first time ever that an episode of the Holocaust was publicized in the Soviet Union. Yevtushenko attributed the silence about the Holocaust in the Soviet Union to Stalinism and anti-Semitism in Soviet society. The poem appeared on the front page of the *New York Times. Novy Mir* produced another domestic and international sensation on November 16, 1962, when the journal published a story under the title *One Day in the Life of Ivan Denisovich,* by the completely unknown Alexander Solzhenitsyn. The author, a teacher from the provincial Russian city of Ryazan, wrote about a Russian muzhik in the Stalinist camps. This novel, for all the horrors it described, focused on a traditional Russian character, the same "little person" who was the object of Pushkin's and Tolstoy's curiosity. In the West, this novel was acclaimed as a crucial, perhaps decisive, step toward de-Stalinization in the Soviet Union.

The publication of Solzhenitsyn's story was attributable to Alexander Tvardovsky, the editor of *Novy Mir*. When he had read the novel in manuscript a few months earlier, its message was irresistible to him. Russian people would outlive the hell of Stalinism and preserve their spiritual integrity. Solzhenitsyn appeared to Tvardovsky to be a long-awaited literary prophet, a new Tolstoy. He sent the manuscript to Khrushchev's assistant Lebedev, who read the short story to Khrushchev while he was on vacation at a Black Sea resort in September 1962. Khrushchev immediately liked it, especially the peasant protagonist, and shared his first impressions. Still, only after all the presidium members read and "unanimously approved" the publication could the novel go into print. On October 20, 1962, Khrushchev invited Tvardovsky to his office to discuss Solzhenitsyn's piece and the future of Soviet literature. The euphoric Tvardovsky asked him to repeal party censorship of literature. Whereas it had been natural to control progressive literary journals under Tsars Nicholas I and Alexander II, he told Khrushchev, "*Novy Mir* and the Soviet government belong to the same camp." Why was he, the editor appointed by the party Central Committee, subordinate to a state censor who lacked any qualifications for this job? Could censors run roughshod over literature simply because they were armed with Stalinist decrees from the 1940s, which "in essence, have already become outdated"? Khrushchev nodded sympathetically and, according to Tvardovsky, expressed his "complete agreement" with the writer.[17]

People all over the Soviet Union besieged libraries and waited for months in line to read the *Novy Mir* volume. In every library, Solzhenitsyn's story stood out because of its dog-eared pages, darkened from "heavy" use by hundreds of readers. With the publication of *One Day*, the whispered truth about Stalin's gulag issued not from the mouth of the party leader, but from the pen of a writer. Two thousand blue-colored volumes of *Novy Mir* were distributed among delegates to the party plenum, and some of them complained that they could not get a copy! In his speech at the plenum, Khrushchev cited Solzhenitsyn's story. Solzhenitsyn took other stories and a play about camp life out of his cache. The expectations of Moscow intellectuals and cultural figures soared: it seemed the sky was the limit. All who had

Two "generals" of the Soviet literary establishment, the poets Alexander Tvardovsky (left) and Alexei Surkov. During the sixties, Tvardovsky, the son of a peasant, transformed the journal *Novy Mir* into the flagship of the new intelligentsia (Courtesy of Memorial, Moscow).

suffered during Stalin's terror regarded Solzhenitsyn as their hero. Anna Akhmatova believed that everything she had written about the Great Terror would soon be published.[18] The director and actors of the Sovremennik Theater begged Solzhenitsyn to authorize rehearsals of a play based on his earlier novel about life in the camps. *One Day* shook many readers to the core, much more than Dudintsev's novel in 1956 had or the still largely unread *Doctor Zhivago*. In their collective diary, the "Commune-33" circle of middle-aged intellectuals indulged in unwanted starry-eyed idealism. They jubilantly anticipated that *One Day* would produce an upheaval equivalent to that following Khrushchev's secret speech. Everyone who had served Stalin would be completely discredited; the pseudoculture of socialist realism would go into the dustbin, along with all the boastful and mendacious propaganda. In addition, "from that moment on, people would begin to speak and think freely, and not a single scoundrel would be able to indict them for anti-Soviet speeches."[19]

In Moscow, the self-proclaimed *shestidesiatniki* scored one victory after another. Writers planned meetings to commemorate the poet Marina Tsvetaeva and various other writers, all of them victims of Stalinism. On November 26 hundreds of leading Moscow artists, literary critics, theater directors, and filmmakers attended the opening day of a conference, Traditions and Innovations in the Art of Socialist Realism, organized by the

Institute of Art History in conjunction with the Theater Society. It would be a pitched battle between the advocates of cultural liberalization against the Stalinist stalwarts, and victory was in sight. The literary critic Lev Kopelev, who had worked in the same gulag lab as Solzhenitsyn, recalled the opening speech by the president of the Academy of Art, Vladimir Serov. "The self-contented and servile courtier Serov," recalled Kopelev, "briefly condemned the cult" of personality under Stalin "and then lashed out with the habitual wrath against the formalists and abstractionists who were allegedly 'on the payroll of [American] imperialists.'" Kopelev stood up and reminded Serov that Hitler and the Nazis had treated modern art in similar terms. The next day, Kopelev in his address to the conference defended the freedom of experimental art. "It is wrong to prohibit any kind of art or drive it underground. Such practices should be banned forever."[20]

In this euphoric atmosphere, the younger Moscow artists, the leaders of the severe style, were waiting for the opening of an exhibition called Thirty Years of the Moscow Union of Artists. They hoped that it would become a milestone in the public recognition of their work and mark the end of the monopoly over official art by the Stalinist old guard. Like their predecessors from the 1920s, these artists dreamed of becoming the cultural mentors of the masses. The artists even traveled to Leningrad in November to gain support for their cause among their much more timid colleagues in that city. In front of their paintings (they brought them, too), they staged a public discussion. Their speeches gave an art critic in the audience "the impression of participating in an anti-Soviet conspiracy." This was foolhardy radicalism comparable to Khrushchev's secret speech, only this time not authorized from above. A widow of former Hermitage director Iosif Orbely, a fearless woman, publicly supported the Moscow artists. She confirmed that the so-called art of socialist realism was worthless.[21] In the same month, Eli Beliutin, with the help of influential sponsors, most of them nuclear physicists, unveiled a New Reality exhibition in the Teachers' House on Greater Communist Street, Moscow. Crowds of intellectuals flocked to it. The sculptor Ernst Neizvestny and his friends who were experimenting with abstract art decided to display their controversial works there as well.

The heady weeks in fall 1962 induced the more daring writers to lower their guard. The poet Voznesensky was especially reckless. In *Literaturnaia Gazeta* on May 1, 1962, he equated the commemoration of May Day with celebration of the "new art" of his friend Neizvestny and Pablo Picasso and with "passing the torch" to the young generation of artists.[22] He had gone to the United States in 1961 and visited France and Italy for the first time in the fall of 1962. The discovery of those new worlds, the air of freedom, and his international fame exhilarated the young writer. When the American socialist Michael Harrington attended Voznesensky's reading at Le Vieux Colombier theater, he was struck by his outspoken, almost brazen demeanor. He thought that Voznesensky was a "sort of politician of poetry." The savvy Ehrenburg, who was traveling with Voznesensky, told the young poet to be more cautious. "I have read your interviews. I cannot decide whether you are daring or crazy. Watch what you say."[23] Voznesensky was not alone in his daredevil attitude. Paustovsky, speaking to professors and students at the Sorbonne, called Pasternak, Akhmatova, and Isaac Babel the best Soviet writers. An Italian journalist who interviewed Vasily Aksyonov in early 1962 wrote about the inexplicable "fascination" the Russian writer felt for the United States. Soviet embassies sent a series of warning signals to the Kremlin about "reckless" pronouncements of Soviet poets and writers abroad.[24]

The most active and politicized intellectuals of the new generation, mostly party members, hoped to use Khrushchev's latest anti-Stalin salvo to settle scores with their enemies. These intellectuals succumbed to the temptation of "leftist" politics, perceiving themselves as doing battle against the Stalinist villains, whom the young iconoclasts considered to be the right. Some survivors of the 1920s era spearheaded this trend. At the conference Traditions and Innovations in Art, Romm identified the conservative bloc, whose members opposed the "contemporary" art, as the same group of anti-Semitic officials who had enthusiastically perpetrated Stalin's anticosmopolitan purges. "These creatures must be cut down to size." Romm's speech quickly appeared in samizdat, was broadcast on Radio Liberty, and received ample attention in Western media.[25] At a meeting of the party organization of the writers' union, one speaker suggested punishing the people who had collaborated in Stalin's crimes, including those who wrote reports on their colleagues to the NKVD. The critic Lev Kopelev and his wife Raisa Orlova believed that there would be no turning back after a few more victories for cultural glasnost. "Stalin stalwarts seemed to have been completely routed. It was sufficient to laugh them off."[26]

Even the leaders of the writers' union believed that tight party control over the content of Soviet art had to be repealed.[27] Alexander Tvardovsky was convinced that it was still possible to save the ideals of "socialist order, the dream of many great intellects and the goal of struggling millions." Only decisive social and political reforms, he believed, could prevent "global disillusionment in communist ideology and practice," which otherwise would be inevitable.[28] Naturally, the abolition of censorship and glasnost or public discussion of social and economic problems were the preconditions for any reforms. Making them happen was the mission of the intelligentsia.

The intellectuals in the vanguard seemed to forget the moral of Daniel's story "This Is Moscow Speaking." Punishing the Stalinist enemies did not resolve the need for cultural and spiritual emancipation. And in any case, the new generation could not just embrace the Russian cultural legacy without digesting what had happened after the Revolution. The two Tarkovskys, father and son, revealed the gap that continued to exist in this regard between the wizened "fathers" from Pasternak's generation and the still optimistic children of Zhivago. Arseny Tarkovsky, after experiencing decades of war and violence (he had been crippled in World War II) viewed human life as an ineluctable tragedy that only art and mystical faith could alleviate. His son was no stranger to tragedy, yet he was full of the social optimism that marked the young artists and intellectuals of his generation. Andrei Tarkovsky was convinced that the new vanguard, people like him, could transform Soviet society. What was good for art was good for Russia. In *Literaturnaia Gazeta* Andrei expressed the wish to establish a network of cinema clubs where only "thinking," highbrow cinema would be screened. These clubs, he wrote, "would elevate and educate" those who view cinema "as true art, rather than entertainment." The younger Tarkovsky was convinced that in time "ordinary movie theaters [would] disappear" and the viewers "who take cinema lightly [would] disappear as well." He announced his intention to set an example in his next film, about an artist of the Russian Renaissance, the icon painter Andrei Rublev. Tarkovsky concluded his reflections by citing the motto of his milieu: "The artist does not exist in and of himself. He represents the conscience of society, the pinnacle of its imaginative powers, and an expression of its talent."[29] It was this belief system that had led many intellectuals and artists from Pasternak's milieu to embrace the Revolution and then perish from it. In 1961–62 faith in the power of high culture and their own pivotal role in healing Russian society from the Stalinist legacy led creative leaders and the idealists of the sixties to stray far beyond realistic possibilities. Like many times before in Russian history, the intelligentsia's dreamers were bound to find their idealistic expectations dashed by a very cold shower.

Fathers and Children

The growing autonomy and freethinking among intellectuals and artists left the KGB and party authorities at a loss. Arrests and other warnings did not help. And at the top of the Soviet power pyramid Khrushchev did not set clear rules, but confused everyone by constantly breaching established boundaries, especially with the publication of Solzhenitsyn's piece. It was difficult for the party hard-liners to pit Khrushchev against Tvardovsky and *Novy Mir*. The chairman, in contrast to Stalin, did not read or understand serious literature; developments in art did not much concern him.

The official party line in 1962 remained the same as before: it was necessary to "consolidate" the "Soviet intelligentsia." In reality, party officials found it more and more difficult to contain the vibrant and expanding Soviet cultural life. And in the absence of instructions from Khrushchev, these officials were often left to their own devices. There were "humans and bureaucrats" in the party apparatus, as Tvardovsky noted in his diary.[30] The "humans" favored a more flexible approach and sympathized with talented writers, artists, and musicians. An instructor at the department of culture of the party Central Committee, Igor Chernoutsan, for instance, was a graduate of IFLI and had extensive personal contacts in literary and artistic circles from his student days there.[31] Khrushchev's personal assistant Vladimir Lebedev was another "enlightened" apparatchik with a keen personal interest in literature and art. Even Alexander Solzhenitsyn, a harsh judge of character, called him "an intelligentsia type" and "a Chekhovian angel attached to the wayward Khrushchev." Alexei Adzhubei, the editor of *Izvestia*, was regarded, with some reservations, as belonging to the same category.[32] The anti-Thaw "bureaucrats" who resented the norms and values of the intelligentsia were infinitely more numerous. Most prominent among them were the majority of the members in the party Politburo and the secretariat, most notoriously Mikhail Suslov, the party secretary in charge of ideology. Suslov feared and resented Adzhubei, who was rumored to be in line to succeed him. Most of the "bureaucrats" had gained their experience during the purges and campaigns of the 1930s and the 1940s. Anything fresh and innovative evoked in them automatic resistance and fear of "loss of control" over the cultural domain, something akin to loss of power. Besides, they were anti-Semites, and many of the innovative cultural figures of the day were of Jewish origin. There were also ambitious younger bureaucrats—for instance, Sergei Pavlov, the new head of the Komsomol—who were concerned about the "penetration of Western influences" into Soviet culture. Pavlov resented Tvardovsky's *Novy Mir* and began to wage an open war against the journal and the "rotten liberalism" of the new intelligentsia.

The bureaucrats and their clients in cultural institutions were in visible retreat between 1960 and 1962. The situation changed, however, when they managed to get Khrushchev involved in a public debate about "fathers and sons." This debate, which took place in Moscow literary circles, focused on several questions: Who was the new young hero of Soviet literature? What generational changes could one perceive between the young people of the 1960s and their parents? What did the younger generation believe in? Would they support and pursue the revolutionary cause of 1917 with the same sacrificial energy as the previous cohorts of true believers? Would the "children" defend the country with the same patriotism as their fathers had during the Great Patriotic war? The debate about fathers and children had radical historical, social, and political resonances and connotations for Russia, going back to the 1860s and Ivan Turgenev's novel *Fathers and Sons*. The rejection of the authorities and the "nihilism" regarding established ideas described by Turgenev could be found again among the Moscow youth of the early 1960s.

In November 1962 Moscow writers gathered to discuss the meaning of generational changes in literature and culture. The primary goal of the discussions was to publicize fresh literary and artistic works, including Aksyonov's novels, Yevtushenko's and Voznesensky's poems, and Khutsiev's film about Moscow youth. Some speakers looked on that youth as the next cohort that would join the resurgent intelligentsia, already being restored by the joint efforts of the postwar generation of intellectuals and the survivors of Pasternak's generation. The speakers viewed them in the same way that Khutsiev did in his film. David Samoilov wrote in his diary in October 1962, after a meeting with high school students, "Their minds are totally free of poison. They are full of contempt for the generations that tolerated Stalinism. They hate war and do not see any civic foundations in it. They are the harbinger of the future."[33] Ehrenburg, curiously, expressed doubt. In an interview with a young journalist from the *Komsomolskaia Pravda* he called the youth of the early 1960s the most enigmatic generation since the Revolution. "I think your generation has no wings," he said teasingly. "You seek to stay in major cities after graduation, find the best niches. This narrow utilitarian outlook is a disease of contemporary youth."[34]

Polls conducted by the Institute of Public Opinion at *Komsomolskaia Pravda* showed a variety of reactions and attitudes among the young respondents, but no distinct generational profile. The so-called nihilists featured in novels and plays remained a small fraction of educated youth. The overwhelming majority could not even articulate their opinions and used newspaper clichés and other forms of Soviet "newspeak." Still, the polls found that the alienation and emphasis on individuality among some young men and women, already visible a decade earlier among *stiliagi,* had deepened. Apparently, sophisticated and educated youth in Moscow and Leningrad were beginning to grow tired of Khrushchev's erratic crowing about the "construction of communism" and his boastful reflections, as mirrored in Soviet media. One anonymous Leningrad student wrote to *Komsomolskaia Pravda* in early 1961 that it was not enough just to learn from "our fathers and grandfathers." The student pointed out, "Each one of us and our generation must develop our own character, our own ideas, on the basis of a careful reappraisal of the achievements and errors of previous generations."[35]

The domestic debate about "nihilists" and "angry young men" did not remain an internal affair of Russian writers and filmmakers. The *Komsomolskaia Pravda* polls, letters, and articles elicited a spate of comments from Western observers and pundits. It seemed natural to Western liberal observers that educated Soviet youth would test the limits of the old dogmatic, xenophobic system. Marvin Kalb wrote in the *New York Times* that the poll did not reveal "flaming revolutionaries . . . those who would call for a national liberation war in Laos or for a rebellion on Wall Street. A common Russian lad or girl absolutely does not appear as a destroyer of the world."[36] Another journalist speculated whether the appearance of "angry young Ivans" was a sign of hidden opposition within the Soviet Union. And Russian émigrés hoped that the generational shift would provide momentum for the "liberation of Russia from the communist yoke." One émigré presenter at a conference on Soviet youth in Munich in November 1962 concluded that "unofficial associations," such as Mayak and other circles of young intellectuals, were "a very serious phenomenon." They were, he said, "the harbingers of secret anti-communist parties, of open political battles lying ahead."[37]

The Western and émigré commentators grossly exaggerated the significance and scale of the nihilism, and ignored the sources of contemporary social optimism and Marxist-Leninist idealism among the postwar generation and even younger people, students in the early 1960s. And the observers mistook the appearance of a literary-artistic milieu influenced by the spirit of the intelligentsia for the rise of an anticommunist opposition. The parallels with the Russian past, when the "children" of Turgenev had produced leftist revolutionary movements, made these commentators expect something similar now. The same parallels, however, occurred to senior KGB officials, who read foreign commentary in analytical intelligence reports and information bulletins. They could not help noticing Western speculations that the "children" would soon replace the "fathers," first in the sphere of culture, then in the halls of power. The anti-Thaw officials and proponents of socialist realism realized that it was a golden opportunity to catch Khrushchev's attention and arouse his ire against artistic innovators.

The intrigue proceeded with startling rapidity in late November 1962, in the aftermath of the Cuban Missile Crisis. The Kennedy administration forced Khrushchev to remove practically all Soviet forces from Cuba on terms deeply humiliating for the Soviet military. Khrushchev's concessions infuriated and alienated Castro and the entire Cuban leadership. Exploiting this situation, the Chinese communist leadership assailed Khrushchev for giving in to "the United States' imperialist attempt to browbeat the people of the world into retreat at the expense of Cuba." Chinese newspapers compared Khrushchev to Neville Chamberlain appeasing Adolf Hitler in Munich.[38]

On the surface, the crisis that ended in a fiasco for Khrushchev's nuclear brinkmanship had nothing to do with the dynamics of the Thaw. Nobody among the enthusiastic left-leaning intellectuals in Moscow realized that Khrushchev's international defeat posed grave dangers to the liberalization in Soviet society. The chairman needed psychological compensation for his colossal loss of face vis-à-vis President John F. Kennedy. At home, Khrushchev's economic plans and endeavors were collapsing, as everyone could see from the empty Soviet stores. Food riots broke out in Novocherkassk and a number of Russian provincial cities in June 1962, after the government had to raise the prices of meat and dairy products by 25 to 30 percent. The revolts were put down harshly by the military, and hundreds of the "ringleaders" in the protest were executed or imprisoned. The KGB registered widespread disaffection with Khrushchev's policies among party members.[39] In this situation, Khrushchev's instinctive inclination, as it had been at the end of 1956, was to crack down on domestic laxity and present himself as a defender of the Soviet state and ideology.

The Stalinist officials picked a perfect moment for their counterattack against the artistic vanguard. On November 20, as the Soviets were retreating in humiliation from Cuba, Khrushchev received a letter from Serov, Vuchetich, and forty other academicians, advocates of socialist realism. They warned the party's Central Committee that the "aggravated international situation put forces into motion that [sought] to infiltrate our state in order to undermine our ideology from within." This infiltration, the letter went on, had been conducted for a number of years "through cinema, television, literature, music, art, tourism, and so on." The academicians blamed Adzhubei's *Izvestia* and its weekly supplement *Nedelia* for becoming "a pulpit" for the "revisionist" ideological agenda. In conclusion, the authors appealed to the Central Committee to implement once again the Stalinist cultural policies that had been in effect from 1946 to 1953.[40]

The expected opening of the exhibition at Manege, where a number of young artists planned to exhibit their innovative work, gave the party faithful an ideal chance to show Khrushchev what how ideological "revisionism" played out on canvas. As chance would have it, the art exhibition by Beliutin's New Reality, which opened in Moscow on November 26, received extensive attention from Western media. Western journalists and television cameramen accosted the young artists, whose heads were spinning with this sudden fame. Western media reported on "abstract art on Greater Communist Street" and speculated that "abstract art had finally been recognized in the USSR." Reports about it appeared on Eurovision news and American television. All this could not avoid angering Khrushchev.[41] The KGB promptly interpreted the reports in Western media as a revision of the party line, as an ideological retreat, a cultural liberalization—obviously under the impact of the American "victory" in the Cuban missile crisis. The KGB's Shelepin added a sensitive detail for Khrushchev's attention. He informed him that "abstract" artists were the same people who invented and spread disparaging jokes about the Soviet leader. The implications were obvious. Was this indeed the beginning of a transition in power from "fathers" to "children" not only in Soviet visual arts, but also in the political realm? Khrushchev, who was sixty-eight, could not help getting the message.

At the Politburo meeting on November 29 Khrushchev exploded. According to the semiofficial notes, he "spoke out sharply" against the "penetration of formalism into art" and railed against Adzhubei and his media outlets. He also threatened to revoke the results of the elections of the writers' union and offered "to make some arrests, if necessary." And he ordered that the filmmaker Romm be brought to party headquarters for interrogation. The chairman told party secretaries Mikhail Suslov and Leonid Ilichev "to sort out this exhibition business." He praised Suslov, apparently for bringing this issue to his attention.[42] On November 30, Beliutin and his followers received a surprise call from Polikarpov, head of the party department of culture, with the request that they transfer their paintings immediately to the Manege Exhibition Hall, where they would be inspected by the Soviet leaders. Beliutin's friends from *Izvestia* told him (they were apparently genuinely misled themselves) that the party leadership had decided to legitimize the new schools of art. Soviet newspapers and the propaganda journal the *Soviet Union*, published for American readers, had allegedly received instructions to report on this event. Beliutin's artists, drunk with joy, hugged each other, not realizing that they were walking into a trap.[43]

There was no chance that Khrushchev would find a common language with the new generation of artists. Khrushchev helped Tvardovsky with Solzhenitsyn's novel. He liked Chukhrai's films and sent them to international festivals.[44] Yet, like the vast majority of the Russian public, Khrushchev detested unconventional art, and especially abstract art. Igor Chernoutsan recalled that "Khrushchev had zero preparation and sensitivity in aesthetics." In this regard, it was "easy to unleash him against the young intelligentsia."[45] At Manege he was acting like an aged, ill-tempered peasant father trying to discipline his sophisticated urbanite children. According to the official minutes, Khrushchev told the young artists, "You believe that we old men do not understand your art. No! We and the people understand what is good and bad."[46] Khrushchev's unstable personality might have contributed to his behavior at Manege. Even his entourage did not expect such an outburst. The president of the Academy of Art, Vladimir Serov, a leading Stalinist stalwart, jubilantly shouted to his secretary as they were leaving the Manege Exhibition Hall: "An incredible thing has happened! We won!" Khrushchev's ire sealed the fate of Beliutin's New Reality as well as the severe style by up-and-coming artists in the official union. Most of the criticized artists lost their jobs and were ostracized. Their paintings disappeared from Manege without a trace. The works of David Shterenberg and Robert Falk, but also Kasimir Malevich, Vasily Kandinsky, Marc Chagall, Vladimir Tatlin, Alexander Rodchenko, Naum Gabo, and other vanguard artists would not be exhibited at Manege for decades to come. It was the innovative output of the artistic intelligentsia of the Thaw, and not Stalinist art, that ended up gathering dust in Russia's storage vaults.

Leaders of the Moscow intelligentsia did not realize at first what had happened; wild rumors circulated through the grapevine. Nothing happened to Solzhenitsyn, Yevtushenko, Aksyonov, and other icons of the Thaw. Tvardovsky confessed his confusion in his diary: "First [the publication of] Solzhenitsyn, now this—does not make any sense. I only wish to avoid getting caught up in this mess."[47] Khrushchev's cultural crackdown, however, was just beginning. He ordered the party apparatus to "purge" the press and television, art institutes, and the guild of graphic artists and book illustrators. He also threatened to scrutinize "all universities and colleges." And he decided that he had a personal responsibility to explain to the cultural and artistic elites what kind of art the party expected from them. On December 17, 1962, he addressed four hundred writers, artists, filmmakers, critics, and apparatchiks in charge of Soviet culture in the reception hall in Lenin Hills, the secluded residential area for the party leaders. The meeting was arranged as an informal discussion, with everybody sitting at restaurant tables eating and drinking. The entrance to the meeting room was "decorated" with samples of Neizvestny's sculptures which, in Khrushchev's opinion, showed everybody the degenerate nature of the "new" art. Khrushchev gave a long and rambling speech.[48]

Just as during the previous meetings with "Soviet intelligentsia," the party leader did not follow the script prepared for him by his speechwriters, yet did not come up with any precise formulas on his own. He began with praise for Solzhenitsyn, who was reluctantly present in the audience, and took personal credit for publishing his story. Then, Khrushchev spoke as a defender of simple, popular, working-class Russia against the young, cosmopolitan, elitist, and Westernized cultural vanguard. His disjointed speech, rude didacticism, and lower-class lexicon automatically suggested a cultural gap between him (and the "working-class" people of Russia)

December 17, 1962, at a meeting with the so-called Soviet intelligentsia. Khrushchev reaches out to sculptor Ernst Neizvestny (on the right, with fist clenched), making a point about socialist realism. The poet Yevgeny Yevtushenko (back row, center) looks on, bemused by the scene (Courtesy of Sergei Smirnov).

and the intelligentsia types. Khrushchev pounced on Neizvestny's abstract sculptures. Unable to understand or evaluate them, the party leader ordered the KGB to investigate where the sculptor had "found copper for this trash." If copper had been stolen, Neizvestny could be indicted as a criminal. After Khrushchev finished, Yevtushenko stood up. He tried to defend the right of artists and writers to decide on their own what art was, by claiming that these were people loyal to communist ideals and opposed only to Stalinism. He also explained Neizvestny's sculptures as the "sins of youth." The sculptor would correct them through his creative evolution. This triggered Khrushchev to remark, "If a person is born ugly, only the grave will correct him." Yevtushenko bravely retorted: "Nikita Sergeevich, we live in a time when mistakes are corrected not by graves, but by live, honest, and truthful Bolshevik words." The poet finished his remarks amid ominous silence in the audience. Khrushchev apparently did not know what to say and announced a break.[49] The next day "all Moscow" was quoting Yevtushenko's words. Yet it had become clear that the party leadership was determined to call the shots in the cultural sphere, and hopes for an autonomous role and a great future for the intelligentsia were dashed.

In March 1963 Khrushchev gathered the cultural elites again, this time more formally, in the amphitheater of the House of the Unions inside the Kremlin. Hundreds of party apparatchiks gathered in rows there as well, like birds of prey waiting for the leader's signal to attack. This time the invited intellectuals expected the worst, including arrests. Some young artists who were invited to the meeting had their wives accompany them to the Kremlin gates. They did not know if they would return home.[50] All witnesses of the March meeting testified that Khrushchev, initially almost amiable, quickly became irritated and got carried away. The KGB and the Soviet embassies abroad had produced more information on the growing contacts of popular young writers and poets with foreigners, and on the interviews given to foreign media, against Khrushchev's policy. Some young intellectuals, including Yevtushenko, had shared with foreign correspondents the hypothesis that the Soviet leader had attacked artists and writers in order to deflect attention from the problematic situation in agriculture. At the start of the March meeting Khrushchev suggested that "all volunteer informants for foreign agencies" leave the hall. The audience erupted in cries of treason, demanding that he name the culprit and punish him. Yevtushenko's hands went cold with fear. Khrushchev, however, remembering the poet's courageous stand at the previous meeting, decided not to throw Yevtushenko to the wolves just yet.[51]

Wanda Wasilewska, who had been Stalin's protégé and was Khrushchev's close friend, took the floor at the March meeting to complain about the writers' interview with the Polish magazine *Polytika*. Working herself into hysterics, Wasilewska claimed that Voznesensky and Aksyonov had undermined communist propaganda in Poland and encouraged Polish "revisionists." She mentioned in particular that Voznesensky had spoken about the generational shift. In reality, Voznesensky had said, "In a political sense we are the children of the Twentieth and Twenty-second congresses of the CPSU, the generation that sees itself in the image of the revolutionary twenties, the traditions of Leninism." He had implied that the generation of the sixties was closer to Lenin than the intermediate cohorts that had grown up under Stalinism.[52] Khrushchev immediately called on the poet, who was in the audience. Voznesensky wanted to explain that he had merely repudiated to a Polish journalist the notion that "our generation was spitting on the fathers' generation." There were "remarkable, revolutionary people" in each generation. He said that he liked Mayakovsky and, although he was not a party member. . . . At that very instant Khrushchev exploded, "Why are you so proud that you are not a Party member? We will sweep you off clean! Do you represent our people or slander our people?" Voznesensky tried to continue but the omnipotent first secretary interrupted him again: "I cannot listen calmly to those who lick the feet of our enemies. I cannot listen to the agents. Look at him. He would like to create a party of non-communists. Well, you are a member of the party, but it is not the same one I am in." Then Khrushchev shouted at the top of his lungs. "The Thaw is over. This is not even a light morning frost. For you and your likes it will be the *arctic* frost [long applause]. We are not those who belonged to the Petöfi Club. We are those who helped smash the Hungarians [applause]."[53]

"You are slaves!" Khrushchev rails at the poet Andrei Voznesensky and the younger artists at a meeting in the Kremlin in March 1963. On the chairman's right sit his associates Frol Kozlov, Leonid Brezhnev, and Mikhail Suslov (Courtesy of Sergei Smirnov).

Voznesensky, in a state of shock, reiterated that he had said "nothing anti-Soviet." Khrushchev, however, heard only what he wanted to hear. He kept harping on the ambitions of left-wing art and artists. Voznesensky, he shrieked, was "a nothing, a zero" and "only one of the three and a half million" who were born in the Soviet Union annually. "Your mouth is still wet from mother's milk. He dares to teach us! Do not think you are another Pasternak. We offered Pasternak the right to leave. If you want, you will get your passport tomorrow. Go to the devil's mother—join your friends abroad." In a complete frenzy, with saliva flying and clenched fist raised high, he continued, to roars of applause from the assembled apparatchiks and many establishment figures in Soviet culture, "They think that Stalin is dead and anything is allowed. . . . No, you are slaves! Slaves! Your behavior shows it. Ehrenburg says that he kept his mouth shut, but when Stalin died, he loosened his tongue. No, gentlemen, we will not allow it!!!"[54]

Entire rows of party functionaries and numerous cultural figures joined Khrushchev's hysterical shrieks at Voznesensky, "Mister Voznesensky—out of this country! Shame! Shame!" Voznesensky, who was wearing his habitual dark turtleneck, heard Shelepin, former KGB head, yell at him from the front row, "In the Kremlin without a white shirt, without a tie! Damn beatnik!"[55] Khrushchev and his chorus of apparatchiks came down on the cultural vanguard in the same way the Komsomol vigilantes had attacked *stiliagi* in the streets of Moscow and Leningrad during the 1950s. The majority of the "Soviet intelligentsia" in the hall became part of a mob ready to lynch a dissident on a cue from their leader. According to one witness, who had gone through war, artillery fire, and frontal attacks, "I never experienced such horror in my life. I had a feeling, if somebody objected, his neighbors would beat him to death, tear him to pieces. The audience wanted to destroy those who had come to believe in the Twentieth and Twenty-second Congress." Never before had the members of the artistic avant-garde felt so isolated and humiliated. Instead of presenting the image of an influential intelligentsia speaking with moral authority to the party leaders, the artists were caught like moths in the flame of Khrushchev's irascibility. Perhaps Khrushchev realized that he was unleashing another orgy of Stalinist witch-hunting. Or perhaps he saw the look of mortal fear on Voznesensky's face. His raised fist opened up, and his shrill cry turned into the loud grumbling of an angry grandfather who concluded by telling the poet, "You may continue to work."[56]

The first secretary's ax also fell on Marlene Khutsiev's film *The Ilyich*

Gate. The director Mikhail Romm inadvertently had brought the film into the discussion by trying to explain the scene when the hero's father refuses to tell his son how to live. Khutsiev, said Romm, wants to let the young contemporaries make up their own minds. "No, no, no," Khrushchev interrupted. "You're interpreting it incorrectly, Comrade Romm. The meaning is just the opposite. Even a cat doesn't discard its kitten, but at a difficult moment, this father turns away from his son. That's what it means."[57] In Khrushchev's opinion, the party had to remain the collective "father" to Soviet youth, properly organized by the Komsomol. In the edited version of *Pravda* published two days later, the Soviet leader wondered why one should feature young men and women who did not know how to live and what to live for. "These are not the sort of people our society can rely upon. They are not fighters, not revolutionaries. They are morally sick people, who have grown old while still young, who have no high aims or vocation in life." Neizvestny, Yevtushenko, Voznesensky, and Aksyonov, he claimed, could be redeemed through the party's "fatherly" care. Others, especially unrepentant artists, had to be ostracized and above all "kept away from Soviet youth."[58]

Khrushchev's rambling harangues produced a tsunami that swept through all institutions of culture, education, and art. This wave threatened to bury the emerging networks of people of the sixties, and the reborn ethos of the intelligentsia. Many "enlightened" functionaries in the Komsomol who had helped the young vanguard artists now lost their jobs, became marginalized, or just defected and adopted the hard line. The head of the Moscow branch of the writers' union who had promoted Yevtushenko, Aksyonov, and their friends was forced to step down. The party organization of the writers' union was dissolved because it was seen as revisionist. Inside the Union of Soviet Artists, the followers of the severe style lost their influential posts and were pushed to the margins. Members of the Beliutin movement and many other innovative artists went underground or found jobs in industrial and media graphics outside the world of "high art." Some stopped painting altogether. Western jazz disappeared from Soviet airwaves. The poetic concerts in the Luzhniki Sports Arena ended abruptly. Instead, newspapers printed speeches by the heroes of the masses, the cosmonauts Gagarin and Titov, in which they criticized Yevtushenko and other leaders of the cultural vanguard.

All the hopes of the avant-garde lay shattered. The Stalinist "varnishers" among writers, "machine-gunners for the party" in literary journals, were back in the saddle and triumphant. Nostalgic Stalinists came to the fore, along with unprincipled careerists and a host of petty souls, including colleagues of the fallen vanguard who were jealous of their talent and above all fearful of being associated with them. The incipient solidarity among intellectuals appeared to go up in smoke, to be replaced by fear and a self-serving attitude, familiar to accomplices of the Stalinist campaigns. Yevtushenko noticed people who had been active in anti-Semitic campaigns under Stalin reappearing on numerous podiums "like devils out of a magic box."[59] Terror returned to the circles and networks of Russian intellectuals and artists. The linguist Koma Ivanov conducted a workshop on semiotics at one of Moscow's academic institutes soon after the Manege disaster. Semiotics was an innovative discipline at the intersection of cybernetics, social science, and the humanities; yet it stemmed from the formalist school of Russian linguistics of the 1920s that had been banned under Stalin. When Academician Mstislav Keldysh, an earlier supporter of semiotics, learned about this, he panicked, as did other sponsors of Ivanov's works. Soon Ivanov realized he could not publish anything on semiotics in Moscow. He moved to the provinces, to Tartu University in Estonia.[60]

All intellectual and cultural elites had to go through a humiliating and self-debasing process of criticism and self-criticism *(prorabotki),* based on the Stalinist blueprint of the 1930s and 1940s. For the Moscow cultural vanguard this inquisitorial process was organized by a specially created Ideological Commission, headed by Party Secretary Ilichev. The rest of the intellectuals, especially members of the party and official unions, were at the mercy of local committees (replicas of the main commission), headed by their vengeful and terrified colleagues. An atmosphere of witch-hunting left no place for logic, rationality, dignity, or legal rights. Even though no arrests took place, many feared they would start at any time. According to a witness, the Stalinist-style *prorabotki* marked "the pinnacle of the informer's art, giving free rein to malice and envy. It was the culmination of evil, the triumph of all manner of foulness, when people even strove to gain the reputation of villains, seeking consolation in the horror that was suggested by what surrounded them. It was, in a way, a mass spiritual sickness. People weren't ashamed of being informers, but even hinted at their special power." The whole process was incredibly demoralizing both for the accused and for the accusers, as well as the large audience of students and readers who were present at such meetings.[61] Those artists and intellectuals who had been too young to experience Stalinist *prorabotki* received a rude lesson in 1963.

Fear was pervasive: Who would dare oppose the party and risk the ostracism of terrified colleagues? At the meeting of the Moscow Union of Artists in the spring of 1963, Leonid Rabichev, a participant in the Beliutin exhibition, was interrogated by the art historian Sarah Valerius, the former wife of the sculptor Yevgeny Vuchetich. She asked Rabichev if he considered himself an abstractionist. When he said he never engaged in abstract art, she pinned him down, "Then you disagree with Nikita Sergeevich Khrushchev?" Rabichev was terrified: if he said no, he would be "merely" expelled from the union; if he chose yes, he could be arrested. He chose the former option. Rabichev was a war veteran, yet he gave in to uncontrollable fear and lost his dignity and self-respect. For twenty years after this incident, he was unable to return to art.[62] Arkady Strugatsky recalled another inquisitorial session, held in late March 1963 for science fiction writers. One well-known writer, Alexander Kazantsev, began to denounce his colleague as "abstractionist" and attributed fascist ideas to him. Nobody dared to protest, and Arkady Strugatsky realized, cold perspiration beading his forehead, that he too was paralyzed by fear. Here was "his majesty Idiot in search of revenge," but what if Kazantsev's attack was approved by the party organization? As shame and rage overwhelmed him, Strugatsky stood up and challenged the raving denouncer. His passion broke the ice of common fear, and everybody began to speak and shout. From the meeting Strugatsky went straight to a bar to calm his nerves with strong drink.[63] It was painful for the post-Stalin artists and intellectuals to admit that their enemy was not only ignorant bureaucrats, but above all cowardice and baseness among the educated elite itself. This realization was a huge blow to faith in the eventual triumph of the intelligentsia's ethos, in a brotherhood of honest and cultured people who would overcome the Stalinist legacy.

Some targets of the backlash held their ground, among them artists of the severe style, but the majority succumbed to the pressure. Ernst Neizvestny, who had stood up bravely to Khrushchev at Manege, afterward sent a letter of repentance, thanking the first secretary for his "fatherly criticism."[64] Voznesensky, after recovering from a nervous breakdown, began to work on a poem about Lenin in emigration. Beliutin buckled under pressure and pleaded guilty. Even Yevtushenko, who had acted courageously at the December meeting with Khrushchev, chose to distance himself publicly from the arrested nonconformist poets and intellectuals and those who produced samizdat. Aksyonov also emphatically rejected claims by the "bourgeois reactionary press in the West" that "we do not respect our fathers, that Soviet youth in general allegedly oppose their fathers." He concluded, "We want to talk to our fathers, and argue with them, but we do not want our fathers to think that we have something up our sleeves against them."[65] The proud cultural vanguard of the sixties intelligentsia, having been forced to its knees, lost its integrity and moral authority in the eyes of many admirers.

Privately, the humiliated writers and artists, who felt disgusted by their own conformism, indulged in emotional outbursts. As Yevtushenko, Aksyonov, and Neizvestny left the Kremlin after the disastrous March 1963 meeting with Khrushchev, Aksyonov began to rave, "Don't you understand that our government is a gang, with no holds barred?"[66] Ernst Neizvestny, as he wrote later in his memoirs, felt that events had confirmed his earlier realization that the "force of history" was in reality represented by good-for-nothing pygmies. Instead of the revolutionary terror unleashed by epic forces, there was the terror in the style of a communal kitchen, perpetrated by "gnomes and goblins" living a fraudulent, repellent life. "Human trash" had been elevated straight from lower, uneducated social classes to commanding positions at all levels of the state. And the chasm between "historical truth, the truth of victory, the sea of blood—and the vulgarity, banality, and pettiness of the 'representatives' of history" wounded Neizvestny's artistic ego. This chasm, as he it summed up, also "laid the basis for the major, inner conflict between me and established power," as well as all those who embodied that power at all levels of society.[67] This realization that oppression originated not only with the bureaucrats above, but with the common people below, continued to deepen the alienation and diminish the social optimism of the sixties intellectuals in the years to come.

Sobering Conclusions

Khrushchev's general hostility to Zhivago's children and his rejection of their claim for social and cultural autonomy and status remained constant. Speaking at the Central Committee (CC) plenum in June 1963, Khrushchev took an anti-intellectual stand. He proposed out of the blue to abolish salary increases for scholars and scientists with degrees. He compared the holders of honorific titles in science and academia to lords in Great Britain. He also asserted that Stalin's approach to intellectuals and artists was "a kind of bribe . . . to create a certain strata of intelligentsia around him." Khrushchev concluded that he relied, instead, "on the working class, on the people."[68] Yet the Soviet leader was inconsistent, as usual. One day he blamed everything on "this crook" Ehrenburg who invented "the Thaw" and even wanted to limit his trips abroad. He threatened to ban the production of shortwave radios in order to prevent Soviet people from listening to the "enemy" broadcasting from abroad. And he frowned at the free-minded filmmakers and threatened to close their association. On another, he changed his mind, encouraged Ehrenburg to work, and allowed the filmmakers' association to exist (after the party secretariat already voted to close it). At one time he professed to be the defender of traditional Russian culture; at another moment he was angry at Paustovsky for his defense of the Russian countryside against the destructive effects of industrial development.[69]

Radio and television resumed, albeit cautiously, the transmission of jazz music. Soviet industry continued to produce millions of shortwave radio sets. Most notably and unexpectedly, Tvardovsky's *Novy Mir* survived the onslaught. In March 1963 the Komsomol boss Sergei Pavlov, backed by powerful conservative forces, had lashed out at the magazine for publishing "with inexplicable consistency" works that "smacked of pessimism and moldy despair." Yet Ilichev, the head of the Ideological Commission, told Tvardovsky, "Take it easy. Continue to work as before."[70] The struggle to interpret the party line on culture continued among the competing apparatchiks. In August, when Khrushchev vacationed at the Black Sea, Adzhubei and Lebedev read him Tvardovsky's banned poem, "Tyorkin in the Other World." Written soon after Stalin's death, it ridiculed Stalinist bureaucracy, regimentation, and servility. Khrushchev read it to all his guests, and two days later Adzhubei's *Izvestia* published it in five million copies. This episode revealed Khrushchev's quandary: although he resented the intelligentsia as a "class" and crushed its ambitions for autonomy, he agreed with the antibureaucratic message of the left-wing writers and poets.

The controversy about fathers and children that had sparked Khrushchev's wrath was almost forgotten in the general assault on the left-wing cultural vanguard. Yet this controversy continued to fuel the search for imaginary conspirators who were allegedly driving a wedge between the party apparatus and Soviet youth. Months after Khrushchev's confrontation with the artistic vanguard, regional party bureaucrats continued to watch for evidence of the cultural and ideological subversion perpetrated by intellectuals. Party investigators appeared one day at Akademgorodok in Novosibirsk to inspect the work of sociologists. When the commissioners found that the scholars were trying to measure the educational level of high school students and their parents, they complained about "ideological sabotage," a plot "to pit the generations of fathers and children against each other." The investigators explained, "It is obvious that the current generation is better educated than their parents. Does it follow from this that parents must hand power over to their children? This is what you want to say?"[71]

Against the ripples of this ideological-cultural witch-hunting the infamous "Brodsky affair" played out in Leningrad. The Leningrad KGB had the young poet Joseph Brodsky in its sights as early as the 1950s. A passionate fan of everything British and American, Brodsky belonged to the cultural underground of Leningrad and was not a member of the writers' union. His poems appeared in samizdat almanacs, and he was not afraid to meet with American tourists. The KGB also discovered his connection to a group of arrested youth that planned to hijack an aircraft and fly abroad. There was no evidence to involve Brodsky in this criminal case. Still, the authorities decided to create a different "case," devised to "cleanse the rot" from educated circles in the former Russian capital. In November 1963 a group of local Stalinist vigilantes and KGB stooges published an article in the local newspaper presenting Brodsky as a literary "sponging parasite" potentially dangerous to "Soviet society." In February 1964 Brodsky was arrested and thrown into prison.[72]

Many cultural figures in Moscow regarded the Brodsky affair as a mere distraction from larger concerns. Tvardovsky refused to intervene in this case. At first, only a tiny group of Leningrad writers and intellectuals rushed to fight for Brodsky's liberation.[73] Soon, however, they received support from Moscow intellectuals active in samizdat. Women were at the forefront: Frida Vigdorova, a friend of Anna Akhmatova and Lidia Chukovskaia, used her position as a staff member of the *Literaturnaia Gazeta* to attend Brodsky's trial, which took place in a district people's court. She took notes on the proceedings, which strongly resembled a kangaroo court. One witness recalled his impressions of the trial: "At that time I was a young man, in great shape, hardened by army service and my work in the Far North. I believed I could not suffer a nervous breakdown. Yet after five hours of surreal impudence and slap-in-the-face lawlessness I returned home ready to vomit."[74] Along with Khrushchev, the Leningrad authorities were determined to show the "rotten" intellectuals that they were "nothing, zero, slaves" when they confronted the state and "common people."

The decision of the people's court was predetermined. Brodsky was sentenced to five years of exile from Leningrad and forced labor in the Archangelsk region. The "common people" brought to the courtroom participated in the scripted political play: they fulminated against the intelligentsia and "parasitic writers." Yet toward the end of the trial a greater number of artists and intellectuals, including Dmitry Shostakovich, Anna Akhmatova, Kornei Chukovsky, and dozens of young writers and poets from Leningrad signed collective letters to the authorities in defense of Brodsky. For these people the Brodsky affair seemed to replicate the earlier persecution of Pasternak. This time, they did not remain silent and passive. Vigdorova's notes were spread through samizdat and leaked to the Western press. People from circles of companions in Moscow, including Ludmilla Alexeyeva, learned about the Brodsky trial from samizdat and began to realize that it was important to find ways to help current victims of repression. The campaign to defend Brodsky produced the first documents in the emerging democratic movement, also known as a movement of human rights defenders.[75]

The abrupt end of Khrushchev's Thaw left believers in the intelligentsia's mission more uncertain of their fate than they had been since 1953. The old writer Chukovsky hoped that even if those in the forefront of intellectual liberalization were crushed, it would be a temporary phenomenon. "It was easy under Stalin," he wrote in his diary. "Crush the intelligentsia, destroy all independent thinkers! Now, however, there are masses of technical intelligentsia, and the state cannot get by without them. These masses have assumed the role of defenders of the humanities and have formed some kind of public opinion."[76] The science fiction writer Boris Strugatsky, however, was less hopeful. By spring 1963, he recalled, "one thing had become quite painfully clear to us. No more illusions and dreams of a better future. We are governed by the enemies of culture. They will always be around and against us. They will never allow us to say what we believe is right, because their sense of correctness is different. While communism is

The poet Joseph Brodsky (sitting to the left of the driver), future winner of the Nobel Prize, in exile in the Russian North, 1964. His arrest for "parasitism" in 1964 triggered the first campaign by the intelligentsia in defense of human rights (Courtesy of Memorial, Moscow).

the world of freedom and creativity for us, for them communism is a society where the population immediately carries out all instructions of the party and the government with relish."[77] The Strugatsky brothers transformed their frightening revelation into the allegorical novel *It Is Hard to Be God*. In this novel, young scholars from Earth, where the ideal communist society has been built, arrive on another planet, where cynical tyrants, fascistlike burghers, and ecclesiastical fanatics seek to destroy educated people who represent the only hope for enlightenment and progress. Despite all the attempts of the scholars, masquerading as local nobles, to end the butchery, they fail to stop the descent into darkness. Their principles prevent them from using force, even to stop the bloodbath. They give up and return to Earth sobered and humiliated.[78]

In his memoirs David Samoilov wrote about the significance of Khrushchev's confrontation with the cultural vanguard. "Khrushchev mistook a struggle over taste for a struggle of ideas." He failed to recognize "that new forms could help cover up the ideological vacuum" of his regime. Instead of incorporating the energy of the young cohorts initially loyal to his course and sympathetic to his illusory new frontiers, he "declared an ideological war on the new generation."[79] In fact, the historical significance of this episode went far beyond a struggle over taste. Khrushchev could indeed have co-opted the cultural vanguard of the early 1960s, for its members still shared the revolutionary-romantic mythology. Instead, abetted by the party stalwarts, he preferred to crush the first intimations of intellectual freedom and cultural autonomy in post-Stalin society. The youngest members of the cultural vanguard were shocked to discover that the witch-hunting atmosphere could return as if there had been no de-Stalinization, *Novy Mir*, "honest" journalism, novels and films, or revelations by Solzhenitsyn. The crackdown had far-reaching consequences for the future of the Soviet society. Without it, some chance for growth and consolidation of reformist forces might have existed under the guise of glasnost and a more "humane" socialism (just as would transpire in 1968 in Czechoslovakia). Instead, the revival of an intelligentsia that could be *both freethinking and morally committed to the Soviet communism* was nipped in the bud. Believers in high culture as a vehicle that could save the Soviet project were isolated and humiliated. The momentum for the Moscow Spring was dead. Not until Gorbachev's glasnost would such a moment come again, when people who believed in the social and cultural mission of the intelligentsia could act in alliance with the Kremlin leadership in the name of reform and the amelioration of society.

The unresolved confrontation between the artistic avant-garde and its antagonists turned into a festering wound afflicting the cultural and intellectual elites of Moscow. As a result, inside the shell of the official Soviet intelligentsia, mutually hostile trends and movements continued to spread. As the pro-Thaw forces evolved from straightforward anti-Stalinism to bolder and more critical interpretations of the Soviet past and present, the enemies of the Thaw experienced their own evolution. A growing number of writers and artists from the post-Stalin generation began to develop an ideological and cultural alternative to the cosmopolitan left inspired by the Revolution and the 1920s. They sought to rehabilitate select elements of Stalinist propaganda, especially the idea of Russian patriotism and Russian imperial greatness. They rediscovered a trove of Russian illiberal, chauvinist, and anti-Semitic concepts to support their stance. On both sides a frantic search for group cultural identity was taking place. Both sides increasingly turned to a different "usable past," from before and beyond the Soviet revolutionary experience. By 1965, nationalism, ethnic and nationalist identities, and anti-Semitism had begun to play a central role in widening the rift between the camps. These developments left Zhivago's children not only at loggerheads with the regime, but at war with themselves.

I was proud of Israel. I am a Russian writer
and I don't know a single word in Hebrew.
But the Jews are my people!

—Anatoly Rybakov, recalling his feelings in
    the 1960s

seven

Searching for Roots
1961-1967

SOMETIME IN the early 1960s, the writer Vladimir Soloukhin went, as
always, to have lunch in the Union of Soviet Writers' exclusive restaurant.
Then he discovered that he had to choose carefully where to sit. At one
table sat the people of the right, all party members, the writers who had
vehemently resisted the Thaw and the liberalization of cultural policies. At
another table dined the people of the left, the cultural vanguard of the time:
Okudzhava, Yevtushenko, Akhmadulina, Aksyonov, and others. Some of
them were party members, but they stood for liberalization of culture and
relaxation of party supervision of it. Up to that point Soloukhin had not
been particularly interested in cultural politics or ideological differences.
He felt enormous sympathy for Dudintsev and Yashin, the "sincere" writers
of the early Thaw. Suddenly, he realized that his place was at the table of the
rightists. Later he recalled that he had instinctively made the correct choice.
His new friends explained to him that the right-left division in Soviet literature "was really about" the division between genuine Russian writers, on
the one hand, and Jews or those who were related to Jews, on the other.[1]

The double trauma of Jewish suffering in the Second World War and Stalin's anti-Semitic campaigns made the Jewish Question a festering wound
in Soviet society. Stalin's postwar campaign to stigmatize and purge the
Jews as "cosmopolitans" had hit the cultural and intellectual elites especially
hard. The poets Slutsky and Samoilov, the journalist Agranovsky, numer-

ous avant-garde artists and literary critics and others in the liberal arts, not to mention lawyers and physicians, had their nationality registered as "Jewish" on their Soviet passports. Many others were registered as "Russians," yet had one parent or some relatives of "Jewish nationality." The anti-Semitic harassment clashed with their Soviet convictions, made them feel set apart from other Soviet citizens. At the same time, during Stalin's anti-cosmopolitanism campaign, some young ethnic Russians who had come to universities from the Russian countryside and later became intellectuals, like Soloukhin, learned to identify assimilated Jews as a hidden minority that was poisoning "the national spirit" of Russian culture. They also began to feel that Russians, the Russian Orthodox Church, and Russian culture were consistently victimized after the Revolution, and that the destruction of Russian peasant life was a terrible crime. It was only a step from there to blaming Jews for what had happened.[2]

The Jewish Question and the Thaw

Anti-Semitic sentiments were "especially strong among the so-called creative literary and artistic intelligentsia, for this group embodies the quintessence of the national spirit, yet also has a high concentration of Russified Jews."[3] In fact, anti-Semitism and opposition to it had played a central role in the formation and evolution of the Russian intelligentsia from the nineteenth century onward. Numerous young Jews were, in the words of Vladimir Jabotinsky, "madly, shamelessly in love with Russian culture" but hated the Russian state and resented Russian social and economic backwardness. Many of those who sought to abandon the world of the shtetl found their new community and religion in the radical-revolutionary and cosmopolitan wing of educated Russian society. Some became involved in politics. Others, like Pasternak's father, devoted themselves to European and Russian art and culture. The discrimination against Jews in tsarist Russia, the waves of anti-Semitic pogroms, the prominent role of secularized and assimilated Jews in Russian revolutionary-democratic movements, and the aversion of progressive intellectuals to "reactionary" expressions of Russian ethnic-nationalism—all these factors nourished philo-Semitism among Russian writers, artists, scientists, intellectuals, and students. In the left-liberal and socialist circles, anti-Semitic sentiments were considered a disgrace and grounds for excommunication. At the same time, the nationalist-minded people in the professions—in law and journalism, for instance—expressed concern about the rapidly growing presence of assimilated and nonassimilated Jews in their fields. They were afraid that with the growth of social mobility Russians would in their own empire be put at a decisive disadvantage to Jews.[4]

The perception, shared by the regime and its enemies, of the special role of Jews in the Bolshevik Revolution was bolstered during the 1920s by the enthusiasm that many educated secular Jews showed for the communist project: they filled many niches in Soviet political, cultural, and propaganda institutions. These Jews moved from the abolished Pale of Settlement to Moscow, Leningrad, and other major Russian cities, where they blended into multiethnic urban communities like the Arbat and mingled with the elements of the prerevolutionary Russian educated classes. They were an essential part of the postrevolutionary melting pot where many of Zhivago's children developed.[5] This Jewish migration to Russian cities, however, produced anti-Semitic ripples.

The Nazi policy of exterminating the Jews after the German attack on the Soviet Union aggravated the Jewish Question in Russia. In 1941–42 the Soviet media wrote about German atrocities against Jews, and even Stalin spoke in December 1941 about "Jewish pogroms." The evidence of German atrocities began to pour in to the Jewish Antifascist Committee (JAC), set up as an affiliate of the Sovinformburo and as one of the tools of the Kremlin's international propaganda. The JAC created a commission to collect evidence on the extermination of the Jews on Soviet territory and publish a "black book" about it. It became an enormous collective project under Ilya Ehrenburg's direction, and many writers collaborated on it. In 1944–45 the JAC, with the consent of Soviet authorities, made arrangements to publish the black book in the United States in English. There was also a Yiddish version, serialized in part in the Soviet newspaper *Der Emes* (Truth).[6]

During the war, anti-Semitism burgeoned in the Soviet army. It also spread through the congested communal apartments and kitchens of Moscow, and among groups of educated professionals.[7] It gradually dawned on the authors of the black book that the Soviet authorities did not want to recognize the Holocaust but rather insisted on treating Jewish suffering as part of the tragedy of the Soviet people as a whole. Stalin remained silent about the project. In May 1947, when the Soviet government suddenly supported the idea of an independent Jewish state in Palestine, the JAC leadership appealed to the Kremlin to publish the black book in Russian and other languages. In response, the command came down to close the project. In 1948 the head of the JAC, the actor Solomon Mikhoels, was murdered on Stalin's orders. Then, angered by the display of solidarity among Soviet Jews for the new state of Israel, Stalin disbanded the JAC and put its leaders, a group of Yiddish writers, poets, and intellectuals, on trial. Most of them were executed. Only Ehrenburg survived unscathed.[8]

The work on the black book and rise of state-sponsored anti-Semitism in the Soviet Union challenged the communist beliefs of a number of Russian-Jewish intellectuals. Among them was the writer Vasily Grossman. Born in 1905 in Berdichev, in the Jewish Pale of Settlement, Grossman belonged to the milieu of the educated and assimilated Jews who had embraced the Russian Revolution and Leninism. He continued to believe in communism during the years of Stalin's terror. Working as a war correspondent for *Krasnaia Zvezda* (Red Star), he observed scenes of anti-Semitism inside the Soviet army, yet these did not prepare him for the Holocaust. When he returned to Berdichev with the Soviet troops, he found no Jews remaining. The shtetls, their population, and their vibrant Yiddish culture were gone. Even Jewish cemeteries were destroyed. In September 1944 Grossman published an essay about Treblinka, a German camp for the mass extermination of Jews. In that essay, Grossman still explained the Holocaust as a product of "imperialism," the ultimate stage of capitalism. Yet the facts in the black book showed how easily genocidal anti-Semitism spread among the Soviet population, especially among Ukrainians and Cossacks. The growing persecution of Jews in the later years of Stalinism caused Grossman to compare the regimes of Hitler and Stalin. In 1956, after Khrushchev's denunciation of Stalin's crimes, Grossman began to write his epic book *Life and Fate,* in which he focused on the Jewish tragedy in the era of totalitarian regimes.[9]

During the Thaw, a large percentage of the urban-educated groups and cultural elites in the Soviet Union came from Jewish families. In 1959, according to the Soviet census and the passport system, there were 240,000 people of "Jewish nationality" in Moscow and 169,000 in Leningrad.[10] Most of them were highly educated and assimilated into Russian culture. Yet, the period of 1941–1953 left deep scars within these groups and drew deep lines between them and the rest of the society. Poet Boris Slutsky wrote about the effect of anti-Semitism during the last decade of Stalin's life on the assimilated Jews of the USSR, "We, the Jews, were lucky. We had no illusions about the evil we faced."[11] The lawyer Dina Kaminskaia wrote in her memoirs, "Anti-Semitism made us Jews distinct" from the rest of Soviet society. "It pushed us into the line of fire."[12] The sociologist Vladimir Shlapentokh recalled that the Jewish Question became pivotal to his selection of friends and colleagues. It meant estrangement from the Russians who were not philo-Semitic.[13]

At the same time, fear induced many educated and assimilated Jews to blend in with the Russian mainstream. They registered their children as Russians on their internal passports, especially when one parent.was ethnically Russian. Cultural figures, writers, and journalists concealed their Jewish names behind Russian pseudonyms and lived in constant fear of being "caught" and "unmasked" because of revived anti-Semitic sentiment.[14] Many Jews chose, as a survival tactic, to move to the forefront of Soviet orthodoxy. Among them were the infamous literary critic David Zaslavsky, who had lambasted Pasternak in 1958, and Sarah Valerius, who expelled abstract artists from the union in 1963.

The Thaw brought an immediate and personal improvement in the life of Soviet Jews. The parting of the Iron Curtain enabled them to restore contacts with their numerous relatives abroad, those who had left Russia's Jewish Pale in the early twentieth century and headed for the West or Palestine.[15] Although most Jews could not get permission to travel abroad because of their suspect "nationality," a growing number of artists and intellectuals of Jewish origin could, because of Khrushchev's "public diplomacy."[16] Maia Plisetskaia, the young star of the Bolshoi Ballet, had Jewish relatives in America, among them an uncle in New York. For years, she was excluded from the Bolshoi's trips abroad, but in 1959, after Khrushchev's intervention, Maia was able to dance with the Bolshoi in the United States and could finally embrace her American relatives.[17]

In 1955–56 a group of Jewish intellectuals and cultural figures petitioned the party authorities to rehabilitate the murdered members of the Jewish Antifascist Committee.[18] After Khrushchev's "secret speech" at the Twentieth Party Congress, the JAC members were rehabilitated, along with some other victims of Stalin's terror. The party department of culture recommended the gradual restoration of Yiddish cultural institutions.[19] Yet nothing came of its proposals. Khrushchev remained indecisive on this issue at best, having imbibed anti-Semitic stereotypes in the Ukraine, where he had grown up and worked for years. The restoration of Yiddish culture was also seen as a complication for the Soviet nationalist-ethnic policies in the cities, where many Jews lived, as well as in the multiethnic borderlands (western Ukraine and the Baltic republics), where the genocidal pogroms had taken place during the war. Another significant consideration was the Soviet alliance with Egypt, Syria, and other Arab regimes hostile to Israel that espoused blatant anti-Semitism.

Yiddish language and culture, not religion, had been the defining factor in a separate Jewish nationality and identity within Soviet society until the late 1940s. The disappearance of this culture turned Soviet Jews "invisible," prominent in Russian literature and history, but unmentionable in the present. Assimilated Jews were generally sophisticated urbanites who were not too enthusiastic about the restoration of Yiddish cultural institutions, the world of Sholom Aleichem, and the memories of the old shtetl. Like the Jews of Berlin and Vienna in the 1900s who had worshipped German-language *Kultur,* Moscow's assimilated Jews associated themselves with Russian high culture: Pushkin and Tolstoy, Dostoevsky and Chekhov, the Bolshoi Ballet, and Tchaikovsky's and Shostakovich's symphonies. Mikhail Agursky, a future ardent Zionist, recalled that in his formative years "the influence of Russian culture was the strongest. There was no Jewish culture as a separate phenomenon."[20] Many assimilated Jewish intellectuals, often the children of Old Bolsheviks and revolutionaries, continued to be inspired by Leninism and the principles of socialist internationalism.

Ehrenburg was the most important advocate for Jewish assimilation into Russian culture and the internationalist revolutionary tradition. The Holocaust and anti-Semitism in the Soviet Union made Ehrenburg feel responsible for Soviet Jewry. In early 1953 he sent a letter to Stalin, trying to dissuade him from deporting Jews.[21] In August 1960 Ehrenburg raised the issue of the Holocaust in the Soviet edition of *The Diary of Anne Frank.* The world-famous testimony about the Holocaust was published in the Soviet Union in two hundred thousand copies.[22] Jews and non-Jews who were exposed to anti-Semitism looked up to Ehrenburg as the highest moral authority. In 1958 Stalin's daughter Svetlana, a philo-Semite and a close friend of the Russian-Jewish poet Samoilov, sent a letter to Ehrenburg, thanking him for his attempts to show a way of truth to "the contemporary Soviet fake intelligentsia."[23] In January 1961, when he celebrated his seventieth birthday and was lionized by the government, the audience at the writers' union celebrated him as a hero of the Russian intelligentsia. Ivan Maisky, an Old Bolshevik with Jewish roots, compared him to Alexander Herzen. Paustovsky called him "our present-day conscience . . . who struggled against anti-Semitism," the greatest vice in any nation. Ehrenburg embraced Paustovsky and called anti-Semitism "the international language of fascism." He concluded, "I am a Russian writer. But as long as a single anti-Semite remains on earth, I will answer the question of nationality with pride: I am a Jew."[24]

Hearing the last words, many in the audience rose and applauded furiously. Ehrenburg was not happy with this reaction. He did not claim his Jewish identity to mobilize what he regarded as "the ghetto mentality" of his listeners. For him, an assimilated Jew, the liberation of Russian culture from Stalinist shackles, its reconnection to European culture, and the spread of culture from the intelligentsia to the masses became a new personal project. He lobbied for the translation and publication of Ernest Hemingway, William Faulkner, François Mauriac, and other foreign writers. Ehrenburg's project could give a new social identity to the intellectuals and artists in Russia, emancipate them from the past, and prevent them from experiencing future divisions along ethnic and religious lines.[25]

The older Russian intellectuals who had managed to preserve the ethos of the intelligentsia during the revolutionary era and Stalin's reign applauded Ehrenburg's program as well. Kornei Chukovsky recorded in his diary in April 1962 that "the struggle between the intelligentsia and the Black Hundreds"—the anti-Semitic conservative nationalists—was again at the center of Russian cultural politics. Another writer, Varlam Shalamov, who had returned from Stalin's camps, wrote in 1961 in his private notes, "Anti-Semitism and the intelligentsia belong to different worlds."[26] In fact, the clear-cut division between the *entire* intelligentsia and bigoted, ignorant anti-Semites was a myth, one that adapted the past to new political and social needs. This perception, however, became the credo of the leaders and followers of the cultural and artistic avant-garde of the early 1960s, among them many assimilated Jews. It was easier for them to explain public anti-Semitism of 1949–1953 as a brutal pogrom by a tyrannical ruler and the "dark masses," directed against intellectuals and people of high culture, everybody who stood out in appearance and manners from the crowd. It seemed that "enlightenment" of Soviet society was the only way toward freeing it from this terrible legacy.[27] During the scare over the supposed

Kremlin Doctors' Plot in early 1953, for the street mob any intelligent and educated person had been branded as a Jew. During the Thaw this equation resurfaced again: the supporters of Ehrenburg seemed to claim that most assimilated and educated Jews in Moscow and Leningrad were natural candidates for the intelligentsia.[28]

The publication of Yevtushenko's poem "Babi Yar" in the *Literaturnaia Gazeta* on September 19, 1961, solidified this growing perception. The poet pointed to the gap between the message of proletarian internationalism on the banners of the Soviet state and the anti-Semitic practices and sentiments of many card-carrying members of the Komsomol and the Communist Party. In his *Precocious Autobiography,* published in the West in 1963, Yevtushenko recalled that back in 1953 he broke off his friendship with Vladimir Kotov, a young poet and Komsomol activist, when Kotov revealed his anti-Semitism. During the Thaw, Yevtushenko wrote, he "came to realize that those who speak in the name of communism but in reality pervert its meaning are among its most dangerous enemies, perhaps even more dangerous than its enemies in the West."[29] Yevtushenko not only broke with Kotov. He excommunicated him from the ranks of both the Russian intelligentsia and "true" communists. It was typical of left-leaning intellectuals and artists while their identity was still evolving that a person could be both a party member and a part of the intelligentsia, as long as he or she stood against Stalinism and anti-Semitism.

"Babi Yar" evoked extremely passionate reactions from both sides of the divide. The poet received thirty thousand enthusiastic letters, from Jews and from Russians, who felt shame at the anti-Semitism in Russian history. The poem also stirred up anti-Semites, including Suslov and some other officials in the party's ideological apparatus. The editor of *Literaturnaia Gazeta* who published "Babi Yar" was fired. The journal *Literatura i Zhizn* (Literature and Life), the mouthpiece of the Russian branch of the writers' union, published a response by the poet Alexei Markov. He wrote, "As long as even one cosmopolite continues to trample Russian cemeteries / I am saying: I am Russian / And the ashes of my people are in my heart."[30] Anti-Semitic colleagues of Yevtushenko, puzzled that a "pure" Russian poet had sided with the Jews, explained the choice as stemming from his vanity and desire for international fame. Others "discovered" that Yevtushenko was "half-Jewish" (the poet himself claimed that he had no Jewish lineage). At a Komsomol conference of young poets, a group of nationalists attacked Yevtushenko like a pack of wolves. One of them reminded Yevtushenko that he lived on Russian soil and ate Russian bread. Immediately, another poet, a 1957 graduate of the School of Journalism at Leningrad University, came to Yevtushenko's defense: "This wretched tradition of anti-Semitism still lives and serves as a reservoir of fascism."[31]

In the early 1960s Ehrenburg, Yevtushenko, and other successful writers and poets from the left-wing cultural vanguard sought to stigmatize anti-Semitism and turn the tables on their enemies. These writers broke the public silence about the tragic fate of Jews during World War II and reminded Russians of the disgraceful harassment of Jews during Stalin's last years. People of Jewish lineage and those without united around this common cause. The Gentiles Anatoly Kuznetsov and Viktor Nekrasov and the Jew Boris Slutsky published novels, articles, and poems describing the Nazi massacres of Jews in Kiev, Berdichev, and other places in Ukraine. Most famously, the Gentile Dmitry Shostakovich composed music to the words of "Babi Yar" and included the poem in his Thirteenth Symphony. The first performance was scheduled for December 18, 1962, at the Moscow Conservatory. This event took place in the shadow of Khrushchev's crackdown on the younger artists at Manege. Yevtushenko bowed to the pressure of party authorities and changed some lines in the poem. Still, the cultural communities in Moscow feared a last-minute cancellation of the performance. The final rehearsals attracted huge crowds, many of them assimilated Jews. The premiere of the symphony electrified the tense hall of the Moscow Conservatory, where it was performed without television crews or radio microphones. As the last chords died away, the jubilant audience acclaimed two Russians, the fifty-year-old Shostakovich and the twenty-eight-year-old Yevtushenko, with thunderous applause, not only for their art, but for their brave decision to identify with the persecuted Jews.

The project of re-creating the Russian intelligentsia in accordance with the principles of philo-Semitism, however, raised difficult questions. Which parts of Russian cultural and historical legacy could be deemed acceptable and laudable, and which had to be condemned or even excised? During the 1920s the merging of assimilated Jews into the revolutionary Soviet intelligentsia had accompanied attempts to eradicate the old intelligentsia, especially the "reactionary" Russian imperial legacy in historiography, literature, music, and other fields. Starting in the mid-1930s, and especially during World War II, expunged figures and elements of the Russian past were restored to public prominence and became part of the Russocentric interpretation of official Soviet history and culture. It is a telling comment on the early sixties that some older mentors of Zhivago's children, in their struggle against Stalinists and anti-Semites, made approving reference to the controversial radical attempts of the 1920s to excise parts of the past. At the conference on the art of socialist realism in November 1962 the film-maker Mikhail Romm, who had been born into a family of assimilated Jews and Bolsheviks, spoke from the heart against the threat of anti-Semitic Russian nationalism. He alluded to "certain traditions that were imposed in our country," among them "the one of playing the Overture of Tchaikovsky's Symphony 1812 twice a year." This musical opus, Romm explained, expresses "the idea of the triumph of orthodox religion and autocracy over the Revolution." Romm asked, "Why should the Soviet power humiliate the Marseillaise, the marvelous hymn of the French Revolution, by drowning it out with the noise of church bells? Why should it celebrate the triumph of Czarist ideology, the ideology of the 'Black Hundreds'"?[32] Following this logic, the sixties intelligentsia would have had to banish many of Dostoevsky's works, the entire legacy of Russian conservative-religious and nationalist philosophers, writers, and journalists, and perhaps even the Russian ballet.

Not surprisingly, enemies of the left-wing intelligentsia immediately saw an opportunity to "defend Russian culture" against these awkward attacks. They wrote that Romm "rejected all of Russia's traditions aside from revolutionary internationalism." In his response, Romm brought the Jewish Question to the center of discussion. He referred to Khrushchev's revelation that Stalin was "an anti-Semite at the bottom of his soul." He admitted that "after the October Revolution I forgot for a long time that I am Jewish by passport." He was reminded of this only in 1943 when his brother was hounded by prejudice to the point of committing suicide. Romm concluded his letter with the assurance that "times have changed" and added, "We have distanced ourselves considerably [from the Stalinist past]." Nevertheless, the ideological and cultural departments of the CC CPSU accused Romm of making pronouncements with a "blatantly tendentious, nationalist [that is, Jewish] character."[33]

The authorities reacted to Ramm's speech with anger. Khrushchev, the ideological bureaucrats, and state censors insisted that the Jewish Question did not exist in the USSR and viewed every expression of Jewish identity as a sign of Zionist influence.[34] In April 1964 the editorial board of the journal *Nash Sovremennik* (Our Contemporary) attempted to publish a poem by Rimma Kazakova, "Reflections on the Grave of My Grandfather in Sevastopol." A 1954 graduate of the history department at Leningrad State University, Kazakova wrote that her family was Jewish-Russian and asserted that there was no Jewish Question for her or other "children of mixed blood." Internationalism was "in their blood." Kazakova expressed the feelings of many intellectuals and artists of her generation, "half-Jews" and "half-Russians" whose Soviet identity was the product of education and choice. The censors, arguing that the poem was "imbued with the idea of some kind of superiority of people of 'mixed blood' over others," banned the poem.[35]

At the meeting with the intelligentsia in December 1962 in Lenin Hills, Khrushchev, probably primed by anti-Semitic colleagues, linked "rotten liberalism" to the Jewish influence. Khrushchev singled out Ehrenburg and Romm, whose Jewish lineage was known to everybody, for criticism. After denying the rumors about anti-Semitism in the Soviet Union, the premier said that among "the enemies of the people" in Stalin's day the leading group had consisted of members of the "Jewish nation." Then, turning to the 1956 events in Hungary and Poland, he alleged that Jews had played a "fateful role" there. Khrushchev's ramblings, his attribution of subversive qualities to the "Jewish nation," which were reminiscent of Stalin's anti-Semitic campaign, drove Ehrenburg into a deep depression and dismayed even some of Khrushchev's advisers.[36] Khrushchev's reaction was dictated not only by crude stereotypes. He also sincerely hoped to sweep the Jewish Question under the rug, for fear that public recognition of it would open a Pandora's box. Despite official Soviet optimism, many powerful and dangerous nationalist undercurrents existed, including Russian nationalism, that threatened to divide the Soviet Union.[37]

"Russian Patriots"

The Jewish Question became a major factor cementing the solidarity of the left-wing cultural vanguard and its mass following in the early 1960s. At the same time, the issue remained a source of permanent tension that generated ambiguity at best, and Russian nationalist resentment at worst.

It was inevitable that during the Thaw Russian intellectuals would attempt to search for a new version of nationalism that would stand "in contrast to the official Stalinist version of the people and patriotism."[38] Modern nationalist ideas came to Russia relatively late from Europe. During the second half of the nineteenth century, attempts to create a national Russian art and to compose "authentic" Russian music and opera were popular among the liberal, secular, and socialist Russian intellectuals, who viewed them as steps toward cultural reunification of educated and Westernized elites with the common people who preserved ancient Russian traditions. Very quickly, however, conservative-religious, national-ethnic, and messianic trends began to sprout. Nikolai Danilevsky, Fyodor Dostoevsky, Vasily Rozanov, Konstantin Leontiev, Vladimir Solovyov, and Georgy Florensky had thought of Russians as a superior community of Orthodox Christians, as opposed to the "Latinized" West. During the revolution of 1905, with the rise of democratic politics, mass-based Russian nationalism assumed anti-Western, antiliberal, xenophobic, and anti-Semitic overtones. The infamous Black Hundred movement represented a grassroots phenomenon similar to anti-Semitic protofascist movements emerging at the same time in Europe—above all in Germany, France, and the Austro-Hungarian Empire. Rejected by the liberal and socialist segments of the Russian intelligentsia, Russian nationalism attracted more conservative and religious-conservative intellectuals. Most of them rejected the Black Hundred pogroms and barbarism, yet they began to discuss the need for a new "Russian idea" to replace the outdated absolutism—some combination of reformed Orthodoxy and constitutional monarchy with Russian communitarian traditions.[39]

The Bolshevik triumph in the Revolution and the Civil War did not end the division. Numerous Russian poets, novelists, and philosophers—among them Nikolai Berdiaev, Andrei Bely, Sergei Bulgakov, Fyodor Stepun, and Semyon Frank—sought to find a third way between Russian "fascism" and the Bolshevik ideology. They believed it could be a Russian version of Christian socialism or Christian democracy. In 1922 the Bolsheviks, fearing the subversive power of these ideas, expelled the thinkers from Soviet Russia.[40] The search for a liberal-nationalist Russian idea was brutally aborted. For the next several decades, only the regime itself decided how and when elements of Bolshevik "internationalism" should be combined with Russian nationalistic themes. And among Russian anti-Bolshevik émigrés there was an enormous reservoir of anti-Semitic sentiment. Many held Lenin and Trotsky responsible, along with other revolutionaries who came from the milieu of assimilated Jews, for the misfortunes of émigrés and imparted to European fascists and Nazis their hatred of the Jews.[41]

Initially, communist internationalism, propagated by the Bolsheviks, succeeded in driving Russian national feelings underground. There seemed to be no room for Russian identity in Soviet culture and ideology. The Bolshevik regime favored other ethnic groups over the Russians. While being discriminated against culturally, economically, and politically, the Russian peasantry had to carry the main burden of the Soviet "affirmative action empire."[42] Yet a powerful nationalist undercurrent continued to grow among Russians, above all among the survivors of the intelligentsia. Stalin skillfully made use of it, first in the struggle against his Jewish and left-wing opponents in the party, and then in the consolidation of his regime after collectivization. Eventually, Stalin placed Russians at the center of the Soviet empire, as "big brother" to other ethnic groups in the empire.[43] In reality, Stalin feared Russian nationalism as a potential political threat and continued to react harshly to the danger of "Russian opposition" to his regime. In 1949 he arrested and executed hundreds of party officials of Russian ethnic background, mostly in Leningrad (the so-called Leningrad affair), on trumped-up charges of Russian nationalism and separatism.[44] Ultimately, Stalin succeeded remarkably: while he paid lip service to Russian patriotic themes, his regime squeezed the last resources from the Russian peasantry. He channeled Russian nationalist sentiments into his imperial project. Long after his death, Russian nationalists among artists, intellectuals, historians, and writers continued to believe that Stalin had begun toward the end of his life to transform the USSR into Great Russia. Even some nationalist Russian émigrés came to view Stalin's autocracy and imperialism as a necessary evil, the only way to revive Russia's greatness.[45]

During the Thaw some Russian émigrés managed to return to Russia and brought with them a variety of nationalist ideas. One of them was Alexander Kazem-Bek, who clashed with Ehrenburg in 1957 on the pages of the *Literaturnaia Gazeta*. In his earlier days in emigration, Kazem-Bek had advocated the transition of the Soviet Union into a "Russian federation" with the tsar leading the Soviets and the proletariat. This tsar, he hoped, would liberate the people "from the yoke of Red and Yellow parasites," that is, Jews and Asians.[46] Another famous returnee, Vasily Shulgin, had been a prominent monarchist before the Revolution, a fierce enemy of the liberal and socialist intelligentsia.[47] Kazem-Bek and Shulgin became mentors of the so-called Russian patriots in the ranks of the sixties intelligentsia.

During the Thaw a number of Stalinist stalwarts, notorious for their participation in the anticosmopolitan campaign, formed the right flank of the Soviet intelligentsia and posed as the defenders of Russian culture from Western influences and their agents. In the world of letters the hub for the Russian patriots was the Russian branch of the Union of Soviet Writers, established with Khrushchev's permission in December 1957. Its weekly *Literatura i Zhizn* and the journal *Nash Sovremennik* fiercely opposed "cosmopolitan" influences and the Thaw in general. The leading figures of the right, Mikhail Sholokhov and Leonid Sobolev, once promising writers, were cynical and opportunistic operators who sponsored younger writers with a nationalistic and anti-Semitic bent.[48] Some Russian patriots of Stalinist vintage also met at the house of the sculptor Yevgeny Vuchetich, an anti-Semite who used disparaging expressions about Jews even in his correspondence with party officials.[49] The Russian patriots sought to warn the party leadership about the Jewish influence in Soviet art and literature. Even the writers who had no Jewish roots, such as Konstantin Simonov, were suspect in their eyes.[50] In 1962 Ivan Shevtsov, the notoriously anti-Semitic journalist from Vuchetich's circle, penned the novel *Plant Louse (Tlia)*. In it he described how a handful of Russian "realists" had to fight against a host of experienced art critics, all of them Jews, who sympathized with abstract art. The main authority in the eyes of these Jews was a character called Lev Barselonsky, obviously modeled on Ehrenburg. After Khrushchev's crackdown on the artists in December 1962, *Plant Louse* was published in one hundred thousand copies, which immediately sold out. Shevtsov received hundreds of letters of support. *Plant Louse* was the first anti-Jewish, anti-intelligentsia, xenophobic novel in the history of Soviet literature.[51]

Many in the bureaucracy shared the anti-Semitism of the rightists, but their crude expressions were embarrassing, and their unsanctioned activism violated party rules. The Kremlin reacted negatively to Shevtsov's tract, especially after Western European communist parties, notably in France and Italy, protested to Moscow that such publications damaged their ties to intellectuals and hurt them politically. Shevtsov's nefarious novel quickly became a source of parodies and bitter jokes among the Moscow intellectuals and artists.

A great many of the older Russian intellectuals brought up in the prerevolutionary liberal milieu were scandalized by Shevtsov's anti-Semitic tract. One of them, the academician Dmitry Likhachev, a senior scholar at the Institute of Russian Literature in Leningrad, began to achieve public prominence in the early 1960s as the leading expert on ancient Russian literature and the defender of the Russian cultural patrimony, including the cathedrals and churches scheduled for destruction. Likhachev's idea of Russian patriotism stood in sharp opposition to xenophobic anti-Semitism. He believed that Russia had always been part of European culture, through ancient Greece, Rome, and the Byzantine Empire. Much like the intellectuals expelled in 1922, he dreamed of blending the best European cultural traditions with Russian "spirituality," into some kind of tolerant and modern social Christianity. During the Thaw Likhachev and other Russian Slavists joined the international network of Slavic studies and corresponded with numerous Western scholars. These Slavists brought up a new generation of scholars, passionate patriots devoted to prerevolutionary Russia, who rejected xenophobic and anti-Semitic mythology.[52]

Yet there were not enough mentors of Likhachev's type. Instead of evolving in the direction in which Russian national thinkers of 1922, as well as Likhachev, had pointed, a number of the postwar intellectuals chose the chauvinist, anti-Semitic type of Russian nationalism. This group of Russian nationalists were far more educated and sophisticated than Shevtsov. They were also different from their Stalinist predecessors and the émigrés. Above all, they belonged to the same generation and sometimes same milieu as their future antagonists on the left. These nationalists were war veterans and postwar graduates of Moscow and Leningrad universities who joined the fresh cohorts of professionals—among them scientists, engineers, writers, and journalists.[53] When they discovered that many places in the professions were occupied by Jews, these Russians reacted by resorting to an anti-Semitism of convenience.[54] The new generation of Russian patriots had numerous sponsors and followers within the party, the KGB, the Komsomol, and other branches of the Soviet bureaucracy. Those people challenged the right of the cultural "leftists" of the early 1960s to call themselves an intelligentsia. The result was a contest for predominance in the private and semipublic cultural sphere in Russia, no longer completely controlled by the state.[55]

In the memoirs and assessments of their opponents on the left, the Russian patriots were often treated as oddballs or apostates with inadequate education and Russian peasant roots. Otherwise, how was it possible to explain why somebody like Vladimir Soloukhin, who was not a cynical careerist and who possessed some literary talent, was not on their side?[56] In fact, the younger Russian patriots had different social and cultural roots. Many of them had not grown up surrounded by the culture and myths of St. Petersburg's and Moscow's intelligentsia. Born rather in villages and provincial towns around Russia, they felt marginal among the urbanites and began to develop their own networks. And they gravitated toward different cultural and ideological landmarks. They did not belong to the *stiliagi,* nor did they worship American jazz or dream American dreams. Trips abroad and the parting of the Iron Curtain made a strong impression on them but also accentuated their sense of marginalization, resentment, and alienation from the West.

During the Thaw some of the younger Russian patriots began to publish their first novels and poems in the spirit of "sincerity in literature." The most articulate ideologues of Russian nationalism came from the cohort of Moscow and Leningrad university students that had been politically awakened by Khrushchev's secret speech, Dudintsev's novel, and other shocks of 1956. Yet gradually they came around to a different cultural and ideological platform. They felt attracted to Russian philosophers and writers, rather than to Hemingway, Remarque, or translated Western novels. Many of them admired the poetry of Boris Pasternak, but Pasternak's spiritual hero from the sophisticated cosmopolitan milieu remained alien to them. They also looked for scapegoats who could be made responsible for Russia's tragic past. When they read Russian classical literature, they considered their most influential author Fyodor Dostoevsky and valued especially his long-suppressed work *The Writer's Diary,* in which he lashed out at Jews and other enemies of Russian Orthodoxy. Another influential book would be Ivan Bunin's *Accursed Days,* in which the embittered writer, a future Nobel Prize winner, castigated Jews for the Red Terror and the destruction of the Russian nation.[57]

Russian Orthodoxy began to attract many Russian patriots, even though most of them had been educated as atheists and become members of the party. Silhouettes of ancient Russian cloisters and churches that had survived destruction under Stalin and Khrushchev, old cemeteries, the liturgy, and church music touched them. Mikhail Lobanov, a Moscow university graduate from a large peasant family in southeastern Russia and a future ideologue of xenophobic Russian nationalism, recalled that he first went to churches out of curiosity. Gradually, he realized that Russian Orthodoxy was a core part of his identity. At the end of 1962 he had a "born again" epiphany and came to the Christian faith.[58] Khrushchev's campaign of militant atheism and the new wave of destruction of Russian churches angered and alienated such Russian patriots.

For nationalist-minded Russian intellectuals and artists, trips to the Russian countryside, rather than trips to the West, often became the starting point in the search for identity. Stalin's repression of the peasantry had resulted in a striking segregation, almost a form of apartheid, between urban and rural life. Children of peasants who moved to Moscow and Leningrad tried at first to burn their bridges and repress their origins. A rural accent and country manners evoked contempt among the sophisticated urbanites.[59] These attitudes, however, began to change during the 1950s and early 1960s. New city dwellers began to acknowledge their peasant roots and suddenly felt pangs of guilt at the sight of village misery and degradation.

A star of the new crop of Russian nationalists in the early 1960s was the young artist Ilya Glazunov. He had grown up in Leningrad in a family with roots in the Baltic nobility and the class of wealthy merchants. In contrast to many young intellectuals, who read Marx and Lenin, Glazunov passionately hated the Soviet regime and Marxism-Leninism. He was one of the first among educated young Russians to meet and talk with the returned émigrés Kazem-Bek and Shulgin. His wife Nina Vinogradova, a relative of the famous art critic Alexander Benois, was an equally passionate Russian nationalist. The couple traveled to the Russian countryside and ancient Russian cities (at that time in neglect and disrepair), collected and restored old icons (thus saving them from destruction), and propagated Russian religious art. At the time of the state atheistic campaign and the fascination of many young intellectuals with Western avant-garde art this behavior was a striking form of dissent. Glazunov's artistic talent was quite modest, but he excelled at networking and became a tireless self-promoter. In 1957, when he was still a student at the Art Institute in Leningrad, he had already arranged an exhibition for himself in Moscow. Soon Ilya and Nina moved to the Soviet capital and made many influential friends there.[60] Thanks to his friends in the Komsomol and the party, who found Glazunov's paintings consonant with their cultural and ethnic roots, the artist made connections with Western communists. The latter also liked his paintings *à la russe*. In 1961 Mikhail Gorbachev and his wife Raisa, with Komsomol delegates and a group of Italian communists, came to Glazunov's apartment to view his works. They became admirers of the artist.[61]

Invited to the party's forum on the future of Soviet arts and literature,

The artist Ilya Glazunov, who promoted the resurgence of Russian nationalist ideas. He passionately hated Marxism-Leninism and the leftist cultural vanguard. Glazunov proposed to rebuild the Moscow cathedral, destroyed under Stalin (Courtesy of V. Gritsiuk, Moscow).

Glazunov took advantage on December 26, 1962, of Khrushchev's attack on abstract artists to address the party leadership and the cultural establishment with a program for the restoration of Russian pride and Russia's cultural heritage. He said that Soviet youth was tired of didacticism and hackneyed, syrupy socialist realism, and as a consequence they were searching for something new outside Russia. The core problem was that young Russians were "separated from their roots." In Glazunov's opinion, the only antidote to the spread of Western cosmopolitan influences and nihilism was the revival of national Russian culture. After articulating his entire agenda for the restoration of Russian historical monuments and churches, Glazunov concluded with the appeal—and this was the most important part— to rebuild the colossal cathedral of Christ the Savior in downtown Moscow. The cathedral had been demolished in 1934, in accordance with Stalin's plans for the reconstruction of Moscow, but the Russian patriots blamed the demolition on Jewish influences within the Kremlin leadership. Glazunov's words were drowned out by applause from the audience. The proposal to restore an important cathedral in Moscow was extremely bold, for he made it in the wake of Khrushchev's atheistic campaign and the destruction of hundreds of churches.[62]

For the party ideological authorities Glazunov's art appeared to be a healthy antidote to underground abstract art. In early 1963, at the official invitation of the Italian Communist Party, Glazunov took his works to Italy. There, he began to criticize modernism and advocated the "restoration of Russian art" based on "national values." While in Italy, he organized (without asking permission of Soviet authorities) an exhibition of his works. It became a sensation. Glazunov became an international star, permitted, like Yevtushenko, to travel abroad and participate in Soviet public diplomacy.

Glazunov's public stand in favor of restoration of Russian churches reflected the demands of the growing movement among Moscow artists and intellectuals to protect the historic downtown from Khrushchev's modernization plans. At that time the Arbat district was targeted by the Moscow authorities for demolition, with the aim of creating a broad avenue from the Kremlin to the government country houses. The impending disappearance of the historic area, considered by many educated Muscovites to be their "small motherland," galvanized people to protest and petition the government.[63] Simultaneously, hundreds of Russian painters, architects, academicians, and historians of art and ancient history began to protest the barbaric destruction of Russian churches and cathedrals by zealous party officials in the course of Khrushchev's atheistic campaign. The protesters sent petitions to the authorities, demanding that they "stop the criminal nihilism toward our cultural heritage," and noted that vandalism of Russian historical objects contrasted with the preservation of similar objects in Georgia and other non-Russian republics. One of the petitions concluded, "The construction of religious buildings was the only way our ancestors had to memorialize their labors and heroes. And we must not be 'Ivans who forget their kin,' but rather, as respectful children and zealous owners, use these monuments for our patriotic and aesthetic education."[64]

Glazunov became one of the public leaders of this movement. Few at that time were familiar with his ideological views. Vladimir Soloukhin in his fictionalized autobiography, published in the West in the 1980s, wrote that his conversations with Ilya Glazunov and his wife Nina had transformed his views. In the late 1950s Soloukhin had remained a Soviet patriot and believed Khrushchev's rhetoric about a "return to true Leninism." Glazunov "opened his eyes" to the amazing wealth and potential of imperial Russia, allegedly aborted by the Revolution. He also brought him around to the idea that monarchy was the only "organic" and natural form of government for Russia, by contrast with Western-style democracy or socialism. "We were brainwashed from childhood on," recalled Soloukhin, to think "that Russia had been the most backward and pitiful state in the world, the poorest and most ignorant one. Yet from various readings, clippings, and books that [Glazunov] pressed into my hands, I began to perceive that it had been a powerful, technically advanced, cultured, and flourishing country." Soloukhin began to wonder, Why had it become necessary to destroy such a country and its peasantry? And who had done it? Among his friends and trusted students, Glazunov tirelessly denounced Lenin, Trotsky, and the Bolshevik Revolution. One of his students wrote in his diary in August 1963, "I do not know any other person besides Ilya Glazunov who speaks in such a way about Lenin and his 'gang' causing innumerable woes to Russia. Bronstein-Trotsky, Sverdlov, Stalin, and the currently ruling Nikita Khrushchev—all of them are in Glazunov's profound conviction servants of the devil."[65]

Indeed, the Russian patriots ended up detesting Khrushchev as much as their enemies on the left flank of the nascent intelligentsia did. The nationalists scorned the party bureaucracy's attempts to bring the opposing sides of the cultural elites together. The party secretariat, in turn, was quick to let the overzealous "patriots" know that they should march to its tune, not the other way around.[66] The importance of preserving good relations with Western communists overruled the temptation to crush the cultural underground and "Zionist tendencies" in the intelligentsia. The publication of anti-Semitic literature was forbidden, in order to offset allegations of anti-Semitism in the USSR.[67] Gradually, the Russian patriots concluded that the Soviet regime was encouraging Zionist elements in their struggle against the "true" Russian intelligentsia. The Russian nationalists believed, however, that the future would bring them more victories. In addition to legalizing the movement for the preservation of historical monuments in Russia, they took over the editorial board of the literary journal *Molodaia Gvardia* (Young Guard), where in the next several years they would prepare their ideological attack against the party's cultural policies and against the "cosmopolitan" tendencies in literature, the arts, and social life.[68]

The Intelligentsia United?

The emerging split between the philo-Semitic left and the anti-Semitic right still appeared to many educated men and women in the post-Stalin generation a vestige of the past, rather than a harbinger of the future. These people rejected xenophobia and wanted cultural freedoms but still felt a moral commitment to the Soviet communist project. Even those who experienced increasing alienation from the official ideology and rhetoric were still reluctant to take a decisive leap, whether toward liberal democracy on the left or toward neo-Nazism or blatant chauvinism on the right. The vast majority of Zhivago's children still clung to their Soviet identity.

This ambivalent state of mind gave rise to perhaps the greatest cultural undertaking of the Soviet sixties: an attempt to reassert the ethos of the prerevolutionary intelligentsia in the realm of literature. Tvardovsky's *Novy Mir* was at the forefront of this effort. The motto of the journal was simple: "We publish only high-quality literature," yet the simplicity was deceptive. In fact, Tvardovsky and the circle of writers, poets, and critics that emerged around *Novy Mir* challenged the regime's monopoly on defining what was true literature and what was trash. This stance did not require any dangerous political confrontation with the authorities, and yet it reaffirmed the intelligentsia's moral authority and its special mission to enlighten and guide the Russian reading public.[69] Equally important, given the vital role of the Jewish Question and Russian nationalism, was that *Novy Mir* offered a cultural and moral common ground for those writers and other intellectuals who represented divergent ideas and narratives.

From a distance of many years, it is apparent that Tvardovsky's *Novy Mir* did not intend to discard the Soviet identity. Rather, the journal and its numerous followers hoped to save this identity by filling it with non-Bolshevik and anti-Stalinist values, above all the "democratic and humanist" traditions of socialist and left-liberal intelligentsia of the previous century.[70] One of the key elements in this attempt was the profound conviction that only a sincere and "truthful" exploration of the Stalinist era could provide the basis for the future existence of *Soviet* internationalist and humanist society. Tvardovsky gradually came to a firm conclusion: the ill-educated bureaucracy needed the intelligentsia as a mediator between the state and the people. Only true artists and writers could help to prepare the moral and spiritual ground for communism.

Tvardovsky's background as a Russian muzhik and the personal wounds inflicted by the tragedy of collectivization seemed to make him a natural ally of the Russian patriots. He felt that the world of the Russian countryside had been more vibrant, spiritual, and rich with remarkable human characters than the world of his young urban contemporaries was. He realized that collectivization had obliterated that world forever, and this realization distressed him.[71] Tvardovsky did not share the fascination of many young people in the left-wing cultural vanguard with Europe and the United States. He did not speak any foreign languages and whenever he had to join official delegations going to the West, he felt alien and lonely abroad.

Initially, Tvardovsky regarded with cold reserve the attempts of Ehrenburg, Paustovsky, and other intellectuals to place the issue of anti-Semitism at the center of the intelligentsia's agenda. In 1960, on reading the manuscript by the Russian-Jewish writer Vasily Grossman, Tvardovsky was of two minds. Grossman's novel *Life and Fate* was about the tragic fate of Jews caught between the Nazi and Soviet regimes. Tvardovsky wrote in his diary that the novel shook him, and yet he felt "bizarre spiritual resistance" to the central message of the novel. For Tvardovsky not the fate of Jews in World War II but the tragedy of the Russian Revolution and the destruction of the Russia peasantry loomed as the primary focus of his thinking. He did not believe that it was possible to find a solution "for all the complications of global bloodletting, the clash of socialism and fascism, in the light of this special, all-determining problem [of anti-Semitism]."[72] In February 1961 the KGB seized the manuscript of Vasily Grossman's novel *Life and Fate*. It was a terrible loss for Russian literature, yet not for Tvardovsky, who refused to accept the centrality of the Holocaust theme.[73] Tvardovsky realized that many on the staff of his journal disagreed with him. In September 1961 he wrote in his diary, "After all, [they] do not like me too much, although they need me as an influential figure. Their sympathies are with Pasternak, Grossman, etc."[74] Tvardovsky's sympathies were with Solzhenitsyn, and the two men shared instinctive mistrust of cosmopolitan intellectuals, indifferent to the fate of traditional Russian culture and the peasantry.[75]

Nevertheless, it was Tvardovsky who turned *Novy Mir* into a cultural space where radically different, potentially conflicting narratives coexisted, instead of encouraging mutually hostile camps. The semifascist ideas of the Russian patriots, with their virulent anti-Semitism, repelled Tvardovsky. By contrast with Solzhenitsyn, he was rather indifferent to the Orthodox faith. And he disliked Dostoevsky's *Writer's Diary* and Ivan Bunin's anti-Semitic and anti-Bolshevik vituperations.[76] Tvardovsky firmly believed in focusing on high-quality literature, no matter who wrote it and what the ideology behind it was. During the 1960s the journal published Ehrenburg's memoirs and the works of Aksyonov and other stars from the leftist camp during the Thaw. At the same time *Novy Mir* published the Russian "village writers" Fyodor Abramov, Alexander Yashin, Vasily Shukshin, Viktor Astafiev, and Boris Mozhaev. These writers were horrified by Khrushchev's agricultural policies, which had killed the traditional Russian peasant spirit. In 1963 Abramov published in *Novy Mir* a bold critique of Khrushchev's policies and urged the authorities to provide peasants with equal rights, such as freedom to travel around the country. Abramov showed that the regime of apartheid had led peasants to abandon the countryside and migrate to the cities or descend into alcoholism. Alexander Yashin, the hero of the early literary Thaw, published a story about a peasant wedding. It portrayed the peasantry as second-class citizens, denied a good education, addicted to drink, mired in poverty, and completely at the mercy of local authorities, who exploited the peasants' labor. Yashin moved beyond the 1950s criticism of the Stalinist bureaucracy to question the promises and performance of the Soviet regime from Stalin to Khrushchev. Chernichenko and other "honest" journalists of the sixties, who had observed the mistakes made in the Virgin Lands, contributed similar critical publications to *Novy Mir*.[77]

In the absence of *Novy Mir*, one can hardly imagine these authors conversing with jazz-loving imitators of Hemingway in Moscow. Some of the writers might otherwise have joined ranks with anti-Semitic Russian nationalists (indeed, Viktor Astafiev would do so later). The journal's humanistic umbrella allowed for coexistence of separate narratives of tragedy and resentment, one related to the Jews, another to the Russians. One of the literary critics writing for *Novy Mir* attended the celebration for the anniversary journal and later remarked that he had never seen so many talented people representing such a variety of experience, views, and ideological orientations in one room. "It was bizarre to see them at one table."[78]

Eventually, Tvardovsky succeeded, because he amended Ehrenburg's concept of the Russian intelligentsia. *Novy Mir*'s audience was a multiethnic community steeped in the common love of Russian language and culture, with various ethnic and racial biases, yet not fixated on them. The mission of the journal was to disclose the truth about Stalinist crimes against Russians and non-Russians, intellectuals and peasants. And the journal paid a price for its success. *Novy Mir*, as a towering literary and moral authority among the reading public, became the favorite target of Stalinists and xenophobic Russian patriots, with justification. The editors of the journals *Oktiabr* (October) and *Ogonyok* (Little Light), Kochetov and Sofronov, tried hard to attract village writers and even Solzhenitsyn to their side, by appealing to their "Russian instincts" and estrangement from the left-wing cultural agenda. Yet only *Novy Mir* could offer a writer a genuine public recognition and an aura of moral authority and cultural independence.[79] In his public attack on *Novy Mir* in March 1963 the Komsomol secretary Sergei Pavlov specifically criticized works by Ehrenburg, Solzhenitsyn, Aksyonov, Voinovich, Nekrasov, and Yashin.[80] Khrushchev, although he liked Tvardovsky and had authorized the publication of his anti-Stalin poem, could not consistently sponsor the journal. In the spring of 1964, attacks against *Novy Mir* rose to new heights. Tvardovsky suffered a painful defeat when his favorite writer, Solzhenitsyn, lost the competition for the Lenin Prize for literature in 1964. Khrushchev, whose domestic position was weakening daily, decided not to throw his weight behind Solzhenitsyn's candidacy.[81]

The attacks from the right and from the bureaucracy drove *Novy Mir* to seek support among its audience. The readership of the journal in the mid-1960s amounted to at least three to five million, an extraordinary figure for a highbrow literary journal. Even with the cap on its circulation placed at 1.2 million copies, the journal was very hard to obtain. The authorities limited subscriptions for ideological reasons; people signed up in public libraries weeks, sometimes months, in advance to read the latest issue. *Novy Mir* became a kind of membership card. Alexeyeva recalls that "the light blue cover of *Novy Mir* sticking out of a coat pocket became a cultural marker of the liberal intellectual." Two strangers reading *Novy Mir* on a bus no longer regarded each other as strangers. "If you talked for a few minutes, you discovered that you had mutual friends."[82] Vera Novoselova, a high school teacher, wrote in May 1964 after reading a new issue of *Novy Mir,* "What have these scoundrels [Soviet bureaucrats and grassroots Stalinists] done to the country! How they have defiled our humanity and soul!"[83] The volume of the letters that readers sent to *Novy Mir* was tremendous. They shared the most intimate and terrible stories from their past, as if they were confessions. The journal became the place where all the dreams and myths of glasnost as an honest public discussion, of the intelligentsia as a civic-minded community, seemed to materialize.[84]

The most passionate supporters of *Novy Mir,* however, were the followers of the left-leaning cultural vanguard in Moscow and Leningrad, the scientists and technical-engineering groups who had rediscovered the ethos of the intelligentsia in the late 1950s and early 1960s. The journal's most talented critics, Vladimir Lakshin, Igor Vinogradov, and later Yuri Burtin, became the darlings of these readers. Every meeting between readers and the journal team was a memorable event. At conferences of the editorial team with readers in Novosibirsk and nearby Akademgorodok, the scientists from the Siberian branch of the Academy of Sciences demonstrated their loyalty and public support for the journal. "Furiously engaged audience," wrote Tvardovsky in his private journal.[85] At a meeting with readers in Leningrad on March 4, 1964, the audience, according to witnesses, expressed unanimous adoration of Tvardovsky, Solzhenitsyn, and the journal. This audience met any hint of criticism of the journal with hisses and boos.[86]

The willingness of *Novy Mir* to explore the Stalinist past, including anti-Semitism, tapped into an enormous wellspring of public emotion. Tvardovsky rejected the claim that *Novy Mir* was a journal for a narrow circle of left-wing intelligentsia and those obsessed by the Jewish Question.[87] Yet educated and assimilated Jews made up a sizable segment of the journal's enthusiastic fans and sought their identity and spirituality in Russian culture. Tvardovsky was aware of this connection, and its political implications troubled him. He was afraid that they would make the journal more vulnerable and erode its support inside the party leadership. His sense of impending danger proved justified. The secret police and party sources reported that at a conference in Akademgorodok a scientist with a "Jewish" name had compared *Novy Mir* to Chernyshevsky's journal *Sovremennik* (The Contemporary), the flagship publication of the democratic opposition in Russia after the abolition of serfdom. The audience wildly applauded this comparison.[88] Well-trained in party politics, Tvardovsky made sure to pay a courtesy visit afterward to the first party secretary of the Novosibirsk region.[89]

The anti-Semitic elements among the party's ideological and cultural authorities, as well as in the KGB and the Komsomol, never missed a chance to present *Novy Mir* as a "Jewish journal." At one point the assistant to Khrushchev, Lebedev, a staunch supporter of *Novy Mir,* told Tvardovsky that, according to KGB reports, the journal was turning into the leading publication of the Jewish intelligentsia and that Vladimir Lakshin, its principal editorialist, was a Jew. Lakshin remembered Tvardovsky suddenly asking him, "Are you Russian Orthodox?" It was a bizarre question for one member of the atheistic party to ask another party member. Yet Lakshin immediately understood its meaning. He responded, "If I were Jewish I would not have been ashamed to admit it. Yet, I am a pure-stock Russian." Tvardovsky was clearly embarrassed. He groomed young Lakshin as his successor (Lakshin joined the party to qualify for the position).[90] The journal, regardless of Tvardovsky's personal reservations, promoted a vital point in Ehrenburg's agenda of creating a composite identity in which assimilated Jews were accepted as part of the intelligentsia, the community rejecting anti-Semitic nationalism.

Novy Mir's attempts to find a balance between the advocates of philo-Semitism and Russian nationalists succeeded in part because many educated people still perceived the main struggle at the time as that between the intelligentsia and its Stalinist enemies. Tvardovsky wrote at the end of 1963 that contrary to his earlier illusory expectations, the publication of Solzhenitsyn's "truth" had not disarmed the "dark army" of the enemy, but instead had primed it for the fight. He concluded that the main enemies of truth and sincerity were Stalinists in the party apparatus and among the censors. They were more dogmatic than Khrushchev and ignored his instructions, while Khrushchev lacked the resolve to get rid of them. "And the only thing left is to try to dismantle this wall brick by brick, prying them loose one after another."[91] Tvardovsky would remark broodingly in August 1965, after Khrushchev's fall, that the bureaucracy in the Soviet Union was not just a phenomenon, a force opposed by other forces; it was the essence "of our life, of our system."[92]

Novy Mir was not the only focus of educated people in Russia, assimilated Jews among them. At this time they also developed a growing fascination with Russian icons, church bells ringing, and the spiritual beauty of pre-Petrine culture and art. The turning point was 1965–66. In July 1965 the preservation enthusiasts obtained political authorization to create the All-Russian Voluntary Society for the Protection of Monuments of History and Culture (VOOPIK, in its Russian acronym). Soon it numbered seven million members, mostly from educated strata. In 1966 Vladimir Soloukhin published an essay, "From the Russian Museum," promoting Russian religious art, which had been destroyed or neglected during the previous decades. He lovingly described the process of restoring an icon blackened by time and neglect. In the same year Andrei Tarkovsky finished his film *Andrei Rublev*. This grandiose philosophical panorama of medieval Russia placed the role of Christianity squarely at the center of Russian history and Russian fate.[93]

Even some of Zhivago's children on the left began to discover Russian Orthodox culture. Starting in the mid-1960s, Muscovite Jews combined their veneration of Alexander Solzhenitsyn and *Novy Mir* with a keen interest in Holy Russia and its Orthodox tradition. Although many Moscow intellectuals still clung to their communist idealism and continued to read Marx and Lenin, a few others began to feel a strange longing for spiritual values they could not find in the tomes of the materialistic, atheistic revolutionaries. Some urban intellectuals, admirers of Solzhenitsyn, shared his nostalgia for the vanished Russia. One journalist later recalled the motives behind his nostalgic spirituality:

> How did it happen that I, born in Moscow and loving this city, who became interested in Sartre and Anouilh, Kafka and Salvador Dalí, suddenly began to feel such a pull toward simple village people? I felt that literature, art, culture, all that I valued and accumulated, was not sufficient. I was looking for a spirit coming from the depths of history and from peasant life. It seemed that this spirit still lived there, in the peasants' midst, in the primeval origins of their morals and ethics. Villages are older than cities; the nation is born there, on the ancestral lands.[94]

A number of assimilated Jews, to their own amazement, discovered that they shared a fascination with Russian icons and churches with their anti-Semitic antagonists. One of them, Mikhail Agursky, even traveled to the Russian North to "search for his roots," as he put it.[95] This search led Agursky to undergo baptism and embrace Orthodox Christianity. The man who helped him to come to Russian Orthodoxy was Father Alexander Men, a remarkable spiritual figure. He was ordained as a priest in the midst of Khrushchev's antireligious campaign.[96] By 1966 his parish in the vicinity of Moscow had become a place of pilgrimage for the newly baptized Moscow intelligentsia, Jews and non-Jews alike. They found Men's blend of intellectualism and spiritualism captivating. In contrast to many other Orthodox priests, Men deemphasized the narrow ethnic Russian nature of the church and removed all anti-Semitic overtones from the liturgy. In contrast to the xenophobic message of the Russian Orthodox hierarchy, formulated during Stalinism in adaptation to official cold war policies, Men's preaching showed

Father Alexander Men. The priest was "sent by God" to some of Zhivago's children, to help reconcile the values of the intelligentsia with Russian Orthodoxy (Courtesy of Memorial, Moscow).

an openness to Western Catholicism, as well as to the spiritual experience of other great religions. In other words, Men played the same ecumenical, humanistic role in the church as Tvardovsky did in the sphere of literature. Among Men's spiritual children were Nadezhda Mandelstam, widow of the famous poet, and the popular bard Alexander Galich, along with members of the Union of Soviet Writers, the Soviet Filmmakers' Union, academic institutes, and agencies of propaganda and education. Years later, the Russian medievalist Sergei Averintsev, another remarkable spiritual figure of this generation, remembered Father Men as "the man sent from God to be a missionary for the wild tribe of the Soviet intelligentsia."[97]

The phenomenon of the "Men church" was an important sign of growing cultural diversity and intellectual uncertainty. As in the late nineteenth and early twentieth centuries, when Boris Pasternak and his generation grew up, in the 1960s the limitations of materialistic socialism and Western cultural influences caused some intellectuals and artists to seek new outlets and communities, in addition to "contemporary" theater, cinema, and art and their favorite literary journal. The conversion of Zhivago's children to Christianity was not a mass phenomenon. Some of them would later change their views and religious orientation and emigrate to Israel, Western Europe, or the United States—among them Mikhail Agursky, who would go so far as to expunge his episode of Christianity from his memoirs published in Israel.[98]

The search for the intelligentsia's roots and meaning could not avoid the issue of national-ethnic identities and languages. Tvardovsky's unifying agenda could stave off fragmentation into nationalities, but only for a time: the solidarity among members of the intelligentsia on the cultural front against the excesses of Stalinism was by its nature impermanent and subject to erosion. Even some of the people around Tvardovsky and other followers of the journal began to criticize *Novy Mir*'s platform of unification. Alexander Solzhenitsyn, privately at first, accused the journal staff, and Lakshin in particular, of associating with cosmopolitan and philo-Semitic groups in the intelligentsia. The author of *One Day* rejected both Soviet and democratic-humanist components of the journal's agenda. His position was increasingly based on his Orthodox faith and conservative-religious thinking borrowed from prerevolutionary Russian sources. He also began to think about the Jewish Question, and not as a problem of anti-Semitism. Borrowing arguments from Shulgin and other anticommunist Russian nationalists, Solzhenitsyn came to the conclusion that the radical, secular, socialist groups among the assimilated Jewry had been guilty in siding with the Bolsheviks and destroying the old Russia. Solzhenitsyn despised the leftist intelligentsia around *Novy Mir* as a group that had lent legitimacy to collectivization and the horrors of the Bolshevik regime, even while denouncing Stalinism. He also believed that the exclusive focus on anti-Semitism under Stalin masked the unwillingness of the descendants of the Jewish Bolsheviks to own up to the responsibility of "their people" for communist crimes.[99]

In 1963 *Novy Mir* published Solzhenitsyn's short story "Matriona's House," in which the author presented the lifestyle of a vanishing Russian peasantry as an ethos to be emulated by the entire country. He emphasized the deep religiosity of a peasant woman, the heroine of the story, and described her as "a righteous person" *(pravednik)*. As one later reviewer pointed out, Solzhenitsyn was groping "for his psychological and spiritual roots, for the manner of how best to live in conformity with his nature as a Russian. He believes that this process requires leaping backwards over the disjuncture of Stalin's regime and of the whole Soviet experiment. It involves digging below the surface of Soviet culture to the base soil of the ancient Russian culture, and below that, to the ideal of that culture." For Solzhenitsyn it was not the cosmopolitan urban intelligentsia but rather the "righteous people" of the Russian peasantry who represented the only hope for salvation of the land.[100]

These views of Solzhenitsyn still could not be published, and therefore remained unknown to his readers. They still thought of him only as the author of *One Day*, fearlessly speaking out about Stalinist crimes. Solzhenitsyn's struggle from 1965 to 1967 against the official literary establishment evoked growing admiration from disillusioned intellectual and cultural figures, especially those of Jewish origin. It is a sad irony that, at a time when Russian-Jewish intellectuals lionized Solzhenitsyn as a hero of the new intelligentsia, the writer had privately adopted views close to the anti-Semitism of the so-called Russian patriots.

At the same time, a few left-wing admirers of *Novy Mir*, among them many assimilated Jews, began to move beyond the journal's unifying agenda. Although a few Russian-Jewish intellectuals converted to Orthodoxy, others felt they could not escape the emotional, psychological challenge of being Jews in a society where pogroms had taken place many times in the past and might still happen in the future. Zionism, although it was banned in the Soviet Union, was a continual temptation and an alternative path to take.[101] Pro-Zionist sympathies exploded among educated groups in Moscow and other major Soviet cities in June 1967, after Israel's triumph over the Arab armies in the Six-Day War.[102] Assimilated Jews in Moscow and Leningrad experienced an unfamiliar and exhilarating feeling. Their Jewishness was no longer identified only with victimhood (and in the anti-Semitic interpretation, with cowardice or lack of military prowess). Numerous writers and literary critics with Jewish ancestors felt with new intensity the dual loyalty to Russian culture and to the Jewish heritage now represented by the Israeli nation.[103] In November 1967, according to a KGB report, thousands of "people of Jewish nationality" gathered at the Moscow synagogue for a Simchat Torah celebration. Among them were students from Moscow State University, the Auto and Road Institute, the Institute of Transportation Engineers, and several other colleges. The KGB analysts attributed this event to the success of Zionist propaganda "against assimilation, for the purity of Jewry." Some hotheads, according to the report, had praised the Israeli military leader Moshe Dayan and shouted, "We want to go to Israel with submachine guns! Long live Jewish students! Long live the Jews!" One scientist asked a small circle of Jewish youth, "What would the Soviet Union have done without us, how great would have been the loss to Soviet science, technology, and culture?" The KGB reported on the "analogous facts of nationalist and chauvinist manifestations in Leningrad during this celebration." Many students who celebrated Simchat Torah were quickly expelled from their universities on the grounds of having participated in a Zionist rally.[104]

The nascent Jewish pride among a considerable number of Moscow intellectuals not only raised Jewish morale, but also generated fears. On July 25, 1965, the poet David Samoilov confided them to his diary. He still worshipped the Russian Revolution and believed in *Novy Mir*'s message and the Russian intelligentsia, but he also was increasingly alarmed by Russian nationalism. In his opinion, anti-Semitism and the appeal to the Black Hundreds were no aberration; they were only a foretaste of what was to come. Looking back to that time in his memoirs, Samoilov admitted that he was afraid of the masses of Russian migrants who were flocking to major cities from the Russian countryside.[105] In 1967 the philosopher Grigory Pomerants, a staunch proponent of Jewish assimilation, compared the Israeli victory on the Sinai Peninsula to "the Greek victory at Marathon." At the same time, he viewed the activities of Glazunov and other Russian patriots to "save and restore the ancient Russian culture" as a thinly veiled threat: "The Russian people can be aroused easily to massacre the Jews." The surmise of the Soviet authorities, he wrote, ran like this: "The uproar about holy Russia won't hurt, but will fit in rather nicely; at present it is the red-bilberry jam which garnishes the military-patriotic chicken, and perhaps later it will be something else: the unofficial reconnoitering for an ordinary official pogrom."[106] Fear of "Russian fascism" would continue to spread among the philo-Semitic intelligentsia. A few years later this fear, among other motives and issues, would lead many assimilated Jews, passionate fans of Russian literature and members of the intelligentsia, to begin to think about emigrating from the Soviet Union.

A very realistic fear among educated Russian-Jewish strata arose from recognition of the growing competition for the best positions in Soviet Russian cultural, educational, and scientific institutions. The sociologist Viktor Zaslavsky wrote that this fear was the result of Soviet policies to distribute slots in the educated professions according to the national-ethnic representation. Because of these policies, Jews, no matter how talented they were, could no longer hold a disproportionate number of jobs in the scientific and cultural elites. As the growing numbers of Russians and other ethnic groups began to join the professional classes, Soviet officials afforded them preferential treatment over Jews. Not all those officials were ideological anti-Semites.[107] Yet the rise in anti-Semitism at the grassroots level and in the bureaucracy—propelled by many factors, including the propaganda of the Russian patriots—was palpable. As a result, many highly educated Soviet Jews discovered that their children could not get into universities, postgraduate studies, or the institutions in academia, art, and science.[108]

The revived Russian intelligentsia in the sixties, like its prerevolutionary European and Russian predecessors almost a century earlier, could not avoid a painful rift. World War II and postwar Stalinist anti-Semitism had provided a powerful boost to distinctly *Jewish* and *Russian* identities within the confines of the Soviet communist project. The zigzags of the Soviet regime between the language of class and revolution on one hand and ethnonationalism and anti-Semitic campaigns on the other had produced cracks in Soviet society that particularly affected the expanding number of educated people. The Thaw, with its questioning of ideological certainties and traumatizing discoveries about the past, began to produce two conflicting narratives of history, tragedy, and martyrdom. On the left the intellectuals and artists, many of them related to the Bolsheviks and communist idealists of the previous era, denounced the state-driven anti-Semitism, and some of them focused on the suppressed memory of the Holocaust. On the opposite end of the spectrum were those who focused on another tragedy, collectivization and the destruction of the Russian peasantry and its way of life. Primed by prerevolutionary and émigré literature, the second group blamed Jewish revolutionaries for the radical socialist experiments that had caused this tragedy. These feelings and perceptions began to affect the thinking and practices of literary and artistic figures from the post-Stalin generation.

In a historical and moral sense, there was no equivalency between the "right" and the "left." The former defended the honor and ethos of the Russian intelligentsia against the semifascist anti-Semitic preachings of the "Russian patriots." It was a great moral tragedy that Russian national feelings that began to be articulated more freely after Stalin's death remained fatally contaminated by xenophobia and anti-Semitism. It was a shame that Russian patriots, in contrast to Pasternak in *Doctor Zhivago*, refused to see the post-1917 history of Russia as the common tragedy of Russians and non-Russians. Instead, they scapegoated Jews. A few figures—above all, the assimilated Jew Ehrenburg and the Russian Tvardovsky—recognized the corrosive effects of anti-Semitic Russian nationalism. These two devoted great efforts to forming a broader identity, in which cosmopolitan and socialist elements could coexist with national and patriotic ones. Ehrenburg's writings pointed to the cosmopolitan, antibourgeois, antinationalist culture of the European left as a model for the future collective community. Tvardovsky's *Novy Mir* harked back to the traditions of Russia's left-leaning democratic intelligentsia of the nineteenth and early twentieth centuries, and above all to its rejection of anti-Semitism, its humanistic values, and its secularism. Both men associated anti-Semitism with the main symbolic enemy of their time, Stalinist bureaucracy.

The efforts to unite the intelligentsia brought temporary success. Yet even under *Novy Mir*'s unifying umbrella, the stand-off continued between defenders of the intelligentsia's ethos and Russian nationalists. And after the last surge of communist illusions ended in 1968, the right and the left within the Soviet intelligentsia would begin to gravitate toward ethnic-national identities, the product of an imagined past as well as of present-day issues and conflicts. The rift produced by the rise of anti-Semitic nationalism and its scapegoating of Jews fractured and weakened the sixties intelligentsia as a whole. That schism also lessened the chances for the formation of a new democratic movement where the ideals of enlightened social responsibility, moral integrity, and political freedom could find an acceptable "national" form and acquire a mass following among Russian people. During the 1970s this failure would greatly contribute to the isolation, political impotence, and eventual demise of the elements of civic consciousness that had begun to emerge in Soviet Russia in the 1960s.[109]

The role of intelligentsia, its method of
thinking and acting, will grow immeasurably
around the world.

—Andrei Sakharov, 1967

Between Reform and Dissent
1965-1968

I N September 1965 the KGB arrested the writers Andrei Siniavsky and
Yuli Daniel and blamed them for publishing "anti-Soviet" works abroad
under the pseudonyms Abram Tertz and Nikolai Arzhak. The KGB made
other arrests of intellectuals and young artists as well, as part of the crackdown by the secret police on the growing role of the private and underground semipublic culture in Soviet society. Unexpectedly, this time the
trial of Siniavsky and Daniel produced a reaction against the gap between
the letter of Soviet law and the state's punitive practices. A new movement
emerged, largely among the generation of postwar students, now intellectuals and artists—the movement for human rights, which would openly and
publicly challenge the Soviet authorities over the interpretation of constitutional rights.[1]

This momentous development occurred almost a year after the party
apparatus, together with the military and the KGB, removed Khrushchev
from power. This action portended a review and a possible revision of the
Kremlin's attitude toward Khrushchev's de-Stalinization. The cohort of
leaders who came to power in Khrushchev's wake believed that his spasmodic attacks on Stalin had destabilized the Soviet regime, jeopardized Soviet control over Eastern Europe, and divided the world communist movement. Prominent figures linked to the de-Stalinization under Khrushchev,
including *Izvestia*'s Alexei Adzhubei, were fired. Tvardovsky and *Novy Mir*

lost political friends at the top. The new Soviet leader, Leonid Brezhnev, secretly admired Stalin; he had never forgotten the victory parade in 1945, when he, along with thousands of other victorious officers and soldiers, had marched across Red Square, past Lenin's Tomb, where Stalin had stood. Two years later Stalin canceled the celebration of Victory Day. In May 1965 Brezhnev addressed the senior military and announced that from then on the victory parade would be an annual ceremony. He also mentioned the "great services" rendered by Stalin during the war. The audience responded with enthusiastic applause. This applause provided a rude jolt to Stalin's hundreds of thousands of victims, their children and family members, and everyone else who had believed that de-Stalinization was irreversible. Instead of remembering and repenting for the terrible past, many Soviet citizens wanted to repress and forget it, while glorifying the war victory.[2]

The creeping "re-Stalinization" attempted by the new regime combined with other, quite contradictory trends. At first, the Kremlin leaders, Leonid Brezhnev among them, took steps to win popularity among educated classes, the most rapidly growing sector of Soviet society. The Politburo abolished certain punitive measures, attributed to Khrushchev, against the artistic milieu, such as the campaign against abstract art. Some films that had previously been banned appeared on the screen. After October 1964 *Pravda* began to publish editorials and articles calling for the reform of Soviet communism in the spirit of "eternal human values," and even for "expanding the ethos of the intelligentsia *(intelligentnost)* among the entire Soviet people."[3]

In September 1965, simultaneously with the arrests of intellectuals, the Kremlin launched the long-debated economic reforms announced with pomp and circumstance at the party plenum. These reforms pledged to give Soviet society the improvement in living standards that Khrushchev had promised but failed to deliver. The economists who took part in the preparation of the economic reforms were "part of the sophisticated and enlightened sector of the intelligentsia whose moods and opinions" exerted influence on at least some high-level administrators and political officials.[4] The sociologist Vladimir Shlapentokh remembered that as a result of these reforms and the great expectations they evoked, "the officially recognized role of the intellectuals" was greater than it had ever been before in Soviet history.[5] Once again, Moscow and Leningrad intellectuals hoped for greater autonomy, freedom of self-expression, and greater tolerance on the part of the regime, and actively entered into public negotiations with the authorities, thus acting as a reformist faction within the party and the state.

Most Western media and observers at that time focused their attention on the resistance to "re-Stalinization," and especially on a few public human rights defenders, who were quickly dubbed dissidents. Heroic acts and statements by "dissidents" made great news during the Cold War.[6] The movement for human rights, however, concealed a growing rift between the left and right wings of Soviet intellectuals. In fact, Solzhenitsyn and Sakharov were antagonists on the Jewish Question and, like others glorified in the West as "freedom-fighters," had no intention of challenging the political authority of the Communist Party. The majority of intellectuals, including the so-called dissidents, still hoped for a reformist evolution of the Soviet project and expected to play a major role in that evolution. Virtually nobody, on the left or on the right, expected or wanted a "return to capitalism" with a free market, private entrepreneurship, and property. Instead, they wanted dialogue, not confrontation, with the state bureaucracy and the communist regime.

The Birth of Public Dissent

Sporadic arrests for "anti-Soviet activities" had continued throughout Khrushchev's decade in power, despite the official de-Stalinization. And after Khrushchev's ouster the arrests went on. In 1965 the KGB arrested dozens of people, including a group of young scholars in Leningrad belonging to the Bell who were spreading leaflets demanding "true socialism" in the USSR, instead of a bureaucratic dictatorship.[7] The arrest of Siniavsky and Daniel for publishing their books abroad under pseudonyms, however, made a difference. Hundreds, even thousands, from Moscow's educated stratum knew these writers. Daniel's apartment was one of the social hubs of the Moscow left-wing intelligentsia. Siniavsky was known for his books and essays in *Novy Mir* and had composed an introduction to the first posthumous volume of Pasternak's poetry (it appeared shortly before Siniavsky's arrest). Semichastny, the head of the KGB, planned to use the trial of Siniavsky and Daniel as a warning to those Soviet intellectuals who "had become internal émigrés, agents of our ideological enemies." In fact, the warning was intended for Tvardovsky's *Novy Mir* and his admirers as well. In September 1965 the KGB seized the private archive Solzhenitsyn kept at the apartments of several of his trusted friends.[8]

The arrest of the two writers shocked the intellectuals of Moscow and Leningrad. Those who had privately taken "progressive" positions calling for reforms and cultural freedom were once again seized by fear, as they had been during the attacks on Pasternak and the assaults on abstract artists.[9] Yet this time not everyone was paralyzed by panic. The young actor Vladimir Vysotsky wrote to a friend, "Andrei Donatovich Siniavsky has been arrested. During the search in his apartment they [the KGB] seized all the tapes with my songs and more serious things—short stories. So far, I have not noticed any police shadowing me, and I do not abandon my optimism. Times are different; we are not afraid of anything."[10] Maria Rozanova and Larisa Bogoraz, the wives of two arrested poets, were convinced, as were their friends, that a return to Stalinism was in the making. Yet for the first time fear pushed them toward collective public action, rather than passive collaborationism. They decided to fight. "We imagined that if we managed to stick together as a group, the scientists and the intelligentsia, then perhaps our resistance would stop the inevitable slide back into Stalinism," recalled Nina Voronel, a friend of Daniel.[11]

What was to be done? In the early 1960s several friends of Alik Ginzburg and Yuli Daniel had come to the conclusion that violent struggle against the Soviet regime was not only futile, but morally degrading to those who practiced it. The philosopher Grigory Pomerants, coming from that milieu, remarked that his friends had developed an aversion to the "revolutionary underground." The calls for vengeance, usually coming from the children whose parents had been killed or mutilated by Stalinists, began to bear an eerie resemblance to the pronouncements of Stalinists themselves. Thus, "there came a cry from the heart: enough blood-letting!"[12] This new mood had inspired Yuli Daniel's story "This Is Moscow Speaking!" about the announcement of a day of open murder.

The intellectuals who rejected retaliation had been influenced by the parting of the Iron Curtain and a feeling of affinity with Western humanist culture. They were, as Ludmilla Alexeyeva later put it, a "brotherhood" of people who "met regularly for evenings of Gershwin at the Conservatory, Fellini retrospectives at the House of Film, French impressionist exhibits at the Pushkin Museum, and, of course, Bulat Okudzhava concerts."[13] They also read and discussed everything *Novy Mir* published. Instead of denouncing "Stalinist bureaucracy," they designed novel forms of public protest that fell within the bounds of Soviet legality. One was the defense of glasnost, or freedom of public speech, as a civil right. On December 3, 1965, Grigory Pomerants and the philosopher-historian Vitaly Rubin challenged the post-Khrushchev official silence on Stalin's crimes by publicly denouncing Stalinism at the Institute of Philosophy in Moscow. In the face of attempts to gag them, the men repeated Khrushchev's line that true Leninists should not support the cult of personality.[14]

An even bolder idea, proposed by the mathematician and logician Alexander Yesenin-Volpin, was to use the constitutional right to rally to advocate for a fair trial for the writers. Volpin was an intellectual and social oddball. A libertarian and an anti-Marxist, he was indifferent to issues such as creative freedom and the historical role of the writer in Russian society. He was interested instead in the problems of a computerized language and logic and their application to the study of Soviet law. Many of Volpin's friends, especially those who remembered the Stalin era, feared that a rally would lead only to a new wave of arrests and terror. One of them told Volpin that an individual could not go against history. It was the position that many from the old intelligentsia had assumed after the victory of the Bolsheviks. Volpin brushed the idea off: "To hell with history! We are talking about a legal fact."[15] On December 5, 1965, the official birthday of the Soviet Constitution, the "brotherhood" of the writers' supporters and students who had learned about the rally from leaflets gathered at the Pushkin statue in Moscow. Volpin's wife remembered that "the wind of liberty was whistling in her ears" and "the feeling of danger and freedom made [her] head spin." There was little fear among the young poets of Moscow's underground who also joined the rally. They were the veterans of Mayak and those belonging to a group called SMOG (the acronym for "daring, thought, image, and profundity").[16]

The demonstrators unfurled their banners: "Glasnost in the trial of Siniavsky and Daniel," and "Honor the Soviet Constitution." The KGB took about twenty people into custody but quickly released them.[17] And foreign correspondents had enough time to take snapshots of the demonstrators. The *New York Times* front page reported "a *glasnost* meeting" on Pushkin Square. Western intellectuals, members of the international writers' club PEN, petitioned for the release of the writers. More information and eventually the unofficial transcript of the trial reached Western media. The BBC,

VOA, Radio Liberty, and other "radio voices" broadcast it to the Soviet audience.[18] Acting on the ideas of glasnost and legalism, Alexander Ginzburg, the father of samizdat, put together *The White Book,* an unauthorized compilation of documents about the Siniavsky-Daniel trial.[19]

The authorities, taken aback by the unusual form of protest, which conformed to the Soviet law, had to make tactical concessions. The trial of Siniavsky and Daniel was opened to the public, and the arrested writers were defended by lawyers (Sophia Kallistratova and Dina Kaminskaia, who later became important figures in the movement for human rights). Nevertheless, in February 1966 the writers received prison sentences: seven years for Siniavsky and "only" five years for Daniel (in recognition of his war record). The harshness of this verdict shocked the Moscow and Leningrad intelligentsia. Tvardovsky wrote in his diary that the sentences evoked "the horrible memory" of Stalinist purges. Quite a few readers of *Novy Mir* thought similarly. But Alexeyeva and her circle of human rights activists celebrated the fact that the authorities had to recognize their demands. And the arrested writers did not admit any guilt.[20]

Many more people, who had not participated in the legal protest, joined a spontaneous campaign to support the prisoners' families. The idea of an informal "Red Cross" for political prisoners in the Soviet Union had emerged for the first time to help the poet Joseph Brodsky when he was exiled in 1964. Over the course of 1966, friends and strangers, usually women, began to come to Daniel's wife Larisa Bogoraz and offer her clothes, food, and other donations, as well as information about other people imprisoned for political motives. They used the word "society" *(obshchestvo, obshchestvennost)* to refer to themselves, a word from the lexicon of the prerevolutionary intelligentsia. "This society," recalled Siniavsky's wife Maria Rozanova, "was something unprecedented and beautiful. It was anonymous assistance from the heart."[21] Later the poet Okudzhava used the term "union" in a song to describe the new social phenomenon. He sang, "Keep holding hands, my friends, keep holding hands / Do not allow any break in our ranks." It was also the start of a charity fund to help political prisoners in Soviet camps. From that moment on, those who were blacklisted and unemployed, owing to their samizdat publications, human rights work, or other unsanctioned activities, could live without hunger or fear for their children. Educated and socially active women, postwar university graduates who for the most part came from families with a revolutionary pedigree, played a leading role in

Andrei Siniavsky (center) at his birthday party in the late 1950s. In 1965 the KGB arrested Siniavsky and Daniel for having their works published in the West. Siniavsky's wife Maria Rozanova (second on the right) and Daniel's wife Larisa Bogoraz (left) organized a campaign to help them. This campaign evolved into the human rights movement in Soviet Russia (Courtesy of Memorial, Moscow).

building the social charity fund along with the rest of the infrastructure for the dissident movement.[22]

The birth of the human rights movement was a remarkable breakthrough in the resurgence of the idea and ethos of the intelligentsia in Russia. It was a milestone in the transformation of left-leaning cultural activities into a *liberal* opposition. This was a novel concept for people who had grown up in a Soviet society where people would have hesitated to call themselves liberals. Initially, they had rejected political violence and revolutionary politics as a matter of principle, and now they developed novel forms of protest. Most of them were no longer young. Two of them, Raisa Orlova (Liberson) and her husband, Lev Kopelev, linked this breakthrough to a shift in consciousness: from the idealization of the "golden age of Bolshevism" and praise of "Leninist norms" to the embrace of "universal moral principles." The best people in the human rights movement, Orlova and Kopelev later recalled, were motivated by the "spiritual culture" of the nineteenth-century Russian intelligentsia, with its "notions of good and evil, of beauty and jus-

Yuli Daniel in Soviet labor camp after 1966. The "society" of Moscow intelligentsia helped him survive there and start a new life after his release (Courtesy of Memorial, Moscow).

tice." But they had also been believers in the socialist ideals. It was precisely because in their youth they "had believed deeply, sincerely, and purely" that in their later years they began to feel the gulf between the ideal and reality so painfully.[23] Orlova and Kopelev had experienced this transition themselves. Orlova had been a passionate and even fanatical Stalinist in her youth. And Kopelev had taken part in collectivization and convinced himself that its brutality was justified by revolutionary necessity.

To add to the complexity of this transition, many members of the human rights movement remained party members. The life of Yelena Bonner, who would play a great role in the history of the human rights movement, illustrates this complexity. Born into the family of a high-placed Bolshevik, she grew up believing that her country was "the best in the world, and the world needed a world revolution." Then both her parents were arrested during Stalin's Great Terror. She later realized that of the twenty-three pupils in her school class, eleven had parents who had been arrested. Yelena, despite being "a child of enemies of the people," attended a university and joined the Komsomol. The war with the Nazis, in which she volunteered as a nurse, roused her from dreams of world revolution and introduced her to anti-Semitism. She took part in the victory parade on Red Square in June 1945. She became a student of medicine and in 1953 was expelled from the Komsomol for defending a "cosmopolitan" professor of medicine. During the Thaw she combined medicine and journalism; her essays appeared in *Yunost* and *Literaturnaia Gazeta*. In 1959–60 she worked on a Soviet medical team for a year in Iraq fighting smallpox. This first trip abroad allowed her, like many of Zhivago's other children, to compare Soviet society with others. Yet she did not lose her ideals completely. In 1961, when Khrushchev attacked Stalin again, she decided to join the party, and did so in 1964. Her motivation was "to correct the Soviet system." Two years later, she joined the charity network of the human rights movement. At that time Bonner still did not see a conflict between her affiliations. She had joined the party to change it for the better. Other women in the movement called her "everybody's Liusia" for her big heart and unflagging readiness to help.[24] In the years 1965–1967 people like Bonner, Kopelev, and Orlova still expected that "common sense" would win out in the Soviet bureaucracy and the more enlightened and pragmatic party apparatchiks would be forced by the logic of historical progress to turn to professionally skilled and morally honest intellectuals and scientists for advice and assistance.[25]

The fledgling movement mobilized the established cultural elites to sign collective appeals to the Kremlin leadership to pardon the writers. Eventually the number of signatories reached a thousand. Sixty-three members of the Union of Soviet Writers, including Ehrenburg, Kopelev, Chukovsky, Akhmadulina, Okudzhava, Rassadin, and Samoilov, were among them. Neia Zorkaia, a student from VGIK during the stormy years 1956 and 1957 and by now a film critic, also signed the petition. She felt happy and empowered—as if she had grown a pair of wings. Numerous scientists, including those who worked on the nuclear project, were in sympathy with the movement. Pyotr Kapitsa and Igor Tamm signed the petition to Brezhnev warning him that the arrests and a return to Stalinism would have major negative consequences for the Soviet Union, including a split in the intelligentsia.[26]

Another petitioner was Andrei Sakharov, the leading designer of Soviet thermonuclear weapons. His biographers emphasize ethical motives in his transition from secret scientist and designer of the first Soviet thermonuclear bombs to human rights activist. Sakharov emblematized a crucial connection between the emerging public dissent and the idea of the Russian intelligentsia. Sakharov's ancestors on both sides came from this imagined community. On his mother's side, his relatives had been involved in the revolutionary People's Will. On his paternal side, his grandfather Nikolai Sakharov, from a priest's family, had joined the movement among the intelligentsia against capital punishment that included the writer Vladimir Korolenko and the followers and friends of Lev Tolstoy. The musician

Alexander Goldenweiser, a friend of the Tolstoy family, stood godfather to the future designer of the Soviet thermonuclear bomb. By birth Sakharov therefore came from the same milieu as Pasternak and his fictional Dr. Zhivago.[27] Sakharov came to activism because of his profound concern that a confrontation between great powers and ideologies could bring the world to the brink of thermonuclear catastrophe. In 1966–67 he already believed that the intelligentsia on both sides of the Cold War divide, and above all scientists, could "help cause the escalation of peace." In previous years the "international campaign of the intelligentsia" to end nuclear tests had been, for Sakharov, a demonstration of its real influence. Like most scientists and figures in the leftist cultural vanguard, he imagined the intelligentsia in Marxist terms, as a new social class. He spoke about "the historic responsibility of the American intelligentsia at a critical moment in world history" to oppose the preparations for nuclear war. He believed that "the role of the intelligentsia, its method of thinking and action, will keep growing all over the world. Following the working class, the intelligentsia must realize its strength as one of the major pillars of the idea of peaceful coexistence."[28]

At the same time, another powerful form of public dissent, called *magnetizdat,* was gaining currency. It became possible after tape recorders became an essential item in the early 1960s. The songs of Bulat Okudzhava about love and solidarity of the Arbat intelligentsia reached thousands, and then millions, thanks to unauthorized tapes, freely distributed.[29] Alexander Galich, a playwright and bard, became another hero of *magnetizdat* and a powerful voice of dissent. He had been born into a family of assimilated Jews and, like his parents, adapted to Soviet realities with remarkable success. He became a member of the writers' union and later the filmmakers' union, earned considerable income from his film scripts, and even received an award from the KGB for the script of a patriotic film. From 1962 to 1967 he produced a cycle of songs about the gulag, the fate of Soviet Jews, and the long shadow cast by the cult of Stalin. Galich felt complicit in Stalinist crimes and urged his audience not to go along passively. Addressing Soviet conformists, he sang sarcastically: "Keep mum and you will end up being one of executioners!" His most famous song was "In Memory of Pasternak." Revisiting the witch hunt against the great poet and the circumstances of his funeral, one tongue-in-cheek verse ran, "How proud we all are that he died in his own bed." The poet warned that all those who voted to expel Pasternak from Russia would be "remembered by name." In March 1968 Galich was a guest at a "festival of bard songs" in Akademgorodok, near Novosibirsk. The organizers of the festival were young physicists from the Integral club. Hundreds of people crowded the hall as Galich began to perform. After he sang about Pasternak, the entire audience stood up in silence and then erupted into thunderous applause. The scientists awarded Galich a prize, not only for his talent but also "in admiration of [his] courage."[30]

The vast majority of the signatories to the petition in defense of Siniavsky and Daniel came from the left flank of the post-Stalin intelligentsia.[31] The authorities noticed a high percentage of "people of Jewish nationality" among the defenders of human rights. Bonner was Jewish. So were Bogoraz, Oriova, Kopelev, and many others. Alexander Voronel, a member of this network, recalled that the human rights movement in Russia "was made up so overwhelmingly of Jews" that it seemed to justify the claim of the radical role of Jews in Russian history, "which the anti-Semites have been ascribing to them since the Russian Revolution."[32] The Russian nationalists and their sympathizers in the KGB and the Komsomol were quick to brand the human rights movement a Zionist conspiracy against the state. Viacheslav Molotov, in a later conversation with the "Russian patriot" Felix Chuev, disagreed. The Jews, he commented, "are undoubtedly more active on average" than the Russians. "There are hotheads among them that sit on both sides of the aisle. Under the conditions of the Khrushchev period, those who nourished a bitter hatred for Stalin raised their heads."[33] Indeed, the "active Jews" in Molotov's categorization were the heralds of a new phase in Soviet history: the leftist network of intellectuals was about to lose faith in the Soviet project.

Historical Revisionists

Yelena Bonner regretted that the human rights movement attracted "disproportionately large numbers of physicists, mathematicians, engineers and biologists, and almost no historians or philosophers."[34] This listing neglects members active in the arts or many other liberal arts. From 1965 to 1967 the most important phenomenon of the emerging movement was the public demand for revision of the Stalinist past and Marxist-Leninist dialectical materialism. The interpretation of Soviet history and Marxism-Leninism itself, once the monopoly of the regime, had suddenly become explosive material in the hands of writers, historians, and philosophers.[35]

For many intellectuals, the revelations about Soviet history called for a reconsideration of their deeply felt patriotism. In 1966 Yelena Bonner received permission to work in the archives of Soviet Armenia, to produce an essay about her famous father-in-law, the Armenian Bolshevik Alikhanov, who had perished in Stalin's terror. Her archival discoveries destroyed her romantic vision of the Revolution and the Civil War. The documents told a tale of immeasurable cruelty, dirty intrigues, and suffering. Later, she would, like her husband Andrei Sakharov, reject revolutionary violence or any other sort in favor of the defense of human rights.[36] Many other writers and intellectuals, while gathering materials about the past, found their beliefs shattered. Konstantin Simonov, who collected reminiscences about Stalin's statesmanship, came to the conclusion in 1965 that the near-destruction of the Soviet Union in 1941–42 was the result of Stalin's Great Terror, when fear paralyzed the Soviet leadership and turned its mighty army into a sitting duck for the aggressors. "Without 1937 there would not have been the summer of 1941," Simonov concluded.[37] At about the same time the biologist Zhores Medvedev and his brother the historian Roy Medvedev were writing revelatory works about the Stalinist past. Typical members of the left-wing intelligentsia, socially as well as biographically, the Medvedev brothers were initially very optimistic about Khrushchev's course and the Thaw.[38] Zhores Medvedev, who had witnessed the destruction of Soviet biology by Lysenko and his hacks, wrote and distributed the first study of those tragic events via samizdat. Roy Medvedev embarked on a bigger project: a history of Stalinism. In 1965–66 Medvedev began to share some of the completed chapters of this book with his friends. He also began to write a samizdat "political journal" monitoring the hidden dynamics within the Soviet leadership after Khrushchev's ouster.[39]

Even the established historians at the Institute of History of the Academy of Sciences, the main academic center for historical research in the Soviet Union, joined the debate on Stalin as a statesman.[40] The institute scholars had prepared for publication two volumes on the history of collectivization, criticizing this calamitous event in Russian history as a violation of Lenin's tolerant policies toward the peasantry. The volumes cited numerous official documents on the disastrous destruction of cattle and other resources, and lethal famine in Ukraine, the Northern Caucasus, and the Volga basin. The party censors prevented publication of this work. Left-leaning historians, however, did not give up. In November 1965 a group of party members, war veterans and anti-Stalinists, won a majority in the institute's administration. The boldest and most energetic were the group of postwar graduates of Moscow State University. "The atmosphere at the institute," one researcher asserted, "improved almost daily." The reformed institute invited the leading authors from *Novy Mir* to its workshops for official discussions of the recent past. Moscow party authorities were concerned about their loss of control and the prominence of historians "of Jewish descent" in the institute's leadership, yet could not stop the trend toward liberalization.[41]

In April 1965, Alexander Nekrich, a historian from the Institute of History, published a book entitled *June 22, 1941*. It became a sensation because of its revelation of numerous facts that challenged the official lies about the Soviet entry into World War II. Not only historians, but many physicists, mathematicians, and scholars from the humanities learned about the book and read it.[42] Nekrich was an assimilated Jew, a war veteran and party member who had a personal moral stake in the Soviet communist project. He was shattered by the revelations of Stalin's crimes and felt alienated from the party he had joined during the war.[43] Still, Nekrich had no illusions about a possible backlash and remained very cautious. Nowhere did he step beyond the anti-Stalinist proclamations and resolutions officially sanctioned under Khrushchev's rule. The military censors approved the book for publication. Even its reviewers, veterans of the KGB and the GRU (Main Intelligence Directorate) agreed with Neckrich's conclusions.[44]

The growing debate about Stalin's direct responsibility in the disastrous defeats of 1941 reached the Kremlin's attention. Nekrich's book challenged official attempts to appeal to Russian chauvinism and to rehabilitate Stalin as a wartime leader. The officials instructed the conservative military historians to attack Nekrich. In February 1966, just after the sentencing of Siniavsky and Daniel, *June 22, 1941* came under scrutiny at the Institute of Marxism-Leninism. Unexpectedly, instead of a witch-hunting session, the meeting of historians and philosophers turned into a demonstration of solidarity for Nekrich on the part of a number of left-leaning intellectuals. Leonid Petrovsky, the son of an Old Bolshevik who was executed by the NKVD in 1941, took the floor and exclaimed, "When will we stop raising our youth with the name of this criminal [Stalin] on their lips?" His record of the discussion made it into samizdat. At the same time, the party committee at the Institute of History closed ranks and backed Nekrich and his work. The committee, after an institute-wide discussion, prepared an unprecedented report to the higher authorities demanding the opening of archives and free access to classified documents. The party committee also organized a discussion at which numerous historians supported the right to do research and publish historical studies on Stalinist crimes. The institute made an attempt to publish the report and the transcripts of the debates around it, but the state censors banned it.[45]

The vast majority of the revisionist historians did not stray beyond the bounds of Marxist-Leninist theory, positing the "progressive change of formations" from feudalism to capitalism to socialism and communism. The historians argued that their appeal for liberalization would not hurt, but rather benefit, the Soviet communist project, would help foreign communists "succeed better and faster, with lesser waste," and would increase "the educational impact" of Soviet historical studies. Nekrich and his backers were careful to indicate that they saw the enemy not in the party bureaucracy, but in Russian anti-Semitic "nationalists, who camouflage themselves with the Marxist banner." The discussants at the Institute of History proclaimed with proud idealism, "Our duty as party-minded communists requires that we learn the whole truth and nothing but the truth" about the past.[46]

The various trends of 1966–67, from the human rights movement to the growing rebellion of historians, were the vocal and visible response of the sixties intelligentsia to a threat of a "return to Stalinism" under the new Kremlin leadership. Dozens of "rebellious" party committees at academic and research institutes in Moscow, Dubna, and Novosibirsk favored further liberalization for intellectuals. According to Roy Medvedev, the two years following fall 1966 were "the peak of the dissident movement and its broadest influence. It enjoyed support among large groups of the intelligentsia, Old Bolsheviks, and even some people in the central party apparatus." Solzhenitsyn wrote a few years later, "Samizdat gushed like a spring flood, new names joined the protests. It seemed that we would start breathing freely with one more push."[47]

Like Khrushchev before him, party leader Leonid Brezhnev had no idea what to do with this commotion among the intellectuals. Brezhnev had some artistic talents himself and did not seek a quarrel with the "creative intelligentsia." Yet he was nervous about historical revisionism, and the tremendous ability of literature and cinema to alter people's perceptions of the past alarmed him. He longed for the days when everyone had learned and discussed only one version of history, the infamous "Short Course" on party history edited by Stalin. At a Politburo discussion on November 10, 1966, Brezhnev complained that some "scholars' works and literary opuses, films, and even media" were "discrediting the history of our party and our people." The hard-liners took a cue from Brezhnev. "We deluded, depraved intelligentsia," declared the party ideologist Suslov. Others proposed to shut down *Novy Mir* or fire Tvardovsky as its editor.[48] From that time on, the state censors began slowly to strangle the journal, by excising some of its best manuscripts and delaying the publication of subsequent issues. It was a war of nerves—and a war for survival—that would consume the last years of Tvardovsky's life. On January 27, 1967, Brezhnev and the Politburo discussed a report by the KGB and the attorney general on Nekrich and his vocal supporters. The report placed them among "thirty-five to forty people who carry out their politically harmful activities by forging and disseminating anti-Soviet literature and organizing all kinds of gatherings and manifestations." In March 1967 when West Germany's *Der Spiegel* wrote that Nekrich and other Soviet historians had resisted Brezhnev's attempts to rehabilitate Stalin, Brezhnev was infuriated. Repressive state mechanisms were set in motion against the revisionist historians, and eventually Nekrich and his defender Petrovsky were expelled from the party.[49] Nevertheless, in 1966–67 nobody could predict how long the war between the government and the dissidents would last and how many casualties it would claim.

Intellectuals and Economic Reforms

In late 1966–67, a great number of leftist intellectuals, albeit depressed by the arrests and censorship, were greatly encouraged by the announcement of economic reforms. Lev Kopelev recalled that he and some of his friends in human rights circles or on the Moscow left wing "still hoped, in a Marxist way, for the development of a material base and the scientific-technical revolution." They expected that computerization would rid the Soviet society of the "grassroots Stalinism" of informers and intriguers in all spheres of social life.[50] These views were not exceptional. In fact, they represented a combination of receding moral commitment to communism and contemporary technocratic illusions—the last bulwark of optimism for the sixties intelligentsia.

A coalition of reform-minded professionals who were intimately linked to the left-leaning cultural network and working within a socialist utopian framework debated and developed the blueprints for the 1965–1968 economic reforms. The academician Vasily Nemchinov, a veteran of Soviet statistics, who was thus privy to economic information, became a key senior mentor of reform-minded intellectuals. His social origins were in the Russian rural intelligentsia formed in the early twentieth century on the basis of the socialist cooperative movement in the Russian countryside. Miraculously, he preserved some values and aspirations from his vanished milieu (ruthlessly destroyed by Stalin).[51] During the Thaw, Nemchinov's practical mind recognized the potential of cybernetics and sociological studies to transform the Soviet economy. He teamed up with Leonid Kantorovich, from circles in the educated Leningrad elite. A mathematical genius who worked on the optimization of economic resources in planned systems, Kantorovich later received the Nobel Prize for his theories.[52]

The reformers had quietly rehabilitated ideals and concepts developed at the time that NEP was crushed by Stalinism.[53] Most economic reformers were mathematicians, specialists in cybernetics, and "honest" journalists. They were at loggerheads with the coterie of Soviet economists but found support in Soviet planning agencies and industrial management. In 1958 Nemchinov and Kantorovich organized a laboratory for mathematical-economic studies at the Academy of Sciences in Moscow. With the support of the proreform majority at the Academy of Sciences, they conducted a number of roundtables discussing ways to "optimize" the Soviet planned economy. In 1963 they founded the Central Institute for Economics and Mathematics (CEMI). Nemchinov and the CEMI experts resumed the pioneering research of Russian economists of the 1920s on theoretical and practical issues of the planned economy, research that had been aborted during the Stalin era. The CEMI scholars discovered the works of Gaetano Pareto, the Russian-born Vasily Leontiev, and John Maynard Keynes. A British economist who visited CEMI in 1964 saw a group of institute researchers, young men and women with an academic background in math, reading Paul Samuelson's *Foundations of Economic Analysis* with the help of English-Russian dictionaries.[54]

In the early 1960s Kantorovich moved to Akademgorodok. There he gave support and inspiration to a group of ambitious young economists and sociologists who were challenging Stalinist orthodoxy. Abel Aganbegyan became a leader of this group. Akademgorodok provided a fertile ground for development and study of economic reforms. Abel Aganbegyan, Tatiana Zaslavskaia, Vladimir Shubkin, and Vladimir Shlapentokh, all from the cohort of postwar students, undertook a series of studies exploring the real economic structures in Soviet society and were among the first to grasp that Khrushchev's attacks on the peasant way of life had triggered a second wave of peasant migration to the cities and created acute imbalances in all spheres of production and consumption.[55]

By the end of the Khrushchev era, a sense of urgency, even despair, prevailed in government and bureaucratic circles. The food riots of 1962 were still fresh in everyone's memory, and similar disturbances could occur any time, for the Soviet Union suffered from acute shortages of food and consumer goods. One member of *Novy Mir*'s editorial staff wrote in his diary in early November 1963, "The country is nearing a catastrophe. There is a lack of bread; peasants are slaughtering cattle; people stand in kilometer-long lines to buy anything."[56] The search for a way out of the fiasco created by Khrushchev produced a "technocratic moment" among Soviet elites; some political leaders and bureaucrats turned to scientists who advocated econometric methods and other changes in economic planning. It seemed that the long-awaited hour had finally arrived for advocates of cybernetics and economic reforms.

The economic discussion revolved around a fundamental question: What was to be done with the centralized system of command and control handed down from the Stalin period? Khrushchev dismantled the system's most odious elements, such as the slave labor armies of the gulag and prison-like labor discipline, and began to combine the enforced "total employment" with elements of a welfare state, by raising minimum wages and pensions, guaranteeing social benefits, and reducing work hours. At first, these measures increased labor productivity and efficiency, yet in the early 1960s the incentives no longer worked. The essence of the economic system remained the same, only more egalitarian; it still discouraged innovation, flexibility, efficiency, and hard work.[57] In the early 1960s nobody among Soviet economists, managers, and bureaucrats understood the deep structural sources of the problem, yet the decline in labor productivity and the enormous waste of resources were impossible to overlook. Against this backdrop, the cyber-enthusiasts suggested comprehensive computerization of the planned economy and in fact of the entire society. And the Kremlin leadership began to listen.

In 1962 the top Soviet economic manager, Alexei Kosygin, asked Viktor Glushkov, the thirty-nine-year-old director of the Ukrainian Institute of Cybernetics, to develop blueprints for a national automatic information system (OGAS). Glushkov wrote in September 1962 that computers could not yet plan the "entire material-technical supply" in Ukraine. Yet he confidently concluded that it would become possible within five to ten years to do so. "In the area of economic management cybernetics fits our socialist planned economy like a glove."[58] Glushkov studied thousands of Soviet plants, mines, railroads, and airports, as well as the major state planning agencies, and in 1964 presented his concept of a computerized brain for the Soviet economy. It was designed to connect to one hundred computer centers, some of which would be located in every major industrial city. These centers, in turn, would reach out to twenty thousand enterprises via special broadband communication lines. Glushkov dreamed of using "electronic money" for payments between enterprises as well as individuals; in this way, he hoped, it would be possible to solve the issue of reliance on "unearned" income, corruption, and the black market. Had this project been realized, the Soviet Union would have become a computerized socialist utopia, the motherland of the Internet and also possibly of the ATM.[59]

Nemchinov and other reform-minded intellectuals were enthusiastic about the prospect of computerization. At the same time they understood the need to upgrade the role of money as a regulator of production and exchange. They even dared to talk about "market elements" in socialist planning, namely about profits, fewer price controls, liberalization of wholesale trade, and competition. In 1960 Nemchinov had published a pamphlet, *Value and Prices under Socialism.* This pamphlet launched a public discussion in *Pravda, Izvestia,* and other leading Soviet newspapers. In the West the discussion became known as the Soviet economic renaissance. In 1962 Professor Yevsei Liberman of Kharkov, one of Nemchinov's protégés, claimed at a public seminar in Moscow that only a combination of profit and autonomy for state enterprises would breathe new life into the Soviet planned economy. These ideas found influential supporters on the State Committee for Science and Technology and the Central Department of Statistics. The reformers published several articles in *Kommunist, Pravda,* and the *Economicheskaia Gazeta* propagating the idea of regulated trade among state enterprises.[60]

Nemchinov died on November 5, 1964, shortly after Khrushchev's ouster.

His brochure, published a year earlier, contained a prophetic prediction about the Soviet economy: "An economic system so fettered from top to bottom will put a brake on social and technological progress, and will break down, sooner or later, under the pressure of the real processes of economic life."[61] In 1965 the economic preparation for reforms entered a final stage. Kosygin, the chairman of the Council of Ministers, was the most senior and earnest supporter of reforms. Even Brezhnev appeared to have had more economic common sense than Khrushchev. To everyone's relief, the government abolished the absurd restrictions on private plots for peasants and on the construction of private dachas, thus giving back to millions of Russians, both peasants and city dwellers, the possibility of living off the land and benefiting from additional food and income.[62]

Public economic discussion reached unprecedented heights of boldness. *Pravda,* with Alexei Rumiantsev at the helm, was at the forefront of the discussion. Gennady Lisichkin argued on the pages of *Pravda* for the introduction of "free prices." The agrarian reporter Yuri Chernichenko, reacting to the growing dependence of the Soviet Union on imported grain, suggested extending market elements to collectivized agriculture. Others offered to develop "socialist" competition, allow the bankruptcy of inefficient state enterprises, and use bank credits to regulate the economic process. Numerous intellectuals read these articles, collected the clippings, and discussed the economic proposals with great excitement.[63]

In the following decades reformist thinkers would claim that their economic ideas had not been properly implemented and that the Brezhnev leadership had smothered economic innovations. While this is true, it is also obvious that none of the reformist intellectuals of 1965 had really grasped the meaning of a market economy. They also did not admit that the Soviet political system was as inconsistent with the market system as oil was with water. Even the boldest reformers remained under the spell of economic orthodoxy and, equally important, believed that the world of private entrepreneurship and private property belonged to the past. One of the reform-minded economists, Viktor Belkin, wrote in his dissertation that state prices should reflect the balance of payments between enterprises. After reading this innocuous statement, the deputy head of Gosplan, the State Planning Committee, claimed that Belkin "seeks to restore capitalism." This statement was enough to make all Belkin's supporters, among them Nemchinov and Kantorovich, retreat and cancel the dissertation defense.[64]

In the mid-1960s all economic reformers—in fact, the entire intellectual class—believed that the Russian Revolution had liberated society, culture, and politics from the tyranny of money, once and for all. For them "genuine" socialism meant emancipation from philistinism and from the bourgeois materialism now embodied by the "new class" of communist nomenklatura.[65] The contempt of the *shestidesiatniki* for capitalist wealth and the capitalist ethos as a source of development and innovation had much in common with the anticapitalist attitudes of the majority of the old prerevolutionary intelligentsia. Postwar students had grown up feeling antipathy toward the well-to-do Stalinist elite and for careerists who aimed to achieve material gains. "Petty bourgeois values" *(meshchanstvo)* to these intellectuals represented the antithesis of the intelligentsia's ethos.[66] Even the members of the human rights movement did not suggest including the right to private property into their agenda. Many of them regarded property owners as a natural constituency of reactionary regimes, including fascism.[67] This shortsightedness would have fatal consequences for the Soviet Union twenty years later, during Gorbachev's perestroika. Igor Birman, one of the reform-minded economists in the 1960s, admitted in his memoirs that the orthodox economists had a point in their resistance to the changes. They "sensed that real reforms would destabilize the system and everything would collapse."[68]

Paradoxically, while Russians in tune with the intelligentsia rejected property and money, and some of them even sought to live according to their beliefs, in the eyes of the people intellectuals were part of the upper class, together with the nomenklatura.[69] Established scientists, the *institutchiki* in Akademgorodok and other scientific centers, did very well by Soviet standards. They had something akin to American tenure, a high level of job security and comfort, access to information and often to travel abroad. In the smoke-filled lobbies they could exchange samizdat and discuss the latest Western intellectual and cultural trends. *Institutchiki* could even deviate from the official ideological tenets within their professional areas, provided their conclusions were published in specialized journals and couched in nonprovocative language. The academic elite had considerable material privileges. Akademgorodok and the town of physicists at Dubna, not to mention the "secret cities," were islands of privileged comfort. The sociologist Vladimir Shubkin recalled that at Akademgorodok top academicians lived in two-story villas with many rooms and special servants.

The families of other senior scientists (who held the rank of corresponding members of the academy) occupied nice townhouses. Less-distinguished scientists and their families lived in apartments, smaller yet still much more comfortable than standard Soviet housing. At the bottom of the hierarchy were junior scientists, lab assistants, and engineers, living, as they said, in "our Harlem," in low-quality apartments. The same hierarchy of perks affected the supply of food and medical services.[70]

The cultural elite also fared well by comparison with the masses. Orchestra, opera, and ballet performances were subsidized. State funds for film productions kept increasing, even though some films were subsequently banned or emasculated by censorship. State television and radio paid hefty sums of money for scripts, music, and production.[71] In 1960 the writer Vladimir Voinovich received an honorarium for a popular song about the Soviet cosmonauts, together with an advance for his short story to be published in *Novy Mir*. He had never seen so much money before. He bought all the luxuries he had only been able to dream about until then, including a television set, a motorcycle, and new coats for his wife and himself.[72] Membership in the "creative" unions, which conveyed life-long fellowship and subsidies, was a much-contested commodity. The top stratum in the union could take out loans from the Litfond, the Literary Foundation started in 1934 by Maxim Gorky. From this source, Soviet writers paid for their vacations, financed their cooperative apartments and dachas, and solved other monetary problems. Union members also could get huge royalties by printing their books in hundreds of thousands of copies. Royalties in the Soviet Union did not depend on sales; they were a fixed percentage.[73] In the Union of Soviet Artists the struggle over resources underlined the aesthetic battles between the defenders of socialist realism and their young formalist critics.[74]

At first, many idealists from the postwar generation continued to frown on privileges and high salaries. When somebody from their milieu openly chose the path of material comfort and career, instead of staying "honest and poor," the "sellout" occasioned surprise and moral indignation.[75] As former idealistic students turned into middle-age professionals, however, the exceptions became the norm. Toward the end of the 1960s it became clear that the anti-Stalinist attack on material privileges had utterly failed. Tvardovsky recorded in 1968, "Money has been rehabilitated in earnest and for a long time."[76] Around the same time, the poet Joseph Brodsky, penniless and hungry in his apartment in Leningrad, lamented: "Money alone is on my mind / The economy today is central."[77] Already in the early seventies, the young American journalist Hedrick Smith found that the Soviet Union fostered a sprawling system of special stores, secret rations, and privileged hospitals intended not only for the party elite, but also for most professionals and intellectuals employed by the state. This system had emerged under Stalin but continued to expand after his death. "Russian intellectual friends" of Smith's from the left-leaning and human rights–oriented intelligentsia in Moscow expressed exasperation at the system, "because it so brazenly flouts the proclaimed ideals of socialist equality." At the same time, as Smith learned, the Russians did not want to change this system. They just wanted the exceptions made for them personally.[78] This was true of many who felt they belonged to the intelligentsia, and at the same time welcomed any opportunity to benefit from the established systems of perks and benefits. Mikhail German, an art historian from Leningrad, recalled in his memoirs that during the second half of the 1960s he had begun to behave and feel like a person with a stronger stake in his material comfort and position, as opposed to his moral autonomy and ideals. He engaged in endless petty compromises and acts of conformism, in order not to lose his personal privilege of traveling abroad, to get "deficit" goods, and to use connections (in Soviet newspeak—*blat*) to obtain the services he needed for his comfortable life. Looking back from the post-Soviet era at his actions, he experienced sadness and shame. His desire to escape from the humiliating misery of Soviet existence into a private comfortable world was understandable, as was his wish to break through the Iron Curtain to see Paris and London. Still, according to his own description, the happiness he felt after achieving his goals was the "happiness of a slave," humiliating and degrading for a genuine *intelligent*.[79]

In paradoxically Marxist fashion, the material background of the scientific reformers in Russia conditioned and set the limits on their economic horizons. In Akademgorodok, one of the major laboratories for the economic reforms, this outcome was appeared with startling clarity. The city of scientists near Novosibirsk experienced its golden age in 1965–1967. It was, as one veteran recalled, "the most liberal-minded spot in the country," with forty-seven academicians, eighty-five doctors of science and over a thousand younger scientists. A witness relates, "Soviet power was relegated to the kennel. Scientists were convinced of their impunity."

Outside their private apartments, scientists could also debate economic and cultural news in their clubs, Sigma and Integral. They patronized poetry and art by inviting famous poets and songwriters and organizing exhibitions of formalist artists, among them Robert Falk, Pavel Filonov, and Kuzma Petrov-Vodkin. Humor and erudition were the norm in this "brotherhood of liberal intellectual solidarity." A journalist from Moscow who managed to visit one of the secret cities in 1963 was struck by the scientists' ability to organize a rudimentary civil society with "discussion clubs" where everyone could talk about political and cultural topics freely and without fear.[80]

In this special milieu, scientists discussed the introduction of a technocratic socialist democracy that would represent a third way between Stalinism and Western capitalism. Some of them believed that the Soviet system could be improved "scientifically" by an alliance of scientists and enlightened party apparatchiks. Those who were involved in economic reforms were thriving. In 1966 Aganbegyan became director of the Institute for Economics and Industrial Organization. In 1968 Zaslavskaia was inducted into the Academy of Sciences. A member of Aganbegyan's team of economic reformists, Shlapentokh himself admitted that he was one of those who lacked the courage to join the human rights movement and publicly challenge the party authorities. "Joining them would have meant a radical change of my life, above all the termination of my professional activities. This would have been a major calamity for me."[81] Gersh Budker and other scientific leaders at Akademgorodok, though highly critical of the party authorities, believed it was possible to milk the Soviet system for funding to build the world's largest labs and particle accelerators, and to make scientific discoveries that would promote "social progress." Scientists' needs were taken care of within the framework of a propertyless, centralized economy. Why wish for its destruction?[82]

People's common stake in the existing (and expanding) system of hierarchical privileges contributed to the demise of the 1965–1968 economic reforms. After a number of pilot projects in select industries were initiated in accordance with the new rules, including sharply reduced indicators and regulators and the right to retain some of the profits and readjust salaries to reflect merit, the reforms bogged down. The early converts to the revised methods enjoyed preferential access to state supplies, a modification that guaranteed improved results with fewer employees. But if continued, the reforms would have brought about mass unemployment among the managerial and working classes. The sociologist Viktor Zaslavsky observed that this process "threatened two important social groups—the lower and middle bureaucracy and semiskilled workers whose status, privileges, and lifestyle were endangered." Soon this inefficient majority swamped the hardworking, educated, and motivated minority. Eventually, such a system was bound to bring stagnation.[83]

The Spring That Never Came

In the history of the post-Stalin Russian intelligentsia, 1968 was the milestone year. The outside world was in a great turmoil. In the East, the "cultural revolution" in China was entering its third year. In the West, "New Left" radicalism raged on and around university campuses from West Berlin and Paris to Berkeley, California. The rapid growth of the anti-Vietnam protest movement, the assassination first of Martin Luther King in April, then of Robert Kennedy in June, plunged the United States into radical politics: urban ghettoes burned, and the anti-Vietnam protesters numbered in the millions. In May radical students built barricades in Paris, and workers went on a national strike. Women's liberation was mobilizing support in the West.[84]

Zhivago's children observed these revolutionary developments with keen interest, although with a sense of detachment. All of them, from the enlightened apparatchiks to the dissidents, repudiated China's Cultural Revolution. Many who had been students immediately following World War II remembered their Chinese classmates as dogmatic Stalinists. The consensus among the human rights advocates and in broader circles of intellectuals of leftist sympathies was that Mao Zedong had unleashed the fanatical mob against the Chinese intelligentsia. This time, they believed the reports in Soviet media, which (though sometimes exaggerated) described the humiliation and torture of Chinese intellectuals and artists. Soviet intellectuals were horrified at the destruction of China's historical legacy. They saw the Red Guards toting the Little Red Book of quotations from Chairman Mao as enemies and fervently hoped that nothing similar could ever happen in Russia.[85] Among Moscow and Leningrad intellectuals, reactions to events in the West varied. Some people were excited by the students' revolt and saw in it a confirmation of the thesis that the intelligentsia, both in the West and in the Soviet Union, was in the vanguard of change. Western intellectuals wanted to refresh the Marxist revolutionary perspective and encourage rebellion against bureaucracy, and the emphasis on individual rights also appealed to many Russian intellectuals. Western rock, the music of cultural protest, spread among Soviet youth with the same speed as the popular lyrics and songs of Russian poets. At the same time, in the disabused view of Zhivago's children, the Western protesters were too naive and extreme. They sympathized with Maoist destructive violence and overlooked the cruel side of Third World guerrillas from Vietnam to Latin America. They demanded an end to authoritarian and "reactionary" practices within Western pluralist democracy. For their Soviet counterparts, this freedom to express protest was in itself an impossible dream. As Zhivago's children watched the clashes between riot police and Western protesters, they were struck not by the police brutality, but rather by the fact that such mass protests were a daily reality. In the Soviet Union the mass riots of 1962 had ended in execution or imprisonment.[86] One Moscow intellectual, a correspondent for *Literaturnaia Gazeta,* who happened to be in Europe in 1968, discovered that he could no longer identify with students at the Sorbonne who carried images of Mao and Che Guevara but also of Lenin, Trotsky, and even Stalin. He was sick of the leaders' portraits on Red Square at home. At the same time, Western protesters were completely ignorant of the tragic communist experience and realities.[87] Some Russian Jews among the observers felt threatened by the mass radicalism, which reminded them of Stalinism and Nazism. Any radical movement, they came to believe, inevitably turned toward violence and scapegoating of Jews.

The film critic Maia Turovskaia, when she traveled to West Germany in 1968, was one who felt this way. Three years earlier, Turovskaia had assisted the filmmaker Mikhail Romm in producing a documentary film, *Ordinary Fascism*. When Romm and she had looked through captured Nazi archives, they had been struck by the similarities between the Nazi and Stalinist methods of orchestrating mass hatred. Like Vasily Grossman, they came to perceive any radical movement anywhere in the world as the prelude to anti-Semitic totalitarianism. All these conclusions colored Turovskaia's perceptions of the radical rallies of West German students. She came back home convinced that Western radicals and the intelligentsia in Moscow were "on different trains going in opposite directions."[88]

Russian society had been isolated for too long from the realities in the West to understand the significance and motivation of the protests there.

Meanwhile, the dramatic events in Central Europe in 1968 had great reso-
nance for the leftist vanguard of Russian intellectuals. Extensive cultural
connections existed between Central European and Russian intellectuals.
During the 1960s not only did the left wing of the Moscow intelligentsia
continue to be influenced by cultural and intellectual life in Poland,
Czechoslovakia, Hungary, and other European countries of the Soviet bloc,
but increasingly cultural influences from Moscow reached those countries.
Many Polish intellectuals who returned from Stalin's camps studied at
Soviet universities, worked there, and brought home the tapes of the songs
of Okudzhava, Galich, Vysotsky, and other sixties poets and singers. Intellectuals throughout Eastern Europe came to know and love the poetry of
Yevtushenko and Voznesensky, the novels of Aksyonov, the films of Chukhrai, Romm, and Tarkovsky. Transnational friendships and alliances were
formed.[89] For left-wing Moscow iconoclasts, the cultural space encompassing Warsaw, Prague, and Sofia was "their Europe," more relevant to them
and their agenda than capitalist and democratic Western Europe.

In March 1968 Polish students demanded *socialist* democracy and intellectual freedom in Warsaw, Lublin, and other Polish cities. The communist
government reacted with an anti-Semitic campaign, expelling students
and forcing Polish Jewish intellectuals to emigrate.[90] In contrast to the Polish regime, Czechoslovakia's reform-minded communist leader Alexander
Dubček, embracing the agenda of socialism with a human face, encouraged
peaceful reforms along the same lines. In May 1968 intellectual activists in
Moscow were focusing on the Prague Spring, rather than on the Western
protest movements. The KGB repressions and arrests, which intensified in
the first half of 1968, rapidly narrowed the circle of human rights advocates.
At the same time, those who remained were in an exalted mood. Ludmilla
Alexeyeva believed that the Czech reforms would soon spill over into the
Soviet Union. She thought that "it was easier to transform Soviet reality
into socialism with a human face than into bourgeois democracy." She and
her activist friends still believed in the linear progression of history: capitalism had preceded socialism, and therefore it represented the past, not
the future. Some of the Russian activists knew Czech, and they informed
others of every revelation about the Czechoslovak glasnost. The background,
the aspirations, the style, and the very language of the Prague reformers
seemed a carbon copy of Zhivago's left-wing children. It appeared that the
Czech intelligentsia of 1968, a more Westernized version of the Russian six-

ties intelligentsia, was demanding the same cultural and intellectual freedoms that the historians, physicists, writers, and artists from Moscow and Leningrad to Novosibirsk dreamed of winning for themselves.[91]

Alexander Tvardovsky also closely followed the news of the Prague Spring struggles. Meanwhile, *Novy Mir* was slowly being strangled by censorship. Tvardovsky attempted to meet with Brezhnev, only to discover that the general secretary of the party was preoccupied by the Czechoslovak crisis. On July 18 Tvardovsky heard on Radio Liberty the declaration "Two Thousand Words," signed by many Czech reform communists and intellectuals. The document concluded: "Again we have the chance to take into our own hands our common cause, which for working purposes we call socialism, and give it a form more appropriate to our once-good reputation and to the fairly good opinion we used to have of ourselves."[92] Tvardovsky admitted that he would have signed this declaration himself. During the tense Soviet-Czechoslovak talks in early August Tvardovsky, for the first time in his life, spent days glued to his shortwave radio set listening to the foreign news broadcasts. He felt euphoric when he learned that the Czechoslovak reformers enjoyed national support and would not bend to Soviet pressure. "I could never have imagined I would feel such joy at the political and moral setback of my country in the eyes of the whole world."[93] A number of Soviet journalists in Prague, all from the "honest" media of the early 1960s (some of them had worked earlier at *Izvestia* under Adzhubei or on the journal *Problems of Peace and Socialism*), rooted for the Czech reformers.[94]

High expectations at the height of the Prague Spring seemed to revive the spirit and hopes of the early 1960s in Moscow. Reform-minded communists, incipient liberals, and technocratic scientists, Jews and non-Jews, regained a common hope for social and cultural renovation. Whenever one of them traveled to Prague and came back, "all Moscow" came to listen to him or her.[95] Mikhail Agursky, who vacillated at the time between Russian Orthodoxy and Zionism, later remembered: "The Prague Spring of 1968 briefly brought me back to the eschatological expectations of a good communism. I still shared the hope that salvation would come from the outside: from Poland, Hungary, the Italian Communist Party—and now from Czechoslovakia."[96] In April through June of 1968 Andrei Sakharov became world-famous for his essay "Reflections on Progress, Peaceful Coexistence, and Intellectual Freedom." During the 1960s Sakharov had concluded that the only way for humankind to avoid a thermonuclear catastrophe was

Andrei Sakharov. He believed in the late 1960s that the intelligentsia, and above all scientists, on both sides of the Cold War divide could "help bring about the escalation of peace" (Courtesy of Memorial, Moscow).

through rapprochement—cultural, social, and political—between the Soviet Union and the West, which would require each side to make compromises. Like the majority of left-leaning intellectuals, he realized that the main obstacle for the Soviet Union was the new bureaucratic elite that put its own interests ahead of "progress." Sakharov saw a link between the idea of domestic change and the danger of nuclear war. For this reason, as well as because of his pacifist values, Sakharov rejected violence and revolutionary change. He feared that any political coup or revolution in Soviet society would cause a retreat into violent chaos. The only alternative was "scientific-democratic" reforms brought about by a gradual evolution in politics, economics, and culture. Sakharov believed that the intelligentsia, in this case scientists and artists, could play a crucial role in such a transformation, but they could do so only if they were allowed freedom of information, travel, and speech. In the spring of 1968 those scientists and other intellectuals who shared the values of the leftist intelligentsia found Sakharov's piece a revelation. Alexeyeva, who retyped the copies of Sakharov's essay for samizdat distribution, was pleased to notice that the author, like her, combined his call for intellectual and cultural freedom with "socialist" views.[97]

Despite growing cynicism and disillusionment, the dream of a Moscow Spring remained a powerful cultural catalyst. Many prominent artists still believed that the vision of freedom under Soviet socialism was a viable option. Yevtushenko was one of them. In 1963–64 the poet, smarting after

Khrushchev's crackdown in 1963, went on a trek around Siberia. There, the thirty-year-old Yevtushenko wrote his best epic poem, *Bratskaia GES* (Bratsk Dam), which took its title from a major power plant on the Angara River. The poem began with a sermon: Yevtushenko appealed to his great poetic predecessors from Pushkin to Pasternak and Mayakovsky to grant him prophetic vision, for "a poet in Russia is never just a poet." He also wrote of the striking continuities between the tsarist regime and Stalinism, of the misery of the Russian people and their patience, punctuated by disastrous rebellions against the autocratic state, such as the peasant revolts of Razin and Pugachev. Yevtushenko also wrote about his contemporaries, the builders of the enormous dam on the Angara River in Siberia. He described the Russian peasant girl Niushka, who fled her demolished village to hold trysts at the construction site with a *stiliaga,* who left her with a baby. Yevtushenko wrote about the Bolshevik Kartsev, who after going through hellish torture, wound up in the gulag, after refusing to betray his comrade. Another protagonist in the poem was Izia Kramer, a Jewish electrician who survived the Nazi extermination camps only to see his beloved Riva humiliated and tortured to death. The poem posed the question whether Russia, despite the Revolution, had returned to a despotic system, with its division into rulers and slaves. No, answered Yevtushenko. He praised Lenin as a genius who had transformed Russia. The Bratsk Dam was not a variation on the Egyptian pyramids, those monuments to tyranny and slavery. Rather, it was a symbol of progress, built by free women and men. Yevtushenko wanted to give the vision of communism with a human face another chance. The poem appeared after heavy censorship, cuts, and revisions in the journal *Yunost* in April 1965.[98]

The Sovremennik Theater also remained loyal to the dreams of socialist emancipation. In 1967 the theater's director, Oleg Yefremov, responding to the regime's pressing demands, decided to stage a trilogy about the Russian revolutionaries, from the aristocratic Decembrists to the Bolsheviks. The official preparations for the celebration of a half-century of communist rule omitted all inconvenient facts from the portrayal of the tragic past. Not wishing to attack the regime, the actors of the Sovremennik Theater aimed to defend the "genuine" origins of the Revolution, as they imagined them, and to protect it against the mendacious official propaganda. The playwrights for the trilogy, Bulat Okudzhava, Alexander Svobodin, and Mikhail Shatrov, were all children of Bolsheviks who had been murdered during

Stalin's terror. They had tried and failed to carry out a world revolution. In the last play, about Lenin and the Bolsheviks, Shatrov "used every means at his command to try to prove that the wellsprings of the Revolution were crystal clear and it was only Stalin and his satraps who had muddied them and brought Lenin's ideas into disrepute." This was the main message of the Thaw.[99]

The authors, the director, and the actors were united in their effort to re-create and interpret the history of the Russian intelligentsia during the preceding century and a half, beginning with the Decembrists and continuing with the revolutionary terrorists of the People's Will. Yet the real interest of Sovremennik's director and artists was in post-1917 Soviet history. They did not doubt that the Revolution itself was morally and historically justified. What they did question was why and at what point it had led to the terror that destroyed the Bolshevik party, including many of their fathers. At what point had the Revolution turned into a catastrophe for the country? Yefremov focused on the problem of ends and means. In the last play of the trilogy on the Bolsheviks, the Sovremennik had the revolutionaries debate the use of Red Terror on the day after an attempt on Lenin's life in July 1918. In reality, the Bolsheviks had unleashed their terror many months earlier, in order to crush and subdue the "former" ruling classes, as well as the non-Bolshevik intelligentsia and peasantry. In Yefremov's mythologized version, Lenin's friends agonized for days before deciding to kill others in order to defend themselves and the Revolution. The message to the audience was that in voting for Red Terror, they inadvertently set in motion the forces that would later devour them. After the fatal vote, the Bolsheviks on the Sovremennik stage stood up like a doomed band of brothers and, staring into the audience, began to sing "The Internationale." The members of the audience rose from their seats and joined in the anthem. The Sovremennik seemed to point to the conclusion that violent politics lead to disaster and should be rejected by the intelligentsia. Yet the issue continued to torment them. How could intellectuals change the repressive autocratic state without becoming part of it or being destroyed by it? The Sovremennik actors and audience found no way out of this dilemma.[100]

The Taganka Theater, established in 1963, surpassed the Sovremennik in boldness and innovation. The theater's founder, the actor Yuri Liubimov, was a latecomer to the left-wing cultural scene.[101] Watching the staging of

Peter Brook's version of *Hamlet* and the plays of Bertolt Brecht, performed in Moscow by a German cast in 1956–57, he had experienced them as a revelation. Liubimov's passion for poetry, especially the poetry of Boris Pasternak (whom he met), made him rebel against socialist realism. At the age of forty-six, Liubimov, with a group of students from a Moscow theater school where he taught, staged Bertolt Brecht's play *The Good Woman of Szechuan*. The biting satire about evil, conformism, and avarice, which Brecht aimed at capitalist society, became in Liubimov's production a reflection on Soviet realities. The play hit Moscow like a bombshell. Boris Slutsky translated Brecht's songs. Adzhubei and Simonov published glowing reviews of the play in *Nedelia* and *Pravda,* respectively. The Soviet Filmmakers' Union, the Union of Soviet Writers, the Academy of Sciences, and the nuclear physicists in Dubna invited Liubimov's group for informal performances. As a result of this public support, Liubimov obtained a license and a home for his theater in the Taganka district of Moscow.[102]

The Taganka Theater addressed an embarrassing issue for Soviet Russian intellectuals: How could they dream of living free and creative lives in a country full of slavishness? While *Novy Mir* spoke to its readers of common values, Liubimov's theater created a public space for joint performances by the actors and the audience, a bit like the democratic agora of Athens. Liubimov was not satisfied with plays written by the leading playwrights of the Thaw. Instead, he patched together his performances from poetry, prose, historical documents, or film scripts. His performances were based on the verses of Andrei Voznesensky, Vladimir Mayakovsky, and Sergei Yesenin, and on John Reed's description of the Russian Revolution. Liubimov invited the poet David Samoilov to produce *The Fallen and the Living,* commemorating the idealistic young poets killed during World War II, and Boris Pasternak as a victim of "another war" against the Russian intelligentsia. The Taganka reveled in exposing an obvious fact: the Brezhnev regime and Soviet society were betraying the ideals in whose name the Revolution had been fought. Still, Liubimov and his actors hesitated to acknowledge that the Revolution itself had occasioned the obliteration of the Russian intelligentsia.[103]

The Ministry of Culture repeatedly banned the Taganka's plays. The officials vociferously objected to the commemoration of Mayakovsky and Pasternak as victimized poets.[104] Liubimov defended his plays by claiming that they restored "socialist values." In April 1968, at the height of the Prague

Spring, ministry officials attempted to fire Liubimov. Liubimov survived because of a few enlightened apparatchiks from the party's Central Committee, speechwriters for Leonid Brezhnev.[105]

The enlightened apparatchiks who saved the Taganka in the spring of 1968 had also followed the events and progress of the Prague Spring. Many of them had worked earlier on the Prague-based *Problems of Peace and Socialism*, a journal, according to Georgy Shakhnazarov, that "played the same kind of role in politics that *Novy Mir* did in literature and the Taganka Theater did in art." Among this group was Alexei Rumiantsev, the editor of *Pravda* in 1965. These people did not share the sentiments of the human rights advocates or take part in the protests. Instead, the defenders of the Taganka believed that they could bring about change by working within the state system and the power structures of the party.[106] The group owed its rise to de-Stalinization and the demand for highly educated "consultants" in the central party apparatus, primarily to deal with global foreign policy issues and the increasingly fractured international communist movement. Many of the enlightened bureaucrats were war veterans and postwar graduates of Moscow State University. They often combined their positions in the party apparatus with senior posts at academic institutes. Above all, these people believed that Marxism-Leninism was not a "dead letter" of official ideology, but a living scientific theory. In particular, they believed that the task of managing society and the economy had become more and more complex and that armed with the theoretical skills, they could help the party and the country adapt to this complexity.[107]

The enlightened apparatchiks rooted for the cultural left. It was a matter of generational identity, politics, and taste. Extensive connections between these bureaucrats and leftist artists and writers often went back to the years when they had studied together during the late Stalinist period and the early post-Stalin years. They were allies in the struggle against numerous xenophobic and anti-Semitic attacks by Russian patriots. After Khrushchev's ouster, the enlightened officials saw themselves as defenders of the policies of de-Stalinization, which had been proclaimed at the Twentieth Party Congress but were now being gradually eroded.[108] In contrast to the anti-intellectual majority in the party apparatus the enlightened apparatchiks were true patrons of high culture. The sculptor Ernst Neizvestny would later admit that they often "acted selflessly and went out on a limb, contrary to their personal interests."[109] In 1968 these communist officials were the only group who received information from many channels and could influence the course of events. They did warn the party leadership that military intervention in Czechoslovakia would cause a split with Western communist parties and damage the Soviet position in the world.[110] People in the highest quarters could not reach a verdict on the Prague Spring. The Czechs did not offer an easy pretext for Soviet military intervention: in contrast to the Hungarian Revolution of 1956, their changes were peaceful, and the Communist Party remained in power in Czechoslovakia. One writer who worked in the party Central Committee in 1968 said that never before had he seen such room for difference of opinion on any issue. "One could walk along the corridor inside the Central Committee and shout at the top of one's lungs: 'It is impossible to send tanks into Czechoslovakia!' And somebody could walk from the other direction and shout back: 'It is time to send tanks into Czechoslovakia and clean up this mess!'"[111] An enlightened speechwriter for Brezhnev, Alexander Bovin, wrote in his diary on August 19: "In our department, in International, in the foreign ministry, the prevailing mood is sharply critical. [Intervention] is considered an unjustified step, [or] at least a premature one."[112]

Finally, Brezhnev and rest of the Politburo concluded that the "creeping counterrevolution" was as dangerous as an armed uprising, and on August 21, the armed forces of the Soviet Union, the GDR, Poland, Hungary, and Bulgaria invaded and occupied Czechoslovakia. In the invading force were 170,000 Soviet troops. The news of the invasion took everyone in Russia by surprise. Yet the KGB and party reports invariably reported "absolute calm" in all Soviet regions and cities. The vast majority of Russian people accepted the invasion as a necessity for Soviet security interests in the split world of the Cold War. Many ordinary Russians had lost relatives in World War II. For them, the fact that Czechoslovakia bordered on West Germany was enough to justify the invasion. "What occupation?" said many people. "Czechoslovakia? But we liberated them in 1945. Two hundred thousand Russian soldiers died there. And now they stage this counterrevolution? We could not give up Czechoslovakia and leave it to the Americans."[113]

The hopes and illusions of Zhivago's children had come face to face with a brutal reality check. Even in comparison with the protest in the Soviet Union over the invasion of Hungary in 1956, the protest over the invasion of Czechoslovakia was remarkably insignificant. In Prague several Russian journalists, sympathizers with the Prague Spring, refused to write lies about the invasion. They were quickly fired by their superiors in Moscow. The only spectacular public protest took place on Red Square on August 25. There were seven protesters, all of them from the human rights movement: Konstantin Babitsky, Larisa Bogoraz, Vadim Delone, Vladimir Dremliuga, Pavel Litvinov, Natalia Gorbanevskaia, and Vladimir Fainberg. Gorbanevskaia, a young poet from Alexeyeva's circle of friends, was an editor of the first samizdat chronicle of human rights violations in the Soviet Union. She brought a baby carriage with her little son inside to the square. In the carriage, she had small Czech flags and posters. One poster read: "Long live a free and independent Czechoslovakia!" On another poster was the famous slogan of Polish national revolutionaries of the nineteenth century: "For your freedom and ours!" The protesters tried to unfurl the flags and posters, but KGB agents charged at them. "Beat the anti-Soviet agents! They're all Jews." It was a secret police trick to identify members of the intelligentsia as "Jewish-looking" and incite the anti-Semitism of the bystanders. The trick did not work this time; however, neither were the bystanders capable of grasping the ideas and slogans of the protesting intellectuals. The KGB quickly arrested the protesters. They continued to behave heroically during the investigation and trial. Larisa Bogoraz stated to the court: "I do not consider myself to be a public person. Public affairs, much less politics, are not the most important aspect of my life. But I faced a dilemma: to protest or keep silent. For me silence would have meant a lie. If I had not protested, I would have held myself responsible for all the activities of the government. In the same way, all the people should be held responsible for Stalin-Beria camps and death sentences." The Soviet court, on the instructions of the party authorities, sentenced the dissidents for "spreading slanderous information about the Soviet state and social system" and for "disrupting social order and transportation." Six protesters were sent to the camps, and one, Fainberg, was committed to a mental asylum.[114]

Few other attempts at protest were made among the left-leaning intelligentsia. Yevtushenko and Aksyonov, on vacation in the Crimea, railed in private against the criminal act of the Soviet regime. Yevtushenko shed "the tears of a deceived idealist," then rushed to the local post office and fired off two cables: one to Brezhnev protesting the invasion, another to the Czech embassy in Moscow, expressing moral solidarity. Aksyonov drowned his rage in alcohol. Alexander Galich, a guitar-toting sixties poet and singer, wrote a song with the refrain: "And you, would you dare to walk out onto the square at the designated hour?" Galich was alluding not only to the protesters on Red Square, but also to the Decembrists who had sacrificed themselves to demonstrate their love of freedom to the people of Russia.[115]

Boris Pasternak had made such a sacrifice, although in a different way, in the late fifties. The majority of the children of Zhivago, however, were not ready for it. Among freethinking scientists and scholars only a few, very timid voices were raised in protest. Nowhere did the "rebellious" party committees resign in protest. At the Institute of History and other think tanks, no strikes or sit-ins took place. In fairness, by that time many prominent activists had already been expelled from the Party and fired from their jobs. Still, the submissiveness of the educated elite was depressing. Even at Akademgorodok, most of scientists promptly "changed the tape" and fell in step to the hard-line patriotic music. In contrast with 1956, no student movement arose in support of the Prague Spring. The lack of response in Moscow to the self-immolation of the Czech student Jan Palach in January 1969 underlined this shocking fact. Some students met the news by raising glasses of vodka—the old Russian tradition for mourning the dead. That was, however, the extent of their courage. One of the writers for *Novy Mir,* Igor Dedkov, who had been a student activist in 1956, wrote in dismay in his journal: "A Czech student died yesterday. Our radio stations and newspapers are silent. They report on anything but Czechoslovakia. All we have been writing makes no sense: cheap, cowardly acts, boot-licking, and prostitution."[116]

The myth of a socially engaged and morally potent intelligentsia collapsed in August 1968, smashed by the brutal force of the authoritarian state. Above all, intellectuals were again afraid of the increasing KGB repression. In January 1967 the KGB had arrested Alexander Ginzburg, the poet Yuri Galanskov, and two other people for the distribution of samizdat, including the *White Book* on the Siniavsky-Daniel trial. The same year, Yuri Andropov was appointed to replace Semichastny as head of the secret police. Andropov created a special KGB directorate to deal with the intelligentsia. Its head, Philip Bobkov, came from the Leningrad school of SMERSH, had worked in Stalin's military counterintelligence, and shared with Andropov some knowledge of intellectual and cultural life. During 1968 the KGB called thousands of intellectuals and students, one by one, for a "prophylactic" interrogation, warning them that continued participation in the human rights movement or samizdat activities would jeopardize their future careers and might lead to arrest. The KGB also subjected dissidents to forced psychiatric treatment on the grounds that they were "mentally unstable."[117]

The Soviet invasion of Czechoslovakia destroyed the last hope linking the pursuit of intellectual and artistic freedom with the Soviet communist project. Yelena Bonner was in Paris visiting Jewish relatives when she watched and read the Western coverage of the Soviet invasion, with pain and dismay. It had finally become clear to her that the Soviet system could not be "corrected" or changed by intellectuals inside the party. The Kremlin leaders would never relinquish their power and their empire. She returned to Moscow with a feeling that her party membership had been a great mistake. The shock of the invasion devalued her previous commitments, and she needed some time to reappraise her life.[118] What cause was now worth fighting and protesting for? Aksyonov had also lost his last remaining illusions. Back in the 1950s he and his friends, *stiliagi* and jazz fans, had been "drunk with the damp breeze from Europe that suddenly started blowing in our direction." Now Aksyonov had had enough of the obedient majority that cared neither for democracy nor for artistic freedom. It dawned on him that the Soviet tank drivers who had invaded Czechoslovakia were "our boys, who applauded us, who read our books."[119] In 1969 the Taganka Theater performed a remarkable new play based on a Maxim Gorky story. At the end the chorus of actors sang a famous prerevolutionary song, "Dubinushka," that used to be sung by the workers who hauled the river barges and towed heavy weights. "The day will come, and the people will arise," sang the actors. Before the Revolution, the artists of the Wanderers school and great opera singer Fyodor Chaliapin had used "Dubinushka" to call the Russian people to revolution. In the Taganka performance, a recording of Chaliapin's mighty bass blended with the chorus from the amplifiers, as the actors moved toward the audience, as if pulling a barge. The actors were not calling for another Revolution, but rather mounting a protest against Russia's eternal lack of freedom.[120]

A tiny enlightened minority in the party apparatus were also angry, yet they did not resign in protest. Before August 1968, a coalition had seemed feasible between them, the economic reformers, reformist scientists, and the left wing of artistic groups. Could it have led eventually to a Moscow Spring? Who might have been the Soviet Alexander Dubček? These questions remained unanswered.[121] The invasion was a painful reminder of how powerless and vulnerable were the friends of reform in Soviet Russia. Gorbachev, at that time the regional party boss of the Stavropol region, later wrote: "From August 21 on, the ideological 'toughening' began, repression of any free thinking." The party Central Committee ordered the regional committees to "take decisive actions in the ideological sphere. The struggle against the dissident movement took on a pervasive character."[122] Numerous reform-minded communists, people involved in the human rights movement, and advocates of more far-reaching de-Stalinization were expelled from the party. The very word "reform" became taboo for almost two decades.

In 1968 Zhivago's children witnessed a new wave of revolutionary events around the world. With their past and experience, they had much to contribute to the global change around them. Their moral fervor, commitment to human rights, and determination to come to terms with the Soviet past, as well as their enduring anticapitalist convictions, placed them in the company of the reformers of the Prague Spring, as well as intellectual dreamers from Berkeley to West Berlin. And from the Stalinist past they had already learned lessons that most left-liberal intellectuals in the West were still reluctant to grasp. All the Moscow intellectuals on the left rejected the mythology of the Cultural Revolution in China. They understood that behind the radical youth in China and the peasant guerrillas in Vietnam stood ruthless manipulators, who would bring only more tyranny, not increased freedom.

Was there a chance in 1968 for a transnational movement of intelligentsia, as Sakharov and other human rights activists in Moscow seemed to expect? The Cold War divide and the Iron Curtain proved too insuperable. The transnational links between Western and Russian intellectuals were almost nonexistent. The agenda of the Western New Left was too different from the immediate agenda of the Prague reformers and Moscow intelligentsia. Western protesters wanted to improve their pluralist democracy, to eradicate racism, discrimination against minorities, and hierarchical authority in society and in academic life. The left-wing intelligentsia in Soviet Russia could hope only to make the omnipotent party and the state observe their own Soviet laws.

The Prague Spring produced the illusion of a reformist solidarity that could unite disparate groups in the intelligentsia with technocrats and enlightened party apparatchiks and initiate a Moscow Spring. The end of the Prague Spring not only left the prospect of a Moscow Spring in ruins but underscored the political and moral sterility of the dream of socialism with a human face—of the attempt to marry the Soviet project to freedom without a return to private property and capitalism. In the absence of that dream, the very idea of an intelligentsia in Russia began to seem like the figment of a naive imagination. And so began the long decline of Zhivago's children and the death throes of their dreams.

The crisis emerged, above all, in the realm of
spirit. The people of the sixties began to lose their
position as the spiritual leaders of the nation.

—Viktor Slavkin, aging *stiliaga*, 1996

nine

The Long Decline
1968-1985

O N JANUARY 22, 1969, a lieutenant in the Soviet army, Viktor Ilyin,
made an attempt to assassinate Leonid Brezhnev. Ilyin had been born in
Leningrad and had joined the military after graduating in March 1968 from
the Leningrad topographical technical school. The Prague Spring and the
Soviet invasion of Czechoslovakia radicalized his thinking. Ilyin boarded
a plane from Leningrad to Moscow, taking with him two Makarov pistols.
On the next day Brezhnev was scheduled to meet with the cosmonauts after
their successful space flight. Ilyin waited for the government cortege near
the Borovitsky Gates of the Kremlin and, aiming at the second car, opened
fire from both guns. He killed the driver. Two cosmonauts were wounded
by broken glass.[1]

A writer for *Novy Mir*, Igor Dedkov, learned about the incident from the
Western radio and compared the event to Karakozov's attempt to assassinate Tsar Alexander II in 1866. Other antiregime intellectuals compared
Ilyin to the nineteenth-century group of radical intellectuals of the People's
Will, who saw regicide as a means to liberate Russia from despotism.[2] Both
historical analogies involved terrorist actions undertaken by intellectuals in
response to the failure of revolution to emancipate the Russian people.[3] Did
it mean that the sixties intellectuals, heartbroken by the failure of the Prague
Spring, were ready to resort to violence? Just the opposite. Ilyin was not the
precursor of the revolutionary intelligentsia. Human rights advocates and

the left-wing intellectuals felt revulsion at an idea of revolutionary terror. They wanted changes to occur, but without bloody coups, revolutions, or turmoil.[4]

Ilyin was committed to a mental asylum. Instead of a return to Stalinism, much feared by many in the left-leaning intelligentsia, Brezhnev continued Khrushchev's New Deal with the Soviet people, including the educated elites. Now, the thrust of Soviet policies was not to achieve a return to Leninism or to support national liberation movements around the world, but rather to usher in détente with the West and ensure domestic conservatism. A joke captures the mood of the time: Stalin, Khrushchev, and Brezhnev are sitting in a train compartment. Suddenly, the train comes to a halt. Stalin gives the order to shoot the engineer. The train continues to stand still. Khrushchev rehabilitates the engineer—still no movement. Brezhnev draws the curtains over the windows and says: "At last, we're moving again." Under Brezhnev, it was no longer necessary to prove that one believed in the Soviet communist project. There was no debate about what this project meant or how to bring it to fruition. It was enough just to accept its existence and to mind one's own business. The KGB watched carefully to make sure everyone observed the ritualized rules of public behavior, and it often conducted "prophylactic measures" to warn and intimidate possible transgressors.

Before August 1968 the Brezhnev leadership still paid grudging respect to intellectuals—the scientific and cultural elites. Even the decision to send troops into Czechoslovakia was dictated by the Kremlin's recognition of the power of intellectuals, whether as instigators of a popular uprising or as promoters of a "quiet revolution." During the next decade, however, the Brezhnev leadership became more certain of its control over educated society. Consequently, the status of intellectuals declined in the eyes of the political leaders. And in a context where no reforms were discussed, there was no place for intellectuals and their advice; nor was there any need for scientific miracles, social science research, investigative media, or interactive television journalism. The continuing expansion of higher education and cultural institutions, along with greater investments in scientific and academic endeavor, did not necessarily lead to the growth of civic society, ideals of democracy and freedom, or simple moral integrity. Those who had in previous decades believed in the power of the "honest" word, the resurgence of Russian literature, or the influence of scientific and scholarly expertise suddenly lost traction. Even the belief in the Marxist version of historically determined progress, almost an article of faith in the 1960s, seemed to have been shattered. Intellectuals and writers became demoralized by the loss of positive common guidelines and goals in the new political and social reality.

Those who had remained convinced of the purpose and significance of the intelligentsia discovered several options that had not existed before. It was possible to express public dissent and turn for support to world public opinion. It was also possible to emigrate from the Soviet Union. And last but not least, it was possible simply to live on without revolutionary ideals or big dreams, making small compromises, and carving out a niche for daily creative and spiritual activities, in the increasingly pragmatic and cynical environment of Brezhnev's Soviet Union.

Dissidents: Living the Intelligentsia's Ideals

The invasion of Czechoslovakia set in motion the group defection of many intellectuals and cultural figures from the Soviet communist project. The earlier optimism and idealism, the hope for a purified, humane socialism that would rescue the revolution, evaporated rapidly in Moscow vanguard circles. There was a widespread sense among leftist intellectuals that history had betrayed them. Those who had assiduously studied the writings of Marx and Lenin before, seeking in them some theoretical magic formula for reforming the Soviet society, ceased searching after the Prague Spring.[5] Dmitry Furman, a Moscow intellectual who graduated from MGU in 1965, recalled that among his friends and colleagues the fad of Marxism-Leninism "died a quiet death sometime during the reign of Brezhnev." Among Furman's friends were Westernizers, Zen Buddhists, Russian Orthodox believers, Russian neo-Nazis, and Zionists. Although many of those people were party members, genuine Marxists were a vanishing breed.[6] In the Russian provinces, far from the cultural urban centers, one could still find people who were true believers in Lenin and Marxism; however, the provinces in Russia were intellectually behind the urban cultural centers by at least a decade.

The heroic form of exodus from the Soviet communist project was to join the dissident movement. A few intellectuals, among them Alik Ginzburg, Valery Chalidze, and Ludmilla Alexeyeva, grasped the potential of forming a constitutional movement, or simply behaving as if Soviet laws and constitutional rights were not a fiction but a reality. It had been Alexander Volpin's idea that had inspired the first public demonstration in December 1965, after the arrest of Siniavsky and Daniel. The dissidents believed they could benefit from the fact that in 1966 the Soviet Union ratified the United Nations Covenant on Human Rights. The Soviet state reacted by issuing amendments to the criminal code, under which people could be arrested and imprisoned for spreading "anti-Soviet slander," but it could not prevent new forms of public dissent. During the Prague Spring a number of dissidents, including Alik Ginzburg, Roy Medvedev, and Ludmilla Alexeyeva, began to put together a samizdat periodical digest, the *Chronicle of Current Events.* In 1969–70 a group of Moscow intellectuals, many of them former party members, established the Committee for Human Rights. At first, the human rights movement remained deliberately nonideological and welcomed people of starkly different views, from reform Marxists to liberals, "Russian patriots" and non-Russian nationalists.[7]

It is difficult to capture the full and remarkable variety of the forms of public dissent and the samizdat publications that appeared during the 1970s. The debate, however, continues on the place and role of the human rights movement in the story of the Russian intelligentsia. For the majority of dissidents, participation in the movement was intimately linked to the ethos of the intelligentsia, the moral as well as intellectual need to be independent from the autocratic state. Some authors presented "dissidents" as the only real *intelligenti* of that time, the people who came closest to embodying the Russian intelligentsia's moral standards and ideals. And the so-called dissidents themselves, all types and descriptions of them, consistently imagined themselves to be the "true" intelligentsia, in contrast to Soviet establishment scientists, physicians, academic scholars, artists, and so on, who refused to participate in their activities. It was notable that most of the dissidents no longer sought their spiritual forebears in post-1917 intellectual and cultural history, even the first post-Revolutionary decade. In a break with their previous beliefs from the time when they belonged to the leftist avant-garde in the early 1960s, they now sought their roots in prerevolutionary Russia, above all among the radicals who opposed the state and addressed society as moral and social prophets.[8]

The dissidents originated in the same social circles that had spawned the Moscow *kompany* during the previous decade. The majority of them belonged to the postwar student generation. They continued to gather at one another's apartments, often in the kitchens, where tea and modest snacks were served, and engaged in endless conversations about literature, art, politics, and the accursed questions of Russian life. Consumption of high culture—fine arts, classical music, along with samizdat—continued to be the highlight of their existence. Women played a particularly prominent role in the movement: they helped the families of the arrested activists, and educated children in the spirit of honesty and intellectual freedom. The joke at the time ran: "Why are you retyping *War and Peace* on your typewriter?—I just want my son to read Tolstoy, and he reads only samizdat."[9] The mutual trust and affection, the habit of intense intellectual and spiritual interaction, characteristic of the earlier bands of companions, remained a vital part of the ethos of the dissident movement. In 1970 Yelena Bonner, an activist in the human rights movement, met Andrei Sakharov when he joined her friends in a Moscow courthouse to attend the trial of a person arrested for "anti-Soviet activities." The two hit it off and quickly discovered they had much in common, above all their love for classical Russian literature, especially the poetry of Alexander Pushkin, an aversion to conformism, and a sense of moral commitment expressed in Goethe's *Faust:* "He only earns his freedom and existence / Who daily conquers them anew!" Sakharov and Bonner were both captivated by the youthful and romantic spirit of this verse. It helped establish a spiritual bond between the two of them that led to their marriage in January 1972.[10]

This romantic and moral ethos of the dissidents was enhanced by a sense of the risk involved in public dissent. They reached out to and assisted victims of state oppression and legal injustice. Anatoly Cherniaev, an enlightened party apparatchik who had friends and schoolmates in the circles frequented by dissidents, in 1974 recorded his envy and admiration for the solidarity within the community *(obshchestvo)* of human rights activists. He learned that poet Yuli Daniel, sentenced with Siniavsky in the infamous trial of 1965–66, had returned from camps and was receiving assistance from the "community." Its networks and connections in Moscow enabled Daniel to make a living by supplying translations under a pseudonym. He even built a house in Moscow and found a new wife among the young women of the community. Cherniaev commented that this assistance revealed "a high level of solidarity, unusual for the present-day state of human relations" in Moscow. "This community is outside the system."[11] In other

Andrei Sakharov and Yelena Bonner. They both admired the same quotation from Goethe's *Faust:* "He only earns his freedom and existence / Who daily conquers them anew!" Their activities in the human rights movement brought them together, and they were married in 1972. Standing behind them (left to right) are the writers Viktor Nekrasov and Vladimir Voinovich (Courtesy of Memorial, Moscow).

words, the dissidents built a civic milieu for themselves, separate from Soviet society.

At first, the dissidents studiously avoided taking political and ideological stands against the Soviet regime. Sakharov, a leading authority among the human rights activists, never believed in a violent overthrow of the Soviet regime. And he continued to hope for free cooperation, even if in some distant future, between the intelligentsia and an enlightened Soviet leadership. In 1970–71 the KGB reported, citing the tapped conversations among the dissidents, that Sakharov wanted to meet with Brezhnev or someone in the Soviet leadership, to explain the goals and purposes of the human rights movement and to reach some kind of understanding. Sources among the dissidents do not corroborate this assertion. The KGB's Yuri Andropov at that time might have viewed such a meeting as a way to separate Sakharov from the dissident movement. In any case, Brezhnev and his colleagues were not prepared to enter into any negotiations with Sakharov. They suspected that the content of such negotiations would be publicized in the

West, and did not want to be embarrassed. Such a meeting would also have meant recognizing Sakharov's status as the leader of an independent intelligentsia.[12]

Inevitably, the initial success of the dissident movement in withstanding state pressures through courage and solidarity, pushed them to perceive themselves as an elite within the intelligentsia or even the only true intelligentsia, in contrast to the conformist majority, including many of their former friends and contacts inside and outside the party. This view, in turn, set them apart from most people in the scientific and cultural elites, who were not ready to join the movement. Active public dissent almost always entailed the revocation of party membership, the loss of professional position and all concomitant privileges, and the loss of "access"—that is, the ability to lobby the authorities through the usual Soviet channels. A new psychology had emerged, observed Sakharov, "when people began to value very highly nonessential needs, such as travel abroad, which thirty years ago had been considered an unimaginable luxury."[13]

Those who had permission to travel abroad considered it not a luxury, but a necessity. Numerous prominent intellectuals and artists still believed they could do more by living out their intellectual dreams inside the system. Bonner and Sakharov discovered this phenomenon in 1970, when they began to collect signatures for a public petition to abolish capital punishment in Soviet law. Yevtushenko and Okudzhava refused to sign the petition, because by doing so they would forfeit the chance to publish, obtain funds for a new journal, and promote young poets. Dmitry Likhachev, a famous historian of ancient Russian art and literature, refused to sign, because he needed to convince the authorities in Leningrad to preserve the old city and suburban parks. Gersh Budker, a physicist from the Akademgorodok, said that his signature would make things more complicated for numerous scientists at his institute.[14] A few courageous artists, among them the cellist Mstislav Rostropovich and his wife, the opera diva Galina Vishnevskaia, supported dissidents with money and signatures, and (in the Rostropoviches' case) even provided a living space in their country house for Alexander Solzhenitsyn. Yet many other artists refused to do so. In the jargon of the seventies, they remained "semidissidents"—that is, they were against the regime but did not dare to take part in public dissent for fear of losing their ability to pursue their professional careers in science, the humanities, or art. Yuri Temirkanov, a world-famous conductor, later confessed: "I have never been a fighter against the communists. I was afraid of them."[15]

The more the community of human rights activists met with rejection from the larger circles of educated society, the greater became the divide between them and the majority in intellectual-artistic circles and broader groups of educated professionals.[16] Estranged from their natural social-cultural base and facing unceasing arrests and harassment from the KGB, the public activists turned to the democratic West as the last straw. Specifically, many of them viewed Western journalists and Western media as the main audience for their activities. They passed materials to them about Soviet repression and violation of legal norms not in order to expand public dissent and to arouse Russian public opinion; rather, they wanted to use the pressure of Western public opinion on the Soviet government to help the friends who were in prisons and psychiatric hospitals and to protect the dissident movement from even harsher reprisals. "The West will help us," became a favorite toast among "defectors-in-place." For dissidents, friendship with Western journalists became essential. Foreigners who resided in Moscow with their families, the hordes of Western officials who came to Moscow and Leningrad during the years of détente, exchange scholars, and participants at scientific conferences carried information in and out of the Soviet Union, helping spread the news about the arrests and persecutions.[17]

During the 1970s the circle of Moscow human rights activists focused attention primarily on the defense of individuals and groups who suffered from the injustices of the Soviet regime. There were many such individuals and groups among the non-Russian ethnic and religious groups—for instance, the Crimean Tatars and Volga Germans who had been evicted from their homelands, various Catholic and Protestant religious groups, western Ukrainian and Baltic nationalists, and increasingly Jews who wanted to emigrate from the Soviet Union. This focus was a logical continuation of the growth in liberal beliefs among former leftist dissidents. It was also a follow-up to the slogan "For your freedom and ours" raised by the protesters on Red Square in August 1968. Among the minorities more manifestations of ethnic solidarity took place than among Russians themselves. Moreover, some followers of the dissident movement (and even more people within bohemian circles and groups of semidissidents in Moscow and Leningrad) began to take a negative view of the Russian people, because they had served as the backbone of the Soviet regime. Of course, Andrei Sakharov and the leading human rights defenders never agreed with this anti-Russian "nationalism in reverse," and they rejected elitist views. Nevertheless, such dicta as "There are only despots and slaves in Russia" and "Slavery is in the Russian genes" could be heard in the dissident milieu.[18]

Historically, nonrevolutionary groups who promoted the idea of the Russian intelligentsia had had to negotiate with the state or influence the bureaucracy to promote change. It was the only alternative to revolutionary violence and underground political activities. The dissidents, however, sought a third way of advancing their moral agenda, and it led them into self-isolation. Their reliance on Western officials, diplomats, and media to spread their message, as well as their apparent emphasis on defending the rights of non-Russians, made the dissidents more vulnerable to attacks by Soviet propaganda and KGB disinformation specialists. At universities, academic institutes, and other cultural institutions, the KGB disseminated materials and sponsored lectures in which the human rights defenders were presented as "non-Russians" and traitors who worked for the West. This campaign did not fall on deaf ears. Many potential sympathizers of the dissidents considered it inappropriate to help the West in its propaganda warfare against the Soviet Union during the Cold War. They felt that the majority of dissidents had a biased agenda that gave them no right to claim to be the moral vanguard of the Russian people. Many of Sakharov's colleagues believed that he went too far and ascribed his outspokenness to the influence of his Jewish wife. Numerous scientists, artists, and other intellectual figures signed the collective letters denouncing the most prominent dissidents, above all Solzhenitsyn and Sakharov. The party authorities generated these letters as a test of loyalty for intellectuals, but also as a weapon to drive a wedge between them and the dissidents. And again this policy worked. More and more of the dissidents became, as Elena Bonner put it, "foreigners at home."[19]

The dissident intellectuals, including Sakharov, appealed to the U.S. Congress in 1973 to link détente and economic relations with the Soviet Union with Soviet domestic reforms, above all the right of emigration. These appeals translated into the Jackson-Vanik amendment to the U.S.-Soviet trade bill, linking trade relations between the superpowers with the right of emigration for Soviet Jews. The human rights activists also took heart in the signing of the Helsinki Final Act in August 1975 by Leonid

Living the intelligentsia's ethos in the 1970s: a circle of dissident friends. Among them were Ludmilla Alexeyeva (second from left), Larisa Bogoraz, and her second husband, Anatoly Marchenko (on right) (Courtesy of Memorial, Moscow).

Brezhnev. This international document, approved by the United States, Canada, and all European countries, obligated the Soviet Union to respect freedom of speech, conscience, and free travel. By that time the struggle for the right to emigrate from the Soviet Union had become the primary goal of the human rights activists. Dissidents in Moscow and some other Soviet cities launched Helsinki Watch groups to monitor Soviet violations of the Helsinki Act. In January 1977 Jimmy Carter became the U.S. president and sent a personal letter to Andrei Sakharov, as a member of the Helsinki Watch group in Moscow. Ludmilla Alexeyeva, another member of this group, recalled that "our most optimistic predictions now seemed within reach. . . . The alliance of Western politicians and Soviet dissidents was starting to emerge." The euphoria was short-lived. The movement, isolated from the broader intellectual circles in Moscow, and Russia as a whole, dwindled rapidly. The KGB retaliated by arresting activists in the Helsinki Watch groups.[20]

During the 1970s the human rights movement had faced mounting attacks not only from the Soviet state, but also from Russian nationalists among the dissidents themselves and in the right wing of Soviet literary circles. The Russian patriots, a growing network of intellectuals and artists from the post-Stalin generation who had embraced Russian nationalism and chauvinism during the 1960s, saw the Prague Spring as a danger, not an opportunity. After 1968 their ideological hatred focused on cosmopolitan party intellectuals, believers in Marxism-Leninism and socialism with a human face. Those, in their opponents' opinion, were the children of the people who had ruined Russia during the Revolution.[21] The patriots celebrated the disappearance of Tvardovsky's *Novy Mir* as their big victory. In 1969 they also published programmatic articles in the Moscow literary journal *Molodaia Gvardia* (Young Guard). These articles adopted the theses of the conservative Slavophile intellectuals of the second half of the nineteenth century, who had opposed the Westernization of Russia and criticized the "Westernized intelligentsia."[22] Now, they wrote, we have the Moscow intelligentsia that sold out to the West opposed to the "national spirit" and "stringently active" in undermining the "foundations of national culture." The Russian patriots urged party authorities to take urgent measures to support and preserve the vanishing Russian peasantry. They also exhorted the government to purge cosmopolitan (that is, Jewish) intellectuals, in the way the Polish regime had done after March 1968.[23]

While applauding the Brezhnev leadership for its newfound toughness after the intervention in Czechoslovakia, Russian patriots criticized the Kremlin's détente policies. In their eyes, these policies opened the gates to Western influence on Russian society, and the eventual triumph of their cosmopolitan and liberal enemies. Driven by these fears, even Russian nationalists who admired *Novy Mir* and initially believed they had to form a united front with liberal human rights activists and reform-minded communists began to distance themselves from them. Gennady Shimanov wrote in his diary in the early 1970s: "Should we as Russian patriots join ranks with the so-called democrats against Soviet power? If tomorrow this power collapses, who will become the masters of Russia? Given the overwhelming supremacy of the anti-Russian forces even in Russia itself, not to mention the power of the West that will come to assist its appointees and allies, those who would come to power would be much worse than the current regime. Therefore, we should firmly take the side of this regime, as bad as it is, by supporting it against the Westernizers."[24]

Numerous scholars, journalists, and Komsomol functionaries shared the nationalist angst and met to discuss a nationalist agenda. Some writers and intellectuals met informally in what they called the Russian Club, in Moscow, Novgorod, and other historic cities. They were particularly carried away by the views of Lev Gumilyov, a brilliant historian and the only son of the poets Anna Akhmatova and Nikolai Gumilyov. During the Stalin era Gumilyov was arrested twice and spent years in the camps. There he became interested in the study of the great nomadic migrations from Asia to Europe. He also developed the concept of a "passionary ethnos" capable of spectacular expansion and conquest. Gumilyov was influenced by thinkers of the Eurasian movement whom he met in the camps, Russians who had returned to the Soviet Union during the 1930s from emigration, believing that Stalinism could transcend the Red-White divide and build a great Eurasian empire. In the spirit of Oswald Spengler, Gumilyov believed that Europe was in a state of permanent decline and that rejuvenation could come only from the East. Gumilyov's view of the Jews in medieval Europe as a parasitic, mercantile class, not a nation, made some authors accuse him of anti-Semitism.[25] His writings, derivatives of the ethnoracial nationalist philosophies of the 1920s, would play the central role in the resurgent Russian nationalist movement. Gumilyov gained many followers among better-educated Russian nationalists, who no longer limited their reference frame to Stalinism. They claimed that Russia, having inherited the baton of a great Eurasian "superethnos," was destined to oppose the declining West. Their discussions invariably zeroed in on the Revolution and the role Jews had played in it. The myth of a Judeo-Masonic conspiracy spread from Muscovite intellectual circles to the provinces through the networks of Russian patriots, especially the Russian branch of the writers' union. The anti-Semitic theorists credited Stalin with trying to liberate Russia from the Jewish yoke and claimed that the Brezhnev leadership was under the control of the hidden Judeo-Masonic cabal.[26] Fortunately, the Soviet leadership never intended to implement the anti-Semitic dreams of the extreme Russian nationalists.

Alexander Solzhenitsyn complicated the venomous intellectual politics in dissident and semidissident circles even more during the 1970s. From 1969 to 1973 the author of *One Day* still remained a moral exemplar to hundreds of thousands of disaffected Russian and non-Russian intellectuals and artists. In 1974 he attracted world attention again when his monumental work *The Gulag Archipelago* was published in the West, unsurpassed collective testimony to the crimes of the communist regime. He was awarded the Nobel Prize. Yet Solzhenitsyn used this fame to promote an agenda that was at sharp variance with the views and values of most of his intellectual admirers. He was an Orthodox believer and a conservative Russian nationalist who idealized premodern Russian history and the Russian peasantry and preached isolationism from the West and Western influences. Solzhenitsyn believed that the intelligentsia in any shape and form was a vehicle for those influences, and hence the intrinsic enemy of the Russian people.

In 1973 Solzhenitsyn began to express his views more clearly than he had before. At first, he rejected the idea that the large educated class that had emerged after Stalin's death could be in any way compared with the Russian intelligentsia. Instead, he wrote, the rapid expansion of higher education in the postwar times had produced a class of "dabblers" without real knowledge or principles. How, he wondered, could Moscow intellectuals be so duplicitous? They "see clearly the flabby weakness of the Party Lie," he wrote, "they ridicule it, and yet they cynically, vocally, and craftily repeat this Lie, contributing to it with their eloquence and stylish embellishments!"[27] Solzhenitsyn seemed to be defending the religious and conservative Russia of his imagination from usurpers who had absorbed the Western cosmopolitan value of intellectual freedom. No wonder that Solzhenitsyn began to criticize the "society" of dissidents. He blamed Sakharov and his colleagues for their unwillingness to defend the Russian people, and eagerness to fight for the rights of Jews and other minorities who wanted to emigrate and "abandon Russia" to its fate. Sakharov, who admired Solzhenitsyn's literary and political contribution to public dissent, realized by the mid-1970s that the writer of *The Gulag Archipelago* adhered to very different philosophies and ethical principles than he did. For Solzhenitsyn, the moral salvation of the Russian people was a quasi-religious concept that he passionately believed in. The fate of specific individuals, Russians and especially non-Russians, was of no interest to him; anyone could be sacrificed for a great cause. Solzhenitsyn, like the KGB, believed that only Sakharov's marriage to the Jewish Yelena Bonner made him act in an anti-Russian and anti-patriotic manner. In February 1974 the Politburo, in an effort to decapitate the dissident movement, expelled Solzhenitsyn from the Soviet Union. In the West, however, Solzhenitsyn fully revealed his true ideological colors. Jewish intellectual admirers of Solzhenitsyn who had lauded his courage in the fight against the Soviet regime turned away from him. The anti-Semitic tone of his interviews and writings, and their implications for Soviet Jews, became an embarrassment to many of his Russian friends. He chose a remote place in Vermont to live, where he worked in isolation from the Russian émigré community. From this haven in the United States he continued to criticize the "Westernized" intelligentsia of Moscow for lack of true national sentiments. At the same time, calling for repentance and moral renewal, he appealed to the Kremlin leadership and bureaucracy and the Russian population at large.[28]

Solzhenitsyn's writings of the 1970s and the polemics surrounding them contributed to further blurring of the intellectual contours of the Russian intelligentsia. Instead of looking to the future, many antiregime intellectuals squabbled and split over historical and ideological narratives from the prerevolutionary past.

Exodus from the Utopia: Emigration

Solzhenitsyn's forced emigration was part of a larger phenomenon that also helped account for the rapid dwindling and fragmentation of the idea of the Russian intelligentsia. Individual intellectuals and artists, dancers, and musicians had defected to the West before the Prague Spring. The exodus from the Soviet Union became a mass phenomenon with the so-called Jewish emigration, the result of a complex set of causes and policies, among them the escalating anti-Semitic rhetoric and the ideology of Russian nationalists, as well as the resurgent Jewish spirit. Among the most important international factors were the U.S.-Israeli campaign to "liberate Jews" in the Soviet Union. The catalyst for this campaign was an affair involving airplane hijackers in June 1970, a group of Soviet Jews led by an adventurous-minded Zionist who wanted to leave the Soviet Union at any cost; they were captured by the KGB before they could escape, and two of them were sentenced to death.[29] Human rights activists in the USSR launched an international campaign in support of the condemned hijackers. Jewish activists abroad harassed Soviet offices in Western capitals. Under pressure, the Politburo decided to commute the death sentences to long prison terms. Still, the Jewish protests and demonstrations continued in Moscow, Tbilisi, and other cities.[30]

In fact, the Kremlin leaders had decided even earlier to authorize a quiet

Jewish emigration from the Soviet Union. The idea allegedly came from the KGB's Andropov, who believed it would be an ideal safety valve, helping to reduce the growing domestic tension around the Jewish Question and at the same time getting rid of many Russian-Jewish intellectuals, who were activists in the human rights movement.[31] The new policy allowed Soviet citizens to emigrate for the first time, but only on an Israeli visa and without the right of return to the Soviet Union. In 1971, 13,711 Soviet Jews emigrated to Israel. In 1972, almost 30,000 were allowed to leave the Soviet Union—five times more than the total number of Jewish émigrés in the years from 1945 to 1968. In 1973–74, the number of people who emigrated topped 50,000. In all, during the 1970s over two hundred thousand Jewish émigrés left the Soviet Union.[32] The first wave of them came from the Baltic States and Georgia, but educated Jews from Moscow, Leningrad, and Kiev found it easy to obtain exit visas as well.[33]

The emigration of Jews was limited in scope, and most Jews stayed in the Soviet Union. Nevertheless, this emigration was bound to be a huge brain drain on recruits to the intelligentsia. Jews constituted just 1 percent of the Soviet population (2.1 million) but had held 7 percent of the posts in science, 20 percent of the positions in established literary circles and journalism, 8 percent in art, and 6 percent in medicine. In 1971–72 there were 105,000 Jewish students in Soviet universities, two times more than the number of university students in Israel. Among sixty thousand Soviet Jews were employed in the sciences, and twenty-two thousand of them had Ph.D.'s. There were nine times more college graduates among the Jews than among those who claimed Russian nationality.[34] And that figure does not take into account the numerous "half-Jews" who had assumed Russian identity and registered themselves as Russian on their domestic passports. Many educated Jewish émigrés who were assimilated into Russian culture had been true believers in the Soviet communist project, and party and Komsomol activists in their youth. During the Thaw and the 1960s they enthusiastically supported left-wing literature, theater, and art, along with its idea of a renascent intelligentsia.[35] During the 1970s, however, a disproportionately high number of them decided to emigrate.

Why did they decide to leave? Most émigrés, when interviewed, pointed to the rising anti-Semitism in Soviet society and their fear for a future for their children in the USSR. This fear related to a long history of sporadic anti-Semitic outbursts, purges, and executions that denied Jews a sense of security or stability in Soviet society. The older émigrés' memories of the Holocaust and Stalin's campaigns made their fears almost palpable. Still, fear of lethal anti-Semitic pogroms in Soviet Russia was *not* the primary reason behind the decision to emigrate. Many Soviet Jews emigrated for reasons other than those they stated. Ample evidence supports this conclusion. The majority of Soviet Jews decided, while they were residing in the émigré camps in Vienna or near Rome, to go to the United States, instead of Israel, for purely pragmatic reasons.[36] Some of them had noticed, in the growing competition for positions in intellectual and scientific strata of Soviet society, the preference being given to non-Jews over Jews in the fields of culture, science, and education. Many publicly active dissidents had children who either had been expelled from universities or had been failed on entrance exams. As Sakharov put it in his reminiscences, it gradually dawned on them that their children "were becoming hostage to [their parents'] public activity." Emigration began to appear the best available option.[37] Another, largely unstated, reason was that after 1968 the widespread belief in the peaceful transformation of the Soviet communist project that had reconciled so many intellectuals to other disadvantages of living in the USSR evaporated. It was particularly true for the Russian-Jewish intellectuals who emigrated from Moscow, Leningrad, and Kiev. Soviet Russia had seemed like the "Promised Land" to their grandparents and parents during the 1920s. It had become a ruined utopia for them and their children. Why tolerate an uncertain future in which they and their children might be scapegoated for Soviet misrule by the growing number of Russian anti-Semitic nationalists?[38]

The emigration had a snowball effect: when one person or family would decide to leave the Soviet Union, others from the same circle or professional group would follow suit. Yelena Bonner recalled that at the end of the 1960s and in the early 1970s a rather negative attitude toward emigration prevailed in Moscow intellectual circles, especially among the idealists of the postwar student generation, as they discussed it during their endless "kitchen debates." The people involved in dissident activities believed that young, educated, and assimilated Jews had to stay and join the movement of democratic intelligentsia. Yet by the middle of the 1970s many in these circles began to regard emigration as the best option for themselves and for others.[39] Rumors circulated from group to group in Moscow and Leningrad, "Everybody's leaving! The best and brightest are leaving!" The decision to emigrate meant burning all bridges, rejecting the identity of a loyal Soviet citizen, and this decision in turn helped to crystallize Jewish identity among the urban educated classes. It began to alienate non-Jews from assimilated Jews in intellectual circles. Those Jews began to imagine their future outside the Soviet and communist framework—a revolutionary development. Voice of America and Israeli radio played up sometimes idealized expectations about American and Israeli society to those who were disillusioned with the Soviet experiment. The media promoted intellectuals' growing desire to belong to a democratic Western culture, to be part of Western civilization. For the émigrés the free world, replacing the discredited Soviet utopia of their parents and grandparents, became the next idealized frontier.[40]

The attitudes of Soviet authorities on Jewish emigration were the product of contradictory impulses. The KGB created the new category of Jewish "refuseniks"—that is, Soviet Jews who were denied the right to emigrate to Israel. To protect the party and the state, the KGB, according to its records, intimidated and harassed tens of thousands of people.[41] At the same time, allowing and encouraging the emigration of Russian-Jewish intellectuals (or expelling them if necessary, as in Solzhenitsyn's case), helped the KGB check domestic Zionism and weaken the base of the dissident movement. It also let Brezhnev off the hook: he could pursue détente with Western powers without jeopardizing domestic stability. The KGB forced many non-Jews from the human rights movement to choose emigration as Jews, at the invitation from the fictional "relatives" in Israel. An increasing number of prominent non-Jewish semidissident intellectuals and artists decided to emigrate after prolonged harassment, KGB provocations, and loss of jobs and income.[42] Ultimately, the "Jewish emigration" was a highly successful strategy for the KGB against the human rights movement and the "society" that supported it. For each dissident arrested by the KGB several hundreds of supporters left the country. During the 1970s Andropov could report a rapid amelioration in the "operational situation" from the point of view of the secret police. Dissidents who refused to emigrate were arrested and incarcerated. Only Sakharov, his wife, and a handful of the founding activists of the human rights movement stayed in the Soviet Union. Ludmilla Alexeyeva supported the right of Jews to emigrate but felt that "the West focused on one theme, Jewish emigration," and failed to provide assistance to the democratic movement inside Soviet Russia.[43]

For many assimilated Jews and "half-Jews" emigration was a very painful act, separating them from their circles of friends and their familiar milieu. A number of Russian-Jewish activists disapproved of emigration. Yefim Etkind, a linguist from Leningrad, wrote in samizdat, "Our culture gets dispersed," and urged young Jews to stay in Russia and continue the struggle for liberalization and democratization. Etkind was harassed by the KGB to such an extent, however, that he chose emigration in 1974.[44] Other Russian-Jewish intellectuals left the Soviet Union with tears and a sense of tremendous loss. They tried to take with them the books and the sounds of the sixties—their tapes with the songs of Okudzhava, Galich, and Vysotsky.[45] Among those who left was Natasha, the daughter of Yuri Timofeev, who in the early 1950s had been the host for a circle of Moscow poets and artists. She emigrated to the United States not so much out of fear of anti-Semitism, but rather because the hope for political and social change after 1968 was dead. She never forgot the brilliant circle of her father's friends, whom she imagined to be the true and only intelligentsia.[46]

For many other educated émigrés from Moscow and Leningrad who ended up in Israel or in the West, and even for their children, the Russian intelligentsia remained a key cultural model. Yet some of them began to claim that emigration might be the only way to preserve the values of this community. In June 1968 Arkady Belinkov, a writer, escaped to the West with his wife during a tourist trip. His dreams for an emancipation of intellectual and cultural life in Soviet Russia had been shattered, and he hoped to emulate Alexander Herzen, the nineteenth-century Russian socialist, and found a "free Russian press" in exile. Belinkov settled in the United States and began to work for Radio Liberty. In December 1969 he wrote, "I never departed from Russian literature. I simply moved elsewhere to work. In the new place one can do much more for the cause of freedom. . . . From the first line of my first book I was always with those who hate black, brown, yellow and red fascism and who fight against it." Belinkov, like Solzhenitsyn, claimed that a community of Russian intellectuals was unrealizable in the Soviet Union. The real choice was between struggle and surrender. Belinkov hoped that his activities abroad would shame the Russian intellectuals who stayed in the Soviet Union into active opposition to the regime.[47]

Some other émigrés sought to act as an intelligentsia-in-exile and hesitated to blend into the intellectual and cultural life in their new countries.[48]

A few émigré intellectuals followed Belinkov's example and began to work for Western propaganda channels, including VOA and Radio Liberty. Back in the Soviet Union they had claimed to be an apolitical and moral opposition to the regime, yet in the West they plunged into Cold War politics, allied themselves with Western cold warriors, and became paid employees of the Western propaganda organizations.[49] Some extended their claims of expertise into international affairs. They believed that Western liberal democracies grossly underestimated and misunderstood the nature of the Soviet threat in the Cold War. These people were united in their hatred and resentment of the country they had left behind. One émigré of prerevolutionary vintage who was close to the dissidents was struck by "the lack of affection for Russia" among them. "In Russia they love only the 'intelligentsia' and everything related to this notion."[50]

Attempts at transplanting the idea of the intelligentsia abroad were illusory. Gradually, émigré intellectuals, writers, poets, musicians, educators, and scholars changed the focus of their lives. Instead of living amid culture and the fine arts, they had to find a job, secure a mortgage, and pay the bills. The factional and ideological divisions smoothed over at home by a common opposition to the regime came to the surface in the free air of the West. Aksyonov, one of the writers who was forced by the Soviet authorities to emigrate in 1980, admitted that the West "unwittingly did more to undo the dissident movement than the KGB."[51] A Western observer wrote about the atmosphere of intolerance and bickering in the émigré literary journals: "At the present time the Russian periodical press, for all its variety and vigor, is still a long way from providing an ideal cultural environment for the free development of uncensored Russian literature."[52]

The New Generation without Rebels or Cause

Even before the exodus, while the leftist intellectuals were still debating the meaning of the Revolution, the religious and national reawakening, the economic reforms, and the Prague Spring, a new generation of Soviet Baby Boomers was arriving on the scene. The cohorts of Moscow students of 1968, potentially the future of the Russian intelligentsia, were the primary beneficiaries of left-wing culture. The Soviet authorities were nervous that this latest group of educated youth would prove fertile ground for anti-Soviet activities. A number of them were investigated and arrested by the

KGB.[53] The father of the leftist avant-garde, Ehrenburg, already sick with terminal cancer, placed his hopes in the next generation of educated youth. "I believe that the legacy of our frightening years can end only when people who were brought up during those years physically disappear from our society. I have high hopes for the youth that did not receive such an up-bringing."[54]

The students of the late 1960s were indeed markedly different from their predecessors, Zhivago's children. Soviet Baby Boomers, born between the late 1940s and the early 1950s, were the first Soviet generation to grow up in peacetime, without war, terror, famine, or violent dislocations. And they did not remember Stalin.[55] This generation was better educated than previous cohorts. The number of university students climbed from 2.4 million in 1960–61 to 3.9 million five years later and reached 4.5 million at the end of the 1960s. Theirs was also a generation of relative gender equality.[56] But what did they think and feel? Were some of them ready to pursue the same moral, cultural, and social mission that the old Russian intelligentsia, from Herzen to Pasternak, had cherished and fostered?

A group of sociologists conducting opinion polls among young readers of *Komsomolskaia Pravda* registered a continuing decline in romanticism and idealism among this cohort, and the spread of cynical conformism. By comparison with the data of the early 1960s, the newspaper found that many more young men and women seemed to have become more material-istic and indifferent to ideas, principles, and big social issues. The sociolo-gists drew a depressing conclusion: "The young intelligentsia has been con-taminated by cynicism."[57] Boris Grushin, the newspaper's main pollster, detected two prevailing trends among the youth. First, there was a new emphasis on freedom, substance, and efficiency as important values. An overwhelming majority of respondents expressed "stormy criticism" of all aspects of Komsomol activities. (This intense criticism so disturbed the Komsomol leaders that they refused to repeat the poll in succeeding years.) Second, the youth expressed total loyalty to the Soviet system, the party, the state, and the Komsomol itself. Nobody suggested any fundamental changes. Nobody advocated dissent. The young critics, as Grushin summa-rized it, "displayed a remarkable *sense of limits* and *did not overstep the es-tablished boundaries* even when they resorted to very sharp expressions and when they criticized the top leadership" of the Komsomol. The new young cohort, to put it simply, accepted the status quo as the norm. They just wanted to improve their own lot.[58]

In January 1966 the head of the Komsomol, Sergei Pavlov, acknowledged as much in his report to his organization. He said that the about seventy million people in the Soviet Union who were born after 1945 had had their worldview shaped by "excessive emphasis on the issues of peaceful development and peaceful coexistence" between Soviet socialism and Western capitalism. Khrushchev's criticism of Stalin, concluded Pavlov, had "created doubts in the eyes of some young men and women about the eternal values of the socialist order."[59] Pavlov and his Komsomol apparatchiks worked hard to invent a "Soviet youth culture" that would serve as a firewall protecting educated Soviet youth from Westernization and liberalism. The logic of their search led them to turn to the "patriotic values" of Russian history and nationalism.[60]

A year before the Prague Spring, an American observer of Russia, John Scott, found that social activism among the young had decreased sharply. Education, a valued ticket to upward mobility during Stalinism, now "stimulate[d] one's desire for more privacy and mobility—one's own room or apartment; the right to turn off the cliché-ridden political program on television; the desire for one's own car; the chance to visit Paris."[61] Never before, Scott concluded, had Soviet youth been "more ideologically alienated, cynical, bitter," and vulnerable to Western influences. Nevertheless, he continued, they would not protest against the regime. They naturally adapted to the existing system.[62] William Taubman, who was an American exchange student at Moscow State University in 1965–66, came to similar conclusions. He found great interest among students in Western movies, books, plays, and radio broadcasts. Similarly, he observed the popularity of such cultural icons of the 1960s as Yevtushenko and Okudzhava. Yet neither of these influences decisively shaped the mood of the students. It was hard to spot idealistic rebels or truth seekers among them. The Komsomol activists Taubman met were loyal to the state and the socialist project and prepared to "work in their own way to improve their society and the quality of their lives."[63]

"Almost every student I met at MGU," wrote Taubman, "praised Soviet progress, which they spelled out as the new industrial might, the achievements in space, free education and medical care, low-cost housing and transportation. They attributed this progress to the country's socialist system." Whereas in 1956 some students had been ready to fight for freedom and glasnost, Taubman's dorm mates enjoyed the limited liberties they had and hoped that gradual progress would yield more. There was little vocal support for Siniavsky and Daniel among students. Taubman's student friends told him, "A lot of kids are tired of politics if it means empty speeches and crusades," and they rejected sacrifices from a practical standpoint.[64] Recent Russian sociological research confirms these observations. The student milieu of the 1940s–50s was a natural breeding ground for rebels and dissenters. By contrast, among the later cohort of dissidents born after 1950 only 10 percent were students and former students.[65] The army of students had too much to lose from participating in dissent of any kind. Half a million relatively well-paid jobs were created during the 1960s in the intellectual and scientific spheres for men and women of high academic qualifications. Everybody expected this trend to continue.

Western influences, much feared by party authorities and the KGB, did not automatically generate liberal and democratic values among students in the late 1960s. Exposure to Western radio, films, and other cultural productions did tend to erode commitment to the Soviet communist project. Increasing numbers of students regarded *Das Kapital* as a turgid "Talmudic" text, irrelevant to their needs. These groups of students believed there were "no true communists." At the same time many students regarded the West not as the realm of democracy and freedom, but rather as a consumer wonderland. Students associated the Western way of life with fashionable clothes on the black market, rock and roll, and Hollywood adventure films featuring the cult of the strong hero.[66] As they realized that the West enjoyed a higher living standard, they determined to achieve at least some minimal level of material comfort in the Soviet Union. For numerous students the disillusionment with Soviet myths enhanced the sense of nationalist identity. In Odessa, a KGB source wrote in 1968, a mixture of dislike and envy of the West was evident.[67]

The shattering revelations about the past under Khrushchev had a lesser impact on younger cohorts than did the greater freedoms and opportunities of the post-Stalin era. Instead of rebelling against their parents for their collaboration in the "evil" perpetrated in the past, as had West German students in 1968, Russian students took advantage of the end of the collectivist frenzy by turning to their individual needs. They had grown up at a time when the "forging and reforging" of socialist identities was over, but the official structures of the bureaucratic system remained intact. This situation produced a decline in idealistic nostalgia and a growth in pragmatism and individualism. The Russian students of 1968 were accustomed to the fact that private and public lives could not and should not be mixed.

None of this portended an intellectual renaissance or any radicalism. Instead, increasing numbers of students and young professionals preferred to accept the immutable nature of the Soviet order and the permanent division between "real life" and the public language and promises of the socialist state. Noticing the glaring contradictions between the realities and the slogans was no longer taboo, and expecting the two to converge in the future became a sign of hopeless naïveté. The Baby Boomers could no longer be true believers, but they did not want to live like bitter cynics, either. This cognitive dissonance generated an insatiable appetite for irony and tongue-in-cheek humor. Whereas for Zhivago's children humor and satire had been a way to soften the impact of the Stalinist past and prepare for social and cultural emancipation and reform, for the Baby Boom generation humor and satire became an organic part of the Soviet conformist existence. The transition from tragedy to farce for most of them was not a means to social engagement, but quite the opposite. Television studios, with the help of Komsomol officials, exploited this trend and launched a national competition of erudite young comics that came to be known as the club of the joyful and resourceful (KVN). As a scholar of KVN has written, "the interest of the authors and the competing teams gradually moved toward satire." Puns, wit, wordplay, and the artful confusion of cultural and linguistic context were based on constant hints and allusions to Soviet cultural realities.[68] The best and the brightest mastered the map of existing ideological and political minefields and managed to skirt them and entertain themselves in public at the same time.

Short satirical stories and jokes that were passed around by word of mouth (anekdoty) became a kind of oral supplement to samizdat. After the late 1960s anekdoty proliferated, becoming the most striking expression of Soviet cultural life. It was customary for the Komsomol and even party bosses to share these jokes in the presence of their subordinates and rank-and-file members as a form of bonding and common entertainment.[69] Foreigners who stayed in the Soviet Union returned with an endless supply of these jokes. Satire and sarcasm functioned as a form of escapism from the immutable, stagnant present, a substitute for the vanished social optimism and idealism. For an increasing number of intellectuals anekdoti marked the middle ground between Stalinist ideological fanaticism and the intelligentsia's so-called accursed questions about Russia's past, present, and future. Joking replaced the need to reflect and take responsibility for economic, political, moral, and cultural problems. As the poet Robert Rozh-

The poet Robert Rozhdest-vensky, a hero of the Thaw poetic renaissance, who remained a Komsomol idealist. He later said, "We reflected less than we laughed" (Courtesy of Memorial, Moscow).

destvensky, a cultural icon of the early 1960s who was recognized as the favorite official poet of the Komsomol, remarked years later, "We reflected less than we laughed."[70]

It became fashionable among the intellectuals of the seventies to treat the sixties' leftist intelligentsia and dissidents as naive and irrelevant Don Quixotes. In the Brezhnev years, acting passionately and heroically became gauche and unfashionable. The notion of a vanguard was replaced by a sense of the irrelevance of any public action. The younger cohort of intellectuals lacked an "inaugural event," such as Stalin's death or Khrushchev's secret speech, to animate their spirit and mobilize their energies for social and political activities. Instead, their common identity was one of intense alienation from the absurd and tedious routine of the Brezhnev years.[71]

Members of the younger generation made their careers within Komsomol and party ranks—participating and voting at public gatherings while behaving as pragmatic individualists in private. Most of them were not cynical and even took pride in their Soviet identity. There were also some who did not want to take part in the conventional and obligatory public rituals. Those people escaped from the white-collar milieu into the lower class: they worked as boilermakers or museum guards, or in other menial jobs. In contrast to their contemporaries in the West who invented new forms and spaces for politics, young Russian intellectuals and artists of the 1970s were not at all interested in issues of power. They rejected traditional politics yet did not create new strategies for civic reform. The "escapists" fostered new expressions of underground culture that appeared absurdist to an uninitiated audience. The most prolific creative forces of this new generation were young artists and writers from Leningrad. Marginalized during the Thaw, this erstwhile cultural capital of Russia now produced social and cultural forms different from those of the Moscow-centered sixties intelligentsia and its leftist circles. Conformist Leningrad Komsomol members and the bohemian underground had had nothing to do with dreams of changing the Soviet communist project from within. They did not participate in the dissident movement. Instead of living and acting like intelligentsia, in opposition to the Soviet bureaucracy, they lived out their private dreams inside boiler rooms, where they worked for minimal wages, and in private apartments, where they invented their absurdist jokes and private rituals.[72]

The appearance of the new cohorts of intellectuals and artists with a pragmatic and escapist outlook revealed that the emergence of the Russian intelligentsia during the Thaw and in the early 1960s had been a passing generational phenomenon. The tragedies and shocks of war, terror, and revelations of Stalinist crimes, the burning moral and psychological necessity of breaching the wall between the private search for truth and the public lie—all these factors had shaped the activities of many intellectuals born in the 1920s and 1930s. For younger Russians, it was all history. The people who had once believed themselves to be the sixties intelligentsia now began to feel like relics in the presence of their own children. In 1975 Viktor Slavkin wrote a play that was staged in a Moscow theater four years later. The hero of Slavkin's play was autobiographical: he had been a *stiliaga* in the 1950s, a fan of American style and jazz, Hemingway, and Vasily Aksyonov's novels. At the end of the seventies, as an already middle-aged man, he meets a former classmate who had been expelled from a university for singing "Chattanooga Choo-Choo." The two enthusiastically reminisce about the old days, while the hero's teenage girl quizzically and slightly ironically observes them "acting young." As Slavkin realizes, the daughter of his hero is as alien to him and his friend as they had once been in relation to the majority of their countrymen in the 1950s.[73]

"Intelligentsia-in-Captivity"

The majority of Zhivago's children survived the Brezhnev period in cultural and intellectual niches or oases that they created for themselves. Unwilling to protest Soviet policies and realities directly, this group participated in them while pursuing their intellectual and artistic lives.[74] Of course, the

KGB never left them alone. The KGB's Fifth Directorate in charge of ideology and culture, headed by General Philip Bobkov, could call on many informants and collaborators among Moscow artists and academics. In contrast to Stasi archives in East Germany, the KGB archives remained closed after the collapse of communism. Therefore, the extent of the KGB's infiltration and recruitment of intellectuals, as well as the tally of their collaboration and denunciations of one another, cannot be yet told.[75] Thus, "terror in the soul" could return to these people and even threaten them with loss of work and status.[76] At the same time, similar to their Central European colleagues, Russian intellectuals and artists in the seventies practiced what Czeslaw Milosz called *Ketman,* the art of dissimulation. They practiced escapism into fine arts and history, and passed responsibility for the lamentable state of affairs on to the communist state and some vague "them."[77] Those from the former left blamed the situation on the Russian people and Russian history. The Russian patriots blamed it on the remaining Jews, those who had not emigrated, on Western cosmopolitan influences, and increasingly on the Bolsheviks and their Revolution.

The repudiation of the Revolution after the Prague Spring went hand in glove with the justification of apathy and conformism. David Samoilov had observed the initial phase of this process as early as 1967, when he wrote, "The wholesale repudiation of the Revolution leads to the worst kind of amoral conformism."[78] Many former idealists from the post-Stalin generation changed their spots and turned coat, as their community fragmented and dissipated in the wake of 1968, new repressive measures by the state, and massive emigration.[79] Neizvestny, the sculptor, observed such changes in his generation before he emigrated from the Soviet Union in 1976: "In the atmosphere of lies and camouflage," he wrote, "a certain cynical brotherhood emerged." Its members had only contempt for unreconstructed Stalinists and naive provincials stuck in the past. "The people in this brotherhood are everywhere, from politicians to performers, 'scientists,' 'journalists,' 'physicians,' 'cinema people,' 'artists,' the usual suspects at numerous international congresses, guests at embassy receptions, usually present at all events attended by foreigners. They recognize one another instinctively."[80]

Nevertheless, "oases" in the state and social structures allowed some of Zhivago's children to live without completely betraying the ideals of their youth. Above all, such oases existed in Moscow during the détente of the 1970s, when the Soviet capital became even more than before a showcase city presenting the more benevolent face of Soviet communism to the world. Such oases could be found in various branches of the state propaganda and information services, including state television and radio, newspapers, and literary journals. The educational and cultural institutions, including big universities, the Sovremennik and Taganka theaters, literary journals and major newspapers, scientific institutes and labs, some museums and big libraries, also afforded Zhivago's children a haven. Even within the Academy of Sciences, and the unions of Soviet writers, composers, and cinematographers, refugees from the sixties intelligentsia could find secure jobs in some professional niches without losing their self-respect. Outside Moscow the most important oasis was Akademgorodok, with its conglomeration of privileged institutions of theoretical science and research labs.[81]

At the academic and scientific institutes, public dissent died out after the Prague Spring, as a result of the repression and emigration of the intellectual elite. Still, some nonconformists and "truth seekers," mostly war veterans, survived there. In 1978 the philosopher Yevgeny Plimak, a research fellow at the Institute of the International Workers Movement in Moscow, spoke up at the discussion of the new party program organized by the institute's party organization. Plimak said that the program's conclusion about the universal crisis of capitalism could not be sustained by facts. He proposed revisions to the program to the party congress. The director of the institute, dismayed by this act of nonconformism, moved that his suggestions be ignored. All Plimak's colleagues supported this motion, out of fear that otherwise their oasis would be endangered and exposed to investigation by the KGB or the party. At the same time, Plimak continued to work at the institute and to pursue his intellectual interests.[82] Another example is the activities of the academician Dmitry Likhachev at the Institute of Russian Literature in Leningrad. During the 1970s Likhachev refused to support petitions by dissidents, but he also refused to sign the collective letters denouncing Sakharov and Solzhenitsyn. This caused him problems: he was beaten by an unidentified attacker, and there was an attempt to set his apartment on fire. For years he could not get the authorities' permission to travel abroad. Nevertheless, Likhachev managed to preserve a niche for relatively independent research and academic freedom in his division at the institute. One protégé of Likhachev recalled that his seminars "gave [one] an impression of being present in a separate, non-Soviet world."[83]

The separation of intellectuals and artists, on both the former left and right wings, from the rest of the Soviet population by a network of privileges and special access to material benefits was, paradoxically, a contributing factor in the continuation and preservation of their oases. They shopped and dined together, and even had apartments and country dachas in a socially homogenous elite environment, similar to Western gated communities. The old elites clustered in dacha settlements to the West of Moscow: Nikolina Gora, Peredelkino, and Zhukovka remained the analogues of such communities in the West. American journalist Hedrick Smith wrote in the 1970s that "Zhukovka is . . . the heart of the dacha country of the high and mighty of Soviet politics, science, and culture. It epitomizes the surprising narrowness of Soviet society at the apex." Smith was guided around Zhukovka's privileged microcosm by Lev Kopelev and Raisa Orlova, who had many friends and enemies in that neighborhood.[84] Intellectuals and artists sought, whenever they could, to buy the property in those communities or at least to rent their dachas nearby. When they could not join the older settlements, they formed one of their own.

The détente policies that the Kremlin leadership, and above all Brezhnev personally, pursued actively during the first half of the 1970s also created a favorable atmosphere for the preservation and even multiplication of oases of relatively unhindered intellectual and cultural life. Between 1967 and 1972, when détente was in ascendancy, new academic institutions emerged in Moscow, among them the Institute for the United States (later Institute for the United States and Canada) and the Institute of Africa. These institutions, along with the Institute of World Economy and International Relations and the Institute of the Economy of World Socialist System (established during the Thaw), gathered knowledge about the outside world. They modeled themselves after Western think tanks, as the source of allegedly nonideological "objective and scientific" information about Western policies, economic life, and social and cultural developments. Quite a few reform-minded intellectuals in the party, unable to continue their careers after the Prague Spring, found academic jobs there.[85] As long as détente flourished, the role of these institutions grew. The party journalist Georgy Arbatov was especially successful in selling the think tank oasis model to party and state institutions. Arbatov, who had been a war veteran and then a postwar student, chose party journalism and consulting work during the Thaw. Despite his Jewish background, he had a spectacular career. In the early 1970s he was a member of the party's Central Committee, a full member of the Academy of Sciences, a veteran of the advisory circle of the KGB's chairman Andropov, and a member of the speechwriting team for Leonid Brezhnev. Arbatov, using his clout and connections, brought to his institute numerous old friends and acquaintances from the intellectual circles of the Thaw who had been connected with left-leaning intellectuals and even the dissidents. Thus, his institute, cosponsored by the KGB and the party leadership, became an oasis where researchers and analysts could discuss many international and domestic issues without fear of repression and denunciation.[86]

Inside the party apparatus there were oases, too. Some enlightened apparatchiks, above all in the divisions dealing with international affairs, were not complete cynics and careerists. Their cynicism was checked by a sense of shame for their country and what had happened to it under Brezhnev's conservative and corrupt rule.[87] A most remarkable case is that of Anatoly Cherniaev, a senior official in the party's international department. He left a record of his intellectual agony and cultural double life in his diaries. Cherniaev's private views and values during the 1960s were remarkably close to those of artists and intellectuals in left-wing circles. He was viscerally opposed to anti-Semitism, supported the Taganka Theater, and never missed a good novel. At the same time, he was proud to see the Soviet Union as a great power. He found new social meaning in détente. Solzhenitsyn and the dissidents repelled him with their blatant alliance "with the other side," the United States and the West in general. He deplored emigration of intellectuals during the 1970s. Some of them he knew and respected.[88] Even after 1968, Cherniaev preserved his illusions about the Revolution. In 1974 he wrote in his diary, "What an era it was! What a powerful spirit lived in our Revolution and the Soviet republic! In no other place could there be anything similar. What a great nation!" Cherniaev deplored the loss of ideological messianism, something that he had believed in in his youth. He did not want the Soviet Union to become an average country, just like all others.[89] And it was his firm conviction that not the dissidents like Sakharov and Solzhenitsyn, but people like him, the enlightened apparatchiks, preserved the best traditions of the Russian intelligentsia in acting as a force for reform.[90] He did not see a conflict between this conviction and his double life, including his party privileges, access to special stores, resorts, and exclusive information denied to other Soviet citizens.

During the 1970s, members of the Union of Soviet Artists learned to coexist with the ideological regime and to practice increasingly diverse styles of art without attracting the authorities' ire. Graphic design and book illustration were a profitable business for artists, and carried no risk of ideological opprobrium. One graphic designer recalled that he and his colleagues "could afford to feed their families, rent several studios, a dacha near Moscow, a village house, and a summer cabin on the shores of the Black and Baltic seas, or in the Carpathian Mountains." The availability of extra money and the bohemian style made successful artists appear like gentry among plebeians. The memoirist recalls nostalgically: "What a marvelous sexual revolution reigned in studios and the vacation houses of the creative unions! Young women loved those free-style men, the artists."[91] Artistic life during the Brezhnev years remained dominated by male attitudes and preferences, although among the artists were some talented women.

Even formalist, abstract artists driven underground after 1962 were able to create cultural oases for themselves. One dramatic event helped them. On September 17, 1974, overzealous Moscow bureaucrats sent three bulldozers and hundreds of plainclothes policemen to destroy an open-air exhibition of the underground artists' work in one of the city's parks. Its organizers were the underground artists Yevgeny Rukhin and Oscar Rabin, along with Alexander Glazer, a collector of abstract art. Many participants were from the Lianozovo group or the veterans of Khrushchev's crackdown at Manege.[92] The bulldozers and their water jets damaged and destroyed many paintings. The police had some foreign journalists who had been invited by the organizers beaten. The international scandal made the Russian underground artists' reputation. As a result, Alexander Glazer recalled, "the whole world learned about the existence of free art in Russia." The scandal also made "Russian free art" marketable. At the same time, it embarrassed the Kremlin, which was keenly interested in détente. A number of "enlightened" speechwriters and advisers complained to Brezhnev about the crassness of the Moscow authorities, and very soon another exhibition of abstract art opened in the same place, but this time without any harassment.[93] The same atmosphere of détente justified a growing artistic and cultural exchange. Soviet and French art museums put together an international exhibition called Moscow-Paris, in which the avant-garde art of the 1920s was prominently displayed. Other similar exhibitions followed. The old aesthetic taboos of the Stalin years, reaffirmed by Khrushchev in December 1962, were no more.

The concept of a free literature ceased to exist with Tvardovsky's *Novy Mir*. In February 1970 Tvardovsky was forced to resign as the editor of the journal. His deputy Lakshin wrote in his diary: "For many the end of the journal is like the death of someone very close."[94] On December 18, 1971, Tvardovsky died. No longer was there any common measuring stick for a "good" and "bad" literature. Any attempt to organize independent literary almanacs outside the bounds of censored literature could lead to reprisals, loss of membership and privileges in the Union of Soviet Writers, and emigration. Nevertheless, numerous niches of relative intellectual autonomy existed and even multiplied during the 1970s for the literary figures of Moscow, members of the Union of Soviet Writers. Outwardly, the prestige of high culture and education remained supreme, and subscriptions to literary magazines continued to grow. Some talented writers quietly pushed aside the boundaries of socialist realism.[95]

The poets Okudzhava and Samoilov discovered what Boris Pasternak had written two decades earlier in *Doctor Zhivago:* that of all things Russian he love most "the childlike Russian quality of Pushkin and Chekhov, their modest reticence in such high-sounding matters as the ultimate purpose of mankind or their own salvation." In contrast to other Russian writers and thinkers, including Tolstoy and Dostoevsky, who "looked restlessly for the meaning of life, and prepared for death and drew conclusions," Pushkin and Chekhov remained to the end of their lives "absorbed in the current, specific tasks imposed on them by their vocation as writers" and as a result "lived their lives quietly, treating both their lives and their work as private, individual matters, of no concern to anyone else."[96] Immersion in the history of the age of Pushkin, the Russian cultural milieu of the early nineteenth century with its "momentary particularities," now became an oasis for the most lyrical poets of the left-wing avant-garde of the early 1960s. Both Okudzhava and Samoilov wrote beautiful pieces about Pushkin and freethinking young aristocrats-turned-radicals. Both these men preferred the muse to the risk of political radicalism.[97]

Another writer who turned the past into an escape for himself and many others was Nathan Eidelman.[98] During the 1970s he became the darling of Moscow intellectual and artistic circles, especially among Russian Jews, because of his inspiring books about the Decembrists and their circles, where Russian high culture had flourished in the early nineteenth century. For Eidelman the cultural icons from the distant past were objects of admira-

The poet David Samoilov, one of Zhivago's older children. Before World War II he dreamed of becoming "a prophet of world revolution." Three decades later he escaped from Soviet life into the world of Russian history and high culture (Courtesy of Memorial, Moscow).

tion and contemplation and offered a quiet escape from the contemporary spiritual vacuum.[99]

A very important kind of noninstitutional oasis for former sixties people was trips abroad. The worlds outside the Soviet Union, despite the gradual opening of the Soviet borders to select travelers, remained unattainable frontiers for the great majority of intellectuals and artists. Therefore, these worlds "over there" retained their quasi-mythical quality and powerful effect on the imagination. Among those fortunate intellectuals and artists who passed all the loyalty tests and obtained permission to travel abroad, the favorite destination was Western Europe, especially France, Britain, and Italy. For these people, travel abroad became more than a bright spot in their lives: it became an addiction. The trips gave the temporary effect of euphoria, liberation, and excitement at the discovery of the wealth of world culture, while offering an escape from the squalor, humiliation, and fear of everyday Soviet life. At the same time, the trips made the return home a slow agony and brought a growing realization of how oppressed and miserable Russian society had become, how degraded the fabric of spiritual existence there. Many of Zhivago's children spent months and years reminiscing nostalgically about their last trip to the West and waiting for the next one. These trips became the essential substitutes for the vanished social optimism and spiritual communities of their younger years. Losing the privilege to travel, jeopardizing it by nonconformist behavior, was an irredeemable loss and a personal tragedy for many.[100]

In the increasingly fragmented strata of intellectuals and artists one of

the few common refuges was theaters and balladeer's songs. Bulat Okudzhava continued to fill the souls of an entire generation with his poetry,
music, and haunting voice. In the 1970s Okudzhava offered a salve for ethical wounds by praising simple human virtues. In a song dedicated to the
writer Yuri Trifonov, he sang,

> Let's allow ourselves to bathe in mutual admiration.
> The words of kindness serve as natural compensation.
> Life's happy moments are in short supply,
> As days go fast and years fly by.

In another song Okudzhava sang that Hope, the muse of the sixties intelligentsia, had "promised wonders and golden castles." Although these promises remained unfulfilled, Hope did not fade away entirely but remained a
"sister" tending the spiritual wounds of the postwar generation.[101]

If Okudzhava provided balm to the soul of the aging intellectuals of the
sixties, another balladeer, Vladimir Vysotsky, gave voice to their anguish.
One of the leading Taganka actors, Vysotsky was influenced by Okudzhava's art.[102] He wrote about love, death, betrayal, and sincerity with unprecedented forcefulness. He articulated memories of the Great Patriotic War
with extraordinary poignancy. People who were unfamiliar with his biography were convinced that he was a war veteran, but Vysotsky had been a
child during the war, and he never served in the army. His war was one of
soldiers, not generals, a genuine people's tragedy. "Battalions keep marching and marching westwards. And women back home keep wailing in fune-
real grief."[103] His son later recalled, "He made cynics understand the war,
and they had tears in their eyes. He explained the life of sportsmen to pilots, and the life of seamen to sportsmen. He told intellectuals about crooks,
and told the crooks about intellectuals. He brought an understanding of
our life that nothing else—not documentary cinema, not popular lectures—
could achieve."[104] During the seventies, Vysotsky's songs not only expressed
the anger of the cheated generation of intellectuals, but also the fatigue of
Russian society, lashed for decades by the forces of history.

Those who listened to these songs belonged to the army of intellectuals
and artists who did not want to be dissidents, yet suffered from the macabre stasis of Soviet life. They had already realized that their past ideals were
a fraud and a cover for horrible crimes. At the same time, Vysotsky's appeal
reached far beyond the social and cultural confines of the intelligentsia. Re-

markably, none of Vysotsky's records were published and sold in stores until the late 1970s. People listened to his unofficial recordings on their tape recorders. His audience was practically the entire adult population of Russia. It included the KGB head Yuri Andropov, academics, scientists, writers, peasants, industrial workers, miners, clerks, taxi drivers, and criminals. People in Eastern Europe from Poland to Bulgaria who disliked Russians as occupiers listened to his songs. Everyone in the Soviet Union knew his songs by heart and sang them on every occasion, within their circles of friends, at weddings and funerals.

The decline of the spirit of the intelligentsia and the fraying of its social and cultural boundaries during the years after 1968 exacerbated the fears of former leftist intellectuals, especially Russian Jews who did not emigrate, that the old communist utopia would be replaced by the virulent and aggressive form of Russian nationalism. Indeed, the extremist anti-Semitic groups of Russian patriots on the right flank of the literary establishment continued to develop their own networks and oases in various structures and institutions, including those sponsored by the state. The literary cultural space was increasingly occupied by Russian village writers who became famous during the 1960s after their work was published in Tvardovsky's *Novy Mir*. In the 1970s, however, they broke with Tvardovsky's line and adopted a conservative nationalist identity.[105] They too addressed the past, although their time frame and cultural referents were different. The village writers described the anxiety of the first generation of intellectuals to have come from the peasantry and looked back at the devastated countryside with horror and nostalgia. They also denigrated urban life, viewed sophisticated urbanite intellectuals with suspicion, and rejected their "Western" values. These novels, written with varying degrees of honesty and talent, began to gain popularity with millions of Russian readers.[106]

A constant struggle went on between the allies of the Russian nationalists in the party apparatus and in the KGB, who favored selective inclusion of nationalist myths in the official ideology, and the enlightened apparatchiks who considered anti-Semitic Russian nationalism shameful and dangerous. Any offensive from one side triggered a counteroffensive from the other. In November 1972 Alexander Yakovlev, acting head of the Propaganda Department of the party, attacked the leading group of Russian patriot journalists and philosophers in an article in *Literaturnaia Gazeta*. Yakovlev belonged to the party intellectuals who, despite their careerism, had studied in the United States during the Thaw and been influenced by left-leaning literature, theater, and journalism. Brezhnev, however, did not want to be drawn into such an argument, on top of other problems with intellectuals. The Politburo demoted Yakovlev and sent him to Canada as an ambassador.[107] During the 1970s, according to Nikolai Mitrokhin, "the majority of the party apparatus, including the members of the Politburo, shared to some extent the ethnonationalist mythology." At the same time, Brezhnev and his Politburo also looked at the extreme Russian nationalists as troublemakers who were challenging the party monopoly on cultural politics. In 1979 the journal *Nash Sovremennik,* run by a group of Russian patriots, published a historical novel about the years leading up to the Russian Revolution. It featured Grigory Rasputin and set down the White Russian émigrés' worst anti-Semitic stereotypes, depicting the Revolution as a Jewish conspiracy. This time, the KGB chief Andropov made the case to the Politburo that "under the slogans of defending Russian nationalist traditions" a new anti-Soviet movement had been born, potentially more massive and dangerous than the "so-called human rights activists who suffered defeat and discredited themselves in the eyes of public opinion." Andropov pointed to the connection between Russian nationalists and Russian émigrés and "Western secret services." According to KGB informants, Sergei Semanov, a nationalist writer and editor of journal *Chelovek i Zakon* (People and Law), had allegedly said to his friends: "The peaceful period of winning souls is over. We must adopt revolutionary methods of struggle. Otherwise, we are lost."[108] Semanov was fired, as a warning to other established Russian patriots who remained untouched in their institutional oases—in this instance, numerous journals and publishing houses.[109]

In December 1979 the Soviet Union invaded Afghanistan. Again, the intellectuals and artists failed the test of history. Out of hundreds of thousands, only a handful of dissidents, above all Andrei Sakharov, protested the invasion. In February 1980 the Soviet leadership stripped Sakharov of all his awards and exiled him to the city of Gorky, which was closed to foreigners. Hundreds of people, among them many established intellectuals loyal to the regime, cabled the party authorities in support of this measure. The Academy of Sciences buckled under the political pressure and denounced the dissident physicist (although it did not officially expel him). Most of Sakharov's colleagues, as well as scientists and intellectuals who had privately respected and admired him, believed that he had gone too far this time. Seeing the invasion of Afghanistan as a justification of their escape from political and social engagement, they stayed within their oases.

Surprisingly, the only exceptions were a few enlightened party apparatchiks and *institutchiks*. They felt frustrated and enraged that the fatal decision to send troops into the mountainous Asian country had been made without any consultation with them. Cherniaev expressed their common feeling in his diary: "I do not believe that ever before in Russian history, even under Stalin, was there a period when such important actions were taken without a hint of discussion, advice, or deliberation. We are entering a very dangerous period, when the ruling circle cannot fully appreciate what it is doing or why."[110] Yet another cause for anger and despair was that the invasion killed the dreams of détente, a cornerstone of the agenda the enlightened apparatchiks advocated, their main *Ketman*.[111] Some *institutchiks* belatedly signaled their reservations to the leadership in confidential letters. Georgy Arbatov went even further. In June 1980 he met with Andropov, his former boss, and attempted to convince him that the Soviet Union should withdraw its troops from Afghanistan. In the atmosphere of pervasive careerism, cynicism, and conformism, it was a courageous act. Andropov informed the Politburo seniors about it, adding pointedly, "Such is the mood in the intelligentsia."[112] It was strange that the KGB chief used this word in a context suggesting the existence of autonomous public opinion within the state structures.

The mood did not improve during the Olympic Games that took place in Moscow in July 1980. The United States and a number of American allies and Arab countries boycotted them. The KGB tightly controlled contacts with foreigners during the games, and nothing like the spontaneous mass enthusiasm and catharsis that had marked the World Youth Festival in 1957 manifested itself. People bitterly joked that the Olympics were "the substitute for the communism" that Khrushchev had promised to construct by 1980. A moment of sorrow and further loss of spirit came during the Olympics when Vladimir Vysotsky, the most popular singer of the sixties, died on July 25, 1980. For Russian intellectuals and artists, it was another loss that depleted their ranks and separated them from the days of optimism. By the end of Brezhnev's era the list of losses was long. All the mentors of Zhivago's children and some of their leaders had passed away, including Anna Akhmatova, Ilya Ehrenburg, Konstantin Paustovsky, Kornei Chukovsky, and Alexander Tvardovsky. The former *Novy Mir* literary critic

Vladimir Vysotsky, the balladeer and actor of the Taganka Theater. Vysotsky wrote in 1965 after the KGB arrested two writers: "I do not abandon my optimism. Times are different; we are not afraid of anything." His songs made him the darling of all Zhivago's children, and his death in 1980 overshadowed the Moscow Olympics (Courtesy of V. Gritsiuk, Moscow).

Vladimir Lakshin lamented in his diary, "The generation of people that embodied a living link with the old culture and the tradition of the nineteenth century have been departing from the scene. Only tasteless clowns remain. Frightening thought."[113] In a metaphorical sense, another of the casualties was Boris Slutsky. His stern poems no longer inspired the younger generation of readers. The death of his beloved wife from cancer in 1977 was the last straw. Slutsky developed manic depression and could not write anymore.[114] His breakdown was caused also by the disappearance of the leftist avant-garde in which he had played the role of the idealistic commissar.

Vysotsky's funeral united Moscow intellectuals with the rest of Russian society in an outpouring of grief. It was truly a national mourning. The line of people waiting to pay their last respects to Vysotsky stretched for three miles to the little Taganka Theater where his coffin was displayed. His funeral overshadowed the Moscow Olympic Games taking place at the same time. From Taganka his coffin proceeded along the Garden Ring, escorted by thousands of policemen (present in the capital for the occasion of the Olympics) to the Vagankovo cemetery.[115] This was the biggest spontaneous public gathering in the Brezhnev years, yet it took place remarkably peacefully and with dignity.

Twenty years earlier, when Boris Pasternak had died, there had been five hundred mourners at his grave. Hundreds of thousands watched the Vysotsky procession. In 1960, though, the future had seemed to belong to the young intelligentsia, whereas in 1980 that dream had faded away, along with the Soviet communist project. Very few could predict that just five years later the conservative reign would come to an end, or that in three years more the streets of Moscow would be filled with huge demonstrations and rallies, led and inspired by writers, journalists, and artists.

The Pharisee claims all, and I'm alone.
This life is not a stroll across the meadow.

—Boris Pasternak, "Hamlet," 1946

epilogue

The End of the Intelligentsia

I N MARCH 1985 the septuagenarian Kremlin rulers loosened their grip
on power. The fifty-four-year-old Mikhail Gorbachev became the general
secretary of the Communist Party. Igor Dedkov wrote in his diary, "A man
of our generation has come to power. A new cycle of Russian illusions is
about to begin."[1] Soon the new leader began to speak of achieving "more
socialism," branded the Brezhnev years a period of stagnation, and finally
began to talk about the need for perestroika (restructuring). Gorbachev
and his wife Raisa, as we have seen, belonged to the postwar Moscow student generation. They had left Moscow for the provincial southern town of
Stavropol in 1955, at the time when the Thaw was becoming noticeable.
Like most of their classmates, the Gorbachevs had an insatiable appetite for
high culture, and a veneration for writers and intellectuals. In the 1950s,
when they had lived in Moscow in the Stromynka dorm, they had spent
all their free time at museums, theaters, and poetry readings. These habits
continued when the couple left Moscow. Gorbachev was the only one
among the rising party leaders who read books on philosophy, sociology,
and history, as well as Lenin's early works. In the summer of 1967 he had
long off-the-record discussions with his former university roommate,
Zdeněk Mlynář, by then a senior official in the Czechoslovak Communist
Party, who had come to Stavropol to see his old friend. Like Mlynář, Gorbachev became convinced of the need to search for a more human and

liberal model of socialism. A few months later Mlynář came out in support of the Prague Spring, and he later emigrated to the West.

Gorbachev never revealed that his sympathies lay with the party reformers at that time; he continued his successful career. Yet Mikhail and Raisa managed to escape the cynicism of many in their age cohort who became unprincipled careerists. Moreover, the Gorbachevs remained untouched by the disillusionments and bitter divisions that profoundly affected their Moscow-based classmates, the former idealistic students. In 1985 the Gorbachevs continued to believe in the ideas most of Zhivago's children had cherished thirty years before. The two neither abandoned their Marxist-Leninist views nor resorted to cultural escapism. Above all, they continued their self-education. They read and discussed the ideas of Jean-Paul Sartre, Martin Heidegger, and Herbert Marcuse. They read *History of the USSR*, written by the Italian communist Giuseppe Boffa, the works of Palmiro Togliatti, the books of Antonio Gramsci, and the articles of socialists Willi Brandt and François Mitterrand. Also, while remaining Soviet Russian patriots, Mikhail and Raisa rejected the anti-Semitism of the Russian nationalists as a shameful betrayal of the socialist ideals of their youth. They were curious to see the world outside the borders of the USSR. They traveled together across Western Europe as tourists, and these trips, together with their reading, made them question Soviet realities without losing hope in a "better socialism." When the Gorbachevs went to live in Moscow in 1978 (the year Gorbachev joined the secretariat and the Politburo), they tried to make up for two decades of life in the provinces. The couple spent every Sunday in museums, methodically explored the city's historical monuments, attended exhibitions and theaters. Raisa reconnected with her classmates from the 1950s, by that time renowned philosophers or sociologists.[2]

Gorbachev was the first Soviet leader since Lenin who was friendly to intellectuals. Determined to return the Soviet Union to the path of reform, he was driven, like other enlightened apparatchiks, by a sense of shame at the inferiority of Soviet social and economic conditions by comparison with the West. In 1983, during his official visit to Canada, Gorbachev conversed with the Soviet ambassador Alexander Yakovlev, who was living out an honorable exile there after his clash with Russian nationalists. Yakovlev showed Gorbachev around prosperous Canadian farms, knowing well that they would greatly impress a former country boy from "black-soil" Russia. Gorbachev gazed at them and muttered to himself, "Even after fifty years we will not be able to reach this level of efficiency." Yakovlev said later to his friend, a veteran of Thaw-era "honest" journalism, "You won't believe it, but he was attacking the system more vigorously than I would or even you."[3] Gorbachev had no sympathy for the dissidents or the circles that supported them; however, he made an exception for Andrei Sakharov (whom he brought back in November 1986 to Moscow from exile in Gorky) and ended up sharing Sakharov's views on the danger of nuclear war and the need for thinking globally about international security. Gorbachev also believed that the best elements of the intelligentsia could be an important force for reform and could supply him with advice. Publicly claiming that the Brezhnev years had been a time of stagnation, Gorbachev turned to "the best forces of his generation," including Moscow intellectual and artistic circles, in hopes of re-creating the cultural and intellectual vanguard of the sixties.[4] He met regularly with the most distinguished writers. His brain trust consisted of international scientific and economic experts and enlightened party apparatchiks like Alexander Yakovlev and Anatoly Cherniaev.[5]

In 1986–87 Gorbachev began to lift the Iron Curtain and, like Khrushchev, invited writers and artists to promote the new "human face" of the Soviet Union abroad. To assist in Gorbachev's exercise of public diplomacy, they accompanied him on his foreign trips. In March 1987 an official delegation of Soviet writers, journalists, and historians for the first time met with ex-Soviet émigré writers, at a conference in Denmark. Almost all of them had belonged to the same generation and lived through the hopes and illusions of the post-Stalin decade. Among the émigrés were Aksyonov, Siniavsky, and Etkind. The first day ended in scandal. When Etkind, by that time a professor at the Sorbonne, made a presentation entitled "Soviet Literature—An Apologia for Violence," a member of the Soviet delegation, Grigory Baklanov, began to shout that he, as a war veteran, would not tolerate such a disgrace. Suddenly the historian Yuri Afanasiev, an MGU student from the class of 1956, took the floor on the Soviet side and said: "We are all from Russia [rossiyane]. Why should we stay divided?" This appeal to Russian cultural identity, instead of the Soviet Union, brought tears to everyone's eyes, including the Russian Jews'.[6] It was a milestone. The postwar generation of intellectuals and artists, the émigrés and those who remained, dissidents and nondissidents, Jews and non-Jews, began to reestablish broken relationships. Afanasiev's appeal to the intellectuals to rally around a reform-oriented Russian identity was a harbinger of great political changes. At the same time, the urge to rally together as the Russian intelligentsia in support of reform was deceptive, considering the internal divisions that had existed over history, identity, cultural preferences, and political agenda.

It became commonplace to explain Gorbachev's reformism as an offshoot of his early affinity with the cultural and intellectual left.[7] The evidence however shows that initially Gorbachev sought to invite all the groups in the divided Moscow intelligentsia and cultural elite to become partners in and backers of his perestroika.[8] In November 1986 at the suggestion of the scholar Dmitry Likhachev, Gorbachev established the Soviet Cultural Foundation, which from 1986 to 1991 raised one hundred million rubles for its projects.[9] The mission of the foundation was to unify and mobilize the best and the brightest to carry out reforms. Gorbachev and his wife had read and liked the books of Likhachev, a scholar of art and literature. In their eyes, Likhachev, who had been educated in St. Petersburg before the Revolution, embodied the qualities of a true Russian *intelligent.* He did not share the negativism of dissident and semidissident "society." He loved the Russian Orthodox tradition and the legacy of the religious thinkers. At the same time, he rejected anti-Semitism and the xenophobia of Russian nationalists and considered Russia to be part of European civilization. As a result, according to James Billington, Likhachev became "a part-time tutor on Russian cultural history to Gorbachev and particularly to his wife Raisa."[10] Likhachev also became the head of the Soviet Cultural Foundation and in this capacity was supposed to serve as mentor to all Zhivago's children, whether on the left or on the right.

At first, experienced Moscow intellectuals, the remnants of the sixties cultural ferment, were skeptical that substantial changes could come from above. Yuri Levada, a sociologist, remembered people's fear that, as had happened many times before, the leader's mood would change or the leader himself would be ousted. "They all placed their hopes in Gorbachev, and tried not to do anything that would drive away the beautiful dream that he brought with him."[11] Alexander Yakovlev, now a member of Gorbachev's political team, pushed his old acquaintances in the cultural elite and the journalists of the sixties into action. "Publish everything, but do not lie," he said to the editors. "The responsibility should be yours."[12] This was the freedom that Tvardovsky had sought so desperately to win. The first ones who appropriated this freedom were journalists, theater directors, and playwrights. Yegor Yakovlev, Otto Latsis, and Len Karpinsky turned an obscure newspaper, *Moscow News*, into the glasnost publication that resuscitated the traditions of "honest" journalism of the early sixties. Oleg Yefremov and the playwright Mikhail Shatrov restaged the sixties plays about revolutionaries, Lenin and the Bolsheviks, which seemed to underscore Gorbachev's slogan "More socialism!"

In 1986 Gorbachev and his reformist lieutenants urged the incorporated writers, artists, and filmmakers to democratize their unions and rid them of the "ballast" of the Brezhnev era. The Filmmakers' Union was the first to take this invitation seriously. Its congress in May 1986 resembled the agitated meetings of spring 1956 and fall 1962. The new leadership of the union consisted of leading cinematic lights of the sixties. The recently appointed head of the Filmmakers' Union, the filmmaker Elem Klimov, promised in his interview for *Pravda* to bar "the path to the screen to hacks, timeservers, and wheeler-dealers" and to clear "a broad path for people of talent and artists" who could "meet the criteria of genuine art." He deplored the spread of entertainment cinema and asserted: "We have to enlighten [people] and make them want to think." The new union leaders released all the films banned by censors during the Brezhnevite "stagnation."[13]

The greatest sensation of glasnost cinema was the film *Repentance* by the Georgian director Tengiz Abuladze. It was an exquisite work of art and a poignant, trenchant denunciation of the Great Terror, secretly produced with the personal authorization of Georgian Party Secretary Eduard Shevardnadze. In October 1986 Gorbachev's colleague Alexander Yakovlev watched the film at home with his family. He recalled: "When it was over, we fell silent for ten minutes. The film took my breath away. It was more than a fresh breeze, it was a hurricane." At that time Gorbachev and the KGB decided to begin releasing political prisoners, as part of the campaign to improve the Soviet image abroad. The unveiling of *Repentance* accorded well with those steps. The Politburo decided at first to send five hundred copies of the film to the provinces, where the KGB monitored the reaction of the audience. In Moscow *Repentance* opened in the midsize screening hall of the Filmmakers' Union in November 1986. For many intellectuals from the postwar generation the event seemed like a replay of fall 1956, when Dudintsev's novel was discussed. The hall was packed; mounted police surrounded the building. After the film many people were weeping.

They knelt before Abuladze and kissed his hands, as if in a trance. Other viewers, however, left the theater, perhaps in protest.[14] Foreign correspondents and television stations waited outside for the crowd to emerge and asked for opinions. And people spoke into the microphones, thus crossing the long-standing divide between private dissent and public conformism.

In 1987 writers and editors from literary journals joined the filmmakers. A season of frank speeches, bold publications, and sensational performances began. The editor of the literary journal *Znamia,* Grigory Baklanov, a war veteran who had belonged to the leftists of the 1960s, published a novel by Anatoly Pristavkin about the murderous deportation of the Chechen people during the Great Patriotic War.[15] In the avalanche of new publications were Anatoly Rybakov's *Children of Arbat,* Vladimir Dudintsev's novel *White Clothes,* and Nikolai Shmelev's fiction and articles. Readers were also hungry for historical, economic, and sociological facts. The circulation of literary journals, no longer limited, grew astronomically, far surpassing the circulation of *Novy Mir* and other journals during the sixties. Finally, the state television channels also began to catch up, showing documentaries on the consequences of the Chernobyl nuclear accident and inviting artists and intellectuals to speak live on issues ranging from Stalinism to the environment. The message in televised discussions was that the entire system, immutable during the years of stagnation, had to change, so that socialism could live up to its potential. The long list of taboo subjects that could not be discussed in the Soviet media shrank rapidly.

Many figures from the leftist avant-garde in the early 1960s did not make it to the front rank during perestroika. Many stayed in emigration and remained highly suspicious and critical of Gorbachev's intentions. Some émigrés pointed to Gorbachev's phrase "more socialism" as proof of his opposition to genuine freedom and democratic reforms.[16] Yevtushenko, Voznesensky, and other poets from the early 1960s published extensively during the perestroika and glasnost years, but their "sincere" lyrical voices were lost in the new environment of public revelations. Slutsky died in 1986, alone and hiding from friends. Samoilov lived in Estonia, far from the politics of perestroika, and died during a poetry reading in 1989. Some scientists, riding the wave of Gorbachev's campaign for nuclear disarmament, gained public visibility. At the same time, by comparison with the early 1960s, in this era scientists were no longer public heroes. In the aftermath of the Chernobyl tragedy, there was a public backlash against nuclear scientists. Many, especially village writers, acted on their resentment over the scientists' earlier preeminence by successfully presenting scientific communities as groups of selfish and arrogant technocrats who sacrificed humanity to their utopian schemes, ignored historical and moral issues, and destroyed the environment. In a word, scientists were now blamed for what they had been admired for just three decades earlier.[17]

At the same time, numerous other figures, among them artists, historians, journalists, and actors, began to claim they belonged to the ranks in perestroika's "progressive intelligentsia." The majority were from the postwar student generation. The Thaw dream of a partnership between a reform-minded political leadership and the progressive intellectual and artistic elites seemed again to be coming to fruition. Yet as in the 1960s, this development revealed a sharp polarization between the "cosmopolitans" and the Russian nationalists, as symbolized by Gorbachev's two lieutenants. Yegor Ligachev favored the Russian nationalists, lacked any rapport with Moscow-based liberal society, and had distinctly conservative and provincial predilections. Alexander Yakovlev, on the contrary, was the archenemy of the Russian patriots and had numerous friends in sixties cultural circles in Moscow. After his demotion as the result of an article against the Russian nationalists, Yakovlev underwent a radical conversion: he began to speak about the ideas and tragic fate of the dissidents, he began to appeal to the émigrés, and he became convinced that the country needed, above all, democratization, glasnost, and cultural liberalization.[18]

Before long the Russian nationalists, who had procured many prominent positions in the rejuvenated and reformed Union of Soviet Writers, took a very negative attitude toward Gorbachev's glasnost. They argued, at first privately and then publicly, that it was a disastrous mistake to let the left-leaning Moscow intellectuals and dissidents define the agenda of reform. Those people, the argument went, did not care about the Russian people and the Russian state, but rather tended only to destabilize and confuse society. The established nationalist writers, journalists, and artists were particularly opposed to the growing assault on Stalinism, which in their eyes represented a period of great achievements when the empire had been built. In late 1986 anti-Semitic Russian patriots began to build up their network of local nongovernment associations, among them antialcohol societies and the "historical-patriotic society" Pamiat (Memory). These associations were especially active in Moscow and Akademgorodok. In Novosibirsk a group of scientists of the Siberian branch of the Academy of Sciences, along with local party officials, organized lectures for students and general public at which the "Protocols of the Elders of Zion" and other supposed evidence of a Judeo-Masonic conspiracy in the Soviet Union were distributed. The patriots targeted the reformist economist Aganbegyan and even the late party leader Yuri Andropov as members of the conspiracy.[19] On March 13, 1988, the newspaper *Sovetskaia Rossia,* one of the havens of Russian nationalists, published a letter by Nina Andreeva, an obscure professor at the Polytechnic Institute in Leningrad. She defended socialist principles but also attacked the notion that one group of intellectuals and artists could be the "leading and mobilizing force" of perestroika. The article claimed that intellectuals who were allegedly promoting "left-wing liberal socialism," were in reality trying to "slaughter socialist values" and undermine the Soviet state. The article specified what was destructive in the activities of the former vanguard of the sixties intelligentsia: "the value placed on individuality, the modernist search in culture, God-seeking tendencies, theocratic idols, sermons on the 'democratic' pleasures of modern capitalism, and genuflection before capitalist achievements, real or false."[20] The article also defended Stalin as a great statesman and linked the adherents of "left-wing liberalism" with the Jewish emigration and "cosmopolitan" trends associated with Jews. The original, unedited letter from Andreeva, which was even more explicitly anti-Semitic, drew ominous parallels between Gorbachev's glasnost and the Prague Spring.[21]

The Andreeva letter gave Russian patriots in the bureaucracy and society as a whole the signal for the counterattack. Ligachev and some members of Gorbachev's Politburo embraced Andreeva's theses. The publication began to look to rank-and-file communists like a new ideological doctrine. Not a single journal dared to publish a rejoinder to Andreeva. The intellectuals of Moscow and Leningrad froze in fearful silence. After painful weeks of waiting, it became clear that Gorbachev interpreted the article as an attack on his policy. In contrast to Khrushchev and Brezhnev, the Soviet leader had taken the Prague Spring as a model for his reformist strategies. He did not fear that a group of freethinking writers and intellectuals would incite a political revolution. He worshipped Lenin as a model politician and was supremely confident that like the Bolshevik founding father, his successor would remain in control of events. *Pravda* published the official rejection of Andreeva's views, condemning her arguments point by point. The rejoinder proclaimed the freedom of cultural and intellectual pursuits. The party issued instructions eliminating the Stalinist policies of party control over the cultural sphere, collectively known as *Zhdanovshchina*. The laws abolishing both censorship and the state monopoly on mass media followed much later, in June 1990, yet de facto the policy of ideological censorship collapsed in spring 1988. The meaning of the past, present, and future, as well as the content of the "new thinking" itself, was open to interpretation not only within the party ranks, but in society at large.[22]

The next year and a half became the golden age of glasnost. The dream of the cultural vanguard of the postwar generation came true. Gorbachev embraced the concept of the intelligentsia as the generator of a reformist climate. He allowed artists and intellectuals to make use of enormous state resources, including state-owned media, to articulate their ideas and ideals to tens of millions of people inside the Soviet Union and abroad. The response from the aging veterans of the sixties was understandably euphoric. It seemed as if the history of their generation had resumed at the point where it had been forcibly arrested in 1968. Soon, however, it became clear to Gorbachev and his reform-minded entourage what the Czechoslovak party reformers had experienced twenty years earlier. Once they had abolished censorship and decided to use the liberalization of the ideological and cultural sphere as a tool to mobilize against the entrenched antireformist forces, it became increasingly difficult to stop that liberalization halfway. And from the revelations of Stalinist crimes, Soviet glasnost inevitably and predictably led to the questioning of the entire foundation of Soviet socialism, including its revolutionary and patriotic myths. In 1988–89 explosive questions about the Revolution and Soviet history emerged in the pages of literary journals and in glasnost-era newspapers, and finally in television programs.[23] The carefully calibrated half-truths of the Khrushchev era were no longer possible. From the special sections of the libraries *(spetskhrany)* opened in 1988–89 thousands of books became available to the general public, books containing a wealth of noncommunist philosophy, political science, history, and economics, and the treasure trove of Russian émigré memoirs and literature. Samizdat ceased to be subversive and became a legitimate part of public media and discussions. In July and August 1988 the first nongovernment newspapers appeared in Moscow. At the same time, former political prisoners organized the group Memorial to document the history of Soviet terror and the persecution of dissidents. In November

1988 the authorities stopped jamming Western radio broadcasts, and the enormous and costly system that had been used for jamming stations was allocated to serve the needs of domestic broadcasting.

From that moment on, glasnost took on a momentum of its own. Writers, economists, sociologists, and even historians issued broadsides against the myths of the Soviet past and present. The new wave of hope and even euphoria among Moscow intellectuals and artists was darkened only by the memory of past setbacks. In a volume summarizing glasnost for Western readers, an elite *institutchik* from the Baby Boom generation expressed the prevailing mood in educated circles in Moscow: "For the first time in my life I feel optimistic and hopeful. For me now my country is the most interesting place in the world. I can barely remember 1956 and the Twentieth Party Congress (I was just six years old at that time), but the atmosphere of enthusiasm in the early 1960s and the ensuing bitterness at the end of that decade are preserved in my memory." For those of Zhivago's children who were entering the fifth or sixth decade of their lives, perestroika was the last chance. This time the reforms could not fail! Eventually, even Gorbachev himself seemed to have been caught up in this "win or perish" attitude. After 1987 he kept repeating that there was no way back and that the failure of perestroika would mean the end of socialism in the Soviet Union.[24]

The founding myths of the regime—the Bolshevik Revolution and the role of Vladimir Lenin—soon came under fierce attack from cosmopolitans and Russian patriots alike. The journalist Vasily Seliunin unmasked Lenin as a violent, doctrinaire fanatic who brought a national catastrophe down on Russia. The historian Yuri Afanasiev denounced the very foundations of the Soviet state and society and wrote about "sixty years of spiritual void and decay."[25] A bit later, the theater director Mark Zakharov publicly proposed that Lenin's body be removed from the mausoleum on Red Square. Vladimir Soloukhin published his anti-Lenin tract in the émigré journal *Posev;* Radio Liberty then broadcast it to all of Russia. The publication of Solzhenitsyn's works in the Soviet Union, along with Grossman's novels, dealt crushing blows to the popular faith in Lenin, the last myth of late Soviet society.[26] The Russian-born American pundit Leon Aron commented, about the cultural and ideological revolution of that time, "Its most original and most dangerous feature is the precision with which the heavy artillery is targeted, and the depth of shell penetration. In Gorbachev's Soviet Union, almost every major legitimizing myth is being shattered." He concluded that Gorbachev, who had set out to create a reformed version of one-party state socialism with a human face, had "unleashed forces that [were] methodically destroying the legitimacy of any such future arrangement. No economic reform, no amount of Western good will, and no brilliant foreign policy stratagems," he added, "can hope to fill this spiritual vacuum."[27] A Moscow intellectual, Lev Osterman, wrote in his diary, "We, the omniscient intelligentsia, should contain our egocentric revelatory passion—in order not to alienate people who might otherwise begin to loathe us for our enlightening mission." Osterman believed that it would be better "to reveal the truth about our past gradually—little by little."[28] Instead, the "perestroika intelligentsia" sponsored by Gorbachev acted with frenzied fervor in attacking the very idols they had recently worshiped and feared.[29] The majority of educated Soviet Russian society experienced disillusionment and demoralization on a large scale. Feeling cheated and claiming to having been hopelessly naive for decades gave rise to a collective inferiority complex. "Homo Sovieticus," the gullible and conformist Soviet citizen, became the target of masochistic social satire, later repeated in public speeches by numerous intellectuals and artists.

Nobody realized that this was the last time that the intelligentsia, as either an idea or a reform-minded community, would play a central role in Russian history. Zhivago's children, because of the cultural differences dividing them and the hatred all of them felt toward the Soviet regime, even though it was now headed by Gorbachev, contributed inadvertently to the self-destruction of the Soviet Union. The squabbling chattering classes, along with Gorbachev himself, dug the grave not only of Soviet communism, but also of the Soviet state. In the spring of 1989 the radical and rapid cultural de-Stalinization of Russian society spilled over into politics. Former dissidents, now skeptical observers of Gorbachev's policies—Sakharov, Bonner, and others—saw the main danger to perestroika as coming from the vast party and bureaucratic apparatus, as well as the KGB. They mistrusted Gorbachev and criticized his vacillations. Their own experience made them believe that radical democratization and peaceful rallies and strikes against the "Stalinist apparatus" could be the only guarantee against the threat of a "Khrushchev scenario," such as the one that had ended in Khrushchev's ouster and the triumph of Brezhnevism. A minority of Gorbachev's advisers, enlightened apparatchiks like Yakovlev and Cherniaev, thought along similar lines. All of them, and the freedom-hungry Muscovite intellectuals, pushed the general secretary toward fundamental democratization, delegitimation of the party, and reliance on peaceful mass rallies. Gorbachev reluctantly followed this advice, and he was also guided by his own reasons. The Kremlin reformer, being confident of his political skills, believed he could ride two horses at once: stay in control of the party apparatus and manage gradual democratization.

In any political revolution, the muses cede the place of honor to political speeches, mass rallies, and public demonstrations. Some intellectuals and nationally known cultural figures sought to ride the crest of radical politics. Dozens of them, mostly established sixties leftists, but also former dissidents, were elected in the spring 1989 to the new national legislative body, the Congress of People's Deputies. Tens of thousands of intellectuals and artists came out of their oases and into the public realm for the first time in their lives. With the passion and devotion emblematic of a reawakened intelligentsia, they helped elect their moral leaders and came to listen to their speeches. When the conservative leadership of the Academy of Sciences tried to prevent the election of Andrei Sakharov to the People's Congress, hundreds and then thousands of scientists and humanitarian scholars from Moscow institutes protested, and the heroic human rights defender was elected. The constituency of intellectuals thus emerged as a factor in the politics in Moscow and Leningrad, and then even in some major provincial cities of Russia.

This constituency included hundreds of thousands of scientists, engineers, librarians, teachers, academic researchers, physicians, and other professionals. The largest and most outspoken contingent among them consisted of the postwar students who had emulated *stiliagi,* read *Novy Mir,* and listened to Western radio and the songs of Okudzhava, Galich, Vysotsky, and other songwriters of the sixties. During all those years, especially in the so-called time of stagnation, they had behaved like conformists and cultural escapists. Now they sought to compensate for the decades of past moral humiliation and doublethinking. Political liberalization and freedom of speech, conscience, and assembly became their watchwords. In their eyes, dissidents like Sakharov and scholars like Likhachev from the semidissident circles embodied the moral and cultural vision of the intelligentsia as they conceived it.

Meanwhile, the political reforms presented new and unfamiliar challenges to both leaders and followers of this movement. The leader of pere-

The academician Dmitry S. Likhachev among the delegates to the Congress of People's Deputies, May 1989. Instead of bringing about a cultural renaissance, the intelligentsia's politics contributed to the demise of the Soviet Union (Courtesy of the Likhachev Foundation, St. Petersburg).

stroika, Gorbachev, was the object of international admiration elicited by his initiatives in disarmament, security cooperation, and above all rapprochement with the West. One by one the Soviet satellites of the Warsaw Pact began to overthrow their communist regimes. On November 9, 1989, the Berlin Wall was breached and the two German states began to move toward reunification. At the same time, Gorbachev and the Politburo were increasingly divided and overwhelmed by domestic changes and processes. Economic and financial crises loomed large in the Soviet Union. From 1986 to 1989, the salaries and honoraria of the creative and scientific elites increased sharply, but soon the collapsing economic and financial system buried those gains under its rubble. Rigidity and disorganization in the state distributive structures and misguided measures to introduce private initiative without changing the centralized system precipitated disastrous consequences, including the disappearance of consumer goods from the stores. Outside Soviet Russia, in the Baltics and in the South Caucasus, non-Russian nationalist forces clashed violently with one another, and with the Soviet state, spilling blood and provoking pogroms and ethnic cleansing. Gorbachev, the rest of the Kremlin leadership, and the more moderate among the experts surrounding them, having been caught unawares, could offer no recipe for reform, no blueprints or consistent strategies. The Soviet Union was sliding into the abyss.[30]

Neither did the best and the brightest have any specific plan for meeting the challenges posed by radical change. Even the best minds in the sixties intelligentsia were not up to the task of reforming Soviet society while preserving sufficient stability in the Soviet Union. In the economic sphere, Gorbachev's advisers were the same sixties reformist journalists and economists who had sought a third path between the centralized Stalinist economy and free-enterprise capitalism. Between 1986 and 1989 they had partially dismantled the existing economic mechanisms. At the same time, nobody, from the reform-minded economists (Aganbegyan, Zaslavskaia, Lisichkin, and others) to the journalists and writers (Seliunin, Shmelev, Latsis, and Chernichenko), knew what to do in the present or in the future about economics and finances. Their schemes for reform revolved around vague notions of an ethical and participatory economy that would somehow combine the promises of the Revolution with the efficiency of modern technological processes. In a word, they diagnosed a terminal illness yet could not prescribe a cure. Some of them proposed "going back to NEP," Lenin's policy of tolerance for the peasantry and small entrepreneurs. Yet at the end of the 1980s the peasantry was as good as moribund, and attempts to create a new class of "cooperators" ran aground because of the abysmal corruption and conflicts between the state apparatus and the new entrepreneurs. The majority of reformist economists claimed that economic reforms required fundamental changes in society, especially a new working-class consciousness of co-ownership and participation in management. These utopian aims emerged under the influence of partial economic reforms in Yugoslavia and Hungary, which had, however, long failed to produce any tangible results. Such programs as workers' councils, socialist cooperatives, and regulation of profit could only generate financial and economic chaos in the Soviet Union.[31] The principal intellectual supporters of perestroika could not imagine the future without some kind of "socialist regulation" in which the state and the technocratic intelligentsia would play leading roles. In many ways, especially in the economic field, the advocates of perestroika remained Soviet to the core. Unable to come up with solutions, glasnost-era economists, supported by the intelligentsia, the politically mobilized educated classes, and later disaffected workers, vented their rage against the managerial and party bureaucracy. In their eyes, it had become the main obstacle to economic transformation. Economists and sociologists concealed their own lack of intellectual vision behind such populist accusations.[32]

In the sphere of national politics the advice of politicized intellectuals was equally problematic and inadequate. On the liberal flank former dissidents, including Sakharov and Bonner, demanded immediate reform of the Soviet Union to offer the complete right of national self-determination. In pursuit of freedom, many Moscow intellectuals automatically supported and promoted any form of ethnic separatism and any movement against the Soviet Russian center. When the Kremlin used military force to put down the ethnic violence that broke out (in Georgia, Armenia, and Azerbaijan), many of them denounced any use of force and appealed to international public opinion. The American Sidney Drell was bewildered when he observed Yelena Bonner lecturing Gorbachev on what to do about the Armenian-Azeri conflict in Nagorno-Karabakh. The dissident refused to listen to the general secretary and insisted that her own solution was the only one that would work. "For her there was no such thing as getting it 99 percent correct. Only 100 percent," he recalled. "She rejected compromises." Even the U.S. ambassador in Moscow, Jack Matlock, who admired Sakharov, believed that the proposals he and Bonner put forward for a territorial solution to the Nagorno-Karabakh issue "could be dangerous" and were likely to lead to violence and loss of life.[33] That was exactly what happened. The dissidents, guided by a traditional aversion to government-sponsored violence and by moral sympathy for nationalist movements in Armenia, Georgia, the Baltics, and elsewhere, helped destabilize and undermine the Soviet Union.

In the Russian Federation, the main constituent part of the Soviet Union, Gorbachev was still trying to balance the radicalized groups in major cities with more conservative segments of Russian society. Many people were humiliated by the revelations of glasnost and increasingly angry about the economic disarray. The Kremlin leader sought to keep these people within the perestroika coalition. This effort did not endear him to the increasingly impatient and fearful liberal intellectuals in Moscow and Leningrad. Panic was growing among Russian Jews, and figures of cosmopolitan and supposedly Westernized cultural background, that Gorbachev's loss of control might bring Russian fascists to power and into the streets. In December 1989 liberal-minded deputies in the congress, the so-called interregional group, decided to call on the people of the Soviet Union to stage a two-hour symbolic strike. When Gorbachev's lieutenants objected that it would further destabilize the country, Andrei Sakharov replied that, on the contrary, it would be the only way to support perestroika, under attack by rightist forces, anti-Semitic and chauvinist Russophile groups united "under the White slogan of a single and indivisible Russia."[34]

On December 14, 1989, after a stormy session in congress, Andrei Sakharov suddenly died of a heart attack. On the eve of that session, he had clashed with Gorbachev and demanded the immediate abolition of the constitutional clause about the leading role of the party. His parting words were: "There will be a fight tomorrow!" His funeral in Moscow was an event reminiscent of the funeral of Vysotsky in 1980. The academician-turned-dissident was mourned as the last true Russian *intelligent,* and it seemed as if the entire intellectual and artistic elite of Moscow had turned out to bid him farewell, along with tens of thousands of other Muscovites. The death of Sakharov, who had always professed his loyalty to Gorbachev, was the tipping point.[35]

The union between left-leaning intellectuals and the Gorbachev leadership began to disintegrate, and their mutual irritation grew. Liberal Moscow politicians, both former party members and former dissidents, criticized Gorbachev for lack of democratic convictions and for adherence to the methods of authoritarian rule. The end of the political romance with Gorbachev represented for many intellectuals and artists the severing of the last link connecting them with the dream of socialism with a human face. Many of them began to proclaim publicly that any kind of socialism in Russia was doomed and that the Soviet communist project could not be redeemed. It could only, like ancient Carthage, be razed to the ground. These members of the perestroika intelligentsia abandoned their onetime creed with a remarkable ease—a result of the long process of erosion of socialist ideals and the accumulation of anger and frustration during the time of radical politicization. At the same time, Gorbachev's "enlightened" assistants, including Anatoly Cherniaev, were appalled by how mean and ungrateful "the upper crust of the Moscow intelligentsia" acted toward the father of perestroika. They saw this group (except for Sakharov, a man of enormous integrity) as elitist and overweening, in that it claimed to have supreme authority over public morality and political matters as well.[36] In the course of 1990 the Moscow interregional group and thousands of its followers began to leave the party and shift their allegiance and aspirations over to Gorbachev's rival, Boris Yeltsin. Yeltsin, guided by ambition and iconoclastic populist instincts, had at first been seen by Sakharov and other intellectuals as a dangerous demagogue. In 1990, however, Yeltsin began to appear like the only leader who could grapple with the situation and at the same time remain open to the ideas and advice of intellectuals. In the spring of 1991 he was elected, in the first free elections, as president of the Russian Federation, still subordinate to the Soviet Union and Soviet leader Gorbachev, but thereafter increasingly autonomous.[37] The more Gorbachev felt abandoned by the intelligentsia and threatened by the forces of chaos, both national-separatist and economic, the more he remained hostage to the same party apparatus and to the KGB he wanted to manage and control. Indecisive in every sphere, he antagonized the majority of Russians, and only a few intellectuals and enlightened apparatchiks remained his true admirers.

The attempts of hard-line members of the Gorbachev team, including the head of the KGB and the minister of defense, to halt the disintegration of the empire led to a feckless coup on August 19, 1991. The putschists placed Gorbachev under house arrest, and he was pushed off the center stage of history. Boris Yeltsin, who displayed defiant resistance in the face of the takeover attempt, remained as the only legitimate leader of Russia. During the three days of uncertainty, when the coup plotters could have stormed the White House, the seat of government for the Russian Federation, thousands of Moscow intellectuals, old and young, converged on it to form a living shield against the attack. It was a moment of mythic redemption for the educated Russian elite for the decades of collaboration with the Bolsheviks and Stalin, for its long passivity and egocentric existence "in captivity," and for its resignation in response to the Soviet invasion of Czechoslovakia and other ignominious pages in its history. The former human rights defenders, including Yelena Bonner, stood next to the triumphant Yeltsin and spoke to the cheering, exultant masses. It seemed as if the dream of the Russian intelligentsia, a leader in the national reformation, had miraculously materialized.

This was, however, the beginning of the end for the grand intellectual dreams. The Soviet Union was crumbling, and new developments, following in rapid succession, left the basic structures and conditions for the existence of the social milieu of the intelligentsia and the mythology of its leading role in shambles. In December 1991 Yeltsin, along with the leaders of Ukraine and Belarus, dissolved the Soviet Union and removed Gorbachev from the political scene. And in January 1992 radical economic reform was launched, shock therapy to bring Russia into capitalism. These developments would have been impossible without the mass conversion of the proliberal intellectuals, the former leftist cultural vanguard, and the politically active dissidents. By then, many of them had abandoned the idea of a third path, of socialism with a human face, in favor of the institutions of Western democracy and market capitalism. At one point the economic reformers, sociologists, and journalists practically stampeded in their haste to make the shift from a model of some kind of socialism (preferably Swedish) to the American version of a deregulated economy. Many intellectuals and artists labored under the illusion that once they took Russia in that direction, the West out of gratitude would provide a new Marshall Plan for them, and all the hardships and humiliations would be over. Most scientists, writers, filmmakers, and other groups of the former Soviet intelligentsia took state support for granted and never imagined the consequences of a collapse of the socialist system. They grossly exaggerated their ability to flourish under conditions of "freedom," including a free market. George Faraday, who observed the turmoil among Soviet filmmakers, recognized that they had "rejected the bureaucratic devil they knew for the capitalist devil they didn't."[38]

Had there been a Russian Rip Van Winkle who went to sleep in 1988 and woke up just four years later, he would have been amazed. The Soviet Union was no more, and the omnipotent state, the Communist Party, and political oppression no longer existed either. There also remained no visionary vanguard promoting enlightenment and reform, and no public veneration for the idea of the intelligentsia. What was left instead was a pathetically weak state and a powerful group of criminalized nouveau riche oligarchs and bureaucrats who stole or embezzled the national wealth. There was also the miserable, impoverished, and degraded population, ignored and despised by the elite groups. The cohorts of liberal intellectuals and cultural gurus who had dominated the earlier national debates either emigrated or joined the small army of timeservers and hacks who attempted to please the new regime in order to get a chunk of former state property. Hundreds of think tanks and research labs, including the ones in Dubna, Academgorodok, and other hubs of advanced scientific research, went virtually bankrupt. The so-called creative unions vanished, along with their entire material base of perks, privileges, and cultural production. The budgets of the Literary Foundation and the Soviet Cultural Foundation disappeared into the pockets of unscrupulous officials. The filmmaking industry practically collapsed, along with the nationwide system of film distribution and screening. Many filmmakers had to switch to the production of mass-culture B-quality movies, instead of the highbrow auteur films they had previously been engaged in. The moral and spiritual downsizing of nationally known writers, those "engineers of human souls," was breathtaking. Literary journals, theaters, opera, musical collectives, all teetered on the brink of bankruptcy. Their circulation dropped from millions to thousands, largely because of the drastic impoverishment of subscribers from the educated strata, who could no longer afford the luxury of reading and discussing ideas.[39]

The intellectual, spiritual, and moral collapse of the early 1990s was unrivaled in Russian history. The rise of the concept of intelligentsia as a moral authority during the perestroika and glasnost years began to falter once intellectuals went into politics. With their abandonment of socialist ideals in favor of Western liberal freedoms and institutions, and then market capitalism and private property, they lost moral and intellectual ground. After all, they were not experts in those areas, and the numerous Western advisers who flocked to Russia eclipsed them. These advisers actually knew what capitalism and democracy were and how they worked. The Moscow cultural elites had inadvertently sawed off the bough on which they were all sitting, not only in an economic and financial sense (they lost their state subsidies), but also in the moral sense. The search for humane socialism had been a form of ethical and moral exercise. Andrei Sakharov had written in the early versions of his memoirs, around 1981–82, "I see in the ideas of socialism a certain (albeit limited) contribution to the socioeconomic development of humanity. I appreciate the moral pathos and attraction of these ideas. And I believe that the presence of socialist elements in the life of democratic countries is important and necessary."[40]

The spasmodic and total rejection of these ideals in the early 1990s by some of the leading representatives of the intellectual and cultural vanguard led to a paradoxical situation. The majority of the Russian population, stripped of its savings and thrown into a state of uncertainty during the plunge into capitalism, began to view the Brezhnev period of supposed stagnation as a better time. Everybody could see the visible excesses of wild Russian capitalism, ridden with criminality and conspicuous consumption, millionaires and billionaires, and obscene cynicism toward Homo Sovieticus, the idealistic Soviet person, who was relegated to the dustbin of history.

In this environment, the Russian Communist Party quickly came back from the shadows and began to score successes in free elections. Another winner was a new ultranationalist party led by Vladimir Zhirinovsky, who proposed publicly to exile the entire perestroika intelligentsia that had allegedly brought the country to such humiliation and misery. At the same time, leading Moscow and Leningrad artists and intellectuals looked to Yeltsin as the only guarantor that the Soviet times would not return and that Russian fascism would not take to the streets. The dangers of a communist victory and the fascist threat of Russian nationalism blended in their imagination to produce the image of a "red-brown menace." In October 1993, when the coalition of communist and nationalist forces tried to force Yeltsin out of power, many Moscow intellectuals supported violent suppression of the coup. When troops loyal to Yeltsin fired at followers of the opposition, cultural icons of the sixties and later times, among them Bulat Okudzhava, Sergei Averintsev, Dmitry Likhachev, and Bella Akhmadulina, applauded the October massacre as the lesser evil. Fear of the ghosts of the past drove many figures from the former intelligentsia to support Yeltsin, even after his government began to lose its early liberal-radical luster and to become mired in corruption and oligarchic schemes. Also, filmmakers, theater directors, and scientists had to turn to Yeltsin and the financial gurus and oligarchs in his entourage for money. It was at first shocking for them to trade their old dependence on the Soviet bureaucracy in for new forms of financial dependence, but many quickly began to see it as the only option, and a profitable one at that. Yeltsin and the recently elected mayor of Moscow, Yuri Luzhkov, could be very generous patrons of the arts. And the oligarchs supporting the Yeltsin regime against the communists were even more generous. As a result, increasing numbers of people from the perestroika intelligentsia began to serve new masters, and were well paid for their service. Smeliansky described how it looked in December 1995, when free elections to the Russian Parliament were held. "As a bait to catch voters, most of the forty-three parties put up actors, pop singers, and television gameshow presenters as candidates. Actors were as sought after as generals. Each party, according to its taste, had video shorts made which were then run on all the television channels every day for two months. Only one party produced no video shorts and did not flash across our screens. This was the Russian Communist Party. It won."[41] Intellectuals and artists found themselves in the service of a regime and its oligarchs that the majority of Russian people hated.

The rapid parting of the Iron Curtain and the new freedom of travel for all, constrained only by economic problems and Western visa restrictions against Russians, destroyed the notion of the captivity of the intelligentsia. Yet the same development also devalued the views and ideas that intellectuals and artists had been promoting for decades through samizdat and Western radio. As had happened earlier to Russian intellectual émigrés, the free market of ideas, intellectual production, and art made the old notions look primitive and outdated. In the world of the late twentieth century, art was a commodity, literature and cinema were a form of entertainment, and mass culture triumphed everywhere. The notion of high culture for connoisseurs and highbrow intellectuals survived only as an elitist phenomenon, unrelated to primary social, economic, and political issues. This change was as destructive to the ethos of the intelligentsia as the structural and spiritual collapse was. The networks that had formed the cultural underground of the Soviet era, an essential part of the intelligentsia's "imagined community," disappeared. A brief boom in Soviet nonconformist art in the West began to wane after 1991. It became clear that the underground culture owed its existence to the unique centrality of high culture in Soviet society, in combination with the state support and pressure to channel this culture within prescribed boundaries. With the advent of democratization and marketization, the artists and intellectuals of the semidissident milieu, who used to thrive on their elitism, had to search for new niches and identities in the emerging post-Soviet order. Many of them—for instance, rock musicians—began to condemn the new order with the same vehemence with which they had denounced the old. The majority, however, emigrated to the West or joined the rapidly expanding mass culture.

Between 1988 and 1993 another mass emigration occurred in Russia, much larger than during the Jewish emigration of the 1970s. It began with the panic among the assimilated Jewish intellectuals in Moscow, Leningrad, and other cities; they were afraid of Russian fascism and took advantage of the opening of borders to emigrate to Israel or the West. Then, as the financial crisis led to the collapse of the cultural and scientific infrastructure, thousands began to look for jobs abroad. In all, 1.5 million people left the Soviet Union, many of whom were highly educated and identified with the intelligentsia. The intellectual and cultural hemorrhage would have been even more terrible had it not been for the large-scale assistance program to scientists and intellectuals organized by the billionaire George Soros, an American financier of Jewish-Hungarian origin who was fascinated by Russian high culture. Western governments and most private foundations, however, provided very limited help.

The unique centrality of high culture, inherited from nineteenth-century tsarist Russia and Central Europe, and reproduced in the late Soviet era, was no more. At the end of 1991 the writer Daniil Granin expressed his fear that in the "new commercial life" there would be "no room for the sublime movements of the soul, for free art for art's sake." He felt that "the intelligentsia in the sense that our history and literature have given us" would soon be gone. "The West has its intellectuals and respects them," Granin went on. "Yet it has never known such an intelligentsia as ours, with its idealism, rejection of profit in the name of public ideals, acute moral sensitivity."[42] In June 1993 the physicist Lev Osterman, an assimilated Jew and an ardent supporter of the left-wing high culture of the sixties, wrote to his son, who had emigrated with his family to the United States: "My chosen and beloved milieu (perhaps through literature) is the Russian intelligentsia and its spiritual heirs in our times. This milieu is unique in the world, owing to Russia's unique history." He noted that post-Soviet existence, especially the gigantic, commercialized mass culture, "has been drying out the soil" for the regeneration of the ethos of the intelligentsia.[43]

The story of Zhivago's children ended in the 1990s. It is a story about the struggle of intellectuals and artists to regain autonomy from an autocratic regime seeking to control society and culture. Yet it is also a story about the heavy price they paid for this autonomy, and above all about the slow and painful disappearance of their revolutionary-romantic idealism and optimism, their faith in progress and in the enlightenment of people, beliefs and values inherited from the milieu of the Russian intelligentsia of the nineteenth century. With the exception of a few courageous public dissenters, like Andrei Sakharov, Yelena Bonner, and Alexander Solzhenitsyn, the intellectuals and artists in Soviet Russia remained an intelligentsia-in-captivity, with all the social and moral consequences that implied. Only a tiny minority consistently sought to live by the intelligentsia's ethos and implement its high principles. Most had to compromise, living a double life, exercising freethinking in private and remaining party conformists in public. Still, for all the justified reproaches aimed at this community during the 1970s and 1980s, time has shown that their cultural and spiritual work in the immediate post-Stalin decades was not in vain. The dazzling entrance of the intelligentsia onto the stage of world history took place during the years of glasnost, when Mikhail Gorbachev granted educated elites the autonomy to create and the freedom to speak and engage in civic activities.

The death of the Russian intelligentsia during the 1990s ended an important chapter in European intellectual and cultural history. This chapter is both inspiring and troubling. The intellectual milieu attracted many Soviet citizens who graduated from universities after World War II, among them the young veterans who had defeated Hitler but later had to struggle with Stalinism. The Moscow intelligentsia's dreams and expectations reached their peak in the years from 1960 to 1968, at a time when cultural and social protest was changing Western democratic societies. In common with Western protest movements, the reborn intelligentsia in the Soviet Union displayed moral fervor and a commitment to emancipation from authoritarianism and to a coming to terms with the crimes and injustices of the recent past. Like the West, Soviet Russia experienced the rise of technocratic trends among scientists, the avant-garde influence in literature, theater, cinema, and journalism, and the movement in defense of human rights. All these left-leaning groups stood against the legacy of Stalinism, xenophobia, and anti-Semitism. These groups, Zhivago's spiritual children, clashed with xenophobic and anti-Semitic groups of Russian nationalists, who also claimed to be part of the intelligentsia. The death of the intelligentsia was an unintended result of the failure of the communist project. The movement of intellectuals, scientists, human rights activists, and artists contributed to the strange end of the communist empire—or even its suicide. At the same time, bringing down the temple of communism brought to an end the intelligentsia's historical mission. Even earlier, in Central Europe after 1989 both the obsession with high culture and the intense underground artistic life vanished in a similar way. Still, in Poland, the Czech Republic, Hungary, and the former Yugoslavia, intellectuals and artists had a much deeper national identity. They had the luxury of pretending that the communist phase was not their own, that it had been imposed from outside. In Russia, by contrast, few intellectuals and cultural figures could feel or think that way. For many of them the idea of the intelligentsia was not related to the task of national self-determination and liberation. On the contrary, many of them lived in constant fear of resurgent Russian nationalism. The grand dreams of Zhivago's children homed in on the centrality of culture and art in the social life of their people, and on the possibility of building a gentler society based on noncapitalist foundations and free from the perpetual drive for money, property, and the acquisition of material goods. The advent of "wild capitalism" sent these illusions crashing down. Shattered was the dream of a revolutionary transformation that would lead to grassroots social justice. The pretension of the intelligentsia to the status of social oracles and cultural prophets, occupying a seat above the state and the people, quickly dissipated, mocked by history itself.

In the early 1990s many intellectuals of the postwar generation began to look back on the optimism of their youth as naive and unjustified. In Alexei Adzhubei's opinion, "We did not know many things, and this ignorance helped us preserve our optimism."[44] Alexei Kozlov, the jazz musician, regretted his optimism in 1960 and renounced the "purely Soviet illusion" that "people could be raised to a higher cultural level."[45] The last and the staunchest believers in Marxist-Leninist historical determinism began, one by one, to abandon their beliefs. The philosopher Yuri Kariakin wrote that for him personally, parting with the communist faith took more than two decades. "I resisted long and fiercely, until I had to surrender before . . . life itself." A longtime admirer of Fyodor Dostoevsky, Kariakin became an Orthodox Christian zealot.[46] Many other intellectuals from his generation embraced the Christian faith as a last spiritual refuge. The trickle of people who in the mid-1960s had made their way to the church of Alexander Men became a torrent by the early 1990s. Confused by the sudden and unfamiliar lack of purpose, some aging sixties intellectuals forgot their militant atheism and put icons up on their apartment walls instead of photos of Hemingway. In lieu of fantasizing about a cybernetic socialist paradise, they humbly lit candles before the altars of Russian Orthodox churches. Consciously or unwittingly, they turned to the values and images that had saved Boris Pasternak from suicide half a century earlier. Yuri Zhivago's poems began at last to reveal their true mystical meaning in their hearts and souls. In the early 1990s, a new "time of troubles" in Russia, Pasternak's poem "Hamlet" sounded especially poignant:

> I love and cherish it, Thy stubborn purpose,
> And am content to play my allotted role,

But now another drama is in progress.
I beg Thee, leave me this time uninvolved.
But alas, there is no turning from the road.
The order of the action has been settled.
The Pharisee claims all, and I'm alone.
This life is not a stroll across the meadow.[47]

Alexander Men, the first and greatest preacher for many of Zhivago's children, could no longer help them find their bearings in a changed Russia. In September 1990 he died near his church after an unknown assassin split his skull with an ax.

The story of Zhivago's children has no happy ending. Arguments about the role and place of this group in Russian history and culture continue to rage to this day. In the immediate wake of the Soviet collapse, the postwar cohorts of intellectuals and cultural figures became an easy target for criticism. Many hostile darts emanated from within their ranks, aimed by Zhivago's children themselves. From his emigration in Paris, Andrei Siniavsky, the onetime critic of socialist realism, lashed out at the moral bankruptcy of the Moscow intelligentsia. He described the post-perestroika developments as "the bitterest years of my life." For him "nothing is more bitter than unfulfilled hopes and lost illusions." The intelligentsia, according to Siniavsky, succumbed to the temptations of power and lust for money. In his opinion, the calling of the intelligentsia was to love the people and share their misfortunes. Instead, intellectuals in Moscow today, he claimed, were "afraid of those same people."[48] The nationalist thinkers blamed the "liberal" majority of their generation for the destruction of the Soviet Union and the sellout to the West.[49] Increasingly allied with the resurgent Orthodox Church, extremist Russian patriots began to identify the liberal Moscow intelligentsia as an elitist group, primarily the "children and grandchildren of Soviet and party nomenklatura." Leonid Borodin, a religious Russian nationalist and a former student of the class of 1956, wrote about his liberal enemies: "They groped around, discovering shortcomings in the life and order around them, yet because of their clan-bound and half-bohemian mentality, on one hand, and because of a typically Soviet internationalist upbringing, on the other, they could never rise to a 'systematic' understanding of the problem."[50]

Scathing criticism of Zhivago's children came from the younger generations, those who had grown up in the 1970s and 1980s and were unceremo-

Andrei Siniavsky as an émigré in Paris. In the early 1990s he blamed the postcommunist intelligentsia for having succumbed to the temptations of power and lust for money (Courtesy of Memorial, Moscow).

niously beginning to push their predecessors to the sidelines of history. Most of them lashed out at the *shestidesiatniki* from a postmodernist position and blamed them for their participation in the Soviet cultural project. The younger critics refused to draw a distinction between the dissidents, the enlightened apparatchiks, the established left-wing poets, novelists, and artists, and the vast conformist majority of party members and Soviet citizens. Some of them claimed that the *shestidesiatniki* had helped the communist regime get its second wind after Stalin's death and endure for almost three decades.

Czeslaw Milosz had once observed that for him the depth of Russian literature was always suspect, because it was "bought at too high a price." In line with this observation, one may suspect that Russia needed its critical intelligentsia and its high culture only as long as it suffered from tyranny, misery, and backwardness. With the emergence of a free market economy and a free exchange of ideas, in addition to a stable middle class holding entrenched democratic values and property, it is no longer necessary to have the intelligentsia either as a moral vanguard and guardian of intellectual integrity or as a social opposition force. In its stead appear professional educators, intellectuals, artists, and entertainers. They respond to the needs of middle-class "well-fed and industrious people," not the idealistic romantics and truth seekers.[51] For all the setbacks and reverses, Russia has been moving steadily in this direction. The gradual transformation of Russia has rendered the intelligentsia a historical anachronism, a subject for literary and historical recollections only.

Zhivago's children rarely lived up to the ethos and ideals of the old

Russian intelligentsia. Their behavior, with a few exceptions among the principled dissidents, was checkered by conformism, cowardice, mutual denunciations, cynicism, and hypocrisy. Quite a few of them were unable to resist pressures from the secret police, let alone the temptations of self-aggrandizement, vanity, and profiteering. The artistic and literary legacy of the Thaw and the succeeding period does not bear comparison with the classical cultural legacy created by their predecessors, not to mention the great writers and thinkers of nineteenth-century Russia. And yet Zhivago's children deserve empathy, not condemnation. The rebirth of the idea of the Russian intelligentsia in the post-Stalin years was a phenomenon that had one foot in the revolutionary era and the other in the era of unparalleled scientific and technological progress, globalization, and mass culture. The children of Zhivago spent their lives on "a voyage from the coast of Utopia" into the turbulent open sea of individual self-discovery.[52] Their grand illusions, tragic experiences, and enormous vitality compressed the most talented people from several age cohorts into one generation.

The story of Zhivago's children demonstrates the remarkable, and underestimated, centrality of the cultural and idealistic dimensions in the history of Soviet society, and consequently in the history of Europe and the world as a whole. The preoccupations and aspirations in the intellectual milieu remained essentially noncapitalist. Most intellectuals and artists in Moscow did not accept or understand Western notions of liberal democracy but rather thought and acted within the Soviet and communist framework, by seeking to combine individual emancipation with socialism. Few were prepared to denounce the legacy of the Russian Revolution or Leninism. This dream of a freer but still noncapitalist society lasted into the era of Mikhail Gorbachev and perestroika, before being buried under the rubble of Soviet communism. Just as the movements of the sixties profoundly changed Western democratic societies, by addressing their totalitarian, racist, and chauvinist past, the revival of the Russian intelligentsia was a crucial part of the evolution of Soviet society away from its revolutionary myths and totalitarian legacy. Curiously enough, some intellectuals in Moscow (and their counterparts in Warsaw, Budapest, and Prague) had begun this process even earlier than their Western counterparts who lived in "free" and democratic societies.[53] This was an impressive achievement, given the high moral and material costs involved. The ethos of educated civic participation, resistance to the immorality of the communist regime, and belief in humane socialism was a feature common to the efforts of Russian, Polish, and Czech reformers and liberal-minded people of culture. The two phenomena, in the West and in the East, were very different, but together they contributed to building a more peaceful and humane world.

Abbreviations

APRF	Arkhiv Prezidenta Rossiiskoi Federatsii (Archive of the President of the Russian Federation)
AVP RF	Arkhiv Vneshnei Politiki Rossiiskoi Federatsii (Archive of Foreign Policy of the Russian Federation)
CC	Central Committee (of the Communist Party of the Soviet Union).
GARF	Gosudarstvennyi Arkhiv Rossiiskoi Federatsii (State Archive of the Russian Federation, Moscow)
RGALI	Rossiiskii Gosudarstvennyi Arkhiv Literatury i Iskusstva (Russian State Archive for Literature and Art, Moscow)
RGANI	Rossiiskii Gosudarstvennyi Arkhiv Noveishei Istorii (Russian State Archive for Recent History, Moscow)
TsADKM	Tsentralnyi Arkhiv Dokumentalnykh Kollektsii Moskvy (Central Archive of Documentary Collections of Moscow)
TsAODM	Tsentralnyi Arkhiv Obshchestvennykh Dvizhenii Moskvy (Central Archive of Social Movements of Moscow), now TsGAOD
TsKhDMO	Tsentr Khranenia Dokumentov Molodezhnykh Organizatsii (Center for Storage of Documents of Youth Organizations, or the archive of the Komsomol, Moscow), now merged with RGANI

Notes

Prologue

1. Yevgeny Pasternak and Yelena Pasternak, *Zhizn Borisa Pasternaka* (St. Petersburg: Zvezda, 2004), 435; see also Y. B. Pasternak, *Boris Pasternak: Biografiia,* at http:// pasternak.niv.ru/pasternak/bio/pasternak-e-b/biografiya-1-1.htm *(note that this and all other Internet sites mentioned in the notes were last accessed in November 2008);* and Christopher Barnes, *Boris Pasternak: A Literary Biography,* vols. 1–2 (New York: Cambridge University Press, 2004).

2. One might also use the term "imagined communities," as does Benedict Anderson, *Imagined Communities: Reflections on the Origin and Spread of Nationalism* (London: Verso, 1991). Anderson also presented the idea in lectures and conversations at a workshop for Russian historians in St. Petersburg, July 5–17, 2007. Most scholars of Russian and Soviet society use the term "intelligentsia" as a social construct (similar to "class") or prefer to speak about "intellectuals." V. P. Leikina-Svirskaia, *Intelligentsia v Rossii vo vtoroi polovine XIX veka* (Moscow: Mysl, 1971); Leikina-Svirskaia, *Russkaia intelligentsia v 1900–1917 godakh* (Moscow: Mysl, 1981); L. G. Churchward, *The Soviet Intelligentsia: An Essay on the Social Structure and Roles of Soviet Intellectuals during the 1960s* (Boston: Routledge and Kegan Paul, 1973); Nicholas Lampert, *The Technical Intelligentsia and the Soviet State* (New York: Holmes & Meier, 1979); Lynn Mally, *Culture of the Future: The Proletkult Movement in Revolutionary Russia* (Berkeley: University of California Press, 1990); Mark D. Steinberg, *Proletarian Imagination: Self, Modernity, and the Sacred in Russia, 1910–1925* (Ithaca, N.Y.: Cornell University Press, 2002); Katerina Clark, *Petersburg, Crucible of Cultural Revolution* (Cambridge, Mass.: Harvard University Press, 1995); Igal Halfin, "The Rape of the Intelligentsia: A Proletarian Foundational Myth," *Russian Review* 56, no. 1 (Jan. 1997): 90–109. Other scholars emphasize the moral, cultural, and even spiritual characteristics of the Russian intelligentsia,

above all the belief in a mission to help the oppressed Russian people, educate and improve Russian society, and reform or overthrow the autocratic regime. See Vera S. Dunham's review of Churchward's book in the *American Journal of Sociology* 80, no. 2 (Sept. 1974): 573–575; Boris Uspensky, "Russkaia intelligentsia kak spetsificheskii fenomen russkoi kultury," in *Etiudy o russkoi istorii* (St. Petersburg: Azbuka, 2002), 393–413; D. S. Likhachev, ed., *Russkaia intelligentsia: Istoriia i sudba* (Moscow: Nauka, 1999).

3. Guy de Mallac, "Pasternak and Religion," *Russian Review* 32, no. 4 (Oct. 1973): 360–375.

4. A. N. Artizov et al., *"Ochistim Rossiiu nadolgo . . .": Repressii protiv inakomysliashchikh, Konets 1921–nachalo 1923 g.* (Moscow: Materik, 2008); Stuart Finkel, *On the Ideological Front: The Russian Intelligentsia and the Making of the Soviet Public Sphere* (New Haven, Conn.: Yale University Press, 2007).

5. Michael David-Fox, *Revolution of the Mind: Higher Learning among the Bolsheviks, 1918–1929* (Ithaca, N.Y.: Cornell University Press, 1997); Katerina Clark and Evgeny Dobrenko, with Andrei Artizov and Oleg Naumov, *Soviet Culture and Power: A History in Documents, 1917–1953* (New Haven, Conn.: Yale University Press, 2007), 32–33; G. S. Smith, *D. S. Mirsky: A Russian-English Life, 1890–1939* (New York: Oxford University Press, 2000).

6. Cynthia A. Ruder, *Making History for Stalin: The Story of the Belomor Canal* (Gainesville: University Press of Florida, 1998).

7. Jochen Hellbeck, *Revolution on My Mind: Writing a Diary under Stalin* (Cambridge, Mass.: Harvard University Press, 2006), 360.

8. Karl Eimermacher, *Die sowjetische Literaturpolitik, 1917 bis 1972: Von der Vielfalt zur Bolschewisierung der Literatur* (Bochum, Ger.: Brockmeyer, 1994). I cite the Russian edition of this book: Karl Eimermacher, *Politika i kultura pri Lenine i Staline* (Moscow: AIRO-XX, 1998), 140. Yevgeny Gromov, *Stalin: Vlast i iskusstvo* (Moscow: Respublika, 1998), 149.

9. Clark and Dobrenko, *Soviet Culture and Power,* 249–301; Katerina Clark, *Petersburg, Crucible of Cultural Revolution* (Cambridge, Mass.: Harvard University Press, 1996), 288–289.

10. Yelena Osokina, *Our Daily Bread: Socialist Distribution and the Art of Survival in Stalin's Russia, 1927–1941* (Armonk, N.Y.: Sharpe, 2001), 65–66.

11. On the fear of marginalization, see Hellbeck, *Revolution on My Mind,* 295–297, 350–351; Lev Anninsky, "Monologi byvshego stalintsa," in *Perestroika: Glasnost, demokratia, sotsializm: "Osmyslit kult Stalina"* (Moscow: Progress, 1989), 55. See the description by the young "proletarian" writer Alexander Avdeenko of his conversation with Prince Dmitry Mirsky, an aristocratic writer who returned to the USSR. Avdeenko, "Otluchenie," *Znamia* 3 and 4 (1989), as analyzed in Ruder, *Making History for Stalin,* 59–62; and the diary of Andrei Arzhilovsky in Véronique Garros, Natalia Korenevskaya, and Thomas Lahusen, eds., *Intimacy and Terror: Soviet Diaries of the 1930s,* trans. Carol A. Flath (New York: New Press, 1995), 139.

12. Papers of Dmitry S. Likhachev, fond 769, Manuscript Division of the Institute of Russian Literature, St. Petersburg; Dmitry S. Likhachev, *Reflections on the Russian Soul: A Memoir* (Budapest: CEU, 1995), 195–196. On the psychological and moral fallout of the Great Terror years, see Orlando Figes, *The Whisperers: Private Life in Stalin's Russia* (New York: Metropolitan, 2007), 227–315.

13. Lazar Fleishman, *Boris Pasternak i literaturnoe dvizheniie 1930-kh godov* (Moscow: Akademicheskii Proekt, 2005), 9, 51–54, 65, 108, 167, 180; Andrei Artizov and Oleg Naumov, eds., *Vlast i khudozhestvennaia intelligentsia: Dokumenty TsK RKP(b), VChK-OGPU-NKVD o kulturnoi politike, 1917–1953* (Moscow: Mezhdunarodny Fond Demokratiia, 2002), 216, 275; Y. B. Pasternak and Y. V. Pasternak, eds., *Boris Pasternak: Pisma k roditeliam i sestram, 1907–1960* (Moscow: Novoe Literaturnoe Obozrenie, 2004), 572. Interview with Yevgeny Pasternak, the poet's son and biographer, in *Vestnik*, June 23, 1998, at http://www.vestnik.com/issues/98/0623/win/nuzov.htm. See also B. M. Borisov, "Reka, raspakhnutaia nastezh: K tvorcheskoi istorii romana Borisa Pasternaka 'Doktor Zhivago,'" at http://pasternak.niv.ru/pasternak/bio/borisov-reka.htm.

14. Pasternak, *Boris Pasternak* (Internet version).

15. Entry in Afinogenov's diary, published in *Voprosy Literatury* 2 (1990): 113–114; on Afinogenov's background and diary, see Hellbeck, *Revolution on My Mind*, 285–345; on Pasternak's humanist religiosity, see Dmitry Bykov, *Boris Pasternak* (Moscow: Molodaia Gvardiia, 2007), 607–609.

16. Cited, from the NKVD files, in Clark and Dobrenko, *Soviet Culture and Power*, 318.

17. Vera Sandomirsky, "Soviet War Poetry," *Russian Review* 4, no. 1 (Autumn 1944): 47–66; Catherine Merridale, *Ivan's War: Life and Death in the Red Army, 1939–1945* (New York: Metropolitan, 2006).

18. Cited in Pasternak, *Boris Pasternak*.

19. From Boris Pasternak, "Dawn," translation by Vladislav Zubok.

20. Joshua Rubenstein, *Tangled Loyalties: The Life and Times of Ilya Ehrenburg* (New York: Basic, 1996); Benedikt Sarnov, *Sluchai Erenburga* (Moscow: Tekst, 2004).

21. Konstantin Simonov, "Wait for Me," translation by Vladislav Zubok.

22. *Znamia* 8 (1989): 147.

23. See the autobiographical preface in A. Tvardovsky, *Stikhotvoreniia i poemy v dvukh tomakh* (Moscow: Khudozhestvennaia Literatura, 1951); and Regina Romanova, *Alexander Tvardovsky: Trudy i dni* (Moscow: Vodolei, 2006).

24. Evgeny Dobrenko, *Formovka sovetskogo pisatelia: Sotsialnye i esteticheskie istoki sovetskoi literaturnoi kultury* (St. Petersburg: Akademicheskii Proiekt, 1999), 302–347.

25. Sandomirsky, "Soviet War Poetry," 63; fragments from Tvardovsky's war diary, "Iz zapisnoi potertoi knizhki (Zapisi A. T. Tvardovskogo, 1944–45 gg.)," *Druzhba Narodov* 6 (2000): 182.

26. Clark and Dobrenko, *Soviet Culture and Power*, 356, 357, 359.

27. Katerina Clark, *The Soviet Novel: History as Ritual,* 3rd ed. (Bloomington: Indiana University Press, 2000), 191; 199–209; Veniamin Kaverin, *Epilog: Memuary* (Moscow: Russkaia Kniga, 2000), 339.

28. Clark and Dobrenko, *Soviet Culture and Power,* 109–113.

29. Isaiah Berlin, *Personal Impressions,* ed. Henry Hardy (New York: Viking, 1981), 177.

30. Vladislav Zubok, *A Failed Empire: The Soviet Union in the Cold War from Stalin to Gorbachev* (Chapel Hill: University of North Carolina Press, 2007), 59–60; Likhachev, *Reflections on the Russian Soul,* 267–277.

31. Rubenstein, *Tangled Loyalties,* 253–276; Rubenstein and Vladimir P. Naumov, eds., *Stalin's Secret Pogrom: The Postwar Inquisition of the Jewish Anti-Fascist Committee* (New Haven, Conn.: Yale University Press, 2001).

32. On Simonov, see Boris Pankin, *Chetyre ia Konstantina Simonova* (Moscow: Voskresenie, 1999); Natalia Ivanova, "Konstantin Simonov glazami cheloveka moego pokoleniia," *Znamia* 7 (1999); and Lev Anninsky, "Konstantin Simonov: 'Ia prishel vovremia,'" *Svobodnaia Mysl* 7 (2005): 154.

33. As indicated earlier, the phrase "imagined community" is inspired by Benedict Anderson's book *Imagined Communities.*

34. Boris Pasternak, *Doctor Zhivago,* trans. Max Hayward and Manya Harari (New York: Pantheon, 1958), 359.

35. Pasternak and Pasternak, *Zhizn Borisa Pasternaka.*

36. Pasternak, *Boris Pasternak: Biografiia,* 2nd ed. (Moscow: Tsitadel, 1997), 691–692.

37. It was quickly translated into English by Max Hayward and Manya Harari. Patricia Blake, introduction, Max Hayward, *Writers in Russia, 1917–1978* (London: Harvill, 1983), xlix–l.

38. Zapiska sekretaria TsK KPSS Suslova s predlozheniiem mer v sviazi s prisuzhdeniem B. L. Pasternaku Nobelevskoi premii po literature, Oct. 23, 1958, in V. Y. Afiani and N. G. Tomilina, "A za mnoiu shum pogoni . . . ," in *Boris Pasternak i vlast: Dokumenty, 1956–1960* (Moscow: ROSSPEN, 2001), 144–145.

39. Vladimir Semichastny, *Bespokoinoe serdtse* (Moscow: Vagrius, 2002), 72–74; Andrei Voznesensky, *Na virtualnom vetru* (Moscow: Vagrius, 2000), 34–35; William Taubman, *Khrushchev: The Man and His Era* (New York: Norton, 2003), 385.

40. From Boris Pasternak, "Nobel Prize," translation by Vladislav Zubok.

41. Pasternak and Pasternak, *Zhizn Borisa Pasternaka,* 466–467.

42. Kaverin, *Epilog,* 381–382; *Novy Mir* 2 (1990): 172.

43. Grigory Pomerants, *Zapiski gadkogo utenka* (Moscow: Moskovskii Rabochii, 1998), 309.

44. Among the descriptions of the funeral see Lidia Chukovskaia, diary entry of June 2, 1960, in Chukovskaia, *Sochinenia v dvukh tomakh* (Moscow: Gudyal-Press, 2000), 2:263–266; and Kaverin, *Epilog,* 385–387.

45. David Samoilov, *Pamiatnye zapiski* (Moscow: Mezhdunarodnye Otnosheniia, 1995), 360.

46. Pasternak, *Doctor Zhivago,* 508.

47. Ethan Pollock, *Stalin and the Soviet Science Wars* (Princeton, N.J.: Princeton University Press, 2006), 3–4.

48. Igor Vinogradov, "Stalin—ideiny tiran" (on the fiftieth anniversary of the Twentieth Party Congress), *Znamia* 7 (2006), at http://magazines.russ.ru/znamia/2006/7/ko9.html.

49. See http://nobelprize.org/nobel_prizes/literature/laureates/1987/brodsky-lecture-e.html.

1. The "Children" Grow Up, 1945–1955

1. Elena Zubkova, *Russia after the War: Hopes, Illusions, and Disappointments, 1945–1957*, trans. Hugh Ragsdale (Armonk, N.Y.: Sharpe, 1998), 36; Anatoly S. Cherniaev, *Moia zhizn i moe vremia* (Moscow: Mezhdunarodnye Otnosheniia, 1995), 195.

2. For poignant memories of this environment, see Eduard Kochergin, *Angelova kukla: Rasskazy risovalnogo cheloveka* (St. Petersburg: Ivan Limbakh, 2006).

3. Georgy Knabe, "Final: Arbatskaia epopeia," in T. Kniazevskaia, ed., *Russkaia intelligentsia* (Moscow: Nauka, 1999), 342–350; Cherniaev, *Moia zhizn,* 38–44; author's interview with historian Sigurd Shmidt, Jan. 17, 2008, Moscow. See also Stephen V. Bittner, *The Many Lives of Khrushchev's Thaw: Experience and Memory in Moscow's Arbat* (Ithaca, N.Y.: Cornell University Press, 2008), 19–39.

4. P. Gorelik, ed., *Boris Slutsky: Vospominaniia sovremennikov* (St. Petersburg: Neva, 2005), 550; Boris Slutsky, *Things That Happened,* ed., trans., and intro. G. S. Smith (Chicago: Ivan R. Dee, 1998), 61.

5. David Samoilov, *Podennye zapisi* (Moscow: Vremia, 2002), 1:78, 86, 97, 107.

6. Oleg Troianovsky, *Cherez gody i rasstoiania* (Moscow: Vagrius, 1997), 94.

7. Samoilov wrote in his diary in October 1941 that his circle, "still anonymous for the state, offered its services to the state." Samoilov, *Podennyie zapisi,* 1:139.

8. Ibid.

9. Elke Scherstjanoi, "Germaniia i nemtsy v pismakh krasnoarmeitsev vesnoi 1945 g.," *Novaia i Noveishaia Istoriia* 2 (2002): 137–151; Samoilov, *Podennye zapisi,* 1, 209; Slutsky, *Things That Happened,* 71.

10. Vera Sandomirsky, "Soviet War Poetry," *Russian Review* 4, no. 1 (Autumn 1944): 66.

11. Boris Slutsky, *O drugikh i o sebe* (Moscow: Vagrius, 2005); Nikolai Inozemtsev, *Frontovoi dnevnik* (Moscow: Nauka, 2005), 181, 227.

12. This topic was virtually taboo in historical studies until the 1990s. See Norman Naimark, *Russians in Germany* (Cambridge, Mass.: Harvard University Press, 1995); Antony Beevor, *The Fall of Berlin, 1945* (New York: Viking, 2002), 28–31, 108–110; Catherine Merridale, *Ivan's War: Life and Death in the Red Army, 1939–1945* (New York: Metropolitan, 2006), 309–320; Cherniaev, *Moia zhizn,* 132–133, 191–192. See also excerpts from the war diaries of Boris Slutsky, "Iz 'zapisok o voine,'" *Ogonyok,* Apr. 17, 1995; war letters of Viktor Olenev published in

Zavtra 19 (1997); K. I. Bukov, M. M. Gorinov, and A. N. Ponomarev, eds., *Moskva voennaia, 1941–1945: Memuary i arkhivnye dokumenty* (Moscow: Mosgorarkhiv, 1995), 707.

13. Grigory Pomerants, *Zapiski gadkogo utenka* (Moscow: Moskovskii Rabochii, 1998), 95, 202, 212; and see similar observations in Alexander Zinoviev, *Russkaia sudba: Ispoved otshchepentsa* (Moscow: ZAO Tsentrpoligraf, 1999), 218.

14. Cherniaev, *Moia zhizn,* 79; Knabe, "Final," 354.

15. Beevor, *The Fall of Berlin,* 421–423; Pomerants, *Zapiski gadkogo utenka,* 96–97; John Barber and Mark Harrison, *The Soviet Home Front, 1941–1945: A Social and Economic History of the USSR in World War II* (London: Longman, 1991), 209; Robert D. English, *Russia and the Idea of the West: Gorbachev, Intellectuals and the End of the Cold War* (New York: Columbia, 2000), 44–46.

16. David Samoilov and Naum Korzhavin in Gorelik, *Boris Slutsky,* 70, 125–136. See also Samoilov, *Podennye zapisi,* 1:219.

17. On philosopher-veterans see G. S. Batygin and C. F. Yarmoliuk, eds., *Rossiiskaia sotsiologiia shestidesiatykh godov v vospominaniiakh i dokumentakh* (St. Petersburg: Russkii Khristianskii Gumanitarnyi Institut, 1999), 83, 206; Yevgeny Plimak, *Na voine i posle voiny: Zapiski veterana* (Moscow: Ves Mir, 2005), 78–87.

18. Georgy Shakhnazarov, *S Vozhdiami i bez nikh* (Moscow: Vagrius, 2001), 69–70.

19. Samoilov, *Podennye zapisi,* 1:232; Gorelik, *Boris Slutsky,* 86.

20. Timofeev's ancestors were Russian noblemen, and his father was an outstanding specialist in venereal diseases, a prototype for Mikhail Bulgakov's professor Pre-obrazhensky in "The Dog's Heart." Among his patients were senior Soviet officials. The rarefied clientele granted the Timofeev family a rare degree of safety in Stalin's Russia. Isay Kuznetsov, "O, molodost poslevoennaia . . . ," *Voprosy Literatury* 4 (2001); Arkady Vaksberg, *Moia zhizn v zhizni* (Moscow: Terra, 2000), 1:237–239. I also conducted numerous conversations and interviews in Arlington, Va., with Natasha Simes, the daughter of Yuri Timofeev, about her father.

21. Igor Shevelev, "'Vse eto pokhozhe na pritchu . . .': O Davide Samoilove i ego dnevnikakh" (interview with Samoilov's son Alexander Davydov), *Novoe Vremia* 13 (Mar. 30, 2003), at http://www.newtimes.ru.

22. Slutsky, *O drugikh i o sebe,* 194; David Samoilov, *Pamiatnye zapiski* (Moscow: Mezhdunarodnye Otnosheniia, 1995), 165.

23. Kuznetsov, "O, molodost poslevoennaia . . . ," 4.

24. Batygin and Yarmoliuk, *Rossiiskaia sotsiologiia,* 372.

25. *Svobodnaia mysl* 3 (2001): 78.

26. Ludmilla Alexeyeva and Paul Goldberg, *The Thaw Generation: Coming of Age in the Post-Stalin Era* (Pittsburgh: University of Pittsburgh Press, 1993), 19, 29–33, 43, 61, 64.

27. A. I. Volkov, M. G. Pugacheva, and S. F. Yarmoliuk, eds., *Pressa v obshchestve, 1959–2000: Otsenki zhurnalistov i sotsiologov—Dokumenty* (Moscow: Moskovskaia Shkola Politicheskikh Issledovanii, 2000), 20.

28. Mikhail Gorbachev, *Zhizn i reformy* (Moscow: Novosti, 1995), 1:68–69.

29. V. P. Smirnov, "Na istoricheskom fakultete MGU v 1948–1953 godakh (Sugubo lichnye vpechatleniia i razmyshleniia)," *Novaia i Noveishaia Istoriia*, 6 (Nov.–Dec. 2005): 135; S. S. Angelina, "*Vremia, ostavsheesia s nami*": *Filologicheskii fakultet v 1953–1958 gg.—Vospominaniia vypusknikov* (Moscow: MAKS, 2004), 175.

30. Shakhnazarov, *S Vozhdiami i bez nikh*, 47; Vladimir Shlapentokh, *Strakh i druzhba v nashem totalitarnom proshlom* (St. Petersburg: Zvezda, 2003), 104. See also the innovative study of postwar Soviet youth in Benjamin K. Tromly, "Re-Imagining the Soviet Intelligentsia: Student Politics and University Life, 1948–1964" (Ph.D. diss., Harvard University, 2007).

31. Ernest Skalsky, interview with Tatiana Kosinova, Nov. 4, 1992, archive of Memorial, St. Petersburg.

32. Smirnov, "Na istoricheskom fakultete MGU," 144; Mikhail Gorbachev and Zdeněk Mlynář, *Conversations with Gorbachev on Perestroika, the Prague Spring, and the Crossroads of Socialism,* trans. George Shriver (New York: Columbia University Press, 2002), 18–19.

33. Yuri Burtin, *Ispoved shestidesiatnika* (Moscow: Progress-Traditsiia, 2003), 14–20.

34. Ibid.

35. Leonid Gordon in Batygin and Yarmoliuk, *Rossiiskaia sotsiologiia,* 373–374.

36. Rada Adzhubei, as quoted in Volkov, Pugacheva, and Yarmoliuk, *Pressa v obshchestve,* 15.

37. A choryphaeus is the leader of the chorus in Greek theater. For the background of these "discussions," see Nikolai Krementsov, *Stalinist Science* (Princeton, N.J.: Princeton University Press, 1997), 129–184; Ethan Pollock, *Stalin and the Soviet Science Wars* (Princeton, N.J.: Princeton University Press, 2006); "'Delo' molodykh istorikov, 1957–1958," *Voprosy Istorii* 4 (1994): 108.

38. Rada Adzhubei, as quoted in Volkov, Pugacheva, and Yarmoliuk, *Pressa v obshchestve,* 16; Alexei Adzhubei, *Krushenie illuzii: Vremia v sobytiakh i litsakh* (Moscow: Interbuk, 1991), 83–85.

39. Juliane Fürst, "Prisoners of the Soviet Self? Political Youth Opposition in Late Stalinism," *Europe-Asia Studies* 54, no. 3 (2002): 358.

40. Interview with Naum Korzhavin, *Novaia Gazeta–Ex Libris* 20 (2005), at http://antology.igrunov.ru/authors/korzhavin/1118492287.html; Naum Korzhavin, *V Soblaznakh krovavoi epokhi,* vols. 1–2 (Moscow: Zakharov, 2007).

41. Ernst Neizvestny, "Katakombnaia kultura i ofitsialnoe iskusstvo," *Posev* 11 (1979).

42. Joseph Brodsky, "The Spoils of War" (1986), in *On Grief and Reason: Essays* (New York: Farrar, Straus and Giroux, 1995). On the changing landscape of visual propaganda, see Peter Kenez, *Cinema and Soviet Society from the Revolution to the Death of Stalin* (London: Tauris, 2001).

43. The *stiliagi* have recently attracted much attention in Western academic literature. See Richard Stites and J. von Geldern, eds., *Mass Culture in Soviet Russia: Tales, Poems, Songs, Movies, Plays, and Folklore, 1917–1953* (Bloomington: Indiana University Press, 1995); Mark Edele, "Strange Young Men in Stalin's Moscow: the Birth and Life of the Stiliagi, 1945–1953," *Jahrbücher für Geschichte Osteuropas* 50

(2003): 37–61; and Alexei Yurchak, *Everything Was Forever, Until It Was No More: The Last Soviet Generation* (Princeton, N.J.: Princeton University Press, 2006), esp. 170–175.

44. Brodsky, "The Spoils of War," 3–21.
45. Vasily Aksyonov, *In Search of Melancholy Baby* (New York: Random House, 1987).
46. Alexei Kozlov, *Kozel na sakse* (expanded Internet version), at http://www.lib.ru/ CULTURE/MUSIC/KOZLOV/kozel_na_saxe.txt.
47. See the interview with Valentin Tikhonenko and Boris Pustyntsev, in *Pchela* 11 (Oct.–Nov. 1997).
48. Edele, "Strange Young Men in Stalin's Moscow," 37–61.
49. Edward Crankshaw, *Russia without Stalin: The Emerging Pattern* (New York: Viking, 1956), 110.
50. Marvin Kalb, *Eastern Exposure* (New York: Farrar, Straus and Cudahy, New York, 1957), 314–315.
51. Kozlov, *Kozel na sakse*, 96–97.
52. Joseph Brodsky, "The Spoils of War," 13–14.
53. For more on this point see Kristin Roth-Ey, "Kto na piedestale, a kto v tolpe? Stiliagi i ideia sovetskoi 'molodiozhnoi kultury' v epokhu 'ottepeli,'" in *Neprikosnovenny Zapas* 3, no. 36 (2004), at http://www.nlo.magazine.ru/philosoph/inostr/ inostr83.html).
54. Recollections of Viktor Malkin, *Kontinent* 71 (1992); Gorelik, *Boris Slutsky,* 504.
55. M. M. Molostvov, *Iz zametok volnodumtsa* (St. Petersburg: Memorial, 2003), 12.
56. Smirnov, "Na istoricheskom fakultete MGU," 162–163.
57. According to Gorbachev's reminiscences before the party secretaries in April 1988. *Politbiuro TsK KPSS . . . Po zapisiam Anatoliia Cherniaeva, Vadima Medvedeva, Georgiia Shakhnazarova, 1985–1991* (Moscow: Alpina Biznes Books, 2006), 323.
58. Yevgeny Yevtushenko, *A Precocious Autobiography,* trans. Andrew R. MacAndrew (London: Collings and Harvill, 1963), 89–92.
59. Bronislav Kholopov, "Lichnaia zhizn v teni GB," *Druzhba Narodov* 10 (1994): 130.
60. Alexeyeva and Goldberg, *The Thaw Generation,* 69.
61. Smirnov, "Na istoricheskom fakultete MGU," 164–165.
62. On Stromynka and Dedkov, see Zubkova, *Russia after the War;* "XX siezd—sorok let spustia," a program by Vladimir Tolz, at http://www.svoboda.org/programs/ cicles/xx/xx_01.asp.
63. Viktor Slavkin, *Pamiatnik neizvestnomu stiliage* (Moscow: Artist, Rezhisser, Teatr, 1996), 19.
64. See, for Gendler's reminiscences, ibid.; V. I. Fomin, ed., *Kinematograf ottepeli: Dokumenty i svidetelstva ochevidtsev* (Moscow: Materik, 1998), 14.
65. Alexeyeva and Goldberg, *The Thaw Generation,* 83. See also Juliane Fürst, "Friends in Private, Friends in Public: The Phenomenon of the Kompania among Soviet Youth in the 1950s and 1960s," in Lewis H. Siegelbaum, ed., *Borders of Socialism: Private Spheres in Soviet Russia* (New York: Palgrave Macmillan, 2006), 135–153.
66. Alexeyeva and Goldberg, *The Thaw Generation,* 83.

67. Andrei Konchalovsky, *Nizkie istiny* (Moscow: Sovershenno Sekretno, 1998): 76–77.

68. "My prosto byli drug dlia druga: Vsiu zhizn" (interview with Mikhail Gorbachev), *Obshchaia Gazeta,* Oct. 28, 1999.

69. Shlapentokh, *Strakh i druzhba,* 69.

70. G. F. Krivosheev, ed., *Rossiia i SSSR v voinakh XX veka: Poteri vooruzhennykh sil—Statisticheskoie issledovaniie* (Moscow: Olma-Press, 2001); B. V. Sokolov, "The Cost of War: Human Losses for the USSR and Germany, 1939–1945," *Journal of Slavic Military Studies* 9 (Mar. 1996): 172; V. E. Kozol, "The Price of Victory: Myths and Realities," ibid., 417–424.

71. Liudmila Alexeeva v soavtorstve s Polom Goldbergom, *Pokolenie ottepeli* (Moscow: Zakharov, 2006), 94–104, 116. The Russian version of Alexeyeva's memoirs contains additional information, omitted from the English-language publication.

72. Instructor of the CC (RSFSR) Department for Science, Schools, and Culture, Dec. 19, 1956, RGANI, f. 5, op. 37, d. 2, l. 145.

73. Alexeyeva and Goldberg, *The Thaw Generation,* 72–73.

74. Cherniaev, *Moia zhizn,* 219.

75. Katerina Clark, *The Soviet Novel: History as Ritual,* 3rd ed. (Bloomington: Indiana University Press, 2000), 191, 199–209.

76. Vera S. Dunham, *In Stalin's Times: Middle-Class Values in Soviet Fiction* (Cambridge: Cambridge University Press, 1976); Marina R. Zezina, *Sovetskaia khudozhestvennaia intelligentsiia i vlast v 1950-e-1960-e gody* (Moscow: Dialog-MGU, 1999), 97; Vladimir Paperny, *Kultura Dva* (Moscow: Novoe Literaturnoe Obozrenie, 1996); Yevgeny Gromov, *Stalin: Vlast i iskusstvo* (Moscow: Respublika, 1998).

77. Orlando Figes, *The Whisperers: Private Life in Stalin's Russia* (New York: Metropolitan, 2007), 522–523.

78. Lev Anninsky, "Konstantin Simonov: "Ia prishel vovremia," *Svobodnaia Mysl* 7 (2005): 154.

79. "'My bolshe komanduem, chem vospityvaem': Kak videlos A. A. Fadeevu rukovodstvo iskusstvom," *Istochnik* 2 (2000): 88–89.

80. Ibid., 95–98.

81. Zapiska Otdela nauki i kultury TsK KPSS, Feb. 8, 1954, RGANI, f. 5, op. 17, d. 454, ll. 33–36, at *Mezhdunarodnyi Fond "Demokratia" (Fond Alexandra Yakovleva),* http://www.idf.ru/11/.

82. Dina R. Spechler, *Permitted Dissent in the USSR: Novy Mir and the Soviet Regime* (New York: Praeger, 1982); Edith Rogovin Frankel, *Novy Mir: A Case Study in the Politics of Literature, 1952–1958* (New York: Cambridge University Press, 1981).

83. Zezina, *Sovetskaia khudozhestvennaia intelligentsiia,* 131.

84. I have already mentioned Timofeev's excellent library. Anatoly Cherniaev listed in his memoirs what he had read just in a few weeks in early 1946: works by Anatole France, Heinrich von Kleist, William Shakespeare, Johann Wolfgang von Goethe, Gustave Flaubert, Maurice Maeterlinck, Oscar Wilde, August Strindberg, and Blaise Pascal, among others. Cherniaev, *Moia zhizn,* 197–198.

85. On Kronid Liubarsky, see A. V. Kessenikh, "Poema o zhizni molodogo sovetskogo fizika, 40–50-kh godov," *Voprosy Istorii Estestvoznaniia i Tekhniki* 2 (1998): 125; on Gorbachev's relations with Mlynář see Gorbachev and Mlynář, *Conversations with Gorbachev,* 1–2, 22–24.

86. See further details in Vladislav Zubok, *A Failed Empire: The Soviet Union in the Cold War from Stalin to Gorbachev* (Chapel Hill: University of North Carolina Press, 2007), 96–97.

87. William Taubman, *Khrushchev: The Man and His Era* (New York: Norton, 2003), 384; Samoilov, *Pamiatnye zapiski,* 361.

88. A. Tvardovsky, "Iz rabochikh tetradei (1953–1960)," *Znamia* 7 (1989): 125.

89. Entry of Oct. 23, 1954, in R. G. Eimontova, ed., "Iz dnevnikov Sergeia Sergeevicha Dmitrieva," *Otechestvennaia Istoriia* 6 (1999): 128.

90. Sandomirsky, "Soviet War Poetry," 57, 60.

91. Samoilov, *Pamiatnye zapiski,* 247. Slutsky's poems are published in Yevgeny Yevtushenko, ed., *Strofy veka: Antologiia russkoi poezii* (Minsk: Polifakt, 1995), 641, 642, 643.

92. Ibid., 346–347.

93. Yevgeny Yevtushenko, *Volchii pasport* (Moscow: Vagrius, 1998), 11.

94. Her Russian-Italian mother was an interpreter with the rank of major in Soviet intelligence. Her father, from whom she inherited the Tartar slant of her eyes, was an airport customs officer.

95. Mihajlo Mihajlov, *Moscow Summer* (New York: Farrar, Straus and Giroux, 1965), 85; Yevtushenko, *Volchii pasport,* 90.

96. Yevtushenko, *Volchii pasport,* 11

2. Shock Effects, 1956-1958

Epigraph from Boris Slutsky, *Things That Happened,* ed., trans., and intro. G. S. Smith (Chicago: Ivan R. Dee, 1999), 183.

1. For further discussion, see Rudolf Pikhoia, "Medlenno taiushchii led (1953–1958)," *Mezhdunarodnyi Istoricheskii Zhurnal* 7 (Jan.–Feb. 2000), at http://history .machaon.ru/all/number_07/analiti4/ice_print/.

2. Viktor Zaslavsky, *La pulizia di classe: Il massacre di Katyn* (Rome: Il Mulino, 2006).

3. Alexander Yakovlev, *Omut pamiati* (Moscow: Vagrius, 2000), 50.

4. Alexander Yakovlev, *Sumerki* (Moscow: Materik, 2003), 253–255; William Taubman, *Khrushchev: The Man and His Era* (New York: Norton, 2003), 274.

5. "Stenogramma zakrytogo partsobraniia partorganizatsii moskovskikh pisatelei, izdatelstva 'Sovetskiii pisatel,'" Litfonda SSSR i Pravleniia SP SSSR," Mar. 29, 1956, TsAODM, f. 8132, op. 1, d. 5, ll. 106–198; ibid., d. 6, ll. 1–138; Taubman, *Khrushchev,* 283.

6. Lidia Chukovskaia, *Zapiski ob Anne Akhmatovoi, 1952–1962* (Moscow: Soglasiie, 1997), 2:195–196.

7. Cited in Elena Zubkova, *Russia after the War: Hopes, Illusions, and Disappointments, 1945–1957*, trans. Hugh Ragsdale (Armonk, N.Y.: Sharpe, 1998), 185.

8. See Chen Jian, "The Effects of the Secret Speech on China and Sino-Soviet Relations," and Kathleen E. Smith, "Soviet Party Propagandists and the Secret Speech," papers presented at the conference De-Stalinization: The First Fifty Years after Khrushchev's Secret Speech, Feb. 16, 2006, Institute for European, Russian and Eurasian Studies, Washington, D.C.

9. Comments written on Mar. 12, 15, 19, and 25, in "Iz dnevnikov Sergeia Sergeevicha Dmitrieva," *Otechestvennaia Istoriia* 1 (2000): 166–167.

10. *Doklad N. S. Khrushcheva o kulte lichnosti Stalina na XX sezde KPSS: Dokumenty* (Moscow: ROSSPEN, 2002), 257–264, 405–428; V. A. Kozlov, "Politicheskiie volneniia v Gruzii posle XX sezda KPSS," *Otechestvennaia Istoriia* 3 (1997): 33–51. See also the report [not later than May 23, 1956] from the Bureau of the Central Committee of Georgia's Communist Party on the mass disturbances in Tbilisi, Gori, Kutaisi, Sukhumi, and Batumi, in *Prezidium TsK KPSS, 1954–1958*, vol. 2, *Postanovleniia, 1954–1958* (Moscow: ROSSPEN, 2006), 283–303.

11. Vadim Medvedev at the roundtable at the Gorbachev Foundation dedicated to the fiftieth anniversary of the Twentieth Party Congress, Feb. 15, 2006, in stenographic report from the foundation. Ludmilla Alexeyeva and Paul Goldberg, *The Thaw Generation: Coming of Age in the Post-Stalin Era* (Pittsburgh: University of Pittsburgh, 1990), 76–77; Ilya Ehrenburg, *Liudi, gody, zhizn*, vols. 5–7 (Moscow: Khudozhestvennaia Literatura, 2000), 448.

12. TsAODM, f. 8132, op. 1, dd. 6, 72, 74; Zubkova, *Russia after the War*, 188–189.

13. Rudolf Pikhoia, "Medlenno taiushchii led (1953–1958)," *Mezhdunarodnyi Istoricheskii Zhurnal* 7 (Jan.–Feb. 2000), at http://history.machaon.ru/all/number_07/analiti4/ice; the recollections of Orlov and others appear in Lev Lurie and Irina Maliarova, eds., *1956 god: Seredina veka* (St. Petersburg: Neva, 2007), 182–196.

14. Postanovlennie Prezidiuma TsK KPSS, "Ob Otkrytii Plenuma TsK KPSS," May 25, 1956, *Prezidium TsK KPSS: Postanovleniia, 1954–1958*, 305, 308–309, 948; Relazione della delegazione Paietta, Negarville, Pellegrini ad direzione del Partito, July 18, 1956; also the letter from Guiseppe Boffa to Giancarlo Paietta, Oct. 3, 1956, Fondazione Gramsci, Rome.

15. David Samoilov, *Pamiatnye zapiski* (Moscow: Mezhdunarodnye Otnosheniia, 1995), 355–356, 360.

16. Chukovskaia, *Zapiski ob Anne Akhmatovoi*, 2:202.

17. This assertion is based on my analysis of the protocols of the Komsomol committees of different departments (schools) at Moscow State University. TsAODM, f. 478, op. 3, dd. 38, 39, 44. See also Sergei Kara-Murza, *"Sovok" vspominaet* (Moscow: Algoritm, 2002), 134–136.

18. At the Institute of Mining Engineers and the Institute of Technology most of the unrest occurred among Jewish students who were intensely interested in culture and humanities but could not get into those fields because of the state-imposed

enrollment quotas. Instead, they had to study mining engineering, and so forth. Author's interview with Viktor Zaslavsky, a graduate of the Institute of Mining Engineers in Leningrad during the 1950s, Apr. 1, 2006, Rome; V. I. Fomin, ed., *Kinematograf ottepeli: Dokumenty i svidetelstva ochevidtsev* (Moscow: Materik, 1998), 208–217; Dmitry Bobyshev, *Ia zdes (Chelovekotekst)* (Moscow: Vagrius, 2003), 95–112.

19. Marat Cheshkov, "Nas vziali posredi reki . . . ," *Karta,* 17–18 (1997): 71; see also interview by T. Kosinova with Cheshkov, Sept. 28, 1992, oral history collection, archive of Memorial, Moscow.

20. Sofia Chuikina, interview with M. M. Krasilnikov, Oct. 26, 1991, archive of Memorial, Moscow.

21. Vitaly Troianovsky, "Chelovek ottepeli," in Fomin, *Kinematograf ottepeli,* 31.

22. Revolt I. Pimenov, *Vospominaniia,* vol. 1, ed. N. Mitrokhin, at http://www.chronos.msu.ru/RREPORTS/pimenov_vospominaniya_1.html.

23. Protocols and resolutions of the Party Organization of Moscow State University, TsAODM, f. 478, op. 2, dd. 18, 304; ibid., op. 3, dd. 30, 31, 33, 34, 44, 48, 50–52, 62, 63; partially published by Yevgeny Taranov, "'Raskachaem Leninskiie Gory!' Iz istorii 'volnodumstva' v Moskovskom Universitete, 1955–1956," *Svobodnaia Mysl* 10 (1993): 99–101.

24. On this sympathy, see Gennady Kuzovkin, "Partiino-Komsomolskie presledovaniia po politicheskim motivam v period rannei 'ottepeli,'" in *Korni Travy: Sbornik statei molodykh istorikov* (Moscow: Zvenia, 1996), 100–124. The chapter is based on an impressive amount of archival research and oral history.

25. Taranov,"'Raskachaem Leninskiie Gory!'" 100–101.

26. Bronislav Kholopov, "Lichnaia zhizn v teni GB," *Druzhba Narodov* 10 (1994): 131.

27. Taranov,"'Raskachaem Leninskiie Gory!'" 100–101.

28. Yelena Zubkova, *Obshchestvo i reformy, 1946–1964* (Moscow: Rossiia Molodaia, 1993), 139–145; Mark Kramer, "The Soviet Union and the 1956 Crises in Hungary and Poland: Reassessments and New Findings," *Journal of Contemporary History* 33, no. 2 (1998): 195–197.

29. Mikhail Konosov, "Zapiski vechnogo studenta," *Smena,* Sept. 18, 1993; Bobyshev, *Ia zdes,* 133, 144–151.

30. TsAODM, f. 8132, op. 1, d. 5.

31. Avdeenko (b. 1908) was a "proletarian writer" personally devoted to Stalin who glorified the Soviet secret police and slave labor in 1932–33. He fell under suspicion in 1940 and lost his membership in the Union of Soviet Writers and the right to publish his works. On Avdeenko's rise and fall, see Alexander Avdeenko, "Otluchenie," *Znamia* 3 (1989): 5–73, and ibid., 4 (1989): 80–133; Cynthia Ann Ruder, *Making History for Stalin: The Story of the Belomor Canal* (Gainesville, Fla.: University of Florida Press, 1998), 59–66.

32. TsAODM, f. 8132, op. 1, d. 5, ll. 188–196.

33. Ibid., d. 6, ll. 4–9, 60–66, 85–86.

34. Ibid.

35. Ibid., d. 5, ll. 195–196; d. 6, ll. 13–14, 58, 70–73.

36. Raisa Orlova, *Vospominaniia o neproshedshem vremeni* (Moscow: Slovo, 1993), 227; Mariia R. Zezina, *Sovetskaia khudozhestvennaia intelligentsiia i vlast v 1950-e-1960-e gg.* (Moscow: Dialog-MGU, 1999), 178, 170.

37. Stenographic minutes of the meeting for Apr. 5, 1956, RGALI, Fond Literaturnoi Gazety (f. 634), op. 4, d. 1241, ll. 61, 87.

38. Pyotr Gorelik, "Drug iunosti i vsei zhizni," in P. Gorelik, ed., *Boris Slutsky: Vospominaniia sovremennikov* (St. Petersburg: Neva, 2005), 54.

39. Ilya Ehrenburg, "O stikhakh Borisa Slutskogo," *Literaturnaia Gazeta,* July 28, 1956; on the circumstances of this publication, see Gorelik, *Boris Slutsky,* 184-188.

40. David Samoilov, *Podennye zapisi* (Moscow: Vremia, 2002), 1:268.

41. The Fadeev letter was published only in October 1990, in the CC CPSU weekly. "Glasnost," *Izvestia TsK KPSS* 10 (1990): 147-151.

42. By opening up the Soviet Union, Khrushchev argued, it would be possible to undermine NATO and other U.S.-led military-political alliances, improve Soviet security, and reduce the burden of military spending. See Vladislav Zubok, *A Failed Empire: The Soviet Union in the Cold War from Stalin to Gorbachev* (Chapel Hill: University of North Carolina Press, 2007), 103-104.

43. RGANI, f. 5, op. 36, ll. 19, 133-134, posted by Mezhdunarodnyi Fond "Demokratii" (Fond Alexandra Yakovleva), at http://www.idf.ru/11/.

44. I am thankful to William Taubman for sharing excerpts from the memoirs of Igor Chernoutsan with me. See also the published excerpts in "Iskusstvo prinadlezhit narodu," *Vremia Novostei,* Mar. 1, 2005, at http://www.cargobay.ru/news/vremja_novostejj/2005/3/1/id_57653.html.

45. Karl E. Loewenstein, "The Thaw: Writers and the Public Sphere in the Soviet Union, 1951-1957" (Ph.D. diss., Dec. 1999, Duke University); Veniamin Kaverin, *Epilog: Memuary* (Moscow: Russkaia Kniga, 2002), 341-352; Dmitry Bykov, *Boris Pasternak* (Moscow: Molodaia Gvardiia, 2007), 739.

46. Boris Pankin, *Chetyre ia Konstantina Simonova* (Moscow: Voskresenie, 1999), 220-221. Simonov was not the only one to be irritated by Pasternak's Christian humanism. See speech of Sergei Smirnov at the session of the Moscow branch of the Union of Soviet Writers, Oct. 31, 1958, *Gorizont* 9 (1988); see also http://antology.igrunov.ru/50-s/esse/1084533076.html.

47. Vladimir Dudintsev, "Dobro ne dolzhno otstupat," *Trud,* Aug. 26, 1989.

48. Ibid.

49. Pankin, *Chetyre ia Konstantina Simonova,* 219.

50. Stenogramma zasedaniia redkollegii po obsuzhdeniiu statii V. Dorofeeva na roman Dudintseva "Ne khlebom edinym," Oct. 18, 1956, RGALI, Fond Literaturnoi Gazety (f. 634), op. 4, d. 1271, ll. 3-52.

51. Dudintsev, "Dobro ne dolzhno."

52. The translated paragraph comes from Hugh McLean and Walter N. Vickery, *The Year of Protest 1956* (New York: Random House, 1961), 155-159. See also private notes on Paustovsky's speech in the papers of M. A. Perelman, RGALI, f. 2242, op. 1, d. 69. On the *Victory* cruise, see *Literaturnaia Gazeta,* July 10, 1956.

53. From the review of the discussion in *Literaturnaia Gazeta,* Oct. 27, 1956, 4.

54. Kaverin, *Epilog,* 332; Konstantin M. Simonov, "Literaturnye zametki," *Novy Mir* 12 (1956), 239–257.

55. Veniamin Iofe, "Politicheskaia oppozitsia v Leningrade, 1950–1960-kh", *Zvezda,* no. 7 (1997): 212–215; Iofe, "Novye etiudy ob optimizme: Sbornik statei i vystuplenii" (St. Petersburg: Memorial, 1998), 98–99; M. Trofimenkov, "'Malenkii Budapesht' na ploshchadi Iskusstv: Ermitazh, Picasso, 1956 . . ," *Smena,* Jan. 26, 1990.

56. Krasnopevtsev was a passionate believer in Stalin until 1953. In 1955 he became a member of the party in order to change it from within. S. D. Rozhdestvensky, "Materialy k istorii samodeiatelnykh politicheskikh obedinenii v SSSR posle 1945 goda," *Pamiat: Istorichestii sbornik,* no. 5 (Moscow: YMCA, 1981–82), 231–233; Tatiana Kosinova, interview with Lev Krasnopevtsev, Aug. 10, 1992, Moscow; L. V. Polikovskaia, interview with Felix Beleliubsky, a member of Krasnopevtsev's circle; Tatiana Kosinova, interview with Vadim Kozovoi, Sept. 22, 1992, Moscow—all deposited in the archives of Memorial, Moscow and St. Petersburg.

57. RGANI, f. 5, op. 30, d. 141, ll. 13–15, 67–68; Aksiutin in William Taubman, Sergei Khrushchev, and Abbott Gleason, eds., *Nikita Khrushchev* (New Haven, Conn.: Yale University Press, 2000), 177–208.

58. Vladimir Bukovsky, *To Build a Castle: My Life as a Dissenter* (New York: Viking, 1977), 109; interview with Vadim Kozovoi, Sept. 22, 1992, Memorial, Moscow.

59. Zubkova, *Obshchestvo i reformy,* 144; Bronislav Kholopov, "Lichnaia zhizn v teni GB." *Druzhba Narodov* 10 (1994): 132, 133.

60. Lev Lurie and Irina Maliarova, *1956 god,* 406–409, 413–415.

61. RGANI, f. 5, op. 30, d. 236. The letter was sent to the writer Yuri Zbanatsky, who sent it to the CC CPSU on Jan. 2, 1957.

62. Alexander Bovin, *XX vek kak zhizn: Vospominaniia* (Moscow: Zakharov, 2003), 54–55.

63. Tatiana Kosinova, interview with Ernest Skalsky, Nov. 4, 1992, archive of Memorial, St. Petersburg.

64. Recollection of Boris Pustyntsev in Tatiana Kosinova, "Sobytiia 1956 g. v Polshe glazami Sovetskikh dissidentov," in *Korni Travy: Sbornik statei molodykh istorikov* (Moscow: Zvenia, 1996), 194.

65. Mikhail Koposov, who in 1956 was a student at the Herzen Pedagogical School, recalled that in Leningrad the party leader Frol Kozlov personally came with his assistants to peruse the students' wall paper *Lit-Front,* posted at the institute, *Smena,* Sept. 18, 1956. A. A. Fursenko, ed., meetings of the presidium on Nov. 4 and 29, *Prezidium TsK KPSS, 1954–1964,* 1:202, 212, 979–980, 984.

66. RGANI, f. 5, op. 37, d. 2, ll. 95–97. See also Kramer, "The Soviet Union and the 1956 Crises in Hungary and Poland," 198.

67. *Apparat TsK KPSS i kultura, 1953–1957: Dokumenty* (Moscow, 2001), 570–780; *Prezidium TsK KPSS,* 985–986.

68. *Literaturnaia Gazeta,* Nov. 22 and 24, 1956; Zezina, *Sovetskaia khudozhestvennaia intelligentsiia,* 175–176.

69. C. Simonov to N. Khrushchev, Nov. 21, 1956, APRF, f. 3, op. 34, d. 191, ll. 134–159,

published in *Istochnik*, no. 6 (1999): 96-105. In October 1956 the Academy of Sciences held a session that legitimated cybernetics, which had been denounced by Stalinist science and propaganda as a pseudodiscipline. See Slava Gerovitch, *From Newspeak to Cyberspeak: A History of Soviet Cybernetics* (Cambridge, Mass.: MIT Press, 2002), 153-197.

70. The conference started on December 6-7 and, after a weekend, continued on December 10, 1956. RGANI, f. 5, op. 39, d. 12, ll. 161-217.

71. "Soveshchaniie v TsK KPSS po voprosam literatury," RGANI, f. 5, op. 39, d. 12, ll. 11, 23, 42. Also see the version of this document published by Zoia Vodopianova and Tamara Domracheva, "'Dokumenty svidetelstvuiut . . . ' kak partiia rukovodila literaturoi," *Voprosy Literatury* 1 (1996), at http://magazines.russ.ru/voplit/1996/1/docum.htm.

72. On December 19 all party and Komsomol organizations received a secret directive from the CC CPSU, "On the Intensification of Political Work among the Masses and Thwarting the Machinations of Anti-Soviet Enemy Elements." For details see A. A. Fursenko, ed., *Prezidium TsK KPSS 1954-1964*, 1:202, 212, 979-980, 984. On Korneichuk and the Petöfi Circle analogy, see Kaverin, *Epilog*, 353.

73. Alexander Gidoni, *Solntse idet s zapada: Kniga vospominanii* (Toronto: Sovremennik, 1980), 67-72; Viktor Slavkin, *Pamiatnik neizvestnomu stiliage* (Moscow: Artist, Rezhisser, Teatr, 1996), 86-87.

74. Pimenov, *Vospominaniia*, 19. See statistical table in *Istochnik* 6 (1995): 153; see also V. A. Kozlov, S. V. Mironenko, O. V. Edelman, and E. Y. Zavadskaia, eds., *Kramola: Inakomyslie v SSSR pri Khrushcheve i Brezhneve, 1953-1982—Rassekrechennye dokumenty Verkhovnogo suda i Prokuratury SSSR* (Moscow: Materik, 2005), 36-41.

75. Georgy Shakhnazarov, *S Vozhdiami i bez nikh* (Moscow: Vagrius, 2001), 78.

76. Entry of Mar. 16, 1957, in Samoilov, *Podennye zapisi*, 1:272.

77. Taubman, *Khrushchev*, 307, 384, 386; A. I. Volkov, M. G. Pugacheva, and S. F. Yarmoliuk, eds., *Pressa v obshchestve, 1959-2000: Otsenki zhurnalistov i sotsiologov—Dokumenty* (Moscow: Moskovskaia Shkola Politicheskikh Issledovanii, 2000), 23.

78. Vystuplenie N. S. Khrushcheva na soveshchanii pisatelei v TsK KPSS, May 13, 1957, APRF, f. 42, op. 1, d. 255, ll. 47-86, published in "A vy sidite, kak surok, o demokratii govorite," *Istochnik* 6 (2003): 81-82, 84.

79. Letter from Antonina Peterson to Dmitry Shepilov, May 3, 1957; letter from Engineer M. Petrygin to the CC CPSU, Jan. 25, 1957; Colonel P. Nesterov to Nikita Khrushchev, Jan. 30, 1957, RGANI, f. 5, op. 30, d. 189, ll. 1-6, 29-30; ibid., d. 190, ll. 142-162.

80. On Khrushchev's management of culture, see Taubman, *Khrushchev*, 306-310, 384; and Alexander Tvardovsky, "Iz rabochikh tetradei (1953-1960)," *Znamia* 8 (1989): 135-140.

81. Diary for Kommuna 33, July 9, 1960, TsADKM, f. 193, op. 1, d. 1, notebook 1959-1961, ll. 219-220. This is the collective diary of a group of educated Russians.

I rely also on the recollections of my mother, Liudmila Zubok, who attended the meeting at Lenin Stadium.

82. Samoilov, *Podennye zapisi,* 1:275. See also Anatoly Cherniaev, *Moia zhizn i moe vremia* (Moscow: Mezhdunarodnye Otnosheniia, 1995), 221.

83. For instance, Pyotr Ponomarev, Dmitry Polikarpov, and Yekaterina Furtseva.

84. Zezina, *Sovetskaia khudozhestvennaia intelligentsiia,* 129.

85. The statistics on new political prisoners tell the story: in 1959 there were 750, only half the number for the previous year. The decline continued through the rest of the Khrushchev era, with only 20 sentenced in 1965. Iofe, "Politicheskaia oppozitsia v Leningrade," 213.

86. Nail Bikkenin, "Stseny obshchestvennoi i chastnoi zhizni," *Svobodnaia Mysl* 3 (2001): 85–86.

87. Vladimir Kozlov, introduction, in Kozlov and Sergei Mironenko, *Kramola,* 45–46.

88. M. R. Zezina, "Shokovaia terapia, ot 1953–go k 1956 godu," *Otechestvennaia Istoriia,* no. 3 (1995): 133; V. S. Volkov, *Intellektualnyi sloi v Sovetskom obshchestve* (Moscow: Fond Razvitie, 1999), at http://www.swolkov.narod.ru/ins/index.htm.

89. Hilary Pilkington, *Russia's Youth and Its Culture: A Nation's Constructors and Constructed* (London: Routledge, 1994), 70.

90. Zapiska v TsK KPSS Moskovskogo gorkoma KPSS, Dec. 15, 1956, RGANI, f. 4, op. 16, d. 1098, ll. 50–52; recollections of Naum Kleiman and Natalia Riazantseva, in Fomin, *Kinematograf ottepeli,* 209–210, 216–217.

91. TsAODM, f. 478, op. 3, d. 74, ll. 92, 99, and ibid., d. 87, ll. 37, 103, 104, published as Tatiana Maximova, "'Volnodumstvo' v MGU," *Istochnik* 3 (2000): 95.

92. Letter from Boris Pasternak to Konstantin Paustovsky, July 12, 1956, in Boris Pasternak, *Sobranie sochinenii, Pisma* (Moscow: Khudozhestvennaia Literatura, 1992), 5:547; Yelena Pasternak and Yevgeny Pasternak. "Perepiska Pasternaka s Feltrinelli," *Kontinent* 107 (2001). On the fears of Pasternak's wife, Zinaida, see Isaiah Berlin, *The Soviet Mind: Russian Culture under Communism,* ed. Henry Hardy (Washington, D.C.: Brookings Institution Press, 2004), 68. Michel Aucouturie, "Pasternak i sotsialisticheskii realizm," in Sergei Bocharov and Alexander Parnis, eds., *Vittorio: Mezhdunarodnyi nauchnyi sbornik posviashchennyi 75-letiu Vittorio Strady* (Moscow: Trikvadrata, 2005), 656; Yevgeny Pasternak, preface, Vitaly Afiani and Natalia Tomilina, eds., *"A za mnoiu shum pogoni": Boris Pasternak i vlast—Dokumenty, 1956–1972* (Moscow: ROSSPEN, 2001), 15, n. 97.

93. Spravka Otdela kultury TsK KPSS o romane B. L. Pasternaka "Doktor Zhivago" [no later than Aug. 31, 1956]; Zapiska ministra inostrannykh del SSSR D. T. Shepilova o peredache rukopisi romana za granitsu, Aug. 31, 1956; and resolution of Aug. 31, 1956, by V. Malin, about sending it around to presidium members. Published on the Web site of the international foundation Democracy, at http://www.idf.ru/almanah/inside/almanah-doc/15/132.

94. Through young Slavists who studied at MGU, Jacqueline de Proyart, Vittorio Strada, and Georges Nivat, Pasternak encouraged Feltrinelli and other editors to speed up the publication and resist Soviet pressure. See Pasternak's letters to Pro-

yart, *Novy Mir* 1 (1992): 127–189; Yevgeny Pasternak and Yelena Pasternak, *Zhizn Borisa Pasternaka: Dokumentalnoe povestvovanie* (St. Petersburg: Zvezda, 2004), 447.

95. Yevgeny Pasternak, *Boris Pasternak: Biografiia* (Moscow: Khudozhestvennaia Literatura, 1997), 703–777.

96. Pasternak and Pasternak, *Zhizn Borisa Pasternaka,* 462–463.

97. "Stenogramma obshchemoskovskogo sobraniia pisatelei," Oct. 31, 1958, samizdat record published in *Gorizont: Obshchestvenno-politicheskii ezhemesiachnik* 9 (1988).

98. Gorelik, *Boris Slutsky,* 53.

99. Samoilov, *Podennye zapisi,* 1:297. Samoilov apparently destroyed the records covering the most dramatic events in the Pasternak affair.

100. Stanislav Savitsky, *Andeground: Istoriia i mify leningradskoi neofitsialnoi literatury* (Moscow: Novoe Literaturnoe Obozrenie, 2002), 83.

101. Denis Kozlov, "'I Have Not Read, but I Will Say': Soviet Literary Audiences and Changing Ideas of Social Membership, 1958–1966," *Kritika* 7, no. 3 (Summer 2006): 563–571.

3. Rediscovery of the World, 1955-1961

1. For more on the Soviets' "new foreign policy," see Vladislav Zubok, *A Failed Empire: The Soviet Union in the Cold War from Stalin to Gorbachev* (Chapel Hill: University of North Carolina Press, 2007), chap. 4; Also see Eleonory Gilburd, "The Revival of Internationalism in the 1950s," paper presented at The Thaw: Soviet Society and Culture during the 1950s and the 1960s, conference held at the University of California, Berkeley, May 12–15, 2005.

2. On the "conquering of hearts and spirits" of people from the Third World, among other foreigners, see Constantin Katsakioris, "L'Union soviétique et les intellectuels africains: Internationalisme, panafricanisme et négritude pendant les années de la décolonization, 1955–1964," *Cahiers du Monde Russe,* 47, nos. 1–2 (Jan.–June 2006): 15–32.

3. Frederick C. Barghoorn, *The Soviet Cultural Offensive: The Role of Cultural Diplomacy in Soviet Foreign Policy* (Westport, Conn.: Greenwood, 1960), 20; Aleksandr Fursenko and Timothy Naftali, *One Hell of a Gamble: Khrushchev, Castro, and Kennedy, 1958–1964* (New York: Norton, 1997), 344; Frances S. Saunders, *The Cultural Cold War: The CIA and the World of Arts and Letters* (New York: New Press, 2000).

4. Veniamin Kaverin, *Epilog: Memuary* (Moscow: Russkaia Kniga, 2002), 377.

5. Report of the Ministry of the Interior, May 13, 1958, GARF, "Osobaia papka" N S. Khrushcheva (1954–1956): Perepiska MVD SSSR s TsK KPSS (1957–1959), d. 498, ll. 37–38.

6. Reminiscences of Irena Verblovskaia, cited in Tatiana Kosinova, "Sobytiia 1956 g. v Polshe glazami sovetskikh dissidentov," at http://polska.ru/polska/historia/ desid_1956.html. See also Irena Grudzinska Gross, "Pod vliianiem? I. Brodsky i

Polsha," *Staroe Literaturnoe Obozrenie* 2 (2001), at magazines.russ.ru/slo/2001/2/grgr.html.

7. David Caute, *The Dancer Defects: The Struggle for Cultural Supremacy during the Cold War* (New York: Oxford University Press, 2003), 411.

8. Viktor Slavkin, *Pamiatnik neizvestnomu stiliage* (Moscow: Artist, Rezhisser, Teatr, 1996), 150.

9. Daniil Granin, "Chuzhoi dnevnik" (1989), in www.lib.ru/PROZA/GRANIN/strjourn.txt; Fyodor Burlatsky, quoted in Lev Lurie and Irina Maliarova, eds., *1956 god: Seredina veka* (St. Petersburg: Neva, 2007), 111.

10. Boris Polevoi to CC CPSU, RGALI, f. 631, op. 26, d. 3826, ll. 5–46.

11. Alexei Adzhubei, *Krushenie illuzii: Vremia v sobytiakh i litsakh* (Moscow: Interbuk, 1991), 128–135, 216; B. Polevoi, "Amerikanskie dnevniki," *Oktiabr* 2 (1956): 93–143; ibid., 3 (1956): 88–153; ibid., 4 (1956): 86–151. N. Gribachev wrote thirteen articles about this trip, all published in *Literaturnaia Gazeta*.

12. "O rabote sovetsko-amerikanskikh institutov i perepiske Sovetskikh i amerikanskikh grazhdan" (n.d.), RGALI, f. 631, op. 26, d. 3826, ll. 26–30.

13. Giuseppe Boffa, *Memorie dal Comunismo: Storia confidenziale di quarant'anni che hanno cambiato volto all'Europa* (Milano: Ponte alle Grazie, 1998), 17–21.

14. *Vremia, ostavsheesia s nami: Filologicheskii fakultet v 1953–1958 gg. Vospominaniia vypusknikov* (Moscow: MAKS, 2004), 177–178.

15. In August 1953 the Kremlin began to consider resuming foreign tourism on Soviet territory for the first time since the early 1930s. According to the official draft of the decision, this measure was "aimed at the popularization of the Soviet achievements in economic and cultural construction, at strengthening the international authority of the Soviet Union and broadening international connections." Party leaders ordered the Council of Ministers to consider this issue on July 21, 1953. On March 24, 1954, V. Molotov, A. Mikoyan, M. Suslov, S. Borisov, and S. Kruglov reported to Georgy Malenkov with draft proposals.

16. *Apparat TsK KPSS i Kultura, 1953–1957: Dokumenty* (Moscow: ROSSPEN, 2001), 494–493; Slava Gerovitch, *From Newspeak to Cyberspeak: A History of Soviet Cybernetics* (Cambridge, Mass.: MIT Press, 2002), 227–228, 234.

17. Raymond L. Garthoff, *A Journey through the Cold War: A Memoir of Containment and Coexistence* (Washington, D.C.: Brookings Institution Press, 2001), 30–31. Leopold Haimson, the budding Kremlinologist from Columbia University, spent a couple of months in Moscow and Leningrad and felt he could meet "with anybody he wanted to." Leopold Haimson, in conversation with M. P. Zezina, "O vremeni i o sebe," *Otechestvennaia Istoriia* 6 (2006): 185.

18. Bronislav Kholopov, "Lichnaia zhizn v teni GB," *Druzhba Narodov* 10 (1994): 131.

19. Robert Griscom, "Report on Russian Youth," *Ladies Home Journal*, Feb. 1957.

20. Interview with one of Leningrad's first professionals to engage in *fartsovka* (the illegal practice of buying goods and currency from foreigners), Valentin Tikhonenko, "Tarzan v svoiem otechestve," *Pchela* 11 (Oct.–Nov. 1997), at http://www.pchela.ru/podshiv/11/tarzan.htm.

21. Frances S. Saunders, *The Cultural Cold War: The CIA and the World of Arts and Letters* (New York: New Press, 2000).

22. See Zapiska prezidenta Akademii khudozhestv SSSR A. M. Gerasimova ob "ozhivlenii nezdorovykh, formalisticheskikh nastroienii v izobrazitelnom iskusstve," Mar. 10, 1955, in *Apparat TsK KPSS i Kultura, 1953–1957*, 367–370; see also Zapiska v TsK, Mar. 21, 1955, ibid., 376–381. Aside from very substantial state orders, the established "academics" were allowed to sell their art through the Art Foundation of the USSR. In 1957 the sales yielded 160 million rubles. *Apparat TsK KPSS i Kultura, 1958–1964: Dokumenty* (Moscow: ROSSPEN, 2005), 164.

23. See *Apparat TsK KPSS i Kultura, 1953–1957*, 316, 467, 474–475, 484–486.

24. Joshua Rubenstein, *Tangled Loyalties: The Life and Times of Ilya Ehrenburg* (New York: Basic, 1996), 297–298; Caute, *The Dancer Defects*, 585–586. On the factional struggle between "old" and "young" artists, as well as between socialist realists and the rest see *Apparat TsK KPSS i Kultura, 1953–1957*, 198–201, 484–486,

25. P. Gorelik, ed., *Boris Slutsky: Vospominaniia sovremennikov* (St. Petersburg: Neva, 2005), 50–51. On the Picasso exhibition and its significance for the Thaw, see Eleonory Gilburd, "Picasso in Thaw Culture," *Cahiers du Monde Russe* 47, 1–2 (Jan.–June 2006): 65–108.

26. Viacheslav Dolinin, Dmitry Severiukhin, *Preodolenie nemoty: Leningradskii samizdat v kontekste nezavisimogo kulturnogo dvizheniia, 1953–1991* (St. Petersburg, 2003); B. Ivanov and B. Roginsky (eds.), *Istoriia leningradskoi nepodtsenzurnoi literatury, 1950–1980-t gody* (St. Petersburg: DEAN, 2000), 12.

27. Entry for Nov. 10, 1956 (notebook 1), diary for Kommuna 33, TsADKM, f. 193, op. 1, d. 2, l. 24.

28. Caute, *The Dancer Defects*.

29. Ibid., 452–456; Truman Capote, *The Muses Are Heard: An Account* (New York: Random House, 1956), 82–83, 108, 168–171, 175.

30. Barghoorn, *The Soviet Cultural Offensive*, 298–299; *Ezhenedelnik Instituta SSSR*, Jan. 13, 1956, 60–61. This was the publication of the Institute for the Study of the USSR at the Radio Liberation (later Radio Liberty) in Munich.

31. The performers included the violinist Isaac Stern and the Boston Symphony Orchestra playing in the Great Hall of the Moscow Conservatory. Caute, *The Dancer Defects*, 396; Marvin Kalb, *Eastern Exposure* (New York: Farrar, Straus and Cudahy, 1958), 66.

32. State Literary Publishers, the leading publishing house for fiction in the USSR, reported that during 1957–58 the following books by American authors were published in Russian: John Steinbeck, *The Grapes of Wrath* (225,000 copies) and Upton Sinclair, *Jimmy Higgins* (300,000 copies) and *King Coal* (150,000 copies). In 1959 the Soviets published Mark Twain's *Collected Works* (300,000 copies), and *An American Tragedy*, by Theodore Dreiser, and *Babbitt*, by Sinclair Lewis (225,000 copies each). RGANI, f. 5, op. 33, d. 95, l. 11.

33. John Steinbeck, *A Russian Journal* (New York: Viking, 1948). The book contained

marvelous and revealing pictures of Russian people by the photographer Robert Capa.

34. Report of the CC Department, Jan. 31, 1956, in *Apparat TsK KPSS i Kultura, 1953–1957*, 481.

35. *Literaturnaia Gazeta*, Feb. 28, 1957. Alexander Kazem-Bek had emigrated from Russia after the Revolution and in the late 1920s became a leader of a protofascist movement of *Mladorossy* (young Russians) in Western Europe. After his return to the Soviet Union, apparently with the assistance of the secret police, he worked in the Orthodox patriarchate.

36. I. G. Ehrenburg to D. T. Shepilov, before Mar. 23, 1957, APRF, f. 3, op. 34, d. 192, ll. 63–63ob, published in *Istochnik* 2 (1997): 118.

37. *Literaturnaia Gazeta*, Mar. 23, 1957.

38. For more on this split, see Nikolai Mitrokhin, *Russkaia Partiia: Dvizheniie Russkikh natsionalistov v SSSR, 1953–1985 gody* (Moscow: Novoe Literaturnoe Obozrenie, 2003).

39. *Apparat TsK KPSS i Kultura, 1953–1957*, 499, 502.

40. Liudmila Gurchenko, *Aplodismenty* (Moscow: Tsentrpoligraf, 1998), 300.

41. Galina Yerofeeva, *Neskuchnyi sad: Nediplomaticheskie zametki o diplomaticheskoi zhizni* (Moscow: Podkova, 1998), 85.

42. TsKhDMO, f. 3, op. 15, d. 18, l. 120; Mikhail German, *Slozhnoe proshedshee: Passé composé* (St. Petersburg: Pechatnyi Dvor, 2006), 261–262.

43. His teacher at the Juilliard School in New York was Rosa Levine, an émigrée from Russia, who inspired him and prepared him for the stress of the competition.

44. Report of Sergei Kaftanov, deputy head of the Ministry of Culture to the CC CPSU, Apr. 12, 1958. "Urgent and Secret," In *Apparat TsK KPSS i Kultura, 1958–1964*, 47–48; Caute, *The Dancer Defects*, 397–398.

45. Entry for Apr. 18, 1958 (notebook 1), diary for Kommuna 33, TsADKM, f. 193, op. 1, d. 2, l. 114.

46. Caute, *The Dancer Defects*, 397–398; Walter L. Hixson, *Parting the Curtain: Propaganda, Culture, and the Cold War* (New York: St. Martin's, 1997), 156.

47. Report from the Komsomol Central Committee to the CC CPSU, Apr. 16, 1954, RGANI, f. 5, op. 30, d. 81, ll. 66–68.

48. He instructed, among others, young Zoia Kosmodemianskaia, a martyr assassinated by the Germans as an arsonist in December 1941.

49. TsKhDMO, f. 3, op. 15, d. 2, ll. 1, 3–4, 8; ibid., op. 104, d. 30, ll. 169–170.

50. TsKhDMO, f. 4, op. 15, d. 2, l. 30; ibid., f. 34, op. 15, d. 4, ll. 40–43.

51. For the transcripts of the Preparatory Commission for the Festival in the Komsomol, see TsKhDMO, f. 3, op. 15, d. 11, l. 18.

52. *Rossiiskaia Gazeta*, July 21, 2005; Adzhubei, *Krushenie illuzii*, 119–130.

53. TsKhDMO, f. 4, op. 104, d. 3, ll. 13–19.

54. TsKhDMO, f. 3, op. 15, d. 18, l. 119; GARF, f. 9401, op. 2, d. 491, ll. 153, 155.

55. TsKhDMO, f. 3, op. 15, d. 4, ll. 34–37, 95–97.

56. This theme is developed in Kristin Roth-Ey, "'Loose Girls' on the Loose? Sex, Pro-

paganda, and the 1957 Youth Festival," in Melanie Ilič, Susan E. Reid, and Lynne Attwood, eds., *Women in the Khrushchev Era* (New York: Palgrave Macmillan, 2004), 75–95.

57. Vittorio Strada, *Autoritratto autocritico: Archeologia della rivoluzione d'Ottobre* (Roma: Liberal Edizioni, 2004), 33–34.

58. On these preparations and preorganized events, see TsKhDMO, f. 3, op. 15, d. 136. See also daily reports of the Komsomol and the Ministry of the Interior on the festival, TsAODM, f. 4, op. 104, d. 31, and GARF, f. 9401, op. 2, d. 491. I was denied access to KGB reports on the festival that are also stored at TsAODM.

59. Adzhubei, *Krushenie illuzii,* 186.

60. Polish Press Survey no. 208 in *Glos Pracy,* Aug. 3, 1957, "Red Archive" of the Open Society Archive, Budapest.

61. Alexei Kozlov, *Kozel na sakse* (Moscow: Vagrius, 1998), 102.

62. A. I. Volkov, M. G. Pugacheva, S. F. Yarmoliuk, eds., *Pressa v obshchestve, 1959–2000: Otsenki zhurnalistov i sotsiologov—Dokumenty* (Moscow: Moskovskaia Shkola Politicheskikh Issledovanii, 2000), 21.

63. Elena Zubkova, *Russia after the War: Hopes, Illusions, and Disappointments, 1945–1957,* trans. Hugh Ragsdale (Armonk, N.Y.: Sharpe, 1998), 200.

64. Among them were Alexei Kozlov, Georgy Garanian, Alexei Zubov, Konstantin Bakholdin, and Boris Rychkov, to mention a few. Kozlov, *Kozel na sakse,* 112.

65. Anatoly Brusilovsky, *Vremia Khudozhnikov* (Moscow: Magazin Iskusstva, 1999), 3–4; N. Tamruchi, "Iz istorii Moskovskogo avangarda," *Znaniie—sila* 5 (1991).

66. TsKhDMO, f. 3, op. 15, d. 2, l. 132.

67. Ibid., l. 137; Komsomol information, Aug. 3, 1957, and Otchet Tsentralnoi studii televideniia o festivale, Aug. 17, 1957, TsKhDMO, f. 4, op. 104, d. 30, ll. 80, 175.

68. GARF, f. 9401, op. 2, d. 491, l. 276.

69. See Leonid Parfenov's television series, *Namedni (1961–1991), Nasha Era,* part on 1962, produced by NTV, Russia, 1997.

70. TsAODM, f. 4, op. 104, d. 31, l. 134; Daniel Schorr, *Staying Tuned: A Life in Journalism* (New York: Pocket Books, 2001).

71. Garthoff, *A Journey through the Cold War,* 36.

72. In the summer of 1957 the group included, aside from Krasnopevtsev, Nikolai Obushenkov, Nikolai Pokrovsky, Leonid Rendel, Marat Cheshkov, Nathan Eidelman, Vladimir Menshikov, Vadim Kozovoi, Mikhail Semenenko, Mark Goldman, and a few other young intellectuals.

73. Interview with Lasota, Nov. 3, 1992, oral history collection of Memorial, archive of Memorial, Moscow.

74. Informatsiia no. 20, "O khode vsemirnogo festivalia molodezhi i studentov," Aug. 10, 1957, TsAODM, f. 4, op. 104, d. 31, l. 161.

75. "In 1956 I was indignant at Israel for splitting world's public opinion in the days of Budapest crisis." Grigory Pomerants, *Zapiski gadkogo utenka* (Moscow: Moskovskii Rabochii, 1998), 321.

76. Recollections of Arseny Berezin, then a young Leningrad physicist and a partic-

ipant in the festival, author's interview with Berezin, Nov. 15, 2000, Alexandria, Va.

77. TsAODM, f. 4, op. 104, d. 31, ll. 8–9, 67, 81, 110; RGANI, f. 5, op. 30, d. 233, l. 123.

78. Yevtushenko in the CNN Cold War series, at http://www.cnn.com/SPECIALS/cold.war/episodes/14/interviews/yevtushenko.

79. GARF, f. 9401, op. 2, d. 491, 433; Kozlov, *Kozel na sakse*, 106–107. See also Roth-Ey, "'Loose Girls' on the Loose?'"

80. Kozlov, *Kozel na sakse*, 107.

81. GARF, f. 9401, op. 2, d. 491, l. 377.

82. Informatsiia no. 16, Aug. 6, 1957, GARF, f. 9401, op. 2, d. 491, l. 362.

83. Report on the Festival, Aug. 29, 1957, TsKhDMO, f. 3, op. 15, d. 4, l. 105; d. 83, l. 49; RGANI, f. 5, op. 30, d. 233, l. 122.

84. RGANI, f. 5, op. 30, d. 233, l. 162.

85. TsKhDMO, f. 1, op. 5, d. 810, l. 301.

86. Vladimir Bukovsky, *To Build a Castle: My Life as a Dissenter* (New York: Viking, 1979), 139.

87. Maia Turovskaia to the author, June 25, 2000, Moscow.

88. Kozlov, *Kozel na sakse*, 100–101.

89. Adzhubei, *Krushenie illuzii*, 187.

90. Doklad Shelepina, "Ob uluchshenii ideino-vospitatelnoi raboty komsomolskikh organizatsii sredi molodezhi," plenary meeting of the CC VLKSM, RGANI, f. 5, op. 30, d. 233, ll. 6–10.

91. Ibid., l. 12.

92. Caute, *The Dancer Defects*, 457.

93. L. Ilichev, A. Romanov, and G. Kazakov to the CC CPSU, Aug. 6, 1958, "O glushenii inostrannykh radiostantsii," RGANI, f. 5, op. 30, d. 75, ll. 165–167.

94. Kozlov, *Kozel na sakse*, 76–96.

95. Among the pioneers of jazz in Moscow were Oleg Lundstrem and Georgy Garanian. Lundstrem was a Russian expat in China who had organized his jazz band in Harbin and in 1947 was allowed to return to the Soviet Union.

96. Barghoorn, *The Soviet Cultural Offensive*, 22–23; Hixson, *Parting the Curtain*, 151–158.

97. Among them were Alexander Yakovlev and Oleg Kalugin, who matriculated at Columbia University, New York. I found the complete list of this group in TsKhDMO, f. 1, op. 46, d. 249, ll. 58–59.

98. Short Summary of the Talks with the GDR Party-Governmental Delegation on June 9, 1959, from AVP RF, f. 0742, op. 4, papka 31, d. 33, ll. 86–87, trans. Hope Harrison, *CWHIP Bulletin*, no. 11 (Winter 1998): p. 212.

99. Adzhubei, *Krushenie illuzii*, 130–134; R. G. Eimontova, ed., "Iz dnevnikov Sergeia Sergeevicha Dmitrieva," entry for July 21, 1959, in *Otechestvennaia Istoriia* 5 (2000), 168.

100. Hixson, *Parting the Curtain*, 188–189.

101. Ibid., 201, 211.

102. One official of Soviet trade unions wrote in his diary after the exhibition: "There was no system. They cannot present their country, people, industries, agriculture, America as a whole. I have seen the exhibition and still do not believe that America and Americans are really as they were presented. . . . We know America as the country of friendly and talented people, with highly developed culture, who created a lot for mankind. But the America at the exhibition has been presented as a disorganized country," Narodny Arkhiv, Moscow, f. 306, l. 37.

103. Hixson, *Parting the Curtain,* 190; Vladislav Zubok, "'Zato my delaiem rakety': Strasti vokrug amerikanskoi vystavki v Sokolnikakh v 1959 godu," *Rodina* 2 (1998): 76–78; author's interview with Joan Urban, one of the guides at the exhibition, Mar. 9, 1999, Washington, D.C.

104. Dmitry Bobyshev, *Ia zdes (Chelovekotekst)* (Moscow: Vagrius, 2003), 211; Susan E. Reid, "Cold War in the Kitchen: Gender and the De-Stalinization of Consumer Taste in the Soviet Union under Khrushchev," *Slavic Review* 61, no. 2 (2002): 223–224.

105. Hixson, *Parting the Curtain,* 212, 228.

106. Vladimir Shlapentokh, "The Changeable Soviet Image of America," in *Anti-Americanism: The Annals of the American Academy of Political and Social Science* (Newbury Park, Calif.: Sage, 1988), 497:157–171; Eric Shiraev and Vladislav Zubok, *Anti-Americanism in Russia: From Stalin to Putin* (New York: Palgrave, 2000), 10, 13–14.

107. Mikhail Gorbachev and Zdeněk Mlynář, *Conversations with Gorbachev on Perestroika, the Prague Spring, and the Crossroads of Socialism,* trans. George Shriver (New York: Columbia University Press, 2002), 36.

108. Garthoff, *A Journey through the Cold War,* 32.

109. Volkov, Pugacheva, and Yarmoliuk, *Pressa v obshchestve,* 67–78.

110. See more in Odd Arne Westad, *The Global Cold War: Third World Interventions and the Making of Our Times* (New York: Cambridge University Press, 2005), 69–71.

111. Author's interviews and conversations with Alexander Lozhkin, a graduate of the Moscow engineering college who worked in 1956–57 as an "adviser" in China, held between 1997 and 2002, Moscow.

112. Recollections of Yelena Bonner in 2005 at: www.echo.msk.ru/guests/341/; Andrei Sakharov Papers, Houghton Library, Harvard University, folder S.IV.22.17.

113. N. P. Kamanin, *Skrytyi kosmos* (Moscow: Infortekst-IF, 1997), 1:233.

114. B. A. Grushin, *Chetyre vremeni Rossii v zerkale oprosov obshchestvennogo mneniia: Zhizn 1-ia—"Epokha Khrushcheva"* (Moscow: Progress-Traditsiia, 2001), 220.

115. Pyotr Vail and Alexander Ghenis, *60-e: Mir sovetskogo cheloveka,* 2nd ed. (Moscow: Novoe Kulturnoe Obozrenie, 1998), 55.

116. *Yunost* 12 (1960): 3; Yevgeny Yevtushenko, "Mir visel na voloske," *Novaia Gazeta,* Nov. 7, 2005.

117. Yevtushenko, "Mir visel na voloske."

118. TsKhDMO, f. 1, op. 5, d. 824, ll.108–109, 137; Sergei Kara-Murza, *"Sovok" vspomi-naet* (Moscow: Algoritm 2002), 218–244.

4. Optimists on the Move, 1957-1961

1. Georgy Shakhzazarov, *S Vozhdiami i bez nikh* (Moscow: Vagrius, 2001), 71.
2. See results of the 1959 population census in *Naselenie Rossii v XX veke: Istoricheskie ocherki*, vol. 2, *1940–1959* (Moscow: ROSSPEN, 2001), 366; Viktor Perevedentsev, "Strana starikov," *Otechestvennye Zapiski* 4 (2004), at http://magazines.russ.ru/oz/2004/4/2004_4_3.html; Mie Nagachi, "Replacing the Dead: The Politics of Re-production in the Post-War Soviet Union," presentation at the American Associa-tion for the Advancement of Slavic Studies conference, Nov. 17, 2006, Washington, D.C.
3. Aileen Kelly, "In the Promised Land," *New York Review of Books*, Nov. 29, 2001; Juliane Fürst, Polly Jones, and Susan Morrissey, "The Relaunch of the Soviet Proj-ect, 1945–1964: Introduction," *Slavonic and East European Review* (London), 86, no. 2 (Apr. 2008): 206.
4. V. A. Kozlov, S. V. Mironenko, O. V. Edelman, and E. Y. Zavadskaia, eds., *Kramola: Inakomyslie v SSSR pri Khrushcheve i Brezhneve, 1953–1982—Rassekrechennye do-kumenty Verkhovnogo suda i Prokuratury SSSR* (Moscow: Materik, 2005).
5. V. Seliunin and G. Khanin, "Lukavaia tsyfra," *Novy Mir* 2 (1987): 181–201; Philip Hanson, *The Rise and Fall of the Soviet Economy: An Economic History of the USSR from 1945* (London: Longman, 2003), 48–49.
6. Daniel Shorr, *Staying Tuned: A Life in Journalism* (New York: Pocket Books, 2001), 86.
7. *Prezidium TsK KPSS, 1954–1964* (Moscow: ROSSPEN, 2003), 1:397–400.
8. Nikolai Barsukov, "Kommunisticheskiie illuzii Khrushcheva: O razrabotke tretiei programmy partii," and "Mysli vslukh: zamechaniia N. S. Khrushcheva na proekt tretiei programmy KPSS," both cited in William Taubman, *Khrushchev: The Man and His Era* (New York: Norton, 2003), 509–511.
9. Elena Zubkova, *Russia after the War: Hopes, Illusions, and Disappointments, 1945–1957*, trans. Hugh Ragsdale (Armonk, N.Y.: Sharpe, 1998), 175.
10. L. G. Churchward, *The Soviet Intelligentsia: An Essay on the Social Structure and Roles of Soviet Intellectuals during the 1960s* (London: Routledge and Kegan Paul, 1973), 11, 20; S. V. Volkov, *Intellektualnyi sloi v sovetskom obshchestve* (Moscow: Fond Razvitie, 1999), 30–31, 126–127.
11. Taubman, *Khrushchev*, 382; Stephen E. Harris, "Moving to the Separate Apartment: Building, Distributing, Furnishing, and Living in Urban Housing in Soviet Russia, 1950s–1960s" (Ph.D. diss., University of Chicago, 2003).
12. Katerina Gerasimova, "Public Privacy in the Soviet Communal Apartment," in Ga-bor Rittersporn, M. Rolfe, and J. Behrends, eds., *Public Spheres in Soviet-Type Soci-eties* (special edition, 2003); Orlando Figes, *The Whisperers: Private Life in Stalin's Russia* (New York: Metropolitan, 2007), 174–186.

13. Taubman, *Khrushchev,* 372.

14. Alexei Adzhubei, *Krushenie illuzii: Vremia v sobytiakh i litsakh* (Moscow: Interbuk, 1991), 143.

15. Steven Zaloga, *The Kremlin's Nuclear Sword: The Rise and Fall of Russia's Strategic Nuclear Forces, 1945–2000* (Washington, D.C.: Smithsonian Institution Press, 2002); Vladislav Zubok, *A Failed Empire: The Soviet Union in the Cold War from Stalin to Gorbachev* (Chapel Hill: University of North Carolina Press, 2007), 130–132.

16. Nikolai Simonov, *Voenno-promyshlennyi kompleks SSSR v 1930–1950e gody* (Moscow: ROSSPEN, 1996), 249–250, 303, 307; Viktoria Glazyrina, "Krasnoiarsk-26: A Closed City of the Defense-Industry Complex," in John Barner and Mark Harrison, eds., *The Soviet Defence-Industry Complex from Stalin to Khrushchev* (London: Macmillan, 2000), 196; Jakov Ladyzhensky, "Krasnoiarsk-26," *Druzhba Narodov* 6 (1996): 125–151.

17. Slava Gerovitch, *From Newspeak to Cyberspeak: A History of Soviet Cybernetics* (Cambridge, Mass.: MIT Press, 2002), 133.

18. Paul R. Josephson, *New Atlantis Revisited: Akademgorodok, the Siberian City of Science* (Princeton, N.J.: Princeton University Press, 1997), 3–15; RGANI, fond 13, op. 1, d. 528, ll. 13–24; Vladimir Shubkin, "Vozrozhdaiushchaiasia sotsiologiia i ofitsialnaia ideologia," in G. S. Batygin and C. F. Yarmoliuk, eds., *Rossiiskaia sotsiologiia shestidesiatykh godov v vospominaniiakh i dokumentakh* (St. Petersburg: Russkii Khristianskii Gumanitarnyi Institut, 1999), 71.

19. Viktor Kazarin, *Obrazovaniie, nauka i intelligentsia v Vostochnoi Sibiri, vtoraia polovina 40kh–seredina 60kh godov XX v* (Irkutsk: Irkutskii Universitet, 1998), 205–206, 220.

20. Aline Mosby, *The View from No. 13 People's Street* (New York: Random House, 1962), 295.

21. Mikhail German, *Slozhnoe proshedshee* (St. Peterburg: Iskusstvo-SPb, 2000), 383; footage from the TV series produced by Leonid Parfenov, *Namedni* (1961–1991), *Nasha Era,* episode "1961," NTV production, Moscow, 1997.

22. M. V. Shkarovsky, *Russkaia Pravoslavnaia Tserkov pri Staline i Khrushcheve (Gosudarstvenno-tserkovnye otnosheniia v SSSR v 1939–1964 godakh)* (Moscow: Graal, 2000), 360–363.

23. Ibid., 361–385; RGANI, f. 5, op. 33, d. 190, ll. 14–47, 120, 144–148.

24. Alexei Kozlov, *Kozel na sakse* (Moscow: Vagrius, 1998), 139–140.

25. *Narodnoe Khoziaistvo v SSSR v 1958: Statisticheskii Ezhegodnik* (Moscow: Gosstatizdat TsSU SSSR, 1959), 350; Rudolf Pikhoia, "Pochemu Khrushchev poterial vlast," *Mezhdunarodnyi Istoricheskii Zhurnal* 8 (Mar.–Apr. 2000), at http://www.history.machaon.ru/all/number_08/analiti4/khrushchev/1/.

26. Taubman, *Khrushchev,* 305–306, 376–378; Pikhoia, "Pochemu Khrushchev poterial vlast."

27. Pikhoia, "Pochemu Khrushchev poterial vlast."

28. German, *Slozhnoe proshedshee,* 334; Natalia Lebina and Alexander Chistikov,

Obyvatel i reformy: Kartiny povednevnoi zhizni gorozhan v gody Nepa i Khrushchevskogo desiatiletia (St. Petersburg: Dmitry Bulanov, 2003), 234.

29. Ivan Shchegolikhin's diary, June 20, 1960, at http://prstr.narod.ru/texts/num0903/2cheg0903.htm; Lebina and Chistikov, *Obyvatel i reformy,* 232–233.

30. Olshansky, "Byli my rannimi," in Batygin and Yarmoliuk, *Rossiiskaia sotsiologiia,* 183–184.

31. Anatoly Cherniaev, *Moia zhizn i moe vremia* (Moscow: Mezhdunarodnye Otnosheniia, 1995), 238. See also similar recollections in Vladimir Novikov, "Vysotsky," *Novy Mir* 11 (2001), at http://magazines.russ.ru/novyi_mi/2001/11/nov.html.

32. Natasha Simes (Timofeeva), letter to the author, Apr. 6, 2006.

33. Rosalind J. Marsh, *Soviet Fiction since Stalin: Science, Politics and Literature* (Beckenham, Eng.: Croom Helm, 1986), chap. 4.

34. A. V. Beliaev and A. A. Rastorguev, *Istoriia Dubny v eie toponimakh* (1993), at http://www.dubna.ru/rastor/History/History.htm.

35. Yevgeny Pasternak, *Boris Pasternak: Biografiia,* at http://pasternak.niv.ru/pasternak.bio/pasternak-e-b/biografiya-9-3.htm 465.

36. Beliaev and Rastorguev, *Istoriia Dubny.*

37. Matthew Evangelista, *Unarmed Forces: The Transnational Movement to End the Cold War* (Ithaca, N.Y.: Cornell University Press, 1999); Lawrence S. Wittner, *Resisting the Bomb: A History of the World Nuclear Disarmament Movement, 1954–1970* (Stanford, Calif.: Stanford University Press, 1997), 279–283.

38. Boris Slutsky, *O drugikh i o sebe* (Moscow: Vagrius, 2005), 189. For Arkady Vysotsky's recollections of his father, see A. Krylov, ed., *Chetyre chetverti puti* (Moscow: Fizkultura i Sport, 1988), 14.

39. Alexei Batalov, "Kak ia byl Gusevym," in I. G. Germanova and N. B. Kuzmina, eds., *Moi rezhisser Romm* (Moscow: Iskusstvo, 1993), 259.

40. These figures are taken from Josephson, *New Atlantis Revisited,* 23.

41. I. Poletaev, "V zashchitu Yuria," *Komsomolskaia Pravda,* Oct. 11, 1959.

42. The group included Admiral Aksel Berg, the head of the Soviet military electronics program; Sergei Sobolev, the chief mathematician on the Soviet atomic project; Anatoly Kitov, another mathematician who studied the computer applications for the Soviet military; and the MGU professor Alexei Liapunov. Gerovitch, *From Newspeak to Cyberspeak,* 173–179.

43. Ibid.; A. I. Poletaev, "'Voennaia kibernetika,' ili fragment iz istorii otechestvennoi 'lzhenauki,'" at http://vivovoco.rsl.ru/VV/PAPERS/BIO/POLETAEV.HTM.

44. Gerovitch, *From Newspeak to Cyberspeak,* 162, 299; Poletaev, "'Voennaia kibernetika.'"

45. Ludmilla Alexeyeva and Paul Goldberg, *The Thaw Generation: Coming of Age in the Post-Stalin Era* (Pittsburgh: University of Pittsburgh Press, 1993), 96–97.

46. "The Danger of Atomic War and President Eisenhower's Proposal," memorandum

from V. Malyshev to N. Khrushchev, Apr. 1, 1954, RGANI, f. 5, op. 126, d. 126, l. 38; Andrei Sakharov, *Vospominaniia* (New York: Chekhov Press, 1990), 261–269.

47. Evangelista, *Unarmed Forces;* Wittner, *Resisting the Bomb,* 279–283.

48. Gerovitch, *From Newspeak to Cyberspeak,* 183–188; Nikolai Krementsov, *Stalinist Science* (Princeton, N.J.: Princeton University Press, 1997), 158–184.

49. "Stranitsy istorii sovetskoi genetiki v literature poslednikh let," *Voprosy Istorii Estestvoznaniia i Tekhniki* 4 (1987): 113–124; Gerovitch, *From Newspeak to Cyberspeak,* 184.

50. S. S. Ilizarov, "Akademicheskii iiun 1958-go," at http://russcience.euro.ru/. Among the anti-Lysenko physicists supporting genetics were Yakov Zeldovich, Andrei Sakharov, Arkady Migdal, Isaac Pomeranchuk, Vitaly Ginzburg, Moisei Markov, and Abram Alikhanov.

51. V. V. Babkov, E. S. Sakanian, *Nikolai Vladimirovich Timofeev-Resovskii, 1900–1981* (Moscow: Pamiatniki Istoricheskoi Mysli, 2002), 254–256, 257–262, 559–566; Poletaev, "'Voennaia kibernetika.'" Alexei Liapunov created another informal workshop, among biology students, his daughters' classmates at Moscow State University. Liapunov invited to his workshop geneticists, who were persecuted by Lysenko and his acolytes. Gerovitch, *From Newspeak to Cyberspeak,* 183.

52. S. S. Ilizarov, "Ia nizveden do urovnia 'uchenogo raba . . .' (atomnyi proekt—Landau—TsK KPSS)," at http://russcience.euro.ru/papers. On Landau's involvement in the nuclear project, see Rudolf Pikhoia, "Medlenno taiushchii led (1953–1958)," *Mezhdunarodnyi Istoricheskii Zhurnal* 7 (Jan.–Feb. 2000), at http://history.machaon.ru/all/number_07/analiti4/ice_print/.

53. A. S. Grossman, "Iz dossie KGB na akademika L. D. Landau," *Voprosy Istorii* 8 (1992): 112–118; "Genii Landau: K 100-letiiu so dnia rozhdenia," *Priroda* 1 (2008): esp. 22–25 (recollections by S. S. Gershtein); "Po dannym agentury i operativnoi tekhniki . . . Spravka KGB SSSR ob akademike L. D. Landau," *Istoricheskii Arkhiv* 3 (1993): 153–159.

54. David Samoilov, *Podennye zapisi* (Moscow: Vremia, 2002), 1:259; Kora Drobantseva-Landau, *Akademik Landau: Kak my zhili* (Moscow: Zakharov, 1999).

55. Josephson, *New Atlantis Revisited,* 43–53.

56. Gennady Nikolaev, "Moi mnogolikii atom: Cherez vsiu zhizn," *Zvezda* 8 (2006), at http://magazines.russ.ru/zvezda/2006/8/ni5.html.

57. Viacheslav Ivanov, "Goluboi zver (Vospominaniia)," *Zvezda* 3 (1995): 158, 166–167; Gerovitch, *From Newspeak to Cyberspeak,* 227–228, 235.

58. Boris Slutsky, "Fiziki i liriki," *Literaturnaia Gazeta,* Oct. 13, 1959.

59. Boris Strugatsky, *Kommentarii k proidennomu, "Esli"* 11–12 (1998), at http://lib.ru/STRUGACKIE/comments.txt.

60. Mark Hopkins, *Mass Media in the Soviet Union* (New York: Pegasus, 1970): 248.

61. L. Ilichev, A. Romanov, and G. Kazakov v TsK KPSS, Aug. 6, 1958, "O zaglushenii inostrannykh radiostantsii," RGANI, f. 5, op. 30, d. 75, ll. 163–167.

62. Recollections of Rada Adzhubei, in A. I. Volkov, M. G. Pugacheva, and S. F. Yarmo-

liuk, eds., *Pressa v obshchestve, 1959-2000: Otsenki zhurnalistov i sotsiologov—Dokumenty* (Moscow: Moskovskaia Shkola Politicheskikh Issledovanii, 2000), 44.

63. For information on Alexei Adzhubei, see the recollections of a journalist, Ella Maksimova, "Nachalo," in Rada Adzhubei et al., eds., *Alexei Adzhubei v koridorakh chetvertoi vlasti* (Moscow: Izvestia, 2003); and Alexei Adzhubei's two books of memoirs, Adzhubei, *Krushenie illuzii,* and Adzhubei, *Te desiat let* (Moscow: Sovetskaia Rossia, 1989).

64. Recollections of Melor Sturua, in Adzhubei et al., *Alexei Adzhubei v koridorakh,* 263.

65. Stenographic record of *letuchka* (editorial meeting) at *Izvestia,* June 1, 1959, published ibid., 112-113.

66. Stenographic record of *letuchka* at *Izvestia,* June 1, 1959, ibid., 114.

67. Stenographic record of *letuchka* at *Izvestia,* June 8, 1959, ibid., 114-115, 119.

68. On the "five principles," see Alexander Volkov, "Piat glavnykh printsipov," in Adzhubei et al., *Alexei Adzhubei v koridorakh,* 215-216.

69. Adzhubei, *Te desiat let,* 21; Ninel Ismailova, "Uroki na vsiu zhizn," in Adzhubei et al., *Alexei Adzhubei v koridorakh,* 100.

70. Author's interview with Vladlen Krivosheev, May 19, 1999, Moscow; Dmitry Mamleev, "Azart molodosti," in Adzhubei et al., *Alexei Adzhubei v koridorakh,* 86-90.

71. G. F. Agranovsky, ed., *Vospominaniia ob Anatolii Agranovskom* (Moscow: Sovetskii Pisatel, 1988).

72. Anatoly Agranovsky, "Kak ia byl pervym," 1962, at http://www.agranovsky.ru/history/roots/papa.htm.

73. Ibid.

74. Thomas C. Wolfe, *Governing Soviet Journalism: The Press and the Socialist Person after Stalin* (Bloomington: Indiana University Press, 2005), 71-103, esp. 85, 98; Yevgenia Albats, "Pobeda," in I. N. Golembiovsky, ed., *Uroki Agranovskogo* (Moscow: Izvestia, 1986), 53-69.

75. Recollections of Melor Sturua, in Adzhubei et al., *Alexei Adzhubei v koridorakh,* 264.

76. Adzhubei et al., *Alexei Adzhubei v koridorakh,* 118; T. Volkova, "Chelovek epokhi: A. I. Adzhubei—redaktor Komsomolskoi pravdy i Izvestii," at http://www.mediascope.ru/?id_menu=2&id_menu_item=4&id_object=4&id_item=205.

77. Boris Grushin, *Chetyre vremeni Rossii: Epokha Khrushcheva* (Moscow: Progress-Traditsiia, 2001), 44-47, 50. This monograph provides the most valuable primary data on public Soviet thinking at that time. See also Grushin, "Institut obshchestvennogo mneniia—otdel 'Komsomolskoi pravdy,'" in Volkov, Pugacheva, and Yarmoliuk, *Pressa v obshchestve,* 49.

78. Grushin, *Chetyre vremeni,* 69-70, 91-92.

79. Ibid., 76, 79, 96, 98, 102, 107-108.

80. Author's interview with Vladlen Krivosheev, May 19, 1999, Moscow.

81. Adzhubei, *Krushenie illuzii,* 135-136.

82. Volkov, Pugacheva, and Yarmoliuk, *Pressa v obshchestve,* 56.

83. Interview with one of the agrarian journalists, Anatoly Streliany, on Radio Liberty, in "Neizvestnaia Tselina," Feb. 29, 2004, at http://www.svoboda.org/programs/ TD/2004/TD.022904.asp; Chernichenko in *Intellektualnaia Rossia,* Sept. 20, 2007, at http://www.intelros.ru/2007/09/20/velikijj_razdrazhitel_jurijj_chernichenko_ o_predannojj_revoljucii.html.

84. Ilichev, Romanov, and Kazakov v TsK KPSS, Aug. 6, 1958, l. 168.

85. Conversation with Thomas Digen, Feb. 10, 1959; response by L. Ilichev and G. Kazakov to the CC CPSU, Feb. 18, 1959, RGANI, f. 5, op. 33, d. 95, ll. 1, 3.

86. *Kommunist* 8 (1959): 66; *Vestnik statistiki* 4 (1959): 92; *Televideniie i UKV* 49 (1958): 5.

87. Yuri Fokin, Yelena Galperina, and Ksenia Marinina became successful program producers. Tomas Kolesnichenko, Mikhail Zenovich, Yevgeny Ambartsumov, and Georgy Mirsky would continue their careers in journalism and academia, and as "enlightened" apparatchiks at the Kremlin.

88. G. Kuznetsov and N. Mesiatsev, *Zolotye gody otechestvennogo televideniia, 1957-1970,* at http://www.tvmuseum.ru/.

89. Mark Rozovsky and Nikita Bogoslovsky were the creators of the program. In 2001 the recollections of the KVN organizers were posted online at http://www.amik.ru/ page/4.html. See also Bella Ostromoukhova, "KVN—'Molodezhnaia kultura' shestidesiatykh," *Neprikosnovenny Zapas* 3 (2004), at http://www.nlo.magazine.ru/ philosoph/sootech/sootech83.html; *Istoriia Televideniia* 1 (1997), at http://www. nlobooks.ru/.

90. Vladimir Sappak, *Televidenie i my: Chetyre besedy* (Moscow: Iskusstvo, 1963), 46.

91. Ibid., 51, 63, 82–84, 95, 103, 112, 117, 125, 126–127; Nina Zorkaia, "Zapiski mechtatelia (perechityvaia knigu)," *Televidenie: Vchera, Segodnia, Zavtra,* no. 4 (Moscow: Iskusstvo, 1984), at http://www.evartist.narod.ru/text12/89.htm.

92. Kuznetsov and Mesiatsev, *Zolotye gody otechestvennogo televideniia;* for proposals for honoraria from the state television to CC PCUS, see RGANI, f. 5, op. 33, d. 72, ll. 19–30.

93. Kuznetsov and Mesiatsev, *Zolotye gody otechestvennogo televideniia.*

94. Ibid.

95. Naum Korzhavin, *V soblaznakh krovavoi epokhi* (Moscow: Zakharov, 2006), 2:579.

96. Anatoly Smeliansky, *The Russian Theater after Stalin* (Cambridge: Cambridge University Press, 1999), 24–29.

97. Alexeyeva and Goldberg, *The Thaw Generation,* 95.

98. Grushin, *Chetyre vremeni,* 159–160.

99. Ibid., 206; Volkov, Pugacheva, and Yarmoliuk, *Pressa v obshchestve,* 57.

100. Grushin, *Chetyre vremeni,* 186, 191.

101. Ibid., 202; Volkov, Pugacheva, and Yarmoliuk, *Pressa v obshchestve,* 58.

102. Recollections of Nikolai Obushenkov, "'Delo' molodykh istorikov," in *Voprosy Istorii* 4 (1994): 124. In 1956 the number of people arrested and sentenced to prison and camp terms for "anti-Soviet propaganda and agitation" was 384; in 1957 the

number spiked, to 1,964; in 1958 it still came to 1,416. Veniamin Iofe, "Polit-icheskaia oppozitsiia v Leningrade, 50–60-kh," *Zvezda* 7 (1997): 213.

103. Vitaly Ronkin, *Na smenu dekabriam prikhodiat ianvari* (Moscow: Memorial, Zve-nia, 2003), 145, 150.

104. I was able to read the files on the members of the "Bell" group in the archive of Memorial, St. Petersburg, in January 2007.

105. Interview with Len Karpinsky, in Batygin and Yarmoliuk, *Rossiiskaia sotsiologiia,* 190–204; biographical data from *Moscow News,* Nov. 26, 2004.

106. Cherniaev, *Moia zhizn i moe vremia,* 46.

107. Lebina and Chistikov, *Obyvatel i reformy,* 284–286; Vladimir Bukovsky, *To Build a Castle: My Life as a Dissenter* (New York: Viking, 1979), 150–151; Liudmila Poli-kovskaia, ed., *"My predchuvstvie... predtecha": Ploshchad Maiakovskogo, 1958–1965* (Moscow: Zvenia, 1997), 14.

108. Stalin in 1950, quoted in Ethan Pollock, *Stalin and the Soviet Science Wars* (Prince-ton, N.J.: Princeton University Press, 2006), 182.

109. More details in Robert D. English, *Russia and the Idea of the West: Gorbachev, Intel-lectuals and the End of the Cold War* (New York: Columbia, 2000), 70–72.

110. Cherniaev, *Moia zhizn,* 225–236; Shakhnazarov, *S Vozhdiami i bez nikh,* 94–95. In the Prague community were future advocates of "new thinking" in international affairs and of socialism with a human face in domestic policy, including Ivan Frolov, Alexei Rumiantsev, Georgy Arbatov, Vadim Zagladin, Nikolai Inozemtsev, and Oleg Bogomolov, the journalists Yuri Kariakin and Boris Grushin, the philos-opher Merab Mamardashvili, and the historians Yevgeny Ambartsumov and Akhmed Iskenderov.

111. David Samoilov, *Pamiatnye zapiski* (Moscow: Mezhdunarodnye Otnosheniia, 1995), 245.

5. The Intelligentsia Reborn, 1959-1962

1. On the rapid expansion of the "private" and "private public" (as distinct from the "official public") sphere in Soviet life see Viktor Voronkov, "Sotsiologicheskoie pokoleniie 1960-kh," in Liudmila Alexeeva c Polom Goldbergom, *Pokolenie otte-peli* (Moscow: Zakharov, 2006), 379–380.

2. Ludmilla Alexeyeva and Paul Goldberg, *The Thaw Generation: Coming of Age in the Post-Stalin Era* (Pittsburgh: University of Pittsburgh Press, 1993), 96–97.

3. Stanislav Rassadin, "Shestidesiatniki: Knigi o molodom sovremennike," *Yunost* 12 (1960): 58–62. In his memoirs four decades later, Rassadin revised his notion of the new community. He explained that he did not write about young people only, but rather about the reborn intelligentsia, all those who shared hopes for a better, more humane and democratic society. Rassadin, *Kniga proshchanii: Vospominaniia o druziakh i ne tolko o nikh* (Moscow: Tekst, 2004), 16–17.

4. Among the descriptions of the funeral, see Lidia Chukovskaia, diary entry for June 2, 1960, in Chukovskaia, *Sochinenia v dvukh tomakh* (Moscow: Gudyal-Press,

2000), 2:263–266; Veniamin Kaverin, *Epilog: Memuary* (Moscow: Russkaia Kniga, 2002), 385–387.

5. Robert Louis Jackson, "Doctor Zhivago: Liebestod of the Russian Intelligentsia," in Victor Erlich, ed., *Pasternak: A Collection of Critical Essays* (Englewood Cliffs, N.J.: Prentice-Hall, 1978).

6. Fyodor Stepun, "Boris Pasternak," ibid., 121–123.

7. Yelena Kumpan, *"Nashi Stariki" i istoriia Leningradskoi nepodtsenzurnoi literatury, 1950–1980-e gody* (St. Petersburg: DEAN, 2000), 29; Emily Lygo, "The Need for New Voices: Writers' Union Policy towards Young Writers, 1953–1964," in Polly Jones, ed., *The Dilemmas of De-Stalinization: Negotiating Cultural and Social Change in the Khrushchev Era* (London: Routledge, 2006), 193–208.

8. Sergei Averintsev, "Opyt Peterburgskoi intelligentsii—po lichnym vpechatleniiam," in S. Bocharov and A. Parnis, eds., *Vittorio* (Moscow: Tri Kvadrata, 2005), 39.

9. E. Vodolazkin, ed., *Dmitry Likhachev: Vosponinaniia, esse, dokumenty, fotografii* (St. Petersburg: LOGOS, 2002), 181.

10. Mikhail German, *Slozhnoe proshedshee: Passé composé* (St. Petersburg: Pechatnyi Dvor, 2006), 272–273.

11. Ibid., 302–305.

12. E. Berar, "Vokrug memuarov Ilyi Erenburga," *Minuvshee: Istoricheskii Almanakh* 8 (1992): 387–406; Joshua Rubenstein, *Tangled Loyalties: The Life and Times of Ilya Ehrenburg* (New York: Basic, 1996), 335–336.

13. Pyotr Vail and Alexander Ghenis, *60-e: Mir sovetskogo cheloveka*, 2nd ed. (Moscow: Novoe Literaturnoe Obozrenie, 1998), 46.

14. "'Erenburg ne sdelal vyvodov . . . ' O publikatsii memuarov pisatelia," *Istochnik* 2 (2002): 110–111.

15. See Edith Rogovin Frankel, *Novy Mir: A Case Study in the Politics of Literature, 1952–1958* (New York: Cambridge University Press, 1981); on the new interest Tvardovsky took in *Novy Mir* in 1960, see Kaverin, *Epilog,* 447.

16. Diaries published by his daughters Valentina and Olga Tvardovsky: Alexander Tvardovsky, "Iz rabochikh tetradei (1953–1960)," *Znamia* 7–9 (1989); "Rabochie tetradi 60-kh godov," *Znamia* 6–9, 11–12 (2000); ibid., 12 (2001); ibid., 2, 4–5, 9–10 (2002); ibid., 8–10 (2003); ibid., 4–5, 9–11 (2004); and ibid., 9–10 (2005). See also Regina Romanova, *Alexandr Tvardovsky: Trudy i dni* (Moscow: Vodolei, 2006).

17. See, on this point, Andrei Turkov, "'Ia proshel takuiu dal . . . ': Perechityvaia Alexandra Tvardovskogo," *Svobodnaia Mysl* 5 (1996): 67.

18. Tvardovsky, "Iz rabochikh tetradei (1953–1960)," *Znamia* 7 (1989): 144.

19. Tvardovsky, "Iz rabochikh tetradei (1953–1960)," entry for Jan. 1958, *Znamia* 8 (1989), 156.

20. Ibid., 147, 169.

21. Ibid., 135.

22. Tvardovsky, entry for June 3, 1961, "Rabochie tetradi 60-kh godov," *Znamia* 6 (2000): 147–148.

23. Anatoly Smeliansky, *The Russian Theater after Stalin,* trans. Patrick Miles (New York: Cambridge University Press, 1999), 10–11.

24. Ibid., 14–15.

25. Mayakovsky lived in a ménage à trois with his muse Lilia Brik and her husband, Osip Brik. Lilia survived the Stalin era and even enjoyed unique immunity (Lilia's sister Elsa, who married the French communist poet Louis Aragon, lived in Paris). Brik's apartment in Moscow became a gathering place for a bohemian circle, a living reminder of literary salons of the Silver Age and of the 1920s. Benidikt Sarnov, "U Lili Brik: Iz knigi vospominanii," *Kontinent* 124 (2005).

26. Liudmila Polikovskaia, ed., *"My predchuvstvie . . . predtecha": Ploshchad Maiakovskogo, 1958–1965* (Moscow: Zvenia, 1997), 25–26.

27. Ibid., 38, 41.

28. Yevgeny Yevtushenko, interview in the CNN Cold War series, at http://www.cnn.com/SPECIALS/cold.war/episodes/14/interviews/yevtushenko/.

29. Polikovskaia, *"My predchuvstvie . . . predtecha,"* 28–30.

30. Slutsky and Samoilov, the prophetic talents from the cohort of war veterans, did not live up to the new public expectations. Slutsky fell out of favor with the critical-minded audience after he became a hapless accomplice in the persecution of Pasternak. Besides, his verses contained too much private pain and too little of the programmatic anti-Stalinism, obligatory at that time in informal circles. Samoilov still remained unknown to the broad reading public, and his poems, touched with early wisdom as well as bitter irony, did not accord with the optimistic and romantic era.

31. Yevgeny Yevtushenko, "Zima" (Winter), translation by Vladislav Zubok. See Russian version at http://zhurnal.lib.ru/a/as_w/zimast-ru-eng.shtml.

32. Zapiska otdelov TsK KPSS o tvorcheskom vechere E. A. Evtushenko v Literaturnom Muzee, Jan. 27, 1960; Zapiska Glavlita SSSR (P. Romanov), Feb. 25, 1960, in *Apparat TsK KPSS i Kultura, 1958–1964: Dokumenty* (Moscow: ROSSPEN, 2005), 347–349, 356.

33. Yevgeny Yevtushenko, *Volchii pasport* (Moscow: Vagrius, 2001), 64–65.

34. Andrei Voznesensky, "The Parabolic Ballad" and "The Antiworlds," translations by Vladislav Zubok. See Russian versions at http://www.world-art.ru/lyric/lyric.php?id=11806 and http://www.world-art.ru/lyric/lyric.php?id=11745.

35. David Samoilov, *Pamiatnye zapiski* (Moscow: Mezhdunarodnye Otnosheniia, 1995), 369.

36. Okudzhava, "The Soldier Made of Paper" (1959), translation by Vladislav Zubok.

37. Bulat Okudzhava, *Vse eshche vperedi* (1997); Georgy Knabe, "Final: Arbatskaia epopeia," in T. Kniazevskaia, *Russkaia intelligentsia* (Moscow: Nauka, 1999), 342–350; Stephen V. Bittner, *The Many Lives of Khrushchev's Thaw: Experience and Memory in Moscow's Arbat* (Ithaca, N.Y.: Cornell University Press, 2008), chap. 1.

38. Vail and Ghenis, *60-e: Mir sovetskogo cheloveka,* 64–65.

39. *Voprosy Literatury* 2 (1993): 235–239; Nikolai Leonov, *Likholetie* (Moscow: Mezhdunarodniie Otnosheniia, 1995), 52.

40. Vasily Aksyonov, "Zvezdnyi bilet," *Yunost* 7 (1961).

41. John E. Bowlt, interview with Dmitry Sarabianov, former professor of art history at MGU, *Journal of the Cold War Studies* 4, no. 1 (Winter 2002): 84. In the late 1950s the Institute of Art History in Moscow gained a reputation as "the nest of the avant-garde" and a refuge for freethinking young philosophers, all of them admirers of the "young" Marx and his interpreter Georg Lukacs. Yuri Davydov, "Dukh mirovoi togda osel v estetike," in G. S. Batygin and C. F. Yarmoliuk, eds., *Rossiiskaia sotsiologiia shestidesiatykh godov v vospominaniiakh i dokumentakh* (St. Petersburg: Russkii Khristianskii Gumanitarnyi Institut, 1999), 397.

42. Author's interview with Vittorio Strada, Apr. 1, 2006, Rome; Vittorio Strada, *Autoritratto autocritico: Archeologia della rivoluzione d'Ottobre* (Milan: Liberal, 2004).

43. In May 1957 and December 1959 Moscow artists organized small exhibitions of the Russian vanguard artists Robert Falk and David Shterenberg, whose art had been banned in Stalin's day. In January 1960 the artists opened another exhibition of formalist works yet, out of caution, closed it to the general public. See Zapiska Ministerstva kultury SSSR o zakrytoi vistavke moskovskikh khudozhnikov, no later than Jan. 21, 1960, in *Apparat TsK KPSS i Kultura, 1958–1964*, 343–344.

44. The leading "severe style" artists were Nikolai Andronov, Geli Korzhev, Viktor Popkov, Pavel Nikonov, and Pyotr Ossovsky. On the severe style and its artists, see Maria Bulanova, "Soviet Art: A Perspective on a Twentieth-Century Phenomenon," in Joan Lee, ed., *Soviet Dis-Union: Socialist Realist and Nonconformist Art* (Minneapolis: Museum of Russian Art, 2006), 17–18; Alexei Bobrikov, "Surovyi stil: mobilizatsiia i kulturnaia revoliutsiia," *Moscow Art Magazine* 52–53 (2003), at http://xz.gif.ru/numbers/51-52/surovo; on the "stalwarts," see Anatoly Brusilovsky, *Vremia Khudozhnikov* (Moscow: Magazin Iskusstva, 1999), 72.

45. Zapiska otdela nauki, shkol i kultury TsK KPSS po RSFSR, May 31, 1960, and report of June 28, 1960, in *Apparat TsK KPSS i kultura, 1958–1964*, 377–378, 387.

46. Georgy Nissky, "Poiski formy," *Moskovsky Komsomolets,* Apr. 9, 1960.

47. Nina Moleva, "Manezh kotorogo nikto ne videl: K 40-letiiu nashumevshei vystavki," *Moskva* 3 (2003), at http://www.moskvam.ru/2003/03/moleva3.htm; Leonid Rabichev, "Manezh 1962, do i posle," *Znamia* 9 (2001): 126–127.

48. Ernst Neizvestny, *Govorit Neizvestny* (Frankfurt-am-Main: Posev, 1980), 96.

49. Samoilov, *Pamiatnye zapiski,* 363, 366.

50. Andrei Volkonsky, the scion of an aristocratic family (relatives of Lev Tolstoy), returned to the USSR in 1947 with his parents, served time in the gulag, and was then admitted to the Moscow Conservatory. His noble background and manners made him a sensation in circles of Moscow artists and intellectuals. His innovative suite based on lyrics by Garcia Lorca began with the words "Christ holds a mirror in each hand." Ilya Ovchinnikov, "Kniaz muzykalnogo avangarda" (obituary for Andrei Volkonsky, Sept. 17, 2008), at http://www.classicalmusicnews.ru/articles/Knjaz-muzykalnogo-avangarda-Umer-kompozitor-Andrei-Volkonskii/.

51. Mikhail Tal, born in Riga, Latvia, moved to Moscow, where he led a furiously active social life and frequented many Moscow *kompany,* theaters, and poetic readings. He was a darling of the "new" journalists and published many reflections on chess, life, and art. M. Tal and Y. Damsky, *Na altar Kaissy* (Moscow: RIPOL Klassik,

2006); Salli Landau, *Liubov i shakhmaty: Elegiia Mikhailu Taliu* (Moscow: Russian Chess House, 2003); recollections of Garry Kasparov on the radio station Ekho Moskvy, Nov. 11, 2008.

52. Smeliansky, *The Russian Theater,* 16–17, 19.

53. Viktor Rozov, *V poiskakh radosti,* ibid., 24. See also Timo Vihavainen, *The Inner Adversary: The Struggle against Philistinism as the Moral Mission of the Russian Intelligentsia* (Washington, D.C.: New Academia, 2006).

54. Smeliansky, *The Russian Theater,* 16–18; Anatoly Brusilovsky, "Vremia khudozhnikov," *Neprikosnovennyi Zapas* 6 (1999), at http://magazines.russ.ru/nz/1999/6/brusil.html.

55. The cohort included Alexander Alov, Vladimir Naumov, Stanislav Rostotsky, Grigory Chukhrai, Mikhail Shveitser, Marlen Khutsiev, Lev Kulidzhanov, Sergei Paradzhanov, and Yakov Segel. There were also younger directors: Georgy Danelia, Rolan Bykov, Eldar Riazanov, and Igor Talankin. After them came Andrei Tarkovsky, Dinara Asanova, Andrei Mikhalkov-Konchalovsky, Gennady Shpalikov, Kira Muratova, and Larisa Shepitko.

56. Information on manuscript of V. I. Bokovich, "Besedy s sovetskimi rezhisserami novogo pokoleniia," sent to the party apparatus by the GLAVLIT censors Dec. 21, 1959, RGANI, f. 5, op. 36, d. 116, ll. 80–100.

57. Josephine Woll, *Real Images: Soviet Cinema and the Thaw* (New York: Taurus, 2000), 8–9, 22, 38; V. I. Fomin, *Kinematograf ottepeli: Dokumenty i svidetelsva ochevidtsev* (Moscow: Materik, 1998), 11.

58. The young filmmaker Mikhail Shveitser decided to make a film on bad party bureaucrats and the idealistic people who became their victims. The plot was based on a novel by Vladimir Tendriakov that appeared in *Novy Mir* in February–March 1956. Despite the support of many filmmakers and writers, the film was banned. It appeared later in an emasculated and ideologically harmless version. Fomin, *Kinematograf ottepeli,* 112–118.

59. Woll, *Real Images,* 97; S. Rostotsky, "Ot imeni pokolenii," *Iskusstvo Kino* 1 (1960), 66–67; Maia Turovskaia, "Ballada o soldate," *Novy Mir* 4 (1961): 250.

60. In 1957 Kalatozov's *The Cranes Are Flying* received the Palme d'Or at Cannes. In 1958 Raizman's film *The Communist* won a prize at the Venice Film Festival.

61. Romm was born in 1901 in Siberia, into a family of assimilated Jews and Bolsheviks. During the 1930s Romm made hagiographic films about Vladimir Lenin. When the Cold War began, he directed anti-American propaganda films, on Stalin's orders. During the Thaw Romm was stricken with a sense of shame about his past. I. G. Germanova and N. B. Kuzmina, eds., *Moi rezhisser Romm* (Moscow: Iskusstvo, 1993), esp. 189, 205; Fomin, *Kinematograf ottepeli,* 74–75.

62. The authorities wanted to ban the film for many reasons, not least of which was that it contained the first public discussion of atomic radiation. Adzhubei's intervention saved the film: he lobbied Khrushchev directly, and *Izvestia*'s leading columnist, Anatoly Agranovsky, published an op-ed article praising *Nine Days.* Kuzmina, *Moi rezhisser Romm,* 107, 285; Woll, *Real Images,* 128; Alexei Adzhubei, *Krushenie illuzii: Vremia v sobytiakh i litsakh* (Moscow: Interbuk, 1991), 213–214.

63. Like Romm, Khutsiev believed in the Revolution, Leninism, and internationalism. And like many *shestidesiatniki,* Khutsiev had been born in Moscow's Arbat, the cradle of the new intelligentsia. His family of Old Bolsheviks had perished in Stalin's purges.

64. Woll, *Real Images,* 144; also A. Demenok, "Zastava Ilyicha—urok istorii," *Iskusstvo Kino* 6 (1988); Gennady Shpalikov, "Liudei teriaiut tolko raz," *Znamia* (1997–98), special issue, 135–144.

65. For more detailed description of the film, see Woll, *Real Images,* 142–145; Rassadin, *Kniga proshchanii,* 394.

66. Woll, *Real Images,* 143–145.

67. The literature on samizdat is voluminous, including Yuri Maltsev, *Volnaia russkaia literatura, 1955–1975* (Frankfurt-am-Main: Posev, 1976); Viacheslav Dolinin and Boris Ivanov, *Samizdat: Po materialam konferentsii "30 let nezavisimoi pechati, 1950–80 gody,"* Apr. 25–27, 1992 (St. Petersburg: Memorial, 1993); Anatoly Strelianyi, ed., *Samizdat veka* (Moscow: Polifakt, 1997); Ann Komaromi, "The Material Existence of Soviet Samizdat," *Slavic Review* 63, no. 3 (Autumn 2004): 597–618; Wolfgang Eichwede, "The Archipelago Samizdat," paper presented at the international conference Samizdat and Underground Culture in the Soviet Bloc Countries, University of Pennsylvania, Apr. 6–7, 2006.

68. Polikovskaia, *"My predchuvstvie . . . predtecha,"* 65.

69. On Gorbanevskaia, see Alexander Daniel's recollections, at http://antology. igrunov.ru/a_daniel.html. Polikovskaia, *"My predchuvstvie . . . predtecha,"* 126–127.

70. See the early background information on Ginzburg in *The Trial of the Four: A Collection of Materials on the Case of Galanskov, Ginzburg, Dobrovolsky and Lashkova, 1967–1968* (New York: Viking, 1972), 5–7.

71. Vasily Aksyonov, "TsPKO im. Ginzburga," *Moskovskie Novosti,* Aug. 8, 2002.

72. Grigory Pomerants, *Zapiski gadkogo utenka* (Moscow: Moskovskii Rabochii, 1998), 308–310, 325.

73. Kropivnitsky was born in 1893 in Moscow. In 1911 he graduated from the Stroganov school of art. From 1912 to 1920 he studied history at Shaniavsky University, a famous educational hub for democratic and socialist intellectuals. Among the members of his group were the artists Oscar Rabin, Vladimir Nemukhin, Liudmila Masterkova, and Dmitry Plavinsky, and two poets, Genrikh Sapgir and Igor Kholin.

74. Galina Manevich, "Khudozhnik i vremia, ili Moskovskoie 'podpolie' 60-kh," in *Drugoe iskusstvo: Moskva, 1956–1976,* vol. 1 (Moscow: SP Interbuk, 1991); Genrikh Sapgir, "Lianozovo i drugiie (gruppy i kruzhki kontsa 50-kh)," *Arion* 3 (1997), at http://magazines.russ.ru/arion/1997/3/; "Pamiati Alexandra Ginzburga," *Russkaia Mysl,* July 25, 2002.

75. Interview with Liudmila Alexeeva, at http://antology.igrunov.ru/l_alexeeva.html; S. Chuikina, "Uchastie zhenshchin v dissidentskom dvizhenii, 1956–1986," at http://www.a-z.ru/women/texts/chuikinr.htm.

76. For an incomplete list of Russian-language samizdat in the 1950s and later, see the Web site Anthology of Samizdat, comp. Viacheslav Igrunov, ed. Mark Barbakadze,

at http://antology.igrunov.ru/l_alexeeva.html; and *Apparat TsK KPSS i Kultura, 1958-1964,* 777.

77. Alexeeva, *Pokolenie ottepeli,* 108; A. Piatkovsky, interview with Alexander Daniel, at http://antology.igrunov.ru/a_daniel.html.

78. Mikhail German observed in his memoirs that Leningrad's artists and intellectuals existed "alongside the Thaw," not inside it. Some of them were very envious of their Moscow colleagues, but could not emulate them. German, *Slozhnoe proshedshee,* 213, 249, 364, 368.

79. For recollections about this group by Nina Koroleva and Alexander Shteinberg, see P. Gorelik, ed., *Boris Slutsky: Vospominaniia sovremennikov* (St. Petersburg: Neva, 2005), 407, 434; Viacheslav Dolinin and Dmitry Severiukhin, *Preodolenie nemoty: Leningradskii samizdat v kontekste nezavisimogo kulturnogo dvizheniia, 1953-1991* (St. Petersburg, 2003), 30. The group of young poets included Andrei Bitov, Yevgeny Rein, Anatoly Naiman, Leonid Britanishsky, Gleb Gorbovsky, Vladimir Ufliand, Lev Losev, Mikhail Yeremin, Yakov Gordin, Leonid Vinogradov, and Joseph Brodsky.

80. Interview with Yakov Gordin, *Pchela* 11 (Oct.–Nov. 1997), at http://www.pchela.ru/podshiv/11.htm. This episode took place in the fall of 1957.

81. Mikhail Romm, *Kak v Kino: Ustnye rasskazy* (Moscow: Dekom, 2003), 181.

82. For more on "boiler room" intellectuals and artists, see Alexei Yurchak, *Everything Was Forever, Until It Was No More: The Last Soviet Generation* (Princeton, N.J.: Princeton University Press, 2005).

83. Hélène Zamoiska-Pelletier was a French Slavicist. In the late 1940s she had obtained through her father, a French diplomat in Moscow, the rare permission to study at Moscow State University.

84. Biographical information on Andrei Siniavsky by Liudmila Polikovskaia, at http://www.krugosvet.ru/articles/109/1010978/1010978a1.htm; Joseph Frank, "The Triumph of Abram Tertz," *New York Review of Books,* June 27, 1991; Siniavsky file in the archive of Memorial, St. Petersburg.

85. For Alexander Daniel's reminiscences about his father, see http://www.memo.ru/history/DISS/books/daniel/predisl.htm. Daniel file in the archive of Memorial, St. Petersburg; Nina Voronel, *Bez prikras: Vospominaniia* (Moscow: Zakharov, 2003), 126-128.

86. Daniel file in the archive of Memorial, St. Petersburg; Alexeyeva, *The Thaw Generation,* 126.

87. Samoilov, *Pamiatnye zapiski,* 363.

88. *Apparat TsK KPSS i Kultura, 1958-1964,* 390.

6. The Vanguard Disowned, 1962-1964

1. "Vyskazivaniia N. S. Khrushcheva pri poseshchenii vystavki proizvedenii moskovskikh khudozhnikov," Dec. 1, 1962, APRF, f. 52, op. 1, d. 329, ll. 85–111, published in *Istochnik* 6 (2003): 159–167.

2. In 1959 his project of a monument to Soviet victory in World War II scored first in the national competition. Yet the stalwarts of socialist realism impeded his rise to national prominence and stole numerous ideas from him. Neizvestny had to work for the "studio" of the Stalinist sculptor Vuchetich in a subsidiary role.

3. *Istochnik* 6 (2003): 162, 164, 165, 166; Ernst Neizvestny, *Govorit Neizvestny* (Frankfurt-am-Main, Posev, 1980), 10–13.

4. Priscilla Johnson and Leopold Labedz, *Khrushchev and the Arts: The Politics of Soviet Culture, 1962–1964* (Cambridge, Mass.: MIT Press, 1965).

5. On KGB-GRU reports on U.S. plans to attack, starting with Shelepin's on June 29, 1960, see Vladislav Zubok, "Inside the Covert Cold War: The KGB versus the CIA, 1960–1962," *Cold War International History Project Bulletin*, no. 4 (Fall 1994); and A. A. Fursenko, "Neobychnaia sudba razvedchika G. N. Bolshakova," *Novaia i Noveishaia Istoriia* 4 (2005): 94–95.

6. *Apparat TsK KPSS i Kultura: Dokumenty, 1958–1964* (Moscow: ROSSPEN, 2005), 390–391, 395, 396.

7. Y. Ivaschenko, "Bezdelniki karabkaiutsia na Parnas," *Izvestia*, Sept. 2, 1960; Liudmila Polikovskaia, ed., *"My predchuvstvie . . . predtecha": Ploshchad Maiakovskogo, 1958–1965* (Moscow: Zvenia, 1997), 153–156.

8. Grigory Pomerants, quoted in "Dissidenty o dissidentstve," *Znamia* (1997–98), special issue, 173. See also *Zapiski gadkogo utenka* (Moscow: Moskovskii Rabochii, 1998), 308; Polikovskaia, *"My predchuvstvie . . . predtecha,"* 240–244.

9. On October 1, 1961, soon after the arrest of Bokshtein, Osipov, and Kuznetsov, *Komsomolskaia Pravda* published an article defending the organizers of poetry meetings in Tambov who had come into conflict with local authorities.

10. Alexei Kozlov, *Kozel na sakse*, at http://www.lib.ru/CULTURE/MUSIC/KOZLOV/kozel_na_saxe.txt, 156–158, 174–187.

11. David Caute, *The Dancer Defects: The Struggle for Cultural Supremacy during the Cold War* (New York: Oxford University Press, 2003), 461; novyi_mi/redkol/butov/perev/someday.html.

12. Caute, *The Dancer Defects*, 461; L. I. Menaker, *Volshebnyi fonar* (St. Petersburg: Liki Rossii, 1998), 142.

13. This figure is drawn from the report by the Komsomol leader Sergei Pavlov to the Central Committee, Feb. 18, 1963, in *Apparat TsK KPSS i Kultura, 1958–1964*, 582–584.

14. Karl Eimermacher, foreword to *Ideologicheskie komissii TsK KPSS, 1958–1964: Dokumenty* (Moscow: ROSSPEN, 1998), 17; Wolfram Eggeling, *Politika i kultura pri Khrushcheve i Brezhneve, 1953–1970* (Moscow: AIRO-XX, 1999), 125–129.

15. *Literaturnaia Gazeta*, Sept. 20, 1962, 1; Muzei Arseniia Tarkovskogo, at http://a88.narod.ru/ars00.htm; George Faraday, *Revolt of the Filmmakers: The Struggle for Artistic Autonomy and the Fall of the Soviet Film Industry* (University Park: Pennsylvania University Press, 2000), 92–97.

16. Bulat Okudzhava, *Vse eshche vperedi*, Mar. 1997, at http://imwerden.de/pdf/okudzhava_vse_eshche_vperedi.pdf.

17. Alexander Tvardovsky, entries for Oct. 2 and 16, "Rabochie tetradi 60-kh godov," *Znamia* 7 (2000): 129, 131, 136.

18. Kornei Chukovsky, entry for Nov. 19, 1962, *Dnevnik, 1930–1969* (Moscow: Sovremennyi Pisatel, 1995), 328; Lidia Chukovskaia, *Zapiski ob Anne Akhmatovoi* (Moscow: Soglasie, 1998), 2:536–537, 552, 556, 560–562.

19. Alexander Solzhenitsyn, *Bodalsia Telenok s Dubom: Ocherki literaturnoi zhizni* (Paris: IMKA-Press, 1975), 63; diary for Kommuna 33, TsADKM, f. 193, op. 1, d. 3, ll. 91–92; Raisa Orlova and Lev Kopelev, *My zhili v Moskve, 1956–1980* (Moscow: Kniga, 1990), 83–84.

20. The evidence on the dates of this conference is confusing. Yuri Gerchuk, "Pochemu Khrushchev prishel v Manezh," *Politicheskii Zhurnal* 46, no. 49 (Dec. 14, 2004), at http://politjournal.ru/index.php?action=Archive; Orlova and Kopelev, *My zhili v Moskve,* 80–81.

21. Mikhail German, *Slozhnoe proshedshee: Passé composé* (St. Petersburg: Pechatnyi Dvor, 2006), 370–71.

22. Andrei Voznesensky, "My-Mai," *Literaturnaia Gazeta,* May 1, 1962, p. 2; Eggeling, *Politika i kultura pri Khrushcheve i Brezhneve,* 127.

23. Joshua Rubenstein, *Tangled Loyalties: The Life and Times of Ilya Ehrenburg* (New York: Basic, 1996), 350.

24. RGANI, f. 5, op. 55 (Ideological Department of the CC CPSU), d. 46, 29–35, 70; *Apparat TsK KPSS i kultura, 1958–1964,* 503–505.

25. Stenogramma vystupleniia Romma, RGANI, f. 5, op. 55, d. 51, ll. 22–32. See the first translation into English in McMillan, *Khrushchev and the Arts,* 95–100; also V. I. Fomin, ed., *Kinematograf ottepeli: Dokumenty i svidetelstva ochevidtsev* (Moscow: Materik, 1998), 315–321.

26. Orlova and Kopelev, *My zhili v Moskve,* 83–84.

27. *Apparat TsK KPSS i Kultura, 1958–1964,* 474–483, 486–495.

28. Tvardovsky, "Rabochie tetradi 60-kh godov," *Znamia* 7 (2000): 121; similar reflections appear in the diary of Tvardovsky's friend the writer Kornei Chukovsky; see Chukovsky, entry for July 1, 1962, *Dnevnik,* 320.

29. *Literaturnaia Gazeta,* Sept. 20, 1962, 1; Muzei Arseniia Tarkovskogo, at http://a88.narod.ru/ars00.htm; Faraday, *Revolt of the Filmmakers,* 92–97.

30. Tvardovsky, entry for July 4, 1962, "Rabochie tetradi 60-kh godov," *Znamia* 7 (2000): 116–117.

31. On Chernoutsan, see Boris Pankin, *Preslovutaia epokha v litsakh i maskakh, sobitiiakh i kazusakh* (Moscow: Voskresenie, 2002), 201–205.

32. Solzhenitsyn, *Bodalsia Telenok s Dubom,* 71–72.

33. David Samoilov, *Podennye zapisi* (Moscow: Vremia, 2002), 1:306.

34. Yaroslav Golovanov, "Beseda na dache," *Komsomolskaia Pravda,* Sept. 9, 1989, p. 4.

35. B. Grushin, *Chetyre vremeni Rossii v zerkale oprosov obshchestvennogo mnenia: Zhizn 1-ia epokha Khrushcheva* (Moscow: Progress-Traditsiia, 2001), 210.

36. Cited in B. Grushin and V. Chikin, *Ispoved pokoleniia* (Moscow: Molodaia Gvardiia, 1962), 71.

37. Allen Kassof, "Now the Angry Young Ivans," *New York Times Magazine*, Nov. 19, 1961, Harrison E. Salisbury, *A New Russia?* (New York: Harper and Row, 1962); "The Problem of Youth in the USSR," p. 70, paper presented at the Twelfth Conference of the Institute for the Study of the USSR, Munich, 1960; The Youth of the Soviet Union, Fourteenth Conference of the Institute for the Study of the USSR, Munich, 1962, "Red Archive" of the Open Society Archive, Budapest, box 497.

38. Cited in Aleksandr Fursenko and Timothy Naftali, *Khrushchev's Cold War* (New York: Norton, 2006), 495–496.

39. Vladimir Kozlov, *Massovye besporiadki v SSSR pri Khrushcheve i Brezhneve, 1953–nachalo 1980-kh gg.* (Novosibirsk: Sibirskii Khronograf, 1999), 308–383; also see the English version: *Mass Uprisings in the USSR: Protest and Rebellion in the Post-Stalin Years* (Armonk, N.Y.: M.E. Sharpe, 2002); P. E. Shelest, *"Da ne sudimy budete": Dnevnikovye zapisi, vospominaniia chlena Politbiuro TsK KPSS* (Moscow: Edition Q, 1992), 154–155.

40. For the text of the letter, see *Istochnik* 6 (2003): 167–168.

41. Nina Moleva, "Manezh kotorogo nikto ne videl: K 40-letiiu nashumevshei vystavki," at http://www.moskvam.ru/2003/03/moleva3.htm; Leonid Rabichev, "Manezh 1962, do i posle," *Znamia* 9 (2001): 126–127.

42. Vladimir Malin's notes at the CC CPSU presidium, Protocol no. 70, meeting of Nov. 29, 1962, in A. Fursenko, *Prezidium TsK KSS, 1954–1964* (Moscow: ROSSPEN, 2003), 1:648.

43. Moleva, "Manezh kotorogo nikto ne videl"; Eli Beliutin, "1 Dekabria 1962 (otryvok iz dnevnikovykh zapisei)," *Ogonyok* 49 (Dec. 8, 1997). See also Nina Moleva, *Eta dolgaia doroga cherez XX vek: Zhizni tvorchestvo Elia Beliutina* (Moscow: Knizhnaia Nakhodka, 2003).

44. Grigory Chukhrai, *Moe Kino* (Moscow: Algoritm, 2002), 117, 135.

45. Valery Fomin, interview with Igor Chernoutsan, sometime in 1989, in V. M. Fomin, *Kino i vlast: Sovetskoie kino, 1965–1985 gody—Dokumenty, svidetelstva, razmyshleniia* (Moscow: Materik, 1996), 160.

46. *Istochnik* 6 (2003): 162; Dmitry Minchenok, "Kak nam bylo strashno," *Ogonyok* 8 (February 2002).

47. *Prezidium TsK KPSS,* 590–593; Tvardovsky, entry for Dec. 13, 1962, "Rabochie tetradi 60-kh godov," *Znamia* 7 (2000): 146; diary of historian and academician Militsa Nechkina, "Dnevniki akademika M. V. Nechkinoi," *Voprosy Istorii* 11 (2005): 115.

48. William Taubman, *Khrushchev: The Man and His Era* (New York: Norton, 2003), 591–592; Mikhail Romm, *Ustnye rasskazy* (Moscow: Komsomolets, 1991), 152–228.

49. Taubman, *Khrushchev,* 591–592.

50. Ibid.; Romm, *Ustnye rasskazy,* 152–228.

51. Yevgeny Yevtushenko, *Volchii pasport* (Moscow: Vagrius, 1998), 282.

52. For the text of the Polish interview with Voznesensky, see RGANI, f. 5, op. 55 (Ideological Department of the CC CPSU), d. 46, ll. 29–35, 70.

53. As mentioned earlier, the Petöfi Club comprised Hungarian intelligentsia calling for a free Hungary in 1956. Andrei Voznesensky, *Proza* (Moscow: Vagrius, 2000), 194.

54. Ibid.

55. Ibid., 194; Taubman, *Khrushchev,* 595.

56. Taubman, *Khrushchev,* 590–595; Rabichev, "Manezh 1962," 132; Voznesensky, *Proza,* 190–191; Yevtushenko, "Fekhtovaniie s navoznoi kuchei," *Volchii pasport,* 196; for excerpts from official minutes of Mar. 7, 1963, meeting, see *Ogonyok* 8 (Feb. 2002); Chukovskaia, *Zapiski ob Anne Akhmatovoi,* 3:49; Anatoly Smeliansky, *The Russian Theater after Stalin,* trans. Patrick Miles (New York: Cambridge University Press, 1999), 22.

57. Taubman, *Khrushchev,* 594.

58. *Pravda,* Mar. 10, 1963; Josephine Woll, *Real Images: Soviet Cinema and the Thaw* (New York: Taurus, 2000), 146–147.

59. Yevtushenko, *Volchii pasport,* 293.

60. Viacheslav Ivanov, "Goluboi zver," *Znamia* 3 (1995): 167, 174.

61. Dmitry S. Likhachev, *Reflections on the Russian Soul: A Memoir* (Budapest: Central European University Press, 2000), 267–268.

62. Rabichev, "Manezh 1962," 141–142.

63. Boris Strugatsky, *Kommentarii k proidennomu, "Esli,"* no. 11–12 (1998), at http://lib.ru/STRUGACKIE/comments.txt.

64. The text of Neizvestny's letter is reproduced in *Istochnik* 6 (2003): 168.

65. *Ideologicheskie komissi TsK KPSS, 1958–1964: Dokumenty* (Moscow: ROSSPEN, 1998). For the meetings of the commission on Dec. 24 and 26, see 301–302, 309–313, 322–323.

66. Yevtushenko, *Volchii pasport,* 298.

67. Neizvestny, *Govorit Neizvestny,* 28–29.

68. Unedited version of stenographic report of the plenum of the CC CPSU, June 18–21, 1963, RGANI, f. 2, op. 1., d. 658, l. 38ob.

69. See the discussions of the Central Committee presidium on Jan. 2 and Apr. 25, 1963, in *Prezidium TsK KPSS,* 712–714.

70. S. Pavlov, "Tvorchestvo molodezhi—sluzheniu velikikh idealov," *Komsomolskaia Pravda,* Mar. 22, 1963; Tvardovsky, entry for Mar. 24, 1963, "Rabochie tetradi 60-kh godov," *Znamia* 9 (2000): 144.

71. Recollections of Vladimir Shubkin, in G. S. Batygin and C. F. Yarmoliuk, eds., *Rossiiskaia sotsiologiia shestidesiatykh godov v vospiminaniiakh i dokumentakh* (St. Petersburg: Russkii Khristianskii Gumanitarnyi Institut, 1999), 74.

72. The literature on Brodsky and his Soviet years is too voluminous to be listed here. For the KGB report on Brodsky, see *Apparat TsK KPSS i Kultura, 1958–1964,* 710–713, 753. On Lerner see Yakov Gordin, "Delo Brodskogo," *Neva* 2 (1989).

73. Among them were the poets Natalia Grudinina, Yakov Gordin, and Natalia Dolinina, as well as the philologist Yefim Etkind.

74. Gordin, "Delo Brodskogo"; Yefim Etkind, *Zapiski nezagovorshchika* (St. Petersburg: Akademicheskii Proekt, 2001), 96–110.

75. Liudmila Alexeeva, *Pokolenie ottepeli* (Moscow: Zakharov, 2006), 108; Orlova and Kopelev, *My zhili v Moskve*, 104–105.

76. Chukovsky, entry for Dec. 16, 1962, *Dnevnik*, 331.

77. Strugatsky, *Kommentarii k proidennomu*.

78. Boris Strugatsky and Arkady Strugatsky, *Trudno byt bogom: Ponedelnik nachinaetsia v subbotu* (Moscow: Molodaia Gvardiia, 1966). The novel was finished in August 1963 and first published in 1964.

79. David Samoilov, *Pamiatnye zapiski* (Moscow: Mezhdunarodnye Otnosheniia, 1995), 363.

7. Searching for Roots, 1961-1967

Epigraph from the interview of the writer Anatoly Rybakov to Marina Goldovskaia in the 1990s, in the documentary film by Marina Goldovskaia *Anatoly Rybakov: The Russian Story,* 2006.

1. Vladimir Soloukhin's *Posledniaia stupen (ispoved vashego sovremennika)* (Moscow: A. O. Delovoi Tsentr, 1995) was written in 1976 but remained unpublished until after the fall of the Soviet Union.

2. See the exposition of this thesis in Geoffrey Hosking, *Rulers and Victims: The Russians in the Soviet Union* (Cambridge, Mass.: Harvard University Press, 2006).

3. Victor Zaslavsky and Robert J. Brym, *Soviet-Jewish Emigration and Soviet Nationality Policy* (Hong Kong: Macmillan, 1983), 102–114, quotation on 112. This pioneering book presents the sociological and historical background on this phenomenon and the emergence of a new Jewish identity in Soviet society, as well as the underlying causes for the new anti-Semitism.

4. Benjamin Nathans, *Beyond the Pale: The Jewish Encounter with Late Imperial Russia* (Berkeley: University of California Press, 2002), 355–364; Michael Stanislawski, *Zionism and the Fin de Siècle: Cosmopolitanism and Nationalism from Nordau to Jabotinsky* (Berkeley: University of California Press, 2001), chap. 6; Yuri Slezkine, *The Jewish Century* (Princeton, N.J.: Princeton University Press, 2004), 69.

5. Zaslavsky and Brym, *Soviet-Jewish Emigration,* 11–17; Terry Martin, *The Affirmative Action Empire: Nations and Nationalism in the Soviet Union, 1923-1939* (Ithaca, N.Y.: Cornell University Press, 2001); Yuri Slezkine, "The USSR as a Communal Apartment, or How a Socialist State Promoted Ethnic Particularism," *Slavic Review* 53 (Summer 1994): 414–452. See also Judith Deutsch Kornblatt, *Doubly Chosen: Jewish Identity, the Soviet Intelligentsia, and the Russian Orthodox Church* (Madison: University of Wisconsin Press, 2004), 53.

6. Among the writers who collaborated on the black book were Pasternak's friend Vsevolod Ivanov, Vasily Grossman, Lidia Seifullina, Margarita Aliger, Viktor Shklovsky, and Veniamin Kaverin. Ilya Altman, "Memorializatsia Kholokosta v Rossii: Istoriia, sovremennost, perspektivy," *Neprikosnovennyi Zapas* 2-3 (2005), at http://magazines.russ.ru/nz/2005/2/alt28.html.

7. On anti-Semitism at the grassroots level during and after the war, see Yelena Zubkova, ed., *Sovetskaia zhizn, 1945-1953* (Moscow: ROSSPEN, 2003), 456–462; Se-

rhy Yekelchyk, "The Civic Duty to Hate: Stalinist Citizenship as Political Practice and Civic Emotion, Kiev, 1943–1953," *Kritika* 7, no. 3 (Summer 2006): 552–554; Amir Weiner, "The Empires Pay a Visit: Gulag Returnees, East European Rebellions, and Soviet Frontier Politics," *Journal of Modern History* 78 (June 2006): 333–376; and Weiner, *Making Sense of War: The Second World War and the Fate of the Bolshevik Revolution* (Princeton, N.J.: Princeton University Press, 2001).

8. Ilya Altman, *Zhertvy nenavisti: Kholokost v SSSR, 1941–1945* (Moscow: Fond Kovcheg, 2002); G. V. Kostyrchenko, *Tainaia politika Stalina: Vlast i antisemitizm* (Moscow: Mezhdunarodnye Otnosheniia, 2001), 422–474.

9. Vasily Grossman, "Treblinskyi ad," at http://lib.ru/PROZA/GROSSMAN/trebl.txt; John Garrard and Carol Garrard, The *Bones of Berdichev: The Life and Fate of Vasily Grossman* (New York: Free Press, 1996).

10. Zaslavsky and Brym, *Soviet-Jewish Emigration,* 27. The best available definition of "Jewish nationality" in the context of Soviet nationality policy can be found here.

11. Benedikt Sarnov, "A nam, evreiam, povezlo," *Lechaim* 11 (Nov. 2002), at http://www.lechaim.ru/ARHIV/127/sarnov.htm.

12. Dina Kaminskaia, *Zapiski advokata* (Kharkov: Folio, 2000), 35.

13. Vladimir Shlapentokh, *Strakh i druzhba v nashem totalitarnom proshlom* (St. Petersburg: Zvezda, 2003), 132.

14. Ibid., 162.

15. On the consequences of these migrations, see Slezkine, *Jewish Century.*

16. Dmitry Polikarpov, memo to the CC CPSU, Dec. 11, 1963, RGANI, f. 5, op. 55, d. 48, l. 6.

17. Maia Plisetskaia, *Ia, Maia* (Moscow: Novosti, 1994), 21–22, 241–243.

18. *Apparat TsK KPSS i Kultura, 1953–1957: Dokumenty* (Moscow: ROSSPEN, 2001), 364, 374; on Yiddish-Soviet culture, see David Shneer, *Yiddish and the Creation of Soviet Jewish Culture, 1918–1930* (New York: Cambridge University Press).

19. *Apparat TsK KPSS i kultura, 1953–1957,* 490–491. At that time forty writers still wrote in Yiddish in Moscow, ten other writers in Kiev, four in Odessa, one in Kharkov, four in Chernovitsa, six in Birobidzhan, two in Minsk, three in Kishinev, and one in Riga.

20. Mikhail Agursky, *Pepel Klaasa: Razryv* (Jerusalem: URA, 1996), 258–259.

21. Joshua Rubenstein, *Tangled Loyalties: The Life and Times of Ilya Ehrenburg* (New York: Basic), 254–255, 274–276; Kostyrchenko, *Tainaia politika Stalina,* 680–681.

22. Anne Frank, *Dnevnik Anni Frank,* trans. R. Rait-Kovaleva, foreword by Ilya Ehrenburg (Moscow: Izdatelstvo Inostrannoi Literatury, 1960), 5–10.

23. Boris Frezinsky, "Pismo Svetlany Stalinoi Ilye Erenburgu," *Voprosy Literatury* 3 (1995). Earlier, Svetlana was in love with the Jewish filmmaker Kapler and was married to a Jew, a student at Moscow State University.

24. Memorandum of the department of culture of the CC CPSU, Jan. 31, 1961, RGANI, f. 5, op. 36, dd. 133, 29; see also the description of this episode in Rubenstein, *Tangled Loyalties,* 329–330.

25. The Russian-Jewish writer Viktor Shklovsky once said that Ehrenburg tried to be Saul and Paul simultaneously. Viktor Shklovsky, "Zoo ili pisma o liubvi," 1924, cited in Benedikt Sarnov, "Sluchai Erenburga," *Lechaim* 11 (Jan. 2003); Benedikt Sarnov, *Sluchai Erenburga* (Moscow: Tekst, 2004), 356–358.

26. Varlam Shalamov, "Zapisnye knizhki, 1954–1979," at http://www.srcc.msu.su/uni-persona/site/authors/shalamov/zapkn_54–79.htm; Kornei Chukovsky, *Dnevnik, 1930–1969* (Moscow: Sovremennyi Pisatel, 1995), 312.

27. David Samoilov, *Podennye zapisi* (Moscow: Vremia, 2002), 1:268.

28. Mikhail German, *Slozhnoe proshedshee: Passé composé* (St. Petersburg: Pechatnyi Dvor, 2006), 207. The critic Stanislav Rassadin recalled in his memoirs that many people could not believe that he was a Russian, not a Jew. Stanislav Rassadin, *Kniga Proshchanii: Vospominaniia o druziakh i ne tolko o nikh* (Moscow: Tekst, 2004), 58–61.

29. Yevgeny Yevtushenko, *A Precocious Autobiography* (New York: Dutton, 1963), 80–81; Yevtushenko, *Volchii pasport* (Moscow: Vagrius, 1998), 79–80.

30. Pyotr Vail and Alexander Ghenis, *60-e: Mir sovetskogo cheloveka*, 2nd ed. (Moscow: Novoe Literaturnoe Obozrenie, 1998), 299–300.

31. Stenogramma soveshchaniia molodykh poetov v TsK VLKSM, Sept. 27, 1961, TsKDMO, f 1, op. 5, d. 810, ll. 45, 68–70, 94, 106–108, 135–137.

32. Stenogramma vystupleniia Romma, RGANI, f. 5, op. 55, d. 51, ll. 22–32; see English translation in Priscilla Johnson and Leopold Labedz, *Khrushchev and the Arts: The Politics of Soviet Culture, 1962–1964* (Cambridge, Mass.: MIT Press, 1965), 95–100. See also V. I. Fomin, ed., *Kinematograf ottepeli: Dokumenty i svidetelstva ochevidtsev* (Moscow: Materik, 1998), 315–321.

33. RGANI, f. 5, op. 55, d. 51, ll. 2–3, 4–9, 11–16, 33–34, 36–37.

34. Semyon Charny, "Razvitie tsenzurnogo antisemitizma v period 'ottepeli' (na primere sudby knigi B. Marka 'Vosstanie v Varshavskom ghetto')" (Moscow: Assotsiatsia Studentov Iudaiki, 1996), at http://www.jewish-heritage.org/jr1a4r.htm.

35. Glavlit (state censorship), *Spravka Glavlita* (memorandum), May 27, 1964, *Voprosy Literatury* 1 (1995): 327.

36. Recollections of this meeting by Igor Chernoutsan (unpublished manuscript); *Istochnik* 6 (2003): 162. Dmitry Minchenok, "Kak nam bylo strashno," *Ogonyok* 8 (Feb. 2002); William Taubman, *Khrushchev: The Man and His Era* (New York: Norton, 2003), 592; Chukovsky, *Dnevnik*, 338–339.

37. Stenograficheskaia zapis zasedaniia Prezidiuma TsK KPSS, July 1, 1959, A. A. Fursenko, ed., *Prezidium TsK KPSS, 1954–1964: Chernovye protokolnye zapisi zasedanii*, vol. 1, *Stenogrammy: Postanovlenia* (Moscow: ROSSPEN, 2003), 366–367, 380–381; Yelena Zubkova, "Vlast i razvitie etnokonfliktnoi situatsii v SSSR, 1953–1985," *Otechestvennaia Istoria* 4 (2005): 8.

38. Andrei Siniavsky, *Syntaksis* 26 (1988); Siniavsky's file at the archive of Memorial, St. Petersburg.

39. Most notably, this trend revealed itself in the *Vekhi* (Landmarks), a collection of essays by Russian intellectuals published in 1909. See *Vekhi: Sbornik statei o Russkoi*

intelligentsii (Moscow, Kushnerev, 1909); Richard Pipes, *Struve: Liberal on the Right, 1905–1944* (Cambridge, Mass.: Harvard University Press, 1980), 106–113.

40. A. N. Artizov and Z. K. Vodopianova, *"Ochistim Rossiiu nadolgo . . . ": Repressii protiv inakomysliashchikh, Konets 1921–nachalo 1923* (Moscow: Materik, 2008), 78–80; Stuart Finkel, *On the Ideological Front: The Russian Intelligentsia and the Making of the Soviet Public Sphere* (New Haven, Conn.: Yale University Press, 2007), 103–112.

41. Norman Cohn, *Warrant for Genocide: The Myth of the Jewish World Conspiracy and the Protocols of the Elders of Zion* (London: Interlink, 2001); and see the more popular, yet nuanced, version in Tom Reiss, *The Orientalist* (New York: Random House, 2005), 176–179.

42. Martin, *The Affirmative Action Empire,* esp. 20.

43. Ibid., 437–461; David Brandenberger, *National Bolshevism: Stalinist Mass Culture and the Formation of Modern Russian National Identity, 1931–1956* (Cambridge, Mass.: Harvard University Press, 2002).

44. "Rech tovarishcha Khrushcheva na soveshchanii apparata Leningradskogo oblastnogo i gorodskogo komitetov KPSS," May 8, 1954, *Istochnik* 6 (2003): 12.

45. Nikolai Mitrokhin, *Russkaia partiia: Dvizhenie russkikh natsionalistov v SSSR, 1953–1985* (Moscow: Novoe Literaturnoe Obozrenie, 2003), 151–152, 161.

46. Rovel Kashapov, "Sotsialist-monarkhist iz Kazani," Feb. 25, 2005, at http://www.narodru.ru/smi1817.html; John Curtis Perry and Konstantin Pleshakov, *The Flight of the Romanovs: A Family Saga* (New York: Basic, 2002), 299–300, 305–306.

47. Shulgin (1878–1976) was among those who in February 1917 had accepted the abdication of Tsar Nicholas II, and then of his brother Mikhail. Shulgin fought against the Bolsheviks in the Civil War and lost. He finally concluded that the Russian empire and monarchy were gone forever and that Lenin's regime, paradoxically, remained the best option for the restoration of a Russian empire. Arrested by the Soviet secret police in 1944 in Yugoslavia, he spent time in the camps and was released in 1956. The KGB allowed him to settle down in the old Russian city of Vladimir to the north of Moscow. V. V. Shulgin, *Gody, Dni: Memuary* (Moscow: Novosti, 1990), 795–797; Alexander Repnikov, "Vasily Vasilievich Shulgin," at http://pravaya.ru/ludi/450/808?print=1.

48. Yevtushenko, *Volchii pasport,* 284–285; Mitrokhin, *Russkaia Partiia,* 149, 152; N. N. Skatov, ed., *Russkie pisateli, XX vek: Biograficheskii slovar v 2kh chastiakh* (Moscow: Prosveshcheniie, 1998), 370.

49. *Apparat TsK KPSS i kultura, 1953–1957,* 492–493.

50. I. Shevtsov to the Central Committee, July 16, 1957, RGANI, f. 5, op. 30, d. 189, ll. 50–62.

51. Mitrokhin, *Russkaia Partiia,* 66; I. M. Shevtsov, *Tlia: Sokoly* (Moscow: Golos, 2000), 5–6; Shevtsov, "Chto bylo, to bylo" *Zavtra* 6, no. 167 (Feb. 11, 1997).

52. On Likhachev's views, see O. V. Panchenko, *D. S. Likhachev: Vospominaniia, Razdumia, Raboty raznykh let,* vol. 2 (St. Petersburg: Ars, 2006); also his papers in

Fond 769, Manuscript Division of the Institute of Russian Literature (Pushkin House), St. Petersburg.

53. Yitzhak M. Brudny found that a great majority of the Russian nationalists who entered the political arena between 1953 and 1964 represented "two consecutive generations," the wartime generation and the postwar generation. Brudny, *Reinventing Russia: Russian Nationalism and the Soviet State, 1953-1991* (Cambridge, Mass.: Harvard University Press, 1998), 34, 36.

54. See Zaslavsky and Brym, *Soviet-Jewish Emigration,* 111-112.

55. Mitrokhin, *Russkaia Partiia,* 5.

56. Aside from Vladimir Soloukhin, it is worth mentioning the talented writer Yuri Bondarev, a war veteran, whose novels about war and the postwar period were at odds with the official "varnished" literature and attracted enormous interest and respect among the reading public in the early 1960s. Other "Russian patriots" who were university graduates of the 1950s were Vadim Kozhinov, Stanislav Kuniaev, Oleg Mikhailov, Sergei Semanov, Viktor Petelin, and Viktor Chalmaev. Mitrokhin, *Russkaia Partiia,* 152, 200-201.

57. For the incomplete anthology of books that circulated secretly during the 1950s, see the Web site for Viacheslav Igrunov, at http://antology.igrunov.ru/50-s/esse/.

58. Mikhail Lobanov, "Na peredovoi (opyt dukhovnoi avtobiografii)," *Nash Sovremennik* 2 (Feb. 2002): 168-198.

59. For a typical attitude see Alexei Kozlov, *Kozel na sakse,* at http://www.lib.ru/CULTURE/MUSIC/KOZLOV/kozel_na_saxe.txt, 147-149.

60. On Glazunov, see Alexander Prokhanov and Vladimir Bondarenko, "Imperiia Glazunova," at http://zavtra.ru/cgi//veil//data/zavtra/02/457/21.html; Igor Golomshtok, "Fenomen Glazunova," *Syntaksis* 4 (1979): 119-135; and L. Kolodny, *Liubov i nenavist Ilyi Glazunova* (Moscow: Golos, 1998).

61. Mikhail Gorbachev, *Zhizn i reformy* (Moscow: Novosti, 1995), 1:160-161.

62. *Ideologicheskiie komissii, Tsk KPSS, 1958-1964: Dokumenty* (Moscow, ROSSPEN, 2000), 323-333; for background on the cathedral, see Konstantin Akinsha and Grigory Kozlov, with Sylvia Hochfield, *The Holy Place* (Cambridge, Mass.: Harvard University Press, 2007).

63. Pyotr Baranovsky, *Trudy, vospominaniia sovremennikov* (Moscow: Otchii Dom, 1996), 183; Mitrokhin, *Russkaia Partiia,* 301-302; Stephen V. Bittner, *The Many Lives of Khrushchev's Thaw: Experience and Memory in Moscow's Arbat* (Ithaca, N.Y.: Cornell University Press, 2008), 153-164.

64. To the plenum of the CC CPSU on the Ideological Question, June 18, 1963, RGANI, f. 5, op. 55, d. 49, ll. 68-74; for other appeals, see ibid., ll. 39-65.

65. Vladimir Soloukhin, *Posledniaia stupen.* In Soloukhin's novel Glazunov is given the pseudonym Kirill Burenin; V. Desiatnikov's diary, as quoted in Nikolai Mitrokhin, *Russkaia Partiia,* 209.

66. Khrushchev and Ilichev were reacting to suggestions from some writers that they distance themselves from the nefarious clique. See May 1963 letter from Stepan

Zlobin to Khrushchev, in "Stepan Zlobin: Iz arkhiva," *Voprosy Literatury* 4 (1998): 309–320.

67. Taubman, *Khrushchev,* 191; Mitrokhin, *Russkaia Partiia,* 167.

68. Mikhail Lobanov, "Na peredovoi (opyt dukhovnoi avtobiografii)," *Nash Sovremennik* 3 (Mar. 2002): 97–99.

69. Motto cited in Yevgeny Dobrenko, *Formovka sovetskogo pisatelia: Sotsialnye i esteticheskie istoki sovetskoi literaturnoi kultury* (St. Petersburg: Akademicheskii Proekt, 1999), 479; and Lev Gudkov and Boris Dubin, *Intelligentsiia: Zametki o literaturno-politicheskikh illuziiakh* (Moscow: Epitsentr-Folio, 1995); Gudkov and Dubin, *Literatura kak sotsialnyi institut: Statyi po sotsiologii literatury* (Moscow: Novoe Literaturnoe Obozrenie, 1994).

70. The role of Tvardovsky and *Novy Mir* in the 1960s remains contested in Russian publications to this day. See, for instance, Yuri Burtin, "O staliniste Tvardovskom, kotoryi terpel i molchal," *Nezavisimaia Gazeta,* Apr. 8, 2000; Regina Romanova, *Alexandr Tvardovsky: Trudy i dni* (Moscow: Vodolei, 2006); E. Vysochina, ed., *A. Tvardovsky: M. Gefter, XX vek—Gologrammy poeta i istorika* (Moscow: Novyi Khronograf, 2005).

71. Entry for Feb. 17, 1957, Tvardovsky, "Iz rabochikh tetradei (1953–1960)," *Znamia* 8 (1989): 122.

72. Entry for Oct. 6, 1960, Tvardovsky, "Iz rabochikh tetradei," *Znamia* 9 (1989): 201–202.

73. Semyon Lipkin, *Zhizn i sudba Vasilia Grossmana* (Moscow: Kniga, 1990); Anna Berzer, *Proshchaniie* (Moscow: Kniga, 1990); Garrard and Garrard, *The Bones of Berdichev;* Frank Ellis, *Vasily Grossman: The Genesis and Evolution of a Russian Heretic* (Providence, R.I.: Berg, 1994).

74. Entry for Sept. 26, 1961, Tvardovsky, "Rabochie tetradi 60-kh godov," *Znamia* 6 (2000): 134.

75. Chukovsky, *Dnevnik,* 333.

76. Entry for Feb. 1959, Tvardovsky, "Iz rabochikh tetradei," *Znamia* 9 (1989): 143–144, 154.

77. Fyodor Abramov, *Chem zhivem—kormimsia* (Leningrad: Sovetsky Pisatel, 1986), 45–91; Brudny, *Reinventing Russia,* 50–52.

78. Felix Svetov, *Opyt biografii* (Moscow: Memorial-Zvenia, 2006), 354–356.

79. Vladimir Lakshin, *Golosa i litsa* (Moscow: Geleos, 2004), esp. 52–73; Brudny, *Reinventing Russia,* 54. Alexander Solzhenitsyn, however, passed his manuscript to Kochetov, in an effort to publish it. Alexander Solzhenitsyn, *The Oak and the Calf: Sketches of Literary Life in the Soviet Union,* trans. Harry Willetts (New York: Harper and Row, 1975), 121–123.

80. S. Pavlov, "Tvorchestvo molodykh—sluzheniiu velikim idealam," *Komsomolskaia Pravda,* Mar. 22, 1963.

81. Diary entries for Apr. 14 and 15, 1964, Tvardovsky, "Rabochie tetradi 60-kh godov," *Znamia* 11 (2000): 163–165.

82. Ludmilla Alexeyeva and Paul Goldberg, *The Thaw Generation: Coming of Age in the Post-Stalin Era* (Pittsburgh: University of Pittsburgh Press, 1990), 96.

83. Diary for Kommuna 33, TsADKM, f. 193, op. 1, d. 3, ll. 131ob, 242–242ob.

84. Diary of Alexander Pismenny, husband of N. Bianky, member of *Novy Mir*'s staff, TsAODM, fond Pismennogo, op. 3, dd. 97, 98, 99; Denis Kozlov, "The Readers of *Novyi Mir*, 1945–1970: Twentieth-Century Experience and Soviet Historical Consciousness" (Ph.D. dissertation, University of Toronto); I. Brainin, "'Ne mogu ne napisat': Petr Grigorenko—Alexandru Solzhenitsinu o Tvardovskom i 'Novom Mire'" *Obshchaia Gazeta*, Jan. 19–25, 1995.

85. Entries for Aug. 31–Sept. 12, 1965, Tvardovsky, "Rabochie tetradi 60-kh godov," *Znamia* 2 (2002): 144.

86. Mark Kachurin and Maria Shneerson, "Chetyre vstrechi," *Zhurnal Vestnik Online* 12 (June 9, 2004); Vladimir Lakshin, *"Novy Mir" vo vremena Khrushcheva: Dnevnik i poputnoe, 1953–1964* (Moscow: Knizhnaia Palata, 1991), 207–208.

87. Samoilov, *Podennye zapisi*, 2:15–16.

88. Kachurin and Shneerson, "Chetyre vstrechi."

89. Vladimir Semichastny, KGB to CC CPSU, Sept. 30, 1965, RGANI, f. 5, op. 30, d. 462, ll. 106–107.

90. Lakshin, *"Novy Mir" vo vremena Khrushcheva*, 247.

91. Entries for Dec. 21, 1963, and Feb. 27, 1964, Tvardovsky, "Rabochie tetradi 60-kh godov," *Znamia* 9 (2000): 174; ibid., 11 (2000): 148.

92. Entry for Aug. 17, 1965, Tvardovsky, "Rabochie tetradi 60-kh godov," *Znamia* 2 (2002): 140.

93. Jack V. Haney, "The Revival of Interest in the Russian Past in the Soviet Union," *Slavic Review* 32, no. 1 (Mar. 1973): 1–16.

94. Boris Metalnikov, "Ottepel—vremia debiutov," *Iskusstvo Kino*, 5 (1998): 140; ibid., 6 (1998): 149.

95. Agursky, *Pepel Klaasa*, 258–259; Kornblatt, *Doubly Chosen*, 69–79.

96. Alexander (Alik) Men was born in 1935 to Jewish parents. His father, Wolf Men, was familiar with Judaism and became a Zionist, but Alik's mother adopted Orthodox Christianity and had him baptized. Alexander Men could not become a student at MGU, presumably because of his Jewish background, but also possibly because his religiosity became known. He managed to receive a secular education at the Institute of Fur. He also developed into a well-rounded and erudite intellectual, mastering philology, history, and Catholic as well as Orthodox exegesis. For more of his biography, see Yves Hamant, *Alexandr Men: Svidetel svoiego vremeni* (Moscow: Rudomino, 1994); Zoia Maslenikova, *Zhizn ottsa Alexandra Menia* (Moscow: Pristsels-Russlit, 1995).

97. Kornblatt, *Doubly Chosen*, 78–80; Averintsev quoted in Elizabeth Roberts and Ann Shukman, eds., *Christianity for the Twenty-first Century: The Prophetic Writings of Alexander Men* (New York: Continuum, 1996), 11; A. I. Zorin and V. I. Iliushenko, eds., *Vokrug imeni ottsa Aleksandra* (Moscow: Obshchestvo "Kulturnoe Vozro-

zhdenie" Imeni Aleksandra Menia, 1993), 82. For further reminiscences from the converted brethren, see N. F. Grigorenko-Men, P. V. Men, T. A. Zhirmunskaia, M. V. Sergeeva, eds., *I bylo utro . . . Vospominaniia ob ottse Alexandre Mene* (Moscow: AP "Vita-Tsentr," 1992).

98. Kornblatt, *Doubly Chosen.*

99. Solzhenitsyn expounded these views later in his controversial book *Dvesti let vmeste* (Moscow: Russky Put, 2001). Rejected by scholars and denounced as anti-Semitic by Solzhenitsyn's former admirers, this work, however, reflected an evolution of the writer's thinking on the Jewish question that had begun in the 1960s.

100. Robert Louis Jackson, "'Matryona's Home': The Making of a Russian Icon," in Kathryn Feuer, ed., *Solzhenitsyn: A Collection of Critical Essays* (Englewood Cliffs, N.J., 1976); Sheryl A. Spitz, "The Impact of Structure in Solzhenitsyn's 'Matryona's Home,'" *Russian Review* 36, no. 2 (Apr. 1977): 174.

101. On the transition of assimilated cosmopolitan Jews to Zionism in the early twentieth century, see Stanislawski, *Zionism and the Fin de Siècle.*

102. On the antagonism between the cosmopolitan liberals and Russian nationalists, see Solzhenitsyn, *Dvesti let vmeste*, pt. 2, 436–448. On pro-Zionist sympathies, see Boris Morozov, ed., *Evreiskaia emigratsiia v svete novykh dokumentov* (Tel Aviv: Ivrus, 1998).

103. Among the evidence on the rise of Jewish pride in June 1967 see recollections of Leonid Gozman, one of the participants of the rally, in Noah Lewin-Epstein, Yaacov Ro'i, and Paul Ritterband, eds., *Russian Jews on Three Continents* (London: Frank Cass, 1997), 409.

104. KGB to the CC CPSU, Nov. 17, 1967, published in Morozov, *Evreiskaia emigratsiia,* 60–61; Leonid Gozman, ibid.

105. Samoilov, *Podennye zapisi,* 2:15–16; Samoilov, *Pamiatnye zapiski* (Moscow: Mezhdunarodnye Otnosheniia, 2001), 365–366.

106. Grigory Pomerants, *Zapiski gadkogo utenka* (Moscow: Moskovskii Rabochii, 1998), 321–322. See also Pomerants, *Neopublikovannoe* (Frankfurt-am-Main: Posev, 1972), 163; and George L. Kline, "Religion, National Character, and the 'Rediscovery of Russian Roots,'" *Slavic Review* 32, no. 1 (Mar. 1973): 30–31.

107. Zaslavsky and Brym, *Soviet-Jewish Emigration,* 116.

108. Ibid., 110–112.

109. On the role of the intelligentsia as a generator of nationalism, and the special limitations in the Russian case, see Nathaniel Knight, "Was the Intelligentsia Part of the Nation? Visions of Society in Post-Emancipation Russia," *Kritika* 7, no. 4 (Fall 2006): 733–758.

8. Between Reform and Dissent, 1965–1968

1. The literature on this movement, produced mostly during the 1970s and 1980s, is enormous. Among the more authoritative studies are Frederick C. Barghoorn, *Détente and the Democratic Movement in the USSR* (New York: Free Press, 1976);

Abraham Brumberg, ed., *In Quest of Justice: Protest and Dissent in the Soviet Union Today* (New York: Praeger, 1970); Peter Reddaway, *Uncensored Russia: Protest and Dissent in the Soviet Union* (New York: American Heritage, 1972); Marshall S. Shatz, *Soviet Dissent in Historical Perspective* (New York: Cambridge University Press, 1981); Dietrich Beyrau, *Intelligenz und Dissens: Die russichen Bildungsschichten in der Sowjetunion, 1917 bis 1985* (Göttingen: Vanderhoeck und Ruprecht, 1993); Liudmila Alexeeva, *Istoriia inakomysliia v SSSR: Noveishii period* (Moscow: Vest, 1992). Fresh analysis in light of the Soviet collapse can be found in Mario Corti, "O nekotorykh aspektakh dissidentskogo dvizheniia," presentation at the conference Dissidentskoie dvizheniie v SSSR, 1950-e–1980-e, organized by Memorial in Moscow, Aug. 1992, at http://www.mario-corti.com/press/#5.

2. The KGB reported on the overwhelmingly positive reaction of the Soviet military and the "working masses" to Brezhnev's speech. RGANI, f. 5, op. 30, d. 462, ll. 38–39, 58–64; See Catherine Merridale, *Night of Stone: Death and Memory in Modern Russia* (New York: Viking, 2001), 148, 155, 415; Polly Jones, "Memories of Terror or Terrorizing Memories? Terror, Trauma and Survival in Soviet Culture of the Thaw," *Slavonic and East European Review* 86, no. 2 (Apr. 2008), special issue, *The Relaunch of the Soviet Project, 1945–46*, 346–371.

3. Paul R. Josephson, *New Atlantis Revisited: Akademgorodok, the Siberian City of Science* (Princeton, N.J.: Princeton University Press, 1997), 23; L. Churchward, *The Soviet Intelligentsia* (London: Routledge, 1973), 9; Mikhail German, *Slozhnoe proshedshee: Passé composé* (St. Petersburg: Pechatnyi Dvor, 2006), 418.

4. Moshe Lewin, *Stalinism and the Seeds of Soviet Reform: The Debates of the 1960s* (Armonk, N.Y.: Sharpe, 1991), vii.

5. Vladimir Shlapentokh, *Soviet Intellectuals and Political Power* (Princeton, N.J.: Princeton University Press, 1991), 172. See also Rudolf Pikhoia, *Sovetskii Soiuz: Istoriia vlasti, 1945–1991* (Moscow: RAGS, 1998), 283.

6. For an attempted revision of this Cold War interpretation, see Jeremi Suri, "The Promise and Failure of 'Developed Socialism': The Soviet 'Thaw' and the Crucible of the Prague Spring," *Contemporary European History* 15, no. 2 (2006): 139–143.

7. Files on the members of the Bell group can be found in the archive of Memorial, St. Petersburg.

8. KGB to Central Committee, Dec. 11, 1965, RGANI, op. 30, d. 462, ll. 249–256.

9. Nina Voronel, *Bez prikras: Vospominaniia* (Moscow: Zakharov, 2003), 144–145.

10. Letter to Igor Kokhanovsky, Dec. 20, 1965, in Pyotr Soldatenkov, *Vladimir Vysotsky* (Moscow: Olimp, 1999), 144.

11. Voronel, *Bez prikras*, 144.

12. Grigory Pomerants, quoted in "Dissidenty o dissidentstve," *Znamia* (1997–98), special issue, 173. See also Pomerants, *Zapiski gadkogo utenka* (Moscow: Moskovskii Rabochii, 1998), 308.

13. Alexeyeva and Goldberg, *The Thaw Generation*, 122.

14. Pomerants, *Zapiski gadkogo utenka*, 336–337; Vitaly Rubin, *Dnevniki—Pisma*, vols. 1–2 (Jerusalem, Biblioteka Aliya, 1988–89).

15. Benjamin Nathans, "The Dictatorship of Reason: Aleksandr Vol'pin and the Idea of Rights under 'Developed Socialism,'" *Slavic Review* 55, no. 4 (Winter 2007): 636–658; recollections of Alexander Volpin, in A. Daniel and A. Roginsky, eds., *Piatoe dekabria 1965 goda,* at http://www.memo.ru/history/diss/books/5dec/index.htm.

16. The founders of SMOG were Yuri Kublanovsky, Vladimir Aleinikov, and Leonid Gubanov. See "Ochishchaiushchii SMOG," *Molodoi Kommunist* 8 (1989): 79–89; "Pamiati SMOGa," *Strelets,* Dec. 1987; recollections of Viktoria Volpina, in Daniel and Roginsky, *Piatoie dekabria;* Vladimir Aleinikov, *SMOG: Roman-poema* (Moscow: OGI, 2008); and Sergei Pavlov to Central Committee, Dec. 8, 1965, RGANI, op. 30, d. 462, ll. 181–184.

17. Alexeyeva and Goldberg, *The Thaw Generation,* 122–124. See also Alexeeva, *Istoriia inakomysliia v SSSR,* and materials collected in the archive of Memorial; Daniel and Roginsky, *Piatoe dekabria.*

18. Max Hayward, ed., *On Trial: The Soviet State versus "Abram Tertz" and "Nikolai Arzhak"* (New York: Harper and Row, 1966); Alexeyeva and Goldberg, *The Thaw Generation,* 120–124, 127; *New York Times,* Dec. 18, 1965; recollections of the participants at Radio Liberty on Dec. 10, 2005, at the site of the Moscow Helsinki Group, at http://www.mhg.ru/smi/62E2314.

19. Alexeyeva and Goldberg, *The Thaw Generation,* 117–120, 138–141; http://www.mhg.ru/smi/62E2314.

20. Alexander Tvardovsky, entry for Feb. 15, 1966, "Rabochie tetradi," *Znamia* 4 (2002): 145–146; Denis Kozlov, "'I Have Not Read, but I Will Say': Soviet Literary Audiences and Changing Ideas of Social Membership, 1958–1966," *Kritika* 7, no. 3 (Summer 2006): 580–595; Catherine Theimer Nepomnyashchy, *Abram Terz and the Poetics of Crime* (New Haven, Conn.: Yale University Press, 1995); Liudmila Alexeeva, *Pokolenie ottepeli* (Moscow: Zakharov, 2006), 145.

21. Raisa Orlova and Lev Kopelev, *My zhili v Moskve, 1956–1980* (Moscow: Kniga, 1990), 110; recollections of Maria Rozanova (Siniavskaia), in *Znamia* (1997–98), special issue, 175.

22. S. Chuikina, "Uchastie zhenshchin v dissidentskom dvizhenii, 1956–1986," at http://www.a-z.ru/women/texts/chuikinr.htm; author's interview with Natalia Gorbanevskaia, June 10, 2008, Paris.

23. I adapted this quote from an essay about Andrei Sakharov: Raisa Orlova and Lev Kopelev, "The Sources of Miracle," in Alexander Babyonyshev, ed., *On Sakharov,* trans. Guy Daniels (New York: Knopf, 1982), 76–79. In my opinion, however, this characterization of the two influences is an autobiographical reconstruction. The belief can be attributed both to them and to the majority of other activists in the new movement as well.

24. Bonner was of Armenian and Jewish origin. She belonged to the milieu of children of Old Bolsheviks and functionaries of the Communist International. Many decades later she described herself at the time as "a person without an intelligible view of the world." In reality, Bonner had taken her ethical views from Russian

classical literature, as well as the prerevolutionary sentimental stories of Lidia Charskaia. Bonner also, like many victims of Stalinist terror, had a passionate desire to remain a social optimist and bridge the gap that her private tragedy opened between her happy Soviet childhood and the uncertain future. Yelena Bonner, *Dochki-materi* (New York: Chekhov, 1991); biographical data on Yelena Bonner, at http://www.prison.org/personal/boner.htm; Yelena Bonner, "Do Dnevnikov," *Znamia* 11 (2005): 62–128; material in "Rossiiskaia Gazeta," at http://www.rg.ru/Anons/arc_2003/0214/1.shtm; Bonner's recollections appear in *Literaturnaia Gazeta*, May 9, 1995, and in her acceptance speech for the 2000 Hannah Arendt Award, *Sunday Times* (London), Feb. 18, 2001; Andrei Sakharov, *Memoirs* (New York: Knopf, 1990), 283; Houghton Library, Harvard University, Andrei Sakharov Papers, MS Russ 79, box 88, folder S.II.2.6.1.45.

25. Orlova and Kopelev, *My zhili v Moskve*, 111–112.

26. The text of the letter appears in Hayward, *On Trial*, 284–285; Neia Zorkaia, "Nezabyvaemyi 1968-i," in V. I. Fomin, ed., *Kino i vlast: Sovetskoie kino, 1965–1985 gody* (Moscow: Materik, 1996), 434–437. The list of signatories included the writers Paustovsky, Kataev, and Nekrasov; the poet Slutsky; the filmmakers Mikhail Romm and Marlene Khutsiev; the dancer Maia Plisetskaia; the director of Sovremennik Theater, Yefremov; and luminaries from the Soviet atomic project, including Leonid Artsimovich, Igor Tamm, and Andrei Sakharov. "Obrashchenie k L. I. Brezhnevu deiatelei nauki i iskusstva," Feb. 14, 1966, RGANI, f. 5, op. 30, d. 487, ll. 40–42, in V. I. Fomin, *Kinematograf Ottepeli: Dokumenty i svidetelstva ochevidtsev* (Moscow: Materik, 1998), 49–52; Andrei Sakharov, *Vospominaniia* (New York: Chekhov, 1990), 353–354.

27. Babyonyshev, *On Sakharov*, 78–79.

28. Sakharov set forth these views in his interview with Ernst Henri, a correspondent for *Literaturnaia Gazeta*. The interview was never published. Earlier, in July 1964, Sakharov had written to Khrushchev that "young members of the intelligentsia stood firmly in support of the line of the Twentieth and Twenty-second Party Congresses in all ideological battles." Houghton Library, Harvard University, Andrei Sakharov Papers, MS Russ 79, box 51, folders S.IV.2.1.01 and S.III.1.2.28.3. See also Gennady Gorelik and Andrei Sakharov, *Nauka i svoboda* (Moscow: Vagrius, 2004), 427–428.

29. For a conceptual piece on the circulation of audiotapes, see J. Martin Daughtry, "*Magnetizdat* as Cultural Practice," paper presented at the conference Samizdat and Underground Culture in the Soviet Bloc Countries, University of Pennsylvania, Apr. 6–7, 2006; Pyotr Vail and Alexander Genis, "Shampanskoe i politura," *Vremia i My* 36 (1978): 134–142, cited in Daughtry, ibid., 9. Some critics characterize the ballads of *magnetizdat* singers, such as Okudzhava, as "pseudoprotest," to contrast them with the protest of dissident movement. In my opinion, the songs were essential for the emergence of public dissent and solidarity within the sixties intelligentsia.

30. On Galich, see http://agalich.narod.ru/; N. G. Kreitner, *Zaklinanie dobra i zla:*

Alexandr Galich (Moscow: Progress, 1991); Gerald Stanton Smith, ed. and trans., *Alexander Galich: Songs and Poems* (Ann Arbor, Mich.: Ardis, 1983).

31. Peter Reddaway, ed., *Uncensored Russia: Protest and Dissent in the Soviet Union* (New York: American Heritage, 1972), 83–85. An American analyst found that among the signatories were thirty-four civil engineers, twenty-four physicists and mathematicians, twenty-two philologists, twenty writers, seventeen mathematicians, seventeen teachers, fifteen scientific researchers, thirteen undergraduate students, ten literary critics, ten historians, nine editors, nine graduate students, eight physicists, eight philosophers, seven economists, and so on. Paul A. Smith, "Protest in Moscow," *Foreign Affairs* (Oct. 1968): 156.

32. Alexander Voronel, "Twenty Years Later," in Noah Lewin-Epstein, Yaacov Ro'i, and Paul Ritterband, eds., *Russian Jews on Three Continents* (London: Frank Cass, 1997), 422–423.

33. Felix Chuev, *Sto sorok besed s Molotovym* (Moscow: Moskovskii Rabochii, 1990), 274.

34. Bonner, acceptance speech for the 2000 Hannah Arendt Award.

35. See, for instance, R. Markwick, "Catalyst of Historiography, Marxism and Dissidence: The Sector of Methodology of the Institute of History, Soviet Academy of Science, 1964–68," *Europe-Asia Studies* 46, no. 4 (1994): 579–596.

36. Houghton Library, Harvard University, Andrei Sakharov Papers, MS Russ 79, box 88, folder S.IV.22.17, p. 176.

37. Konstantin Simonov, "Stalin i voina: Uroki istorii i dolg pisatelia," Apr. 28, 1965, at http://www.hronos.km.ru/dokum/197_dok/19650428sim.html.

38. These twin brothers were born in 1925 in Tbilisi into the family of a Red Army brigade commissar, who named his boys after famous Indian and French socialists. In 1938 the commissar was arrested and sent to one of Stalin's camps, where he later died. Zhores graduated from the Agricultural Academy and Roy graduated from Leningrad University with a philosophy major. Roy, unable to pursue his career as a historian, instead worked as a schoolteacher. After Khrushchev's secret speech, the father was rehabilitated, and Roy Medvedev joined the party. His friends, surviving Old Bolsheviks and children of Stalin's victims, helped him find a job in Moscow. For Roy Medvedev's biography, see http://antology.igrunov.ru/authors/roy.

39. Zhores Medvedev, "Biologicheskaia nauka i kult lichnosti," manuscript reprinted in 1969 in the West under the title "The Rise and Fall of T. D. Lysenko." The Cyrillic version can be found in a Russian anthology of samizdat, at http://antology.igrunov.ru/authors/zh_medv/razgrom.html. Sakharov, *Vospominaniia*, 359–360, 376–377.

40. For the larger context of the "academic dissent," see A. B. Bezborodov, *Fenomen akademicheskogo dissidentstva v SSSR* (Moscow: RGGU, 1998).

41. Among them were Vladimir Danilov, Yevgeny Plimak, Pyotr Yakir, Aron Avrekh, Pavel Volobuev, Mikhail Gefter, and Konstantin Tarnovsky. L. V. Danilova, "Partii-

naia organizatsiia Instituta istorii AN SSSR v ideinom protivostoianii s partiinymi instantsiiami, 1966–1968 gg," *Voprosy Istorii* 12 (2007): 44–50; and recollections of the historians Lev Slezkine and Nelli Komolova, in *Otreshivshiisia ot strakha: Pamiati A. M. Nekricha: Vospominaniia, statyi, dokumenty* (Moscow: Institut Vseobshchei Istorii RAN, 1996), 23–26, 121; Yevgeny Plimak, *Na voine i posle voiny: Zapiski veterana* (Moscow: Ves Mir, 2005), 135–139.

42. "Delo Nekricha," *Kentavr* 4 (1994): 94–114; ibid., 5 (1994): 82–97.

43. Like so many, Nekrich came from a Jewish family that worshipped communist internationalism. After World War II, despite Stalin's anti-Semitic campaign, Nekrich managed to graduate from Moscow State University, where he later completed his graduate studies. He found a job at the Institute of History of the Soviet Academy of Sciences. He was careful enough to keep a low profile when some of the established Soviet historians (Eduard Burdzhalov and Anna Pankratova) got their fingers burned after attempting to revise the story of Stalin's role in the Bolshevik Revolution. After Khrushchev's secret speech, when some anti-Stalinists, mostly children of Stalin's victims, became party members, Nekrich confided to his friend, "I would gladly leave the party, but it would be suicidal." Recollections of Slezkine, in *Otreshivshiisia ot strakha*, 21–22.

44. See the Aug. 3, 1965, letter of A. M. Nekrich to A. M. Samsonov and G. S. Osipian regarding the criticism of Nekrich's book, in T. M., Goriaeva, ed., *Istoriia sovetskoi politicheskoi tsenzury: Dokumenty i kommentarii* (Moscow: ROSSPEN, 1997), 551–555.

45. "Partiinaia organizatsiia Instituta istorii," *Voprosy Istorii* 12 (2007): 51–52.

46. Ibid., 71–74.

47. Roy Medvedev, "Dissidenty o dissidentstve," *Znamia* (1997–98), special issue, 171; Alexander Solzhenitsyn, "Obrazovanshchina," in *Iz-pod glyb* (Paris: YMCA, 1974), reprinted in D. S. Likhachev, ed., *Russkaia intelligentsia: Istoriia i sudba* (Moscow: Nauka, 1999), 136.

48. "Iz rabochei zapisi zasedania Politbiuro TsK KPSS," Nov. 10, 1966, *Istochnik* 2 (1996): 112–118.

49. See documentary evidence collected by L. P. Petrovsky, in *Otreshivshiisia ot strakha*, 65–75; the quotation from the report to the Politburo appears on p. 73; see also Alexander Tvardovsky, "Rabochie tetradi," *Znamia* 8 (2003): 146.

50. Orlova and Kopelev, *My zhili v Moskve*, 112.

51. On Soviet economic debates, see Lewin, *Stalinism and the Seeds of Soviet Reform*, 134–135; Pekka Sutela, *Socialism, Planning and Optimality: A Study in Soviet Economic Thought* (Helsinki: Societas Scientiarum Fennica, 1984). On Vasily Nemchinov, see www.cemi.rssi.ru/rus/persons/nemchin.htm.

52. V. L. Kantorovich, S. S. Kutateladze, and V. I. Fet, eds., *Leonid Vitalievich Kantorovich: Chelovek i uchenyi* (Novosibirsk: CO RAN, 2002), 1:310–315.

53. Abel Aganbegyan, *Moving the Mountain* (London: Bantam, 1989), 148; Robert D. English, *Russia and the Idea of the West: Gorbachev, Intellectuals, and the End of the Cold War* (New York: Columbia University Press, 2000), 95, 274, n. 57.

54. Philip Hanson, *The Rise and Fall of the Soviet Economy* (New York: Longman, 2003), 97.

55. Vladimir Shlapentokh, *Strakh i druzhba v nashem totalitarnom proshlom* (St. Petersburg: Zvezda, 2003), 167; Aganbegyan, *Moving the Mountain;* Tatiana Zaslavskaia, "Nam ochen khotelos sozdat nastoiashchuiu nauku," in G. S. Batygin and C. F. Yarmoliuk, eds., *Rossiiskaia sotsiologiia shestidesiatykh godov v vospominaniiakh i dokumentakh* (St. Petersburg: Russkii Khristianskii Gumanitarnyi Institut, 1999), 138–139; Igor Birman, *Ia—economist (o sebe, liubimom)* (Moscow: Vremia, 2001).

56. Lev Levitsky, entry for Nov. 5, 1963, "Dnevnik," *Znamia* 7 (2001): 123. On Kosygin's recollections about the living standards of his father, a highly qualified worker, see T. I. Fetisov, ed., *Premier izvesnyi i neizvesnyi: Vospominaniia o A. N. Kosygine* (Moscow: Respublika, 1997), 232–233.

57. A. K. Sokolov, "Prinuzhdenie k trudu v sovetskoi promyshlennosti i ego krizis, konets 1930-kh–seredina 1950-kh gg., in L. I. Borodkin and Y. A. Petrov, eds., *Ekonomicheskaia istoriia: Ezhegodnik* (Moscow: ROSSPEN, 2003), 89–96.

58. V. Glushkov, "Kibernetika, progress, budushchee," *Literaturnaia Gazeta,* Sept. 25, 1962, pp. 1, 2, 3.

59. On Glushkov's project, see the untitled article by Olga Kitova (Glushkov) and Iulia Kapitonova, at http://www.computer-museum.ru/galglory/27.htm; B. N. Malinovsky, *Akademik V. Glushkov: Stranitsy zhizni i tvorchestva* (Kiev: Naukova Dumka, 1993).

60. E. Liberman, "Plan, Pribyl, Premia," *Pravda,* Sept. 9, 1962; www.cemi.rssi.ru/rus/persons/nemchin.htm.

61. V. Nemchinov, "O Dalneishem Sovershenstvovanii Planirovaniia i Upravleniia Khoziaistvom (Moscow: Ekonomizdat, 1963), 53, cited in Lewin. *Stalinism and the Seeds of Soviet Reform,* 157.

62. On Khrushchev's "anti-dacha" campaigns, see RGANI, f. 6, op. 6, d. 1757, ll. 7–17, 42; ibid., d. 1735, ll. 1–50; Alexander Tvardovsky, entry for Nov. 9, 1964, "Rabochie tetradi 60-kh godov," *Znamia* 12 (2000): 141.

63. Gennady Lisichkin, *Plan i rynok* (Moscow: Ekonomika, 1966); Yuri Chernichenko, "Tselinnaia doroga," *Novy Mir* 1 (1961); Chernichenko, "Russkaia pshenitsa," *Novy Mir* 11 (1965). Viktor Starodubtsev, "Ezda k rynku na tormozakh," *Nezavisimaia Gazeta,* Oct. 28, 2005; German, *Slozhnoe proshedshee,* 418.

64. For the documents on these polemics, see *Leonid Vitalievich Kantorovich,* 2:196–197, 331–353.

65. Ilya Ehrenburg, *Liudi, gody, zhizn: Sobraniie sochinenii,* 9 vols., 8:251, cited in Pyotr Vail and Alexander Ghenis, *60-e: Mir sovetskogo cheloveka,* 2nd ed. (Moscow: Novoe Literaturnoe Obozrenie, 1998), 46–47.

66. On students' discussion of privileges in 1956, see "O Partiinom rukovodstve kommunisticheskim vospitaniem studentov na filologicheskom fakultete MGU," TsAODM, f. 4, op. 113, d. 41, l. 94.

67. Report of Martin Schtigler, "The Youth of the Soviet Union," p. 70, Fourteenth

Conference of the Institute for the Study of the USSR, Munich, 1962, "Red Archive" of the Open Society Archive, Budapest, collection box 497; Hanson, *The Rise and Fall of the Soviet Economy,* 97; A. I. Volkov, M. G. Pugacheva, and S. F. Yarmoliuk, eds., *Pressa v obshchestve, 1959-2000: Otsenki zhurnalistov i sotsiologov—Documenty* (Moscow: Moskovskaia Shkola Politicheskikh Issledovanii, 2000), 67–78.

68. I borrowed the arguments in this paragraph from Vladimir Kontorovich, "Lessons of the 1965 Soviet Economic Reform," *Soviet Studies* 40, no. 2 (Apr. 1988): 308–317. See also Hanson, *The Rise and Fall of the Soviet Economy,* 104–108; Birman, *Ia—economist,* 253–254.

69. Khrushchev at the party plenum, June 18–21, 1963, RGANI, f. 2, op. 1, d. 658, ll. 38ob.

70. Batygin and Yarmoliuk, *Rossiiskaia sotsiologiia,* 72.

71. For the high honorarium rates of the State Committee for Radio Broadcasting and Television in 1958, see RGANI, f. 5, op. 33, d. 72, ll. 26–34.

72. Vladimir Voinovich, "Denezhnyi dozhd," a segment of his memoirs serialized in *Novye Izvestia,* Apr. 21, 2006.

73. Vladimir Lakshin. *"Novy Mir" vo vremena Khrushcheva: Dnevnik i poputnoe, 1953-1964* (Moscow: Knizhnaia Palata, 1991), 48; Ivan Shchegolikhin, diary entry for Dec. 12, 1963, at http://prostor.samal.kz/texts/num0903/1cheg0903.htm; R. Romanova, "Kak Partiia rukovodila literaturoi," *Voprosy Literatury* (May–June 1996): 300–302.

74. For an example, see the letter from artists who were members of Moscow Organization of Soviet Artists to Khrushchev, around May 28, 1959, published in *Apparat TsK KPSS i Kultura 1958-1964: Dokumenty* (Moscow: ROSSPEN, 2005), 252–255.

75. Lakshin, *"Novy Mir" vo vremena Khrushcheva,* 30–31. The journalist Lev Levitsky wrote in his diary on May 28, 1963, about his lunch at Adzhubei's *Izvestia:* "What a monstrous division between the chosen and the rest. There is one cafeteria for the top bosses. For the rest of the journalists and editorial workers, including us from *Novy Mir,* another cafeteria, clean and comfortable. Typographical workers, couriers, and guards eat in the basement canteen, incomparably worse than our cafeteria. All this is taking place in a country that calls itself the state of workers and peasants, who allegedly have the power." Lev Levitsky, "Dnevnik," *Znamia* 7 (2001): 118.

76. Alexander Tvardovsky, entry for June 10, 1968, "Rabochie tetradi," *Znamia* 9 (2003): 126.

77. Joseph Brodsky, "Rech o prolitom moloke" (poem, Jan. 1967), at http://www.knigica.ru/poetry6394.html.

78. Hedrick Smith, *The Russians,* rev. ed. (New York: Ballantine, 1984), 30–67.

79. German, *Slozhnoe proshedshee,* 385–398.

80. Shlapentokh, *Strakh i druzhba,* 169–174; letter to the author from the physicist Arseny Berezin, Nov. 15, 2000; Komsomol Secretary Pavlov to CC CPSU, Mar. 5, 1966, RGANI, f. 5, op. 30, d. 490, ll. 76–81. KGB to CC CPSU, Mar. 3, 1965, RGANI

f. 5, op. 30 d. 462. ll. 19–22; Leonid Vladimirov, *Rossiia bez prikras i umolchanii* (Frankfurt: Posev, 1969), 124–125, published in English as Vladimirov, *The Russians* (New York: Praeger, 1968); A. I. Burshtein, "Rekviem po shestidesiatym, ili pod znakom integrala," at http://russcience.chat.ru/memory/burstein.htm.

81. Shlapentokh, *Strakh i druzhba,* 176–177.

82. The physicist Andrei Sakharov wrote in his diary in 1980 that the scientific leader of the Soviet atomic project, Igor Kurchatov, wanted, by using his influential position, "to create a vast science within the framework" of the existing Soviet system. During the 1960s many Soviet scientists, members of the intelligentsia community, continued to think and act in this way. Andrei Sakharov and Yelena Bonner, *Dnevniki: Roman-dokument,* vol. 2, in *Sobranie Sochinenii* (Moscow: Vremia, 2006), 83–85.

83. Viktor Zaslavsky, *The Neo-Stalinist State* (Armonk, N.Y.: Sharpe, 1982), 48–51.

84. On China's Cultural Revolution, see Jing Lin, *The Red Guard's Path to Violence: Political, Educational, and Psychological Factors* (New York: Praeger, 1991); and Paul Clark, *The Chinese Cultural Revolution: A History* (New York: Cambridge University Press, 2008). On 1968 in the West, see Carole Fink, ed., *1968: The World Transformed* (New York: Cambridge University Press, 1998); Kristin Ross, *May '68 and Its Afterlives* (Chicago: University of Chicago Press, 2003); David R. Faber, *The Age of Great Dreams: America in the 1960s* (Chicago: Hill and Wang, 1994); and Tony Judt, *Postwar: A History of Europe since 1945* (New York: Penguin, 2005), 407–421.

85. Georgy Arbatov, *The System: An Insider's Life in Soviet Politics* (New York: Times Books, 1992), 99–102; On the reaction of the party intellectuals to the cultural revolution, see Alexander Bovin, *XX vek kak zhizn: Vospominaniia* (Moscow: Zakharov, 2003). The description of dissidents' reactions is based on author's interview with Natalia Gorbanevskaia, June 10, 2008, Paris.

86. Author's conversation with Maia Turovskaia, June 25, 2000, Moscow.

87. Arkady Vaksberg, *Moia zhizn v zhizni* (Moscow: Terra Sport, 2000), 1:342, 391, 391, 397.

88. Fomin, *Kinematograf ottepeli,* 396–397; author's conversation with Turovskaia, June 25, 2000. See also Judt, *Postwar,* 421.

89. Scholars are only now beginning to study these transnational networks. See Krzysztof Gozdowski, "Ermitazh osmotren, zamechanii net, ili kak vosprinimala polskaia auditoria russkikh bardov," *Novaia Polsha* 12 (2007): 3–9; http://www.strefapiosenki.pl/content/view/476/; and Anthony Kemp-Welch, *Poland under Communism: A Cold War History* (London: Cambridge University Press, 2008).

90. Neal Asherson, "The Polish March: Students, Workers, and 1968," at http://www.opendemocracy.net/article/globalisation/the_polish_march_students_workers_and_1968.

91. Alexeeva, *Pokolenie ottepeli,* 218–219.

92. "Dva tisice slov," *Literarni Listy,* June 27, 1968, reproduced in Jaromir Navratil, ed., *The Prague Spring, 1968* (Budapest: CEU, 1998), 177–181.

93. Tvardovsky, entry for Aug. 10, 1968, "Rabochie tetradi," *Znamia* 9 (2003): 142–143, 149.

94. Vladlen Krivosheev, "'Izvestia' i tanki v Prage," *Izvestia*, Aug. 22, 1998.

95. Vladimir Lukin, "Tanki na zakate leta," *Literaturnaia Gazeta*, Aug. 18, 1993; English, *Russia and the Idea of the West*, 110–111.

96. Mikhail Agursky, *Pepel Klaasa* (Jerusalem: URA, 1988), 328.

97. Andrei Sakharov, "Progress, Peaceful Coexistence, and Intellectual Freedom" (June 1968), in Harrison E. Salisbury, ed., *Sakharov Speaks* (New York: Vintage, 1974), 56–114; *Materialy konferentsii k 30-letiiu raboty A. D. Sakharova "Razmyshleniia o progresse, mirnom sosushchestvovanii i intellektualnoi svobode"* (Moscow: Prava Cheloveka, 1998), 15–21, 41–43; Sakharov's recollections in handwritten version of his memoirs, Houghton Library, Harvard University, Andrei Sakharov Papers, MS Russ 79, box 50, folder S.II.2.5.172. Sakharov wrote that he remained "optimistic and positive regarding Soviet realities and the prospects" for Soviet evolution—more so than many cynics "within the system" whom he met. "In this sense," Sakharov wrote, "I am more a Homo Sovietus than they."

98. The poem was rejected by a few samizdat readers, who had begun to grow tired of "honest" revolutionary pathos. Galina Yevtushenko, the poet's wife, who was close to the human rights activists, even threatened to divorce her husband for praising Lenin and the party. The vast majority of the Russian intellectuals, however, applauded the poet's message. Yevtushenko, *Bratskaia GES, Pervoie sobranie sochinenii* (Moscow: RA Neva Group, 1998), 2:364–465. See also Yevtushenko, *Volchii pasport* (Moscow: Vagrius, 1998), 231, 262, 268–269. On the poem as the monument to illusions, see also Lev Anninsky, "Bez bantikov," *Druzhba Narodov* 8 (2003): 219–223.

99. Smeliansky, *The Russian Theater after Stalin*, 24–25.

100. Ibid., 26–28.

101. Yuri Liubimov, *Rasskazy starogo trepacha* (Moscow: Novosti, 2001), 104–105, 114–115, 160–161, 162–183, 200; Smeliansky, *The Russian Theater*, 32. Liubimov, born in the year of the Russian Revolution, was older than Yefremov. His peasant roots and memories of NEP (his parents were arrested as "NEP-people") also added to his complex memories. He tried to "reforge" himself in the 1930s and even briefly served as a skilled industrial worker. But his early love for theater brought him to a branch of Stanislavsky's Art Theater. His training was influenced by the Russian avant-garde theater directors Vakhtangov and Meyerhold. He also watched the death throes of the old intelligentsia in the clutches of Stalinism. Along with a few talented young people of his generation, like Simonov and Tvardovsky, Liubimov did not perish under Stalinism, but flourished. He became a supporting actor in a play about Lenin during the Revolution. He married a beautiful, nationally known actress. He starred in many popular films, received the Stalin Prize, and belonged to several prestigious boards and committees. Soon after Stalin's death Liubimov joined the party. In contrast to Simonov and Tvardovsky, he never expressed any pangs of bad conscience about his earlier life, at least in writing. "I did not pay attention to politics; I acted," he claimed in his memoirs.

102. Liubimov, *Rasskazy*, 228, 195, 202–203, 229–238; Veniamin Smekhov, *Teatr moei pamiati* (Moscow: Vagrius, 2001), 95–96.

103. Liubimov, *Rasskazy,* 229–239; Smeliansky, *The Russian Theater,* 37–39; Veniamin Smekhov, *Teatr moiei pamiati* (Moscow: Vagrius, 2001), 95–96. Many of the authors for the Taganka were the same as those for *Novy Mir:* Fyodor Abramov, Boris Mozhaev, Alexander Solzhenitsyn, and Yuri Trifonov. Samoilov, Kopelev, Korzhavin, and other literary critics and poets helped with various plays. Shostakovich, Schnittke, and Andrei Volkonsky composed music. Among the members of the Taganka public art council were the physicist Pyotr Kapitsa, Yevtushenko, Akhmadulina, Voznesensky, Okudzhava, Tvardovsky, and the filmmaker Sergei Paradzhanov.

104. Liubimov, *Rasskazy,* 252–256, 259–262.

105. Smeliansky, *The Russian Theater,* 40–41.

106. Supporters of the Taganka from the central party apparatus included Anatoly Cherniaev, Nikolai Inozemtsev, Georgy Arbatov, Alexander Bovin, Nikolai Shishlin, Yevgeny Samoteikin, A. Kozlov (consultant), V. Alexandrov, and Raf Fyodorov from Andropov's department. Also, the party philosopher, academician Alexei Rumiantsev, lobbied to save the theater. Cherniaev, *Moia zhizn i moe vremia,* 242.

107. T. Kosinova, interview with Marat Cheshkov, Sept. 21, 1992, Moscow, Oral History Collection, archive of Memorial, Moscow.

108. Andrei Konchalovsky, *Nizkie istiny* (Moscow: Sovershenno Sekretno, 1998), 161.

109. Neizvestny, *Govorit Neizvestny* (Frankfurt-am-Main, Posev, 1980), 50–57, 117; for similar observations see those of Vladimir Yadov, in Batygin and Yarmoliuk, *Rossiiskaia sotsiologiia,* 48.

110. For more details, see English, *Russia and the Idea of the West,* 70–72; Bovin, *XX vek kak zhizn,* 180–184; Shmelev, "Curriculum vitae," *Znamia* (1997–98), special issue, 112. Shakhnazarov, *S Vozhdiami i bez nikh,* 83, 85–86.

111. Shmelev, "Curriculum vitae."

112. Bovin, *XX vek kak zhizn,* 189.

113. Recollections of Natalia Gorbanevskaia, "Chto pomniu ia o demonstratsii," at http://www.hro.org/editions/karta/nr21/demonstr.htm.

114. Ibid. See also Gorbanevskaia, *Polden: Delo o demonstratsii na Krasnoi ploshchadi 25 avgusta 1968 goda* (Moscow: Novoe Izdatelstvo, 2007), 204–205, 270–275.

115. Yevtushenko, *Volchii pasport,* 299–301; Alexeeva, *Pokolenie ottepeli,* 226–228.

116. Igor Dedkov, "Kak trudno daiutsia inye dni!—Iz dnevnikovykh zapisei 1953–1974 godov," *Novy Mir* 5 (1996): 144; author conversation with Vladimir Pechatnov (a student at MGIMO in 1969), Nov. 11, 2006, Rome; Amir Weiner, "Déjà Vu All Over Again," *Journal of Contemporary European History* 15, no. 2 (June 2006), 190.

117. Leonid Mlechin, *Predsedateli KGB Rassekrechennye sudby* (Moscow: Tsentrpoligraf, 2005), 499—550; Roy Medvedev, *Neizvestnyi Andropov: Politicheskaia biografiia Yuriia Andropova* (Moscow: Prava Cheloveka, 1999), 117–118.

118. Houghton Library, Harvard University, Andrei Sakharov Papers, MS Russ 79, box 88, folder S.II.2.6.1.45.

119. Vasily Aksyonov, *Ozhog: Sobranie sochinenii* (Moscow: Yunost, 1994), 3:26–28, 31–34, 111–117.

120. Smeliansky, *The Russian Theater,* 46.

121. Bovin, *XX vek kak zhizn,* 262.

122. Mikhail Gorbachev, *Zhizn i reformy* (Moscow: Novosti, 1995), 1:119.

9. The Long Decline, 1968-1985

1. A. Zhelezniakov, "Vystrely u Borovitskikh vorot," at http://www.cosmoworld.ru/spaceencyclopedia/index.shtml?jan69.html.

2. Igor Dedkov, "'Kak trudno daiutsia inye dni!' Iz dnevnikovykh zapisei 1953–1974 godov," *Novy Mir* 5 (1996): 144. See also Jay Bergman, "Soviet Dissidents on the Russian Intelligentsia, 1965–1985," *Russian Review* 51, no. 1 (Jan. 1992): 23.

3. For recent research on the prerevolutionary intelligentsia's attraction to terrorism, see Marina Mogilner, *Mifologiia "podpolnogo cheloveka": Radikalnyi mikrokosm v Rossii nachala XX veka kak predmet semioticheskogo analiza* (Moscow: Novoe Literatunoe Obozrenie, 1999).

4. Author's interview with Natalia Gorbanevskaia, June 10, 2008, Paris.

5. Yuri Davydov, a Marxist sociologist from the postwar generation, was influenced by the campaign of petitions from 1965 to 1968.The censors banned his philosophical-sociological anthology. After the end of the Prague Spring Davydov privately abandoned his Marxist views. In G. S. Batygin and C. F. Yarmoliuk, eds., *Rossiiskaia sotsiologiia shestidesiatykh godov v vospiminaniiakh i dokumentakh* (St. Petersburg: Russkii Khristianskii Gumanitarnyi Institut, 1999), 398.

6. Dmitry Furman, "Perestroika glazami moskovskogo gumanitariia," in Boris Kuvaldin, ed., *Proryv k svobode: O perestroike dvadsat let spustia (kriticheskii analiz)* (Moscow: Alpina, 2005), 316–319.

7. Benjamin Nathans, "The Dictatorship of Reason: Alexandr Vol'pin and the Idea of Rights under Developed Socialism," *Slavic Review* 66, no. 4 (Winter 2007): 660. The human rights group included Valery Chalidze, Andrei Sakharov, Igor Shafarevich, Valentin Turchin, Andrei Tverdokhlebov, and a number of other scientists, scholars, and intellectuals.

8. Bergman, "Soviet Dissidents on the Russian Intelligentsia," 18; Boris Kagarlitsky, *The Thinking Reed: Intellectuals and the Soviet State* (London: Verso, 1988), 8–37.

9. Liudmila Alexeeva, *Pokolenie ottepeli* (Moscow: Zakharov, 2006), 154.

10. Andrei Sakharov, *Memoirs* (New York: Knopf, 1990), 283. On literary romanticism and connections as a common background for Bonner and many dissidents, see Yelena Bonner, "Do Dnevnikov," *Znamia* 11 (2005): 64–66, 69–70, 74–78, 89. Johann Wolfgang von Goethe, *Faust: A Tragedy,* trans. Bayard Taylor (Boston: James R. Osgood, 1873), 2:404.

11. Anatoly Cherniaev, *Dnevniki,* Feb. 21, 1974. The original is on file at the National Security Archive, Washington, D.C.

12. Joshua Rubenstein and Alexander Gribanov, eds., *The KGB Files of Andrei Sakharov* (New Haven, Conn.: Yale University Press, 2005), 114–116; Mario Corti, "O nekotorykh aspektakh dissidentskogo dvizheniia," presentation at the conference Dis-

sidentskoie dvizheniie v SSSR, 1950–1980-e gody, organized by Memorial, Aug. 1992, at http://www.mario-corti.com/press/#5.

13. Houghton Library, Harvard University, Andrei Sakharov, Papers, MS Russ 79, folder S.IV.22.17.

14. A. Sakharov and Y. Bonner, *Dnevniki: Roman-dokument* (Moscow: Vremia, 2006), 1:109–110.

15. Yuri Svetov, "Ne ssorias s vlastiu, no ot vlasti v storone," in V. D. Stepanovskaia, ed., *Yuri Temirkanov: Shtrikhi k portretu* (St. Petersburg: Kult-Inform-Press, 1998), 136–137. For a similar position, see also Mikhail German, *Slozhnoe proshedshee: Passé composé* (St. Petersburg: Pechatnyi Dvor, 2006), 445, 546–548.

16. Yelena Bonner was a friend of Bulat Okudzhava, but after he refused to sign a petition against death sentences, their friendship came to an end. When they met by chance in 1972 and Bonner addressed the poet, he responded with defiance: "I am fine. I have earned a lot of money. I have bought a new apartment. We are going to buy a car." Bonner and Sakharov, *Dnevniki,* 1:111–113.

17. In greater detail, the dissident movement and détente was analyzed in Frederick C. Barghoorn, *Détente and the Democratic Movement in the USSR* (New York: Free Press, 1976), esp. chap. 3. Barghoorn, however, does not focus on how the human rights movement used the atmosphere and opportunities of détente.

18. Corti, "O nekotorykh aspektakh."

19. At the same time, some physicists and mathematicians in the Soviet Union, together with Western colleagues, ran an international support network for Andrei Sakharov. This network had agents in major Soviet research centers, including the Leningrad and Moscow institutes for physics, the Kurchatov Institute, and Akademgorodok. Author's interview with Arseny Berezin, Nov. 15, 2000, Washington, D.C.; author's interview with Sidney Drell, June 11, 2007, Bellagio.

20. Alexeyeva and Goldberg, *The Thaw Generation,* 288–289; "The Moscow Helsinki Group, 30th Anniversary: From the Secret Files," National Security Archive Electronic Briefing Book no. 191, at http://www.gwu.edu/~nsarchiv/NSAEBB/NSAEBB191/index.htm.

21. This cohort included Mikhail Lobanov, Viktor Chalmaev, Vadim Kozhinov, Oleg Mikhailov, Anatoly Lanschikov, Sergei Semanov, Vitaly Skurlatov, Stanislav Kuniaev, Sergei Vikulov, Pyotr Palievsky, and Fyodor Karelin.

22. As Russia during the Great Reforms began to open up to the West, the Slavophile movement adopted extremely antiliberal, anticapitalist, and xenophobic views. The conservative Slavophiles (among them Mikhail Katkov, Konstantin Pobedonostsev, and Konstantin Leontiev) believed that imitating European trends would doom Russia as a state and the Russian people as a unique cultural-religious community. The Slavophiles rejected Western concepts of freedom, democracy, and national independence, speaking instead of a religious-spiritual autocratic community in the Byzantine tradition. James Billington, *The Icon and the Axe: An Interpretive History of Russian Culture* (New York: Vintage, 1970); Richard Pipes, *Russian Conservatism and Its Critics: A Study in Political Culture* (New Haven, Conn.: Yale University Press, 2006).

23. Nikolai Mitrokhin, *Russkaia partiia: Dvizhenie russkikh natsionalistov v SSSR, 1953-1985 gody* (Moscow: Novoe Literaturnoie Obozreniie, 2003), 131-135; Alexander Yakovlev, *Sumerki* (Moscow: Materik, 2003), 312-315. See also Geoffrey Hosking, *Rulers and Victims: The Russians in the Soviet Union* (Cambridge, Mass.: Harvard University Press, 2006), 361-365.

24. Cited in Mitrokhin, *Russkaia partiia*, 523.

25. See Victor Yasmann, "Red Religion: An Ideology of Neo-Messianic Russian Fundamentalism," *Demokratizatsiia* 1, no. 2 (1993): 20-40.

26. Sergei Semanov, "Russkii klub," *Moskva* 3 (Mar. 1997), reproduced in Semanov, *Brezhnev: Pravitel zolotogo veka* (Moscow: Veche, 2002), 342-343; Hosking, *Rulers and Victims*, 368-369.

27. Alexander Solzhenitsyn, "Obrazovanshchina" (Jan. 1974).

28. Michael Scammel, *Solzhenitsyn: A Biography* (New York: Norton, 1984); Houghton Library, Harvard University, Andrei Sakharov Papers, MS Russ 79, box 50, folders S.II.2.5, 178 and 181.

29. Eduard Kuznetsov and Mark Dymshits were sentenced to death. Kuznetsov, who had formerly considered himself a Russian, was a veteran of the Mayak gatherings who had been arrested in 1961. In the camps be became a Jewish activist (his father was a Jew). *Khronika Tekushchikh Sobytii* 20 (July 2, 1971), at http://www.memo.ru/history/diss/chr/chr20.htm; Liudmila Polikovskaia, ed., *"My predchuvstvie . . . predtecha": Ploshchad Maiakovskogo, 1958-1965* (Moscow: Zvenia, 1997), 225.

30. Andrei Sakharov, *Vospominaniia* (New York: Chekhov, 1990), 426-433.

31. V. A. Kozlov, S. V. Mironenko, O. V. Edelman, and E. Y. Zavadskaia, eds., *Kramola: Inakomyslie v SSSR pri Khrushcheve i Brezhneve, 1953-1982—Rassekrechennye dokumenty Verkhovnogo suda i Prokuratury SSSR* (Moscow: Materik, 2005), 53. Yelena Bonner, letter to Eduard Kuznetsov, around June 1982, in Houghton Library, Elena Bonner Papers, 2004M-12 (unsorted correspondence).

32. Memorandum of Philip Bobkov, head of the Fifth Directorate of the KGB, May 9, 1973, published in Boris Morozov, *Evreiskaia emigratsia v svete novykh dokumentov* (Tel Aviv: Tel Aviv University, 1998), 169; Zvi Gitelman, "Soviet Political Culture: Insights from Jewish Emigrés," *Soviet Studies* 24, no. 4 (Oct. 1977): 546. See also Leonard Schroeter, *The Last Exodus* (New York: Universe, 1974).

33. Gitelman, "Soviet Political Culture," 546.

34. Leon Onikov, "O vyezde chasti evreiskogo naseleniia iz SSSR," in Morozov, *Evreiskaia emigratsiia*, 201.

35. Schroeter, *Last Exodus*, 377. According to a contemporary observer, among participants in the human rights movement 60 to 70 percent were Jews or married to Jews. Barghoorn, *Détente and the Democratic Movement in the USSR*, 106-112.

36. Between 1971 and 1980, 132,000 Soviet citizens emigrated from the USSR to Israel, and 42,000 to the United States. Mark Tolts, "Demography of the Jews in the Former Soviet Union: Yesterday and Today," in Zvi Gitelman, with M. Glants and M. I. Goldman, eds., *Jewish Life after the USSR* (Bloomington: Indiana University Press, 2003), 177-178.

37. Houghton Library, Harvard University, Andrei Sakharov Papers, MS Russ 79, box 50, folder S.II.2.5.180.

38. James R. Millar et al., *Soviet Interview Project, 1979–1985* (Urbana-Champaign, Ill.: Inter-University Consortium for Political and Social Research, 1989); Yuri Slezkine, *The Jewish Century* (Princeton, N.J.: Princeton University Press, 2004), 340–348.

39. Sakharov and Bonner, *Dnevniki,* 1:136.

40. Genrikh Yoffe, "Operatsiia 'Iskhod': Pismo iz Kanady," *Svobodnaia Mysl* 12 (2002): 91; Noam Kochavi, "Idealpolitik in Disguise: Israel, Jewish Emigration from the Soviet Union, and the Nixon Administration, 1969–1974," *International History Review* 39, 3 (Sept. 2007): 473–554.

41. "K voprosu o vyezde za granitsu lits evreiskoi natsionalnosti," minutes of the Politburo for Mar. 20, 1973, *Istochnik* 1 (1996): 156. See also Morozov, *Evreiskaia emigratsiia,* 164–168; Bovin, *XX vek kak zhizn,* 257–258; Cherniaev, *Dnevniki,* Mar. 9, 1975; and Andropov to Politburo, Dec. 29, 1975, on site of the National Security Archive, at http://www2.gwu.edu/~nsarchiv/ NSAEBB/ NSAEBB191/12–29–1975. pdf.

42. By 1975 most of the theorists and practitioners of the human rights movement had left the Soviet Union, including Alexander Volpin, Valery Chalidze, and Boris Shragin. The writers Alexander Solzhenitsyn, Vladimir Voinovich, Vladimir Maximov, and Andrei Siniavsky, along with the poets Joseph Brodsky and Naum Korzhavin, either were expelled or preferred to emigrate. In 1978 the regime got rid of the world-famous cellist Mstislav Rostropovich and his wife, the opera singer Galina Vishnevskaia, by canceling their Soviet citizenship. In 1976 poet Natalia Gorbanevskaia, one of those who had demonstrated on Red Square against the invasion of Czechoslovakia, emigrated to France with her son, after three years' residence in a prison psychiatric hospital. In 1982 Yuri Liubimov, the Taganka director, did not return to the Soviet Union after taking a trip abroad.

43. Alexeeva, *Pokolenie ottepeli,* 292, 305.

44. Etkind, *Zapiski nezagovorshchika: Barselonskaia proza* (St. Petersburg: Akademicheskii Proekt, 2001), 258–266.

45. J. Martin Daughtry, "*Magnetizdat* as Cultural Practice," p. 2, paper presented at the conference Samizdat and Underground Culture in the Soviet Bloc Countries, University of Pennsylvania, Apr. 6–7, 2006; Vladimir Shlapentokh, *Soviet Intellectuals and Political Power: The Post-Stalin Era* (London: Tauris, 1990), 194; Stanislav Rassadin, *Kniga proshchanii: Vospominaniia o druziakh i ne tolko o nikh* (Moscow: Tekst, 2004), 102; Yoffe, "Operatsiia 'Iskhod,'" 94. Stanislav Rassadin recalled his farewell meeting with poet Naum Korzhavin in 1973, on "one of the bitterest days of my life." "Leaving was like an act of death." There were other reactions. The film director Andrei Konchalovsky, who emigrated to the United States in 1980, later wrote that he wanted to get rid of the Soviet passport, "the passport of a slave." Vladimir Maximov, a writer, told Andrei Sakharov around 1971, "One should carry

this country [Russia] on the sole of one's boots." The people repelled him even more than the regime. Andrei Konchalovsky, *Nizkie istiny* (Moscow: Sovershenno Sekretno, 1998), 157–158; Sakharov, *Vospominaniia,* 480.

46. Natasha Simes (Timofeeva) spoke of her recollections to me in repeated conversations between 1996 and 2008 in Arlington, Virginia.

47. Arkady V. Belinkov, "The Soviet Intelligentsia and the Socialist Revolution: On Yury Olesha's 'Envy,'" *Russian Review* 30, no. 4 (Oct. 1971): 356–358. The posthumously published sequel appeared in *Russian Review* 31, no. 1 (Jan. 1972): 37. Belinkov's starkly negative attitudes toward educated milieus in Moscow can be also seen in his last novel, written between 1965 and 1968. See Belinkov, *Sdacha i gibel sovetskogo intelligenta: Yuri Olesha* (Madrid: Ediciones Castilla, 1976).

48. Tamar Rapoport and Edna Lomsky-Feder, "'Intelligentsia' as an Ethnic Habitus: The Inculcation and Restructuring of Intelligentsia among Russian Jews," *British Journal of Sociology of Education* 23, no. 2 (2002): 233, 241; Paul Ritterband, "Jewish Identity among Russian Immigrants in the U.S.," in Noah Lewin-Epstein, Jaacov Ro'i and Paul Ritterband, *Russian Jews on Three Continents: Migration and Resettlement* (London: Frank Cass, 1997), 339; author's interviews with the Italian Slavist Vittorio Strada, Apr. 1, 2006, Rome, and Apr. 15, 2006, Venice; Rassadin, *Kniga proshchanii,* 106.

49. Andrei Siniavsky published the journal *Syntaxis.* Vladimir Maximov obtained the funds to launch *Kontinent.* Valery Chalidze started a publishing house specializing in émigré literature.

50. Alexander Schmeman, entry for Apr. 19, 1977, *Dnevniki, 1973–1983* (Moscow: Russkii Put, 2005), 360–361.

51. Vasily Aksyonov, quoted in *Znamia* (1997–98), special issue, 152.

52. Arnold McMillin, "Exiled Russian Writers of the Third Wave and the Émigré Press," *Modern Language Review* 84, no. 2 (Apr. 1989): 406–441.

53. RGANI, f. 2, op. 1, d. 62, l. 102.

54. Letter from Varlam Shalamov to Ilya Ehrenburg, Apr. 28, 1966, published by Boris Frezinsky in *Sovetskaia Kultura,* Jan. 26, 1991.

55. Donald J. Raleigh, *Russia's Sputnik Generation: Soviet Baby Boomers Talk about Their Lives* (Bloomington: Indiana University Press, 2006), 4; Donna Bahry, "Politics, Generations, and Change in the USSR," in James R. Millar, ed., *Politics, Work, and Daily Life in the USSR: A Survey of Former Soviet Citizens* (New York: Cambridge University Press, 1987), 74.

56. *Narodnoe khoziaistvo SSSR v 1969: Statisticheskii ezhegodnik* (Moscow: Izdatelstvo "Statistika," TsSU pri Sovete Ministrov SSSR, 1970), 665; B. P. Pockney, ed., *Soviet Statistics since 1950* (New York: St. Martin's, 1991), 43.

57. *Komsomolskaia Pravda,* Dec. 13, 1964; ibid., Mar. 4, 1965.

58. B. A. Grushin, *Chetyre zhizni Rossii v zerkale oprosov obshchestvennogo mneniia: Epokha Brezhneva* (chast 1) (Moscow: Progress-Traditsiia, 2003), 101–115.

59. Pavlov to CC CPSU, information at the plenum of the CC VLKSM, Jan. 21, 1966, RGANI, f 5, op. 30, d. 490, ll. 13–19; *Pravda,* Aug. 29, 1965, p. 2.

60. TsAODM, f. 4, op. 136, d. 111, ll. 17–19, cited in Mitrokhin, *Russkaia partiia,* 290–291.

61. John Scott speech at NYU–Radio Liberty conference Communication with Soviet Youth, Mar. 10, 1967, Open Society Archive, Budapest, 300/80, box 496, 2–6. Scott had worked as an engineer during the construction of Magnitogorsk from 1932 to 1937, became fluent in Russian, married a Russian girl, and managed to return to the United States at the height of the Great Purge. In 1958 Scott returned to the Soviet Union, and in 1965–66 he went on another extensive journey to Siberia, Mongolia, Ukraine, Central Asia, Leningrad, and Moscow.

62. Ibid., 9–10, 14.

63. William Taubman, *The View from Lenin Hills: Soviet Youth in Ferment* (New York: Coward-McCann, 1967), 188–192, 196, 197, 244, 246–249. A graduate of Columbia and Harvard, Taubman, who was fluent in Russian, spent an academic year at MGU between September 1965 and the summer of 1966. He lived in a high-rise student dorm in Lenin Hills, attended student meetings with party lecturers, and took part in the students' social and cultural life. He listened with them to Okudzhava's songs and performed Bob Dylan's songs for them.

64. Ibid.

65. Viktor Voronkov, "Sotsiologicheskoe pokolenie 1960-kh," in Alexeeva, *Pokolenie ottepeli,* 376–377. Voronkov admits that the figure might be lower because the Soviet authorities learned to wean out potential dissidents at an early stage. This does not, however, change the fact that the student body became more conservative after the mid-1960s.

66. KGB to CC CPSU, Nov. 5, 1968, *Istoricheskii Arkhiv* 1 (1994): 181–185.

67. Ibid., 175–207, esp. 175–176, 179–185, 187–188, 190.

68. Bella Ostromoukhova, KVN—molodezhnaia kultura 1960-kh," *Neprikosnovenny Zapas* 4 (2004), 52–59.

69. Alexei Yurchak, *Everything Was Forever, Until It Was No More: The Last Soviet Generation* (Princeton, N.J.: Princeton University Press, 2006), 273–274.

70. Quoted in Yuri Bezeliansky, *Klub 1932* (Moscow: Raduga, 2000), 187. See also Pyotr Vail and Alexander Ghenis, *60-e: Mir sovetskogo cheloveka,* 2nd ed. (Moscow: Novoe Literaturnoe Obozrenie, 1998), 151.

71. Yurchak, *Everything Was Forever,* 32.

72. Ibid., 104, 128.

73. Viktor Slavkin, *Pamiatnik neizvestnomu stiliage* (Moscow: Artist, Rezhisser, Teatr, 1996).

74. Robert D. English, *Russia and the Idea of the West: Gorbachev, Intellectuals, and the End of the Cold War* (New York: Columbia University Press, 2000); Georgy Arbatov, *The System: An Inside's Life in Soviet Politics* (Westminster, Md.: Times Books, 1992) on the concept of "oases."

75. Timothy Garton Ash, "The Stasi on Our Minds," *New York Review of Books,* May 31, 2007, 4, 6, 8.

76. Alexeeva, *Pokolenie ottepeli,* 140–141.

77. Czeslaw Milosz, *The Captive Mind* (New York: Knopf, 1953), esp. 69–77.

78. David Samoilov, entry for Apr. 20, 1967, *Podennye zapisi,* vol. 2 (Moscow: Vremia, 2002).

79. This process, not yet explored by historians, attracted the attention of a writer, Olga Grushin, who was the daughter of the sociologist Boris Grushin. Olga Grushin, *The Dream Life of Sukhanov* (New York: Putnam, 2005; interview with Olga Grushin, at http://www.voanews.com/russian/archive/2006-12/2006-12-30-voa4. cfm).

80. Ernst Neizvestny, *Govorit Neizvestny* (Frankfurt-am-Main: Posev, 1984), 65.

81. One famous "oasis" that was very important for scholars in the humanities, especially linguists, sociologists, and philosophers, was in Estonia, at the University of Tartu. Professor Yuri Lotman, a war veteran, an assimilated Russian Jew, and a brilliant member of the postwar generation of intellectuals, was able to run a seminar there on semiotics and structural and formal linguistics. Hundreds of intellectuals flocked to work with Lotman from Moscow, Leningrad, and other parts of Russia.

82. Yevgeny Plimak, *Na voine i posle voiny: Zapiski veterana* (Moscow: Ves Mir, 2005), 150.

83. E. Vodolazkin, ed., *Dmitry Likhachev i ego epokha: Vospominaniia, esse, dokumenty, fotografii* (St. Petersburg: Logos, 2002), 82, 102, 110, 116.

84. Hedrick Smith, *The Russians* (New York: Crown, 1976), 49–55.

85. English, *Russia and the Idea of the West,* 124–127.

86. Arbatov, *The System.*

87. Neizvestny, *Govorit Neizvestny,* 117–118.

88. Cherniaev, *Dnevniki,* Sept. 18, 1976, and Mar. 12, 1977.

89. Ibid., Mar. 10, 1974, Sept. 24, 1975, and Oct. 19, 1975.

90. Anatoly Cherniaev, *Moia zhizn i moe vremia* (Moscow: Mezhdunarodnye Otnosheniia, 1995), 246.

91. Vladimir Salnikov, "Rasskaz o tom, kak byli sviazani khudozhestvenye printsipy i dengi v sovetskom iskusstve," *Moscow Art Magazine,* no. 46, at http://xz.gif.ru/ numbers/46/rasskaz.

92. Among these veterans were Oleg Tselkov, Eduard Shteynberg, Eduard Drobitsky, Vladimir Nemukhin, Lidia Masterkova, Vitaly Komar, and Alexander Melamid.

93. Alexander Glezer, "Esli kto zabyl, kak ono byvaet," *Moscow News* 35 (Sept. 17, 2004). On the reaction of Brezhnev's assistant Andrei Alexandrov-Agentov, see Cherniaev, *Dnevniki,* Sept. 29, 1974.

94. Vladimir Lakshin, entry for Feb. 10, 1970, "Poslednii akt: Dnevnik 1969–1970 godov," *Druzhba Narodov* 6 (2003): 166–167.

95. See Geoffrey Hosking, *Beyond Socialist Realism: Soviet Fiction since Ivan Denisovich* (New York: Holmes & Meier, 1980), 201.

96. Boris Pasternak, *Doctor Zhivago,* trans. Max Hayward and Manya Harari (New York: Pantheon, 1958), 285.

97. Samoilov, despite the progressive loss of his eyesight, worked in the literary archives. In 1976, after many of his oldest friends emigrated to the West, he bought a

house in Parnu, Estonia, where he stayed most of the time. He returned to Moscow only to read his poetry.

98. Eidelman was born in 1930 in Moscow into an assimilated Jewish family, fervent supporters of the Bolshevik Revolution. His father, a literary critic, passionately criticized Pasternak for his "formalism." Nathan Eidelman graduated from Moscow State University as a historian in 1952, but because of the anti-Semitic campaign (and the arrest of his father) he worked at a high school outside Moscow. Khrushchev's secret speech changed the historian's life; he returned to Moscow and joined the neo-Marxist underground group of Lev Krasnopevtsev. When the group was arrested, Eidelman's house was searched and he lost his job as a schoolteacher. G. M. Hamburg, "Writing History and the End of the Soviet Era: The Secret Lives of Nathan Eidel'man," *Kritika* 7, no. 1 (Winter 2006): 71–109.

99. See the Web site devoted to Eidelman, at http://vivovoco.rsl.ru/VV/PAPERS/NYE/EIDELMAN.HTM.

100. German, *Slozhnoe proshedshee,* 397–415, 447–457, 471–499.

101. Songs by Okudzhava (1975 and 1976), translations by Vladislav Zubok.

102. Vysotsky was born in Moscow in 1937, the son of a Soviet army officer. He had learned from his schoolteacher about Russian poetry, learned to love Boris Pasternak, Velimir Khlebnikov, Marina Tsvetaeva, Alexei Kruchenykh, Igor Severianin, and Nikolai Gumilyov. He also discovered Isaac Babel, a writer banned at the time. In 1955–56 he attended the Institute of Civil Engineering but, sensing his artistic vocation, signed up for the Studio School of the Moscow Art Theater. He graduated as an actor in 1960 and after many trials and errors found a home in the Taganka Theater. Alla Demidova, *Vladimir Vysotsky kakim znaiu i liubliu* (Moscow: Soiuz Teatralnykh Deiatelei RSFSR, 1989), 30.

103. Pyotr Soldatenkov, *Vladimir Vysotsky* (Moscow: Olimp, 1999), 56.

104. Arkady Vysotsky, in *Vladimir Vysotsky: Chetyre chetverti puti* (Moscow: Fizkultura i Sport 1988), 15.

105. Yitzhak M. Brudny, *Reinventing Russia: Russian Nationalism and the Soviet State, 1953–1991* (Cambridge, Mass.: Harvard University Press, 1998), 105, 109, 127.

106. This group of writers included Viktor Astafiev, Vasily Belov, Yuri Bondarev, Valentin Rasputin, Vladimir Soloukhin, Vladimir Chivilikhin, Dmitry Balashov, Pyotr Proskurin, and Sergei Zalygin.

107. The American-Israeli scholar Yitzhak Brudny sees the rise in influence of conservative Russian nationalists as a result of the policy of "inclusion" by the Brezhnev leadership, "an integral part of what might be called the Brezhnev program" that began in early 1966 and peaked in 1968–69. Brudny, *Reinventing Russia,* 57–58, 64–65, 98–102; Mitrokhin, *Russkaia partiia,* 357; Cherniaev, *Moia zhizn i moe vremia,* 370–371, 388. "Protiv anti-istorizma," *Literaturnaia Gazeta,* Nov. 15, 1972.

108. Andropov to CC CPSU, Mar. 28, 1981, RGANI, f. 5, op. 84, d. 1011, ll. 31–35, published in *Istochnik* 6 (1994): 108–110. On the attempts of radical Russian nationalists to organize themselves and spread, see Mitrokhin, *Russkaia partiia,* 537–556.

109. Brudny, *Reinventing Russia,* 123–128.

110. Cherniaev, *Dnevniki,* Dec. 30, 1979.

111. Ibid., Jan. 1, 1977, and Dec. 19, 1980.

112. Ibid., June 21, 1980.

113. Entry for Oct. 28, 1969, in Vladimir Lakshin, "Memuary: Poslednii akt," *Druzhba Narodov* 5 (2003): 177.

114. Gorelik, *Boris Slutsky,* 64–66, 384–385; S. Shcheglov, "Poslednie gody Borisa Slutskogo," *Voprosy Literatury* 4 (1999): 369–372.

115. Cherniaev, *Dnevniki,* July 29, 1980.

Epilogue

1. Igor Dedkov, entry for Mar. 11, 1985, "Novyi tsykl rossiiskikh illiuzii: Iz dnevnikovykh zapisei, 1985–1986 godov," *Novy Mir* 11 (2001): 123.

2. Andrei Grachev, *Gorbachev* (Moscow: Vagrius, 2001), 28–29, 86; Robert D. English, *Russia and the Idea of the West: Gorbachev, Intellectuals, and the End of the Cold War* (New York: Columbia University Press), 182, 202.

3. Andrei Grachev, *Gorbachev's Gamble: Soviet Foreign Policy and the End of the Cold War* (Malden, Mass.: Polity Press, 2008), 46.

4. See Archie Brown, *Seven Years That Changed the World* (Oxford: Oxford University Press, 1997); and Brown, "Gorbachev, Lenin, and the Break with Leninism," *Demokratizatsyia* 15, no. 2 (Spring 2007): 230–244.

5. This brain trust also included Zaslavskaia and Aganbegyan from Akademgorodok, Leonid Abalkin, Oleg Bogomolov, Georgy Arbatov, Yevgeny Primakov, and the physicists Yevgeny Velikhov and Roald Sagdeev. Later, Georgy Shakhnazarov and two MGU classmates of Raisa, Nail Bikkenin and Anatoly Lukianov, joined the brain trust.

6. Galina Belaia, "Ia rodom iz shestidesiatykh . . . ," *Novoe Literaturnoe Obozrenie* 70 (2004): 223–227.

7. Igor Vinogradov, a columnist for Tvardovsky's *Novy Mir,* described Gorbachev as "a typical Don Quixote from the sixties generation" who realized its dream of "democratic socialism." Igor Vinogradov, "Paradoks Mikhaila Gorbacheva," *Kontinent* 107 (2001): 261–263, 270–276.

8. Gorbachev's roots in the rural Russian South made him sympathetic toward village writers and Russian nationalists. See the report on the Politburo meeting on July 3, 1986, in A. Cherniaev, V. Veber, and V. Medvedev, eds., *V Politbiuro TsK KPSS . . . Po zapisiam Anatolia Cherniaeva, Vadima Medvedeva, Georgiia Shakhnazarova, 1985–1991* (Moscow: Alpina, 2006), 60; Alexander Yakovlev, *Omut pamiati* (Moscow: Vagrius, 2000), 264; and Anatoly Cherniaev, *My Six Years with Gorbachev,* trans. and ed. Robert D. English and Elizabeth Tucker (University Park: Pennsylvania State University Press, 2000), 212–214.

9. See http://culture.ru/index.php?section=1&sub=75.

10. Born into a middle-class liberal family from St. Petersburg in 1906, Likhachev studied at the university, was arrested in 1928, and spent six years in the Solovetsky

concentration camp and on the construction of the Belomor Canal. He survived the Great Terror and the blockade of Leningrad and found an intellectual haven at the Institute of Russian Literature (Pushkin House). His admirer Sergei Averintsev believed that Likhachev belonged to "a cultural type that was irrevocably lost" by the end of the Soviet era. See Likhachev, "Sergei Averintsev," in *Literaturnaia Gazeta*, Oct. 12, 1999, 6; E. G. Vodolazkin, ed., *Dmitry Likhachev i ego epokha: Vospominaniia, esse, dokumenty, fogografii* (St. Petersburg: Logos, 2002); biographical materials, at http://likhachev.lfond.spb.ru/memoirs.htm; and James H. Billington, *Russia in Search of Itself* (Washington, D.C.: Woodrow Wilson Center Press, 2004), 60–64.

11. Yuri Levada, "Yuri Burtin: Chelovek i ego vremia—In memoriam," *Novoe Literaturnoe Obozrenie* 48 (2001): 91.

12. Yakovlev, *Omut pamiati,* 256.

13. Elem Klimov, whose name was an acronym taken from the names Engels, Lenin, Marx, was born in Stalingrad in 1933 into a family of communist idealists. He left the burning city, attacked by the Wehrmacht, in the fall of 1942. He graduated from VGIK in 1964. His first film, a satirical comedy, was banned. The first film made by his wife, Larisa Shepitko, was destroyed by the censors. George Faraday, *Revolt of Filmmakers: The Struggle for Artistic Autonomy and the Fall of the Soviet Film Industry* (Philadelphia: Pennsylvania State University Press, 2000), 125–129.

14. Alexander Yakovlev, archive of Radio Liberty, at http://www.svoboda.org/programs/cicles/cinema/russian/Repentance.asp; Lev Osterman, diary entry for Nov. 14, 1986, *Intelligentsia i vlast v Rossii, 1985-1996* (Moscow: Gumanitarnyi Tsentr Monolit, 2000), 20.

15. Pristavkin had graduated in 1959 from the Institute of Literature in Moscow, yet for years he had to write "into the drawer" and could not publish his works.

16. Author's interview with Natalia Gorbanevskaia, June 10, 2008, Paris.

17. On the effects of Chernobyl, see David R. Marples, *The Social Impact of the Chernobyl Disaster* (New York: St. Martin's, 1988); Grigory Medvedev, *The Truth about Chernobyl* (New York: Basic, 1989); and Svetlana Alexievich, *Voices from Chernobyl,* trans. Keith Gessen (London: Dalkey Archive Press, 2005).

18. Yakovlev, *Omut pamiati,* 239–246; Alexander Yakovlev and the Roots of the Soviet Reforms, a collection of documents at the Web site for the National Security Archive, Washington, D.C., at http://www.gwu.edu/~nsarchiv/NSAEBB/NSAEBB168/index.htm.

19. *Universitetskaia zhizn* (newspaper of the University of Novosibirsk), Dec. 23, 1986; Varlen Soskin to D. S. Likhachev, Jan. 16, 1987, in the papers of D. S. Likhachev, fond 769, Manuscript Division of the Institute of Russian Literature (Pushkin House), St. Petersburg.

20. Nina Andreeva, "Ne mogu postupitsia printsipami," *Sovetskaia Rossia,* Mar. 13, 1988. An incomplete English translation appears in Isaac J. Tarasulo, ed., *Gorbachev and Glasnost: Viewpoints from the Soviet Press* (Wilmington, Del.: Scholarly Resources, 1989), 277–290.

21. The head of the editorial board, Viktor Chikin, a veteran of *Komsomolskaia Pravda* and a prominent member of the Russian nationalist network, edited Andreeva's letter before its publication. In one passage edited out of the newspaper version, Andreeva reminded everyone that in Czechoslovakia in 1968, "it all began, too, with the congress of writers and with [Jews]. And how did that end?" Another dropped sentence was: "The Jews in our country have become a nationality apart." Giuletto Chiesa, "Secret History of the Anti-Gorbachev Manifesto," *L'Unità*, May 23, 1988, translated into English in Kevin Devlin, "L'Unità on the Secret History of the Andreeva Letter," RFE/RL Research, RAD background report 93 (USSR), at http://files.osa.ceu.hu/holdings/300/8/3/text/139-3-214.shtml.

22. *V Politbiuro TsK KPSS*, 356–360.

23. Vasily Grossman's novel *Life and Fate,* impounded by the KGB in 1960, did not vanish; three friends of the writer secretly kept a copy for decades, and in 1988 the Moscow literary journal *Oktiabr* published it in full. John Garrard and Carol Garrard, *The Bones of Berdichev: The Life and Fate of Vasily Grossman* (New York: Free Press, 1996), 317–324. Among other shattering publications were the "Requiem" of Anna Akhmatova, about the victims of the Great Terror, the anti-Bolshevik work *We,* by Yevgeny Zamiatin, the poems of Joseph Brodsky, and the novels of Vladimir Nabokov.

24. Andrei Melville, "A Personal Introduction," in Andrei Melville and Gail W. Lapidus, eds., *The Glasnost Papers* (Boulder, Colo.: Westview, 1990), 1. After the collapse of the Soviet Union, Melville, the son of a Soviet philosopher and a senior researcher at the Institute for the United States and Canada Studies, became a very successful educational entrepreneur.

25. Vasily Seliunin, "Istoki," *Novy Mir,* May 1988, 162–189. Seliunin graduated from MGU as a journalist in the early 1950s (in the same cohort as Adzhubei); Dmitry Shalin, interview with Vasily Seliunin, Apr. 30, 1990, Boston, at http://www.unlv.edu/centers/cdclv/archives/Interviews/seliunin.html; Melville and Lapidus, *The Glasnost Papers,* 73–83.

26. The effects of the desacralization of Leninism are described in Alexei Yurchak, *"Everything Was Forever, Until It Was No More": The Last Soviet Generation* (Princeton, N.J.: Princeton University Press, 2006), 295.

27. Leon Aron, *Russia's Revolution: Essays, 1989–2006* (Washington, D.C.: AEI, 2007), 4, 12–13.

28. Lev Osterman, entry for Nov. 8, 1987, in Osterman, *Intelligentsia i vlast v Rossii,* 29, 30.

29. The Italian film director Bernardo Bertolucci brilliantly showed a similar transition in his film *Il Conformista* (1970).

30. Vladislav Zubok, *A Failed Empire: The Soviet Union in the Cold War from Stalin to Gorbachev* (Chapel Hill: University of North Carolina Press, 2007), chap. 10.

31. Seliunin, at http://www.unlv.edu/centers/cdclv/archives/Interviews/seliunin.html; Levada, "Yuri Burtin"; Melville and Lapidus, *The Glasnost Papers,* 189–227.

32. The discussion on economic reforms in glasnost media is analyzed in Melville and

Lapidus, *The Glasnost Papers*, 189–227. Remarks on the reformers' being still "Soviet" in their thinking are based on author's interview with Vittorio Strada, Apr. 1, 2006, Rome.

33. Author conversation with Sidney Drell, June 11, 2007, Bellagio, Italy; Jack F. Matlock, *Autopsy on an Empire* (New York: Random House, 1995), 108.

34. Houghton Library, Harvard University, Andrei Sakharov Papers, MS Russ 79, folder S.II.2.6.1.45.

35. Timothy Colton, *Yeltsin: A Life* (New York: Basic, 2008), 168–170.

36. Cherniaev, *My Six Years with Gorbachev;* K. N. Brutents, *Nesbyvsheesia: Neravnodushnye zametki o perestroike* (Moscow: Mezhdunarodnye Otnosheniia, 2005), 310.

37. Leon Aron, *Yeltsin;* Colton, *Yeltsin,* 177–185, 191–194.

38. Faraday, *Revolt of Filmmakers,* 129.

39. Rosalind Marsh, "The Death of Soviet Literature: Can Russian Literature Survive?" *Europe-Asia Studies* 45, no. 1 (1993): 115–139; N. N. Shneidman, *Russian Literature, 1988–1994: The End of an Era* (Toronto: University of Toronto Press, 1995), 22–23, 26–28.

40. Houghton Library, Harvard University, Andrei Sakharov Papers, MS Russ 79, folder S.II.2.5.172.

41. Anatoly Smeliansky, *The Russian Theater after Stalin* (New York: Cambridge University Press, 1999), 142.

42. Daniil Granin, "Sobratsia s dukhom, chtoby vyzhit: O meste intelligentsii v nastoiashchem vremeni," *Izvestia,* Dec. 19, 1991.

43. Osterman, *Intelligentsia i vlast v Rossii,* 260.

44. Alexei Adzhubei, *Krushenie illuzii: Vremia v sobytiakh i litsakh* (Moscow: Interbuk, 1991), 143.

45. Alexei Kozlov, *Kozel na sakse* (Moscow: Vagrius, 1998), 169.

46. Yuri Kariakin, quoted in Sergei Miturich, ed., *Vittorio: Mezhdunarodnyi nauchnyi sbornik posveshchennyi 75-letiiu Vittorio Strady* (Moscow: Tri Kvadrata, 2005), 24, 25.

47. From Yuri Zhivago's (Boris Pasternak's) poem "Hamlet," trans. Christopher Barnes, *Toronto Slavic Quarterly* 10 (Fall 2004), at http://www.utoronto.ca/tsq/10/barnes10.shtml. Quoted by permission.

48. Andrei Siniavsky, *The Russian Intelligentsia,* trans. Lynn Visson (New York: Columbia University Press, 1997), 1, 12–13.

49. Vladimir Bondarenko, *Deti 1937 goda* (Moscow: Informpechat ITRK, 2001).

50. "Dissidenty o dissidentstve," *Znamia* (1997–98), special issue, 159.

51. Czeslaw Milosz, *Native Realm: A Search for Self-Definition,* trans. Catherine S. Leach (Garden City, N.Y.: Doubleday, 1981), 145.

52. I allude here to a play of Tom Stoppard, *The Coast of Utopia* (New York: Grove, 2003).

53. Tony Judt, *Postwar: A History of Europe since 1945* (New York: Penguin, 2005), 394.

Acknowledgments

Zhivago's Children was not just a scholarly project. I came of age in Moscow after Soviet tanks had crushed the Prague Spring, thus reinstating the Iron Curtain and demolishing the idealistic project of socialism with a human face. In those years the word "intelligentsia" was often on the lips of my parents and their friends, some of them television engineers, others employees in the military-industrial complex, and yet others musicians, artists, or art historians. To them I owe my first interest in the intelligentsia's universe. This interest grew when I began to listen to the ballads of the Russian songwriters of the sixties, whose records my parents played on a bulky tape recorder. Such singing had nothing in common with the saccharine timbre of the crooners we were used to hearing on official Soviet radio and television. I learned from Vysotsky and Okudzhava about the existence of labor camps and anti-Semitism in the Soviet Union, Stalin's use of "penal battalions" of kamikaze units to fight against Hitler's armies, and many other shocking revelations. I also learned about the poet Boris Pasternak, whose writings were not on the Soviet school curriculum. It was the beginning of my discovery of the rich and diverse cultural world that had flourished in Russia after Stalin's death yet was not part of the official culture. It was, in fact, the world of the intelligentsia, which had played such a pivotal role in the thinking and interests of my parents and their friends. *Zhivago's Children* is the acknowledgment of my gratitude to them.

The book could not have been written without the publication of numerous recollections and personal diaries. The cultural and intellectual elites of Russia in the 1950s and 1960s were concentrated in Moscow and to a lesser extent in Leningrad (St. Petersburg). Even more than Paris has in France, or New York in the United States, Moscow held a monopoly on the production of high culture in the late Soviet era. The sources on the period are rich and amazingly varied: fiction and nonfiction publications that reflect the issues, debates, and moods of the time; and manuscripts in samizdat, which was as essential a feature of the Russia of the 1960s as electronic mail is in postcommunist Russia today. Also very useful, although limited, are the published observations of Western scholars, journalists, and diplomats— who visited the USSR or lived there. Diaries were a particularly important source for the book. Memoirs, oral histories, and interviews required very careful treatment, for individuals had altered their views and memories after the collapse of Soviet communism. Many intellectuals and artists were ashamed of their ideals and illusions during the years immediately following Stalin's death. Some of them exaggerated the oppositional, anti-Soviet nature of their earlier views, as if they had grown up already with the wisdom and knowledge that came to them at a later age. Still, these types of sources helped me greatly, and without them *Zhivago's Children* could not have been written.

The archival documentation for the book came from state as well as nongovernmental archives. The bulk of the archival material came from Moscow-based archives, above all the Russian State Archive for Recent History, the Central Moscow Archive of Social Movements, the Central Archive of Documentary Collections of Moscow, the Russian State Archive for Literature and Art, and the State Archive of the Russian Federation. Uniquely helpful was the non-government-based Memorial (Memorial—Historical, Educational, Human Rights and Charitable Society), with branches in Moscow and St. Petersburg. Among the archival collections outside Russia, the most important for my research was the Red Archive at the Open Society Archive in Budapest (the former archive of Radio Free Europe / Radio Liberty). The papers of Andrei Sakharov and Yelena Bonner at Harvard University's Houghton Library helped me overcome a number of misunderstandings regarding the views and values of Soviet dissidents as they evolved during the 1960s and after.

I feel gratitude to many individuals, archivists and scholars, who helped me find what I did and did not expect to find. My special thanks go to Boris

Belenkin, Alexander Daniel, Irina Flige, Tatiana Goriaeva, Boris Ilizarov, Tatiana Kosinova, Vladimir Kozlov, Mark Kramer, Sergei Kudriashov, Sergei Mironenko, Lidia Naumova, Mikhail Prozumenschikov, István Rév, Arseny Roginsky, Natalia Tomilina, Zoia Vodopianova, Tatiana Yankelevich, Olga Zaslavskaia, and Elena Zubkova. I am indebted to Dr. Semyon Ekshtut and Alexander Oldenburg from the journal *Rodina*, Tatiana Khromova from Memorial in Moscow, Alexander Kobak of the Dmitry Likhachev Foundation, Isay and Yevgenia Kuznetsov, and Sergei Smirnov for helping me, on rather short notice, find photographs of some key protagonists of *Zhivago's Children*.

A number of foundations and research centers granted me hospitality and unique aesthetic and intellectual environments for thinking and writing. Incentive grants from Temple University and the Carnegie Corporation of New York funded some of my research time in Russia. During my research fellowship at Collegium Budapest, I not only discussed my project with a diverse group of international scholars but drafted the first chapters of the book. Budapest, with its imperial grandeur and turbulent history, was a perfect setting for my endeavor. Other chapters were drafted in Italy, thanks to generous fellowships at Guido Carli Free International University for Social Sciences in Rome and at the superb Bellagio Center of the Rockefeller Foundation. A good deal of Russian literature and art, from Nikolai Gogol's *Dead Souls* to Maxim Gorky's *Klim Samgin,* was conceived under the Italian sun, and I cannot find any objection to this tradition. A public policy scholarship at the Woodrow Wilson International Center for Scholars in Washington, D.C., afforded me time and resources for the final editorial work.

The friends and colleagues who helped me in the course of this project are numerous. Thomas S. Blanton at the National Security Archive and Beth Bailey, David Farber, and Ralph Young at Temple University encouraged me to compare Zhivago's children, the Russian *shestidesiatniki,* with the men and women of the sixties in the West. Michael David Fox, Stephen Kotkin, Eric Lohr, Benjamin Nathans, Yuri Slezkine, and Richard Stites offered me venues for discussing my manuscript and asked probing questions at the final stage of the project. Vladimir Shlapentokh, Natasha Simes, Konstantin Simis, Ralph Young, and Victor Zaslavsky read earlier drafts of some chapters and commented on them, and Holger Loewendorf labored through the entire manuscript. My particular gratitude goes to the two anonymous reviewers and my fabulous editors Joyce Seltzer and Susan Abel. They helped me correct numerous errors and biases (I am afraid some remain) and see Zhivago's children as a phenomenon in world history that can, after all, be understood by Western readers. Last, my parents, other relatives, and my wife Yelena encouraged me unflaggingly in this endeavor. They gave me the care and love without which the life of the spirit dries up. Also, my children Andrei and Michael were my inspiration. I hoped that one day they would begin their own intellectual journey and discover the cultural legacy that had molded and stimulated their grandparents and parents. As I was finishing the manuscript, Andrei succumbed to terrible trauma after a car accident. The memory of him will stay forever in my heart.

Index